Frommer's®

Thailand

7th Edition

by Charles Agar

Here's what the critics say about Frommer's:

"Amazingly easy to use. Very portable, very complete."
—*Booklist*

"Detailed, accurate, and easy-to-read information for all price ranges."
—*Glamour Magazine*

"Hotel information is close to encyclopedic."
—*Des Moines Sunday Register*

"Frommer's Guides have a way of giving you a real feel for a place."
—*Knight Ridder Newspapers*

WILEY
Wiley Publishing, Inc.

Published by:

Wiley Publishing, Inc.

111 River St.
Hoboken, NJ 07030-5774

ISBN-13: 978-0-471-78470-8
ISBN-10: 0-471-78470-2

Editor: Christine Summers
Production Editor: Eric T. Schroeder
Cartographer: Tim Lohnes
Photo Editor: Richard Fox
Production by Wiley Indianapolis Composition Services

Front cover photo: Bangkok: Wat Phra Keo, gold Kinaree statue in foreground
Back cover photo: Krabi: Ao Nang Beach
For information on our other products and services or to obtain technical support, please contact our Customer Care Department within the U.S. at 800/762-2974, outside the U.S. at 317/572-3993 or fax 317/572-4002.

Wiley also publishes its books in a variety of electronic formats. Some content that appears in print may not be available in electronic formats.

Manufactured in the United States of America

5   4   3   2   1

Contents

10 Central Thailand   274

11 Exploring Northern Thailand   298

12 Chiang Mai   308

13 Touring the Northern Hills   343

14 Exploring Isan: Thailand's Frontier   365

List of Maps

An Invitation to the Reader

In researching this book, we discovered many wonderful places—hotels, restaurants, shops, and more. We're sure you'll find others. Please tell us about them, so we can share the information with your fellow travelers in upcoming editions. If you were disappointed with a recommendation, we'd love to know that, too. Please write to:

Frommer's Thailand, 7th Edition
Wiley Publishing, Inc. • 111 River St. • Hoboken, NJ 07030-5774

An Additional Note

Please be advised that travel information is subject to change at any time—and this is especially true of prices. We therefore suggest that you write or call ahead for confirmation when making your travel plans. The authors, editors, and publisher cannot be held responsible for the experiences of readers while traveling. Your safety is important to us, however, so we encourage you to stay alert and be aware of your surroundings. Keep a close eye on cameras, purses, and wallets, all favorite targets of thieves and pickpockets.

About the Author

In addition to updating this and the last edition of Frommer's Thailand, **Charles Agar** also wrote the first edition of Frommer's Vietnam and updated two editions of Frommer's Southeast Asia, covering Thailand, Laos, Vietnam, Cambodia, and Bali. He would like to thank the many people who have helped him, among them: Alex and Lynn in Chiang Mai; Davies Stamm for sharing the roads of Isan; Alex Z. for the ride through that thunderstorm on the Eastern Gulf; and Jack and Nok on Koh Samui for their kind welcome and friendship. A special thanks to his parents and family, to Connell McGrath, and to Michael, Anna, and young Ryan Deland for their hospitality and support in Bangkok. Contact Charlie through his website: www.charlesagar.com.

Other Great Guides for Your Trip:

Frommer's Southeast Asia
Frommer's Singapore & Malaysia
Frommer's Hong Kong
Frommer's China

Frommer's Star Ratings, Icons & Abbreviations

Every hotel, restaurant, and attraction listing in this guide has been ranked for quality, value, service, amenities, and special features using a **star-rating system.** In country, state, and regional guides, we also rate towns and regions to help you narrow down your choices and budget your time accordingly. Hotels and restaurants are rated on a scale of zero (recommended) to three stars (exceptional). Attractions, shopping, nightlife, towns, and regions are rated according to the following scale: zero stars (recommended), one star (highly recommended), two stars (very highly recommended), and three stars (must-see).

In addition to the star-rating system, we also use **seven feature icons** that point you to the great deals, in-the-know advice, and unique experiences that separate travelers from tourists. Throughout the book, look for:

Finds	Special finds—those places only insiders know about
Fun Fact	Fun facts—details that make travelers more informed and their trips more fun
Kids	Best bets for kids and advice for the whole family
Moments	Special moments—those experiences that memories are made of
Overrated	Places or experiences not worth your time or money
Tips	Insider tips—great ways to save time and money
Value	Great values—where to get the best deals

The following **abbreviations** are used for credit cards:

AE	American Express	DISC	Discover	V	Visa
DC	Diners Club	MC	MasterCard		

Frommers.com

Now that you have the guidebook to a great trip, visit our website at **www.frommers.com** for travel information on more than 3,000 destinations. With features updated regularly, we give you instant access to the most current trip-planning information available. At Frommers.com, you'll also find the best prices on airfares, accommodations, and car rentals—and you can even book travel online through our travel booking partners. At Frommers.com, you'll also find the following:

- Online updates to our most popular guidebooks
- Vacation sweepstakes and contest giveaways
- Newsletter highlighting the hottest travel trends
- Online travel message boards with featured travel discussions

What's New in Thailand

Thailand has something for everyone, from the wild rave baby to the plucky pensioner, from young kids in need of lots of activities to parents hoping to get away from it all. Thailand is not just for backpackers anymore, though backpackers still flock here while enjoying Internet access at every turn, a host of upmarket guesthouses, and VIP tours at cost (hardened overlanders scoff at Thailand these days). Quality adventure companies run great trips to trekking areas, nature preserves, and hill-tribe villages, and light adventure tours take you to the back of beyond in comfort, or you can do it yourself and have a good adventure. Accommodations cover every base. Despite the long and costly flight from the U.S. or Europe, Thailand still sings the siren song of great budget travel accommodation and luxuries at a fraction of prices back home.

Sadly, Thailand is synonymous with the Christmas Tsunami of December 2004. No one can forget the tragic day when a wall of water spawned by a massive undersea earthquake hammered the coastal countries in South Asia along the Indian Ocean and Andaman Sea, and though some areas in the far south of Thailand were devastated by the wave, these days the reconstruction is near completion and Thais are as gracious and eager as ever to welcome foreign visitors. Only parts of the west coast of the Malay Peninsula were hit, namely the west coast of the popular tourist island of Phuket,

parts of Pha Nga and Khao Lak just north of Phuket (some of the worst damage in Thailand), and Koh Phi Phi, a low-lying island that is unlikely to be rebuilt (there is talk of making the once overdeveloped area on Phi Phi Don into a day-access only national park), as well as parts of Krabi and Koh Lanta. Although loss of life was high (regionally over 200,000, with an estimated 6,000 of those people in Thailand alone, many of whom were foreigners), clean-up was prompt, and the Thai government—acting with only limited technical support from international sources—handled the disaster with aplomb, with no reports of looting or unrest. A memorial service is planned throughout the country during the Christmas season in 2006, and there are a number of monuments under construction, notably on Phuket and on Koh Phi Phi. *Note:* There is now a sophisticated seismic alarm system in the Indian Ocean and Andaman Sea, and many hotels have been equipped with special alarm systems and marked escape routes in the event of a repeat of a rogue wave. Many hotels in the region used the setback of damage from the tsunami as a reason to retrench and renovate, upgrading aging properties as a result of the disaster.

Caution: Travelers should be aware of the volatile situation in the far south near the Malay border. Extremist groups among large, disenfranchised Muslim populations, particular in the area of Pattani, Narathiwat, and Sungai Kolok, wage an ongoing subversion of Thai institutions. There have been a number of small-scale bombings and violent clashes. Groups are bidding for autonomy, rhetoric that the conservative Thai government has been fast to squelch. In fact, the international community has criticized the conservative government of Prime Minister Taksin for its often overly brutal response to suspected insurgency. The unrest is in an area far from popular tour sites in the south, but it is a good idea to keep an eye on the situation.

Have no fear for avian influenza, aka "bird flu." There were a few cases in Thailand, but the numbers are insignificant.

Throughout Thailand, visitors will find improved **DSL connection** in Internet shops (and a price increase of often 2B per minute, about $3 per hour), and more wireless connection, often free in public spaces at hotels and restaurants, or accessed with prepaid cards.

Thailand's budget domestic airlines, **Air Asia** (www.airasia.com) and **Nok Air** (www.nokair.com), make it easy and affordable to make short hops in-country (it's best to buy tickets far in advance, and pay careful attention to the stiff penalties for changing dates).

Below are some updates and happenings region by region:

BANGKOK   The big news in Bangkok is the airport under construction. Set to open sometime in 2006, **Suvanabhumi International Airport** will replace longtime international hub Don Muang International as the main arrival point for international flights to Thailand (older Don Muang will become a military and civil airport). There is a planned spur of Bangkok's Skytrain to the Suvanabhumi site, just east of the city center, where **Novotel Hotel** (www.accor.com) is under construction.

Bangkok's **new subway system** is up and running, opening up new areas of town and connecting Hua Lampong Train Station through the center of town and as far as Mo Chit, the Northeastern Bus Station. The subway augments the useful BTS Skytrain, an elevated monorail at town center, meaning that you can always escape Bangkok's chaotic road traffic (aka hours waiting in gridlock at rush hour).

New hotel listings in this edition include the following: **Chakrabongse Villas** (✆ 02622-3356; www.thaivillas. com), three private villas overlooking the Chao Praya River at the heart of historical Bangkok; **JW Marriott** (✆ 02656-7700; www.marriott.com/bkkdt), a luxurious choice on Sukhumvit; **Intercontinental** (✆ 02656-0444; www.intercontinental. com), which recently took over the Le Meridien Hotel, and now adjoins the **Holiday Inn Bangkok** under same management (✆ 02656-1555; www.holiday-inn.com); and **Swissotel Nai Lert Park** (✆ 02253-0123; www.nailertpark. swissotel.com), now reopened under management of Raffles. In the mid-range, look for new (to this edition) **Swiss Lodge** (✆ 02233-5345; www.swiss lodge.com), a popular business address in the heart of Silom; and **Arnoma** (✆ 02255-3410; www.arnoma.com), a comfy, familiar choice across from the World Trade Center shopping complex.

Bangkok dining choices are many and varied, from **Baan Kanitha** and **Lemongrass,** two popular Thai restaurants, to refined hotel dining at the Oriental or the Peninsula. New to this edition is little **Le Bouchon** (✆ 02234-9109), a French bistro in the heart of the red-light district of Patpong. Also try chic **New York Steakhouse** (✆ 02656-9798) at the JW Marriott, or **The Great American Rib Company BKK** (✆ 02661-3801), a popular expat restaurant great for parties. Look for good local specials in the sidebar, "Bangkok Street Eats," in the dining section.

On the entertainment front, check out the **Joe Louis Puppet Theater** (✆ 02252-9683) in the Suan Lum Night Market. For nightlife try chic **Hu'u Bar** (✆ 02676-6677; www.huuinasia.com), along with popular old haunts like the disco at the Novotel or **Bed Supper Club** (✆ 02651-3537). Shopping in Bangkok expands with the likes of ultraluxe **Erawan Plaza,** adjacent to Erawan Shrine and Grand Hyatt Erawan Hotel.

EASTERN GULF New to Pattaya is the luxurious **Sheraton Pattaya Resort** (✆ 03825-9888; www.sheraton.com/pattaya), a collection of fine upmarket rooms, suites, and villas overlooking tiered pools and an ocean vista. Nearby **Cabbages & Condoms** (✆ 03825-0556) is a good mid-range atmospheric choice.

Little **Koh Samet,** a resort island popular for Bangkok weekenders and once home to but a few mid-range and budget resorts, will see a whole new standard when **Paradee** (✆ 02438-9771 in Bangkok; www.samedresorts.com), a cool boutique resort, is completed sometime in 2006.

Koh Chang, the last island before Cambodia as you go east from Bangkok, now plays host to a bevy of upmarket resorts and an increase in services. Many who'd planned vacations in tsunami-damaged regions changed their reservations to Koh Chang. **Aiyapura** (✆ 03955-5119; www.aiyapura.com) was the first luxury resort on the island, and now has stiff competition, the best choice being **Amari Emerald Cove Resort** (✆ 03955-2000; www.amari.com), another stylish offering from this distinctive but affordable Thai chain. White Sand Beach is the center of development on the island, and there you'll find a few good mid-range choices, including the basic bungalows and good services at **Banpu** (✆ 03955-1234), or spartan **Mac Resort** (✆ 03955-1124; www.mac-resorthotel.com). Further afield,

in the far south, find the luxe bungalows of **Nirvana Resort** (✆ 03955-8061; www.nirvanakohchang.com), and nearby is the best island dining on the busy pier at **Bang Bao.** You can go diving from Koh Chang, or take an elephant ride at **Ban Kwan Chang** (✆ 01919-3995; www.bankwanchang.com), and there is even a unique area where you can explore a mangrove swamp by kayak at **Salak Kok Kayak Station** (✆ 07137-2962).

EAST COAST MALAY PENINSULA Heading south from Bangkok, you first reach **Hua Hin,** Bangkok's earliest tour destination and royal retreat, which hosts the annual **King's Cup Elephant Polo Tournament** each September. **Sheraton** (✆ 03244-2531; www.sheraton.com) will open a new resort in Hua Hin in 2006.

Koh Samui, the most popular island in the east, isn't just for backpackers any more; the one-time coconut palm hideaway now hosts a number of upscale resorts. **Santiburi** was the first five-star resort on the island; previously managed by Dusit and now an independent resort, Santiburi has spawned its own more affordable choice nearby, **Bophut Resort and Spa,** as well as a unique golf course in the precipitous hills above the resort. Along with Santiburi, now find **Napasai** (✆ 07743-9200; www.pansea.com) from the folks at Pansea, as well as luxury **Anantara Resort and Spa** (✆ 07742-8300; www.anantara.com), a stylish theme property; as well as **Bandara** (✆ 07724-5795; www.bandararesort.com), all along Bophut Beach in the north of the island. Check out **Sala Samui** (✆ 07724-5888; www.salasamui.com), an upmarket, chic villa property near Choeng Mon Beach, as well as luxury **Sila Evason Hideaway and Spa** (✆ 07724-5678; www.sixsenses.com). Lamai Beach's only five-star property, Buriraya, has just rebranded and will reopen in 2006 as the **Renaissance**

Samui Resort and Spa (© 07742-9300; www.buriraya.com), as part of the Marriot chain. Retirees are flocking to Samui and talk of townhouses and condo developments is all the buzz. You heard it here.

Amari Palm Reef Resort (© 07742-2015; www.amari.com) has just completed an addition to their popular Chaweng Beach resort, and they've just opened a cool freestanding Italian restaurant, **Prego.** Three resorts in Chaweng, none new to Samui but all new to this edition, each follow suit with fine dining open to the main road and outside guests. There's **Central Samui Beach Resort** (© 07723-0500; www.centralhotels resorts.com), which hosts its own freestanding Brazilian-theme restaurant, **Zico's; Chaweng Regent Beach Resort** (© 07744-2389; www.chawengregent. com), with a seafood and grill restaurant, **Red Snapper;** and **Muang Samui Resort** (© 07742-9700; www.muangsamui. com), which runs busy **Samui Seafood Grill.**

In other dining news, **The Mangrove** is still tops, but look for **Bellini** (© 07741-3831; www.bellini-samui.com), a new upmarket version of popular Vecchia Napoli, as well as **Big John Seafood** (© 07741-5537; www.bigjohnsamui. com), an open-air joint on the far western shore of Samui.

For touring, try a trip on the *June Bahtra* (© 07742-2738; www.junebahtra. com), a luxury Chinese junk now available for rent in the waters off of Samui, or take a trip on the large liner owned by the ferry company **Seatrans** (© 07742-6000), out to the **Ang Thong Marine Park.**

Just adjacent to Koh Samui, little **Koh Pha Ngan** is notorious as a place to "ride the snake" at their monthly **Full Moon Party,** but things are a little toned down these days and the island is a good place for families with some far-flung, comfortable resorts (full moon at Haad Rin on Pha Ngan is still a riot). **The Sanctuary** (© 01271-3614; www.thesanctuary thailand.com) is a cool patchouli-wafting health and cleansing retreat reached only by boat from Haad Rin, the party beach, and further afield along the west coast of Pha Ngan find the likes of **Haad Son Resort** (© 07734-9104; www.phangan. info/haadson.), among other affordable, laid-back choices.

Connected by high-speed catamarans run by **Lomprayah** as well as a local ferry, the island of **Koh Tao** can be reached from Samui or Pha Ngan, or the mainland at Chumphon. A diver's island peopled with expats running small businesses, the "Turtle Island" of Koh Tao has a few new upmarket resorts, foremost among them little **Jamahkiri Spa & Resort** (© 07745-6400; www.jamahkiri. com), like a James Bond villain hideaway. Also try rustic **Charm Churee Villa** (© 07745-6393; www.charmchuree villa.com) or **Koh Tao Cabana** (© 07745-6505; www.kohtaocabana.com). The island is not just for divers anymore, and these new resorts and restaurants like slick **Papa's Tapas** herald the beginning of boutique luxuries on Koh Tao.

WEST COAST MALAY PENINSULA

Now synonymous with the tragedy of the tsunami, **Phuket** is still Thailand's premiere resort destination, and the only real effects post-tsunami are the memorials going up, the sense of gratitude among survivors, and the return of tourists. Many of the resorts that were damaged used the time to reinvest and rebuild.

Kata Thani Hotel (© 07633-0124; www.katathani.com), on secluded Katanoi Beach in the far southwest of the island, just reopened in grand form after a major renovation. **Mom Tri's Boathouse** (© 07633-0015; www.boathousephuket. com) was damaged by the tsunami but made lemonade out of lemons and turned their gutted fine dining area into a more open and light space, still a great choice, as well as their new luxury suites at hilltop **Villa Royale.** On Karon Beach the **Hilton Phuket Arcadia Resort and Spa** (℃ 07639-6433; www.hilton.com) just reopened after rebranding, and their inviting spa village alone is worth the trip. Next door, the **Crowne Plaza Karon Beach** (℃ 07639-6139; www.phuket. crowneplaza.com) just opened its doors. New to this edition (but not to Phuket) is **Central Karon Village Phuket** (℃ 07628-6300; www.centralhotelsresorts.com) on the hill above the north end of Karon, with luxury suites overlooking the sea. For budget watchers, little **Karona Resort and Spa** (℃ 07628-6406; www. karonaresort.com) is a real find (right on the cusp of Kata and Karon).

Patong is the busy, overdeveloped beach area in the middle of the island's west coast hit hardest by the tsunami. Only the one hotel directly at beachside has closed. The rest have rebuilt. **Holiday Inn Resort Phuket** (℃ 07634-0608; www.phuket.holiday-inn.com) was just finishing a new wing at the end of 2005, and new to this edition is a good budget choice called **Horizon Beach Resort Hotel** (℃ 07629-2526; www.horizon beach.com), as well as **Royal Palm Resortel** (℃ 07629-2510; www.theroyal palm.com), a longtime budget standby in the heart of Patong, which has completely renovated and reopened after severe tsunami damage.

There are a number of new, high-end resorts scattered about the island. Look for **Treetops Arasia** (℃ 07627-1271; www. treetops-arasia.com), a group of stacked suites high on a hill, as well as new **Trisara** (℃ 07631-0100; www.trisara.com) and its rock-star villas at seaside.

Dining in Phuket is a joy. Longtime popular **The Boathouse** (℃ 07633-0557), a great choice for famous Phuket lobster, now has an upmarket companion in **Mom Tri's Kitchen** in their new hilltop resort. Also new to this edition are **The Cliff** (℃ 07628-6300), a fine dining choice at the Central Resort in Karon, as well as Patong's new **Yin Dee** (℃ 07629-4108; www.baanyindee.com), at the Baan Yin Dee Resort, and tiny **Pan Yaah Thai Restaurant** (℃ 07634-4473), a great choice for real local cuisine north of Patong. Long popular **On the Rock** (℃ 07633-0625; www.marinaphuket. com) just reopened after renovations (a great spot for a romantic meal over pounding surf), and famed **Baan Rim Pa** (℃ 07634-0789; www.baanrimpa.com), a veritable Patong institution, just opened a new Italian outlet next door: **Da Maurizio Bar and Ristorante** (℃ 07634-4079).

Phuket Fantasea (℃ 07638-5111; www.phuket-fantasea.com) is still the island's top nightlife attraction, but also check out the dinner and show in-town at **Sphinx** (℃ 07634-1500; www.sphinx thai.com). For art buffs, don't miss the new gallery, **Soul of Asia** (℃ 07621-1122; www.soulofasia.com), with a main outlet in Phuket Town.

Day trips and overnights from Phuket are minion, best to **Khao Sok National Park** (contact www.paddleasia.com), or by boat to **Phang Nga Bay.** The areas of **Khao Lak** and parts of **Phang Nga Province** on the mainland just north of Phuket were hit hard by the tsunami, but rebuilding is ongoing and there are a number of hotels being finished.

Koh Phi Phi, once a popular backpacker destination, was nearly erased by the tsunami, and the loss of life among tourists there was quite high. The island isthmus at the center of the main island of **Koh Phi Phi,** Phi Phi Don, is just above water at high tide, and the tsunami hit the island with brutal impact, devastating the small bungalow area. There is talk of keeping Phi Phi a day trip destination or limiting development on Phi Phi Don (the islands are protected national park land and original developers built as squatters), but there are still a few resorts scattered on remote beaches, including **Holiday Inn Phi Phi** (© 07626-1860; www.holiday-inn.com) and **Phi Phi Island Village** (© 07621-5014; www.pp island.com).

Krabi, on the mainland just across from Phuket, has lots of good options, newest among them luxurious **Nakamanda** (© 07562-8200; www.nakamanda.com).

On **Koh Lanta,** the predominantly Muslim fisherman's islands off the coast southwest of Krabi, development carries on at a busy pace. **Pimalai Resort and Spa** (© 07560-7999; www.pimalai.com) is still in a class of its own, but new boutique resorts like **Layana** (© 07560-7100; www.layanaresort.com), or affordable **Lanta Casuarina** (© 07568-4685; www.hmhotels-resorts.com), and budget **Andaman Lanta Resort** (© 07568-4200; www.andamanlanta.com), **Moonlight Bay Resort** (© 07568-4401; www.mlb-resort.com), and **Southern Lanta Resort** (© 07568-4175; www.southern lanta.com) are attracting greater numbers of international travelers.

In coastal **Trang,** the **Amari Trang** has recently upgraded to an official five-star hotel.

CHIANG MAI & THE FAR NORTH
There was major **flooding** in the fall of 2005 throughout the far north. Heavy rains caused dangerous flash flooding across the hill-towns of the region, and the town of Pai was hit with a wall of water (some called it the "Mountain Tsunami") that knocked out the large central market area and damaged riverside hotels. The city of Chiang Mai was repeatedly

flooded as the Mae Ping River betrayed her banks, causing great damage (imagine waist-high water in the Night Bazaar, if you've been before).

The big news in Chiang Mai is the rise in upscale accommodation led by the near-completion of the super-luxurious **Mandarin Oriental Dhara Dhevi** (© 05388-8888; www.mandarinoriental.com) on the outskirts of town, a new high standard. Also unique and stylish is luxury **Rachamankha** (© 05390-4111; www.rachamankha.com), within the city walls, as well as the new **Chedi** (© 05325-3333; www.ghmhotels.com) which, though plagued by floods at its riverside location, opened in late 2005. And keep an eye out for **D2 Chiang Mai,** a new luxury brand from Dusit (www.dusit.com) set to open in early 2006. **Central Duangtawan Hotel** (© 05390-5000; www.centralhotels resorts.com) is a good mid-range choice, and little **Downtown Inn** (© 05327-0662; www.empresshotels.com) is a good budget option, both new to this edition. Look for **Oasis Spa** (© 05381-5000), a new luxury garden spa in the heart of the Old City.

Among Chiang Mai's many top dining options, stop by **Mike's Original** (© 01497-1026), a great little hotdog and hamburger stand among the bars, and great for a late-night snack.

In the far northern town of **Pai,** mid-range **Pai River Corner** (© 05369-9049; www.pairivercorner.com) is a cozy new choice, and be sure to have a groovy dinner at **Baan Benjarong** (© 05369-8010).

1

The Best of Thailand

Traffic and tranquility, beaches and bargains, rural roads, ancient palaces, and stunning temples: Thailand has much to offer anyone from the casual visitor in search of affordable luxury to the rugged backpacker hoping to get off the track. What brings visitors back time and again is the allure of the ephemeral: seemingly spontaneous festivals, chance meetings, and whimsical moments in an unpredictable land of ancient culture and elusive wisdom. The kingdom's most notable sites are opulent royal palaces, ancient ruins, and peak-roofed temples housing serene images of the Buddha, places where the past comes alive in architecture and artwork as well as beliefs and practices. In bustling Bangkok, you'll find simple canal and riverside communities, a sprawling Chinatown, an ultra-modern cityscape, and giant outdoor markets that are a heady mix of sights, sounds, and smells. Beyond urban Thailand are flat plains carpeted with rice paddies and dotted with tiny villages, mountains of luxuriant teak forests where elephants once roamed wild, long stretches of white sand beach, and acres of coconut palms and rubber plantations on the southern islands and eastern gulf. Rural life is languid and hospitable, and behind every warm Thai smile there is true kindness and a certain wisdom of the ancients.

In Thailand you'll find adventure of all kinds—extreme sports on land and sea, trekking to tribal villages and rugged roads to bordertowns and outposts. The countryside is ripe for exploration by bus, train, car, motorbike, and boat, and visitors are only limited by their tolerance for hard-earned adventures. Gorgeous tropical island beaches play host to laid-back bungalow guesthouses and posh, Thai-style five-star resorts. The cuisine is captivating, a unique blend of sweet, sour, and salty tastes tempered with fiery spice.

In this chapter we list the best restaurants and hotels, as well as hints on where to find what you're looking for in this dazzling kingdom.

1 The Best Cultural Experiences

- **Celebrate Songkran:** April 13 marks the first day of *Songkran,* the Thai New Year. Traditionally, Thais wash the Buddha images in local temples with water and then sprinkle water on the hands of their elders as a show of filial piety. In recent years, however, *Songkran* has escalated into a nationwide water fight, and Khao San Road, the backpacker street in Bangkok, is the epicenter of water spraying, talc throwing, and good times. It is a riot, but stay inside unless you don't mind being wet to the bone, caked with chunks of powder, and aching from laughter. See p. 303.

- **Get off the "Track":** Whether just a day trip out of busy Bangkok or a ride inland from the beach resort of your choice, Thailand is a great place to explore the back of beyond and learn a little something about slow living and hospitality. In areas like the Mae Hong Son Loop northwest of Chiang Mai, the Golden Triangle near Chiang Rai, or more out-of-the-way locations like Isan, the large northeastern territory near Laos offers adventures around every corner. Narrow roads, hairpin turns, sweltering heat, and unpredictable drivers make for lots of excitement. Jungle terrain supporting little-visited villages, paddy-carpeted valleys dotted with quaint wooden farmhouses, rolling hills green with lush foliage and jutting limestone cliffs are what attract so many. Adventure awaits. See chapters 12 through 15.

- **Make merit:** While many Thai people will "make merit" on a daily basis, it is possible for visitors to participate in this age-old tradition as well. This custom—gestures that secure a better life here and hereafter—can be performed in any number of ways: offer pails filled with necessary daily objects like soaps, food, robes, and a small donation to the abbot of a monastery; contribute to a monk's morning meal with offerings of food; or purchase a caged bird at one of the temple complexes and set it free (a great photo op). It is best to consult a Thai person about formalities and customs beforehand in order to understand complex matters of etiquette. And remember, always thank the receiving monk—he will never thank you. He never begs; only offers you the opportunity to better your life.

- **Pet an Elephant:** Thailand's gentle giants never fail to amaze, and it isn't uncommon to see elephants padding along city streets. If these huge creatures are at first daunting, time spent around them proves their intelligence, grace, and majesty—the very symbols of the nation.

The many elephant camps in and around Chiang Mai are a good entree into the world of elephants, and there are tourist "pony-ride" style attractions and shows in many of the resort areas, but by far the best way to get to know an elephant is to visit or take a trek with the elephants from the Young Elephant Training Center in Lampang (© **05422-9042**).

Officials claim that the practice is coming to an end, but elephants are often used in big cities as ploys to collect donations from diners and shoppers. You'll be asked to buy a 20B (50¢) bunch of sugarcane, and the mahout, often guys who just rent the animals for the night like a livery cab, pockets the difference. It is a pity to see these majestic creatures wandering in traffic, blinking lights hanging from their tails, and it is tempting to buy some sugarcane and get close to the animals, but the real charity would be to buy the animal itself and free it from abusive handlers.

- **Shop 'til you drop:** It is a full-contact sport in Thailand and there are a variety of venues where you can pick up anything from fine local crafts, weaving, and jewelry, to top brand-name items (or copies thereof). The busy markets are certainly the most atmospheric: Chatuchak, the weekend market, and Suan Lum, the night market in Bangkok, the busy Night Bazaar in Chiang Mai, and the many small markets in every small town. Thai towns of any size all support large retail outlets of varying quality, from small discount department stores to luxury malls like the Emporium or Gaysorn Plaza in Bangkok. Bangkok's crazy Mah Boon Krong (MBK) Shopping Center or Siam Square is as reflective of current Thai culture as any temple or tour site, and a visit is a way to participate in Thai pop culture anthropologist-style and pick up affordable gifts for the folks back home. See the "Shopping" section at the end of any destination chapter.

- **Discover Spirit Houses:** Take the time to notice one of these elaborate creations. Like dollhouse-size dainty shrines, some of them quite elaborate, spirit houses are usually set atop an eye-level post and can be seen in nearly every yard or business entry. They are meant to house spirits—family spirits or spirits of former dwellers—and every morning or on auspicious days householders will place offerings of flowers, drinks, and food to care for the spirits and keep them happy. The spirit house is erected shortly after a new occupant enters a home.

Each municipality also has a "city shrine," a larger spirit house maintained for the entire town. These will always be well-tended, draped with colorful garlands and offerings. Thais rarely neglect the shrines, their ancestors, or the spirit world—a tradition that is as alive today as it has been for centuries.

- **Surrender to Fate:** In Thailand, fate works in strange ways—a broken down bus, nobody who speaks English for miles, help in the form of a kind stranger on a motorbike and a friend for life. When faced with big changes on the road (and there are sure to be some), it can either ruin your day or actually make your whole experience. Repeat this phrase often: *mai pen rai* ("never mind"), and you will enjoy Thailand all the more.

2 The Best Super-Luxe Resorts & Spas

- **Amanpuri** (Phuket; ✆ **07632-4333**): If you know Aman you know what comes with the high price. Everything done to a "T." Amanpuri is the first Aman and still one of the best. Great day cruises and a fantastic spa.
- **Banyan Tree Phuket** (Phuket; ✆ **800/ 525-4800** or 07632-4374): With private villas that are pure romantic luxury, Banyan Tree is a favorite for honeymooners—with great options for dining and activities. See p. 247.
- **Rayavadee** (Krabi; ✆ **07562-0740**): The two-story private bungalows at Rayavadee are on a luxury campus that opens to three beaches in different directions and lies in the shadow of some of the most dynamic, precipitous cliffs in the country. Rayavadee is a dynamic property featuring a room standard and service unparalleled anywhere in Thailand. See p. 264.
- **Pimalai Resort and Spa** (Ko Lanta; ✆ **07560-7999**): On a remote stretch of beach far down the west coast of

Ko Lanta, an as-yet little-developed island of budget bungalows and low-end resorts, Pimalai is a shining gem of luxury private bungalows, fine dining, and great service. They offer direct boat connections, and it is the perfect, upmarket escape. See p. 270.

- **Chiva-Som International Health Resort** (Hua Hin; ✆ **03253-6536**): Luxury accommodations and personalized care makes this a popular choice for visiting celebrities. After experiencing Chiva-Som's beauty and health treatments, you'll know how the rich and famous stay so rich and famous, and a visit here can be a good starting over point for a new chapter of health. See p. 183.
- **The Tongsai Bay** (Koh Samui; ✆ **07742-5015**): Casual and classy, the large suites of Tongsai Bay are the model of "outdoor living," overlooking a beautiful, isolated bay from on high. See p. 206

- **Sila Evason Hideaway and Spa** (Koh Samui; ✆ **07724-5678**): A new superluxe campus of designer villas, fine dining, and a great spa. See p. 207.
- **The Santiburi Resort** (Koh Samui; ✆ **07742-5031**): This was the first five-star on the one-time backpacker isle, and today is still a very inviting campus of luxury bungalows amid palm groves at seaside. See p. 204.
- **The Four Seasons Resort & Spa** (Chiang Mai; ✆ **800/545-4000** or 05329-8181): Luxurious Thai-style suites, excellent restaurants, a multitude of activities, and the most amazing swimming pool you've ever seen await you at The Four Seasons. Don't forget to meet their resident water buffalo family—they work the resort's private rice paddies. See p. 312.
- **The Mandarin Oriental Dhara Dhevi** (Chiang Mai; ✆ **05388-8888**): This is a new uber-luxe resort on the outskirts of Chiang Mai. The price is high and for good reason; accommodation and service is over-the-top, and it also houses a unique museum of Thai art and architecture.

3 The Best Mid- & High-end Resorts

- **Bangkok Marriott Resort & Spa** (Bangkok; ✆ **800/228-9290** or 02476-0022): After a day of crazy Bangkok traffic and exhausting sightseeing, you'll be relieved to hop aboard the ferryboat that'll take you to this sanctuary on the other side of the river. A city hotel that looks like a resort, the Marriott is simultaneously convenient and remote. See p. 101.
- **Royal Cliff Beach Resort** (Pattaya; ✆ **03825-0421**): A massive compound made of three distinct properties, this locally owned resort was one of the first and still one of the best, set well away from the Pattaya chaos (but close enough to go visit). See p. 166.
- **Amari Emerald Cove Resort** (Ko Chang; ✆ **03955-2000**): New and meticulous, this stylish gem sets the stage for future development on Ko Chang, an island growing in popularity in the Eastern Gulf. See p. 176.
- **Katathani Hotel** (Phuket; ✆ **07633-0124**): Newly renovated, on quiet Kata Noi Beach, Katathani is a good, affordable, cover-the-bases choice with plenty of quiet and atmosphere. See p. 238.
- **Hilton Phuket Arcadia Resort and Spa** (Phuket; ✆ **07639-6433**): Newly reopened as a Hilton, this sprawling resort has it all, including a great spa. See p. 241.
- **Amari Coral Beach Phuket** (Phuket; ✆ **07634-0106**): A jewel in the Amari crown, this cozy resort overlooks Patong from on high and has all you'll need: great vistas, top services, and quiet. See p. 243.
- **Sheraton Krabi Beach Resort** (Krabi; ✆ **07562-8000**): A self-contained enclave with a great spa, in-house dining, and lots of activities, the resort is set in a unique mangrove forest that daily ebbs and flows with the tide. See p. 267.
- **Hilton Hua Hin Resort and Spa** (Hua Hin; ✆ **03251-2888**): Like a tidy city hotel in the heart of little Hua Hin, but with all the resort facilities and perks associated with the Hilton brand. See p. 184.
- **Laem Set Inn** (Koh Samui; ✆ **07742-4393**): Laem Set is a shining star among the many cookie-cutter developments springing up over the island. In a quiet, isolated location the hotel's charming local decor and good amenities make for the ideal Samui getaway. See p. 213.

- **Peace Resort** (Koh Samui; ℂ **07742-5357**): Modest and affordable, Peace Resort is just that—simple, comfortable, and peaceful. A good choice. See p. 206.
- **Coral Bay** (Koh Samui; ℂ **07742-2223**): Large, semi-luxe, rustic bungalows on a verdant hillside overlooking a coral bay. Great little spa and services. See p. 209.

- **Anantara Resort and Spa Golden Triangle** (Chiang Saen; ℂ **05378-4084**): There's nothing else like this luxurious resort overlooking the Mekong in the heart of a rugged region. Great spa and close to the Hall of Opium. See p. 184.

4 The Best Luxury Hotels

- **The Oriental** (Bangkok; ℂ **800/526-6566** or 02236-0400): One of the world's premier hotels, the Oriental has its roots in the days of romantic steamship travel. On the Chao Praya River, ferries and long-tail boats stop at the pier regularly, making trips to old Bangkok incredibly simple and fun. See p. 100.
- **The Peninsula Bangkok** (Bangkok; ℂ **800/262-9467** in the U.S., 02861-2888 in Bangkok): One of those places where everything is automated and works, where the service is exacting without being effusive, where every detail is taken care of with alacrity. Everything at the Peninsula is new, shiny, and upscale, and the upper floors feature some of the best views of Bangkok. See p. 100.
- **The Sukhothai** (Bangkok; ℂ **02287-0222**): Designed in a seamless

Asian-styled contemporary luxury, Sukhothai's bold architecture successfully combines the best of old and new. See p. 103.
- **Metropolitan** (Bangkok; ℂ **02625-3333**): Bangkok's latest catwalk for international celebs, hip Metropolitan has a sister hotel in London. See p. 103.
- **Sofitel Central Hua Hin Resort** (Hua Hin; ℂ **800/221-4542** or 03251-2021): Recent renovations and additions haven't altered this historic hotel's rich heritage, impeccable service, and fantastic grounds. A royal legacy. See p. 185.
- **Rachamankha** (Chiang Mai; ℂ **05390-4111**): Stylish, sophisticated, a mini-museum of regional culture and style in Chiang Mai, new Rachamankha is one to watch. See p. 319.

5 The Best Hotels with Character

- **The Atlanta** (Bangkok; ℂ **02252-6069**): It is more or less "love it or leave it" at the Atlanta, one of Bangkok's quirkiest, most atmospheric haunts. Rooms are basic, but the hotel lobby is still decorated in the original Art Deco theme of the 1950s (the oldest unrenovated hotel in Bangkok). See p. 112.
- **Mom Tri's Boathouse** (Phuket; ℂ **07633-0015**): Pricier than others

in this category, Mom Tri's Boathouse is a longtime popular choice for long stays and return visitors right on the beach at Kata (also see their luxe hilltop resort). See p. 239.
- **Phra-Nang Inn** (Krabi; ℂ **07563-7130**): From its rustic Thai-style log cabin exterior, to guest rooms with Chinese tiled floors, stucco walls pressed with tiny shells, canopy beds with seashell garlands, and odd slate

tiled bathrooms, the Phra-Nang never fails to delight. See p. 266.

- **Lotus Village** (Sukhothai; ✆ **05562-1484**): An atmospheric guesthouse with fine, raised bungalows of teak and a certain mellow malaise that makes the place appealing (not far from the market and city center). See p. 289.

- **Cabbages & Condoms** (Pattaya; ✆ **03825-0556**): A minihilltop resort with affordable rooms, Cabbages and Condoms touts its rural development and HIV protection mission all the while offering a great atmospheric stay outside of kooky Pattaya. See p. 167.

- **River View Lodge** (Chiang Mai; ✆ **05327-1109**): A longtime Frommer's favorite, this quirky hotel looks over the Mae Ping River at the center of town, close to the Night Bazaar. See p. 317.

- **Tamarind Village** (Chiang Mai; ✆ **05341-8896**): New on the scene and a masterful little escape within an enclosed compound right in the center of the old city in Chiang Mai,

Tamarind Village is budget boutique and quite cozy in a surprisingly pleasant blend of smoothed concrete, rattan matting, and local fabrics and carving. See p. 319.

- **The Golden Triangle Inn** (Chiang Rai; ✆ **05371-1339**): One of the older choices in Chiang Rai, Golden Triangle keeps it simple and personalized. Preserving gardens and maintaining quaint guest rooms, the staff goes out of its way to make your stay enjoyable. See p. 359.

- **Belle Villa** (Pai; ✆ **05369-8226**): On the outskirts of shanti-shanti Pai in the far north of Thailand, Belle Villa is cozy upscale riverside bungalows, a pool, and dining. Private, comfortable, and beautiful views. See p. 347.

- **Fern Resort** (Mae Hong Son; ✆ 05368-0001): You're well off the beaten path, and the place is just a collection of mid-range bungalows, but the setting is lovely and you can go on self-guided hikes with the resort's bevy of dogs. See p. 352.

6 The Best Fine Dining

- **Le Normandie** (Oriental Hotel, Bangkok; ✆ **02236-0400**): The formal service and setting are a bit formidable, the prices are steep, but the food at The Normandie is to die for. See p. 116.

- **Bed Supper Club** (Bangkok; ✆ **02651-3537**): Ever wanted to get in bed with Bangkok's young, hip elite? That's what it is all about at ultra-modern Bed Supper Club. Diners are feted from a limited menu nightly and sit (or lie) on huge, common beds, and nosh and hobnob to the tones of a house DJ. Great food and unique atmosphere. See p. 122.

- **Baan Kanitha** (Bangkok; ✆ **02253-4683**): Authentic Thai tempered to

Western tastes and presented in stylish fashion in a cozy, always busy venue that feels like old Indochina. See p. 122.

- **Sala Rim Nam** (Bangkok; ✆ **02437-2918**): Across the river from and managed by the Oriental Hotel, Sala Rim Nam is the best choice for authentic Thai dance and fine Thai buffet dining. See p. 128.

- **New York Steakhouse** (Bangkok; ✆ **02656-9798**): Just closed the deal and want to celebrate (or impress)? This authentic steakhouse at the JW Marriott is where to do it up right. Imported steaks, wines, and ales. Nothing like it in town. See p. 123.

- **Mom Tri's Boathouse & Villa Royale aka The Boathouse** (Boathouse Inn, Phuket; ✆ **07633-0015**): While there are other more formal dining experiences on the island, the Boathouse Inn has first-class cuisine—so delicious, travelers enroll in their cookery school to learn their secrets. Wine lovers appreciate their fine selection of labels. See p. 251.
- **Le Coq d'Or** (Chiang Mai; ✆ **05328-2024**): Have your French cuisine in a delightful old British country house in northern Thailand. Coq d'Or's menu is limited, but each offering is done to perfection. See p. 321.
- **Le Grand Lanna** (Chiang Mai; ✆ **05326-2569**): Fine Thai dining at affordable prices, this longtime favorite is a stylish setup, complete with live Thai music and dance, and great for a romantic evening. See p. 324.

7 The Best Small Restaurants

- **May Kaidee** (Bangkok; ✆ **02629-4839**): It is just tables in an alley-way, and you choose from a limited picture menu, writing your own order (and the service is hit or miss), but friendly May serves up some of the best authentic Thai food going, and it's all vegetarian to boot. See p. 127.
- **Le Bouchon** (Bangkok; ✆ **02234-9109**): A real find, this hole in the wall fine French restaurant is in the thick of seedy Patpong. Real French, a long wine list, and a hoot to get there down the busy red-light soi.
- **Somboon Seafood** (Bangkok; ✆ **02233-3104**): A unique local spot, four floors of chaos every evening and a crab curry to die for.
- **Lemongrass** (Bangkok; ✆ **02258-8637**): Real Thai served Western-style in an atmospheric storefront just a stone's throw from the Emporium.
- **Ka Jok See** (Phuket Town; ✆ **07621-7903**): A unique one, Ka Jok See—smart decor, chic and elite, and very, very good Thai food. The kind of hush-hush upscale joint that attracts hotel GMs and mafia Dons. See p. 254.
- **Tatanka** (Phuket; ✆ **07632-4349**): Just outside of the luxurious Laguna Beach Complex, Phuket's upscale community of resorts, Tatanka is the answer to dull hotel restaurants, a panoply of international tastes in a constantly evolving menu. Worth the trip from other beaches. See p. 253.
- **The Mangrove** (Koh Samui; ✆ **07742-7584**): With a roster of daily specials dreamed up by a vibrant husband-and-wife team, the Mangrove is the best fine dining choice on the island. Don't miss it (out by the airport).
- **Itsara** (Hua Hin; ✆ **03253-0574**): Set in a 1920s era villa at seaside, this Thai and seafood restaurant is a local favorite and a fun evening. See p. 187.
- **Dream Café** (Sukhothai; ✆ **05561-2081**): With a quiet courtyard out back, and cool indoor seating amid decor that is more like an old carved temple, little Dream Café is a fun find and a great place to relax after a day of temple touring. See p. 290.
- **Khaomao-Khaofang Restaurant** (Mae Sot; ✆ **05553-2483**): As much an oddity as it is a restaurant, the organic-themed decor of the upscale Khaomao-Khaofang would be wonderfully chic in Bangkok or Chiang Mai, but it comes off as somehow otherworldly in tiny Mae Sot, as do the portraits of Thailand's best and brightest who have visited. The place is out in the boonies on the Burmese border and the upscale design couldn't be more out of place, but the food is great

and the atmosphere is laid-back, if a bit surreal. See p. 295.

- **The Whole Earth** (Chiang Mai; ⓒ **05328-2463**): Real Thai, Indian, and great vegetarian food served in a quiet *sala* at the city center. See p. 324.
- **The House** (Chiang Mai; ⓒ **05341-9011**): Stylish and romantic, set in an old villa on the edge of the Old City of Chiang Mai, the cool and candlelit House serves innovative Pacific Rim Fusion cuisine. See p. 322.

- **Golden Triangle Café** (Chiang Rai; ⓒ **05371-1339**): The Thai menu here tops the list—almost a guidebook of Thai cuisine. Outside of Chiang Rai's busy market, this is the best dining going. A great meal, plus an education. See p. 359.
- **Baan Benjarong** (Pai; ⓒ **05369-8010**): Find this little place if you're in far northern Pai: a great feed of authentic local cuisine for very little. See p. 348.

8 The Best Party Beaches

- **Patong Beach** (Phuket): The busiest beachside strip on Phuket, Patong is a great place for shopping, dining, and the nightlife. Though a bit seedy along some side streets, it is a lot of fun and kicks late every night. The beach isn't the greatest, but it is a good area to yip it up at night. See chapter 9.
- **Chaweng Beach** (Koh Samui): If you like the beach, but don't want to feel like you're marooned, then Chaweng has all the action you're looking for. With countless dining options, shopping, nightlife choices, and activities (and lots of tourists enjoying the same), Chaweng can be a lot of fun and parties late into the night with some raucous little clubs and young crowds. Comparisons with Patong (on Phuket island) are apt. See chapter 9.

- **Haad Rin** (Ko Phangan): People still talk about it in hushed tones, but the infamous Full Moon Parties on Ko Phangan's Haad Rin have been attracting crowds of rave babies in the thousands. Drug busts are on the rise and the parties are becoming a more "packaged" experience than the more grass-roots hoedowns they once were, but it is where to get your proverbial "freak on" in Thailand. See chapter 9.
- **Pattaya** (Pattaya, Eastern Seaboard): The infamous red-light capital of Thailand, Pattaya's very origins were as a base for U.S. troops on R and R from fighting in Vietnam, and the city still has a certain "last stop before hell" feel to it. The go-gos and beer bars of Pattaya attract guys from all over the world. See chapter 7.

9 The Best Outdoor Adventures

- **Trekking** (Northern Thailand): A top draw for would-be adventurers, trekking is a great way to get out of the maze and get up among lush jungle terrain and meet with unique cultural experiences in hill-tribe villages. See the many options about Thailand's far north in chapters 11 through 14.

- **Rock Climbing at Raillay Beach** (Krabi): The dynamic karst cliffs above Krabi's Raillay beach make for some of the best sport rock-climbing in the world. But you don't have to be an expert. Beginners are welcome to sign up for an intro course and enjoy the challenge and the breathtaking views from on high. See chapter 9.

- **Scuba Diving:** If you're not certified, Thailand is a great place to do it; scuba services are affordable yet offer a high standard of safety, and many large outfitters have long track-records in the business and experienced expat staff. The most popular centers—Phuket, Ko Phi Phi, Koh Samui, and nearby Ko Tao (almost strictly a divers island)—have the largest concentration of operators to beautiful coral sites with lots of marine life. The best scuba operators offer all levels of PADI courses, daily junkets, and longer stays on liveaboard trips—even short introduction dives for beginners. See chapters 7, 8, and 9.

- **Snorkeling just about anywhere:** With huge living reefs and other odd creatures close to the water's surface, snorkeling in both the Andaman Sea and the Gulf of Thailand opens up under-the-sea wonders to anybody who can swim (or even just float). Check out Phuket's bays, Ko Phi Phi, areas around Krabi, Koh Samui, and islands along the eastern seaboard. See chapters 7, 8, and 9.

- **White-Water Rafting** (Pai): Paddle through protected forests and along canyon walls lined with fossils and be carried over wild rapids as well as beautiful calmer stretches. Thai Adventure Rafting organizes exciting but safe tours from their office in laid-back little Pai. See chapter 13.

10 The Best of Natural Thailand

- **Phang Nga Bay** (near Phuket): Imagine yourself in a Chinese scroll painting. Above you are hundreds of towering cliffs, jagged limestone towers peppered with lonely trees—each one an island in a peaceful bay. This place has gotten so sadly touristy, but it really is very beautiful. You won't believe your eyes. See chapter 9.

- **The Road from Chiang Mai to Mae Hong Son:** Mountaintops open onto views of the misty hills all the way to Myanmar (Burma), while valleys are filled with pleasant farming communities and shimmering rice paddies. The overland route to this Myanmar border town leads you through the foothills of the Himalayas. See chapter 12.

- **Khao Yai National Park** (northeast): Thailand's oldest and most visited park still supports lots of wildlife, from elephants and even tigers to more than 300 species of birds. Hike along nature trails, or camp out and hold a vigil in high watchtowers at night, the best time to see the nocturnal creatures in action. See chapter 6.

- **Khao Sok** (from Surat Thani or Phuket): Best visited by kayak (a few companies arrange custom trips; try Paddle Asia, © **07631-1222**; www. paddleasia.com), the hilly jungles and hidden bays of Khao Sok are your best chance to witness rare jungle animals like tapirs, sloths, bears, and beautiful hornbills. See "Day Trips from Surat Thani" in chapter 8.

11 The Best Offbeat Vacation Activities

- **Northern Thailand by Motorcycle:** Be careful (riding a bike is statistically the most dangerous thing going in the kingdom), but travel by motorbike is a great way to see the countryside. With good paved roads, plenty of gasoline stations and rest stops, and friendly folks along the way to lend a hand, touring the kingdom by motorcycle is exhilarating. It's best around the Mae Hong Son Loop northwest of Chiang Mai, but anywhere will do

(Isan is great to explore). Mountain passes, wandering rivers, small villages and towns, the rural roads of the Thai north pass by natural wonders and temples glorious and pedestrian, and the beauty of riding a motorbike is that you can make your own itinerary, stop and smell the flowers, or hit the accelerator and get bugs in your teeth. Get your motor running. See chapters 11 through 14.

- **Novice monk and meditation programs:** Almost every Thai man enters the sangha, or monkhood, for some period of time, usually just a few weeks as a young man and again later, during marriage. Since the first Western spiritual seekers started coming in droves to Thailand in the 1970s and '80s, many monasteries opened their doors to foreign laypeople interested in practicing meditation. Opportunities abound in Thailand for joining meditation courses of varying length and intensity, most in the Theravada Buddhist tradition of Vipassana, or "Insight" meditation. In the south, try Wat Suan Mohk (near Surat Thani) or Wat Kow Thom (on Ko Phangan). In the north, try Wat Rampoeng (near Chiang Mai). In Bangkok, try Wat Mahathat.

- **Become an Elephant Mahout** (Lampang, near Chiang Mai; © 05422-9042): Sign-up for a homestay or longer trek with the Young Elephant Training Center and you'll get down and dirty with pachyderms; this is not a picnic or pony ride. You'll be given a set of baggy elephant-trainer togs and taught the language of the elephants (a mix of the Thai and Karen languages). Participants spend the better part of the day caring for the animals, feeding and washing them, as well as learning all that you need to hop on the neck (no basket ride here) and steer your own two tons of elephant. On multiday treks, you'll be assigned your own animal and ride alone.

- **One Nose-job or Two?** (Phuket): **Medical Tourism** is all the rage in Thailand, and many folks find that the cost and quality of many procedures (particularly cosmetic work) is so good in Thailand that it is worth the trip, and the savings affords you a groovy recovery on the beach.

12 The Best Shopping

- **Chatuchak Weekend Market** (Bangkok): A tourist attraction in its own right, Thailand's largest market is a never-ending village of bargains—from fighting cocks to clothing, tools, antiques, and so much more. Don't get lost (you will). See chapter 6.

- **Suan Lum Night Market** (Bangkok): Newly set up near Lumpini (and soon a stop on the subway), the Suan Lum Night Market is a better choice, especially with the kids, than a visit to the crazy night market in the red-light area of Patpong. At Suan Lum, you can find similar goods to those at the Weekend Market, as well as some newer high-end shops. See chapter 6.

- **Night Bazaar** (Chiang Mai): Tribal crafts and locally produced items line Chang Klan Road and the giant market building—find bags, clothes, jewelry, and trinkets, plus cheap knockoffs. Don't forget to bargain. See chapter 12.

- **Sankampaeng Road** (Chiang Mai): This 9 kilometer (5½-mile) stretch of highway is home to shops, showrooms, and factories with Thailand's best handicrafts—bronze and silver, furniture, ceramics, antiques, umbrellas, silks and cottons, and paper goods. See chapter 13.

13 The Most Intriguing Archaeological Sights

- **Ayuthaya:** The former capital of Siam was one of the world's largest and most sophisticated cities before it was sacked by the Burmese in 1756. Today it remains one of Thailand's greatest historical treasures, with abundant evidence of its former grandeur. It is easily reached in a day trip from Bangkok. See chapter 6.

- **Sukhothai:** Founded in 1238, Sukhothai (The Dawn of Happiness) was a capital of an early Thai kingdom. Many of the ruins of this religious and cultural center are faithfully preserved and well maintained in an idyllic setting. See chapter 11.

14 The Best Museums

- **The National Museum** (Bangkok): Simply the biggest and best repository of the nation's treasures. Objects from throughout Thailand's long and various history include beautiful stone carvings of Hindu deities, exquisite Buddha images, gold jewelry, ceramics, royal costumes, wood carvings, musical instruments, and more. See p. 135.

- **The Hall of Opium** (Near Chiang Saen at the Golden Triangle): Newly opened to replace a tiny roadside shack that drew tourists for years to the same purpose: explaining the cultivation process and history of opium growth in the Golden Triangle Region. This new museum, supported by the royal family, is a large, luxurious campus overlooking the Mekong and displays are quite hightech and informative. See p. 363.

15 The Best Small Towns

- **Pai:** Not your typical tiny mountain-valley farming village, Pai is a favorite for budget travelers who want to put their feet up and relax. The scenery is gorgeous, bungalows are cheap, food is good—and the nightlife is surprisingly fun. You will want to stay longer than you planned. See chapter 13.

- **Mae Sot:** A charming little border town—you can jump over to Burma on a day pass, or stay and shop for Burmese trinkets in the market on the Thailand side of the river. Small and friendly, this town is very accessible to foreigners. See chapter 10.

- **Nong Khai** (Isan): A busy bordertown perched on the edge of the Friendship Bridge between Thailand and Laos, Nong Khai has a sprawling central market and supports some quiet little neighborhoods where budget guesthouses kind of suck you in. Day trips by bicycle to the unique sculpture gardens near town or, much further afield by car or bus to an ancient archeological oddity will keep you busy, but you may not want to be; this is a good place to put your feet up and reflect while watching the mighty Mekong flow past. See chapter 14.

16 The Most Fascinating Temples

- **Wat Phra Kaeo** (Bangkok): With its flamboyant colors and rich details, this shrine is a magnificent setting for Thailand's most revered image, the Emerald Buddha. Inside the main temple building, a profusion of offerings surrounds the pedestal that supports the tiny image. See p. 137.

- **Wat Arun** (Thonburi/Bangkok): The golden Temple of Dawn shimmers in the sunrise across the Chao Praya River from Bangkok, but the sunset is even better still. As you climb its steep central *prang* (tower), you get a close view of the porcelain pieces that make its floral design. See p. 139.

- **Wat Yai Chai Mongkon** (Phitsanulok): One of the most holy temples in the country, Wat Yai is home to the Phra Buddha Chinarat image, cast in bronze. One of the few remaining Sukhothai images, this one is the prototype for many replicas. Outside, the temple complex hums with activity, and many Thais make the pilgrimage here. See p. 278.

- **Wat Mahathat** (Nakhon Si Thammarat): The city is the center of southern Buddhism in Thailand—the first Thai capital to convert to Theravada Buddhism, and a major influence on the kingdoms to follow. The main *chedi* contains a relic of the Buddha brought from Sri Lanka more than a millennium ago. See p. 278.

- **Wat Ko Keo Suttharam** (Phetchaburi): The walls of the main hall were painted in the 1730s, during the Kingdom of Ayuthaya, and while the murals are fading, you can still make out the images of the earliest Westerners to come to the country. See p. 189.

- **The Erawan Shrine** (Bangkok): Not a site notable for its size or superstructure, the Erawan Shrine is famed for the veracity of its devotees. Located near Chit Lom BTS station in the center of town, few Thai people pass without offering a bow, or *wai,* in reverence. See p. 139.

2

Planning Your Trip to Thailand

Here you'll find all of the nuts and bolts on how to get there, where and when to visit, and what documents you'll need, as well as pointers to other sources of information that can make the difference between a smooth or bumpy ride.

1 The Regions in Brief

The Thais compare their land to the shape of an elephant's head, seen in profile, facing west. Thailand is roughly equidistant from China and India; centuries of migration from southern China and trade contacts with India brought tremendous influences from each of these Asian centers. Located in the center of Indochina, Thailand borders Myanmar (Burma) to the north and west, Laos to the northeast, Cambodia (Kampuchea) to the east, and Malaysia to the south. Its southwestern coast stretches along the Andaman Sea, and its southern and southeastern coastlines border the Gulf of Thailand. Thailand covers roughly 466,200 sq. km (180,000 sq. miles) and is divided into six major geographic zones.

WESTERN THAILAND West of Bangkok, mountains and valleys are carved by the Kwai River, the site of the infamous World War II "Death Railway," named for the 12,000 prisoners of war who died in Japanese labor camps during its construction. A bridge over the river near Kanchanaburi was made famous by the film *Bridge on the River Kwai,* and is a stop on the lists of many travelers who come to learn about this story in the war's history, witness the site, and pay respects to those whose lives were lost. Just to the north of Bangkok (which is in every way the center of the country, along the Chao Praya River banks) is Ayuthaya, Thailand's capital after Sukhothai.

THE SOUTHEASTERN COAST The southeastern coast is lined with seaside resorts; first Pattaya and then the islands Ko Samet and Ko Chang. Farther east, in the mountains, is Thailand's greatest concentration of sapphire and ruby mines. Recently, natural gas deposits were discovered off the southeastern coast, and the government has constructed two new deep-water ports that will soon be accessible by rail, easing some of the industrial pressure on Bangkok.

THE SOUTHERN PENINSULA A long, narrow peninsula (the elephant's trunk) extends south to the Malaysian border, with the Andaman Sea on the west and the Gulf of Thailand on the east. The eastern coastline along the gulf extends more than 1,811km (1,125 miles); the western shoreline runs 716km (445 miles) along the Andaman Sea. This region is the most tropical in the country, with heavy rainfall during the monsoons. The northeast monsoon, roughly from November to April, brings clear weather and calm seas to the west coast; the southwest monsoon, March to October, brings similar conditions to the east coast.

There are glamorous beach resorts here, such as the western islands of Phuket and nearby Ko Pi Pi, Krabi, and Ko Tarutao. Koh Samui, off the east coast, is comparable to Phuket. The south is also interesting as the home of the majority of Thailand's Muslim minority, who have put quite a stamp on the southernmost provinces. The primary industries in this region are tin mining, rubber production, coconut and oil palm plantations, fishing, and, of course, tourism.

THE CENTRAL PLAIN Thailand's central plain is an extremely fertile region, providing the country and the world with much of its abundant rice crop. The main city of the central plain is Phitsanulok, northeast of which are the impressive remains of Sukhothai, Thailand's first capital, and the ancient city of Si Satchanalai; to the south is Lopburi, an ancient Mon/Khmer settlement.

ISAN The broad and relatively infertile northeast plateau (the ear of the elephant), Isan is the least developed region in Thailand, bordered by the Mekong River (*Mae Nam Khong* in Thai). One of the country's four great rivers, the Mekong separates the country from neighboring Laos on the north and northeast boundaries. The people of Isan share a cultural similarity with Laos, but you needn't travel to Isan to meet them. Many young Isan people find their way to the capital city for work. Isan is dusty in the cool winter and muddy during the summer monsoon. The region contains the most ancient Bronze Age village in the country (if not the world), more than 5,600 years old, at Ban Chiang. There are also major Khmer ruins at Phimai, outside Khorat, and outside Surin and Buriram. Other than potash mining and subsistence farming, the region has little economic development, though recently there has been some growth of industry in and around Khorat and Khon Kaen.

NORTHERN THAILAND The north (the forehead of the elephant) is a relatively cool mountainous region at the foothills of the Himalayas, where elephants have traditionally provided the heavy labor needed to harvest teak and other hardwoods. In the past, this region was under control of the powerful and influential Lanna Kingdom. Today it is largely populated by Tai Yai people, the original Thai people who migrated from southern China in the first centuries of the millennium, yet the region is more famous for the colorful hill-tribe people who dwell in the jungles high in the mountains. Like most of Thailand, the cool hills in the north are well suited for farming, particularly for strawberries, asparagus, peaches, litchis, and other fruits. At higher elevations many hill-tribe farmers cultivate opium poppies, though agricultural programs advanced by Thailand's royal family are introducing more productive crops. (The people who grow addictive crops rarely profit in the trade and, like everyone else, they are often ruined by them.) The cooler temperatures also make the north a favorite destination for Thais on holiday, especially from March to May, when the rest of the country is scorching. The major cities in the north are Chiang Mai, Chiang Rai, Lamphun, Lampang, and Mae Hong Son.

2 Entry Requirements & Customs

ENTRY REQUIREMENTS

PASSPORTS & VISAS All visitors to Thailand must carry a valid **passport** with **proof of onward passage** (either a return or through ticket). Visa applications are not required if you are staying less than 30 days and are a national of 1 of 41 designated countries, including Australia,

Thailand

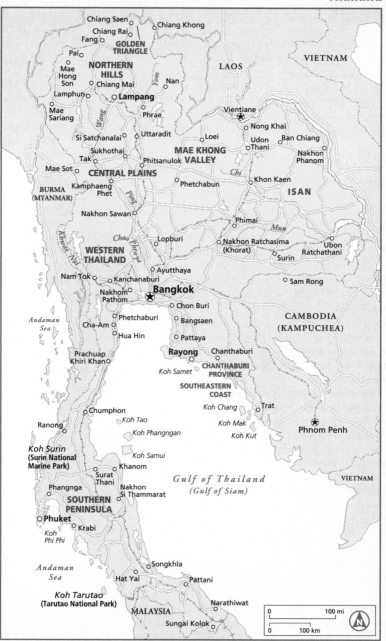

Canada, Ireland, New Zealand, the United Kingdom, and the United States (New Zealanders may stay up to 3 months).

The **Immigration Division of the Royal Thai Police Department** is found at 507 Soi Suan Phu (off Sathorn Tai Rd. South of Silom area and Sala Daeng BTS station); © **02287-3101.** The price of all visa extensions was just raised to 1,900B ($46), an increase of 400%, making 10-day extensions of 30-day visas uneconomical; it is best to always have a proper visa and exit the country by the date stamped in your passport (or make the proverbial "visa-run" over border-points with Myanmar, Laos, Cambodia or Malaysia). Visitors planning to stay for longer than a month can arrange 60-day tourist visas at embassies overseas for a cost of 1,900B ($46; renewable for an additional 30 days for another 1,900B/ $46). If you overstay your visa, you will be charged 200B ($4.90) per day, payable when exiting the kingdom, but overstays are best avoided. Longer overstays are punishable by a 20,000B ($490) fine or a stay in immigration jail. For more information about visas, check this useful site: www.thaivisa.com.

Warning: Many small storefronts and travel agencies offer visa services, saying they will run your passport over the border and arrange a new visa; these companies are disreputable and have been known to supply bogus visas that land customers in jail. Don't let your passport travel without you (it is illegal).

THAI EMBASSIES OVERSEAS In the **United States,** contact the **Royal Thai Embassy,** 1024 Wisconsin Ave. NW, Suite 401, Washington, DC 20007 (© **202/944-3600;** fax 202/944-3611); **The Permanent Mission of Thailand** to the United Nations, 351 E. 52nd St., New York, NY 10022 (© **212/754-2230;** fax 212/754-2535); the **Royal Thai Consulate-General,** 801 N. La Brea Ave., Los Angeles, CA 90038 (© **213/ 937-1894;** fax 213/937-5987); or the **Royal Thai Consulate General,** 35 E. Wacker Dr., Suite 1834, Chicago, IL 60601 (© **312/236-2447;** fax 312/236-1906). In **Canada,** contact the **Royal Thai Embassy,** 180 Island Park Dr., Ottawa, Ontario K1Y OA2 (© **613/722-4444;** fax 613/722-6624); or the **Royal Thai Embassy,** 106-736 Granville St., Vancouver, BC V6Z 1G4 (© **604/687-1143;** fax 604/687-4434). In **Australia,** contact the **Royal Thai Embassy,** 111 Empire Circuit Yarralumla, ACT 2600 Canberra (© **02/6273-1149;** fax 02/ 6273-1518); or the **Royal Thai Consulate General,** 2nd floor, 75-77 Pitt St., Sydney, NSW 2000 (© **02/9241-2120;** fax 02/9247-8312). In **New Zealand,** contact the **Royal Thai Embassy,** 2 Cook St., Karori, P.O. Box 17226, Wellington (© **644/476-8618;** fax 644/476-3677). In the **United Kingdom,** contact the **Royal Thai Embassy,** 29-30 Queens Gate, London (© **171/589-0173;** fax 171/ 823-9695, enquiries@thaiconsul-uk.com).

MEDICAL REQUIREMENTS No inoculations or vaccinations are required unless you are coming from or passing through areas infected with yellow fever. Yellow fever certificates are required for those coming from 14 African and South American countries. Check at the consulate or embassy for up-to-date information about health certificates that may be required for entry.

A NOTE ON PASSPORTS For information on how to get a passport, go to "Passports" in the "Fast Facts" section of this chapter—the websites listed provide downloadable passport applications as well as the current fees for processing passport applications. For an up-to-date, country-by-country listing of passport requirements around the world, go to the "Foreign Entry Requirement" Web page of the U.S. State Department at **travel.state.gov.**

Tips Passport Savvy

Allow plenty of time before your trip to apply for a passport; processing normally takes 3 weeks but can take longer during busy periods (especially spring). And keep in mind that if you need a passport in a hurry, you'll pay a higher processing fee. When traveling, safeguard your passport in an inconspicuous, inaccessible place like a money belt, and keep a copy of the critical pages with your passport number in a separate place. If you lose your passport, visit the nearest consulate or embassy of your native country as soon as possible for a replacement.

CUSTOMS
WHAT YOU CAN BRING INTO THAILAND

It is prohibited by law to bring the following items into Thailand: narcotics, pornography, firearms and ammunition, and agricultural products. Tourists are allowed to enter the country with 1 liter of alcohol and 200 cigarettes (or 250g of cigars or smoking tobacco) per adult, duty free. Photographic equipment (one still, video, or movie camera, plus five rolls of still film or three rolls of 8mm or 16mm motion-picture film—by the way, the film rule is not strictly enforced), and "professional instruments" (typewriter, personal computer, and so on) are allowed, provided they are taken out of the country on departure. Tourists are permitted to take gold out of the country without export duty, unless you are dealing in import/export-related business.

WHAT YOU CAN TAKE HOME FROM THAILAND

Pay more attention to what you can in fact import to your home country, as Thai customs as you exit the kingdom are rather lax. One exception is the following rule about Thai cultural treasures.

EXPORT OF ANTIQUES OR ART FROM THAILAND The government wants to keep track of all pieces of art and antiquity that leave the kingdom, and so special permission is required for removing these items from the country. It is forbidden to take antique or authentic Buddha images, Bodhisattva images, or fragments thereof out of the country.

You will be required to submit the object, two 5-by-7-inch photographs of the front view of the object, your passport, and a photocopy of your passport notarized by your home embassy. The authorization process takes 8 days.

For further details contact the **Department of Fine Arts,** Na Phra That Road, next to Thammasat University (✆ **02221-7811** or 02225-2652), open weekdays 9am to 4pm.

Please note: This is only an issue if the object in question is an antique, especially one that has been removed from a temple or palace, or a piece that has particular historic value to the kingdom. If you purchase a small Buddha image or reproduction, whether an amulet or a statue, you can just ship it or pack it in your bag. Any antique dealer will be able to notify you about which images require special permission.

Returning **U.S. citizens** who have been away for at least 48 hours are allowed to bring back, once every 30 days, $800 worth of merchandise duty-free. You'll pay a flat rate of duty on the next $1,000 worth of purchases. Any dollar amount beyond that is subject to duties at whatever rates apply. On mailed gifts, the duty-free limit is $200. Be sure to keep your receipts or purchases accessible to expedite the declaration process. **Note:** If you owe duty, you are required to pay on your arrival in the United States—either by cash, personal check, government or traveler's check, or money order (and, in some locations, a Visa or MasterCard).

To avoid paying duty on foreign-made personal items you owned before your trip, bring along a bill of sale, insurance policy, jeweler's appraisal, or receipts of purchase. Or you can register items that can be readily identified by a permanently affixed serial number or marking—think laptop computers, cameras, and CD players—with Customs before you leave. Take the items to the nearest Customs office or register them with Customs at the airport from which you're departing. You'll receive, at no cost, a Certificate of Registration, which allows duty-free entry for the life of the item.

With some exceptions, you cannot bring fresh fruits and vegetables into the United States. For specifics on what you can bring back, download the invaluable free pamphlet *Know Before You Go* online at **www.cbp.gov**. (Click on "Travel," and then click on "Know Before You Go! Online Brochure.") Or contact the **U.S. Customs & Border Protection (CBP),** 1300 Pennsylvania Ave., NW, Washington, DC 20229 (© 877/287-8667) and request the pamphlet.

For a clear summary of **Canadian** rules, write for the booklet *I Declare,* issued by the **Canada Border Services Agency** (© 800/461-9999 in Canada, or 204/983-3500; www.cbsa-asfc.gc.ca). Canada allows its citizens a C$750 exemption, and you're allowed to bring back duty-free 200 cigarettes, 50 cigars or cigarillos, 200 tobacco sticks, and 200g manufactured tobacco, 53 imperial ounces of wine, *or* 40 imperial ounces of liquor, *or* 8.5 liters of beer or ale. In addition, you're allowed to mail gifts to Canada valued at less than C$60 a day, provided they're unsolicited and don't contain alcohol or tobacco (write on the package "Unsolicited gift, under $60 value"). All valuables should be declared on the Y-38 form before departure from Canada, including serial numbers of valuables you already own, such as expensive foreign cameras. *Note:* The C$750 exemption can only be used once a year and only after an absence of 7 days.

U.K. citizens returning from **a non-EU country** have a customs allowance of: 200 cigarettes, *or* 100 cigarillos, *or* 50 cigars; or 250 grams of smoking tobacco; 2 liters of still table wine; 1 liter of spirits or strong liqueurs (over 22% volume); *or* 2 liters of fortified wine, sparkling wine or other liqueurs; 60cc (ml) perfume; 250cc (ml) of toilet water; and £145 worth of all other goods, including gifts and souvenirs. People under 17 cannot have the tobacco or alcohol allowance. For more information, contact HM Customs & Excise at © **0845/010-9000** (from outside the U.K., 020/8929-0152), or consult their website at www.hmrc.gov.uk.

The duty-free allowance in **Australia** is A$400 or, for those under 18, A$200. Citizens can bring in 250 cigarettes *or* 250 grams of loose tobacco, and 1,125 milliliters of alcohol. If you're returning with valuables you already own, such as foreign-made cameras, you should file form B263. A helpful brochure available from Australian consulates or Customs offices is *Know Before You Go.* For more information, call the **Australian Customs Service** at © **1300/363-263,** or log on to www.customs.gov.au.

The duty-free allowance for **New Zealand** is NZ$700. Citizens over 17 can bring in 200 cigarettes, *or* 50 cigars, *or* 250 grams of tobacco (or a mixture of all three if their combined weight doesn't exceed 250g); plus 4.5 liters of wine or beer, and 1.125 liters of liquor. New Zealand currency does not carry import or export restrictions. Fill out a certificate of export, listing the valuables you are taking out of the country; that way, you can bring them back without paying duty. Most questions are answered in a free pamphlet available at New Zealand consulates and Customs offices: *New Zealand Customs Guide for Travellers, Notice no. 4.* For more information, contact **New Zealand Customs,** The Customhouse, 17–21 Whitmore St., Box 2218, Wellington (© **04/473-6099** or 0800/428-786; www.customs.govt.nz).

3 Money

Travel in Thailand is very affordable, and budget travelers, the "Cheap Charlies" of the world (called *kee neow* in Thai), visit the kingdom as much for the slow pace of life as for the fact that they can get by quite well for just a fraction of living costs in most Western countries. Hotels and restaurants of comparable, if not better, quality than in most areas of the developed West come at a fraction of the price in Thailand.

It is rare that you'll be able to purchase Thai baht from overseas before any trip (and if so at a likely high rate of commission), and airport bank kiosks operate 24 hours to accommodate the myriad flights passing through Bangkok and Chiang Mai, so there is no need to exchange money before leaving.

CURRENCY

The Thai unit of currency is the **baht** (written B) divided into 100 **satang.** Little-used copper-colored coins represent 25 and 50 satang; silver-colored coins are 1B and 5B, and the larger 10B coin is silver with an inset copper center. Bank notes come in denominations of 20B (green), 50B (blue with a clear, plastic window), 100B (red), 500B (purple), and 1,000B (khaki).

There are no restrictions on the import of foreign currencies or traveler's checks, but you cannot export foreign currency in excess of 50,000B ($1,220) per person or 500,000B ($12,195) if exiting to a neighboring country.

CURRENCY EXCHANGE RATES

Before the currency crisis in July 1997, 1 U.S. dollar could buy you 25 Thai baht. During the worst of the crisis, the value was 55B to the U.S. dollar. Recent years have seen the Thai baht fluctuate from 44B per dollar to as little as 39B for a greenback. Amounts listed throughout this book are calculated at **$1 = 41B.** For the most up-to-date figures, see **www.xe.com/ucc.**

Some travelers like to change some money—just enough to cover airport incidentals and transportation to your hotel—before leaving home (though don't expect the exchange rate to be ideal). You can sometimes buy Thai baht at your local American Express or Thomas Cook office or at your bank, but most airport exchange kiosks in Thailand are open 24 hours (and ATM machines are everywhere), and there is rarely a wait at the airport in Bangkok.

ATMs

The easiest and best way to get cash in Thailand is from an ATM. The **Cirrus** (© **800/424-7787;** www.mastercard. com) and **PLUS** (© **800/843-7587;** www. visa.com) networks span the kingdom. Look at the back of your bank card to see which network you're on, then call or check online for ATM locations in Thailand. Be sure you know your personal identification number (PIN) and daily withdrawal limit before you depart. *Note:* Remember that many banks impose a fee every time you use a card at another bank's ATM, and that fee can be higher for international transactions (up to $5 or more) than for domestic ones (where they're rarely more than $2). In addition, the bank from which you withdraw cash may charge its own fee. To compare banks' ATM fees within the U.S., use **www.bankrate.com**. For international withdrawal fees, ask your bank.

What Things Cost in Bangkok	Thai Baht	US$
Taxi from the airport to the city center including expressway toll	250	6.10
Local telephone call (private pay phone) per minute	3	0.07
Double at The Oriental (very expensive)	12,300	300
Double at The Royal Princess (moderate)	3,600	87.80
Double at the Atlanta (inexpensive)	500	12.20
Dinner for one, without wine, at Sala Thip (moderate)	700	17.07
Dinner for one, without wine, at Cabbages & Condoms (inexpensive)	350	8.54
Dinner for one, without wine, at a food court (inexpensive)	100	2.44
Bottle of beer at a hotel bar	150	3.66
Bottle of beer at a local bar	80	1.95
Coca-Cola	15	0.37
Cup of coffee	20–50	0.49–1.22
Roll of ASA 100 Kodacolor film, 36 exposures	120	2.93
Admission to the National Museum	40	0.98
Movie ticket	100–140	2.45–3.41

Most Thai banks are connected to the major ATM networks. The most likely access is at **Bangkok Bank, Thai Farmers Bank, Siam Commercial Bank,** and **Bank of Ayudhya,** each with major branches in every city and many small towns. For specific locations, see each town's "Fast Facts" listing.

You can also get cash advances on your credit card at an ATM. Keep in mind that credit card companies try to protect themselves from theft by limiting the funds someone can withdraw outside their home country, so call your credit card company before you leave home to let them know you'll be traveling abroad. And keep in mind that you'll pay interest from the moment of your withdrawal, even if you pay your monthly bills on time.

TRAVELER'S CHECKS

Traveler's checks are something of an anachronism from the days before the ATM made cash accessible at any time. Given the fees you'll pay for ATM use at banks other than your own, however, you might be better off with traveler's checks if you're withdrawing money often.

You can get traveler's checks at almost any bank. **American Express** offers denominations of $20, $50, $100, $500, and (for cardholders only) $1,000. You'll pay a service charge ranging from 1% to 4%. You can also get American Express traveler's checks over the phone by calling © **800/221-7282;** Amex gold and platinum cardholders who use this number are exempt from the 1% fee.

Visa offers traveler's checks at Citibank locations nationwide, as well as at several other banks. The service charge ranges between 1.5% and 2%; checks come in denominations of $20, $50, $100, $500, and $1,000. Call © **800/732-1322** for information. AAA members can obtain

The Baht, the U.S. Dollar, the Euro, the Australian Dollar & the British Pound

Thai B	US$	Euro€	A$	UK£
1	0.02	0.02	0.03	0.01
5	0.12	0.10	0.16	0.07
10	0.24	0.20	0.32	0.13
20	0.49	0.40	0.65	0.27
50	1.22	1.01	1.62	0.69
100	2.44	2.03	3.25	1.38
500	12.20	10.19	16.30	6.93
1,000	24.39	20.36	32.58	13.85
5,000	121.95	101.87	162.92	69.23
10,000	243.90	203.57	325.63	138.50

Visa checks for a $9.95 fee (for checks up to $1,500) at most AAA offices or by calling ☎ 866/339-3378. MasterCard also offers traveler's checks. Call ☎ 800/223-9920 for a location near you.

American Express, Thomas Cook, Visa, and MasterCard offer foreign currency traveler's checks. You'll pay the rate of exchange at the time of your purchase (so it is a good idea to monitor the rate before you buy), and most companies charge a transaction fee per order (and a shipping fee if you order online).

If you do choose to carry traveler's checks, keep a record of their serial numbers separate from your checks in the event that they are stolen or lost. You'll get a refund faster if you know the numbers.

In Thailand, traveler's checks are easily exchanged in most banks, hotels, tourist-oriented shops, and at the many exchange counters (best rates are at the bank).

CREDIT CARDS

Credit cards are another safe way to carry money. They also provide a convenient record of all your expenses, and they generally offer relatively good exchange rates. You can also withdraw cash advances from your credit cards at banks or ATMs, provided you know your PIN. If you don't know yours, call the number on the back of your credit card and ask the bank to send it to you. It usually takes 5 to 7 business days, though some banks will provide the number over the phone if you tell them your mother's maiden name or some other personal information.

Keep in mind that many banks now assess a 1 to 3% "transaction fee" on all charges you incur abroad (whether you're using the local currency or U.S. dollars). But credit cards still may be the smart way to go when you factor in things like exorbitant ATM fees and the higher exchange rates and service fees you'll pay with traveler's checks.

Nearly all international hotels and larger businesses accept major credit cards. Despite protest from credit card companies, many smaller establishments add a 3% to 5% surcharge for payment by credit card (this above and beyond any fees levied by your credit company). Be sure to ask before proffering your card. Take care when using your card: Don't let it out of your sight, even for a moment, and be sure to keep all receipts. Never leave your cards with others for safekeeping (such as during a trek). If you don't

---

Tips **Dear Visa: I'm Off to Bangkok!**

Some credit card companies recommend that you notify them of any impending trip abroad so that they don't become suspicious of foreign transactions and block your charges. If you don't call your credit card company in advance, you can still call the card's toll-free emergency number (see "Fast Facts," p. 62) if a charge is refused—provided you remember to carry the phone number with you. Perhaps the most important lesson here is to carry more than one card, so you have a backup.

---

want to carry them, put them in a hotel safe. There have been numerous reports of charges having been made while cards were left at guesthouses, or small shops running extra slips against a card. So traveler's checks might be the safest bet. In smaller towns and remote provinces, the baht will be the only acceptable currency.

For tips and telephone numbers to call if your wallet is stolen or lost, go to "Lost & Found" in the "Fast Facts" section of this chapter. To report a lost or stolen credit card in Thailand, call these service lines: **American Express** (© 02273-5544); **Diners Club** (© 02238-3660) **MasterCard** (© 02260-8572); and **Visa** (© 02256-7326).

4 When to Go

Take a close look at the weather information below, as an ill-planned trip can mean rain or seas too rough for diving or beach activity. The high season for tourism throughout the kingdom is the winter period, a cool season from November through February. Prices go up and hotels fill in high season, so be sure to make reservations well in advance. Off-season weather, however, is not intolerable, and some travelers report joyfully trading the crowded beaches and high prices of high season for a bit of off-season discomfort, the odd rainy afternoon or more sultry temperatures, and a significant savings, not to mention some elbow room.

Thailand has two distinct climate zones: **tropical** in the south, and **tropical savanna** in the north. The northern and central areas of the country (including Bangkok) experience three distinct seasons. The **hot season** lasts from March to May, with temperatures averaging in the upper 90s Fahrenheit (mid-30s Celsius),

with April the hottest month. This period sees very little rain, if any at all. The **rainy season** begins in June and lasts until October; the average temperature is 84°F (29°C) with 90% humidity. While the rainy season brings frequent showers, it is rare for them to last for a whole day or for days on end. Daily showers will come in torrents, usually in the late afternoon or evening for maybe 3 or 4 hours—many times bringing floods. Trekking in the north is not recommended during this time. The **cool season,** from November through February, has temperatures from the high 70s to low 80s Fahrenheit (26°C), with moderate and infrequent rain showers. In the north during the cool season (which is also the peak season for tourism), day temperatures can be as low as 60°F (16°C) in Chiang Mai and 41°F (5°C) in the hills.

The **southern Malay Peninsula** has intermittent showers year-round, and daily ones during the rainy season (temperatures average in the low 80s/30°C). If you're traveling to Phuket or Koh Samui, it will be helpful to note that the two islands alternate peak seasons somewhat. Optimal weather on Phuket occurs between November and April, when the island welcomes the highest numbers of travelers and the most expensive resort rates. Alternately, Koh Samui's great weather lasts from about February to October. Refer to each destination's section for more information about peak seasons and weather patterns.

HOLIDAYS

Many holidays are based on the Thai lunar calendar, falling on the full moon of each month; check with the Tourism Authority of Thailand (TAT; www.tat. or.th) for the current year's schedule. Chapter 11, "Exploring Northern Thailand," includes a list of festivals and events specific to the north.

On national holidays, all government offices and some shops and offices are closed. All transport still runs on holidays, and restaurants and nightlife establishments are open with the exception of the beginning of Buddhist Lent in July, HM Queen Sirikit's birthday in August, and HM King Bhumibol's birthday in December, when almost all bars stop serving alcohol for the day.

January

Thailand celebrates New Year's Day the same as the rest of the world (nursing a hangover). In **late February or early March** (depending on the lunar cycle) is **Makha Bucha Day,** when temples celebrate the day 1,250 disciples spontaneously gathered to hear the Buddha preach his doctrine.

April

Chakri Memorial Day (Apr 6) commemorates the founding of the Chakri dynasty (the reigning dynasty).

Songkran is the New Year according to the Thai calendar, an event that begins on April 13 and lasts from 3 to 10 days. After honoring local abbots and family elders, folks hit the streets for massive water fights. Be warned—foreigners are the Thais' favorite targets, and areas like Khao San Road become playful, messy war zones where everyone gets soaked (police included) and then covered in colored powder. Water guns are available at all markets—arm thyself and have a blast!

May

National Labor Day falls on the 1st, **Coronation Day** (celebrating the coronation of HM King Bhumibol in 1950) is on the 5th, while the 14th is **Royal Ploughing Day,** the first day of the rice-planting cycle, which is celebrated with a traditional Brahman parade. **Visakha Bucha Day**—marking the birth, enlightenment, and death of the Buddha—will fall in **mid-May,** depending on the lunar calendar.

July

Thais celebrate the **Buddhist Lent** immediately following Asarnha Bucha Day in mid-July (depending on the Lunar Calendar) signaling the beginning of the rains' retreat and the 3-month period of meditation for all Buddhist monks—this was the day that the Buddha delivered his first sermon to the first five disciples.

August

August 12 honors the birthday of HM Queen Sirikit and also Mother's Day.

October

On **October 23, Chulalongkorn Day,** the country's favorite king, Rama V, is remembered.

November

Loy Krathong, in early **November,** is Thailand's most beautiful holiday, honoring the water spirit and serving as a day to wash away sins committed during the previous year. The most spectacular celebrations are in Ayuthaya, Sukhothai, and Chiang Mai.

December

December 5 marks HM King Bhumibol's birthday and Father's Day. And finally, December 10, Constitution Day, recognizes Thailand's first constitution in 1932.

Check with the Tourist Authority of Thailand (the TAT, hot line ℂ **1672;** www.tat.org, and listings in each chapter) for more information on the events listed below, as well as for other holidays celebrated by local people of various regions throughout Thailand; also see specific chapters for regional information and local schedules.

THAILAND CALENDAR OF EVENTS

January/February

Chinese New Year, Bangkok. Head for Chinatown to celebrate the New Year with a Chingay parade—complete with Lion Dance. Celebrated everywhere, but most raucous in Bangkok's Chinatown or Chinese neighborhoods in any city (during the end of the lunar year in Jan or early Feb).

February

Flower Festival, Chiang Mai. When all of the north is in bloom, Chiang Mai springs to life with parades, floats decorated with flowers, and beauty contests (first weekend).

March

Poi Sang Long, Mae Hong Son. An auspicious day preceding Buddhist Lent (different every year, so check

with TAT at ℂ **1672**). Young monks are paraded through the streets and feted with offerings to celebrate their ordination.

April

Pattaya Festival, Pattaya. Parades and fireworks accompany a food festival and lots of partying (first week).

International Kite Festival, Bangkok. The place to see this national pastime, with contests and displays (third week).

June/July

Phi Ta Khon, Loei. This Buddhist festival features a procession of masked dancers and recitations from monks. Celebrated on the arrival of the fifth or sixth lunar month (check with the TAT, ℂ **1672**, for details).

September/October

Boat Races, Phitsanulok, Narathiwat. Races, country fairs, and parades to mark the end of the rains (first week of each month).

October

Vegetarian Festival, Phuket. Chinese religious festival with parades, temple ceremonies, and athletic competitions (second week for 9 days).

November

Elephant Roundup, Surin. Elephant parades, demonstrations, and cultural performances (third weekend).

December

King's Cup Regatta, Phuket. Global competitors race yachts in this international event (Dec 7–13).

5 Travel Insurance

Check your existing insurance policies and credit-card coverage before you buy travel insurance. You may already be covered for lost luggage, cancelled tickets, or medical expenses.

The cost of travel insurance varies widely, depending on the cost and length of your trip, your age and health, and the type of trip you're taking, but expect to pay between 5% and 8% of the vacation itself. You can get estimates from various providers through **InsureMyTrip.com**. Enter your trip cost and dates, your age, and other information, for prices from more than a dozen companies.

TRIP-CANCELLATION INSURANCE

Trip-cancellation insurance will help retrieve your money if you have to back out of a trip or depart early, or if your travel supplier goes bankrupt. Permissible reasons for trip cancellation can range from sickness to natural disasters to the State Department declaring a destination unsafe for travel. (Insurers usually won't cover vague fears, though, as many travelers discovered when they tried to cancel their trips in October 2001.) In this unstable world, trip-cancellation insurance is a good buy if you're purchasing tickets well in advance—who knows what the state of the world, or of your airline, will be in 9 months? Insurance policy details vary, so read the fine print—and make sure that your airline or cruise line is on the list of carriers covered in case of bankruptcy. A good resource is **"Travel Guard Alerts,"** a list of companies considered high-risk by Travel Guard International (see website below). Protect yourself further by paying for the insurance with a credit card—by law, consumers can get their money back on goods and services not received if they report the loss within 60 days after the charge is listed on their credit card statement.

Note: Many tour operators, particularly those offering trips to remote or high-risk areas, include insurance in the total trip cost or can arrange insurance policies through a partnering provider, which is a convenient and often cost-effective way for the traveler to obtain insurance. Make sure the tour company is a reputable one, however, and be aware that some experts suggest you avoid buying insurance from the tour or cruise company you're traveling with. They contend it is more secure to buy from a "third party" than to put all your money in one place.

For more information, contact one of the following recommended insurers: **Access America** (© 866/807-3982; www.accessamerica.com); **Travel Guard International** (© 800/826-4919; www.travelguard.com); **Travel Insured International** (© 800/243-3174; www.travelinsured.com); and **Travelex Insurance Services** (© 888/457-4602; www.travelexinsurance.com).

MEDICAL INSURANCE For travel overseas, most health plans (including Medicare and Medicaid) do not provide coverage, and the ones that do often require you to pay for services upfront and reimburse you only after you return home. Even if your plan does cover overseas treatment, most out-of-country hospitals make you pay your bills up front, and send you a refund only after you've returned home and filed the necessary paperwork with your insurance company. As a safety net, you may want to buy travel medical insurance, particularly if you're traveling to a remote or high-risk area where emergency evacuation is a possible scenario. If you require additional medical insurance, try **MEDEX Assistance** (© 410/453-6300; www.medexassist.com) or **Travel Assistance International** (© 800/821-2828; www.travelassistance.com; for general information on services, call the company's Worldwide Assistance Services, Inc., at © 800/777-8710). For a budget option, get affordable travel insurance from **Student Travel Agency (STA)** (© 800/781-4040 in North America; www.sta.com or www.statravel.com); it's not just for students.

LOST-LUGGAGE INSURANCE On international flights (including U.S. portions of international trips), baggage coverage is limited to approximately $9.07 per pound, up to approximately $635 per checked bag. If you plan to check items more valuable than what's covered by the standard liability, see if your homeowner's policy covers your valuables, or get baggage insurance as part of your comprehensive travel-insurance package. Don't buy insurance at the airport, where it is usually overpriced. Be sure to take any valuables or irreplaceable items with you in your carry-on luggage, because many valuables (including books, money, and electronics) aren't covered by airline policies.

If your luggage is lost, immediately file a lost-luggage claim at the airport, detailing the luggage contents. Most airlines require that you report delayed, damaged, or lost baggage within 4 hours of arrival. The airlines are required to deliver luggage, once found, directly to your house or destination free of charge.

6 Health & Safety

STAYING HEALTHY

Thailand poses no specific health hazard that requires immunization, but the same cautions for visiting rugged, tropical climes apply to the more remote areas of the Thai kingdom. Most health-care professionals in the West are able to supply you with information about health problems specific to the region, and it is recommended that travelers have current immunizations for hepatitis A and tetanus. Heat and humidity combined with sometimes less sanitary conditions than most are used to in their home countries means that it is important to watch for infections; wash any wound promptly and keep covered.

GENERAL AVAILABILITY OF HEALTH CARE

Dispensaries and hospital facilities in Thailand, especially in urban centers, are on par with most of the West, and even the smallest towns will have some tenable facility or provide transport to a good hospital (see "Fast Facts" in individual destination chapters). Many Thai doctors and health-care professionals receive training abroad, and, in fact, places like Bumrungrad Hospital (© **02667-1000;** www.bumrungrad.com) in Bangkok and the better facilities in Phuket have given rise to a unique phenomenon of what is now termed medical tourism, where visitors take care of medical problems, anything from dental work to plastic surgery, and, because of the affordability of medical care in Thailand (and at the same high standard of quality), are able to combine their recovery with a beach vacation or enjoy the comforts of big-city Bangkok in the process.

Contact the **International Association for Medical Assistance to Travelers** (IAMAT) (© **716/754-4883** or, in Canada, 416/652-0137; www.iamat.org) for tips on travel and health concerns in the countries you're visiting, and for lists of local, English-speaking doctors. The United States **Centers for Disease Control and Prevention** (© **800/311-3435;** www.cdc.gov) provides up-to-date information on health hazards by region or country and offers tips on food safety. The website **www.tripprep.com**, sponsored by a consortium of travel medicine practitioners, may also offer helpful advice on traveling abroad. You can find listings of reliable clinics overseas at the **International Society of Travel Medicine** (www.istm.org).

COMMON AILMENTS

STOMACH TROUBLE Don't drink the water, and watch what you eat. The most common illness in these parts is **diarrhea.** Often, just the abrupt change in climate and diet bring on an uncomfortable bout of Montezuma's Revenge that takes all the fun out of touring temples or riding rural buses. It is a good idea to bring with you a good over-the-counter antidiarrhea medicine such as Imodium A.D., an electrolyte supplement to mix in plenty of water (to prevent dehydration and loss of energy), and, above all, a roll of toilet paper or packet of tissues for while you're away from your hotel. Don't count on public toilets having any. Some cases of diarrhea are caused by bacteria or viruses in either food or drinking water. Be sure to stick to canned or bottled drinks or the bottled water sold everywhere. While food in most restaurants is perfectly safe, be wary of street food. If you eat from a street stall, check ingredients for freshness and cleanliness. Watch the cook prepare food before you, and never eat anything that looks like it has been sitting around. Avoid anything raw—vegetables included—from vendors. If your condition lasts for more than 24 hours and you have painful cramps, chances are you've picked something up and should find a doctor for possible antibiotic treatment.

TROPICAL ILLNESSES **Hepatitis A** can be avoided using the same precautions as for diarrhea. Most Asians are immune through exposure, but people from the West are very susceptible. Talk to your doctor about receiving a vaccine before your trip.

Major tourist areas such as Bangkok, Phuket, Koh Samui, and Chiang Mai are **malaria free.** However, malaria is still a problem in rural parts, particularly territories in the mountains to the north and near borders with Cambodia. If traveling to remote border areas, take a malarial prophylaxis, such as atovaquone/proguanil or doxycycline (see a travel med specialist to confer). Note that Mefloquine is no longer recommended for Thailand. The best way to prevent malarial transmission or catching any other baddy listed below is to cover up with long pants and sleeves after dark, stay indoors, sleep with mosquito netting, and use repellents. Make sure your repellent is specially made for the tropics. DEET works well. If, despite these precautions, you develop a fever within 2 weeks of entering a high-risk area, be sure to consult a physician.

Dengue fever is a problem throughout Southeast Asia, and recent years have seen epidemics in the region. Similar to malaria, the virus is spread by mosquito bites, but the mosquitoes that carry the virus only bite during the day. There is no existing prophylactic, so like malaria your best bet is to avoid being bitten. Symptoms include fever, a skin rash, and severe headaches. Seek medical attention. For foreign visitors, the disease is rarely fatal, but for people who are natives of endemic areas, the internal hemorrhaging caused by the virus often kills.

Japanese encephalitis is a viral infection that attacks the brain and is spread by mosquito bite. Outbreaks have been known to occur in the region, so stay abreast of the most up-to-date CDC information. Like malaria and dengue, the best protection is to avoid being bitten.

BUGS, BITES & OTHER WILDLIFE CONCERNS One of the biggest concerns, as you can see from the list of tropical diseases above, are mosquitoes. Take appropriate precautions. It is not a bad idea to wear long trousers instead of shorts (also more acceptable in Thai culture) as protection against not just mosquito bites, but ticks, snakes, and other pests, as well as to spare yourself cuts and scrapes that can get infected, most important when on jungle treks. Do not get creative about nibbling bush-tucker, even if you think you know what kind of mushroom it is, because there are some really nasty ones in this part of the world. When venturing into thick jungle terrain, do so with a qualified guide, of course, and keep an eye out for the many creepy-crawlies: it is a jungle out there.

Rabies is a concern in Thailand, as are bites from any stray dogs, infected or not. You'll see some pretty miserable canines in your travels in Thailand—sick and diseased, sleeping on the side of the road, limping through markets, hanging around temple complexes where monks do their karmic duty and feed the animals (though they never seem to care for them beyond that). Occasionally, a **rabid** animal makes its way into the mix. Stay clear of stray dogs, and find a doctor fast if you've been bitten. The sooner you receive treatment, the better. All Thai dogs have been whacked with sticks and hit by flying rocks, so even miming those actions is often enough of a deterrent.

Don't swim in **freshwater streams or pools** (other than chlorinated hotel pools), as they are frequently contaminated. Avoid the ocean near the outlets of sewage pipes and freshwater streams, because of contaminated water—poisonous sea snakes often inhabit these areas. Be especially careful of coral reefs (such as those along Phuket), jellyfish, and sea urchins, and treat all cuts or stings immediately by washing with soap and water and applying an antimicrobial preparation. Antihistamines can help with allergic responses. Ear infections are a common problem; those prone to ear infections can use mild boric acid or vinegar solutions to prevent or combat them.

RESPIRATORY ILLNESS   The air in Bangkok is an irritant to anyone with respiratory issues. SARS is long gone from the region (there were no cases in Thailand), and though there have been reported cases of avian influenza, or "bird flu," among poultry workers, the danger of contracting the disease is low. If, however, avian influenza mutates as expected, the flu will spread far and wide internationally, and the risk in Thailand will be no greater than in developed countries.

COPING WITH THE HEAT   Avoid **sunstroke** or **heat exhaustion** by exercising caution when getting active out in the roasting sunlight. Thailand's slower pace of life is in fact dictated by the hot and humid weather, so (when in Rome) take it easy, stay out of the noon-day sun, and drink lots of liquid to avoid dehydration. Bottled water is inexpensive and widely available. Avoid excessive exposure to the sun, use a strong sunscreen, and wear a hat for protection. Restricting alcohol consumption and eating light meals will help you to acclimate.

WHAT TO DO IF YOU GET SICK IN THAILAND

Medical services in Thailand are good, and over-the-counter dispensaries are comparable with standards in the West. Most offer prescription drugs on an as-needed basis, the pharmacist more or less acts as a diagnostician in many parts. Check the "Fast Facts" section of individual destination chapters for hospital listings. In an emergency, do not hesitate to contact your country's embassy. In most cases, your existing health plan will provide the coverage you need. But double-check; you may want to buy **travel medical insurance** instead. (See the section on insurance, above.) Bring your insurance ID card with you when you travel.

If you suffer from a chronic illness, consult your doctor before your departure. For conditions like epilepsy, diabetes, or heart problems, wear a **Medic Alert Identification Tag** (© **800/825-3785;** www.medicalert.org), which will immediately alert doctors to your condition and give them access to your records through Medic Alert's 24-hour hot line.

Pack **prescription medications** in your carry-on luggage, and carry prescription medications in their original containers, with pharmacy labels—otherwise they won't make it through airport security. Also bring along copies of your prescriptions in case you lose your pills or run out. Don't forget an extra pair of contact lenses or prescription glasses. Carry the generic name of prescription medicines, in case a local pharmacist is unfamiliar with the brand name.

Contact the **International Association for Medical Assistance to Travelers (IAMAT)** (© **716/754-4883,** 416/652-0137 in Canada; www.iamat.org) for tips on travel and health concerns in the countries you're visiting and lists of local, English-speaking doctors. The United States **Centers for Disease Control and Prevention** (© 800/311-3435; www.cdc.gov) provides up-to-date information on necessary vaccines and health hazards by region or country. Any foreign consulate can provide a list of area doctors who speak English. If you get sick, consider asking your hotel concierge to recommend a local doctor—even his or her own. You can also try the emergency room at a local hospital; many have walk-in clinics for emergency cases that are not life-threatening. You may not get immediate attention, but you won't pay the high price of an emergency room visit.

STAYING SAFE

Thailand is a very safe destination. You are far less likely to experience the kind of anonymous violent crime so common in the West, for example, but travelers should follow some precautions. Of concern are the kingdom's many pickpockets and scam artists in tour areas. Keep an eye on valuables in crowded places—true anywhere—and be wary of anyone who approaches you in the street to solicit your friendship; however genuine the entreaty, many visitors find more than

they bargain for and waste precious time on "shopping tours" where your "guide" will collect a commission and keep you from getting where you'd like to go (or worse). In general, even in big cities, you are safe to walk at night. Women traveling alone generally find Thailand an amenable place, but should keep on guard, especially at night.

Avoid public conflict in Thailand, something that is just not done and a "face losing" proposition. If, for whatever reason, you find yourself in the middle of something feisty or beyond just a minor disagreement, call the tourist police: The national hot line is © 1155. You cannot win out in altercations in Thailand, and it is best to walk away and get assistance.

That said, Thai police are a political entity and corrupt as they come. In general, the police are not there to protect and serve as much as they are there to harass and collect, so just steer clear of any official or military doings unless in need of help (and in that case, go to the English-speaking tourist police).

Traffic and chaotic road conditions are probably the biggest dangers for visitors to Thailand. Thai drivers pass aggressively and must weave to avoid the many obstacles on busy roads. Self-drive car rental

Avoiding "Economy Class Syndrome"

Deep vein thrombosis (DVT), or as it is known in the world of flying, "economy-class syndrome," is a blood clot that develops in a deep vein. It is a potentially deadly condition that can be caused by sitting in cramped conditions—such as an airplane cabin—for too long. During a flight (especially the long hauls from Europe or North America to Thailand), get up, walk around, and stretch your legs every 60 to 90 minutes to keep your blood flowing. Other preventative measures include frequent flexing of the legs while sitting, drinking lots of water, and avoiding alcohol and sleeping pills. If you have a history of deep vein thrombosis, heart disease, or another condition that puts you at high risk, some experts recommend wearing compression stockings or taking anticoagulants when you fly; always ask your physician about the best course for you. Symptoms of deep vein thrombosis include leg pain or swelling, or even shortness of breath.

Sex for Sale

Every day you're in Thailand, in any part of the country, you will see foreigners enjoying the company of Thai women and men. Although prostitution is illegal, it is tolerated and is as much a tourist draw as the kingdom's hotels and beaches. In poor, uneducated, rural families, where sons are counted on as farm labor, the sex trade has become an income-earning occupation for daughters who have few other job alternatives. It is true that most of the urban sex workers earn more income than their families back home, sending savings back each month to support younger siblings and older parents. While girls sent to the big cities as CSWs (the official term is "commercial sex worker") can sometimes quietly retire and return to their villages, for every happy ending, there are many more sad tales of drug use and physical abuse.

With a legacy of royal patronage and social acceptance, the world's oldest profession has been part of Thailand's economy for centuries. It is hard to get exact numbers for CSWs in Thailand (the number goes from 80,000–800,000 depending on the source), but it is interesting to note that foreigners engaging the services of prostitutes comprises only a fraction of the nationwide industry (Westerners are just more obvious to spot, and areas like Patpong in Bangkok, and Pattaya just east of Bangkok, don't mask the skin trades at all). The dark side is that though efforts at cracking down on prostitution is given much lip-service, and legislation prohibits full nudity in most go-go bars, for example, that just means the more upfront transactions suffer while the many backroom deals—children being bought and sold after being kidnapped and enslaved—carry on.

Thailand has made significant steps to counter the spread of **AIDS** and, through education and the introduction of condoms, has reputedly stemmed the tide of new cases (though statistics are unreliable). A leading force in this effort is the Population & Community Development Association (PCDA), led by the courageous and innovative public health crusader Meechai Viravaidya. The PCDA has enlarged the scope of its rural development programs from family planning and cottage-industry schemes, to distributing condoms and running seminars for CSWs.

Western embassies report numerous cases of tourists who are drugged in their hotel rooms by their chosen girl of the night, awaking 2 days later to find all their valuables gone. There are a shocking number of stories about young Western travelers found dead in their hotel rooms from unexplained causes. Exercise caution in your dealings with strangers. If, in spite of all these warnings, you decide to use the services of Thailand's commercial sex workers, take proper precautions; men should wear a latex condom.

makes sense only in places like the far north, rural Isan in the northeast, or in some of the resort destinations, but extreme caution should be taken and defensive driving skills are key. If you do get in an accident, Thai style is to negotiate a settlement at roadside, but you'll want to contact local officials and go from there.

An old Asia hand I know says that the best insurance policy you could take out in Thailand and elsewhere in the region is to never get on a motorcycle, whether as a driver or passenger on the back of a motorbike taxi. Good advice, but it is apparent from the many banged, bruised, and mummy-wrapped travelers limping around Thai resort areas (not to mention the frightening statistics of the many deaths annually) that few heed the warning. Motorbikes are the most convenient way to get around (and park), and are available for rent in most tourist centers, but exercise great caution.

The political situation in Thailand is quite stable, a constitutional monarchy, but as recently as the early 1990s, Thailand was turned on its ear with a military coup. The national police force, military, and citizenry constantly bounce around the shuttlecock of power, and when one faction gets too big for its britches there is a shift. But you are unlikely to be caught up in any political issues in Thailand.

Since 2003 there has been increased sectarian violence between Thai Muslims and Thai military police in the far southern provinces near the Malaysian border. All Thai institutions, schools, and Buddhist temples have been made targets for small-scale bombs. The Thai government has come under international scrutiny for the brutal force used to quell uprisings. The violence is confined to a few provinces in the far south, far from any tourist areas.

A guaranteed way to get in real trouble in Thailand is to get involved in drugs and prostitution. However tempting, drug use, even a casual toke off of someone's "Thai stick," is to be avoided completely. There is a zero-tolerance policy, and unless you can cough up the right bribe on the spot, you'll find yourself in a grimy cell before you can shout "Embassy!" Many tourists are attracted to Thailand for the loose restrictions on paid sex, and despite some changes in legislation, sex tourism is still a major draw to Thailand. If you indulge, take extreme caution. See the info below.

DEALING WITH DISCRIMINATION

Thai people are very accepting, but there is a certain institutionalized racism in old Siam. Caucasian foreigners are called "Falang" (a bastardization of "France" pronounced by the first colonists and a word that also means "guava") and occupy a high place (no matter their actions) in the scheme of things. Thais follow a codified hierarchy, with niches for Thais of Chinese heritage, who own and operate much of Thai businesses and commerce, and people from Isan, the impoverished northeast of the kingdom, who come to work the more menial jobs in the big cities in Thailand, and all levels in-between.

Foreign visitors are overcharged for all goods and services, and some take this personally, as some form of discrimination, but it is Thai practice that if you have more, you are meant to give more. The rule applies to Thais as well, and, regardless of your budget, you are wealthy in Thailand. Skills in bargaining and getting the "local price" come in time.

7 Specialized Travel Resources

TRAVELERS WITH DISABILITIES

Most disabilities shouldn't stop anyone from traveling. There are more options and resources out there than ever before. Visitors to Thailand will find that short of the better hotels in the larger towns, amenities for disabled travelers are inconsistent.

Many travel agencies offer customized tours and itineraries for travelers with disabilities. **Flying Wheels Travel** (© 507/451-5005; www.flyingwheelstravel.com) offers escorted tours and cruises that emphasize sports and private tours in minivans with lifts. **Access-Able Travel**

Source (© 303/232-2979; www.access-able.com) offers extensive access information and advice for traveling around the world with disabilities. **Accessible Journeys** (© 800/846-4537 or 610/521-0339; www.disabilitytravel.com) caters specifically to slow walkers and wheelchair travelers and their families and friends.

Avis Rent a Car has an "Avis Access" program that offers such services as a dedicated 24-hour toll-free number (© 888/879-4273) for customers with special travel needs; special car features such as swivel seats, spinner knobs, and hand controls; and accessible bus service.

Organizations that offer assistance to disabled travelers include **MossRehab** (www.mossresourcenet.org), which provides a library of accessible-travel resources online; the **American Foundation for the Blind (AFB)** (© 800/232-5463; www.afb.org), a referral resource for the blind or visually impaired that includes information on traveling with Seeing Eye dogs; and **SATH (Society for Accessible Travel & Hospitality)** (© 212/447-7284; www.sath.org; annual membership fees: $45 adults, $30 seniors and students), which offers a wealth of travel resources for all types of disabilities and informed recommendations on destinations, access guides, travel agents, tour operators, vehicle rentals, and companion services. **AirAmbulanceCard.com** is now partnered with SATH and allows you to preselect top-notch hospitals in case of an emergency for $195 a year ($295 per family), among other benefits.

For more information specifically targeted to travelers with disabilities, the community website **iCan** (www.icanonline.net/channels/travel) has destination guides and several regular columns on accessible travel. Also check out the quarterly magazine *Emerging Horizons* (www.emerginghorizons.com; $15 per year, $20 outside the U.S.); and *Open World* magazine, published by SATH (see above; subscription: $13 per year, $21 outside the U.S.).

GAY & LESBIAN TRAVELERS

Thailand is a very gay-friendly destination where "alternative" lifestyles are quite common and accepted. The same kind of red-light district nightlife that caters to heterosexual males is mirrored in places like Bangkok, Pattaya, and Chiang Mai by a large gay go-go club scene as well as gay clubs and bars. Cross-dressers and transsexuals, called "lady-boys" or *Katoeys* in Thai, play an important role in Thai culture and are accepted in mainstream life.

The **International Gay and Lesbian Travel Association (IGLTA)** (© 800/448-8550 or 954/776-2626; www.iglta.org) is the trade association for the gay and lesbian travel industry, and offers an online directory of gay- and lesbian-friendly travel businesses; go to their website and click on "Members."

Many agencies offer tours and travel itineraries specifically for gay and lesbian travelers. **Above and Beyond Tours** (© 800/397-2681; www.abovebeyondtours.com) is the exclusive gay and lesbian tour operator for United Airlines. **Now, Voyager** (© 800/255-6951; www.nowvoyager.com) is a well-known San Francisco–based, gay-owned and operated travel service. **Olivia Cruises & Resorts** (© 800/631-6277; www.olivia.com) charters entire resorts and ships for exclusive lesbian vacations and offers smaller group experiences for both gay and lesbian travelers. (In 2005, tennis great Martina Navratilova was named Olivia's official spokesperson.)

Gay.com Travel (© 800/929-2268 or 415/644-8044; www.gay.com/travel or www.outandabout.com) is an excellent online successor to the popular *Out & About* print magazine. It provides regularly updated information about gay-owned, gay-oriented, and gay-friendly lodging, dining, sightseeing, nightlife, and shopping establishments in every important destination worldwide. It also offers trip-planning information for gay and lesbian travelers for more than 50 destinations, along various themes, ranging from Sex & Travel to Vacations for Couples.

The following travel guides are available at many bookstores, or you can order them from any online bookseller: *Frommer's Gay & Lesbian Europe* (www.frommers.com), an excellent travel resource to the top European cities and resorts; *Spartacus International Gay Guide* (Bruno Gmünder Verlag; www.spartacusworld.com/gayguide/) and *Odysseus: The International Gay Travel Planner* (Odysseus Enterprises Ltd.), both good, annual, English-language guidebooks focused on gay men; and the *Damron* guides (www.damron.com), with separate, annual books for gay men and lesbians.

SENIOR TRAVEL

Mention the fact that you're a senior citizen when you make your travel reservations; you may be able to secure special discounts on tours and airline reservations. Senior citizens, though highly revered in Thai society, will not, however, receive any special discounts at Thai attractions.

Members of **AARP** (formerly known as the American Association of Retired Persons), 601 E St. NW, Washington, DC 20049 (© **888/687-2277**; www.aarp.org), get discounts on hotels, airfares, and car rentals. AARP offers members a wide range of benefits, including *AARP: The Magazine* and a monthly newsletter. Anyone over 50 can join.

Many reliable agencies and organizations target the 50-plus market. **Elderhostel** (© **877/426-8056**; www.elderhostel.org) arranges study programs for those aged 55 and over (and a spouse or companion of any age) in the U.S. and in more than 80 countries around the world. Most courses last 5 to 7 days in the U.S. (2–4 weeks abroad), and many include airfare, accommodations in university dormitories or modest inns, meals, and tuition. **ElderTreks** (© **800/741-7956;** www.eldertreks.com) offers small-group tours to off-the-beaten-path or adventure-travel locations, restricted to travelers 50 and older. **INTRAV** (© **800/456-8100;** www.intrav.com) is a high-end tour operator that caters to the mature, discerning traveler (not specifically seniors), with trips around the world that include guided safaris, polar expeditions, private-jet adventures, and small-boat cruises down jungle rivers.

Recommended publications offering travel resources and discounts for seniors include: the quarterly magazine *Travel 50 & Beyond* (www.travel50andbeyond.com); *Travel Unlimited: Uncommon Adventures for the Mature Traveler* (Avalon); *101 Tips for Mature Travelers,* available from Grand Circle Travel (© **800/221-2610** or 617/350-7500; www.gct.com); and *Unbelievably Good Deals and Great Adventures That You Absolutely Can't Get Unless You're Over 50* (McGraw-Hill), by Joann Rattner Heilman.

FAMILY TRAVEL

If you have enough trouble getting your kids out of the house in the morning, dragging them thousands of miles away may seem like an insurmountable challenge. But family travel can be immensely rewarding, giving you new ways of seeing the world through smaller pairs of eyes.

A visit to Thailand will certainly broaden the horizons of young visitors, and families report great experiences in the kingdom. Most larger resort areas have kid-friendly programs, hotels with kids' clubs, connecting rooms, sports equipment rental, and kid-oriented group activities. Many of the larger hotels offer special deals for families with children. You will find willing and affordable babysitters at every turn, and the Thai people are especially kind, generous, and playful with kids, foreign children attracting special attention. Remember that children will need a valid passport to enter Thailand.

Familyhostel (© 800/733-9753; www. learn.unh.edu/familyhostel) takes the whole family, including kids ages 8 to 15, on moderately priced domestic and international learning vacations. Lectures, field trips, and sightseeing are guided by a team of academics.

Recommended family travel Internet sites include **Family Travel Forum** (www. familytravelforum.com), a comprehensive site that offers customized trip planning; **Family Travel Network** (www. familytravelnetwork.com), an award-winning site that offers travel features, deals, and tips; **Traveling Internationally with Your Kids** (www.travelwithyourkids. com), a comprehensive site offering sound advice for long-distance and international travel with children; and **Family Travel Files** (www.thefamilytravelfiles. com), which offers an online magazine and a directory of off-the-beaten-path tours and tour operators for families.

WOMEN TRAVELERS

Women travelers face no particular discrimination or dangers in Thailand, nor is there anything preventing them entree to Thai culture. Women should, however, be very careful when dealing with monks: Never touch a monk, never hand anything directly to them (it should be set on the floor in front of the monk or given to a man who will hand it to them directly), and don't sit next to monks on public transport. Some parts of temples do not allow women to enter, but there will be signs to that effect.

Thais are rather modest, though current scanty fashion trends would tell you otherwise. Women should avoid short-shorts or going topless at beaches. At Muslim temples, quite prevalent in the south, be sure to wear a long skirt or trousers and have your shoulders covered.

The only other problem single women face in Thailand is the constant questioning: "Are you married?" Friends tell me it is like everyone is that grandmother who is eager for more grandkids. Thais commonly marry quite young and get right to the business of building a family, and anything short of that is, to Thais, somehow pitiable. Don't take it personally.

Check out the award-winning website **Journeywoman** (www.journeywoman. com), a "real-life" women's travel-information network where you can sign up for a free e-mail newsletter and get advice on everything from etiquette and dress to safety; or the travel guide *Safety and Security for Women Who Travel* by Sheila Swan and Peter Laufer (Travelers' Tales, Inc.), offering common-sense tips on safe travel.

AFRICAN-AMERICAN TRAVELERS

The Internet offers a number of helpful travel sites for African-American travelers. **Black Travel Online** (www.blacktravel online.com) posts news on upcoming events and includes links to articles and travel-booking sites.

Agencies and organizations that provide resources for black travelers include: **Rodgers Travel** (© 800/825-1775; www. rodgerstravel.com), a Philadelphia-based travel agency with an extensive menu of tours in destinations worldwide, including heritage and private-group tours. For more information, check out the following collections and guides: *Go Girl: The Black Woman's Guide to Travel & Adventure* (Eighth Mountain Press), a compilation of travel essays by writers including Jill Nelson and Audre Lorde, with some practical information and trip-planning advice; *The African American Travel Guide,* by Wayne Robinson

(Hunter Publishing; www.hunterpublish ing.com), with details on 19 North American cities; *Steppin' Out* by Carla Labat (Avalon), with details on 20 cities; *Travel and Enjoy Magazine* (℃ **866/ 266-6211;** www.travelandenjoy.com; subscription: $38 per year), which focuses on discounts and destination reviews; and the more narrative *Path- finders Magazine* (℃ **877/977-PATH;** www.pathfinderstravel.com; subscrip- tion: $15 per year), which includes arti- cles on everything from Rio de Janeiro to Ghana as well as information on upcom- ing ski, diving, golf, and tennis trips.

STUDENT TRAVEL

Discounts for students in Thailand and the rest of Southeast Asia are better earned by the tenacity of the individual traveler's bargaining skills and tolerance for sub-standard accommodation rather than flashing a student ID. The **Interna- tional Student Identity Card (ISIC),** however, offers substantial savings on plane tickets and some entrance fees. It also provides you with basic health and life insurance and a 24-hour help line. The card is available for $22 from **STA Travel** (℃ **800/781-4040** in North America; www.sta.com or www.statravel. com), the biggest student travel agency in the world. If you're no longer a student but are still under 26, you can get an **International Youth Travel Card (IYTC)** for the same price from the same people, which entitles you to some discounts (but not on museum admissions). (*Note:* In 2002, STA Travel bought competitors **Council Travel** and **USIT Campus** after they went bankrupt. They are still operat- ing some offices under the Council name, but they are now owned by STA.) **Travel CUTS** (℃ **800/667-2887** or 416/614- 2887; www.travelcuts.com) offers similar services for both Canadians and U.S. res- idents. Irish students may prefer to turn to **USIT** (℃ **01/602-1600;** www.usit

now.ie), an Ireland-based specialist in stu- dent, youth, and independent travel.

SINGLE TRAVELERS

Many people prefer traveling alone, and for independent travelers, solo journeys offer infinite opportunities to make friends and meet locals, especially in Thailand where large groups of foreigners are intimidating to locals. Most hotels offer "single" rates; if, however, you like resorts, tours, or cruises, you're likely to get hit with a "single supplement" to the base price. Single travelers can avoid these supplements, of course, by agreeing to room with other single travelers on the trip. An even better idea is to find a com- patible roommate before you go from one of the many roommate locator agencies.

Travel Buddies Singles Travel Club (℃ **800/998-9099;** www.travelbuddies worldwide.com), based in Canada, runs small, intimate, single-friendly group trips and will match you with a roommate free of charge. **TravelChums** (℃ **212/787- 2621;** www.travelchums.com) is an Inter- net-only travel-companion matching service with elements of an online per- sonals-type site, hosted by the respected New York–based Shaw Guides travel service. **The Single Gourmet Club** (www.singlegourmet.com/chapters.php) is an international social, dining, and travel club for singles of all ages, with club chapters in 21 cities in the U.S. and Canada. Annual membership fees vary from city to city.

Many reputable tour companies offer singles-only trips. **Backroads** (℃ **800/ 462-2848;** www.backroads.com) offers more than 160 active-travel trips to 30 destinations worldwide.

For more information, check out Eleanor Berman's latest edition of *Travel- ing Solo: Advice and Ideas for More Than 250 Great Vacations* (Globe Pequot), a guide with advice on traveling alone, either solo or as part of a group tour. (It has been updated for 2003.)

Also look for **Vagabonding** (Villard, 2002), a guide to searching for the pearl while taking care of life back home, including advice spiritual and practical about

consolidating a life in the West and going "vagabonding" as an English teacher, a spiritual seeker, or a nest egg–toting long-time traveler. Good inspiration.

8 Planning Your Trip Online

SURFING FOR AIRFARES

It is not a bad idea to try the bigger online services to get an idea of what's out there or find good specials, especially off-season. The "big three" online travel agencies, **Expedia.com**, **Travelocity.com**, and **Orbitz.com**, sell most of the air tickets bought on the Internet. (Canadian travelers should try expedia.ca and Travelocity. ca; U.K. residents can go for expedia. co.uk and opodo.co.uk.). **Kayak.com** is also gaining popularity and uses a sophisticated search engine (developed at MIT). Each has different business deals with the airlines and may offer different fares on the same flights, so it is wise to shop around. Expedia, Kayak, and Travelocity will also send you **e-mail notification** when a cheap fare becomes available to your favorite destination. Of the smaller travel-agency websites, **SideStep** (www. sidestep.com) has gotten the best reviews from Frommer's authors.' The website (with optional browser add-on) purports to "search 140 sites at once," but in reality only beats competitors' fares as often as other sites do.

Also remember to check **airline websites,** especially with major regional carriers: Thai Airways, Cathay Pacific, EVA Airline, Singapore Air, or Korean Air. Even with major airlines, you can often shave a few bucks from a fare by booking directly through the airline and avoiding a travel agency's transaction fee. But you'll get these discounts only by **booking online:** Most airlines now offer online-only fares that even their phone agents know nothing about. For the websites of airlines that fly to and from your destination, go to "Getting There," p. 48.

Great **last-minute deals** are available through free weekly e-mail services provided directly by the airlines. Most of these are announced on Tuesday or Wednesday and must be purchased online. Most are only valid for travel that weekend, but some (such as Southwest's) can be booked weeks or months in advance. Sign up for weekly e-mail alerts at airline websites or check mega-sites that compile comprehensive lists of last-minute specials, such as **Smarter Travel** (smartertravel.com). For last-minute trips, **site59.com** and **lastminutetravel. com** in the U.S. and **lastminute.com** in Europe often have better air-and-hotel package deals than the major-label sites.

If you're willing to give up some control over your flight details, use what is called an **"opaque" fare service** like **Priceline** (www.priceline.com; www. priceline.co.uk for Europeans) or its smaller competitor **Hotwire** (www.hotwire. com). Both offer rock-bottom prices in exchange for travel on a "mystery airline" at a mysterious time of day, often with a mysterious change of planes en route. The mystery airlines are all major, well-known carriers—and the possibility of being sent from Philadelphia to Chicago via Tampa is remote; the airlines' routing computers have gotten a lot better than they used to be. Your chances of getting a 6am or 11pm flight, however, are still pretty high. Hotwire tells you flight prices before you buy; Priceline usually has better deals than Hotwire, but you have to play their "name our price" game. If you're new at this, the helpful folks at **BiddingForTravel** (www.biddingfor travel.com) do a good job of demystifying

Priceline's prices and strategies. Priceline and Hotwire are great for flights within North America and between the U.S. and Europe. But for flights to other parts of the world, consolidators will almost always beat their fares.

Note: In 2004 Priceline added non-opaque service to its roster. You now have the option to pick exact flights, times, and airlines from a list of offers—or opt to bid on opaque fares as before.

SURFING FOR HOTELS

Shopping online for hotels is generally done one of two ways: by booking through the hotel's own website or through an independent booking agency (or a fare-service agency like Priceline; see below). These Internet hotel agencies have multiplied in mind-boggling numbers of late, competing for the business of millions of consumers surfing for accommodations around the world. This competitiveness can be a boon to consumers who have the patience and time to shop and compare the online sites for good deals—but shop they must, for prices can vary considerably from site to site. And keep in mind that hotels at the top of a site's listing may be there for no other reason than that they paid money to get the placement.

Bidding for hotels online is not a bad option for the larger properties in big cities or resort areas. There are lots of sites offering booking options in Thai hotels, many offering significant discounts from usual services of the big international hotel booking sites (below). Try www.asia rooms.com among the many local online booking agents. Most regional online booking and ticket consolidators in Thailand work through Diethelm Travel (www.diethelmtravel.com).

Important Note: If you book a budget room online, you'll likely be given a "run of the house" room, which means the least desirable, without view, near the elevator, etc.

Of the "big three" sites, **Expedia** offers a long list of special deals and "virtual tours" or photos of available rooms so you can see what you're paying for (a feature that helps counter the claims that the best rooms are often held back from bargain booking websites). **Travelocity** posts unvarnished customer reviews and ranks its properties according to the AAA rating system. (**Trip Advisor** [www.tripadvisor.com] is another excellent source of unbiased user reviews of hotels around the world. While even the finest hotels can inspire a misleadingly poor review from a picky or crabby traveler, the body of user opinions, when take as a whole, is usually a reliable indicator.)

Other reliable online booking agencies include **Hotels.com** and **Quikbook.com**. An excellent free program, **TravelAxe** (www.travelaxe.net), can help you search multiple hotel sites at once, even ones you may never have heard of—and conveniently lists the total price of the room, including the taxes and service charges. Another booking site, **Travelweb** (www.travelweb.com), is partly owned by the hotels it represents (including the Hilton, Hyatt, and Starwood chains), and is therefore plugged directly into the hotels' reservations systems—unlike independent online agencies, which have to fax or e-mail reservation requests to the hotel, a good portion of which get misplaced in the shuffle. More than once, travelers have arrived at the hotel, only to be told that they have no reservation. To be fair, many of the major sites are undergoing improvements in service and ease of use, and Expedia will soon be able to plug directly into the reservations systems of many hotel chains—none of which can be bad news for consumers. In the meantime, it is a good idea to **get a confirmation number** and **make a printout** of any online booking transaction.

In the opaque website category, **Priceline** and **Hotwire** are even better for

Frommers.com: The Complete Travel Resource

For an excellent travel-planning resource, we highly recommend **Frommers. com** (www.frommers.com), voted Best Travel Site by *PC Magazine*. We're a little biased, of course, but we guarantee that you'll find the travel tips, reviews, monthly vacation giveaways, bookstore, and online-booking capabilities thoroughly indispensable. Among the special features are our popular **Destinations** section, where you'll get expert travel tips, hotel and dining recommendations, and advice on the sights to see for more than 3,500 destinations around the globe; the **Frommers.com Newsletter,** with the latest deals, travel trends, and money-saving secrets; our **Community** area featuring **Message Boards,** where Frommer's readers post queries and share advice (sometimes even our authors show up to answer questions); and our **Photo Center,** where you can post and share vacation tips. When your research is finished, the **Online Reservations System** (www.frommers. com/book_a_trip) takes you to Frommer's preferred online partners for booking your vacation at affordable prices.

hotels than for airfares; through both, you're allowed to pick the neighborhood and quality level of your hotel before paying. Priceline's hotel product even covers Europe and Asia, though it is much better at getting five-star lodging for three-star prices than at finding anything at the bottom of the scale. On the down side, many hotels stick Priceline guests in their least desirable rooms. Be sure to go to the BiddingforTravel website (see above) before bidding on a hotel room on Priceline; it features a fairly up-to-date list of hotels that Priceline uses in major cities. For both Priceline and Hotwire, you pay upfront, and the fee is nonrefundable. *Note:* Some hotels do not provide loyalty program credits or points or other frequent-stay amenities when you book a room through opaque online services.

SURFING FOR RENTAL CARS

For booking rental cars online, the best deals are usually found at rental-car company websites, although all the major online travel agencies also offer rental-car reservations services. Priceline and Hotwire work well for rental cars, too;

the only "mystery" is which major rental company you get, and for most travelers the difference between Hertz, Avis, and Budget is negligible.

TRAVEL BLOGS & TRAVELOGUES

More and more travelers are using travel web logs, or **blogs,** to chronicle their journeys online. To read a few blogs about Thailand, try **Thingsasian.com**, a comprehensive site with some spirited contributors, many travel journalists among them.

You can search for other blogs about Thailand at **Travelblog.com** or post your own travelogue at **Travelblog.org**. For blogs that cover general travel news and highlight various destinations, try **Written road.com** or Gawker Media's snarky **Grid skipper.com**. For more literary travel essays, try Salon.com's travel section (**Salon. com/Wanderlust**), and **Worldhum.com**, which also has an extensive list of other travel-related journals, blogs, online communities, newspaper coverage, and bookstores.

9 The 21st-Century Traveler

INTERNET ACCESS AWAY FROM HOME

Travelers have any number of ways to check their e-mail and access the Internet on the road in Thailand. Using your own laptop—or even a PDA (personal digital assistant) or electronic organizer with a modem—is a good choice if you don't mind lugging it around, but the best route is to rely on Thailand's many cybercafes (affordable) and hotel business centers (pricey).

WITHOUT YOUR OWN COMPUTER

Internet cafes are anywhere and everywhere in Thailand. Hotel business centers charge exorbitant rates (usually about 600B/$15 per day), but you can find very affordable service, for as little as 20B (50¢) per hour for dial-up and 60B to 120B/$1.50 to $3 for higher speeds at the country's many cybercafes. Tourist centers, particularly near budget accommodations in places like Bangkok's Khao San Road or on the main tourist strips of beach destinations, are chockablock with cafes set-up especially for foreign visitors. When out in the country, you'll find small shops full of school-kids playing online shoot-em-up games, and most offer acceptable dial-up service. The departure terminal of Don Muang Airport in Bangkok now has **Internet kiosks.**

To retrieve your e-mail, ask your **Internet Service Provider (ISP)** if it has a Web-based interface tied to your existing e-mail account. If your ISP doesn't have such an interface, you can use the free **mail2web** service (www.mail2web.com) to view and reply to your home e-mail. For more flexibility, you may want to open a free, Web-based e-mail account with **Yahoo! Mail** (mail.yahoo.com). (Microsoft's Hotmail is another popular option, but Hotmail has severe spam problems.) Your home ISP may be able to forward your e-mail to the Web-based account automatically.

If you need to access files on your office computer, look into a service called **GoToMyPC** (www.gotomypc.com). The service provides a Web-based interface for you to access and manipulate a distant PC from anywhere—even a cybercafe—provided your "target" PC is on and has an always-on connection to the Internet (such as with Road Runner cable). The service offers top-quality security, but if you're worried about hackers, use your own laptop rather than a cybercafe to access the GoToMyPC system.

WITH YOUR OWN COMPUTER

More and more hotels, cafes, and retailers are signing on as Wi-Fi (wireless fidelity) "hotspots," from where you can get a high-speed connection without cable wires, networking hardware, or a phone line (see below). Many laptops sold in the last year have built-in Wi-Fi capability (an 802.11b wireless Ethernet connection). In Thailand you'll find wireless services at many **Starbuck's Coffee** branches, as well as at the popular **Black Canyon Coffee;** both have their own pre-paid cards available (service is about 4B, or 10¢ per minute). **TOT** (www.tothotspot.th.com) sells its own wireless services at hotspots everywhere, including in most airport terminals. Some hotels, usually the finer addresses in big cities, offer free wireless connection in common areas and the executive lounge.

For dial-up access, most business-class hotels offer dataports for laptop modems. **Call your hotel in advance** to see what your options are.

In addition, major Internet Service Providers (ISPs) have **local access numbers** around the world, allowing you to go online by placing a local call. Check your ISP's website or call its toll-free

Online Traveler's Toolbox

Veteran travelers usually carry some essential items to make their trips easier. Following is a selection of handy online tools to bookmark and use.

- **Tourist Authority of Thailand** (www.tat.org.) is a comprehensive site with information on locations throughout Thailand.
- The official **Thai government** website (www.thaigov.go.th/index-eng.htm) has good info on current happenings in the kingdom.
- For **transportation information,** try the following sites: for updates on construction of the new airport, see www.airportthai.com; for individual airlines, **Thai Airways International** (www.thaiair.com), **Bangkok Air** (www.bangkokair.com), **Nok Air** (www.nokair.com), **Orient Thai** (www.orient-thai.com or www.onetwo-go.com), **Air Asia** (www.airasia.com.), or **PB Air** (www.pbair.com). Contact the **Thai State Railway** at www.srt.or.th.
- **Useful Health Links: The U.S. Center for Disease Control** (www.cdc.gov/travel) maintains an important database of required immunizations and offers advice and pertinent warnings. Thailand's **Bumrungrad Hospital** (www.bumrungrad.com) is arguably the best in the country, followed closely by **Bangkok Hospital** (www.bangkokhospital.com; with locations throughout the kingdom) and **Bangkok Nursing Home** (www.bnhhospital.com).
- **Thai publications** in English are numerous. The *Bangkok Post* (www.bangkokpost.com) and *The Nation* (www.nationmultimedia.com) are the two major English language dailies, and *Metro Magazine* (www.bkkmetro.com) lists lots of events and happenings.
- It is hard to find any **balanced expat advice** on Thailand (most folks blogging on life in Thailand are either really jaded or have lost their minds), but there are some fun sites out there. **Stickman** (www.stickmanbangkok.com)

number and ask how you can use your current account away from home, and how much it will cost. Thailand has its own popular ISP called **CS Loxinfo,** with handy prepaid cards for dial-up use.

Wherever you go, bring a **connection kit** of the right power and phone adapters, a spare phone cord, and a spare Ethernet network cable—or find out whether your hotel supplies them to guests.

USING A CELLPHONE IN THAILAND

The three letters that define much of the world's **wireless capabilities** are GSM (Global System for Mobiles), a big, seamless network that makes for easy cross-border cellphone use throughout Europe and dozens of other countries worldwide. In the U.S., T-Mobile, AT&T Wireless, and Cingular use this quasi-universal system; in Canada, Microcell and some Rogers customers are GSM compatible, and all Europeans and most Australians use GSM.

If your cellphone is on a GSM system, and you have a world-capable multiband phone such as many Sony-Ericsson, Motorola, or Samsung models, you can make and receive calls across civilized areas around much of the globe, from and **Phillip Williams** (www.philipwilliams.freeservers.com) both maintain extensive catalogues about travel and work in Thailand—lots of good tongue-in-cheek stuff. For information about getting a Thai visa, look for www.thaivisa.com. To find a room for rent for long stays, try www.mrroomfinder.com.

- **Airplane Seating and Food.** Find out which seats to reserve and which to avoid (and more) on all major domestic airlines at www.seatguru.com. And check out the type of meal (with photos) you'll likely be served on airlines around the world at www.airlinemeals.net.
- **Foreign Languages for Travelers** (www.travlang.com). Learn basic terms in more than 70 languages and click on any underlined phrase to hear what it sounds like.
- **Intellicast** (www.intellicast.com) and **Weather.com** (www.weather.com). Gives weather forecasts for all 50 states and for cities around the world.
- **Time and Date** (www.timeanddate.com). See what time (and day) it is anywhere in the world.
- **Travel Warnings** (travel.state.gov, www.fco.gov.uk/travel, www.voyage.gc.ca, www.dfat.gov.au/consular/advice). These sites report on places where health concerns or unrest might threaten American, British, Canadian, and Australian travelers. Generally, U.S. warnings are the most paranoid; Australian warnings are the most relaxed.
- **Universal Currency Converter** (www.xe.com/ucc). See what your dollar or pound is worth in more than 100 other countries.
- **Visa ATM Locator** (www.visa.com), for locations of PLUS ATMs worldwide, or **MasterCard ATM Locator** (www.mastercard.com), for locations of Cirrus ATMs worldwide.

Andorra to Uganda. Just call your wireless operator and ask for "international roaming" to be activated on your account. Unfortunately, per-minute charges can be high—usually $1 to $1.50 in Western Europe and up to $5 in places like Russia and Indonesia.

That's why it is important to buy an "unlocked" world phone from the get-go. Many cellphone operators sell "locked" phones that restrict you from using any other removable computer memory phone chip (called a **SIM card**) card than the ones they supply. Having an unlocked phone allows you to install a cheap, pre-paid SIM card (found at a local retailer)

in your destination country. (Show your phone to the salesperson; not all phones work on all networks.) You'll get a local phone number—and much, much lower calling rates. Unlocking an already locked phone can be complicated, but it can be done; just call your cellular operator and say you'll be going abroad for several months and want to use the phone with a local provider.

For trips of more than a few weeks spent in one country, **buying a phone** becomes economically attractive, as Thailand has a number of cheap, no-questions-asked pre-paid phone systems. The best choice for cellphone service and assistance is at **Mah**

Boon Krong, or **MBK** (© 02217-9111), near the National Stadium BTS station in central Bangkok (but you can get assistance with cellphone service just about anywhere in Thailand). Prepaid programs like the popular **1-2 Call Plan by AIS** let you buy a SIM card for just 800B ($20) and prepaid cards for regional calls as low as 10¢ per minute. With most plans you receive incoming calls for free.

Wilderness adventurers, or those heading to less-developed countries, might consider renting a **satellite phone ("satphone"),** which is different from a cellphone in that it connects to satellites and works where there's no cellular signal or ground-based tower. You can rent satellite phones from **RoadPost** (© **888/290-1606** or 905/272-5665; www.roadpost.com). As of this writing, satphones were outrageously expensive to buy, so don't even think about it.

10 Getting There

BY PLANE

When you plan your trip, consider that Thailand has more than one international airport. While most international flights arrive in Bangkok, you can also fly directly to Phuket, Koh Samui, Hat Yai, and Chiang Mai from certain regional destinations like Singapore or Hong Kong. Check destination chapters for details.

FLIGHTS FROM NORTH AMERICA Thai Airways International (© 800/ 426-5204) flies daily to Bangkok from Los Angeles; also check their new direct flight from New York. **United Airlines** (© 800/241-6522; www.ual.com) and **Northwest Airlines** (© 800/447-4747; www.nwa.com) can connect pretty much any airport in North America to Bangkok via daily flights. **Canadian Airlines International** (© 800/661-2227; www.cdnair.ca) flies to Bangkok from Vancouver via Hong Kong daily. Also check for connecting flights with **EVA, Japan Airline (JAL),** and **Korean Airline.**

FLIGHTS FROM AUSTRALIA Thai Airways (© 300/651-960 toll free within Australia, 7/3215-4700 in Brisbane, or 8/9322-7522 in Perth) services Bangkok from Sydney daily and from Brisbane, Melbourne, and Perth three times a week. **Qantas** (© 131211 toll-free within Australia; www.quantas.com)—in addition to two dailies from Sydney and a daily

flight from Melbourne, both direct—can also connect Adelaide, Brisbane, and Canberra daily. **British Airways** (© 2/ 8904-8800 in Sydney, 7/3223-3123 in Brisbane, 8/9425-7711 in Perth; www.british-airways.com) flies twice daily from Sydney.

FLIGHTS FROM THE UNITED KINGDOM Two or three flights daily, nonstop flights from London to Bangkok, are offered by **British Airways** (© 0345/ 22-21-11 from anywhere within the United Kingdom; www.british-airways.com).

GETTING THROUGH THE AIRPORT

With the federalization of airport security, screening procedures at U.S. airports are more stable and consistent than ever. Generally, you'll be fine if you arrive at the airport **1 hour** before a domestic flight and **2 hours** before an international flight; if you show up late, tell an airline employee and they'll probably whisk you to the front of the line.

Bring a **current, government-issued photo ID** such as a driver's license or passport. Keep your ID at the ready to present at check-in, the security checkpoint, and sometimes even the gate. (Children under 18 do not need government-issued photo IDs for domestic flights, but they do for international flights to most countries.)

In 2003, the TSA phased out **gate check-in** at all U.S. airports. Passengers with e-tickets, which have made paper tickets nearly obsolete, can beat the ticket-counter lines by using airport **electronic kiosks** or even **online check-in** from their home computers. Online check-in involves logging on to your airlines' website, accessing your reservation, and printing out your boarding pass—and the airline may even offer you bonus miles to do so! If you're using a kiosk at the airport, bring the credit card you used to book the ticket or your frequent-flier card. Print out your boarding pass from the kiosk and simply proceed to the security checkpoint with your pass and a photo ID. If you're checking bags or looking to snag an exit-row seat, you will be able to do so using most airline kiosks. Even the smaller airlines are employing the kiosk system, but always call your airline to make sure these alternatives are available. **Curbside check-in** is also a good way to avoid lines, although a few airlines still don't allow it; call for your airline's policy before you go.

Security checkpoint lines are getting shorter than they were during 2001 and 2002, but an orange alert, suspicious passenger, or high passenger volume can still make for a long wait. If you have trouble standing for long periods of time, tell an airline employee; the airline will provide a wheelchair. Speed up security by **not wearing metal objects** such as big belt buckles. If you've got metallic body parts, a note from your doctor can prevent a long chat with the security screeners. Keep in mind that only **ticketed passengers** are allowed past security, except for people escorting disabled passengers or children.

Federalization has stabilized **what you can carry on** and **what you can't.** The general rule is that sharp things are out, nail clippers are okay, and food and beverages must pass through the X-ray machine—but security screeners can't make you drink from your coffee cup. Bring food in your carry-on rather than checking it, as explosive-detection machines used on checked luggage have been known to mistake food (especially chocolate, for some reason) for bombs. Travelers in the U.S. are allowed one carry-on bag, plus a "personal item" such as a purse, briefcase, or laptop bag. Carry-on hoarders can stuff all sorts of things into a laptop bag; as long as it has a laptop in it, it is still considered a personal item. The Transportation Security Administration (TSA) has issued a list of restricted items; check its website (www.tsa.gov/public/index.jsp) for details.

Airport screeners may decide that your checked luggage warrants a hand search. You can now purchase luggage locks that allow screeners to open and relock a checked bag if hand searching is necessary. Look for Travel Sentry certified locks at luggage or travel shops and Brookstone stores (you can buy them online at www.brookstone.com). Luggage inspectors can open these TSA-approved locks with a special code or key—rather than having to cut them off the suitcase, as they normally do to conduct a hand search. For more information on the locks, visit www.travelsentry.org.

FLYING FOR LESS: TIPS FOR GETTING THE BEST AIRFARE

Passengers sharing the same airplane cabin rarely pay the same fare. Travelers who need to purchase tickets at the last minute, change their itinerary at a moment's notice, or fly one-way often get stuck paying the premium rate. Here are some ways to keep your airfare costs down.

- Passengers who can book their ticket either **long in advance or at the last minute,** or who **fly midweek** or **at less-trafficked hours** may pay a fraction of the full fare. If your schedule is flexible, say so, and ask if you can secure a cheaper fare by changing your flight plans.

- Search **the Internet** for cheap fares (see "Planning Your Trip Online").
- Keep an eye on local newspapers for **promotional specials** or **fare wars,** when airlines lower prices on their most popular routes. You rarely see fare wars offered for peak travel times, but if you can travel in the off-months, you may snag a bargain.
- Try to book a ticket **in its country of origin.** If you're planning a one-way flight from Bangkok to Luang Prabang (Laos) or Siem Reap and Angkor Wat (Cambodia), a Thai travel agent will probably have the lowest fares. For multi-leg trips, book in the country of the first leg; for example, book New York–London–Amsterdam–Rome–New York in the U.S.
- **Consolidators,** also known as bucket shops, are great sources for international tickets, although they usually can't beat Internet fares within North America. Start by looking in Sunday newspaper travel sections; U.S. travelers should focus on the *New York Times, Los Angeles Times,* and *Miami Herald.* For less-developed destinations, small travel agents who cater to immigrant communities in large cities often have the best deals. *Beware:* Bucket-shop tickets are usually nonrefundable or rigged with stiff cancellation penalties, often as high as 50% to 75% of the ticket price, and some put you on charter airlines, which may leave at inconvenient times and experience delays. Try the folks at Join Us Travel (www.joinustravel.com) and talk with their Asian specialists.

  Several reliable consolidators are worldwide and available online. **STA Travel** has been the world's leading consolidator for students since purchasing Council Travel, but their

fares are competitive for travelers of all ages. **ELTExpress (Flights.com)** (© 800/TRAV-800; www.eltexpress. com) has excellent fares worldwide, particularly to Europe. They also have "local" websites in 12 countries. **FlyCheap** (© 800/FLY-CHEAP; www.1800flycheap.com) is owned by package-holiday megalith MyTravel and has especially good fares to sunny destinations. **Air Tickets Direct** (© 800/778-3447; www.airtickets direct.com) is based in Montreal and leverages the currently weak Canadian dollar for low fares; they also book trips to places that U.S. travel agents won't touch, such as Cuba.

- Join **frequent-flier clubs.** Frequent-flier membership doesn't cost a cent, but it does entitle you to better seats, faster response to phone inquiries, and prompter service if your luggage is stolen or your flight is canceled or delayed, or if you want to change your seat. And you don't have to fly to earn points; **frequent-flier credit cards** can earn you thousands of miles for doing your everyday shopping. With more than 70 mileage awards programs on the market, consumers have never had more options, but the system has never been more complicated—what with major airlines folding, new budget carriers emerging, and alliances forming (allowing you to earn points on partner airlines). Investigate the program details of your favorite airlines before you sink points into any one. Consider which airlines have hubs in the airport nearest you, and, of those carriers, which have the most advantageous alliances, given your most common routes? To play the frequent-flier game to your best advantage, consult Randy Petersen's **Inside Flyer** (www.insideflyer.com). Petersen and friends review all the programs in detail and post regular updates on changes in policies and trends. Petersen will also field direct questions (via e-mail) if a partner airline refuses to redeem points, for instance, or if you're still not sure after researching the various programs which one is right for you. It is well worth the $12 online subscription fee, good for 1 year.

LONG-HAUL FLIGHTS: HOW TO STAY COMFORTABLE

Long flights can be trying; stuffy air and cramped seats can make you feel as if you're being sent parcel post in a small box. But with a little advance planning, you can make an otherwise unpleasant experience almost bearable.

- Your choice of airline and airplane will definitely affect your leg room. Find more details at **www.seatguru. com,** which has extensive details about almost every seat on six major U.S. airlines. For international airlines, research firm Skytrax has posted a list of average seat pitches at **www.airlinequality.com**.

- Emergency exit seats and bulkhead seats typically have the most legroom. Emergency exit seats are usually left unassigned until the day of a flight (to ensure that someone able-bodied fills the seats); it is worth getting to the ticket counter early to snag one of these spots for a long flight. Many passengers find that bulkhead seating (the row facing the wall at the front of the cabin) offers more legroom, but keep in mind that bulkheads are where airlines often put baby bassinets, so you may be sitting next to an infant.

- To have two seats for yourself in a three-seat row, try for an aisle seat in a center section toward the back of coach. If you're traveling with a companion, book an aisle and a window seat. Middle seats are usually booked last, so chances are good you'll end up with three seats to yourselves. And in the event that a third passenger is assigned the middle seat, he or she will probably be more than happy to trade for a window or an aisle.

- Ask about entertainment options. Many airlines offer seatback video systems where you get to choose your movies or play video games—but only on some of their planes. (Boeing 777s are your best bet.)

- To sleep, avoid the last row of any section or the row in front of an emergency exit, as these seats are the least likely to recline. Avoid seats near highly trafficked toilet areas. Avoid seats in the back of many jets—these can be narrower than those in the rest of coach. You also may want to reserve a window seat so you can rest your head and avoid being bumped in the aisle.

- Get up, walk around, and stretch every 60 to 90 minutes to keep your blood flowing. This helps avoid **deep vein thrombosis (DVT),** or "economy-class syndrome," a potentially deadly condition caused by sitting in cramped conditions for too long. Other preventive measures include drinking lots of water and avoiding alcohol (see next bullet). See "Avoiding 'Economy Class Syndrome'" box under "Healthy & Safety," p. 35.

- Drink water before, during, and after your flight to combat the lack of humidity in airplane cabins—which can be drier than the Sahara. Bring a bottle of water on board. Avoid alcohol, which will dehydrate you.

- If you're flying with kids, don't forget to carry on toys, books, pacifiers, and chewing gum to help them relieve ear pressure buildup during ascent and descent. Let each child pack his or her own backpack with favorite toys.

BY BUS

There are many private buses linking Singapore and Malaysia with Hat Yai in southern Thailand. In Singapore, call the **Singapore Tourism Board** at ℂ **800/334-1335,** and in Malaysia call the **Malaysia Tourism Board** (ℂ **603/293-5188**) for more information. From Laos, regular buses can carry you over the border from any of a number of border crossings along the long Thai–Laos Border. The number to call for **Tourist Information in Vientiane** is ℂ **856-21/212-248.**

BY TRAIN

Thailand is accessible via train from Singapore and peninsular Malaysia. **Malaysia's Keretapi Tanah Melayu Berhad (KTM)** begins in Singapore (ℂ **65/222-5165**), stopping in Kuala Lumpur (ℂ **603/273-8000**) and Butterworth (Penang) (ℂ **604/323-7962**), before heading for Thailand, where it joins service with the State Railway of Thailand. Bangkok's Hua Lampong Railway Station is centrally located on Krung Kasem Road (ℂ **02223-7010** or 1690). Taxis, tuk-tuks (motorized three-wheeled vehicles), and public buses are just outside the station.

The *Eastern & Oriental Express* (www.orient-express.com) operates a 2-night/3-day journey between Singapore and Bangkok that makes *getting* there almost better than *being* there. The romance of 1930s colonial travel is joined with modern luxury in six Pullman cars, seven State cars, a Presidential car, plus two restaurant cars, a bar car, saloon, and observation cars. Along the way, stops are made in Penang (Georgetown) and Kanchanaburi (River Kwai) for light sightseeing. Current fares are per person one-way $1,440 Pullman superior double; $2,130 State double; and $2,900 Presidential Suite. Certain times of the year promotions will include overnights at The Oriental Bangkok and The Oriental Singapore. Call ℂ **800/524-2420** in the U.S., or **65/392-3500** in Singapore.

BY SHIP

Sun Cruises is the biggest name in cruising for the region. Stopping in Singapore, Malacca, and Penang in Malaysia, and Phuket, their floating resort has six restaurants, four Jacuzzis, pool, fitness center, spa, deck games, and seven bars and lounges. For details contact **Pacific Leisure** (Thailand), 156/13 Phang Nga Rd., Phuket, 83000 (ℂ **07623-2511;** fax 07623-2510; www.pacific-leisure.com).

11 Packages for the Independent Traveler

Before you start your search for the lowest airfare, you may want to consider booking your flight as part of a travel package. Package tours are not the same thing as escorted tours. Package tours are simply a way to buy the airfare, accommodations, and other elements of your trip (such as car rentals, airport transfers, and sometimes even activities) at the same time and often at discounted prices—kind of like one-stop shopping. Packages are sold in bulk to tour operators—who resell them to the public at a cost that usually undercuts standard rates.

One good source of package deals is the airlines themselves. Most major airlines offer air/land packages, including **American Airlines Vacations** (ℂ 800/321-2121; www.aavacations.com), **Delta Vacations** (ℂ 800/221-6666; www.delta vacations.com), **Continental Airlines Vacations** (ℂ 800/301-3800; www.co vacations.com), and **United Vacations** (ℂ 888/854-3899; www.unitedvacations. com). Several big **online travel agencies**—Expedia, Travelocity, Orbitz, Site59, and Lastminute.com—also do a brisk business in packages. If you're unsure about the pedigree of a smaller packager, check with the Better Business Bureau in the city where the company is based, or go online at www.bbb.org. If a packager won't tell you where they're based, don't fly with them.

Travel packages are also listed in the travel section of your local Sunday newspaper. Or check ads in the national travel magazines such as *Arthur Frommer's Budget Travel Magazine, Travel & Leisure, National Geographic Traveler,* and *Condé Nast Traveler.*

Package tours can vary by leaps and bounds. Some offer a better class of hotels than others. Some offer the same hotels for lower prices. Some offer flights on scheduled airlines, while others book charters. Some limit your choice of accommodations and travel days. You are often required to make a large payment up front. On the plus side, packages can save you money, offering group prices but allowing for independent travel. Some even let you add on a few guided excursions or escorted day trips (also at prices lower than if you booked them yourself) without booking an entirely escorted tour.

Before you invest in a package tour, get some answers. Ask about the **accommodations choices** and prices for each. Then look up the hotels' reviews in a Frommer's guide and check their rates online for your specific dates of travel. You'll also want to find out what **type of room** you'll get. If you need a certain type of room, ask for it; don't take whatever is thrown your way. Request a nonsmoking room, a quiet room, a room with a view, or whatever you fancy.

Finally, look for **hidden expenses.** Ask whether airport departure fees and taxes, for example, are included in the total cost.

12 Escorted General-Interest Tours

Escorted tours are structured group tours with a group leader. The price usually includes everything from airfare to hotels, meals, tours, admission costs, and local transportation.

- **Absolute Asia** Founded in 1989, Absolute Asia offers an array of innovative itineraries, specializing in individual or small group tours customized to your interests, with experienced local guides and excellent accommodations. Talk to them about tours that feature art, cuisine, religion, antiques, photography, wildlife study, archaeology, and soft adventure—they can plan a specialized trip to see just about anything you can dream up for any length of time. 180 Varick St., 16th Floor, New York, NY 10014; ✆ **800/736-8187;** fax 212/627-4090; www.absolute asia.com.

- **Asia Transpacific Journeys** Coordinating tours to every corner of South and Southeast Asia and the Pacific, Asia Transpacific Journeys deals with small groups and custom programs that include luxury hotel accommodations. They have specific tours for Thailand and their flagship package, the 23-day Passage to Indochina tour, takes you through all of the countries in Indochina. Asia Transpacific tours are fun and promote cultural understanding, a model of sustainable tourism, and are a highly recommended choice. 2995 Center Green Court, Boulder, CO 80301; ✆ **800/642-2742** or 303/443-6789; fax 303/443-7078; www.south eastasia.com or www.asiatranspacific. com.

- **Diethelm** The folks at this Swiss-based tour company, with offices throughout the region (and a popular choice for European tour groups), are friendly and helpful. Diethelm has full tour programs and can help with any details for travelers in-country, arrange car rental or vans for small groups, and offer discount options to all destinations. Kian Gwan Building II, 140/1 Wireless Rd., Bangkok 10330, Thailand; ℂ **662/255-9150;** fax 662/256-0248; www.diethelm-travel.com.

- **Intrepid** This popular Australian operator is probably the best choice to get off the beaten path on a tour of Asia. Intrepid caters tours for the culturally discerning, those with humanitarian goals, and adventure travelers on a budget looking for a group-oriented tour of off-the-map locations. Their motto is their name, and with some of the best guides in Asia, these folks will take you to the back of beyond safely, in style, and with lots of laughs. Box 2781, Fitzroy, DC VIC 3065, 12 Spring St., Fitzroy, Victoria, Australia; ℂ **613/9473-2626,** 877/488-1616 in the U.S.; fax 613/9419-4426; www.intrepidtravel.com.

Many people derive a certain ease and security from escorted trips. Escorted tours—whether by bus, motor coach, train, or boat—let travelers sit back and enjoy their trip without having to spend lots of time behind the wheel. All the little details are taken care of; you know your costs up front; and there are few surprises. Escorted tours can take you to the maximum number of sights in the minimum amount of time with the least amount of hassle—you don't have to sweat over the plotting and planning of a vacation schedule. Escorted tours are particularly convenient for people with limited mobility.

On the downside, an escorted tour often requires a big deposit up front, and lodging and dining choices are predetermined. As part of a cloud of tourists, you'll get little opportunity for serendipitous interactions with locals. The tours can be jam-packed with activities, leaving little room for individual sightseeing, whim, or adventure—plus they also often focus only on the heavily touristed sites, so you miss out on the lesser-known gems.

Before you invest in an escorted tour, ask about the **cancellation policy:** Is a deposit required? Can they cancel the trip if they don't get enough people? Do you get a refund if they cancel? If *you* cancel? How late can you cancel if you are unable to go? When do you pay in full? *Note:* If you choose an escorted tour, think strongly about purchasing trip-cancellation insurance, especially if the tour operator asks you to pay up front. See the section on "Travel Insurance," earlier in this chapter.

You'll also want to get a complete **schedule** of the trip to find out how much sightseeing is planned each day and whether enough time has been allotted for relaxing or wandering solo.

The **size** of the group is also important to know up front. Generally, the smaller the group, the more flexible the itinerary, and the less time you'll spend waiting for people to get on and off the bus. Find out the **demographics** of the group as well. What is the age range? What is the gender breakdown? Is this mostly a trip for couples or singles?

Discuss what is included in the **price.** You may have to pay for transportation to and from the airport. A box lunch may be included in an excursion, but drinks might cost extra. Tips may not be included. Find out if you will be charged if you decide to opt out of certain activities or meals.

Finally, if you plan to travel alone, you'll need to know if a **single supplement** will be charged and if the company can match you up with a roommate.

13 Outdoor Adventures

While for some the ideal holiday is days on end spent rolling around on a beach sucking back juicy cocktails, others want to push themselves to the limit, seeking thrills and adventure. Amazing Thailand's well-developed tourism industry offers lots of backcountry options. Routes have opened up nature's wild side to those who would dare, and many operators have jockeyed into place providing adventure-travel options that are professional, well planned, and safe for everyone, from beginners to experts. The following section will give you an overview of the many options, but for planning details refer to the specific destination.

The first thing many people consider for an active vacation is **scuba diving** or **snorkeling.** Living coral reefs grace the waters of the Andaman Sea, off Thailand's southwest coast, and the Gulf of Thailand. More than 80 species of coral have been discovered in the Gulf, while the deeper and more saline Andaman has more than 210. Marine life includes hundreds of species of fish, plus numerous varieties of crustaceans and sea turtles. With the aid of scuba gear, divers can get an up-close and personal view of this undersea universe. For those without certification, many reefs close to the surface are still vibrant.

From Phuket (see chapter 9) you can organize **long-term scuba trips** on live-aboard boats or you can take a day trip that includes two or three dives. From Ko Phi Phi, Krabi, Koh Samui, Hua Hin, Chumphon, and Pattaya (see chapters 8, "The Eastern Seaboard," 9, "Southern Peninsula: The East Coast & Islands," and 10, "Southern Peninsula: The West Coast & Islands"), many operators schedule frequent trips. All are staffed with PADI-certified dive masters, provide quality gear and decent boats, and are licensed by the Tourism Authority. Many

offer scuba training and certification packages, and can have you ready to dive in 5 days. Pretty much every beach has independent operators or guesthouses that rent snorkels, masks, and fins for the day. A few boat operators take snorkelers to reefs off neighboring islands—especially at Ko Phi Phi, Krabi, Koh Samui, and Pattaya.

Thailand's mountainous jungle terrain in the north has become a haven for **trekkers,** particularly those who wish to visit remote villages inhabited by the tribal people who live there. While the average trek lasts 3 days and 2 nights, some like to go out into the wilds for up to 10 days or more. Trekking usually involves no more than 3 to 4 hours of straight walking on jungle paths. All tours provide local guides to accompany groups, and the guides will keep the pace steady but comfortable for all trekkers involved. Some trips break up the monotonous walking with treks on elephant-back, in four-wheel-drive Jeeps, or light rafting on flat bamboo rafts. Chiang Mai (see chapter 12, "Chiang Mai") has the most trekking firms, while Chiang Rai, Pai, and Mae Hong Son (see chapter 13, "Touring the Northern Hills") also have their share of trekking companies. Our best recommendation for trekking is **Contact Travel** (© **05327-7178;** www.activethailand.com), a reputable outfitter with custom trips starting from their home base in Chiang Mai.

Thai officials are taking steps to preserve the nature and wildlife of its many different ecological zones, from swamp jungles in the south, to mountain forests in the north, to underwater marine parks in the Gulf of Thailand and the Andaman Sea. In more than 80 national parks, the kingdom also tries to teach visitors about not only the local wildlife species in residence, but also the delicate balance of each habitat. Many parks have clearly displayed informational exhibits at their visitor centers, trails with bridges and catwalks, and markers explaining the important elements of the environment and its inhabitants. Others provide rudimentary bungalow accommodations or can rent tents and supplies for campers. For more complete information, get in touch with the **Royal Forestry Department** at © 02579-5734 or 02579-7223.

River rafting in rubber rafts and kayaks is also becoming increasingly popular in Thailand, with operators in Pai (see chapter 13) and Mae Sot (see chapter 10, "Central Thailand"), taking small groups down local rivers. Winding through dense jungles, past rock formations and local villages, these trips include camping and sometimes trekking. Rapids are rarely extreme but are big enough to be loads of fun, and safety measures are taken seriously. If you're a true enthusiast, talk to Thai Adventure Rafting in Pai about accompanying a group in your own kayak or canoe (see chapter 13).

A few lucky folks know that Thailand is home to 1 of the top 10 climbing walls in the world. **Rock climbing** at Raillay beach in Krabi (see chapter 9) is attracting lovers of the sport, who come to have a go at these challenging cliffs. Views are breathtaking—truly amazing scenery out into the Andaman and surrounding islands. A few small outfits accept beginners for training or will organize climbs for more specialized experts, providing all necessary equipment.

14 Getting Around Thailand

Thailand's domestic transport is accessible, efficient, and inexpensive. If your time is short, fly. But if you have the time to take in the countryside, travel by bus, train, or private car. Read carefully the options below.

BY PLANE

Bangkok's **Don Muang International Airport** may not be as glitzy as its neighbors' newer airports, but it works well—services and gates are easy to find, many airport staff speak English, there's convenient transportation to town, and it is relatively safe. Airports in other cities usually tend to have money-changing facilities, information counters, and waiting ground transportation. In the very small places, you'll have to arrange airport pick-up either through your hotel or the airline.

Most domestic flights are on **Thai Airways,** part of Thai Airways International, 6 Larn Luang Rd., Bangkok (© 02535-2084), with Bangkok as its hub. Flights connect Bangkok and 27 domestic cities, including Chiang Mai, Chiang Rai, Mae Hong Son, Phitsanulok, Loei, Surat Thani, and Phuket. There are also connecting flights between many of these cities.

Bangkok Airways, Queen Sirikit Convention Center, New Ratchadaphisek Road, Bangkok (© 02229-3456), has a very convenient flight that links Phuket with Koh Samui directly. It also flies to Ranong, U Tapao (near Pattaya), Sukhothai, and Chiang Mai, with international flights from Singapore and Phnom Penh. **Air Andaman,** 87 Nai Lert Bldg., 4th Floor, Unit 402a, Sukhumvit Rd. (© 02251-4905) handles short domestic hops. Double-check all flights before making arrangements as these routes change frequently.

Check what's on offer from Thailand's latest budget carrier, **Air Asia** (© 02515-9999 in Bangkok; www.airasia.com). They fly between Bangkok and Chiang Mai, Phuket, Hat Yai, and Khon Kaen for super cheap.

Note that for international departures a 500B ($12) airport tax is levied. For domestic flights, airport taxes range between 30B to 150B (75¢–$3.65), but are normally included with your ticket purchase.

BY CAR

Renting a car is a snap in Thailand, although self-driving in Bangkok traffic is discouraged. One-way streets, construction projects, and traffic jams are frequent and frustrating. Outside the city, it is a good option, although Thai drivers are quite reckless, and American drivers must reorient themselves to driving on the left side of the road.

Among the many car-rental agencies, both **Avis** (*C* **02255-5300**) and **Budget** (*C* **02566-5067**) each have convenient offices around the country.

You can rent a car with or without a driver. All drivers are required to have an international driver's license. At press time, self-drive rates started at 1,500B ($37) per day for a small Suzuki four-wheel-drive and much more for luxury vehicles.

Local tour operators in larger destinations like Chiang Mai, Phuket, or Koh Samui will rent cars for considerably cheaper than the larger, more well-known agencies. Sometimes the savings are up to 50%. These companies also rarely require international driver's licenses but will accept your local license from back home as proof you know how to drive. Always ask if you will still be covered by their insurance policy—if you are taken to court for an accident, you may be found guilty for not being properly licensed. Make sure you're covered before you sign.

Gas stations are conveniently located along highways and in towns and cities. Esso, Shell, Caltex, and PTT all have competitive rates. Expect to pay about 400B ($9.75) each time you fill your tank.

BY TRAIN

Bangkok's **Hua Lampong Railway Station** is a convenient, user-friendly facility: Clear signs point the way to public toilets, coin phones, the food court, and baggage check area. A Post & Telegraph Office, Information Counter, police box, ATMs and money-changing facilities, convenience shops, baggage check, and restaurants surround a large open seating area.

From this hub, the State Railway of Thailand provides regular service to destinations north as far as Chiang Mai, northeast to Udon Thani, east to Pattaya, and south to Thailand's southern border, where it connects with Malaysia's *Keretapi Tanah Melayu Berhad* (KTM) with service to Penang (Butterworth), Kuala Lumpur, and Singapore. Complete schedules and fare information can be obtained at any railway station or by calling **Hua Lampong Railway Station** directly at *C* **02223-7010,** or call their information hot line at *C* **1690.**

There are a number of different trains, each running at a different speed and priced accordingly. The fastest is the Special Express, which is the best choice for long-haul, overnight travel. These trains cut travel time by as much as 60%, and have sleeper cars, which are a must for the really long trips. Rapid trains are the next best option. Prices vary for class, from air-conditioned sleeper cars in first class to air-conditioned and fan sleepers or seats in second, on down to the straight-backed, hard seats in third class.

Warning: On trains, pay close attention to your possessions. Thievery is common on overnight trips.

BY BUS

Thailand has a very efficient and inexpensive bus system, highly recommended for budget travelers and short-haul trips. Buses are the cheapest transportation to the farthest and most remote destinations in the country. Options abound, but the major choices are public or private and air-conditioned or non-air-conditioned.

trips usually depart in the ... arrive at their destination ... morning. Whenever you can, opt for the VIP buses, especially for overnight trips. Some have 36 seats; better ones have 24 seats. The extra cost is well worth the legroom. Also, stick to government buses operated from each city's proper bus terminal. Many private companies sell VIP tickets for major routes, but put you on a standard bus. Ideally, buses are best for short excursions; expect to pay a minimum of 50B ($1.25) for a one-way ticket. Longer-haul buses are an excellent value (usually less than $1 per hour of travel), but can be very slow.

Warning: When traveling by long-distance bus, pay close attention to your possessions. Thievery is common, particularly on overnight buses when valuables are left in overhead racks.

BY TAXI

The more expensive, private cars affiliated with hotels and travel agents post their rates, but you'll have to negotiate with public sedan taxis, sometimes even metered taxis, and tuk-tuk (motorized three-wheel trishaw/pedicab) drivers. If you don't know the correct fare, ask a shop owner, hotelier, or restaurateur what you should expect to pay for your destination and negotiate accordingly. Tuk-tuk rides start at 30B/75¢ for short hops; be sure to bargain hard with these guys, and don't let 'em take you for a ride (in other words, shopping trips or to massage parlors). In most provincial areas and resort islands, small pickup trucks called *songtao* cruise the main streets offering group-ride taxi service at cheap, set fees. With taxis, tuk-tuks, or *songtao*, always remember to agree on your fare before engaging a driver. Tipping is not expected but gladly accepted.

15 Tips on Accommodations

The well-traveled areas in Bangkok, Phuket, Chiang Mai, Pattaya, and Koh Samui offer up the widest assortment of accommodation. International chains like Sheraton, Marriott, Westin, Le Meridien, and Holiday Inn have some of the finest hotels and resorts in the country, while the Thai-owned and operated Dusit and Amari chains have numerous properties that can compete with the best. Five-star hotels and resorts spare no detail for the business or leisure traveler, providing designer toiletries, plush robes, in-room stereo systems, in-house videos, and many other creature comforts that will fill your life with luxury. Some of the best restaurants are operated by hotels, and many of the finer properties host a whole range of dining choices. With more facilities, better activity options and services, and well-trained staff, you'll have the time of your life, but plan to spend more than 10,200B ($249) a night for a double room (see the "Very Expensive"

category in any destination chapter). Many hotels in this category have started quoting prices in U.S. dollars.

Most hotels that fall into the "Expensive" category have all the bells and whistles, but feature less deluxe amenities; silk bathrobes, personal stereos, and in-house movies are gone, and room design and furnishings become less luxurious. However, most rooms are handsome and well maintained, and facilities tend to be good quality. Expect to pay around 5,000B ($122) per night.

"Moderate" hotels and resorts start at about 2,000B ($49) and are often quite modern and a good value for the money. Most have swimming pools, good restaurants, toiletries in the room, satellite television with movie channels, in-room safes, and international direct dialing from your room. In smaller cities and towns, this category is about the best you can do, but some of these moderately priced options can have facilities and rooms of surprising quality. And prices are discounted greatly, as little as 1,000B ($24) depending on the season.

Thailand is heaven for the budget traveler and the many mom-and-pop guesthouses or budget hotels and hostels are often as much a part of the experience of travel in country as anything. If you go really inexpensive, expect to rough it. Cold-water showers, fan-cooled rooms, and dormitories are the norm. But sometimes you find inexpensive accommodations that stand out from the pack—quaint beachside bungalow villages, city hotels with good locations, or small guesthouses with knowledgeable and helpful staff.

Expensive and moderately priced hotels add a 10% service charge plus 7% government tax, also called value-added tax (VAT), with the exception of special offers that are mostly inclusive of these fees.

And, finally, a note regarding our amenities listings, some of which are unique to Asian hotels. "Coffee/tea-making facilities" means you have complimentary instant tea and coffee and an electric kettle in your room. Where "satellite TV" is indicated, that means you'll get channels like CNN, BBC, MTV, and possibly a movie channel or two, such as HBO or Cinemax.

Thailand has its own rating system based on the number of amenities in any given hotel, but the system is arbitrary and takes little account of quality. Often the smaller boutique resorts of the highest quality have lower star ratings because they lack the "business center and meeting facilities for 250 or more" required. It's best to go by reputation rather than the Thai ratings system.

SAVING ON YOUR HOTEL ROOM

The **rack rate** is the maximum rate that a hotel charges for a room. Hardly anybody pays this price, however, except in high season or on holidays. To lower the cost of your room:

- **Ask about special rates or other discounts.** Always ask whether a less expensive room than the first one quoted is available, or whether any special rates apply to you. You may qualify for corporate, student, military, senior, or other discounts. Mention membership in AAA, AARP, frequent-flier programs, or trade unions, which may entitle you to special deals as well. Find out the hotel policy on children—do kids stay free in the room or qualify for a special rate?

- **Dial direct.** When booking a room in a chain hotel, you'll often get a better deal by calling the individual hotel's reservation desk rather than the chain's main number.

- **Book online.** Many hotels offer Internet-only discounts, or supply rooms to Priceline, Hotwire, or Expedia at rates much lower than the ones you can get through the hotel itself. Shop around. And if you have special needs—a quiet room, a room with a view—call the hotel directly and make your needs known after you've booked online.

- **Remember the law of supply and demand.** Resort hotels are most crowded and therefore most expensive on weekends, so discounts are usually available for midweek stays. Business hotels in downtown locations are busiest during the week, so you can expect big discounts over the weekend. Many hotels have high-season and low-season prices, and booking the day after "high season" ends can mean big discounts.

- **Look into group or long-stay discounts.** If you come as part of a large group, you should be able to negotiate a bargain rate, since the hotel can then guarantee occupancy in a number of rooms. Likewise, if you're planning a long stay (at least 5 days), you might qualify for a discount. As a general rule, expect 1 night free after a 7-night stay.

- **Avoid excess charges and hidden costs.** When you book a room, ask whether the hotel charges for parking. Use your own cell phone, pay phones, or prepaid phone cards instead of dialing directly from hotel phones, which usually have exorbitant rates. And don't be tempted by the room's minibar offerings: Most hotels charge through the nose for water, soda, and snacks. Finally, ask about local taxes and service charges, which can increase the cost of a room by 15% or more. If a hotel insists upon tacking on a surprise "energy surcharge" that wasn't mentioned at check-in or a "resort fee" for amenities you didn't use, you can often make a case for getting it removed.
- **Book an efficiency.** A room with a kitchenette allows you to shop for groceries and cook your own meals. This is a big money saver, especially for families on long stays.

Note that there has been a large boom in construction of private villas and timeshare properties in places like Koh Samui and Phuket, and many travelers fall in love with Thailand and buy in right away.

LANDING THE BEST ROOM

Somebody has to get the best room in the house. It might as well be you. You can start by joining the hotel's frequent-guest program, which may make you eligible for upgrades. A hotel-branded credit card usually gives its owner "silver" or "gold" status in frequent-guest programs for free. Always ask about a corner room. They're often larger and quieter, with more windows and light, and they often cost the same as standard rooms. When you make your reservation, ask if the hotel is renovating; if it is, request a room away from the construction. Ask about nonsmoking rooms, rooms with views, rooms with twin, queen- or king-size beds. If you're a light sleeper, request a quiet room away from vending machines, elevators, restaurants, bars, and discos. Ask for a room that has been most recently renovated or redecorated.

If you aren't happy with your room when you arrive, ask for another one. Most lodgings will be willing to accommodate you.

In resort areas, particularly in warm climates, ask the following questions before you book a room:

- What's the view like? Cost-conscious travelers may be willing to pay less for a back room facing the parking lot, especially if they don't plan to spend much time in their room.
- Does the room have air-conditioning or ceiling fans? Do the windows open? If they do, and the nighttime entertainment takes place alfresco, you may want to find out when show time is over.
- How far is the room from the beach and other amenities? If it is far, is there transportation to and from the beach, and is it free?

16 Tips on Dining

One of the greatest joys of visiting Thailand is the plethora of dining options in any area. From high-class hotel restaurants and power-lunch points, to street-side noodle stands, you'll find it all, and in this volume we list the whole range.

Storefront restaurants and street vendors, apart from those in a specified night market area, are open early morning to late at night. Restaurants catering to tourists also open from morning until late. You're not expected to tip at a Thai restaurant, but rounding up the bill or leaving 20B (50¢) on top of most checks is acceptable. A 15% to 20% tip will shock and awe in smaller restaurants, but will be accepted (sometimes even tacked on) at fine-dining outlets.

The larger cities and towns play host to a whole range of Western and international restaurants. Bangkok in particular covers all the bases, but going for authentic Thai is usually a far better option than the bland, faux-Western dishes served at many budget traveler restaurants (the same place that serves soggy hamburgers on sweet rolls probably makes a great pad thai).

One-dish meals like noodle soup or fried-rice or noodles are popular for solo travelers, but Thai meals are best when shared family style. There are many regional variations, but the most notable are the barbecue, sticky-rice, and spicy papaya salads in Isan (the northeast), and the fiery coconut curries of the south; always ask about regional specials. Most family meals consist of a meat or fish dish (often a whole fish), fried or steamed vegetables, a curry, stir-fried dishes of meat and vegetables, and a soup, such as fiery Tom Yam. Meals are lengthy and boisterous affairs, and food is picked-at slowly. Drink flows freely in Thailand, and local beer, as well as rice whiskey, accompanies most meals.

Thais are very practical about table manners. If something is best eaten with the hands, then feel free. If there are seeds or bones to spit out, you just go ahead and spit 'em out. Single-serve noodle soups are usually eaten with chopsticks and a Chinese spoon, but you won't be bothering anyone to ask for a fork. Rice dishes are eaten with a spoon and fork, the spoon commonly held in the right hand, and the fork in the left is used only to load the spoon for delivery; follow local customs if you wish, but do whatever you're comfortable with.

17 Recommended Books, Films & Music

Anna and the King, the original work of Anna Leonowens, the late 19th century governess for the children of King Rama IV, Thailand's most progressive leader, who, with the help of Anna's feisty insight, brought the kingdom into this century. Don't miss the film of the same name starring Jodie Foster (though due to gross historical inaccuracies the film was banned from public release in Thailand).

The Beach, by Alex Garland, and the popular film featuring Leonardo DiCaprio, tells the story of young backpackers in search of the perfect hideaway. Following a map given them by a man on the edge, the searchers swim to a remote island (not far from Samui) and join a community of dropouts living in bliss on a beautiful, secluded beach, the sea providing the food and nearby fields full of all the ganja they can smoke. The story has become a popular model for the modern Utopia, and travelers in Thailand seem to enjoy the idea of a heaven on earth in the Thai south (and most find that today's overdeveloped beachfronts come up short). I like the way Khao San Road, the neon-lit backpacker ghetto of Bangkok, is depicted as mysterious and exotic—quite the contrary. For another Utopia, check-out Emily Barr's *Backpacker,* another model for idealistic travel and soul-searching in Thailand.

I really like Tiziano Terzai's book, *A Fortune-Teller Told Me.* Though not about Thailand exclusively, Terzai offers a well-crafted portrait of the interlocking cultures of Asia, telling how China's diaspora affects the region and painstakingly relating the interesting minutia of Southeast Asian culture in an autobiography of his search for personal destiny.

Also look for the popular *Bangkok 8,* an internationally acclaimed thriller.

For help in understanding what the heck is going on around you in Thailand, pick up a copy of *Culture Shock! Thailand* by Robert and Nanthapa Cooper. Most bookstores in the West and in Thailand sell a host of useful phrase-books and Thai/English dictionaries. For more comprehensive study of the basics of Thai writing and speaking, pick up a copy of *Thailand for Beginners* by Benjawan Becker.

Asia Books, a Thai bookseller with outlets throughout the country, is also a small press publisher and offers some interesting and informative writing about Thailand and Asia in general. Stop by any of their stores in Bangkok or the larger tourist centers, and look for their titles in small kiosks at beachside convenience stores in resort towns. Carol Hollinger's *Mai Pen Rai Means Nevermind* is a personal history of time spent in the kingdom some 30 years ago, but the cultural insights are quite current. *Patpong Sisters* by Cleo Odzer and *Sex Slaves* by Louise

Brown are both interesting exposés of the Thai sex industry. These are but a few of the many titles published by Asia Books.

The full list would be long, but below are just a few of the many books about Buddhism and the Thai Theravadan traditions: For the word straight from the horse's mouth, try any of the writing by Ajahn Buddhadasa, a widely published Thai monk and founder of Wat Suan Mohk, an international meditation center in the south of Thailand. Buddhadasa's *Handbook for Mankind* and *The ABCs of Buddhism* are good introductions to meditation practice. Also look for writing by Jack Kornfield, an American who writes about meditation practices in works like *A Path With Heart*. Phra Peter Parrapadipo's *Phra Farang,* literally "the foreign monk," tells the story of an Englishman turned Thai Buddhist monk. A unique read.

FAST FACTS: Thailand

American Express There is no specific agent that handles American Express services in Thailand anymore, but they have an **American Express** office at 388 Pahonyothin Rd. in Bangkok. You can reach the office at ☎ **02273-5296** during business hours (Mon–Fri 8:30am–4:30pm) or call their customer service hot line (☎ **02273-5544**) with any problems or questions.

ATM Networks Most major banks throughout the country have ATMs. In general, you can get cash with your debit card at any Bangkok Bank, Thai Farmers Bank, Siam Commercial Bank, or Bank of Ayudhya—provided your card is hooked into the MasterCard/Cirrus or Visa/PLUS network. See the "Money" section, earlier in this chapter.

Business Hours Government offices (including branch post offices) are open Monday to Friday 8:30am to 4:30pm, with a lunch break between noon and 1pm. Businesses are generally open 8am to 5pm. Shops often stay open from 8am until 7pm or later, 7 days a week. Department stores are generally open 10am to 7pm.

Car Rentals See "Getting Around," earlier in this chapter.

Currency See "Money," earlier in this chapter.

Driving Rules See "Getting Around," earlier in this chapter.

Drugstores Throughout the country, there are excellent drugstores stocked with many brand-name medications and toiletries, plus less expensive local brands. Pharmacists often speak some English, and a surprising number of drugs that require a prescription elsewhere can be dispensed at their discretion.

Electricity All outlets—except in some luxury hotels—are 220 volts AC (50 cycles). Outlets have two flat-pronged or round-pronged holes, so you may need an adapter. If you use a 110-volt hair dryer, electric shaver, or battery charger for a computer, bring a transformer and adapter.

Embassies & Consulates While most countries have consular representation in Bangkok, the United States, Australia, Canada, and the United Kingdom also have consulates in Chiang Mai. See chapters 4, "Introducing Bangkok," and 12 for details. Most embassies have 24-hour emergency services. If you are seriously injured or ill, do not hesitate to call your embassy for assistance.

Emergencies Throughout the country, the emergency number you should use is ⓒ **1699** or ⓒ **1155** for the Tourist Police. Don't expect many English speakers at normal police posts outside the major tourist areas. (Ambulances must be summoned from hospitals rather than through a central service.) You should also contact your embassy or consulate, the Tourist Police, or the local Tourist Authority of Thailand (TAT) office.

Etiquette & Customs Practicing cultural sensitivity is very important in Thailand, and even longtime visitors are bound to come up against new and different faux pas to trip them up. Pay close attention to what Thai people do, especially in temples and at the table, and you'll be fine.

Appropriate Attire: You wouldn't know it by the current fashion trends in urban Bangkok, where tiny miniskirts and bare midriffs are common, but Thai people are quite modest. Longer shorts and even sleeveless tops are permissible for foreigners of both sexes, but short-shorts or miniskirts are not really appropriate. You'll see Thai men wandering about without shirts, and while many foreign visitors take this as a cue to strip down and beat the heat, it is not acceptable anywhere but the beach—foreigners, strangely, are held to a different set of expectations.

Gestures: The traditional Thai greeting is called the *wai*. To perform this, place your hands together at chest or chin level as if you are praying, bow your head to your hands, and bow your upper body slightly. The *wai* is also used to say thank you and goodbye. It is good to return the greeting if you're given it, but when entering hotels and restaurants, where everyone is strictly business, visitors are not expected to return the gesture. In a business setting, a handshake is more appropriate.

From traditions as old as the Buddha in Thailand, the head is considered the most sacred part of the body, and the feet are the lowliest; therefore, do not casually touch another person's head or even nonchalantly tousle the hair of a child, and don't sit with your legs crossed or otherwise point your feet at someone and particularly not toward Buddhist images. If you are seated on the floor, men may sit with the legs crossed, but women should tuck them to one side. In crowded places, on buses and trains, for example, it is common to make room (even when you think there is none) for others to pass rather than inviting them to go over and thus expose the bottoms of their feet toward you. As in most cultures, pointing with the finger is also considered rude; Thais use a palms-up hand gesture when signifying direction or indicating a person or thing. Beckoning is done with what looks to Westerners like a wave goodbye.

Men and women should avoid public displays of affection, though these rules are changing with the generations, and it is more and more common to see young couples snuggling. Women should never try to shake hands with or even hand something directly to a monk, and it is common that bus or train seating arrangements change when a monk gets on board so that monks are separate from women. Similar rules apply to Muslim temples, where women should remember to wear appropriately modest attire.

Avoiding Offense: Funny, but the best way to avoid offending anyone in Thailand is not to show your offense and express anger, a "face-losing" proposition for you and very embarrassing for the Thai people around you. Most Thai people are Buddhist, and a person showing violence or ill temper is regarded with surprise and disapproval. A gentle approach will take you farther, and patient persistence and a smile will achieve more, especially when haggling, than an argument. It is important to haggle, of course, but just one or two go-rounds are usually enough, and "no" means no. If you have a disagreement of any kind, keep your cool.

It's also important to remember the concept of "Thai time," and that appointments are loosely kept and offense at someone's tardiness is met with confusion. If you make an appointment with someone who doesn't deal with many other international visitors, be ready to wait (or come late yourself).

A common greeting in Thailand is to ask, "Have you eaten yet?" *(Kin kao laew reu yang?),* telling of the importance, common in many cultures, of offering and accepting hospitality whenever possible. Western visitors are often asked to join impromptu feasts. Hospitality is one thing, but don't feel pressed into drinking rice wine (I've had offers at breakfast); if something looks unsavory or really turns you off, it is okay to politely decline an offer (but just a taste will make your host happy).

Be sensitive, particularly in Buddhist temples, Muslim mosques, and among hill-tribe people in the far north, and ask before taking photographs. Hill-tribe spirit gates in particular should not be photographed at all.

Holidays See "Calendar of Events," earlier in this chapter.

Hot lines There are regular meetings of **Alcoholics Anonymous (AA)** in Bangkok and around Thailand. Check their regional website at www.aathailand.org or call the AA hot line at ⓒ **02231-8300.**

Information See "Visitor Information," earlier in this chapter.

Internet Access You'll find Internet cafes everywhere in Thailand. See the Fast Facts sections in specific destination chapters for details.

Language Central (often called Bangkok) Thai is the official language. English is spoken in the major cities at most hotels, restaurants, and shops, and is the second language of the professional class, as well as the international business language. (For more information on the Thai language, see "The Language," in appendix A.)

Liquor Laws The official drinking age in Thailand is 18, but laws are loosely followed—you can buy alcohol in most areas any time of day or night, with exceptions for certain Buddhist holidays. All restaurants, bars, and nightclubs sell booze, and you can pickup take-away-size packages from just about anywhere. Nightlife spots now close at 2am at the latest (and the rule is being policed vigorously).

Lost & Found Be sure to tell all of your credit card companies the minute you discover your wallet has been lost or stolen and file a report at the nearest police precinct. Your credit card company or insurer may require a police report number or record of the loss. Most credit card companies have an emergency toll-free number to call if your card is lost or stolen; they may be able to wire you a cash advance immediately or deliver an emergency credit card in a day or two. Visa's U.S. emergency number is ✆ 800/847-2911 or 410/581-9994. American Express cardholders and traveler's check holders should call ✆ 800/221-7282. MasterCard holders should call ✆ 800/307-7309 or 636/722-7111. For other credit cards, call the toll-free number directory at ✆ 800/555-1212.

To report a lost or stolen credit card in Thailand, call these service lines: **American Express** (✆ 02273-5544); **Diners Club** (✆ 02238-3660); **MasterCard** (✆ 02260-8572); and **Visa** (✆ 02256-7326).

If you need emergency cash over the weekend when all banks are closed, you can have money wired to you via **Western Union** (✆ 800/325-6000; www.westernunion.com).

Identity theft or fraud are potential complications of losing your wallet, especially if you've lost your driver's license along with your cash and credit cards. Notify the major credit-reporting bureaus immediately; placing a fraud alert on your records may protect you against liability for criminal activity. The three major U.S. credit-reporting agencies are **Equifax** (✆ 800/766-0008; www.equifax.com), **Experian** (✆ 888/397-3742; www.experian.com), and **TransUnion** (✆ 800/680-7289; www.transunion.com). Finally, if you've lost all forms of photo ID call your airline and explain the situation; they might allow you to board the plane if you have a copy of your passport or birth certificate and a copy of the police report you've filed.

Mail You can use *poste restante* as an address anywhere in the country. For those unfamiliar with this service, it is comparable to General Delivery in the United States, whereby you can receive mail addressed to you, care of Poste Restante, GPO, Name of City, and the mail is held for you at the post office or GPO until you pick it up. You need either a valid passport or ID card, must sign a receipt, and pay 1B (2¢) per letter received. Hours of operation are the same as the post office. Airmail postcards to the United States cost 12B to 15B (30¢–35¢), depending on the size of the card; first-class letters cost 19B (45¢) per 5 grams (rates to Europe are about the same). Airmail delivery usually takes 7 days.

Air parcel post costs 610B ($15) per kilogram. Surface or sea parcel post costs 215B ($5.25) for 1 kilogram (3 or 4 months for delivery). International Express Mail (EMS) costs 440B ($11) from 1 to 250 grams, with delivery guaranteed within 4 days. See individual chapters for local post offices and their hours.

Shipping by air freight is expensive. Two major international delivery services have their main dispatching offices in Bangkok, though they deliver throughout the country; these are **DHL Thailand,** Grand Amarin Tower Building, Phetchaburi Road (© **02207-0600**), and **Federal Express,** at Rama IV Road (© **02367-3222**). **UPS Parcel Delivery Service,** with a main branch in Bangkok at 16/1 Soi 44/1 Sukhumvit Road (© **02712-3300**), also has branches elsewhere in Thailand. Many businesses will also package and mail merchandise for a reasonable price.

Maps The **TAT** gives out regional and city maps at their information offices, and there are a number of good privately produced maps, usually free, available at most hotels and many businesses.

Newspapers & Magazines The major domestic English-language dailies are the *Bangkok Post* and *The Nation,* distributed in the morning in the capital and later in the day around the country. They cover the domestic political scene, as well as international news from AP, UPI, and Reuters wire services, and cost 20B (50¢). Both the *Asian Wall Street Journal* and *International Herald Tribune* are available Monday to Friday on their day of publication in Bangkok (in the provinces a day or two later). *Time, Newsweek,* the *Economist, Asiaweek,* and the *Far Eastern Economic Review* are sold at newsstands in the international hotels, as well as in bookstores in all the major cities.

Passports **For Residents of the United States:** Whether you're applying in person or by mail, you can download passport applications from the U.S. State Department website at **travel.state.gov.** For general information, call the **National Passport Agency** (© **202/647-0518**). To find your regional passport office, either check the U.S. State Department website or call the **National Passport Information Center** (© **900/225-5674**); the fee is 55¢ per minute for automated information and $1.50 per minute for operator-assisted calls.

For Residents of Canada: Passport applications are available at travel agencies throughout Canada or from the central **Passport Office,** Department of Foreign Affairs and International Trade, Ottawa, ON K1A 0G3 (© **800/567-6868;** www.ppt.gc.ca).

For Residents of the United Kingdom: To pick up an application for a standard 10-year passport (5-year passport for children under 16), visit your nearest passport office, major post office, or travel agency or contact the **United Kingdom Passport Service** at © **0870/521-0410,** or search its website at www.ukpa. gov.uk.

For Residents of Ireland: You can apply for a 10-year passport at the **Passport Office,** Setanta Centre, Molesworth Street, Dublin 2 (© **01/671-1633;** www.irl gov.ie/iveagh). Those under age 18 and over 65 must apply for a €12 3-year passport. You can also apply at 1A South Mall, Cork (© **021/272-525**) or at most main post offices.

For Residents of Australia: You can pick up an application from your local post office or any branch of Passports Australia, but you must schedule an interview at the passport office to present your application materials. Call the **Australian Passport Information Service** at © **131-232,** or visit the government website at www.passports.gov.au.

For Residents of New Zealand: You can pick up a passport application at any New Zealand Passports Office or download it from their website. Contact the

Passports Office at © 0800/225-050 in New Zealand or 04/474-8100, or log on to www.passports.govt.nz.

Police The **Tourist Police** (© **1699** or **1155**), with offices in every city (see specific chapters), speak English (and other foreign languages) and are open 24 hours. You should call them in an emergency rather than the regular police because there is no guarantee that the regular police operator will speak English.

Restrooms The better restaurants and hotels will have Western toilets. Shops and budget hotels will have an Asian toilet, aka "squatty potty," a hole in the ground with foot pads on either side. Near the toilet is a water bucket or sink with a small ladle. The water is for flushing and cleaning the toilet. Don't count on these places having toilet paper. Some shopping malls have dispensers outside the restroom—2B (5¢) for some paper. Dispose of it in the wastebasket provided, as it will clog up rudimentary sewage systems.

Safety Anonymous violent crime in Thailand is rare; however petty crime such as purse snatching or pickpocketing is common. Overland travelers should take care on overnight buses and trains for small-time thieves. In remote parts of the country and near the Burmese and Laos borders, local bandits or rebel groups have been known to rob travelers.

Beware of credit card scams; carry a minimum of cards, don't allow them out of your sight, and keep all receipts. Never leave your cards with others for safekeeping (such as during a trek). If you don't want to carry them, put them in a hotel safe. Don't carry unnecessary valuables, and keep those you do carry in your hotel's safe. Pay particular attention to your things, especially purses and wallets, on public transportation.

A special warning: Be wary of strangers who offer to guide you (particularly in Bangkok), take you to any shop (especially jewelry shops), or buy you food or drink. This is most likely to occur near a tourist sight. Be warned that this kind of forward behavior is simply not normal for the average Thai. There are rare exceptions, but most likely these new "friends" will try to swindle you in some way. This often takes the form of trying to persuade you to buy "high quality" jewelry or gems (usually worthless) at "bargain" prices. Also, beware of anyone inviting you to his or her home, then offering to show you a famous Thai card game or engage you in any sort of gambling. You will lose. If you are approached about such schemes, call the Tourist Police immediately (see above for more information).

For those who contemplate bringing a prostitute to their hotel room, be advised of the danger of food or drink laced with sleeping potions. There are many incidents with victims waking up 2 days later to find their valuables gone.

Smoking Thailand has just recently imposed a ban on smoking in restaurants and it looks like it is going to stick. Quite surprising, really. If the restaurant is attached to a bar, though, there are both smoking and non-smoking sections.

Taxes & Service Charges Hotels charge a 7% government value-added tax (VAT) and typically add a 10% service charge; hotel restaurants add 8.25% government tax. Smaller hotels quote the price inclusive of these charges.

Telephones Major hotels in Thailand feature convenient international direct-dial (IDD), long-distance service, and in-house fax transmission. Hotels charge a surcharge on local and long-distance calls, which can add up to 50% in some cases. Credit card or collect calls are a much better value, but most hotels also add a hefty service charge for them to your bill.

Most major post offices have special offices or booths for overseas calls, as well as fax and telex service, usually open 7am to 11pm. There are Overseas Telegraph and Telephone offices (also called OCO or Overseas Call Office) open 24 hours throughout the country for long-distance international calls and telex and fax service. In addition, several guesthouses and travel agents in tourist areas offer long-distance calling on their private line or using very affordable net-to-phone connections of varying quality. Local calls can be made from any red or blue public pay telephone. Calls cost 1B (2¢) for 3 minutes, with additional 1B (2¢) coins needed after hearing multiple beeps on the line. Blue public phones are for long-distance calls within Thailand. Card phones can be found in most airports, in many public buildings, and in larger shopping centers. Cards can be purchased in several denominations at Telephone Organization of Thailand (TOT) offices or in any convenience store. Yellow TOT cards are sold in denominations of 300B and 500B ($7.30 and $12) and are specific for domestic or international phones that are clearly marked as such. Also, **Hatari PhoneNet** offers prepaid cards where you access an account via a toll-free number (the best deal going). All phone cards are available at convenience stores everywhere.

To call Thailand: If you're calling Thailand from the United States:

1. Dial the international access code: 011
2. Dial the country code: 66
3. And dial the number. So the whole number you'd dial for Bangkok would be 011-66-2-000-0000.

Important note: When making domestic calls to Thailand, be sure to omit the "0" that appears before all phone numbers in this guide (thus you will only dial 8 digits after the "66" country code).

To make international calls: To make international calls from Thailand, first dial 00 and then the country code (U.S. or Canada 1, U.K. 44, Ireland 353, Australia 61, New Zealand 64). Next you dial the area code and number. For example, if you wanted to call the British Embassy in Washington, D.C., you would dial 00-1-202-588-7800.

For directory assistance: Dial ℂ **1133.**

Time Zone Bangkok and all of Thailand are 7 hours ahead of GMT (Greenwich Mean Time). During winter months, this means that Bangkok is exactly 7 hours ahead of London, 12 hours ahead of New York, and 15 hours ahead of Los Angeles. Daylight saving time will add 1 hour to these figures.

Tipping If no service charge is added to your check in a fine dining establishment, a 10% to 15% tip is appropriate. In local shops, a small tip of 10B (25¢) or so is common. Airport or hotel porters expect tips, but just 20B to 50B (50¢–$1.25) is acceptable. Feel free to reward good service wherever you find it. Tipping taxi drivers is not expected, but it is accepted. Carry small bills, as many cab drivers either don't have change or won't admit to having any in the hope of getting a tip.

Useful Phone Numbers U.S. Dept. of State Travel Advisory ℂ **202/647-5225** (manned 24 hr.); U.S. Passport Agency ℂ **202/647-0518**; U.S. Centers for Disease Control International Traveler's Hotline ℂ **404/332-4559**.

Water Don't drink the tap water, even in the major hotels. Most hotels provide bottled water in or near the minibar or in the bathroom; use it for brushing your teeth as well as drinking. Most restaurants serve bottled or boiled water and ice made from boiled water, but always ask to be sure.

3

Suggested Itineraries in Thailand

Thailand is your oyster! A great place to explore, follow a passion, or connect with locals, and a place where itinerary planning often goes out the window in favor of "trail magic" and spontaneous occurrences. Most trips begin in **Bangkok,** the country's capital and largest international hub, and most travelers include some beach time along with any other cultural or adventure agendas. When flying directly to Thailand from the U.S. or Europe, be aware that you'll be dazed and confused with jetlag for the first few days. It is best to go easy at the start. Arrival in busy Bangkok, with its traffic, heat, and humidity, can be a bit overwhelming—it all takes a little bit of getting used to, and you might just be settling in and enjoying things by the time you leave if you're doing a 1 week tour. So do yourself a favor and carve out more time than less, and factor in rest time at the beginning and end of your trip.

And plan your trip around a passion! Like Thai food? Start at the **Blue Elephant** cooking school in Bangkok, or try the **Chiang Mai Cooking School** in the north and learn how to make it; chase down local specialties, explore the markets to learn about produce, and try some of Thailand's many upmarket Thai restaurants. Interested in massage? Start at **Wat Po Massage School** or the **International Training Massage** in Chiang Mai and learn the nuts and bolts of this fascinating ancient tradition. Is adventure your thing? Get your motor running and light out for one of Thailand's many national parks, **Khao Yai** just north of Bangkok or **Khao Sok** in the south, or connect with adventure tour and trekking operators in Chiang Mai. Interested in Thai history and architecture? Start at Bangkok's many temples and the **National Museum** and explore the country's many ancient sites. Want to get enlightened? Learn about Buddhism? Find a meditation course or talk with a teacher. Try **Wat Mahathat** in Bangkok, **Wat Rampoeng** in Chiang Mai, **Wat Suan Mokkh** in Surat Thani, or **Wat Kow Tahm** on Koh Pha Ngan; all great places to learn about the "inside job" of Buddhist practice. These are just a few of the many focused trips possible in Thailand. Find yours and go for it!

Multiple-week trips mean opportunities to both explore the back of beyond by bus and train as well as get some time with your toes in the sand at the beach somewhere along the way. With shorter itineraries, you might want to limit yourself to Bangkok, a short hop by plane up to rural parts near Chiang Mai, and then a flight to one of the beaches in the south. Be sure to factor in a few days for shopping in Bangkok or Chiang Mai at the end of your route.

Weather plays an important part in trip planning. The winter months, November to February, are generally the best time to go, but it is the tourist high season with attendant high prices and crowds, especially in December. In the far north, in and around Chiang Mai, the weather is cooler, while summer months bring heavy rain. In the Malay Peninsula to the south the best time to visit Phuket and areas on the western coast of the peninsula is from November to April; while for Koh Samui and beach destinations on the eastern coast, the best time to visit is from February to October (the result of opposing monsoon systems). Check destination chapters for more weather specifics.

You might want to plan your trip around a Thai holiday. **Songkran** is the Thai New Year, celebrated for a week starting April 13. It is more or less a prolonged water fight, and young travelers love it. Also **Loy Krathong,** celebrated in early November, is a magical holiday celebrated throughout Thailand (though best in the north at Sukhothai or Chiang Mai) where small bamboo floats are released on the rivers to let go of the previous year's sins and make good wishes for the future.

Thailand also makes a great base for exploring the rest of Southeast Asia, and Bangkok's many air connections make it a great hub for side trips to Laos (fly to Luang Prabang in the north), Cambodia (don't miss an opportunity to visit Angkor Wat), or Vietnam.

1 Begin (or End) in Bangkok: 2 or 3 Days

The Thai capital is a trip. Traffic is chaos and the city's pollution leaves your skin covered in grit after even the shortest stroll, but Bangkok has much to offer by way of not only the familiar, but also unique culture, comforts, and corruption.

Tack this short itinerary on at the beginning or the end of any trip in Thailand. Many visitors split it up, spending a day or two touring the city sites at the beginning of their journey, and a day or two filling suitcases with booty on shopping tours of the city at the end of their trip.

Day ❶: Bangkok's Riverside Sites

If your budget allows, stay at one of the finer hotels along the riverside: The Oriental, the Peninsula, or the Shangri-La. From any of these hotels it is just a matter of hopping the hotel shuttle boat out front to the Saphan Taksin (Taksin Bridge) boat pier and riding the local riverboats for the day. Another good option is to stay on Silom or Sukhumvit and connect with the boat pier by convenient BTS Skytrain (cabs are ubiquitous and affordable, but be sure to avoid rush hour on the roads).

You can buy a day pass on the tourist boats of the **Chao Phraya Express Company** (© 02222-5330) for just 100B ($2.45) that will afford on-and-off access to any boat chugging along the Chao Praya. Going from Saphan Taksin north along the S-curve of the river through the heart of Bangkok and Rattanakosin Island (where you'll find the bulk of the city's historical sites), good stops include the **River City Shopping Complex; Chinatown** (take a good long wander through chaotic market streets); the famous **Wat Po** and its **Giant Reclining Buddha** (get off at Tha Tien, "Tha" means "pier"); then on to the **Grand Palace;** and the famed **Wat Phra Kaew,** the temple with the famed **Emerald Buddha** (be sure to wear trousers and shirts with sleeves, no shorts and no cutoff shirts). Cross from Tha Tien by local ferry to **Wat Arun,** the "Temple of the Dawn." You could carry on to the **National Museum** and even stop in at busy **Khao San Road,** the city's busy backpacker ghetto at the end of the boat line in Banglampoo. Wat Po, the Grand

Palace, and Wat Phra Kaew are the highlights of this trip, and there is a lot to see in 1 day (enough for 2 days, really). You might want to arrange this day with a private guide (contact **World Travel** at ✆ **02233-5900**) or **Sea Tours** (✆ **02216-5783** or 02237-3702).

Also consider a **tour of the** *klongs* (canals) of Thonburi, the sprawling area on the west shore of the Chao Praya, by longtail boat. You can arrange for a tour of the klongs at riverside anywhere (the touts will approach you); best at booths near the boat departure point at Saphan Taksin, River City Shopping Complex, or the busy drop-off point near the Wat Po Temple at Tha Thien.

Boat back to your hotel and collapse. Long day, no? If you've got energy, see the nightlife suggestions on Days 2 & 3 (below).

Days ❷ & ❸: Bangkok

Explore the downtown area. If you are an early riser, make your way to **Lumpini Park** for a stroll and maybe even join in for Tai Chi or an aerobics class (you might even spot the Thai prime minister on his morning constitutional). What to see in Bangkok is up to your own tastes. Shoppers have any number of choices, as do temple aficionados and culture vultures (then there are those who see shopping *as* culture). Start with the **Jim Thompson House,** home of the American silk magnate, right in the city center (near the Siam stop on the BTS Skytrain); then, if your tastes run to good shopping, hit the likes of **Mah Boon Krong** or **Siam Square** among the city's mall-rat set, or go upscale at the **Erawan Plaza** (don't miss a visit to the powerful **Erawan Shrine**), **Gaysorn Plaza, The Emporium,** or the new **Playground** at Thong Lor. Techies love a visit to **Panthip Plaza,** the city's biggest computer and electronics bazaar. If it is a weekend, make the trip (by Skytrain or subway) to

the **Weekend Market,** otherwise hit the **Suan Lum Night Market** near Lumpini Park (best after 6pm).

Culture junkies will want to return to the riverside to visit any sites they missed on day 1 or to further explore Chinatown (take a cab after rush hour or hop back on the riverboats for more exploring). Other good finds include **Benchamabophit** near Dusit Park, or **Wat Suthat** and its giant swing (near Chinatown), as well as **Wat Sakhet,** the Golden Mount among the many. Other opportunities for cultural connection include a day of **Thai cooking lessons** at **Blue Elephant** (at the Surasak stop on the Skytrain) or the **Oriental Thai Cooking School** (at the Oriental Hotel), meditation study at **Wat Mahathat,** or learning Thai massage at **Wat Po.**

And most important: **Get a massage!** You may have had a long flight, and temple touring takes it out of you. Bangkok's many affordable day spas or luxurious hotel spa treatments are affordable (compared with the West) and very professional. Try a real Thai massage, like having yoga done "to you."

Got any more energy in the evening? Bangkok awaits. **Sala Rim Nam** (operated by the Oriental Hotel) and the **Supatra River House** are both good choices for Thai dance and cultural shows including dinner. **The Joe Louis Puppet Theater** (in the Suan Lum Night Bazaar) is an entertaining show of traditional Thai puppetry. **Thai Boxing** at the Lumpini or Ratchadamnoen Stadiums makes for a gritty and exciting evening.

Dining choices run the gamut. I highly recommend **Baan Kanitha** or **Lemongrass** for classic Thai, but dining choices, from the local to the luxurious, are many. Check the nightlife section in the Bangkok chapters, but for an ultra-chic evening hit **Bed Supperclub,** or for a shot and a beer look for the little outdoor alley bar (also on Sukhumvit Soi 11 near

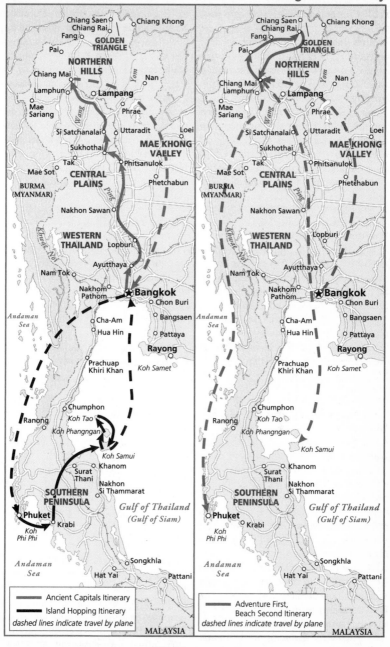

Bed) **Cheap Charlie's** (two extremes, really). Red-light nightlife is everywhere (it finds you, really). If that's your thing, hit **Nana Plaza** or **Soi Cowboy** (gotta see it once), or go to the busy night market area lining the streets of **Patpong,** Bangkok's busiest red-light district, which is now sanitized a bit for tourists and even popular with families. One night in Bangkok usually leads to more.

If you have extra time, good day trips from Bangkok include going by boat to the former capital of **Ayuthaya;** taking an early morning tour of the **Damnoen Sadek Floating Market;** or going further afield to the likes of **Kanchanaburi,** home of the "Death Railway" and bridge made famous in the film *Bridge of the River Kwai;* or up to **Khao Yai National Park.**

If your time in Thailand is limited and you want to hop to the beach, try **Hua Hin,** the royal retreat just 3 hours south of Bangkok, or **Pattaya,** Thai's "sin city," just a few hours east along the gulf, both easy overnights from the capital.

2 Ancient Capitals Tour: 6 Days

Start in Bangkok and take in the major sites in the current Thai capital, then trace the legacy of the ancient capitals. First, north to Ayuthaya, capital until the late 18th century, then via tiny Lop Buri (best by train) to Phitsanulok, then Sukhothai, and Sri Satchanalai, the very origins of the Kingdom of Thailand, and on to the ancient Lanna capital of Chiang Mai. The tour is a short course in the evolution of Thai architecture, and many get hooked and make a trip to the archaeological sites further afield in Isan, the Northeast, like Phimai, or even to the ancient Khmer ruins of Angkor Wat in Cambodia.

Pack to be fast and light for this journey, as you'll be carrying your own kit quite often along the way (unless you arrange a private car or tour for the whole itinerary).

Day ❶: Bangkok to Ayuthaya
There are a number of good day-trip options by boat from Bangkok to Ayuthaya (see section 8, "Side Trips from Bangkok," in chapter 6), and you could even arrange for a one-way journey with one of these companies (they usually make one leg by boat, one leg by bus). More fun and adventurous, though, is going by local train from Bangkok's Hua Lampong Train Station (now easily accessed by subway). In Ayuthaya, **Krungsri River House** is the best hotel (though basic) and convenient to the train station. From there cross by rickety local ferry to the center of old Ayuthaya and hit the highlights: the city museums include the **Ayutthaya Historical Study Center** and the **Chao Sam Praya National Museum,** both with good historical info

and artifacts; don't miss **Wat Mahathat** at the city center and the most striking of the Ayuthaya ruins; also **Wihaan Phra Mongkol Bopit,** which contains one of the largest Buddha images in Thailand. Take an elephant ride at the city center, or take a late afternoon boat ride tour, by longtail boat, around the city island. In the evening, catch a meal at the colorful night market or at one of the city's little floating restaurants.

Day ❷: Ayuthaya to Phitsanulok (via Lop Buri)
Get an early start and hop the first train to little Lop Buri (just an hour or so north of Ayuthaya). Leave your bags at the Lop Buri station and find the little TAT office just down an alley (well marked) from there and grab a map. Visit **King Narai's Palace** and the various ruin

sites of little Lop Buri, and keep an eye out for the town's mischievous monkeys. Catch the afternoon train to Phitsanulok. Overnight at **Topland Hotel** in the center of Phitsanulok and enjoy a good meal at the riverside night market or one of the city's floating restaurants.

Day ❸: Phitsanulok to Sukhothai

Get an early start and visit Phitsanulok's **Wat Yai,** then go by road to Sukhothai, the very origin of Thai culture and dynastic rule. You can go by local bus, but from Phitsanulok it is best by rented vehicle with driver, as this gives you freedom to explore rural sites along the way and to get to and from the temples. There are a number of small tour and rental agencies in Phitsanulok. Make your way to Sukhothai and explore the ancient city. Spend the night at **Lotus Village** (✆ 05562-1484), a collection of cozy bungalows, or the more familiar (but not luxurious) **Pailyn Sukhothai Hotel** (✆ 05561-3310). Be sure to dine at unique **Dream Café** (✆ 05561-2081).

Day ❹: Sukhothai to Lampang (via Si Satchanalai) or Chiang Mai

This is a long-haul day and there are a few options for doing it. You can go back to Phitsanulok and unload your rented vehicle and go to Lampang (or on to Chiang Mai) by local transport (bus or train), or keep the rented vehicle and carry on to Lampang or Chiang Mai. Hit the temples of **Si Satchanalai** north of Sukhothai in the morning, then carry on to **Lampang** or **Chiang Mai.** You can make an extended stop in Lampang, and, time permitting, visit the **Elephant Conservation Center,** where guests learn the ins and outs of being an elephant mahout.

Note: From Sukhothai, you could also take a different tack, going west from Sukhothai to the Burmese border town of **Mae Sot** for an overnight, then up along the rugged border of Burma to little **Mae Sariang** (a stop on the Mae Hong Son Loop) before Chiang Mai. A rugged, adventurous route.

Day ❺: Chiang Mai

Explore the city. Get a bicycle and ride around to the temple sites along small cobbled alleys in the heart of the Old City of Chiang Mai. In the evening have a groovy dinner along the Mae Ping River, and shop and party 'til you drop in the downtown Night Bazaar area. For continued adventure in the north, add on from Day 2 in the itinerary "Adventure First, Beach Second," below.

Day ❻: Chiang Mai to Bangkok

Last-minute shopping in both of these shopping meccas. See destination chapters for more information on shopping options.

---

3 Island Hopping & Adventure in the Malay Peninsula: From 12 Days to Eternity (Your Choice)

This itinerary is the bare bones of what might be a prolonged stay. Each of these beach destinations alone could suck you in for good, really, and below we've listed a number of side trips and options for further exploration. Find a great spot? Stay for a while.

Day ❶: Bangkok to Phuket

A 30-minute flight and short taxi transfer from the airport brings you to the resort of your choice, anything from the luxurious to the affordable, and you can be in that hammock or baking in the sun before you can say "staff meeting."

Days ❷ & ❸: Phuket

These 2 days could turn into many as the languid rhythms of Phuket take you in. Spend time at the beach; choose from great restaurants—**The Boathouse** is a good place to try famed (and pricey) Phuket lobster; or head to **Patong** for some wild nightlife and a glimpse of red-light Thailand. **Phuket Fantasea** is a kitschy show popular with families, or you can enjoy a quiet candlelit dinner at your resort of choice. Take an extra day or so here if possible and find adventure by ship and kayak in **Pha Nga Bay,** or a multiday trip to **Khao Sok National Park.** If you are a diver, make a multiday trip to the **Similan Islands,** now accessible by luxury live-aboard dive boats.

Days ④ & ⑤: Phuket to Krabi

Depart by boat from the pier near Phuket Town and you'll stop for part of the day at **Koh Phi Phi,** a one-time popular backpacker island devastated by the 2004 Christmas Tsunami (there are still some options for an overnight stay). Climb the small peak on Phi Phi Don and get a view of the barbell-shaped isle. Then take an afternoon boat on to **Krabi Town.** You can also do the trip easily by road, with stops in **Pha Nga Bay** along the way. Leaving Krabi Town, stay in one of Krabi's hideaway resorts like the **Sheraton** or **Rayavadee** on **Raillay Beach** (accessible only by boat). Hit Raillay and its high karst towers for a day of **rock climbing,** or lounge in the shadow of limestone majesty overlooking Happy Island. This is a good place to squeeze in an extra day in this itinerary, or consider a side trip to tiny **Trang** (stay at luxury **Amari Trang**) or to one of the new resorts on the fishing island of **Koh Lanta.**

Day ⑥: Krabi to Koh Samui

Hop a short flight from Krabi to **Koh Samui.** Stay at one of the new luxury resorts on **Bophut Beach,** or hit the busy **Chaweng** area; a midrange choice like **Coral Bay** keeps you close to the action but in relative quiet. Samui now boasts some very luxurious choices: **Tongsai Bay, Sila Evason Hideaway, Santiburi, Renaissance Samui,** and **Sala Samui.**

Get caught up in Koh Samui! Find out what live acts are playing at hip **Coco Blues Bar** in Chaweng, sign up for a cooking course at **Sitca,** sign up for scuba, a day trip to **Angthong Marine Park,** a round of golf at the new Santiburi golf course, arrange a trip aboard a yacht, or find a good hideaway spa (I recommend the fasting and health programs at **Spa Samui** in Lamai). Nightlife in Chaweng is as wild as you want it.

Day ⑦: Samui

Take a day to sink in to the languid rhythms of this tropical isle (or recover from last night in Chaweng). A good day for spa treatments or a romantic evening meal at **The Mangrove,** the island's best little fine-dining outlet.

Day ⑧: Samui to Koh Pha Ngan

You've heard of the wild Full Moon Parties on Koh Pha Ngan, and the festivities go on (even at "half moon" and "no moon"), but little Pha Ngan is a good, affordable escape with lots of far-flung resorts, your own slice of tropical heaven. Haad Rin is the center of the party and the best place for dinner and a night out, but you can also live the quiet life on the isle.

Days ⑨ & ⑩: Koh Pha Ngan to Koh Tao (Optional)

If diving is your bag, then be sure to get out this far. The "Turtle Island," Koh Tao, is a simple connection from Koh Samui (via Koh Pha Ngan) by high-speed catamaran ferry. Take a few days to get certified or upgrade your skills underwater. If you're not an aquanaut, there is still plenty to do on the island at upmarket resorts and spas.

Day ⑪: Rest Day

Wherever you are, stay. Take a day trip. Enjoy some rest time, whatever your feeling on this last day in paradise.

Day ⑫: Koh Samui to Bangkok

Return by flight to the capital, making any required boat connection, and giving yourself some time to shop in Bangkok.

4 "Adventure First, Beach Second" Tour: 10 days

Many visitors like to "earn" their toes-in-the-sand lounging time. Here's a good way to do that: Starting from Bangkok, hit the far north, using Chiang Mai as a hub for rugged trips into the back of beyond. Rent a motorbike and get muddy, take a trek, go rafting, and then, tired and bedraggled, hop a flight to one of the beach destinations in the south, Phuket or Koh Samui, for example, and put your feet up, spin some tall tales, and catch up with that journal writing or get into that novel you've been toting around. This can be anything from a 10-day to a 1-month proposition.

Day ❶: Bangkok to Chiang Mai

Fly from the capital to the old Lanna Thai capital in the far north in the morning. Set yourself up in one of the good, centrally located choices (I like **Tamarind Village**), or one of the town's new ultra-luxe properties (some far out of town). Hit a few sites inside the Old Walled City of Chiang Mai, and if the weather is good, dash up to the mountaintop temple of Doi Suthep. In the evening engage in some kingly dining (try one of the fun riverside restaurants) and wander the busy **Night Bazaar.**

Days ❷ & ❸: Chiang Mai to Pai

Light out into the beautiful, hilly boondocks. Go by self-drive rental car (motorcycle for the adventurous), or arrange a tour with guide and driver. Explore the hills around little **Pai,** a cozy town, and stay at **Belle Villa** outside of town or **Pai River Corner.** From Pai, arrange a 1- or 2-day trekking trip or rafting adventure.

Days ❹ & ❺: Adventures Outside of Pai

If you are rafting from Pai to Mae Hong Son or your trek ends near there, you can visit the villages of **Long Neck Karen people** and have a night's stay in laid-back **Fern Resort** or comfy in-town **Imperial Tara.** If going by road between Pai and Mae Hong Son (a scenic drive), be sure to stop at the cool **Lod,** or **Spirit, Caves,** about half-way.

Days ❻ & ❼: From Pai (or Mae Hong Son) to Chiang Rai

Hop a flight from Mae Hong Son via Chiang Mai to little Chiang Rai (you can also do this as an overland trip via the little town of **Chiang Dao** and **Fang**), and take a day exploring the **Golden Triangle,** a one-time opium smuggling region bordering Laos and Burma. Stay in Chiang Rai at one of the luxe riverside resorts, or laid-back **Golden Triangle Inn** in town (a good place to arrange tours and trekking), or up in the Golden Triangle proper at **Anantara** or the mid-range **Imperial Resort.** Don't miss the **Hall of Opium** and a visit to the main temple sites in Chiang Saen. Shoppers for the bizarre like the border market (or even cross over into Burma for a few hours) in the farthest northern area of **Mae Sai.**

Note: If your feet are still itchy, Thailand's rugged Northeast, **Isan,** is ripe for exploration: fly to **Udonthani** from Chiang Rai or Chiang Mai and rent a vehicle or join a tour (see chapter 14, "Exploring Isan: Thailand's Frontier," for details). To extend your adventure trip even further afield from Chiang Rai, make the overland journey from Chiang Rai east to the border, then cross into Laos and take the 2-day down-river trip to **Luang Prabang,** a memorable journey (see the *Frommer's Southeast Asia* guide for more info).

Days ⑧ to ⑩ (or Until Your Time & Money Run Out): From Chiang Rai to the Beach

You earned it, now hit the beach! Go for somewhere with direct flights, likely a stopover in Bangkok from Chiang Rai or Chiang Mai, but either **Koh Samui** or **Phuket** are good choices. Take all the time you have, and rehash with your mates the stories of your northern derring-dos.

4

Introducing Bangkok

With a population of over 10 million in a country of only 60 million, Thailand's capital is the urban and cultural heart of the land: where all trends originate, where all roads meet, an exaggeration of every aspect of life in the kingdom. Choked with traffic, polluted, and corrupt, the city is also the financial capital of one of the fastest-growing economies in the world. Bangkok is a city on the rise, with new construction starts at an all-time high. Central Bangkok is all columns of glass and steel, hulking shopping complexes, and hotels. Linked at the city center by the useful elevated rail line, the BTS Skytrain, Bangkok now also boasts a convenient subway line, both good options to avoid Bangkok's notorious 2-hour gridlocks. Suvanabhumi Airport was near completion and had even experienced a few ceremonial landings at the time of publication, but this new airport, which will eventually be connected by Skytrain with downtown Bangkok, is not set to open until well into 2006.

Founded when King Rama I moved the city across the river from Thonburi in 1782, Bangkok is not a particularly ancient capital, but a cool mix of modern and traditional. Stunning temples and mendicant monks share space with cellphone-wielding socialites and Starbucks; luxury condominiums stand stridently just a stone's throw from labyrinthine slums along dirty canals; glittering shopping malls and modern buildings rise in a city whose heart is still the Grand Palace and the Temple of the Emerald Buddha.

What strikes many upon arrival in the Big Mango is the highly developed infrastructure, high-end shopping, world class accommodation, and heavy pollution. Many are disappointed that the city is less mysterious than their preconceptions, but there are still gems to find in and among the new construction and urban sprawl, and exploring Bangkok is still a highlight of any trip to Thailand.

Bangkok has a concentration of luxury hotels unrivaled in the region, and visitors can find anything from the most basic 120B ($2.95) cell to a ritzy high-rise suite. Whatever your budget, lodging is affordable and Bangkok is a good place to splurge for far more comforts than the same prices afford you back home. And food? They've got it all in the Thai capital: fine dining on par with any large city, as well as great atmospheric local joints.

And Bangkok is safe. Visitors should take care to guard valuables from pickpockets as anywhere, but you are unlikely to experience the kind of anonymous crime so common in the West. You can wander in a day from busy, luxury shopping districts to quiet temple compounds, cacophonous markets to tiny alleyways. Get lost and explore. Even in a city choked by traffic, pollution, and acres of concrete, you can find moments of serenity and are sure to experience a warm welcome from kind Thai folks.

Rivaled only by Chiang Mai in the north, Bangkok is a shopper's heaven with anything from name-brand luxury items (and, of course, knock-offs) to fine local handicrafts, antiques, silk, and jewels. For nightlife, the proverbial "One Night in Bangkok" still delivers the same old kick.

The Real Bangkok

Referred to as "Krung Thep" by Thais and sometimes called "The Big Mango" or "The City of Angels," the official name of Bangkok is the world's longest: Krungthepmahanakhon Amonrattanakosin Mahintharayutthaya Mahadilokphop Noppharatratchathaniburirom Udomratchaniwetmahasathan Amonphimana-watansthit Sakkathattiyawitsanukamprasit, which is a proud description of Bangkok's royal legacy.

1 Orientation

ARRIVING

Bangkok's Don Muang Airport is still the main hub for international travelers to Thailand until the completion of Suvanabhumi International Airport (sometime in late 2006). The city has three bus terminals, and a centrally located train station. Within the city, taxis and tuk-tuks (three-wheeled, motorized trishaws/pedicabs) cruise the broad avenues and provide inexpensive, reliable transportation. The BTS Skytrain, the city's elevated rail line, as well as a slick new subway line make for direct connection between the domestic train station, downtown, and far-flung reaches of this sprawling burg.

BY PLANE

Bangkok is a major hub for air travel in Southeast Asia, with more than 70 airlines providing service. Currently, international and domestic flights come and go from Bangkok's **Don Muang International Airport,** but the city promises a new facility, **Suvanabhumi International Airport,** to open its doors sometime in late 2006. Construction on the new airport is at a fever pitch and Suvanabhumi, which is 25km directly east of the city center, will eventually connect with the city center by a special spur of the city's Skytrain. The airport has already welcomed test flights, but plans for formal opening are still not set. **Novotel** (www.accor.com) will host a new airport hotel adjacent to Suvanabhumi. The current hub, Don Muang International, will become a military airport. For information and ongoing updates about Suvanabhumi, see **www.airportthai.co.th**.

Dong Muang International Airport is 22 kilometers (14 miles) north of the heart of the city. International and domestic flights arrive at different terminals, a short kilometer (⅔-mile) walk or a free shuttle ride away.

Travelers arriving at the international terminal at Don Muang will find a wide range of services awaiting them, available 24 hours unless otherwise noted: luggage storage for 90B ($2.20) per day with a 3-month maximum; currency exchange banks with the same rates as in-town banks; ATMs; a post office with overseas telephone service; **Airport Information booths** and **Tourism Authority of Thailand (TAT) booths** (Terminal 1, ✆ 02504-2701; and Terminal 2, ✆ 02535-2669), open 8am to midnight; a Thai Hotel Association desk that will assist you in finding available accommodations; restaurants serving both Thai and international food; a minimarket; and the first-class **Amari Airport Hotel** (see "Accommodations," in chapter 5, "Where to Stay & Dine in Bangkok"), a short walk or free shuttle ride away.

The domestic terminal offers most of these services, though on a more limited schedule: luggage storage, for 90B ($2.20) a day with a 14-day limit, open 6am to 11pm; a post office in the departure wing with overseas telephone service; a foreign exchange bank; the Hotel Association desk open 24 hours; and a cafeteria-style coffee shop.

The airport provides **free shuttle service** between the international and domestic terminals, with buses every 15 minutes. If you have light luggage, you might find it more enjoyable (and sometimes faster) to walk.

Passengers on domestic flights pay 50B ($1.20) departure tax, which is always included in the price of your ticket at the point of purchase, while those on international flights must purchase a 500B ($12) departure tax ticket from either vending machines or sales booths just after check-in before you enter immigration. Make sure you have adequate funds; there aren't any ATMs once you pass the ticketing point. Children under 2 years are exempt.

GETTING TO & FROM THE AIRPORT   To get from the airport to points in central Bangkok takes about a half-hour with no traffic, up to 2 hours at rush hour. Most of the larger hotels offer pickup service for a fee. You can easily arrange for an air-conditioned minibus, taxi, or limousine to your hotel; these are found outside the arrival hall of both the international and domestic terminals (ground floor level).

When exiting the terminal, don't be tempted by the many taxi touts; it's best to press on to the **taxi stand** in front of both the domestic and international terminals. There is usually a long queue of riders, but taxis arrive regularly and the line moves fast (standing in line is your first taste of Bangkok heat). Charges will be according to the meter, plus a 50B ($1.20) service charge for airport service. The driver will ask if you would like to take the expressway. **Chalerm Mahanakhon Expressway** connects the airport with downtown Bangkok and is a good bet to beat the traffic. The driver will ask for 40B ($1) at two tollbooths, so make sure you get change ("small money") before leaving the airport. Expect to pay between 250B and 300B ($6.10–$7.30) to hotels downtown.

Private limousine services have air-conditioned sedans for hire from booths in the arrival halls of both international and domestic airports. Trips to town start at 650B ($16). Advanced booking is not necessary.

The Airport Bus (𝄢 **02995-1252**) is a convenient and inexpensive alternative with service every 15 minutes from 4:30am to 12:30am, stopping regularly at international and domestic terminals. Three bus routes serve the city's various well-traveled points—Silom and Charoen Krung Road near the river and in the business district, Khao San Road in the historic district, Sukhumvit in the shopping/embassy area, and many other destinations. At bus stops outside the arrival halls, helpful staff wait to advise travelers. Tell them your hotel, and they'll direct you to the correct bus. Buy a ticket at curbside for just 100B ($2.45).

Public bus and train service connect the airport to the city for a nominal cost but are both inconvenient. Hop a cab or airport bus and save yourself the grief.

BY TRAIN

The Thai rail network is extremely well organized, connecting Bangkok with major cities throughout the country. (You can also travel by train to Bangkok from Singapore, via Kuala Lumpur and Butterworth, Malaysia.)

All trains to and from the capital stop at **Hua Lampong Railroad Station** (𝄢 **02223-7010** or the hot line at 𝄢 **1690**), east of Chinatown, at the intersection of Rama IV and Krung Kasem roads. Inside the station, clear signs point the way to public toilets, pay phones, the food court, and baggage check area (one bag just 20B/50¢ per day). A Post & Telegraph Office, Information Counter, police box, ATMs and money-changing facilities, convenience shops, baggage check, and restaurants surround a large open seating area.

Bangkok at a Glance

American Embassy **5**
Australian Embassy **4**
BNH Hospital **3**
British Embassy **7**
Bumrungrad Hospital **8**
Canadian Embassy **2**
General Post Office **1**
New Zealand Embassy **6**

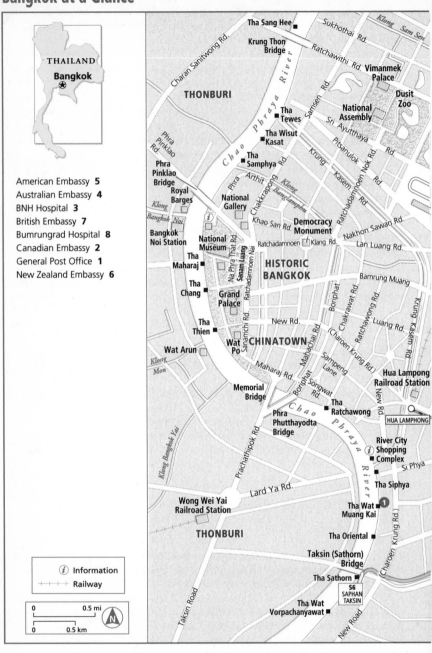

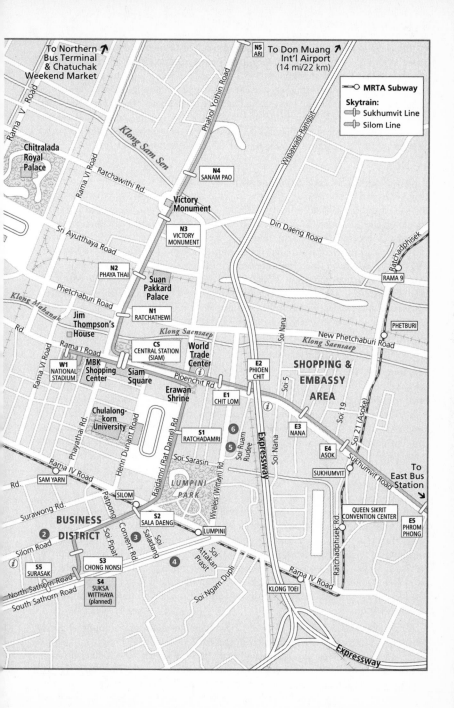

Officials will approach you in the station offering help—directing you to trains, ticket booths, and ground transportation. It is quite a useful service and quite helpful, but be careful—not all are officials, and if you are nervous about these or any other strangers, proceed to the ticketing counter or information booth directly.

As the station is centrally located, metered taxis cost about 100B ($2.45) to most hotels; a tuk-tuk should be no more than 80B ($1.95). A spur of the new subway system connects with the station, and it is a good way to get to the Silom area (directly) or to Sukhumvit (via transfer to Skytrain at the Asoke station).

BY BUS

Bangkok has three major bus stations, each serving a different part of the country. All air-conditioned public buses to the west and the southern peninsula arrive and depart from the **Southern Bus Terminal** (© 02434-7192) on Nakhon Chaisi and Phra Pinklao Road (near Bangkok Noi Station), west of the river over the Phra Pinklao Bridge from the Democracy Monument. Service to the east coast (including Pattaya) arrives and departs from the **Eastern Bus Terminal,** also known as **Ekkamai** (© 02391-2504), on Sukhumvit Road opposite Soi 63 (Ekkamai BTS Skytrain station). Buses to the north arrive and leave from the **Northern Bus Terminal,** aka **Mo Chit** (© 02936-2841), Kampaengphet 2 Road, near the **Chatuchak Weekend Market,** and a short taxi or bus ride from the Mo Chit Skytrain or subway stations. VIP buses leave from locations in town and can be booked at private offices anywhere along Sukhumvit Road or Khao San Road.

VISITOR INFORMATION

The **Bangkok Tourist Bureau** has offices at major tour destinations throughout the city. Call them with any questions at © 02225-7612 (www.bma.go.th). They provide basic information services, maps, brochures, good recommendations, and can even give you bus directions and some creative day-trip itineraries: a useful resource. Their main office is at 17/1 Phra Athit Road, just under the Phra Pinklao bridge near Khao San, but they also operate out of both terminals at the airport, with no fewer than 16 information kiosks around the city: opposite the Grand Palace, in front of Mah Book Krung shopping mall, at the World Trade Center, River City Shopping Center, and along Sukhumvit (all are open Mon–Sat 9am–4:30pm).

The **Tourism Authority of Thailand (TAT)** offers general information regarding travel to other provinces in Thailand and operates a useful hot line reached from anywhere in the kingdom: © **1672.** They have a counter in the international terminal of Don Muang Airport, open 8am to midnight. Their main office, at Le Concorde Building, Ratchadaphisek Road (© 02694-1222; www.tat.or.th), doesn't make for an easy stop for information—far more convenient is the branch office at Ratchadamnoen Nok Avenue (© 02282-9773), not far from the Grand Palace and other sites in historic Bangkok. Their regional offices are often quite helpful, but rarely have convenient locations.

USEFUL PUBLICATIONS   The TAT produces an enormous amount of glossy tourist brochures on every destination in the country, including Bangkok. Bangkok also has a ton of free magazines, most of which are available in hotel lobbies throughout the city. Look for the *Thaiways* maps and thin guides, produced bimonthly with maps, tips, and facts (about Pattaya, Chiang Mai, and Phuket as well), plus articles on Thai culture. *Bangkok Dining & Entertainment,* another slim volume, specializes mostly in restaurant write-ups and nightlife coverage. On sale in bookstores, pickup a copy of *Metro Magazine* (100B/$2.45) for the best nightlife and restaurant listings, what's happening, plus funny and fascinating social commentary. For a peek into the lives of Thailand's highbrow hobnobbers, *Thailand Tattler* covers the charity ball and art gala set in between Madison Avenue adverts (100B/$2.45).

CITY LAYOUT

Vintage 19th-century photographs of Bangkok tell of the busy life on the **Chao Praya River,** where a ragtag range of vessels, from humble rowboats to royal barges, crowded the busy port. This was the original gateway for early foreign visitors who traveled upriver from the Gulf of Siam. Rama I, upon moving the capital city from Thonburi on the west bank to Bangkok on the east, dug a series of canals fanning out from the S-shaped river. For strategic reasons, the canals replicated the moat system used at Ayuthaya, Siam's previous capital, in the hopes of protecting the city from invasion. The city waterways represented the primordial oceans that surrounded the Buddhist heavens. A small artificial island cut into the land along the riverbank became the site for the Grand Palace, Wat Phra Kaeo (the Temple of the Emerald Buddha), and Wat Po. To this day the island is still known as **Rattanakosin.** This is the historical center of the city and the main tourist destination for day trips.

The canals, or klongs, continued eastward from Rattanakosin as the city's population grew. Chinese and Indian merchants formed settlements alongside the river to the southeast of the island. The **Chinatown** of today still bustles with commerce, now along back alleys instead of canals. The main thoroughfare through Chinatown, Charoen Krung Road (sometimes called by its former name, New Road), snakes southward, following the shape of the river. On the eastern edge of Chinatown find **Hua Lamphong Railway Station,** the hub for rail travel in Thailand.

Just beyond Chinatown along the river bank, in an area called **Bangrak,** foreign diplomats built European-style buildings to house their embassies. The Oriental Hotel, the grande dame of Bangkok's plush hotels, sits along the riverbank in this early cosmopolitan neighborhood. Bangrak's main thoroughfares, Surawong Road, Silom Road, and Sathorn Road, originate at Charoen Krung and run parallel all the way to Rama IV Road. Within Bangrak you'll find many embassy buildings, fine hotels, and high-rise office buildings, restaurants and pubs, plus the Patpong nighttime entertainment hub and market.

Back to Rattanakosin, as you head north upriver in the other direction from Chinatown, you'll hit **Banglampoo,** home to Bangkok's National Museum, Wat Suthat, The Giant Swing, and Klong Phu Khao Thong (Golden Mount). The center point, the huge Democracy Monument, marks the traffic circle where the wide Ratchadamnoen Klong Road intersects Dinso Road. But Banglampoo's biggest claim to fame these days is Khao San Road, a small street that, over the years, has become the main congregation center for backpackers—with budget accommodations, inexpensive restaurants, lots of tour agents, and good nightlife.

Further north of Banglampoo, the area known as **Dusit** is home to Wat Benchamabophit, Vimanmek Palace, the Dusit Zoo, and wide city parks.

As Bangkok spread on the east shore of the river, **Thonburi,** the brief site of the former capital across the river from the Grand Palace, continued in relative isolation. While Bangkok was quick to fill in canals to usher in the age of the automobile, residential Thonburi's canals remain, and a long-tail boat ride through the area is a high point of a trip here. Thai riverside houses, both traditional and new, and neighborhood businesses (some housed in floating barges) reveal glimpses of life as it might have been 200 years ago. On dry land, you'll have to cross the Phra Pinklao Bridge from Banglampoo to reach **Bangkok's Southern Bus Terminal** in this area.

Meanwhile back on the other side of the river, Bangkok was thriving. Over the 2 centuries since its founding, the city fanned eastward. From Rattanakosin, beyond Banglampoo and Bangrak, the area called Pathumwan became home to many residences, the most famous of which is Jim Thompson's house, a stunning Thai-style house open to visitors. Nowadays this area is better known as **Siam Square,** named for the huge shopping malls that draw locals and visitors day and night. The area's hotels, cafes, and nightclubs glitter with modern style—many come here to stroll along Rama I and Ratchadamri roads to see and be seen.

Beyond Pathumwan, **Wireless (Witthayu) Road** runs north to south between Rama IV Road (at the edge of Bangrak) and Rama I Road (at the edge of Pathumwan). Here, huge embassy complexes and exclusive hotels cater to diplomats, business people, and well-heeled travelers.

From the Siam Square area, **Sukhumvit Road** extends to the east and north, its length traced by the convenient Skytrain. Many foreign residents live along the small numbered streets, or *sois,* that branch-out from Sukhumvit. With foreign residents come demand for good restaurants, entertainment spots, shopping, and services. Along Sukhumvit, you'll find luxury hotels alongside inexpensive accommodations, fine dining and cheap local eats, first-rate shopping malls, and street-side bazaars. While Bangkok's major attractions are elsewhere in the city, Sukhumvit's fine accommodations and dining options are connected by the BTS Skytrain to all points in town (just 15 min. by train to the Chao Praya River). Sukhumvit Road leads all the way to Pattaya along the east coast, and, fittingly, you'll find **Bangkok's Eastern Bus Terminal,** at Ekkamai BTS Skytrain stop on Sukhumvit Soi 63.

Until completion of the Suvanabhumi International Airport just east of the city, most visitors arrive via **Don Muang International Airport,** a 40-minute drive north of the city center off the Chalerm Mahanakhon Expressway. Nearby, the Chatuchak weekend market and Bangkok's **Northern Bus Terminal** provide good excuses for visitors to venture here.

FINDING AN ADDRESS Note that even-numbered addresses are on one side of the street and odd-numbered on the opposite side. Most addresses are subdivided by a "/" symbol, as in 123/4 Silom Rd., which is a variation on sequential numbering that accounts for new construction. Be aware that 123 and 124 Silom Rd. will be on opposite sides of the street, but not necessarily close to each other. You'll find the term *soi* frequently in addresses. The term *soi* simply means "street" in Thai, but numbered *sois* are usually small lanes off of major streets. So, 45 Soi 23 Sukhumvit (sometimes written 45 Sukhumvit Soi 23) is found at number 45 on Soi 23, a lane that runs perpendicular to Sukhumvit Road. Even-numbered *sois* will be on the north side, and

---

⸂Tips Obtain a Taxi Card

It's a good idea to ask the staff at your hotel to write the address of your destination in Thai, to assist taxi drivers. Many drivers do not speak English, or if they do, may not understand your pronunciation of a street address. Even more are unfamiliar with following directions from a map. Most hotels have a "taxi card" with their address in Thai to assist guests.

odd-numbered on the south side; closely numbered *sois* are not necessarily close by (for example, Soi 21 and Soi 20 may be far apart along the same longer boulevard).

STREET MAPS   There are a number of excellent Bangkok maps. Nancy Chandler's "Map of Bangkok" is an extremely detailed, fun, colorful source, great for finding specific hotels, restaurants, and shopping, and chock-full of good recommendations (it even comes with a short handbook). It costs just 160B ($3.90) and is well worth it. For good bus route specifics, the "Latest Tour Guide to Bangkok and Thailand"—affectionately called "The Bus Map"—as well as the "Bangkok Thailand Guide Map" both have good details and are available at bookstores for just 60B ($1.45). The free "Thaiways Map of Bangkok" and "Metropolitan Map" are both chock-full of adverts and good detailed city maps with specific insets (available in most hotels).

NEIGHBORHOODS IN BRIEF
Hotels, restaurants, and attractions have been subdivided into smaller regions within the city.

On the River   This is the territory of Bangkok's grand riverside hotels, fine shopping at the River City Shopping Complex, as well as the many upmarket stops along Charoen Krung Road.

Chinatown   Also along the riverside, just west of the Grand Palace area and Banglampoo, Chinatown is a maze of shopping streets and home to a few little atmospheric hotels.

Banglampoo and Historic Bangkok Home to the **Grand Palace,** this area is the site of the original Bangkok capital The area lies within the confines of **Rattanakosin Island,** created as a defense measure by King Rama I. The area contains the city's most important historical sites, beginning with Wat Po, the Grand Palace, and Wat Phra Kaeo, then continuing north to the **Dusit Zoo** and Vimanmek Palace Museum. There are numerous historic wats (temples), the National Museum, and the National Theater and Library. **Khao San Road** is the city's backpacker ghetto, and there are first-class and moderate hotels among the many budget guesthouses. The only drawback here is that, short of the slow riverboats, you're cut off from central Bangkok and faster modes of public transport (the BTS Skytrain, and the subway).

The Business District   The Business District, also called **Bangrak,** is bounded by Rama IV Road on the east, Chinatown on the north, Charoen Krung Road (or New Rd., near the river) on the west, and South Sathorn Road on the south. Silom Road and Surawong Road run east–west through the center. As its name implies, many banks, businesses, and embassies have offices in this area, but it is also a good choice for vacation travelers with its many shops and malls, good restaurants, high-quality hotels, and the famous Patpong nightlife area.

Sukhumvit Road and the Shopping/Embassy Area   This includes the neighborhoods on either side of the thoroughfare called Rama I Road on its western end, then Ploenchit Road as it runs east and crosses Ratchadamri Road, and finally, Sukhumvit Road as it crosses under the airport freeway. Here are several deluxe hotels, many first-class and moderate hotels, numerous shopping complexes, the newer office buildings, most of the Western embassies, and a large concentration of the expatriate community: a convenient central area with access to all of Bangkok's activities.

2 Getting Around

It can take more than 2 hours by taxi to get from one side of town to the other during rush hour. The good news is that, with the convenient BTS Skytrain and soon-to-open subway line (as well as the convenient Chao Praya boats, and even speedy, but dirty, sewer-canal barges), you can avoid the standstill at city center. Access to the town's modern and effective public transport is now a defining factor in visitors' choices of accommodation and dining, and areas like Khao San Road, detached from the better modes of transport, are giving way in popularity to places like Sukhumvit and Silom. Bangkok's taxis are quite affordable and the best choice for door-to-door transportation.

BY SKYTRAIN   The **Bangkok Mass Transit System (BTS),** known as the "Skytrain," is the best way to get around Bangkok. The elevated railway system brilliantly whisks you above the maddening traffic. While coverage is limited, the trains provide good access to Bangkok's central areas. The Silom Line runs from the Chao Praya river at the Taksin Bridge through the Silom area and to the Siam Square shopping area. Siam is the interchange point, and the Sukhumvit Line connects from here north to the Chatuchak Weekend Market or east along the length of Sukhumvit road. Single-journey tickets cost from 10B to 40B (25¢–$1). For single trips, buy tickets at platform vending machines: You choose your numbered destination on the map and pay in a slot (get small change at the information booth as needed). Ticket cards let you through the turnstile and are required for exit, so be sure to hang on to them during the ride. You can buy 1-day and 3-day unlimited passes for 100B/$2.45 and 280B/$6.85 respectively (the pass comes with a useful little city guide and map). Stored-value cards are also available and don't come with any discount, but save you from fumbling for change at the vending machines. If you are in town for any length of time and make lots of trips, it is worth it to buy any of a number of multi-trip cards that give you discount rates as low as 18B/45¢ per ride (for a prepaid 30-ride ticket). Hours of operation are between 6am and midnight. See **www.bts.co.th**.

BY SUBWAY   Bangkok's new subway, completed in 2002, is a great addition to the city. Beginning at Hua Lampong Train Station, the subway cuts a wide backward C swath through town, connecting with the Skytrain at the Sala Daeng stop (on Silom Road) and at Asoke (Sukhumvit) before its terminus near the Mo Chit Bus Station in the far north. Trains run from 6am to midnight and a ride along the full length of the system costs just 36B (90¢) for now. For more information see their website: **www. bangkokmetro.co.th**.

BY PUBLIC RIVERBOATS   Efficient and scenic, the public riverboats on the Chao Praya are a great way to get around the sites in the city center and are a remarkable window on local life.

The **Chao Phraya Express Company** (*©* **02222-5330**) boats trace the river's length, with stops at many piers (*tha* in Thai) on both the Thonburi side (west) and in central Bangkok (east). The popular commuter service even continues out to the suburbs north of the city (there are good maps available at BTS, and route maps posted at each stop). Most sightseers will board near Saphan Taksin BTS station, the last stop on the Silom Line as it meets the river. The major stops going into town from Saphan Taksin are: Tha Ratchawong (in Chinatown off Ratchawong Rd.), Tha Thien (near Wat Po), Tha Chang (near the Temple of the Emerald Buddha), and Tha Maharaj (near Wat Mahathat). There is a range of boats available.

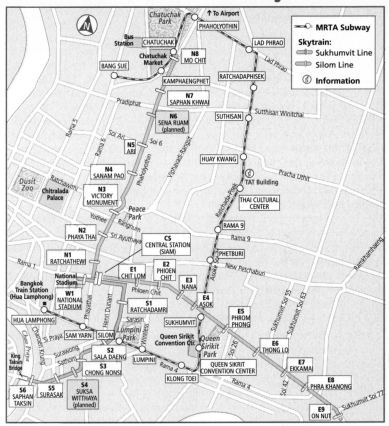

Tourist Express Boats are the fastest and most convenient. These make regular stops along the river and have guides talking over a microphone about the sites you'll pass at riverside (and also helpful, directions on where to go). Short trips start at 15B/35¢, and you can also buy an all-day pass, good for all riverboats, for 100B/$2.45. Boats take about 30 minutes to go from Taksin Bridge to Banglampoo, a real Bangkok must see.

Express boats are long, white boats with a pointed bow bearing the Chao Phraya Express logo on the side, and have bench seats and open sides. Tell them your destination when you board, and the attendant will tell you if it is the right boat (basically avoid the long-haul boats with colored flags on top). Trips start at just 6B/15¢, and you won't pay more than 15B/35¢ to go the length of town.

Cross-river ferries are another category and are useful for getting to places like Wat Arun or other sites in Thonburi.

BY CHARTERED LONG-TAIL BOAT   Private boats are a great way to see the busy riverside area in style and to tour the narrow canals of neighboring Thonburi. Boat charter is available anywhere, really, and the touts will find you, especially at the

---

Finds Surfing the Sewage Canals

Here's a fun little adventure and a great way to cross Bangkok from near the Grand Palace area back to Sukhumvit and the commercial center of town (and the best way to beat rush hour traffic). A narrow, dirty canal, Klong Saen Saep, the last of the many that were long ago filled in to "modernize" Bangkok, runs the length of Phetburi Road with stops in central Bangkok (and all the way to Ton Lor, after a change at Krung Kasem Road). These long, low boats are designed to fit under bridges and are fitted with tarps that are raised and lowered by pulleys to protect passengers from any toxic splashing. Rides start at just 8B/20¢. Board the boats just north of Wat Mahathat. These canal buses really zip along and churn-up a stink, but it is a unique perspective on the last vestiges of what was once the Venice of Southeast Asia, and gets you back to civilized central Bangkok without having to inhale bus fumes in motionless traffic. A fun adventure at day's end.

---

main sites. But it is best to arrange hourly trips at the riverfront kiosk near the **River City Shopping** or at the **Grand Palace** (✆ **02225-6179**), where guides have TAT licenses and are less likely to overcharge or give you any runaround. **L and H Travel Company** (✆ **02630-6663**) operates a small kiosk at the riverside exit of the BTS Skytrain. Trips of varying length cost 500B/$12.20 per hour, per boat, though drivers will want to negotiate this. Be specific about destinations and times.

BY PUBLIC BUS   Bangkok buses are very cheap, frequent, and fairly fast if a little bit confusing and less rider-friendly in terms of helpful ticket-takers and simply marked routes and stops. Be especially careful of pickpockets and artful characters adept at literally cutting into a bag on a crowded bus. Air-conditioned buses are just a few baht extra and save you from inhaling lots of pollution. The Bus Map ("Latest Tour Guide to Bangkok") provides route information. The most practical air-conditioned routes are: A1 (looping from the Grand Palace area to Rama IV Rd., Siam Square, then east down Ploenchit and Sukhumvit rds.); A2 (running a loop through the Business District [Bangrak] area along Silom and Surawong rds.); A3 (connecting the Dusit area near the zoo and Khao San Rd. before crossing the Chao Praya); and A8 (running the length of Rama I, Ploenchit, and Sukhumvit rds.). Fares are collected onboard—even for air-conditioned routes, fares are cheap—between 6B and 20B (15¢–50¢). Try to have exact change or "small money."

BY TAXI   Taxis are everywhere, affordable and helpful. Just flag them down, and be sure they use the meter—it is 35B ($1.95) for the flag-fall and the first 3km (2 miles), thereafter it is about 5B (10¢) per kilometer. You can hail taxis along any road at any time, or join queues in front of hotels and shopping malls. Most drivers are from Thailand's rural northeast, Isan, and few speak English; it is good to have your hotel concierge or a Thai friend write out any destination in Thai. At night, especially around Patpong, taxis will try to barter a flat fare (usually much higher than what the metered fare would be). Insist they use the meter, or get out and find a moving cab (taxis that loiter are usually out to soak you). Few drivers carry enough cash to break a 1,000B ($24) or even a 500B ($12) note, but you should be able to get exact change from 100B ($2.45) notes, and remember that drivers will often claim that they have no change in the hopes of getting a bit extra. In the case of a big bill, have them take you to a convenience store or hotel where you can break a bill. Tipping is not expected but appreciated.

BY CAR & DRIVER   You'd have to be a bit mad to drive yourself around Bangkok, what with the crazy traffic, left-side driving (if you're not used to it), and aggressive tactics of cabs and trucks. If you're in search of your own wheels, it is best to hire a car with a driver. Reputable companies provide sedans with drivers who know the city well, some of whom speak English. They also offer the option of an accompanying tour guide—professionals or students who can take you around each sight. The best hotels provide European luxury vehicles with an English-speaking driver for at least 300B ($7.30) for any single trip and far more per hour or by day (up to 2,000B/$49 per day).

Diethelm Travel (✆ **0255-9150;** www.diethelm-travel.com), a leader in the region, can arrange tours of any length. **World Travel** (✆ **02233-5900**) and **Sea Tour** (✆ **02216-5783**) both arrange English-speaking guides to lead you on customized tours at affordable rates. **Avis** (2/12 Wireless Rd.; ✆ **02255-5300**) and **Budget** (Don Muang Railway St., near the airport; ✆ **02566-5067**) also offer chauffeured cars, but at rates from 3,000B/$73 per day for a car with a driver.

BY TUK-TUK   As much a national symbol as the elephant, the tuk-tuk, a small three-wheeled open-sided vehicle powered by a motorcycle engine, is noisy (named for the putt-putt sound it makes), smoky, and good fun. Drivers whip around city traffic like kamikazes. Note tuk-tuk decor: bright colors, gilded ornamentation, and flashing lights. They're not recommended for long hauls or during rush hour—if you get stuck behind a bus or truck, you'll be coughing up exhaust fumes for days to follow—but for short trips or off-peak hours they're convenient and a real kick, especially for first-time visitors to Thailand.

All tuk-tuk fares are negotiated, usually beginning at 40B ($1) for short trips. Bargain hard, but remember you'll always end up paying more than locals.

One word of warning: Tuk-tuk drivers are notorious for trying to talk travelers into shopping trips and sex-massage parlors that pay commissions. Drivers will offer you a very low fare (even just 10B/25¢), but will waste your time by stranding you at small, out-of-the-way gem and silk emporiums, or big massage palaces, all places that scam you and where the driver gets a cut. Insist on being taken where you want to go directly: Say, "No shopping!"

BY MOTORCYCLE TAXI   On every street corner, packs of drivers in colored vests play checkers, motorcycles standing by, waiting to shuttle passengers around the city. Though they get you around fast when you're in a hurry (weaving through traffic jams and speeding down straightaways), they're also incredibly unsafe. These guys will get you there fast, but take all sorts of strategic risks on the road a la Evel Knievel. Use them only in a pinch and strictly for short distances (they're popular for short hops to the end of longer *sois,* or side streets). They charge from 10B (25¢) for a few blocks to 60B ($1.45) for greater distances. Hold on tight and keep your knees tucked in.

ON FOOT   For a city of this size, Bangkok's pedestrian traffic, particularly in the city center and at rush hour, moves at a collective mosey, frustrating to New York–style strutters or folks in a hurry. *A hint:* Don't hurry. It sounds crazy, but it works. It is easy and safe to walk around some sections of town, but Bangkok is so spread out and the vehicle traffic generates so much air pollution that you'll want to pick your battles and limit your walking to certain neighborhoods and smaller streets. Bangkok sidewalks can be gauntlets of buckled tiles, loose manhole coverings, and tangled wires, so take care. When crossing busier streets, look for pedestrian fly-over walkways or, if you have to cross at street level, find others who are also crossing and follow them when they head out into traffic. Otherwise, you could be left standing on the corner forever, not sure when to jump out.

FACTS FACTS: Bangkok

Airport See "Arriving," earlier in this chapter.

American Express There is no specific agent that handles American Express services in Thailand anymore, but they have an **American Express** office at 388 Pahonyothin Rd. in Bangkok. You can reach the office at $©$ **02273-5296** during business hours (Mon–Fri 8:30am–4:30pm) or call their customer service hot line ($©$ **02273-5544**) with any problems or questions.

ATMs See "Fast Facts: Thailand," in chapter 2, "Planning Your Trip to Thailand."

Banks Many international banks maintain offices in Bangkok, including **Bank of America,** next door to the Hilton at 2/2 Wireless Rd. ($©$ **02251-6333**); **Chase Manhattan Bank,** Bubhajit Building, Sathorn Nua Rd. ($©$ **02234-5992**); **Citibank,** 82 Sathorn Nua Rd. ($©$ **02232-2000**); **National Australia Bank,** 90 Sathorn Rd. ($©$ **02236-6016**); and **Standard Chartered Bank,** Abdulrahim Place, 990 Rama IV Rd. ($©$ **02636-1000**). However, even if your bank has a branch in Thailand, your home account is considered foreign here—conducting personal banking will require special arrangements before leaving home.

Bookstores You'll find a number of bookstores offering a wide variety of English-language books. One of the best for an extensive selection of books on Thailand and Asia is **Asia Books,** with a main branch at 221 Sukhumvit Rd. between Soi 15 and 17 ($©$ **02252-7277**). Asia Books has outlets all over Thailand (they even sponsor small racks in retail stores) and in Bangkok at the following locations: **The Emporium** on Sukhumvit at Soi 22, **Landmark Plaza Building** on Sukhumvit at Soi 4; on the third floor of **Thaniya Plaza** off Silom Road; second floor of Times Square on Sukhumvit Road between Soi 12 and 14 ($©$ **02250-0162**); and in the Peninsula Plaza mall near the Regent Hotel on Ratchadamri Road, south of Rama I Road ($©$ **02253-9786**). All are open daily from 10am to 8 or 9pm.

You'll find a good selection of English-language paperbacks at **Bookazine,** in Patpong on the 1st floor at CP Tower, 313 Silom Rd. ($©$ **02231-0016**); in Ploenchit on the 3rd floor at Amarin Plaza 494–502 Ploenchit Rd. ($©$ **02256-9304**); and Siam Square, 286 Siam Square opposite Siam Center, Rama I Road ($©$ **02619-1015**).

Another large and gorgeous bookstore, **Books Kinokuniya** has shops in Pathumwan at Isetan Department Store, 6th floor, World Trade Center, Ratchadamri Road ($©$ **02255-9834**), and on Sukhumvit at Emporium Shopping Complex, 3rd floor, 622 Sukhumvit Rd. Soi 24 ($©$ **02664-8554**).

Dasa Books, 710/4 Sukhumvit (east of the Emporium btwn. Soi 26 and 28; $©$ **02661-2993**), is a great place to grab a coffee, exchange that old novel for a new one, and chat with friendly American owner Don Gilliland and get his good insights into Bangkok and travel in Thailand.

For secondhand books, visit **Elite Used Books,** 593-5 Sukhumvit Rd. ((℃ **02258-0221**). Almost every international-class hotel has a newsstand with papers and a few books.

Business Hours Government offices (including branch post offices) are open Monday to Friday 8:30am to 4:30pm, with a lunch break between noon and 1pm. Businesses are generally open 8am to 5pm. Shops often stay open from 8am until 7pm or later, 7 days a week. Department stores are generally open 10am to 7pm.

Car Rentals See "Getting Around: By Car & Driver," above.

Climate See "When to Go," in chapter 2.

Currency Exchange Most banks will exchange foreign currency Monday to Friday 8:30am to 3:30pm. Exchange booths affiliated with the major banks are found in all tourist areas, open daily from as early as 7am to as late as 9pm.

Dentists & Doctors Thailand has an excellent medical care system. Most medical personnel speak English, and many were trained overseas. Most of the better hotels have doctors and/or nurses on staff or on call who can treat minor maladies. Check first with your concierge for assistance, and then contact your country's consulate if you need further help.

Embassies & Consulates Your home embassy in Thailand can help you in emergencies—medical and legal (to an extent), and is the place to contact if you've lost your travel documents and need them replaced. The following is a list of major foreign representatives in Bangkok: **Embassy of the United States of America,** 120-22 Wireless Rd. ((℃ **02205-4000**); **Canada Embassy,** 15th floor, Abdulrahim Place, 990 Rama IV Rd. ((℃ **02636-0540**); **Australian Embassy,** 37 South Sathorn Rd. ((℃ **02287-2680**); **New Zealand Embassy,** 93 Wireless Rd. ((℃ **02254-2530**); and the **British Embassy,** 1031 Wireless Rd. ((℃ **02253-0191**).

Emergencies In any emergency, first call **Bangkok's Tourist Police**—which is a direct-dial four-digit number (℃ **1155,** or call **02678-6800.** Someone at both numbers will speak English. In case of **fire,** call either (℃ **199** or **191,** both of which are direct-dial numbers. **Ambulance service** is handled by individual private hospitals; see "Hospitals," below, or call your hotel's front desk. For operator-assisted **overseas calls,** dial (℃ **100.**

Eyeglass Repair You'll find optical shops in all the major shopping areas of the city, most of which can provide replacement glasses within 24 hours at reasonable prices. For eye problems, try the **Rutnin Eye Hospital** at 80 Sukhumvit Soi 21 (Soi Asoke) ((℃ **02259-0812**).

Hospitals All hospitals listed here offer 24-hour emergency room care and ambulance service. Be advised that you may need your passport and a deposit of up to 20,000B ($488) before you are admitted. Bills must be settled before you leave. Your domestic medical insurance policy will probably not be accepted for payment, though major credit cards are. The best facility going is luxurious **Bumrungrad Hospital,** 33 Soi 3, Sukhumvit Rd. ((℃ **02667-1000**), which is, for some, the destination of choice in Bangkok for cosmetic surgeries and affordable, high-quality procedures. **BNH Hospital** (formerly the Bangkok Nursing Home) is at 9 Convent Rd., between Silom and Sathorn roads, south of Rama IV Road (© 02632-0052).

Hot Lines There are regular meetings of **Alcoholics Anonymous (AA)** in Bangkok and around Thailand. Check their regional website at www.aathailand.org, or call the AA hot line at © 02231-8300.

Information See "Visitor Information," earlier in this chapter.

Internet Most shopping malls and even the smallest hotels these days have at least a few terminals, and you can't take a step in places like Khao San Road, the backpacker area, or along Sukhumvit Road without spying an Internet storefront. Prices range from 1B to 5B per minute (that's about $1.20–$7.20 per hr.). Big hotels charge exorbitant rates and are not worth it; just take a walk in any direction and you'll find affordable services (as low as 40B/$1 per hr.). Here are just a few: The folks at **BKK Express** (1/18 Sukhumvit Soi 11; © 02651-3621) are very helpful (can even set up *post-restante* service for you—where your mail is held for you at a post office or GPO until you pick it up) and have good Internet connections for 1B per minute (near Suk 11 Guesthouse). **Time Internet Café** (Time Square, Sukhumvit Soi 12 at Asoke BTS; © 02653-3636) is near the city center. In Khao San, **Hello Internet** has been around as long as the Internet, and has good service if you can find their sign out of the many (they're on the 2nd floor). On Silom, near Patpong, find the city's most expensive connections. One good choice near the Patpong sois is **WorldNet** (64 Silom © 02632-8686), with 3B/7¢ per minute service from their little kiosk near Kentucky Fried Chicken.

Lost Property If you have lost anything or have had your valuables stolen, call the national police hot line at © **1155**. Believe it or not, there have been several reports of lost items being returned to the appropriate consulate by taxi drivers or bus attendants.

Luggage Storage Both the domestic and international terminals of **Don Muang Airport** offer luggage storage for 90B ($2.20) a day—7am to 10pm in the domestic terminal, 24 hours a day in the international terminal. Most hotels will allow you to store luggage while away on trips in the countryside.

Mail See "Fast Facts: Thailand," in chapter 2 for rates. If shipping a parcel from Bangkok, take advantage of the Packing Service offered by the **GPO (Post and Telegraph Office),** Charoen Krung Rd. (© 02233-1050), open 24 hours. Small cardboard packing cartons cost from just 10B (25¢), and packing service is available during normal office hours.

Maps See "Visitor Information," earlier in this chapter.

Newspapers & Magazines Bangkok Post and *The Nation,* English-language dailies, both cover local, national, and international news, plus happenings around town, TV listings, and other useful information (just 20B/50¢). *Metro Magazine* (100B/$2.45), found at most bookstores, is a good source of current information about what's happening in Bangkok, especially the entertainment and social scene. *Falang* spins tales of backpacker debauch and daring-do and, like Metro, has a listing section in the back with advice for travel in Thailand (100B/$2.45). *Where, Look East,* and *Thailand Magazine* are slick monthly English-language magazines distributed free and emphasizing events and features about Bangkok, with lesser coverage of other Thai cities and provinces.

Pharmacies Bangkok has a great many pharmacies, though the drugs dispensed differ widely in quality. Thailand is notorious for producing generic knockoffs of name-brand drugs and selling them at a discount. Be warned that these drugs are not checked for quality. Bring with you any prescription medications you require. If something new arises that calls for a prescription, the treating hospital or clinic will be able to provide reliable drugs from its dispensary.

Police Call the **Tourist Police** at © **1155** or 02678-6801, open 24 hours, for assistance. English is spoken.

Post Office The General Post Office (GPO) Post and Telegraph Office, Charoen Krung Road (© **02233-1050**), is open 24 hours. Telegraph and telephone service are available in the north end of the building. Ask at your hotel for branch offices located closer to you.

Radio & TV In Bangkok, **88FM** is hip "Radio No Problem"; **GET 102.5FM** is pop music spun by Western DJs, and **Smooth 105FM** and **Easy FM 105.5** play adult-oriented contemporary music. Every day at 8am and 6pm, every radio station plays the national anthem; at 8pm they broadcast the daily news.

Television channels all broadcast either local Thai programs or English-language programs dubbed in Thai. **UBC (United Broadcasting Company)** provides satellite programming for the entire country. Most hotels, even those in rural areas, carry UBC channels such as CNN, CNBC, Star Movies, HBO, MTV, and Star Sports, plus other channels.

Safety In general, Bangkok is a safe city, but be careful of pickpockets as you might anywhere (especially on public buses). Don't seek out trouble—avoid public disagreements or hostility (especially with locals), and steer clear of gambling activities. You are generally safe, even alone at night in most parts of the city, but rely on your gut instincts—if you get a bad feeling about a place or situation, remove yourself from the scene to avoid getting caught up in someone else's drama.

Taxes See "Fast Facts: Thailand," in chapter 2.

Taxis See "Getting Around," earlier in this chapter.

Telephone, Telegrams & Telex Beware of hotel surcharges on international calls, usually 25% to 40% (check with the operator before dialing). A credit card or collect call placed from your room also carries a service charge. See "Fast Facts: Thailand," in chapter 2 for additional information.

The main government telephone office occupies a separate building on the grounds of the GPO (General Post Office) on Charoen Krung Road (New Road) between the Oriental and Royal Orchid Sheraton hotels and is open daily 24 hours. This office is for international calls.

All post offices and 7-Elevens sell prepaid phone cards for use with the domestic or international, orange or yellow (respectively) Lensko, or TOT, **public phones**—usually outside the nearest 7-Eleven. These phones will also charge calls to credit cards and AT&T calling cards. **Hatari Phonenet** is another prepaid card plan for overseas calls. Buy the cards at 7-Eleven (in 300B/$7.30 or 500B/$12.20 denominations), and call a toll-free number from any phone for overseas direct (the best deal going, really).

Coin phones (either blue or the newer silver in color) are available for local and long-distance calls (with rates from 6B/15¢ per min.). You will need a pile of 5 baht coins and can observe your running total on the meter, putting in more coins as needed. For **information** within the Bangkok metropolitan area, dial © **1133,** or find an English-language copy of the *Greater Bangkok Business Listing.*

Telegraph services, including fax service and telegram service, are offered in the telephone and telegraph office of the GPO, open daily 24 hours. The same services (except for telegram *restante*) are offered at the telephone and telegraph offices at Don Muang Airport. A fax to the United States costs about 400B ($9.75) and must be prepared on an official form.

5

Where to Stay & Dine in Bangkok

Crash a tuk-tuk in the Thai capital and there's a good chance you'll hit a five-star hotel. The city hosts some luxurious properties, and Bangkok lodging at all levels comes with great amenities and service at a fraction of what you'd pay in Europe or the U.S. Bring your appetite too, as dining in Thailand's capital is alone worth the trip; find everything from superb Thai banquet meals to hole-in-the-wall noodle shops, from gourmet French to familiar pizza and pasta, all for very little.

1 Accommodations

Bangkok offers fantastic bang for your buck, and many hotels have great promotional packages with unique inclusions (breakfast, airport transfers, laundry, or local calls). Check chapter 2 for information on finding discounts in Bangkok and elsewhere in the kingdom. Remember—the hotel prices listed in this book are the *published rack rates*—with the exception of guesthouses, these rarely represent the actual rates you should pay. Contact hotels directly about special deals, and see chapter 2 for more budget advice. Unless otherwise noted, the prices listed are subject to a 7% government value-added tax and 10% service charge. In the high season (Dec–Feb), make reservations well in advance.

Note: Bangkok hotels, especially those in the "Moderate" category, offer significant discounts when booked directly through hotel websites.

THE AIRPORT AREA

Don Muang International Airport is anywhere from 30 minutes to 1 hour (or more) by car from the center of Bangkok, depending on your destination and traffic. Traffic is lighter going into town in the evening, but if you have just a quick overnight or a long layover, you might want to stay at either the **Amari Airport Hotel** (© **02566-1020**) just across from the international terminal with rooms from $250, or, if you're on a budget, the **Asia Airport Hotel** (© **02992-6999**), just 3 kilometers (2 miles) down Phaholyothin Road from Don Muang International Airport, with rooms from $75. Don Muang will close its doors in 2006, and both hotels will become convention hotels. **Suvanabhumi International Airport** (www.suvarnabhumiairport.com) will opens its doors sometime in 2006, and the new facility will be serviced by a **Novotel** (www.accor.com) now under construction.

ON THE RIVER

This is one of the most convenient and picturesque parts of the city. The river hotels offer great views and access to the fascinating Chao Praya River, the birthplace of

Where to Stay in Bangkok

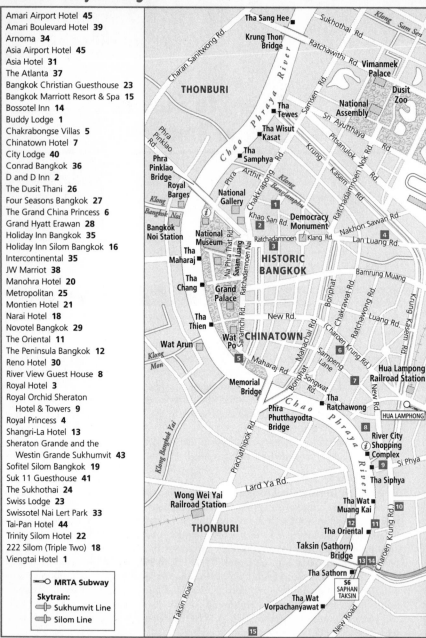

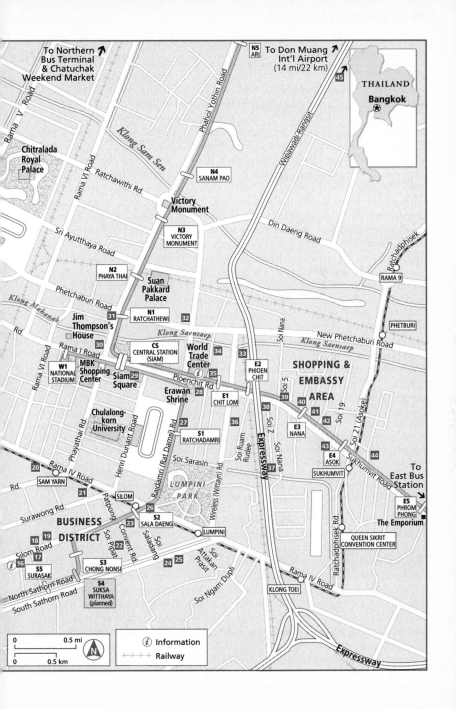

To Northern
Bus Terminal
& Chatuchak
Weekend Market

N5 ARI

To Don Muang
Int'l Airport
(14 mi/22 km)

45

THAILAND

Bangkok

Chitralada
Royal
Palace

N4 SANAM PAO

Klong Sam Sen

Rama V Road

Rama VI Road

Ratchawithi Rd.

Phahol Yothin Road

Wipawadi-Rangsit

Din Daeng Road

Ratchadphisek

RAMA 9

Sri Ayutthaya Road

Victory
Monument

N3 VICTORY MONUMENT

N2 PHAYA THAI

Phetchaburi Road

Klong Mahanak

Suan
Pakkard
Palace

N1 RATCHATHEWI

32

Klong Saensaep

Soi Nana

New Phetchaburi Road

Klong Saensaep

PHETBURI

Jim
Thompson's
House

Rd.

31

30

CS CENTRAL STATION (SIAM)

World
Trade
Center

34

33

E2 PHIOEN CHIT

SHOPPING &
EMBASSY
AREA

Rama I Road

Rama VI Road

W1 NATIONAL STADIUM

MBK
Shopping
Center

Siam
Square

29

28

Erawan
Shrine

Ploenchit Rd.

35

E1 CHIT LOM

38

39

40

Soi 5

Soi Nana

41

Soi 19

Soi 21 (Asoke)

42

Chulalong-
korn
University

Phayathai Rd.

Henri Dunant Road

Rajdamri (Rat Damri) Rd.

27

36

S1 RATCHADAMRI

Soi Ruam
Rudee

Soi Z

Soi Nana

Expressway

E3 NANA

43

E4 ASOK

44

Sukhumvit Road

To
East Bus
Station

Soi Sarasin

20

Rama IV Road

SAM YARN

Rd.

21

LUMPINI
PARK

Wireless (Wittayu) Rd.

37

SUKHUMVIT

E5 PHROM PHONG

The Emporium

Surawong Road

18 **19**

Silom Road

17

16

S5 SURASAK

SILOM

26

S2 SALA DAENG

23

Convent Rd.

Soi Pibat

22

Patpong

Soi Saladang

LUMPINI

24 **25**

Soi Attakan Prasit

QUEEN SIKRIT
CONVENTION CENTER

Ratchadaphisek Rd.

BUSINESS
DISTRICT

S3 CHONG NONSI

S4 SUKSA WITTHAYA (planned)

North Sathorn Road

South Sathorn Road

Soi Ngam Dupli

KLONG TOEI

Rama IV Road

Expressway

| 0 | 0.5 mi |
| 0 | 0.5 km |

N

(i) Information

Railway

Bangkok. View and access don't come cheaply though, and you'll pay the highest prices at the most centrally located facilities.

VERY EXPENSIVE

The Oriental ✿✿✿   A stay at The Oriental, the city's oldest and most atmospheric hotel, is a delight and sure to make memories, and you might even catch a glimpse of Thai royalty or glitterati. The hotel history dates from the 1860s when the original Oriental, no longer standing, was established by two Danish sea captains soon after King Mongkut (Rama IV) reopened Siam to world trade. The hotel has withstood occupation by Japanese and American troops, and has played host to a long roster of Thai and international dignitaries and celebrities, including adventurous authors Joseph Conrad, Somerset Maugham, Noël Coward, Graham Greene, John Le Carré, and James Michener. Rooms in the older wing, built in 1876, pack the most colonial richness and charm. Rooms in the newer buildings (ca. 1958 and 1976) are more spacious, some with better views of the river, but they sacrifice some of that Oriental Hotel romance. It is the level and range of service, however, that distinguishes the Oriental from the other riverfront hotels, and everyone from honeymooners and corporate execs to the well-heeled tourist is treated like a diplomat. Even if you don't stay, stop by for high tea in the oldest building, now called the Author's Wing, which houses luxury suites. The area was recently renovated and is one of the best-preserved pieces of old Bangkok. A small buffet and tea service costs 942B ($23) and is as atmospheric as it gets in old Siam. The Oriental's Bamboo Bar hosts the city's hippest jazz acts, the hotel's Le Normandie is a benchmark of fine dining in the city, and their new restaurant, The Verandah, is cool and casual. Private riverboats make regular connections with the Saphan Taksin stop on the Skytrain, as well as the River City shopping complex. The hotel has a luxury spa compound, as well as a luxury Thai-style dining venue and cooking school in a shaded area just across the river.

48 Oriental Ave., Bangkok 10500 (on the riverfront off Charoen Krung Rd. [New Rd.]). ✆ **800/526-6566** or 02236-0400. Fax 02236-1937. www.mandarin-oriental.com. 393 units. 14,000B–16,800B ($340–$410) double; from 19,200B ($468 suite). AE, DC, MC, V. 5-min. walk or boat ride to Saphan Taksin BTS station. **Amenities:** 5 restaurants; lounge w/world-class live jazz performances; 2 outdoor pools; 2 lighted outdoor tennis courts; state-of-the-art fitness center; luxurious spa w/sauna, steam, massage, and traditional Thai beauty treatments; concierge; tour desk; car-rental desk; limousine service; helicopter transfer service; tour boats for river excursions; business center; upmarket shopping arcade; salon; 24-hr. room service; babysitting; same-day laundry service/dry cleaning; nonsmoking rooms; executive-level rooms; cooking school. *In room:* A/C, satellite TV, minibar, fridge, hair dryer, safe.

The Peninsula Bangkok ✿✿✿   Whether you land on the helicopter pad and promenade into the exclusive top-floor lounge, roll in from the airport in one of the hotel's Rolls-Royce limousines, or step lightly off the wood-decked, custom barges that ply the Chao Praya River, you'll feel like you've "arrived" however you get to the Peninsula, one of Bangkok's most deluxe accommodations. Any possible amenity is available here, from elegant dining to great activities and top-of-the-line business services. Some of the largest in town, all rooms have river views and are done in a refined Thai and Western theme, a good marriage of Thai tradition and high-tech luxury with wooden paneling, silk wallpaper, and attractive carpets. The technical features of each room may make you may feel like you've walked into a James Bond film, as each room is digitized in ways that only Agent Q could've conceived of: Each bedside features a panel control that operates everything, including from the three phones, voice-mail, climate control, TV, and even the mechanized room curtains. The large marble bathrooms have separate vanity counters and a large tub with a hands-free telephone and

TV monitor built-in. "Ask and it will be done," seems the rule about service, and the multilingual staff is friendly and very accommodating. Their dining outlets, including the award-winning Mei Jang for Chinese, atmospheric riverside Thiptara for real Thai, and Jester's for international fare, are tops, and they have some great boutique shopping.

333 Charoennakorn Road, Klongsan, Bangkok 10600. (just across the Chao Praya River from Saphan Taksin Station) ℂ 800/262-9467 in the U.S.; 02861-2888 in Bangkok. www.peninsula.com. 370 units. 7,600B ($185) superior double; 10,400B–12,000B ($255–$290) deluxe; from 18,400B ($450) suite. AE, DC, MC, V. **Amenities:** 3 restaurants; 2 bars; 60m 3-tiered pool; tennis court; state-of-the-art fitness center; full spa service w/sauna, steam, massage and aromatherapy; concierge; tour desk; car-rental; fleet of Rolls Royce limousines; rooftop helicopter pad; tour boats and complimentary ferry service; business center; fine shopping; extensive salon; 24-hr. room service; babysitting; laundry/dry cleaning; executive check-in. *In room:* A/C, TV w/satellite programming, minibar, hair dryer, safe, CD player.

EXPENSIVE

Bangkok Marriott Resort & Spa ⟨⟩⟨⟩ ⟨Kids⟩ On the banks of the Chao Praya across the river and a few miles downstream from the heart of riverside Bangkok, the resort is accessed by a 15-minute boat cruise on the Marriott's frequent shuttle barges (when returning to the resort in the afternoon, you're given a cold scented towel and bottled water, a nice touch). Some don't like to be so far removed, but most find the short departure from crazy Bangkok a real relief, and once at the resort, the big city seems a distant memory. The three wings of the hotel surround a large landscaped pool area with lily ponds and fountains, and there is a wonderful spa for a very uniquely calming Bangkok experience. They have good sports and recreation options, and dining and activity choices are many, including a new school of spa cuisine, and familiar restaurants like Trader Vic's and Benihana, as well as their popular Riverside Terrace restaurant with a nightly buffet and culture show (see the "Dinner with Thai Dance" section, p. 128). Choose the Bangkok Marriott if you want to explore Bangkok and at the same time escape it.

257/1–3 Charoen Nakhon Rd., at the Krungthep Bridge, Bangkok 10600 (on the Thonburi [east] side of the Chao Praya River, 15 min. by boat from River City). ℂ 800/228-9290 or 02476-0022. Fax 02476-1120. www.marriott hotels.com. 413 units. 7,200B ($175) deluxe double; 8,800B ($215) executive double; from 14,400B ($350) suite. AE, DC, MC, V. **Amenities:** 5 restaurants; bar and lounge; dinner cruise; large, landscaped pool w/Jacuzzi; 2 outdoor lighted tennis courts; fitness center w/sauna; new spa w/massage and beauty treatments; children's recreation programs; concierge; tour desk; limousine service; business center; adjoining shopping arcade; salon; 24-hr. room service; babysitting; same-day laundry service/dry cleaning; nonsmoking rooms. *In room:* A/C, satellite TV, dataport, minibar, fridge, safe, IDD phone.

Royal Orchid Sheraton Hotel & Towers ⟨⟩ Set on a curve in the river, the Royal Orchid offers great views of the magnificent Chao Praya. Though a bit far from public transport—a longer ride by riverboat from the Sathorn pier than to the other riverside addresses—the Sheraton is a good base for shopping or sightseeing. The rooms are spacious, pastel hued, and trimmed with warm teakwood, lending a refined and distinctly Thai ambience. The Sheraton Towers, a hotel within a hotel on the 26th through 28th floors (with its own check-in desk and express elevator), offers more ornate decor and a higher level of service for a premium; Sheraton Tower suites, for example, have personal fax machines in the sitting room, and all rooms are staffed by 24-hour butlers. Recent renovations added the luxurious Mandara spa and state-of-the-art fitness center. The large pool area makes it easy to forget the big, crowded city. The hotel is a good home base for exploring the riverfront, and they have a walkway leading to the popular River City Shopping Complex.

2 Captain Bush Lane, Siphya Rd., Bangkok 10500 (next to River City Mall). ℂ 800/325-3535 or 02266-0123. Fax 02236-8320. www.royalorchidsheraton.com. 740 units. 8,000B–11,300B ($195–$275) double; from 13,000B ($320)

suite. AE, DC, MC, V. 15-min. walk to Saphan Taksin BTS station. **Amenities:** 4 restaurants; lounge; 2 outdoor pools open 24 hr.; outdoor lighted tennis court; brand-new 24-hr. fitness center w/sauna; new and luxurious spa w/private plunge pools, steam, massage, and beauty treatments; concierge; tour desk; car-rental desk; limousine service; 24-hr. business center; small shopping arcade; 24-hr. room service; babysitting; same-day laundry service/dry cleaning; executive-level rooms. *In room:* A/C, satellite TV w/pay movies, minibar, fridge, hair dryer, safe, IDD phone.

Shangri-La Hotel ★★   The modern, opulent Shangri-La, on the banks of the Chao Praya, boasts acres of polished marble, a jungle of tropical plants and flowers, and two towers with breathtaking views of the river. All rooms are decorated with lush carpeting and teak furniture and have marble bathrooms. The views are terrific from the higher-floor deluxe rooms, and most have either a balcony or a small sitting room, making them closer to junior suites and a particularly good value for on-the-river upscale accommodations. For such an enormous place, the level of service and facilities is surprisingly good. The luxurious Krung Thep Wing adds another 17-story, riverview tower to the grounds, as well as a riverside swimming pool, restaurant, and breakfast lounge. Guests register in their spacious rooms, surrounded by colorful Thai paintings and glistening Thai silk.

89 Soi Wat Suan Plu, Charoen Krung Rd. (New Rd.), Bangkok 10500 (adjacent to Sathorn Bridge, w/access off Charoen Krung Rd. [New Rd.] at south end of Silom Rd.). (℃ **800/942-5050** or 02236-7777. Fax 02236-8579. www.shangri-la.com. 850 units. 8,000B–12,300B ($195–$300) double; from 13,500B ($330) suite. AE, DC, MC, V. Next to Saphan Taksin BTS station. **Amenities:** 6 restaurants; lounge and bar; dinner cruise; 2 outdoor pools w/outdoor Jacuzzi; 2 outdoor lighted tennis courts; 2 squash courts; fitness center w/Jacuzzi, sauna, steam, massage, and aerobics classes; concierge; tour desk; car-rental desk; limousine service; helicopter transfer; city shuttle service; business center; small shopping arcade; salon; 24-hr. room service; same-day laundry service/dry cleaning; nonsmoking rooms; executive-level rooms. *In room:* A/C, satellite TV, dataport, minibar, fridge, coffee/tea-making facilities, hair dryer, safe.

MODERATE

Chakrabongse Villas   Here's a real find. The three luxury units of the Chakrabongse Villas are in the heart of the riverside area, just across from Wat Arun, and are the very picture of old-style Thai living. A good, high-end choice, these antique edifices are usually booked well in advance, so be sure to call ahead.

396 Maharaj Rd., Tatien, Bangkok 10200. (℃ **02622-3356.** Fax 02225-3861. www.thaivillas.com. 3 units. 4,000B–8,000B ($100–$195). MC, V. **Amenities:** 1 restaurant and bar; tour desk; limited room service; laundry and dry cleaning. *In room:* A/C, TV, minibar, safe, IDD phone.

INEXPENSIVE

Bossotel Inn ⟨Value⟩   It's not on the water and there are no views, but the spiffy little Bossotel is convenient to the Saphan Taksin BTS stop and close to the river. The hotel attracts folks on a budget (ask about discount rates for longer stays). Rooms are large but very basic, the furniture and decor a monotone gray, and the staff is helpful but few speak any English. They have good, affordable massage on the second floor.

55/12–13 Soi Charoen Krung 42/1, Bangrak, Bangkok 10500 (5-min. walk to Saphan Taksin BTS station just off Charoen Krung Rd., on Soi 42, near Shangri-La Hotel). (℃ **02630-6120.** Fax 02237-3225. 46 units. 1,000B–1,800B ($25–$45) double. AE, MC, V. **Amenities:** Coffee shop; tour desk; small business center; limited room service; massage; same-day laundry service. *In room:* A/C, satellite TV, minibar, fridge.

THE BUSINESS DISTRICT

Sure, this area is convenient for business travelers whose appointments are concentrated in nearby office buildings and banks, but if you're here on leisure, don't be put off by the "Business District" name, which is merely to distinguish this area from the others. You'll find some good values in the high-end range around Silom Road. It is an easy taxi ride to the river area, and a 30-minute trip to the Palace area (depending on the time of day).

VERY EXPENSIVE

Metropolitan Located on the site of the old YMCA, the Metropolitan is fashioned after the famed property in London and is Bangkok's newest house of style, a haven for pop stars and wannabes. The chic, modular lobby and crisply dressed staff could easily be mistaken for the velvet rope crowd at an upscale urban club. Rooms are elegantly angular but not minimalist (minimalism is "out," of course); there are lots of warm touches like earth-toned fabrics and overstuffed pillows to offset the crisp, contemporary lines. Bathrooms are large with big sunken tubs. A stylish little getaway with some cool new fine-dining choices. The pool is right out of a fashion mag glamour spread, and they have some très chic dining outlets. The staff is hip to what's going on in town and can always point you in the right direction to special events and parties.

27 South Sathorn Rd., Tungmahamek, Sathorn, Bangkok 10120 (a short cab-ride from Sala Daeng BTS station, soon just a short walk to the Lumpini subway stop). © **02625-3333.** Fax 02625-3300. www.metropolitan.como.bz. 171 units. 9,600B–10,400B ($235–$255) double; from 12,000B ($290) suite. AE, MC, V. **Amenities:** 2 restaurants; bar; outdoor pool; great fitness center; spa w/massage, Jacuzzi, sauna and steam; tour desk; airport transfer; business center; Internet; salon; shopping arcade; 24-hr. room service; same-day laundry/dry cleaning. In room: A/C, satellite TV w/DVD and CD, minibar, fridge, safe, IDD phone.

The Sukhothai ✿✿✿ Inside the Sukhothai, visitors find a welcome, if studied, serenity. Avoiding the hype of high-rises, the hotel's maze of low pavilions combines crisp, contemporary lines with earthy textures and tones. Broad, colonnaded public spaces surround peaceful lotus pools. Symmetry and simplicity form the backdrop for brick *chedis* (stupas or mounds), terra-cotta friezes, and celadon ceramics evoking the ancient kingdom of Sukhothai. Large guest rooms carry the same signature style in fine Thai silk, mellow teak, and celadon tile. Gigantic luxurious bathrooms feature oversize bathtubs, separate shower and toilet stalls, plus two full-size wardrobes. Technologically up-to-date, these smart rooms also have personal fax machines and Internet connections. The Sukhothai is second to none in excellent service and assures a sense of privacy. Their adjoining spa complex is stellar.

13/3 South Sathorn Rd., Bangkok 10120 (south of Lumphini Park, near intersection of Rama IV and Wireless rds., next to the YWCA). © **02287-0222.** Fax 02287-4980. www.sukhothai.com. 220 units. 7,800B–8,600B ($190–$210) double; from 11,600B ($285) suite. AE, DC, MC, V. **Amenities:** 4 restaurants; bar and lobby lounge; 25m outdoor pool; outdoor lighted tennis court; air-conditioned racquetball court; state-of-the-art fitness center w/Jacuzzi, sauna, steam, massage, and aerobics classes; concierge; limousine service; 24-hr. business center w/cutting edge technology; salon; 24-hr. room service; babysitting; executive-level rooms. In room: A/C, satellite TV and in-house video, fax, dataport w/direct Internet access, hair dryer, safe, IDD phone.

EXPENSIVE

The Dusit Thani ✿✿ "The Dusit" was once Bangkok's grandest address (and tallest building), but Bangkok has built around the old girl—now the Dusit lies in the shadow of the Skytrain and a hulking highway flyover, but the location is still one of the best, just at the edge of the busiest part of Silom Road and a short walk from both the Skytrain and the subway (also quiet Lumpini Park). The lobby is grand, with splashing fountains and exotic flowers, and the large outdoor pool is surrounded by thick foliage and provides a great escape after a day of sightseeing. Newly renovated rooms, though smaller than most in this category, are a classy international chic, with built-in blonde wood paneling and subdued indirect lighting. Their popular royal restaurant, Benjarong, is still a fine traditional dining experience (see "Dining," later in this chapter).

Rama IV Rd., Bangkok 10500 (near Sala Daeng BTS station on the corner of Silom and Rama IV rds. opposite Lumpini Park). © **02236-0450.** Fax 02236-6400. www.dusit.com. 532 units. 6,000B–7,600B ($145–$185) double; from 10,000B ($245) suite. AE, DC, MC, V. **Amenities:** 8 restaurants; lounge; bar; library w/high tea service; small land-scaped pool; driving range and chipping green; fitness center; spa w/massage, sauna, steam and spa cafe; concierge; limousine service; business center; shopping arcade; salon; 24-hr. room service; babysitting; same-day laundry service/dry cleaning; executive-level rooms. *In room:* A/C, satellite TV w/VCR, minibar, fridge, hair dryer, safe, IDD phone.

Holiday Inn Silom Bangkok ✯
Yup, it is the same old Holiday Inn of roadside American fame, and this Bangkok address offers fair rates and is popular for families. Comfortable guest rooms are done in tidy striped fabrics and floral prints, quite cozy. Superior rooms in the Plaza Tower are an especially good value, though smaller than those in the Crowne Tower, which have high ceilings and a spacious feel. Deluxe rooms have fine dark wood appointments and oversize porthole windows framed by heavy drapery and overlooking the city. Bathrooms are tidy but a bit cramped. It is just a short walk to the river (and the Shangri-La and Oriental) in one direction and a long walk to busy Silom Road in the other, and the hotel is in the middle of the gem-trade district. The large lobby seating areas are always abuzz with travelers who are either resting from a day's adventure, or waiting to begin a new one.

981 Silom Rd., Bangkok 10500 (1 block east of Charoen Krung Rd., or New Rd., and the river; also just a 10-min. walk to Surasak BTS station). © **02238-4300.** Fax 02238-5289. www.bangkok-silom.holiday-inn.com. 700 units. 4,300B–4,900B ($105–$120) double; from 6,800B ($165) suite. AE, DC, MC, V. **Amenities:** 3 restaurants; lounge; small, outdoor pool; outdoor lighted tennis court; small fitness center; Jacuzzi; concierge; tour desk; limousine service; business center; salon; 24-hr. room service; babysitting; same-day laundry service/dry cleaning; executive-level rooms. *In room:* A/C, satellite TV w/in-house video, dataport, minibar, fridge, hair dryer, IDD phone.

Montien Hotel ✯
The Montien is a slick and comfortable business hotel in the very heart of Silom, right at the terminus of the two busy Patpong *sois*. Set up in two large wings, each with dark teak hallways and bright, pleasant rooms, the Montien has seen some good upgrades in recent years and offers lots of services and upmarket amenities at a cost that would put you in a dull cell in other parts of the world. Unique here, too, are the resident psychics at the mezzanine level's Astrologer's Terrace, open daily from 10:30am to 7pm. A glimpse at your future is just 500B ($12).

54 Surawong Rd., Bangkok 10500 (near Patpong). © **02233-7060.** Fax 02236-5218. www.montien.com. 475 units. 5,000B–8,000 ($120–$195) double; from 9,000B ($220) suite. AE, DC, MC, V. 10-min. walk to Sala Daeng BTS station. **Amenities:** 3 restaurants; bar; lounge, and karaoke; outdoor pool; fitness center w/sauna; tour desk; limousine service; business center; 24-hr. room service; babysitting; same-day laundry service/dry cleaning; executive-level rooms. *In room:* A/C, satellite TV, minibar, fridge, hair dryer, safe, IDD phone.

Sofitel Silom Bangkok ✯
If you know other Sofitel properties in Asia, you will know what to expect from the Sofitel Silom: a high-end, modern, stylish, efficient city hotel. The location is great, just past the chaos of busy Silom Road in the Patpong area but not too far to commute. Chic, contemporary Thai-style rooms are done in dark wood with rich striped hangings and clean, minimalist lines. Baths are large, with separate shower and bath, and slick granite countertops. They have good executive services, and though they cater mostly to business people, the high standard at Sofitel Silom attracts more and more families and individual travelers looking for the familiar. They offer good spa services, but only a small pool and minimal fitness center.

188 Silom Road, Bangrak, Bangkok 10500. © **02238-1991.** Fax 02238-1999. www.sofitel.com. 454 units. 7,200B ($175) deluxe double; from 8,800B ($215) suite. AE, MC, V. **Amenities:** 5 restaurants; 2 bars; small outdoor pool;

fitness center; tour desk; limousine service; business center; 24-hr. room service; same-day laundry service/dry cleaning. *In room:* A/C, satellite TV, minibar, fridge, hair dryer, safe, IDD phone.

MODERATE

Manohra Hotel   This bright old standby, a 5-minute walk from the river and the famed Oriental, has a glitzy glass-and-stone lobby that faces a small indoor swimming pool. Guest rooms are compact and rather dimly lit, but the hotel has a full range of amenities. Often booked-out with European tours.

412 Surawong Rd., Bangkok 10500 (between Charoen Krung [New Rd.] and Mahesak Rd.). © 02234-5070. Fax 02237-7662. 250 units. 2,000B–2,600B ($50–$65) double (big discounts always available from prices listed). AE, DC, MC, V. **Amenities:** Restaurant; lounge; pool; small fitness center w/massage; tour desk; business center; salon; 24-hr. room service; same-day laundry service/dry cleaning. *In room:* A/C, satellite TV, minibar, fridge.

Narai Hotel and 222 (Triple Two) ✦   Just a short walk west of the Chong Nonsi stop of the Skytrain (and not far from busy Silom Rd.), Narai Hotel is a clean, comfortable business standard and popular with tour groups. There is nothing particularly stylish about the staid lobby and dull but adequate rooms, but everything works and service is efficient. If it is style you want, step just next door to their newest venture, a cool little boutique hideaway called the Triple Two (referring to the Silom street address). Rooms here are ultra-chic, done with silk appointments and traditional Thai fixtures that provide good contrast with the clean, ultra-modern lines. The hotels share amenities like the large pool and a small fitness area. Triple Two has a great indoor-outdoor dining venue, and Narai has lots of shopping and dining options.

Narai Hotel: 222 Silom Rd. Bangrak, Bangkok 10500 (just east of Chong Nonsi BTS station). © 02237-0100. Fax 02236-7161. www.narai.com. 469 units. 3,000B–6,000B ($75–$150) double; from 14,000B ($340) suite. AE, MC, V. **Amenities:** 4 restaurants; bar and lounge; outdoor pool; small fitness center; car rental; business center w/Internet; shopping arcade (jewelry); 24-hr. room service; same-day laundry/dry cleaning. *In room:* A/C, satellite TV, minibar, fridge.

Triple Two Silom: 222 Silom Rd. Bangrak, Bangkok 10500 (just east of Chong Nonsi BTS station). © 02627-2222. Fax 02627-2300. www.tripletwosilom.com. 75 units. 5,000B ($120) double; from 6,000B ($145) suite. AE, MC, V. **Amenities:** Restaurant; bar; shared facilities w/adjoining Narai Hotel (pool and so on); 24-hr. room service; same-day laundry/dry cleaning. *In room:* A/C, satellite TV w/DVD player, dataport, minibar, fridge, safe, IDD phone.

Swiss Lodge   Just a short skip down Convent Road off of Silom near the Sala Daeng Skytrain station brings you to this cozy, convenient hotel. Swiss Lodge started out as a small guesthouse and is now a popular choice for business folks (many Europeans on long-stay) and travelers. Though near the red-light district of Patpong, there is no sleazy vibe to the place, and front desk staff is friendly and efficient. Rooms are large and very plain, in a faded blue carpeting and simple furnishings, but everything is clean, and there are lots of good amenities (including in-room wireless). They have a good restaurant with daily buffet, and the swimming pool is but a postage stamp but not a bad escape.

3 Convent Road, Silom, Bangkok 10500. © 02233-5345. Fax 02236-9425. www.swisslodge.com. 46 units. 4,400B ($110) standard single; 4,900B ($120) superior double; 5,300B ($130) deluxe double (discounts available when booking directly). AE, MC, V. **Amenities:** Restaurant and bar; small outdoor pool; business center with Internet; 24-hour room service; same-day laundry; dry cleaning. *In room:* A/C, satellite TV, dataport, minibar, fridge, safe, IDD phone.

INEXPENSIVE

Bangkok Christian Guesthouse   A wholesome yin to the debaucherous yang of the nearby red-light district, the Bangkok Christian Guesthouse is on a small *soi* just one street back from Sala Daeng BTS station and is a convenient, quiet, and comfortable choice (just a short walk from sin to salvation, or vice-versa). This tranquil two-story guesthouse, originally a Presbyterian missionary residence, was converted into a lodge in the late 1960s, and is now operated by the Church of Christ in Thailand. Large, recently refurbished rooms are simple. The best rooms are on the second floor overlooking the large lawn with its sitting area, goldfish pond, and teak pavilion. There's a large, cozy lounge and library, an affordable canteen restaurant, and a friendly and helpful staff.

123 Saladaeng, Soi 2, Convent Rd., Bangkok 10500 (1 block south of Silom Rd. off the corner of Convent Rd. Near Sala Daeng BTS station). © 02233-6303. Fax 02237-1742. 30 units. 1,000B–1,400B ($24–$34) double; 1,800B ($44) triple; 2,200B ($54) quad. No credit cards. 10-min. walk to Sala Daeng BTS station. **Amenities:** Restaurant; laundry service. *In room:* A/C, no phone.

Trinity Silom Hotel ⚘ The hotel itself is small, but has good services and is a good location for the price. Guest rooms feature floral pattern prints and dark-wood headboards for a homey feeling. The staff is charming, friendly, and helpful. What sets the Trinity apart is its location within the Trinity Complex, a convenient shopping area. Easy access to both the Silom Road business area and shopping activity and the Skytrain make this a good choice in this class for both comfort and convenience.

425/15 Silom Soi 5, Bangkok 10500 (behind Bangkok Bank, 2 short blocks south of Silom Rd. on Soi 5, near Patpong). © 02231-5333. Fax 02231-5417. 104 units. 1,700B–2,300B ($40–$57) double; from 2,500B ($60) suite. AE, MC, V. 5-min. walk to Chong Nonsi BTS station. **Amenities:** Accessible to all guests within the Trinity Complex building: 4 restaurants; outdoor pool; outdoor lighted tennis court; fitness center w/sauna and massage; business center; limited room service; babysitting; same-day laundry service/dry cleaning. *In room:* A/C, satellite TV, minibar, fridge.

SUKHUMVIT ROAD: THE SHOPPING/EMBASSY AREA

Accessed along its entire length by the convenient Skytrain, Sukhumvit Road is the heart of upscale, commercial Bangkok. Here you'll find many of the town's finest large shopping complexes and restaurants, as well as busy street-side shopping and dining stalls. Many businesses now house offices in the numbered side streets, called *sois,* that extend from this main thoroughfare, and tourists as well as business travelers will find this the most convenient location with many comfortable hotel options. There are few good budget choices (much better than busy and inconvenient Khao San Rd.), and direct access to the BTS Skytrain means you can get anywhere you need to go in town at any time of day.

Hint: Siam, the Skytrain's main hub and center of the shopping area, is pronounced with a long "see" instead of "sigh." Say "*See*-yam" if you want to tell the taxi driver how to get to the area.

VERY EXPENSIVE

Conrad Bangkok ⚘⚘ The Conrad rises out of a large shopping compound in the area just adjacent to the U.S. Embassy. The hotel is Bangkok's hippest house of style, a medley of angular and austere as well as rounded edges, and rich, earthy colors: distinctly Asian, contemporary, luxurious, and chic. Rooms are compact and finely appointed with every modern convenience, alongside Thai touches like Dong San Drums for coffee tables and Thai artwork. Baths have freestanding tubs and are done in granite, marble, and glass, some with large sliders so the tubs can open to sleeping areas. Service is over-the-top. The ultra-chic lobby is often full of partiers from the adjoining Diplomat Bar as well as "87," the hotel's club and the latest place to see and be seen in town. They host many conventions and are one of the best business standards in town. All Seasons Place, the adjoining mall, hosts high-end shops.

Sukhumvit Road

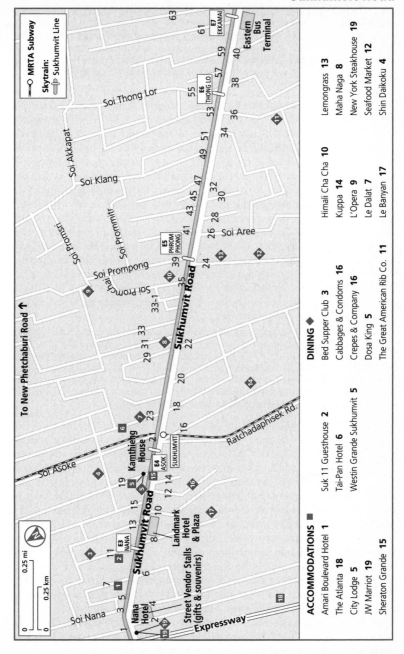

MRTA Subway

Skytrain:
Sukhumvit Line

To New Phetchaburi Road ↑

Soi Thong Lor

Soi Akkapat

Soi Klang

Soi Promsri

Soi Prommitr

Soi Prompong

Thai Prom

Soi Prom

Soi Aree

Sukhumvit Road

Ratchadaphisek Rd.

Soi Asoke

Kamthieng House

Soi Nana

Nana Hotel

Street Vendor Stalls (gifts & souvenirs)

Landmark Hotel & Plaza

Sukhumvit Road

Expressway

E3 NANA

E4 ASOK

SUKHUMVIT

E5 PHROM PHONG

E6 THONG LO

E7 EKKAMAI

Eastern Bus Terminal

0.25 mi
0.25 km

ACCOMMODATIONS ■

Amari Boulevard Hotel **1**
The Atlanta **18**
City Lodge **5**
JW Marriott **19**
Sheraton Grande **15**

Suk 11 Guesthouse **2**
Tai-Pan Hotel **6**
Westin Grande Sukhumvit **5**

DINING ◆

Bed Supper Club **3**
Cabbages & Condoms **16**
Crepes & Company **16**
Dosa King **5**
The Great American Rib Co. **11**

Himali Cha Cha **10**
Kuppa **14**
L'Opera **9**
Le Dalat **7**
Le Banyan **17**

Lemongrass **13**
Maha Naga **8**
New York Steakhouse **19**
Seafood Market **12**
Shin Daikoku **4**

All Seasons Place, 87 Wireless Rd., Bangkok (just across from the U.S. Embassy). © **02690-9999**. Fax 02690-9000. www.conrad.com. 392 units. 9,600B–12,000B ($235–$295) double; from 16,000B ($390) suite. AE, DC, MC, V. **Amenities:** 5 restaurants; 2 bars; large outdoor pool; 2 lighted tennis courts; outdoor running track; tip-top fitness center; spa w/massage, Jacuzzi, sauna, steam; concierge; tour desk; car rental; business center w/Internet; set in a large, high-end shopping complex (All Seasons Place); salon; 24-hr. room service; same-day laundry/dry cleaning; non-smoking floors; executive check-in; large meeting and banquet facilities. *In room:* A/C, satellite TV, fax and dataport, minibar, fridge, coffeemaker, hair dryer, safe, IDD phone.

The Four Seasons Bangkok 🏵🏵🏵 The Bangkok Four Seasons (formerly the Regent) is a modern palace. The entry is grand and the eye is led to the sweeping staircase, giant Thai murals, and gold sunbursts on the vaulted ceiling. The impeccable service begins at the threshold, and an air of luxury pervades any stay in this modern city resort. Rooms are some of the largest in town and feature traditional-style Thai murals, handsome color schemes, and plush carpeted dressing areas next to each large tiled bath. The more expensive rooms have a view of the Royal Bangkok Sport Club and racetrack. Cabana rooms and suites face the large pool and terrace area, which is filled with palms, lotus pools, and all sorts of tropical greenery. If you can ignore the new condominium blocks overlooking the area, it is a real hideaway. The Four Seasons has one of the finest hotel spas in Bangkok, and their **Spice Market** and Biscotti restaurants merit a visit even if you don't stay here (see "Dining," later in this chapter). There are fine executive services (a 24-hr. lounge area with business center and buffet) available to all room standards for an upgrade of just 1,435B ($35). Close to the center of town and the Ratchadamri Skytrain stop, you can get anywhere from here (though you may not want to leave).

155 Ratchadamri Rd., Bangkok 10330 (adjacent to Ratchadamri BTS station, just south of Rama I Rd.). © **02251-6127**. Fax 02253-9195. www.fourseasons.com. 358 units. 11,500B–12,300B ($280–$300) double; 17,200B–20,000B ($420–$490) cabana room/suite; from 15,500B ($380) suite. AE, DC, MC, V. **Amenities:** 7 restaurants; lobby lounge serving high tea and live jazz; landscaped outdoor pool; state-of-the-art fitness center; spa w/massage, sauna, and steam; concierge; limousine service; 24-hr. business center; shopping arcade (w/Jim Thompson Silk); salon; 24-hr. room service; babysitting; same-day laundry service/dry cleaning; nonsmoking rooms; executive-level rooms; meeting rooms. *In room:* A/C; satellite TV, dataport, minibar, hair dryer, safe, IDD phone.

Grand Hyatt Erawan 🏵🏵🏵 Bangkok's old grande dame and the choice of royalty and dignitaries (Bush slept here), the Grand Hyatt is in the best location in town and is tops in comfort, convenience, and style. Don't miss the hotel shrine, a monument to prosperity and good luck dating from the 1956 construction of the hotel (see the Erawan Shrine listing in "The Wats," in chapter 6). The hotel layout is on a grand scale with giant columns and balustrade staircases reminiscent of colonial architecture. The lobby and its lush indoor landscaping is a perfect setting for afternoon tea, and worthy of a visit in and of itself. The works of dozens of contemporary Thai artists grace hallways and spacious rooms, where earth-toned silks, celadon accessories, antique-finish furnishings, parquet floors, Oriental rugs, large bathrooms, and city views abound. Rooms have just been given a technological upgrade and now feature individual reading lights, Internet access, and compact control panels. In addition to the facilities one expects from a five-star hotel, there is a delightful fifth-floor pool terrace, where a waterfall tumbles down a rocky wall into a full-size hot tub. Their in-house dining is some of the best in the city: Try Spasso for great Italian (see "Dining" later in this chapter). The hotel has just added a luxury shopping center, with high-end outlets like Burberry and Cartier overlooking the small Erawan shrine.

494 Ratchadamri Rd., Bangkok 10330 (corner of Rama I Rd.). © **800/233-1234** or 02254-1234. Fax 02254-6308. www.hyatt.com. 387 units. 11,500B–12,500B ($280–$300) double; from 19,200B ($470) suite. AE, DC, MC, V. 5-min.

walk to Chit Lom BTS station. **Amenities:** 8 restaurants; lounge, disco, and wine bar; rooftop pool and garden; outdoor grass tennis court; 2 squash courts; fitness center w/Jacuzzi, sauna, steam, and massage; spa; concierge; tour desk; limousine and helicopter service; 24-hr. business center; shopping arcade; salon; 24-hr. room service; babysitting; same-day laundry service/dry cleaning; nonsmoking rooms; executive-level rooms. *In room:* A/C, TV w/satellite programming, dataport, minibar, hair dryer, safe.

Intercontinental ★★

Formerly Le Meridien, the new Intercontinental has a great location near Chit Lom BTS Station and downtown shopping. Rooms are immaculate, done in a bland but familiar high-end business hotel and set in a glass-and-steel tower block with unobstructed views of the city. You pay a premium here, but you get perks like wireless Internet, excellent services, and fine dining; don't miss their branch of the popular Shin Daikoku Japanese restaurant (see "Dining," later in this chapter).

973 Ploenchit Rd., Pathumwan, Bangkok 10330 (adjacent to Chit Lom BTS station, near intersection of Rama I and Ratchadamri rds.). ✆ **800/225-5843** or 02656-0444. Fax 02656-0555. www.intercontinental.com. 381 units. 9,850B–11,000B ($240–$270) double; from 11,900B ($290) suite. AE, DC, MC, V. **Amenities:** 3 restaurants; tower lounge w/live music daily; karaoke; outdoor pools; fitness centers; spa w/Jacuzzi, sauna, steam, massage, and beauty treatments; concierge; tour desk; car-rental desk; limousine service; business center; shopping arcade; salon; 24-hr. room service; babysitting; same-day laundry service/dry cleaning; nonsmoking rooms; executive-level rooms. *In room:* A/C, satellite TV, minibar, fridge, coffeemaker, hair dryer, safe, IDD phone.

JW Marriott ★★

A luxe downtown property, right in the heart of the busy Sukhumvit Road area, the JW Marriott is a cozy house of style, service, and convenience. A great choice for the business traveler, with extensive executive services and efficient staff covering any eventuality, and for the vacationer looking to explore the downtown shopping area or access the whole of the city by convenient Skytrain connection. The hotel has great dining choices, including the city's popular **New York Steakhouse** (see "Dining," later in this chapter), and their lobby cafe and streetside **Bangkok Baking Company** are good quiet nooks (all served by good wireless Internet connection). Tops is the 16th floor health club with extensive fitness and health facilities (popular with outside guests and members), as well as a professional spa and cozy outdoor pool: a real oasis. Upper floors of the hotel overlook the busy Nana area and Sukhumvit Road. Rooms are tasteful upmarket contemporary with ultra-comfortable soft beds, cozy office areas overlooking the cityscape, and large baths done in marble and granite with separate shower and large bath tub. Suites are vast and stunning. The hotel's Mandara spa is tip-top. Service is very efficient, and the hotel is popular with Marriott membership awards members. The Marriott offers great dining options: Chinese, Thai, and a popular Japanese dining area with teppanyaki grill, sushi, and separate sake bar, as well as their popular New York Steakhouse. Their small coffee shop is a popular stop along Sukhumvit.

4 Sukhumvit Road, Soi 2. ✆ **02656-7700.** Fax 02/656-7711. www.marriott.com/bkkdt. 441 units. $180 deluxe double; From $220 suite. AE, DC, MC, V. **Amenities:** 5 restaurants; 3 bars; health club; spa with massage; Jacuzzi; sauna; concierge; car-rental; business center; shopping arcade; 24-hr. room service; massage; babysitting (available on request); laundry; dry cleaning; designated non-smoking rooms; executive level rooms. *In room:* A/C, satellite TV, dataport, minibar, fridge, coffeemaker, hair dryer, iron/ironing board, safe, IDD phone.

Sheraton Grande and the Westin Grande Sukhumvit ★★

Just catty-corner to one another along busy Sukhumvit near the Asoke BTS Skytrain station, these sister brand properties are both luxurious, efficient, and convenient. There is a certain formulaic quality to these two chains, but it is a high-end formula and quite comfortable and familiar. Each tower room is nicely appointed, and the beds are the most comfortable in Thailand, hands down. The Sheraton Grande is the more luxurious of the two, and has a more upmarket style and popular fine dining choices that appeal to the discerning. The Sheraton's 10th floor pool will make you think you've been airlifted to the islands; popular 1st floor **Rita's** has regular live acts and attracts a hip after-work crowd; and the 3rd floor **Living Room** shakes with jazz nightly, even some very popular international acts. Across the street, the Westin begins on the seventh floor above the popular Robinson's department store and is a more affordable but similarly comfortable choice. Both properties offer deluxe business service, in-house spa treatments, and tip-top fitness centers. Direct Skytrain access at the nearby Asoke BTS station means that the city is at your disposal.

Sheraton Grande: 250 Sukhumvit Rd. (between Sois 12 and 14). 🕻 **02649-8888.** Fax 02649-8000. www.starwood hotels.com/bangkok. 445 units. 10,250B–11,900B ($250–$290) double; from 18,500B ($450) suite. AE, DC, MC, V. **Amenities:** 4 restaurants; bar; jazz club; outdoor pool; fine fitness center; spa w/Jacuzzi, sauna, and hydrotherapy; concierge; tour desk; car rental; business center w/Internet; shopping; 24-hr. room service; same-day laundry/dry cleaning; nonsmoking floors. *In room:* A/C, satellite TV, minibar, fridge, coffeemaker, safe, IDD phone.

Westin Grande: 259 Sukhumvit Rd. Bangkok 1011. 🕻 **02651-1000.** Fax 02255-2441. 364 units. 6,150B–8,200B ($150–$200) double; from 11,900B ($290) suite. AE, DC, MC, V. **Amenities:** 2 restaurants; 2 bars; karaoke; outdoor pool; fitness center; concierge; tour desk; car rental; limo service; business center w/Internet; shopping arcade; salon; 24-hr. room service; same-day laundry/dry cleaning. *In room:* A/C, satellite TV, minibar, fridge, safe, IDD phone.

EXPENSIVE

Amari Boulevard Hotel 🖈   Right in the heart of the busy Nana area of Sukhumvit Road (near the BTS Nana station), the city's best shopping and dining options are at your disposal from the Amari Boulevard, and the nearby Watergate (🕻 **02653-9000**) is a real upscale gem, the crowning jewel of the popular Amari chain in Thailand. The Boulevard offers an excellent facility at good value, and the newer Krung Thep Wing has spacious rooms with terrific city views, while the original wing has attractive balconied rooms that are a better value. When rooms are discounted 40% to 60% in the low season, this hotel is a very good bargain.

2 Soi 5, Sukhumvit Rd., Bangkok 10110 (north of Sukhumvit Rd., on Soi 5). 🕻 **02255-2930.** Fax 02255-2950. www. amari.com. 315 units. 6,800B–8,400B ($165–$205) double; from 8,800B ($215) suite. AE, DC, MC, V. 5-min. walk to Nana BTS station. **Amenities:** Restaurant; rooftop pool; fitness center; concierge; tour desk; limousine service; business center; 24-hr. room service; massage; babysitting; same-day laundry service/dry cleaning. *In room:* A/C, satellite TV, minibar, fridge, safe, IDD phone.

Holiday Inn Bangkok   Adjacent to Gaysorn Plaza and accessed directly via the Chit Lom BTS stop (right next to the Intercontinental, above), the new Holiday Inn Bangkok on Sukhumvit is a real find, but it seems like everyone else has found it too (the place is always booked). Rooms are a comfortable mid-range contemporary, and everything is brand spankin' new after major renovations (this used to be the President Hotel). Rooms have eye-swirling pattern carpets (appeals to some) and large spaces decked in wood and tile. Bathrooms are good sized, with granite sink stands and shower-bath combos in most. The hotel shares facilities with the Intercontinental next door, and is a very convenient address.

971 Ploenchit Rd., Bangkok 10330. 🕻 **02656-1555.** Fax 02656-1666. In the U.S.: 800-HOLIDAY (800-465-4329). www.holiday-inn.com. 379 units. 7,600B ($185) standard, 8,000B ($195) superior, from 10,000B ($245) executive rooms and suites. AE, DC, MC, V. **Amenities:** 2 restaurants; 1 bar; outdoor pool; sauna; health and fitness center; kid's club; business center; laundry; dry cleaning. *In room:* A/C, satellite TV, fridge, minibar, coffee/tea, IDD phone.

Novotel Bangkok 🖈🖈   This elegant and opulent high-rise hotel in the Siam Square shopping area is one of this French chain's best. The marble-and-glass entrance leads to an expansive gray stone interior, complemented by soft leather-upholstered sofas and chairs. Pastel tones carry over into guest quarters, where the rooms are spacious and fully equipped. Novotel is perfect for business or shopping trips and close to the Skytrain. Don't miss their popular disco.

Siam Square Soi 6, Bangkok 10330 (in Siam Square off Rama I Rd.). (C) 02255-6888. Fax 02254-1328. 465 units. 5,100B–6,300B ($125–$155) double; from 7,200B ($175) suite. AE, DC, MC, V. Siam BTS station. **Amenities:** 4 restaurants; huge popular disco; outdoor pool; fitness center w/massage; concierge; tour desk; limousine service; business center; shopping arcade; salon; 24-hr. room service; babysitting; same-day laundry service/dry cleaning; nonsmoking rooms; executive-level rooms. In room: A/C, satellite TV, minibar, fridge, safe, IDD phone.

Swissotel Nai Lert Park ✦

Managed by the folks from Raffles, the famed Singaporean hotelier, Swissotel Nai Lert was once a popular Hilton hotel. Set in the verdant Nai Lert Park, the Swissotel is a great little inner-city oasis. Rooms are cozy and kept to a high standard, but not particularly luxurious, overlooking either a central courtyard area or the park. A popular choice for regional travelers and for large weddings and functions. The hotel is a short ride north of Sukhumvit from the central Chit Lom Skytrain stop.

2 Wireless Rd., Bangkok 10330. (C) 02253-0123. www.nailertpark.swissotel.com (or www.rafflesinternational.com). 338 units. 6,000B–8,000B ($145–$195) double. **Amenities:** 4 restaurants; 2 bars; outdoor pool; tennis courts; health club; tour desk; business center; 24-hr. room service; massage; laundry; dry cleaning. In room: A/C, satellite TV, fridge, minibar, safe, IDD phone.

MODERATE

Arnoma

Plunked right in among the many shopping outlets, from the sprawling World Trade Center Mall to next door Narai Phand craft center to nearby Big C complex on Rajdamri Road, Arnoma is a convenient address. Rooms are contemporary and comfortable, and very tidy but not special (be sure to ask for nonsmoking). The place is big and busy, but the staff seem to handle it well. Good discounts are available from the rates listed below.

99 Rajdamri Road, Pathumwan, Bangkok 10330. (C) 02255-3410. Fax 02255-3456. www.arnoma.com. 369 units. 3,200B–4,600B ($80–$115) double; from 5,000B ($125) suite. **Amenities:** 3 restaurants (international, Chinese, buffet); 1 bar and cafe; outdoor pool; health club; spa; Jacuzzi; sauna; car-rental; business center; limited room service; massage; babysitting; laundry; dry cleaning. In room: A/C, satellite TV, fridge, minibar, safe, IDD phone.

Asia Hotel

With a second floor connection directly to the Skytrain (just one stop away from the central Siam station), Asia Hotel wins out over others in this category by virtue of location and affordability, but certainly not for style. The lobby is always busy with tour groups but has a worn feel; an old Chinese-style hotel that needs a facelift, really. With the Skytrain station hovering above and a covered parking lot in front, you'll feel as if you've entered a cave. However, it is its location, near the main shopping boulevard housing Bangkok's best and largest shopping malls, that attracts (not too far from historic attractions either). Rooms are like those at a simple and clean American roadside motel. Five restaurants serve up everything from standard Chinese to Vietnamese—even Brazilian. But you're so close to the cafes of Rama I, you probably won't hang around the hotel too much.

296 Phayathai Rd., Bangkok 10400 (between Phetchaburi and Rama I rds. w/direct BTS access at Ratchathewi). (C) 02215-0808. Fax 02215-4360. www.asiahotel.co.th. 650 units. 3,000B–5,000B ($75–$125) double (with Internet discounts as low as 1,400B/$35); from 5,000B ($125) suite. AE, MC, V. Ratchathewi BTS station. **Amenities:** 5 restaurants; lobby lounge; 2 outdoor pools; small fitness center w/Jacuzzi, sauna, and massage; tour desk; car-rental desk; limousine service; business center; 24-hr. room service; babysitting; same-day laundry service/dry cleaning. In room: A/C, TV w/satellite programming, minibar, IDD phone.

City Lodge *☆ Value*   Budget-watchers will appreciate the two small, spiffy City Lodges. Both the newer lodge on Soi 9, and its nearby cousin, the older, 35-room City Lodge on Soi 19 (© 02254-4783; fax 02255-7340), provide clean, compact rooms with simple, modern decor. Each has a pleasant coffee shop (facing the bustle on Sukhumvit Rd. at Soi 9; serving Italian fare on Soi 19) and facility-sharing privileges at the more deluxe Amari Boulevard Hotel on Soi 5 (see above). Rooms are large, with some major furniture mismatching going on, but are clean and not musty. No frills here, but still a lot of comfort for your money and very convenient to the Skytrain (at Asoke) and shopping.

137/1–3 Sukhumvit Soi 9, Bangkok 10110 (corner of Sukhumvit and Soi 9). © **02253-7705** (also at Soi 19; © 02254-4783). Fax 02255-4667. www.amari.com. 28 units. 2,300B–3,400B ($55–$85) double. MC, V. Nana or Asoke BTS stations. **Amenities:** Excellent coffee shop; access to Amari Boulevard's rooftop pool, fitness center, and business center; 24-hr. room service; babysitting; same-day laundry service/dry cleaning; *In room:* A/C, satellite TV, minibar, fridge.

Tai-Pan Hotel   This mid-size tower hotel rises above a quiet *soi* in a neighborhood that's convenient to Sukhumvit shopping and dining and close to the Skytrain at Asoke station (which means the city is your oyster). The staff is attentive and helpful, and the carpeted rooms have comfortable sitting areas and city views and all the facilities you'd expect from a more expensive hotel. The excellent coffee shop has bargain buffet breakfasts and lunches. A good value.

25 Sukhumvit Soi 23, Bangkok 10110 (1 block north of Sukhumvit Rd. on Soi 23). © **02260-9888**. Fax 02259-7908. www.tai-pan.com. 150 units. 3,400B–4,400B ($85–$110) double; from 6,000B ($150) suite. AE, DC, MC, V. 10-min. walk to Asoke BTS station. **Amenities:** Coffee shop; small pool; small fitness center; business center; 24-hr. room service; same-day laundry service/dry cleaning. *In room:* A/C, satellite TV, minibar, fridge, IDD phone.

INEXPENSIVE

The Atlanta *Finds*   A great budget choice, the Atlanta is chock-full of history and atmosphere. The oldest "original" hotel in the city (without renovation) and the first in Bangkok to have a swimming pool, the Atlanta was built in 1952 by Dr. Max Henne, a renaissance man and early expat, and is now managed by his son, Dr. Charles Henne. For years it was *the* foreign visitor's address of note in Bangkok. If you don't believe it, have a look at the photo in the canteen of a young King Bhumibol playing saxophone along with a trumpeting Louis Armstrong look-alike, with Benny Goodman on clarinet, while a grinning George Bush Sr. looks on from the background. Surreal. The lobby is original Art Deco and quite unique. The dining area serves great Thai treats and features a small library and occasional film screenings. There is a small pool out back and the hotel has a good travel service desk. Rooms are concrete basic and only a few suites have hot water. Service is quirky (there is even a sign that jokingly explains the surly front desk policy: NO COMPLAINTS AT THESE PRICES) but that's part of the charm. The hotel hosts many visiting artists and writers, and the works of journalists- and photographers-in-residence line the walls. They have a good "no drugs and no sex tourism" policy. The location is convenient to town, at the far end of Sukhumvit Soi 2, just a 10-minute walk to Sukhumvit and the Skytrain. They are often full, so it is best to reserve by fax. Popular for long stays.

78 Soi 2 Sukhumvit Rd., Bangkok 10110 (at the very end of Soi 2, a 5-min. walk or a 10B/25¢ motorbike taxi ride). © **02252-6069**. Fax 02656-8123. 49 units. 330B–450B ($8–$11) fan room; 500B–620B ($12–$15) A/C double. Cash only. **Amenities:** Restaurant; small outdoor pool; small gym area; tour desk; Internet corner; library (w/light table for photographers); laundry service. *In room:* A/C, safe (bring your own lock).

Reno Hotel   Just a stone's throw from the Skytrain, the Reno is the best of many hotels down the small quiet road, Soi Kasemsan, near the National Stadium stop of the Skytrain and close to Siam at the city center: a convenient and popular little budget enclave. Reno is nothing special—even with a recent face-lift it offers just basic rooms and limited services—but they do have a nice little coffee shop and Internet nook, and the price is right so they're often full (if so, try any hotel along the road and expect to pay as little as 500B/$12).

40 Soi Kasemsan 1, Rama 1 Rd., Bangkok. *C* **02215-0026.** Fax 02215-3430. 50 units. 840B–1,200B ($20–$29) double; from 1,500B ($37) suite. MC, V. **Amenities:** Coffee shop; outdoor pool; tour desk; Internet; laundry. *In room:* A/C; upper standards have TV.

Suk 11 Guesthouse ★★   For budget convenience in Bangkok, Suk 11 finds few rivals. With convenient access to the Skytrain at Nana and prices more befitting the budget spots on Khao San Road, this family-owned gem is often fully booked so call ahead (or book on their useful website). Rooms are basic: just plain linoleum floors and large beds in double rooms. Bathrooms are small, the shower-in-room variety, but clean. They have rooms with shared bathrooms for very little, but the single and double rooms with bathroom are the best bet. Common areas and hallways are done in a faux rustic style with wood-plank floors and are meant to look like old Thai streets. There are some quiet sitting areas and even a yoga room. It is a popular spot for folks studying Thai massage and a friendly camaraderie pervades. Walls are thin, though. A healthy Thai buffet breakfast is included, and the staff couldn't be more friendly.

1/13 Soi Sukhumvit 11 Sukhumvit Rd. (behind 7-Eleven), Bangkok 10110. *C* **02253-5927.** www.suk11.com. 75 units. 500B ($12) single; 600B ($15) double. Cash only. **Amenities:** Restaurant; game-room; laundry; yoga room; Internet terminals; library. *In room:* A/C.

BANGLAMPOO & KHAO SAN ROAD

Most of the major tourist sights are located here, making sightseeing on foot more feasible, though it is quite a long ride from commercial Bangkok. For budget travelers, the widest range of low-price accommodations is found in this area, and budget means as low as 120B ($3) for ultra-simple windowless cells.

MODERATE/INEXPENSIVE

Buddy Lodge   This is the newest in what is a likely trend of more upscale, air-conditioned accommodations, like mini-hotels really, in and around the Khao San Road backpacker area. You pay a lot more than you would for the usual airless cell in the area, but you get some comforts like air-conditioning, TV, and more security. Rooms are not big, but all are new and clean, with wicker furnishings and hard, but comfy, beds. Rooms are styled like old Thai houses, an effect that works and almost improves with the nicks and scrapes of use (the hotel is just a few years old now and always busy). This is "party town" for young backpackers going and coming from places all over Asia, and the spill-over from crazy Khao San just out front can get pretty raucous in the echoing hallways. There is a small pool, a popular restaurant, and lots of shopping and services in the plaza at the hotel entrance or on busy Khao San out front.

265 Khao San Rd., Bangkok 10200 (on the eastern end of the Khao San strip). *C* **02629-4477.** Fax 02629-4744. www.buddylodge.com. 75 units. 2,000B–2,500B ($50–$61) double. MC, V. **Amenities:** Restaurant; bar; outdoor pool; tour desk; large adjoining shopping arcade (and busy Khao San out front); laundry. *In room:* A/C, satellite TV, minibar, fridge, safe, IDD phone.

D and D Inn   A long-time "high end" favorite for Khao San, D and D has nothing to do with dungeons or dragons, but lots to do with affordable, clean, basic rooms with air-conditioning. The place is often full, and service is characterized by a calm and calculated "Next!" because the rooms are in such demand. The hotel is always expanding (that means hammering all day long), but there are some newer upgraded rooms in the most recent incarnation, and the lobby and small shopping area out front have been expanded beyond recognition.

68-70 Khao San Rd., Phranakorn, Bangkok 10200 (right in the middle of Khao San). © **02629-5252.** Fax 02629-0529. 230 units. 750B–1,350B ($18–$33) double. Cash only. **Amenities:** Numerous restaurants and shopping in adjoining atrium and on the road out front; laundry. *In room:* A/C, TV, fridge.

Royal Hotel ⚘ Near Thammasat University along the big, busy boulevard of Ratchadamnoen, the cozy Royal Hotel is just a 5-minute walk from the Royal Palace. It is good for the budget-minded sightseers who don't want to stay on crazy Khao San, but short of being near some of the major sites, the Royal isn't particularly convenient for getting around Bangkok. The glitzy lobby, with polished marble floors, chandeliers, and massive modern white Corinthian columns, was built in the 1950s and is a fun architectural pastiche from the Art Deco era (the hotel gained fame as the major field hospital during the May 1991 Democracy demonstrations). Clean, kitschy rooms have lots of overly florid filigree and pink, ruffled dusters, but are spacious and have high ceilings. With a small pool and all the basic amenities, you're just a short walk to the useful tour services on Khao San, but this place is quiet and a bit more "grown-up."

Ratchadamnoen Ave., Bangkok 10200 (2 blocks east of National Museum). © **02222-9111.** Fax 02224-2083. 300 units. 1,300B ($32) double; from 4,000B ($98) suite. AE, MC, V. **Amenities:** 2 restaurants; lobby bar; outdoor pool; tour desk; car-rental desk; courtesy car or limo; salon; 24-hr. room service; same-day laundry service/dry cleaning. *In room:* A/C, TV w/satellite programming and in-house video programs, minibar.

Viengtai Hotel One of the oldest hotels in the Banglampoo area, the Viengtai soldiers on, a rather spartan, battered enclave, but rooms are clean, the price is right, and you are just off Khao San Road (on Rambuttri just behind) but close enough to all of the action.

42 Rambuttri Rd., Banglampoo. © **02280-5434.** Fax 02281-8153. www.viengtai.co.th. 230 units. 1,750B–2,350B ($43–$57). V, MC. **Amenities:** Restaurant and bar; tour desk; laundry. *In room:* A/C, TV, fridge.

Budget stops abound in and around Khao San. Ask about any of the following: **New Siam Guesthouse** (29 Soi Chanasongkram, Pra-Athit Rd; © **02282-4554;** www.newsiamguesthouse.com); or **Sawasdee Guesthouse** (35 Soi Rongmain, Chao Fa Rd.; © **02629-2340;** www.sawasdee-hotels.com). All have rooms as low as 200B ($5) and some with good A/C rooms for a hitch more. Great on the budget.

CHINATOWN

It's a trip to the past, really, in the small streets and alleyways of busy Chinatown, one of Bangkok's more out-of-the way destinations and a unique choice for foreign visitors.

MODERATE

Grand China Princess Luxurious yet affordable, close to many attractions, and only a 5-minute walk from Ratchawong pier and the Chao Praya ferry system, standing amid the bustling shop houses and businesses of colorful Chinatown, the Grand China Princess begins 10 stories above a shopping arcade and Chinese restaurant. Recent cosmetic improvements in guest rooms provide all of the contemporary necessities, amenities usually found in more expensive hotels, without sparing Thai-style touches and character. Suites are especially large and done in muted tones of rose and gray. The 25th floor features Bangkok's first revolving lounge, with spectacular views over the city and Chao Praya River. Popular with groups from Hong Kong and Singapore.

215 Yaowarat Rd., Samphantawong, Bangkok 10100 (corner of Ratchawong Rd., just south of Charoen Krung [New Rd.]). © 02224-9977. Fax 02224-7999. www.grandchina.com. 155 units. 3,200B–3,500B ($78–$83) double; from 7,000B ($171) suite. AE, MC, V. **Amenities:** 3 restaurants; rooftop revolving lounge; small rooftop pool; active fitness center w/Jacuzzi, sauna, massage, and aerobics classes; concierge; tour desk; limousine service; business center; 24-hr. room service; same-day laundry service/dry cleaning. *In room:* A/C, satellite TV, minibar, fridge, coffee/tea-making facilities, safe, IDD phone.

Royal Princess This first-class hotel near the Grand Palace in the Rattanakosin Island area is another of the many fine Dusit Hotels and is great for travelers interested in the sights of old Bangkok, popular mostly with Thai travelers. Public spaces are wall-to-wall marble and bustle with activity, yet the scale is intimate. Guest rooms are very tastefully furnished and bright. While higher priced deluxe rooms have balconies overlooking the tropically landscaped pool, the superior rooms of the same style look out over the neighborhood. It is a 10-minute taxi ride to either the Grand Palace or Vimanmek Palace, and though the area lacks a diversity of dining, the authentic flavor of this old neighborhood more than compensates.

269 Larn Luang Rd., Pomprab, Bangkok 10100 (east of Wat Saket). © 02281-3088. Fax 02280-1314. www.royal princess.com. 177 units. 3,000B–4,000B ($73–$98) double; from 7,000B ($171) suite. AE, DC, MC, V. **Amenities:** 4 restaurants; lounge; small landscaped pool; fitness center w/massage; tour desk; shuttle bus service; business center; 24-hr. room service; babysitting; same-day laundry service/dry cleaning. *In room:* A/C, satellite TV, minibar, fridge, hair dryer, safe, IDD phone.

INEXPENSIVE

Chinatown Hotel 😊😊 You're right in the heart of it here, like living among the many storefronts on lower Manhattan's Mott Street or San Francisco's Chinatown. It is a memorable stay for location only: Though bright and tidy compared to other choices in this price category, the facilities are few and both common areas and rooms are compact (though clean). Price variations only reflect room size (there are a few showy, theme suites not worth the upgrade).

562 Yaowarat Rd., Samphantawong, Bangkok 10100 (3 blocks from Grand China Princess Hotel). © 02225-0203. Fax 02226-1295. www.chinatownhotel.co.th. 60 units. 950B–1,400B ($23–$34) double; from 2,100B ($51) suite. MC, V. **Amenities:** Coffee shop; tour desk; limited room service; massage; same-day laundry service/dry cleaning. *In room:* A/C, satellite TV, minibar, fridge, hair dryer, safe.

River View Guest House This special little place is deep in the heart of Chinatown, only 5 minutes from the railroad station, and a stone's throw from the river. It is not particularly comfortable, but the atmosphere of the busy neighborhood and nearby Chinese temples and shops (and, of course, the river views) attract visitors in search of an immersion experience. Part of the appeal is that to get here you'll have to wander through the neighboring *sois*, lanes, and labyrinthine alleys. Rooms are nothing special, just guesthouse basic, but some have great views, and dining at their rooftop restaurant is an experience in itself. *Note:* Be sure to grab a business card at the front desk so you can find your way home once you've checked-in (dropping breadcrumbs won't quite do it).

768 Soi Panurangsri, Songwat Rd., Sanjao Tosuekong, Taladnoi, Bangkok 10100 (500m/1,640 ft. southeast of railroad station, between the intersection of Songwat and Charoen Krung rds. and the river). © 02234-5429. Fax 02237-5428. 45 units. 450B ($11) double w/fan; from 690B ($17) double w/A/C. MC, V. **Amenities:** Rooftop restaurant; laundry service. *In room:* Some w/A/C, TV, fridge.

2 Dining

If you like your local Thai restaurant back home (and Thai cuisine is represented in so many places now), you'll love the many choices in Bangkok, from simple noodle stands to sophisticated, upmarket joints. Prices are reasonable, and you'll be hard-pressed to spend more than 2,000B ($49) for two at some of the town's finest restaurants. The city also offers a spectacular array of excellent European, Chinese, and other Asian cuisine that is expensive by local standards but a bargain compared to back home. Bangkok hotels are famous for hosting world-renowned chefs, so grab a local paper or one of the many city magazines like *Metro* (at bookstores and newsstands) to find out about any fun foodie events. You will not go hungry in the Big Mango, and the adventurous will wander off the beaten track to smaller street-side eateries and the best authentic Thai.

ON THE RIVER
VERY EXPENSIVE
Le Normandie ✿✿✿ FRENCH   The ultra-elegant Normandie, atop the renowned Oriental Hotel, with panoramic views of Thonburi and the Chao Praya River, is the apex in formal dining in Thailand, both in price and quality. The room glistens in gold and silver, from place settings to chandeliers, and the warm tones of golden silks impart a delicious glow. Some of the highest rated master chefs from France have made guest appearances at Normandie, adding their own unique touches to the menu. The menu features a limited selection of daily specials, with classic selections such as pan-fried goose liver, followed by a pan-fried turbot with potato and leek in a parsley sauce. The beef filet main course, in a red wine sauce, is divine. The set also includes cheese, coffee, and a sinful dessert. Order any wine you can imagine from their extensive list.

The Oriental Bangkok, 48 Oriental Ave. (off Charoen Krung [New Rd.], overlooking the river). ✆ **02236-0400.** Reservations required at least 1 day in advance. Jacket/tie required for men. Main courses 1,000B–1,600B ($24–$39); set menu with wine selections 5,000B ($122). AE, DC, MC, V. Daily noon–2:30pm and 7–10pm; closed Sun lunch. 10-min. walk from Saphan Taksin BTS station.

EXPENSIVE
Salathip ✿✿ THAI   Salathip, on the river terrace of the Shangri-La Hotel, is arguably Bangkok's most romantic Thai restaurant. Classical music and traditional cuisine are superbly presented under aging, carved teak pavilions perched over a lotus pond and overlooking the river (there are also air-conditioned dining rooms). Dishes are skillfully prepared and presented artfully. Set menus are a good initiation into Thai cuisine and feature a range of courses. Here's an example: Thai spring rolls, pomelo salad with chicken, a spicy seafood soup, snapper with chili sauce, and your choice of Thai curries. There is live music nightly, as well as Thai dancing and a culture show.

Shangri-La Hotel, 89 Soi Wat Suan Plu (overlooking Chao Praya River, near Taksin Bridge). ✆ **02236-7777.** Reservations recommended. Main courses 200B–450B ($5–$11). AE, DC, MC, V. Daily 6:30–10:30pm. Saphan Taksin BTS station.

MODERATE
Harmonique ✿✿ THAI   A nice little find, Harmonique is set in the courtyard of a century-old mansion and just oozes character. This is a great stop if touring the riverfront or visiting the antiques stores of nearby River City by day. You enter Harmonique through the crook of a dangling banyan tree, and there is courtyard seating

as well as small open-air dining areas, each like a small museum of Thai antiques. The cuisine is Thai, tailored to Western tastes, but it is all still very good—the *tom yam* with fish is delicious, served only as spicy as you like, and with enormous chunks of fish. The sizzling grilled seafood platter is nice and garlicky (chilies on the side). They also feature good Western desserts like brownies, great with a cool tea on a hot day and an atmospheric spot to relax.

22 Charoen Krung (New Rd.) Soi 34. © 02630-6270. Main courses 70B–200B ($1.70–$4.90). AE, MC, V. Mon–Sat 11am–10pm. 15-min. walk from Saphan Taksin BTS station.

Himali Cha Cha Restaurant INDIAN   Mr. Cha Cha, the original owner and proprietor (now deceased), was on Lord Mountbatten's staff in India before he went on to cook for the diplomatic corps in Laos. This, the original restaurant, was built in 1980, and there are now three locations in greater Bangkok run by his children. House specialties include a mutton barbecue, chicken tikka, and chicken masala. The Indian *thali* plates (a large plate with a variety of items to sample—similar to an appetizer plate) are great, especially for lunch. The atmosphere is a bit bland, but the curries are good. Try their other locations: on Sukhumvit Soi 35 (near Phrom Phong BTS), © 02258-8843; or on Convent Road in Silom (near the Sala Daeng BTS station; © 02238-1478).

1229/11 Charoen Krung Rd. (on a side street off Charoen Krung [New Rd.], corner of Surawong). © 02235-1569. Main courses 80B–250B ($2–$6). AE, DC, MC, V. Daily 11am–3:30pm and 6–10:30pm. 15-min. walk from Saphan Taksin BTS station.

THE BUSINESS DISTRICT

Silom road is where you'll find Patpong, the busy red-light district, and tourist night market. It is also a good place for familiar fare, from McDonalds to small coffee shops, as well as good street-side dining (see "Tips on Dining: Bangkok Street Eats," below), and some good, upscale, and atmospheric eateries.

EXPENSIVE

Benjarong ✦ THAI   Named for the exquisite five-color pottery once reserved exclusively for the royal family, Benjarong's fine Thai cuisine focuses on the five basic flavors of Thai cooking (salty, bitter, hot, sweet, and sour) in traditional "royal" dishes. While the a la carte menu is extensive, the most popular dishes are the sweet red curry crab claws and the exotic grilled fish with black beans in banana leaves. The illustrated menu will help you navigate your way through the choices. For after-dinner treats, the *kong-wan* is an ornate selection of typical Thai desserts—distinctive, light, and not too sweet.

The Dusit Thani, Rama IV Rd. (corner of Silom Rd. and Rama IV Rd.). © 02236-0450. Reservations recommended. Main courses 180B–600B ($4.40–$15). AE, DC, MC, V. Daily 11:30am–2:30pm and 6:30–10:30pm; closed for lunch Sat–Sun. Sala Daeng BTS station.

MODERATE

Anna's Café THAI   Anna's Café, named for the governess-cum–cultural diplomat of "Anna and the King" fame, is a great hideaway just a short walk from busy Silom. Anna's serves good Thai and familiar Western cuisine, a comfortable choice all around. I had a green curry with chicken, not too spicy and not too expensive, and the cool courtyard was just the right place to rest from the city heat. In the evening, it is all candlelight and romance.

114 Soi Saladaeng, Silom Rd., Bangkok (off Silom Rd. near Saladaeng BTS station). © 02632-0623. Main courses 90B–230B ($2.20–$5.60). AE, MC, V. Daily 11am–10pm.

Where to Dine in Bangkok

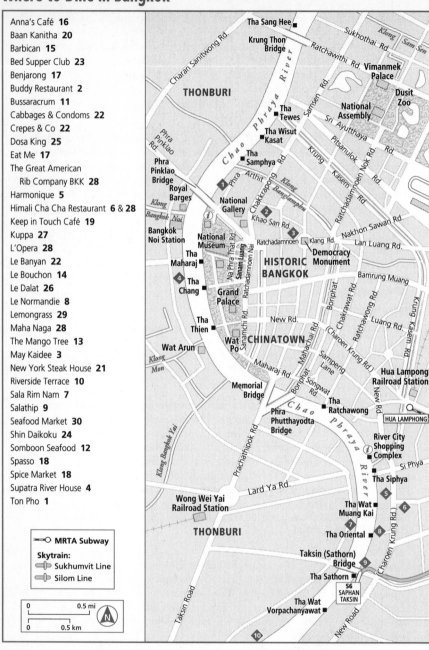

Anna's Café **16**
Baan Kanitha **20**
Barbican **15**
Bed Supper Club **23**
Benjarong **17**
Buddy Restaurant **2**
Bussaracrum **11**
Cabbages & Condoms **22**
Crepes & Co **22**
Dosa King **25**
Eat Me **17**
The Great American
   Rib Company BKK **28**
Harmonique **5**
Himali Cha Cha Restaurant **6 & 28**
Keep in Touch Café **19**
Kuppa **27**
L'Opera **28**
Le Banyan **22**
Le Bouchon **14**
Le Dalat **26**
Le Normandie **8**
Lemongrass **29**
Maha Naga **28**
The Mango Tree **13**
May Kaidee **3**
New York Steak House **21**
Riverside Terrace **10**
Sala Rim Nam **7**
Salathip **9**
Seafood Market **30**
Shin Daikoku **24**
Somboon Seafood **12**
Spasso **18**
Spice Market **18**
Supatra River House **4**
Ton Pho **1**

MRTA Subway

Skytrain:
Sukhumvit Line
Silom Line

0   0.5 mi
0   0.5 km

N

THONBURI

Tha Sang Hee
Krung Thon
Bridge
Krung Thon
Sukhothai Rd.
Klong
Sam Sen
Charan Sanitwong Rd.
Ratchawithi Rd.
Vimanmek
Palace
Dusit
Zoo
Chao
Phraya
River
Samsen Rd.
National
Assembly
Sri Ayutthaya
Tha
Tewes
Tha Wisut
Kasat
Phra
Pinklao
Rd.
Tha
Samphya
Krung
Pitsanulok
Rd.
Kasem Rd.
Phra
Pinklao
Bridge
Royal
Barges
Klong
Bangkok Noi
Phra
Arthit
Chakkrapong
Klong
Banglamphu
National
Gallery
Khao San Rd.
Ratchadamnoen Nok Rd.
Nakhon Sawan Rd.
Bangkok
Noi Station
National
Museum
Ratchadamnoen Nai
Klang Rd.
Lan Luang Rd.
Tha
Maharaj
Na Phra That Rd.
Sanam Luang
Ratchadamnoen Nai
Ratchadamnoen
Klang Rd.
Democracy
Monument
HISTORIC
BANGKOK
Bamrung Muang
Tha
Chang
Grand
Palace
Sanamchi Rd.
New Rd.
Boriphat
Chakrawat Rd.
Ratchawong Rd.
Luang Rd.
Krung Kasem Rd.
Tha
Thien
Wat
Po
CHINATOWN
Sanamchi Rd.
Mahachai Rd.
(Charoen Krung Rd.)
Wat Arun
Maharaj Rd.
Sampeng
Lane
Klong
Mon
Boriphat
Songwat Rd.
Hua Lampong
Railroad Station
Memorial
Bridge
Chao
Phraya
Tha
Ratchawong
New Rd.
HUA LAMPHONG
Phra
Phutthayodta
Bridge
River City
Shopping
Complex
Si Phya
Klong Bangkok Yai
Prachathipok Rd.
Phraya
River
Tha Siphya
Lard Ya Rd.
Wong Wei Yai
Railroad Station
Tha Wat
Muang Kai
Charoen Krung Rd.
THONBURI
Tha Oriental
Taksin (Sathorn)
Bridge
Tha Sathorn
Taksin Road
S6
SAPHAN
TAKSIN
Tha Wat
Vorpachanyawat
New Road

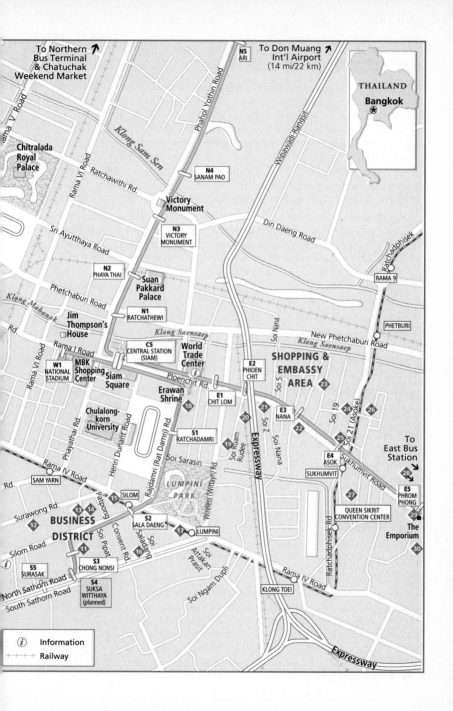

To Northern Bus Terminal & Chatuchak Weekend Market

To Don Muang Int'l Airport (14 mi/22 km)

THAILAND
Bangkok

Chitralada Royal Palace

Klong Sam Sen

Rama V Road

Rama VI Road

Ratchawithi Rd.

N5 ARI

Wipawadi-Rangsit

Ratchadphisek

N4 SANAM PAO

Victory Monument

Sri Ayutthaya Road

Din Daeng Road

RAMA 9

N3 VICTORY MONUMENT

N2 PHAYA THAI

Suan Pakkard Palace

Phetchaburi Road

Klong Mahanak

Rd.

Jim Thompson's House

N1 RATCHATHEWI

Klong Saensaep

New Phetchaburi Road

PHETBURI

Rama I Road

Klong Saensaep

CS CENTRAL STATION (SIAM)

World Trade Center

Soi Nana

SHOPPING & EMBASSY AREA

W1 NATIONAL STADIUM

MBK Shopping Center

Siam Square

Rama VI Road

E2 PHIOEN CHIT

Ploenchit Rd.

23

Erawan Shrine

E1 CHIT LOM

18

Soi 5

Soi 19

Soi 21 (Asoke)

24

26

Chulalong-korn University

Phayathai Rd.

Henri Dunant Road

Rajdamri (Rat Damri) Rd.

21

E3 NANA

22

25

S1 RATCHADAMRI

19

Soi Ruam Rudee

20

Soi Nana

E4 ASOK

Sukhumvit Road

To East Bus Station

Rama IV Road

SAM YARN

Soi Sarasin

Expressway

SUKHUMVIT

E5 PHROM PHONG

28

LUMPINI PARK

Wireless (Witayu) Rd.

27

29

The Emporium

BUSINESS DISTRICT

Surawong Rd.

13 14

SILOM

S2 SALA DAENG

17 LUMPINI

QUEEN SIKRIT CONVENTION CENTER

30

12

15

Patpong

Silom Road

11

Convent Rd.

Soi Saladang

Ratchadphisek Rd.

S5 SURASAK

S3 CHONG NONSI

Soi Pipat

Soi Attakan Prasit

Rama IV Road

North Sathorn Road

South Sathorn Road

S4 SUKSA WITTHAYA (planned)

Soi Ngam Dupli

KLONG TOEI

Expressway

ⓘ Information

＋＋＋＋＋ Railway

119

Tips on Dining: Bangkok Street Eats

Ask any Bangkokian to take you to their favorite restaurant and you'll most likely be eating at street-side or in a small, open-air joint. There are some world-class restaurants in the Big Mango, especially in the big hotels, and the town's many Thai-Western fusion restaurants are all the rage, but for good, authentic Thai in Bangkok, as in most areas of the country, the many night bazaars and hawker stalls are where you'll find the best eats. Eating at street-side will challenge your senses with the pungent aromas of garlic, chili, and barbecued meats, as well as the cacophony of music, lights, and voices at Thai open-air eateries. For the best open-air dining, try the few below:

Thong Lo   The European luxury cars that roll up late at night to pick up take-out orders tells you something about this place. Adjacent to the Thong Lo BTS stop (on the right side as you get off when traveling east/from Siam), you wander around the many open-air stalls, choosing what you want (anything from fried oyster pancakes to a great seafood salad) and then pick a table and sit down. The shop owners miraculously figure out a bill for you (and are always bang-on). The best street eats in town.

Suan Lum Night Bazaar   Just next to Lumpini Park, this sprawling shopping compound also features a grand, open-air food court. Buy coupons for food (about 100B/$2.45 will do it) and choose from the many stalls. Beer hostesses sling the suds, and there is a large central stage with Thai rock bands playing Western cover tunes nightly.

Soi Rang Nam   Here's a find. A short ride on the Skytrain from Siam brings you to Victory Monument. Exit the right side of the station and walk back toward Siam. Rang Nar is the first left and the street is lined with open-air carts and small, storefront restaurants serving authentic Isan (northeastern)

The Barbican ✦ INTERNATIONAL   A happenin' bar as much as anything, Barbican also serves good pasta entrees, goulash, and a tasty "Guinness pie." Everything on the menu is good, and the atmosphere is a cool, steel-and-granite chic. The place is full at happy hour, and there are often live jazz acts.

9/4–5 Soi Thaniya, Silom Rd. (1 block east of Patpong between Silom and Surawong rds.). ✆ 02234-3590. Reservations not necessary. Main courses from 120B ($2.90). AE, DC, MC, V. Daily 11:30am–2am. Sala Daeng BTS station.

Bussaracrum THAI   The menu at this tranquil, teak-paneled royal restaurant changes monthly, a cornucopia of Thai "Royal Cuisine" the likes of which the king or visiting dignitaries might enjoy (popular with small group tours). The *rhoom* (minced pork and shrimp in egg-net wrapping) was a favorite of King Rama II. The *saengwa* (cold shrimp salad with squash gourd) is an unusual dish and complements their good *tom yam* (spicy seafood soup). Ask for suggestions and enjoy a royal meal indeed.

139 Sethiwon Building, Pan Rd. off Silom (between Silom and Sathorn). ✆ 02226-6312. Main courses 150B–350B ($3.70–$8.55). AE, MC, V. Daily 11am–2pm and 5–10pm.

Eat Me INTERNATIONAL   More art cafe than restaurant, Eat Me is all about exposed industrial beams, dark wood, and indirect lighting on walls of an ever-changing fare of sticky rice accompanied by barbecued meat dishes and spicy papaya salad. Try **Tee Sud Isan Inter** (4/11-12 Soi Rang Nam; © **02245-3665**), among the many.

Khao San Road Area   Just 15B (35¢) earns you a pad thai served on Styrofoam and eaten with thin chopsticks. Also grilled satay and fried rice (not to mention the good halal sweet pancakes) make up the diet of many budget travelers, and busy Khao San Road is a good place for good eats at nighttime after a bit of pub crawling.

Silom Road   Just on the edge of the busy night market in Patpong, you'll find lots of noodle stalls, and in places like Convent Road (just across Silom from Patpong) you'll find *Kâo Man Gai*, a delicious boiled chicken on rice and seasoned to taste (and just 20B/50¢).

Note: Many are put-off by seeming unhygienic conditions of street stalls, and for good reason. Even if you are an adventurous eater, take some precautions: Check all ingredients for freshness, and be sure that anything you eat is prepared fresh, not just sitting out.

Food courts are another great way to sample authentic Thai food for very little. Every shopping mall has one, usually on the top floor. You buy coupons redeemable at small outlets lining a cafeteria dining area. Expect to pay as little as 50B ($1.20) for a main-course of something you've never seen before, a drink, and a tasty Thai dessert like bananas on sticky rice in coconut nectar. Try the upscale **Emporium** or **Siam Square** department stores to get you started, or look for **The Lofts** at the top of the Central Department Store just adjacent to the Chit Lom Stop on the BTS Skytrain.

---

exhibition space. They serve light Thai meals, rich and delicious desserts, and good coffee. There's an air-conditioned room, but go for the cozy balcony couch or the tables overlooking a small courtyard. A good, quiet place to get downright metaphysical with that special someone.

Soi Pipat 2, a small street off of Convent Rd. just south of Silom Rd. in the Patpong area. © **02238-0931**. Main courses 80B–480B ($1.95–$12). MC, V. Daily 3pm–1am.

Le Bouchon ✹✹ FRENCH   Find this hush-hush little French bistro, the kind of place packed with French expats on lunch breaks, and a great little candlelit romantic enclave in the evening. It is right in the thick of Patpong, and you'll have to elbow your way past wild-eyed sex show touts and cat-calling bar girls and lady boys to get there, but that is part of the fun. The food is delicious: rich French fare heavy on thick sauces, meat, and seafood. The chalkboard features daily specials and always a few surprises. The wine list is deep, and lunch hours sometimes become days off. Bon appetite.

37/17 Patpong 2 (just off Silom Rd.). © **02234-9109**. Main courses 180B–500B ($4.40–$12.20). MC, V. Daily

The Mango Tree ✹THAI   In a lovely 80-year-old Siamese restaurant house with its own tropical garden, Mango Tree offers a quiet retreat from the hectic Patpong area. Live traditional music and classical Thai decorative touches fill the house with charm, and the attentive staff serves well-prepared dishes from all regions of the country. Their mild, green chicken curry and their crispy spring rolls are both excellent—but the menu is extensive, so feel free to experiment. The only trouble is, the food isn't exactly authentic—but it is still quite good.

37 Soi Tantawan, Bangrak (off west end of Surawong Rd., across from Tawana Ramada Hotel). ✆ 02236-2820. Reservations recommended. Main courses 90B–350B ($2.20–$8.55). AE, DC, MC, V. Daily 11:30am–midnight. 10-min. walk from Sala Daeng BTS station.

Somboon Seafood ✸✸ SEAFOOD   This one's for those who would sacrifice atmosphere for excellent food. Packed nightly, you'll still be able to find a table (the place is huge). The staff is extremely friendly—between them and the picture menu, you'll be able to order the best dishes and have the finest recommendations. Peruse the large aquariums outside to see all the live seafood options such as prawn, fishes, lobsters, and crabs (guaranteed freshness). The house specialty, chili crab curry, is especially good, as is the *tom yang goong* soup (spiced to individual taste).

169/7–11 Surawongse Rd. (just across from the Peugeot building). ✆ 02233-3104. Main courses 90B–300B ($2.20–$7.30); seafood at market prices (about 800B/$20 for 2). No credit cards. Daily 4–11pm.

THE SHOPPING/EMBASSY AREA
EXPENSIVE

Baan Kanitha ✸✸ THAI   With so many fine Thai restaurants popping up around the city, it is getting hard to choose. Look no further than Baan Kanitha for authentic Thai in a comfortable, classy atmosphere. Down busy, traffic-choked Ruam Rudee, Baan Kanitha is an unexpected little oasis. They'll start you off with a free tray of finger foods, the dried condiments for making your own little spicy spring rolls called *mienkham,* and then you'll graduate to shared dishes of curry, from spicy red to mellow yellow and green, light salads, and good seafood as you like it. The pomelo salad is a find. Follow-up with good Thai desserts. Thais actually come here, a rarity for upscale Thai eateries, and the place is always packed: both good signs. Be sure to call ahead.

49 Soi Ruam Rudee. ✆ 02253-4683 (also another location at 36/1 Sukhumvit Soi 23; ✆ 02258-4128). Reservations highly recommended. Main courses 120B–350B ($3–$8.50). AE, MC, V. Daily 11am–2pm and 6–11pm. 5-min. walk from Phloen Chit BTS station.

Bed Supper Club ✸✸ INTERNATIONAL   This is the coolest place in Bangkok, hands down. Come for a drink in the bar, at least, and stick around for when the place busts open into a full-on club. They serve meals nightly for one sitting at 8:30pm, and the best part is that, as the name suggests, you eat in long, shared beds. The building is a giant cylinder, almost a pointed parody of "modern," really, the kind of architecture George Jetson might like. Walking up a concrete gangplank, the velvet rope gang ushers you in via large airplane airlocks. One side is the bar, the other is the dining area where you'll be assigned your slot on one of the two big beds that line the walls. The atmosphere is fun—a two-story, glowing white-and-neon interior: unique. Four-course meals are ordered from a limited menu on weeknights for 790B and weekends for 990B ($19 and $24). The food is fantastic, a constantly changing menu. I shared a tuna sashimi, tomato and basil soup, and a black cod filet artfully stacked on a bed of mashed potatoes and asparagus. All entrees are original. Dessert is pure decadence of rich chocolate specials and cakes. The atmosphere is a kind of comfortable surreal, with cool trance music spun by a DJ, and waitstaff in tight spacesuits and angel wings. Not to be missed.

26 Sukhumvit Soi 11, Klongtoey-Nua, Bangkok 10110 (at the end of Soi 11, near the Nana BTS station) ℂ 02651-3537. www.bedsupperclub.com. Reservations required. Men should wear trousers, not shorts. Set menu: 800B ($20) weeknights; 1,000B ($25) weekends. AE, MC, V. Open weekdays 7:30pm–midnight and until 2am on weekends. Dinner is served promptly at 8:30 (best to be early).

Le Banyan ⚞⚟FRENCH   A spreading banyan tree on the edge of the gardenlike grounds inspires the name. The upscale dining area is warm in tone, furnished with sisal matting and white clapboard walls adorned with Thai carvings, old photos, and prints of early Bangkok. The house special is a dish for two: pressed duck with goose liver, shallots, wine, and Armagnac to make the sauce. Other fine choices include a rack of lamb a la Provençal and salmon with lemon grass. There are daily specials and a list of fine wines. If you come on foot, you'll run the gauntlet of all the girly bars at the entrance of the *soi*, but find this little upscale gem and enjoy an evening of fine dining and effusive service.

59 Sukhumvit Soi 8 (1 block south of Sukhumvit Rd.). ℂ 02253-5556. Reservations recommended. Main courses 350B–1,440B ($8.55–$35). AE, DC, MC, V. Mon–Sat 6–10pm. 10-min. walk from Nana BTS station.

Maha Naga ⚞⚟THAI/WESTERN FUSION   Classy Maha Naga is an oasis of luxurious Thai dining in the heart of the Sukhumvit area. The name means "big snake" or "dragon," and refers to the stylistic caps of many Thai temple roofs. A fountain courtyard surrounded by high-peaked, lavishly decorated, and air-conditioned Thai pavilions makes for a quiet, romantic evening or a fun night for private groups. The food is delicious, a bold marriage of Thai and Western traditions in unique dishes like pork chops with spicy Thai som tam (papaya salad) flavor, whole lobster done in a chili sauce, or imported New Zealand grilled filet with Thai spice and mint. Elsewhere, fusion dishes come out rather bland, but the unique fare at Maha Naga breaks new ground.

2 Sukhumvit Soi 29, Klongtoey, Bangkok 10110. ℂ 02662-3060. Reservations recommended. Main courses 300B–800B ($7.30–$20). AE, DC, MC, V. Daily 11:30am–2:30pm and 6–11pm. A 10-min. walk south from Phrom Pong BTS station.

New York Steakhouse ⚞   A reputation well earned as one of the best steakhouses in the region, the JW Marriott's very mannish New York Steakhouse, with its dark wood and high leather wing chairs, is a posh but casual power dining spot on the second floor of the hotel, the best place in Thailand for a thick juicy imported Aussie steak served with a host of hearty sides (mushrooms, broccoli with cheese, mashed potatoes, and veggies). If money is no object, try their supremely tenderized Matsusaka Beef from Japan (just $160 per cut). Also try their tournedos of beef, grilled lamb chops, fine salads, and excellent seafood choices, from live oyster to Alaskan crab legs, tiger prawns to Phuket lobster. Be sure to start with one of their classic martinis and choose from a wine list as long as your arm (even an in-house sommelier). Dress code is casual (but no shorts or sandals). No kids under 12 allowed. Very professional service and a cool, casual atmosphere guarantee a memorable evening.

At the JW Marriott (second floor), 4 Sukhumvit Road, Soi 2, Bangkok, 10110. ℂ 02656-9798 (direct) or the hotel at ℂ 02656-7700. Main courses 1,600B–6,900B ($39–$168). AE, MC, V. Daily 6pm–11pm. Reservations recommended.

Shin Daikoku ⚞⚟JAPANESE   With a track record of over 30 years as the home away from home for the many Japanese expatriates in Bangkok, Shin Daikoku serves delicious and authentic Japanese dishes, from hot apps and noodle dishes like soba and udon, to sushi, sashimi, and even teppanyaki steaks. Set in a quiet neighborhood off Sukhumvit (near the Asoke Skytrain stop), the restaurant is a sprawling compound of private *tatami* (mattress) rooms, and an open dining area surrounds a cavernous indoor garden and a pond full of koi (Japanese carp). Female staff wear cotton *yukata* (summer kimonos) and pad around politely, hovering over every detail of the meal. The roaring laughter and shouts of "Kampai!" from behind the painted, paper shoji screens of private rooms tells you that they're doing it right here. A la carte dishes are small and rather expensive, but they're worth it. And they have good sushi and sashimi sets. Order some sake, take your shoes off, wrap your tie around your head, and belt out a hearty "Kampai!"

32/8 Soi Wattana, Sukhumvit 19 Klongtoey (a 5-min. walk down Soi 19 from Asoke BTS station and on left after the first intersecting road, Wattana). ⒸⒻ 02254-9981. Reservations for big groups only. Main course 100B–1,600B ($2.45–$39). AE, DC, MC, V. Daily 11:30am–2pm and 5:30–10:30pm. Asoke BTS station.

Spasso ⭐ ITALIAN   Spasso is as well known as a nightlife spot as it is for Italian cuisine. A hip and classy place, the bar is always hoppin' and there is often live music, even people waiting in line, at this artsy modern trattoria with fine decor. The food is a treat: Start with one of their antipastos featuring fine imported treats like carpaccio or smoked salmon, and then choose from their fine pastas, some, like the fusilli with chilies and shrimp, done in a modified Thai style. Thin-crust pizza fans will find a dozen combos, all made with fresh ingredients and baked in a brick oven. Local bands start at around 9:30pm, and the dancing starts not long after.

In the Grand Hyatt Erawan, 494 Ratchadamri Rd. ⒸⒻ 02254-1234. Reservations recommended for dinner. Main courses 300B–820B ($7.30–$20). AE, DC, MC, V. Daily noon–2:30pm, and 7–10:30pm (kitchen closes, but disco stays open). 5-min. walk from Chit Lom BTS station.

Spice Market ⭐⭐ THAI   The theatrical decor reflects the name: Burlap spice sacks, ceramic pots, and glass jars set in dark-wood cabinets around the dining area playfully re-create the mercantile feel of a traditional Thai shop house. The food is artfully presented, authentically spiced, and extraordinarily delicious, with featured regional specialties for a great way to sample dishes from places you may or may not be traveling to in the kingdom. House specialties include a tasty *mienkham* appetizer of coconut, dried shrimp, nuts, and chilies that you assemble yourself, rolling ingredients in a leaf for a tasty little treat. For entrees, try the *poo nim phad prig* (soft-shell crab deep-fried with chili and peppercorn), or *siew ngap* (red curry with roasted duck in coconut milk). The menu's "chili rating" guarantees that spices are tempered to your palate. Sunday brunches here and at the Four Seasons' other fine dining outlets are quite popular.

In the Four Seasons Bangkok, 155 Ratchadamri Rd. (south of Rama I Rd.). ⒸⒻ 02251-6127. Reservations recommended. Main courses 180B–450B ($4.40–$11). AE, DC, MC, V. Daily 11:30am–2:30pm and 6–11pm. Ratchadamri BTS station.

MODERATE

The Great American Rib Company BKK   New on the scene and a real expat favorite, the kind of place to hold a party or celebrate a birthday, The Great American Rib Company is run by two Americans and they've got the formula just right: simple, hearty, rib-stickin' cuisine. The best choice is their Great American Barbeque Feast of a full rack of ribs, a whole roasted "Butt Kickin' Chicken," 1 pound of pulled pork, pepper-coated "Pastramied" pork tenderloin, baked beans, coleslaw, curly fries, and Jalapeño corn bread. Loosen your belt. They have good fajitas and Tex-Mex specials, steaks and burgers, soups and salads. The crispy Buffalo wings are tops. Follow with some really intense apple pie. A huge feed and a nice slice of America in the heart of old Bangkok.

32 Sukhumvit Soi 36, Klongtoey. ⒸⒻ 02661-3801. greatrib@anbs.co.th. Main course 85B–400B ($2.10–$9.75). Set meals (for 3 or 4) 1,000B ($24). MC, V. Daily 11am–10pm.

Kuppa ★★ INTERNATIONAL   This cafe restaurant is worth a visit if only to see the unique space, a former warehouse (reputedly a CIA hangout) now a chic, modern interior, housing the offices of owner and interior designer Robin Lourvanij, a woman who shares her time and heart between Bangkok and Australia. Come for the coffee and don't miss the hulking roaster machine, a centerpiece of the dining area where they roast their own blend weekly. The food is delicious: a healthy sampling of unique Thai and Western fare and good stuff to fill the homesick tummies of expats and visitors. Grilled items are great, and there are lots of daily specials. Dessert is something sinful with good coffee. Kuppa is in a quiet neighborhood and has good couches for kicking back. Look for their new outlet near the Playground shopping center near Thong Lor.

39 Sukhumvit Soi 16, Klongtoey, Bangkok (a long walk down Soi 16 from the Asoke BTS Skytrain station). (✆ 02663-0495. Main courses 165B–495B ($4–$12). AE, MC, V. Daily 10:30am–11:30pm.

Le Dalat ★★ VIETNAMESE   Le Dalat's fine food and lovely garden setting make for a charming evening. The restaurant is casual and understatedly elegant, housed in an old Thai house done up in Vietnamese and Chinese antiques. The excellent food is prepared by Vietnamese-trained Thai chefs. Go for the *bi guon* (spring rolls with herbs and pork), *chao tom* (pounded shrimp laced on ground sugarcane in a basket of fresh noodles), and *cha ra* (fresh filet of grilled fish). In nice weather, you'll enjoy dining in the gracefully landscaped outdoor garden. A very highly recommended restaurant. Don't miss a visit to the men's room to see their unique collection of odd erotic wall art. And look for their new outlet near the hip shopping complex Playground, near Tong Lor.

14 Sukhumvit Soi 23. (✆ 02661-7967 (or at 47/1 Sukhumvit Soi 23 [north of Sukhumvit Rd. near Asoke BTS station]; (✆ 02258-4192). Reservations recommended at dinner. Main courses 150B–650B ($3.65–$16). AE, DC, MC, V. Daily 11:30am–2:30pm and 6–10:30pm.

Lemongrass THAI   Nouvelle Thai cuisine tailored to Western tastes is the specialty of this pleasant restaurant. Just a short walk from the Skytrain (near Phrom Pong) and just across from the hulking Emporium Shopping Center, Lemongrass is set in a small Thai mansion handsomely converted and furnished with antiques, and a visit here makes it easy to forget busy Bangkok outside. Try house favorites pomelo salad or chicken satay. Also excellent is the *tom yang kung* (a spicy sweet-and-sour prawn soup with ginger shoots), and the lemon grass chicken is tender and juicy.

5/1 Sukhumvit Soi 24 (south of Sukhumvit Rd. on Soi 24). (✆ 02258-8637. Reservations highly recommended. Main courses 120B–550B ($2.95–$13). AE, DC, MC, V. Daily 11am–2pm and 6–11pm. Phrom Pong BTS station.

L'Opera ★ ITALIAN   With its sister restaurant in Vientiane, Laos, L'Opera Bangkok has been hosting visitors and expats since they first opened in the 1970s, when Soi 39 was but a dusty little alley with cows grazing out front. Now it is a sophisticated enclave and they've got the formula just right, dim lights in a glassed-in pavilion, cool jazz in the air, and good, affordable Italian. Come with friends and fill the table. We had biscotti appetizers followed by a decadent seafood salad. For a main course, go for the fresh fish done as you like, or any of the grilled items or pastas. I had a delicious squid-ink linguini and clams. Tops!

53 Sukhumvit Soi 39, Klongtoey Bangkok. (✆ 02258-5606. Main courses 200B–880B ($4.90–$22). AE, MC, V. Daily 6–11pm. Near Phrom Phong BTS station.

Seafood Market ★ SEAFOOD   *Warning:* This place is touristy, but I wouldn't recommend it if it weren't good food and fun. Chances are you've never had a dining

---

Cricket, Anyone?

Look for the snack stands along Sukhumvit Road (also Khao San Rd.) that sell all sorts of fried insects. Grasshoppers, beetles that look like cockroaches, scorpions, ants, and grubs are a favorite snack for folks from Isan, in the northeast, where bugs are in fact cultivated for the dining table and are an important source of protein in the region. How does it taste? Crickets are a bit like popcorn, and the beetles are something like a crispy (hate to say it) chicken. A great photo op.

---

experience like this before, and if you're a seafood fan, you'll love it. After you've been seated, look over the list of preparation styles, then walk to the back and take a shopping cart. Peruse the no fewer than 40 different creatures of the sea, either live or on ice, all priced by the kilo. Pay for it all at the cashier, then cart it back to the table. Waiters are skilled at making perfect suggestions for your catch, and what comes out of the kitchen is always good. Cooking charges and corkage are paid separately at the end of the meal. The seafood is market price, the fish incredibly fresh.

89 Sukhumvit Soi 24 (Soi Kasame), Bangkok. © 02261-2071. Reservations suggested for weekend dinner. Market Prices. AE, MC, V. Daily 11:30am–midnight.

INEXPENSIVE

Cabbages & Condoms 🐸🐸 THAI   Here's a theme restaurant with a purpose. Opened by local hero Mechai Viravaidya, founder of the Population & Community Development Association, the restaurant helps fund population control, AIDS awareness, and a host of rural development programs. Set in a large compound, the two-story restaurant has air-conditioned indoor dining—but if you sit on the garden terrace, you're in a fairyland of twinkling lights: quite romantic. Share a whole fish done as you like, or try the *kai hor bai teoy* (fried boneless chicken wrapped in pandan leaves with a dark sweet soy sauce for dipping). There's also a large selection of vegetable and bean curd entrees. Before you leave, be sure to check out the gift shop's whimsical condom-related merchandise. The restaurant hands out condoms instead of dinner mints.

10 Sukhumvit Soi 12. © 02229-4610. Reservations recommended. 70B–200B ($1.70–$4.90). AE, DC, MC, V. Daily 11am–10pm. 15-min. walk from Asoke BTS station.

Crepes & Co 🐸🐸 *Kids* EUROPEAN   Popular among Bangkok foreign residents (and their kids), this is the place to satisfy that sweet tooth. Crepes & Co. serves them up light and fluffy and filled with any of dozens of combinations, both savory and sweet—all of them delicious. They also serve good Mediterranean main courses. Everything is excellent. They have great coffee and a good selection of tea.

18/1 Sukhumvit Soi 12. © 02653-3990. Reservations recommended. Main courses 100B–300B ($2.45–$7.30). AE, DC, MC, V. Mon–Sat 9am–midnight; Sun 8am–midnight. 15-min. walk from Asoke BTS station.

Dosa King 🐸 INDIAN/VEGETARIAN   What is a Dosa, you ask? It is a Punjabi dish of curry or other savory filling folded into a large, lentil-and-flour tortilla or crepe (depending on your orientation), and served with coconut or coriander sauce. Very tasty and all 100% vegetarian, a comfort for some. Dosa King does have other traditional Indian dishes, but stick with the house special and a enjoy a quick, healthy meal for very little while trudging along Sukhumvit.

265/1 Sukhumvit Soi 19, Bangkok 10110. ℂ **02651-1700.** Main courses 65B–135B ($1.60–$3.30). AE, MC, V. Daily 11am–11pm. Near Asoke BTS station.

Keep in Touch Café THAI/WESTERN   Here's a fun little find. Nothing fancy about this little expat joint, but a friendlier cafe there never was. They have good affordable Western and Thai fare, and feature regular live music acts. Popular with expats. They're on the far end of Soi Ruam Rudee, across from Bangkok's biggest Catholic church.

48/10 Soi Ruam Rudee, Pathumwan, Bangkok, 10330. ℂ **02650/9497.** Main courses 60B–180B ($1.50–$4.40). V, MC. Daily 11:30am–2pm and 5–11pm.

BANGLAMPOO & KHAO SAN ROAD

Khao San Road is Bangkok's busy backpacker ghetto and where you'll find every manner of food, from Israeli and halal cuisine to Italian, as well as tasty Thai food served at street-side (and McDonalds). Avoid the budget guesthouses serving bland versions of Western food, but do have a seat somewhere along the busy road, order up a fruit shake, and watch the nightly parade of young travelers. Below are a few good choices near Khao San.

INEXPENSIVE

Buddy Restaurant   A popular bar as much as anything, Buddy Restaurant is part of the growing Buddy Lodge "compound." The second floor restaurant serves good Thai and Western and is always full, even late into the night with the club-going set.

265 Khaosan Rd., Banglampoo. ℂ **02629-4477.** www.buddylodge.com. Main courses 70B–340B ($1.70–$8.30). V, MC. Open 24 hrs.

May Kaidee ★ *Finds* VEGETARIAN/THAI   Find this place. It is my favorite restaurant in Thailand. Don't come for atmosphere—it's more or less tables in a little alleyway—but bring your appetite for healthy and delicious Thai vegetarian dishes. Ms. May (pronounced *My*) has developed a real following, as much for her wry smile and kindness as for the great curries and soups she serves. The best massaman curry in Thailand and an array of dishes from sweet green curry to good stir-fries come with your choice of white or a unique short-grained brown rice. For dessert, don't pass-up the black sticky-rice with mango. May has a good cookbook for sale and also offers cooking classes. May keeps opening up new storefronts around Khao San, none of which seem to go, but this one does.

At the eastern terminus of Khao San Rd. in a small alley behind the first row of buildings (behind Burger King, in fact; ask around—everyone knows this place). ℂ **02629-4839.** Main course 60B–120B ($1.50–$3.65). Cash only. Daily 7am–10pm.

Ton Pho ★ THAI   This is one popular with locals, and a good place to try real Thai food (at real Thai prices). The restaurant is at riverside, but overlooks the busy public boat pier that accesses Banglampoo and the popular Khao San Road area—which means that the view is of groups gathering and departing on smoke-belching river buses rather than a wide riverside landscape. Ton Pho has been around almost 20 years and has a good following. Great stir-fries and classic Thai dishes like Tom Yum Goon and coconut milk–infused soups and curries.

43 Phra-A-Thit Rd., Banglampoo. ℂ **02280-0452.** Main course 50B–250B ($1.20–$6.10). Cash only. Daily 11am–10pm.

DINNER WITH THAI DANCE

Riverside Terrace 𝄢 SEAFOOD BARBECUE   On an al fresco patio beside the river, Marriott stages a Thai cultural show with traditional dance. It is a good option if you'd like to see the stage show but would rather eat international cuisine as opposed to Thai, which is standard for most dinner show venues. The food is good and the buffet quite extensive. Call the hotel for details on how to pick up the hotel's free shuttle ferry on the Chao Praya River.

In the Bangkok Marriott Resort & Spa, 257/1–3 Charoen Nakhon Rd. near Krungthep Bridge. ℭ **02476-0021**. Reservations recommended. 950B ($23). AE, DC, MC, V. Daily 7:15–8:30pm.

Sala Rim Nam 𝄢𝄢 THAI   As you would expect from the folks at the Oriental Hotel, this Thai restaurant is one of Bangkok's special places. Guests sit on pillows at low tables in the glittering, bronze-trimmed, teak-and-marble main hall, and dine on finely crafted Thai dishes. In the evening, classical dancers from Bangkok's Department of Fine Arts perform a 1-hour show of royal dances of the Sukhothai and Ayutthaya periods, as well as various folk dances. They have a free shuttle from the Saphan Taksin pier (on a separate dock connecting with city hotels).

In the Oriental Bangkok (on the Thonburi side of the Chao Praya River). ℭ **02437-2918**. 1,700B ($41) adult, 1,350B ($33) children. AE, DC, MC, V. Daily 7–10pm, performance 8:30pm.

Supatra River House 𝄢𝄢 THAI   Held only on Friday and Saturday nights, the show at Supatra is very interesting, with refreshing and creative interpretations by true performers. Also, you are not locked into a set menu and can order a la carte or just sip a drink and enjoy the show. The one drawback is that while the two-story teak house and river terrace makes a beautiful setting, not all tables have a good view of the performance.

266 Soi Wat Rakhang Arunamarin Rd., Siriraj Bangkoknoi. ℭ **02411-0305**. Reservations recommended. Main courses 120B–380B ($2.90–$9.25). MC, V. Fri and Sat night only. Shows start at 8:30pm. Call ahead to arrange for free ferry transfer across the river.

DINNER & LUNCH CRUISES ON THE CHAO PRAYA

While there are a number of tour operators who offer dinner cruises along the Chao Praya, if you want to eat the finest food, I only have one solid recommendation. The *Manohra,* a reconverted antique rice barge, cruises the river nightly serving a six-course Thai dinner that's delicious (and not overly spicy). The quality of the food is excellent, especially considering most other dinner cruises serve lukewarm indescribable food. The set menu is 1,200B ($29) per person, and *Manohra* sets sail at 7:30pm (but you can pick it up at the Oriental pier, where it stops at about 7:40pm). Be sure to book in advance to make sure the boat isn't rented out for a private party. Call the **Bangkok Marriott Resort & Spa** (ℭ **02476-0021**). The *Manohra* is also available for private itineraries. Also see "Side Trips from Bangkok" in chapter 6, and read about the Marriot's *Manohra II* with its multiday itineraries on the Chao Praya. See www.manohracruises.com.

The *Horizon II* makes daily trips to Ayuthaya and back, as well as evening cruises in town for a romantic candlelit meal. Cruises start at just 1,400B ($34) and leave daily at 8am for all-day trips or 7:30pm for dinner cruises. Contact the **Shangri La Hotel** (ℭ **02236-7777**).

6

What to See & Do in Bangkok

Sprawling and labyrinthine, busy Bangkok holds daytime adventures for the urban explorer, wild nightlife for the party animal, temples and sites for the culture vulture, and a full "fix" for the shopaholic. First-time visitors are often amazed by the luxuries afforded by central Bangkok's shopping areas, and at the same time delighted by the funky back streets and canals, the cacophonous markets, and spectacular temples. This chapter presents the best of many city sites and is arranged by the following sub-headings. Bangkok's Waterways gives you the ins and outs of the city's canals and the pleasures of traveling along these old thoroughfares. Bangkok's Historical Treasures covers magnificent palaces, rich antique homes, and fascinating museums packed with the nation's treasures. Cultural Pursuits lets you in on unique local experiences, and Staying Active is for sports people—both participants and observers. The Shopping section gives you the lowdown on what and where to buy, and Bangkok After Dark lists the details of evening arts and cultural performances, the nightclub scene, and the city's risqué counterculture. Side Trips from Bangkok are listed at the end of this chapter.

1 Bangkok's Waterways

The history of Bangkok was written on its waterways, which until recent years were the essential focus of the city's life. When the 18th-century capital was moved from Ayuthaya to Thonburi, and then across the river to Bangkok, King Rama I dug a canal (now called Klong Ong Ang and Klong Banglampoo) that sliced Rattanakosin Island out of the large bend in the river to strengthen the defensive position of the Grand Palace. Other canals (*klongs*) were added, which became the boulevards and avenues of the city. Boats were the primary means of transportation, with horse-drawn travel reserved for royalty.

As Ayuthaya was before it, Bangkok came to be known as the "Venice of the East," but sadly, many of these *klongs* have been paved over in the last century, although the magnificent Chao Praya River ("the River of Kings") still cuts through the heart of the city and along its length, as well as in neighboring Thonburi. Opportunities abound for exploring small *klong* networks and river arteries linking waterside neighborhoods seemingly untouched by time.

Boats of all sizes and shapes ply the length of **Chao Praya River.** Ferries cross the river when full, and numerous commuter boats carry business people to work, kids to school, and saffron-robed monks to temple. Hulking barges pull mountains of rice, gravel, sand, lumber, vegetables, and the countless families who make them their homes. The **Royal Barges**—long, graceful, gilt crafts—usually seen on display in

Bangkok Attractions

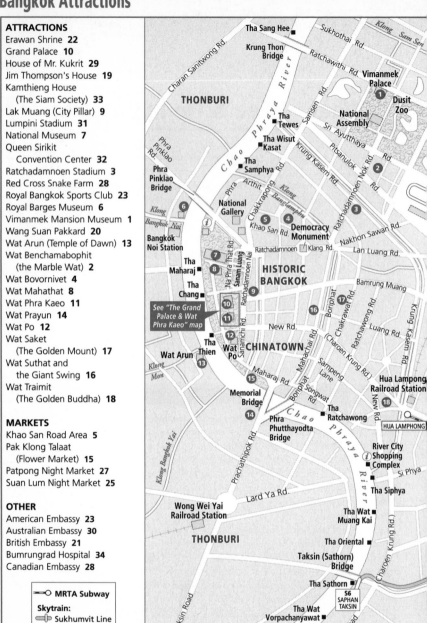

═O MRTA Subway
Skytrain:
⊂⊃ Sukhumvit Line
⊂⊃ Silom Line

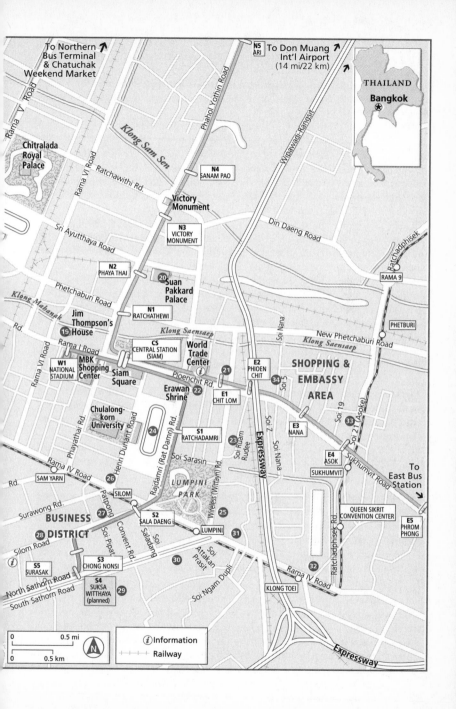

museums only (see "Bangkok's Historical Treasures" below), make infrequent appearances on parade to celebrate the arrival of visiting dignitaries or other special events.

The strangest, most frequently seen boat on the river is the long-tail water taxi, a long, thin, graceful vessel, powered by an automobile engine connected by a long, exposed shaft (tail) to the propeller. These water taxis carry passengers and goods throughout the maze of klongs.

For an intimate glimpse of traditional Thai life, schedule a few hours to explore the waterways. You'll see people using the river to bathe, wash their clothes, and even brush their teeth at water's edge (a practice not recommended for foreigners). Floating kitchens in sampans serve rice and noodles to customers in other boats. Men dance across carpets of logs floating to lumber mills. Wooden houses on stilts spread back from the banks of the river and klongs, each with its own spirit house perfumed with incense and decked out with flowers and other offerings.

There are several ways to tour the *klongs*. **World Travel** (© **02233-5900**) and **Sea Tours** (© **02216-5783** or 02237-3702) both arrange English-speaking guides to lead you on a customized tour at affordable rates. **Diethelm Travel** (© **0255-9150**; www. diethelm-travel.com) can arrange tours of any length.

Better yet, charter a **long-tail water taxi** for about 500B ($12) an hour—expect to negotiate the price, and be sure to agree on the charge before you get in the boat. You'll find boats for hire at the Tha Chang ferry pier near The Grand Palace, the pier at River City Shopping Complex (© **02235-3108**), or at the riverside exit of Saphan Taksin, the terminal station of the BTS at riverside (there's a small kiosk with tour-boat information). Look for the small tour-agent kiosk manned by **LS&H Travel Co.** (© **02589-5553**; www.journeyasia.com) as you exit the Saphan Taksin Station. Any hotel concierge can also make arrangements. Take your time and explore Klong Bangkok Noi and Klong Bangkok Yai, with a stop at the Royal Barges Museum on the way (see "Bangkok's Historical Treasures," below, for information on the Royal Barges Museum). Beware of independent boat operators who offer to take you to souvenir or gem shops.

If you've got the time, take a day to visit the **floating market** at Damnoen Saduak, about 80km (48 miles) southwest of Bangkok in Ratchaburi Province, or ride up to Ayuthaya by boat (see "Side Trips from Bangkok," later in this chapter).

2 Bangkok's Historical Treasures

Thailand is a cultural crossroads, and Indian, Khmer, Chinese, European, and Thai histories collide in the design of the likes of the Grand Palace, Wat Phra Kaeo, and Wat Po. Be sure to wear appropriate attire (no tank tops or shorts) and go with a guide (or hire one on-site) to better experience these wonders.

The Grand Palace ⭐⭐⭐   The number-one destination in Bangkok is also the most touristy. However, you shouldn't let the large busloads keep you away—it's a terrific sight to see, and, if you arrive at 8:30am when the gates first open, you can have the place to yourself. As this is sacred royal ground, visitors are required to wear long pants or skirts, and shirtsleeves that cover the upper arms. The rules are inconsistently enforced, but many have been turned away for inappropriate dress. And remember—it closes at 3:30pm, so don't show up any later than 2:30pm!

The palace as it appears today was greatly influenced by Western architecture, including colonial and Victorian motifs. Anna—tutor to the son of Rama IV and the central figure in the story *The King and I*—lived here. The royal family moved to

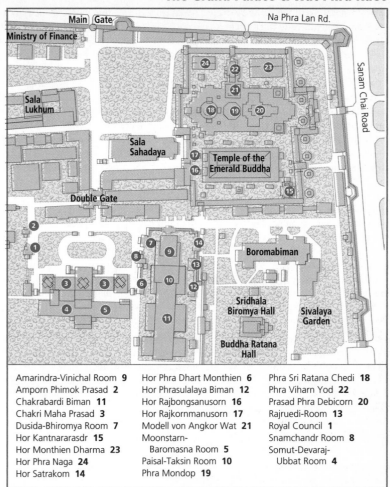

Amarindra-Vinichal Room **9**	Hor Phra Dhart Monthien **6**	Phra Sri Ratana Chedi **18**
Amporn Phimok Prasad **2**	Hor Phrasulalaya Biman **12**	Phra Viharn Yod **22**
Chakrabardi Biman **11**	Hor Rajbongsanusorn **16**	Prasad Phra Debicorn **20**
Chakri Maha Prasad **3**	Hor Rajkornmanusorn **17**	Rajruedi-Room **13**
Dusida-Bhiromya Room **7**	Modell von Angkor Wat **21**	Royal Council **1**
Hor Kantnararasdr **15**	Moonstarn-	Snamchandr Room **8**
Hor Monthien Dharma **23**	Baromasna Room **5**	Somut-Devaraj-
Hor Phra Naga **24**	Paisal-Taksin Room **10**	Ubbat Room **4**
Hor Satrakom **14**	Phra Mondop **19**	

Chitralada Palace after the death of King Ananda in 1946, but it was here, in 1981, that General Chitpatima attempted to overthrow the government in an unsuccessful coup.

As you enter the palace gate, built in the 1780s, you'll see the **Pavilion for Holy Water,** where priests swore loyalty to the royal family and purified themselves with water from Thailand's four main rivers. Nearby is a lacquered-wood structure called the **Arporn Phimok Prasad (Disrobing Pavilion),** built so the king could conveniently mount his palanquin for royal elephant processions (most of the time it served as a kind of elephant parking lot).

Also nearby is the **Chakri Maha Prasad,** designed by Western architects as a royal residence for Rama IV to commemorate the centennial of the Chakri dynasty. The king's advisors urged him to use Thai motifs to demonstrate his independence from growing Western influence: The Thai, temple-style roof rests physically and symbolically on top of an imperial Victorian building. This Thai-Victorian building contains the ashes of royal family members on the third floor, the throne room and reception hall on the main floor, and a collection of weapons on the ground floor.

The whitewashed stone building nearby now serves as the **Funeral Hall,** though it was originally the residence of Rama I and Rama II. The corpse of a deceased royal figure is kept in this building for a year before it is cremated in a nearby field. On each of the four corners of the roof is a **garuda** (the half-human, half-bird "steed" of Rama, an avatar of the Hindu god Vishnu), symbolizing the king, who is considered a reincarnation of Rama. The palace garden was rebuilt under Rama IV in the 1860s, and the highlight here is a section that reproduces the landscape of a Thai mountain-and-woods fable. This structure was used as a ceremonial place for Thai princes to cut their topknot in a coming-of-age ritual.

The Grand Palace also has a harem, the **Forbidden Quarters** (no one other than the king was allowed to enter), where the king's wives lived (King Bhumibol Adulyadej ended the age-old tradition of polygamy and has only one wife, Queen Sirikit). Close by is the Amarin Vinichai Prasad, or Coronation Hall, built by Rama I and added to by subsequent kings. Today, this building is used, like the palace in general, for royal coronations, weddings, and state events only, and it is here that the king makes his grandest appearances.

Near the river on Na Phra Lan Rd. near Sanam Luang. ✆ 02222-8181. Admission 200B ($4.90). Price includes Wat Phra Kaeo and the Coin Pavilion inside the Grand Palace grounds, as well as admission to the Vimanmek Palace (near the National Assembly). Daily 8:30am–3:30pm; most individual buildings are closed to the public except on special days proclaimed by the king. Take the Chao Praya Express Boat to the Tha Chang Pier, then walk east and south.

The House of Mr. Kukrit   An artist, poet, statesman, actor, patron of the arts, and like a vestige of culture himself, Mom Rajawongse (M. R.) Kukrit Pramoj was born in 1911, studied in England, graduated in Oxford, and went on to lead Thailand as prime minister in 1975 to 1976. His legacies include the Khon Thammasat Dance Troupe, which he formed in the 1960s to encourage and keep alive traditions of Thai dance; as well as numerous tombs; and an appearance alongside Marlon Brando in the film *The Ugly American.* The house is a collection of rural wooden buildings he amassed and contain his rooms, his study, and his place of worship, much as he left them when he passed away in 1995 at the age of 84. Young museum docents will show you around and give a good tour in English. The museum is hidden down a small *soi* south of Silom. It's kind of hard to find, but worth it if you are keen on visiting a piece of old Bangkok.

10am–5pm. Admission 50B ($1.20). Open Saturdays, Sundays, and Thai holidays only.

Jim Thompson's House ✹   Jim Thompson was a New York architect who served in the OSS (Office of Strategic Services, now the CIA) in Thailand during World War II and afterward settled in Bangkok. Almost single-handedly he revived Thailand's silk industry, employing Thai Muslims as skilled silk weavers and building up a thriving industry. After expanding his sales to international markets, Mr. Thompson mysteriously disappeared in 1967 while vacationing in the Cameron Highlands of Malaysia. Despite extensive investigations, his disappearance has never been resolved. (The most recent theory, for which some evidence apparently exists, is that he was accidentally struck by a truck and his body hidden to prevent repercussions.)

Thompson's legacy is substantial, as both an entrepreneur and a collector, and his Thai house contains a splendid collection of Khmer sculpture, Chinese porcelain,

Burmese carving (especially a 17th-century teak Buddha), and antique Thai scroll paintings.

The house is composed of six linked teak and theng (harder than teak) wood houses from central Thailand that were rebuilt according to Thai architectural principles, but with Western additions (such as a staircase and window screens). In some rooms the floor is made of Italian marble, but the wall panels are pegged teak. The house slopes toward the center to help stabilize the structure (the original houses were built on stilts without foundations). The busy nearby Klong San Sap and landscaped garden make a lovely spot, especially on a hot day. There is also a gallery space with a revolving collection of local artists.

You can buy silk from the Jim Thompson Thai Silk Company retail shop on-site, at their popular shop near Silom (see "Shopping," later in this chapter), or at outlets throughout the kingdom.

Soi Kasemsan 2 (on a small *soi* off Rama I Rd., opposite the National Stadium BTS station). ✆ **02216-7368.** Admission 100B ($2.45). Daily 9am–5:30pm.

Kamthieng House (The Siam Society)
The 19th-century Kamthieng House, on the grounds of the Siam Society Headquarters, is a rice farmer's teak house transplanted from the banks of Chiang Mai's Ping River. Its collection, organized with financial help from the Asia and Rockefeller foundations, is oriented toward ethnographic objects illustrating the culture of everyday life.

Many agricultural and domestic items, including woven fish baskets and terra-cotta pots, are on display, but we were drawn most to the exhibit about the Chao Vieng, or city dwellers, from the northern Lanna Thai Kingdom. If you plan to trek through that area, you will particularly enjoy this small but informative collection. We also enjoyed walking through the grounds, which are landscaped like a northern Thai garden.

The Siam Society also supports an excellent library and gallery, with information on nearly every aspect of Thai society, concentrating on regional culture. They also publish scholarly texts on Thai culture, which can be purchased.

131 Soi Asoke (north of Sukhumvit on Soi 21). ✆ **02661-6470.** Admission 100B ($2.45) adults, 50B ($1.20) children. Tues–Sat 9am–5pm. 10-min. walk from Asoke BTS station.

The National Museum ★★
The National Museum, just a short (15-min.) walk north of the Grand Palace and the Temple of the Emerald Buddha, is the country's central treasury of art and archaeology (32 branches are located throughout the provinces). Some of the buildings are themselves works of art. It is important to remember that the facility is closed on Monday and Tuesday.

The current museum—the largest in Southeast Asia—was built as part of the Grand Palace complex when the capital of Siam was moved from Thonburi to Bangkok in 1782. Originally the palace of Rama I's brother, the deputy king and appointed successor, it was called the Wang Na ("Palace at the Front"). The position of princely successor was eventually abolished, and Rama V had the palace converted into a museum in 1884. Thammasat University, the College of Dramatic Arts, and the National Theater were also built on the royal grounds, along with additional museum buildings.

To see the entire collection, which is highly recommended, plan to spend a few hours. Start with the **Thai History and the Prehistoric Galleries** in the first building. If you're rushed, go straight to the **Red House** behind it, a traditional 18th-century Thai building that was originally the living quarters of Princess Sri Sudarak, sister of King Rama I. It is furnished in period style, with many pieces originally owned by the princess.

Another essential stop is the **Phuttaisawan (Buddhaisawan) Chapel,** built in 1787 to house the Phra Phut Sihing, one of Thailand's most revered Buddha images, brought here from its original home in Chiang Mai. The chapel is an exquisite example of Buddhist temple architecture.

From the chapel, work your way back through the main building of the royal palace to see the gold jewelry, some from the royal collections, and the Thai ceramics, including many pieces in the five-color bencharong style. The **Old Transportation Room** contains ivory carvings, elephant chairs, and royal palanquins. There are also rooms of royal emblems and insignia, stone carvings, wood carvings, costumes, textiles, musical instruments, and Buddhist religious artifacts.

Fine art and sculpture are found in the newer galleries at the rear of the museum compound. Gallery after gallery is filled with both Thai and pre-Thai sculpture (including some excellent Mon work) and Hindu and Buddhist images from the provinces.

Na Phra That Rd. (about 1km/⅔ mile north of the Grand Palace). ℂ 02224-1333. Admission 40B ($1). Wed–Sun 9am–4pm. Free English-language tours: Buddhism culture, Wed 9:30am; art, culture, religion, Thurs 9:30am; call the museum or check a newspaper for more details and current schedule.

The Royal Barges 𝒻

If you've hired a long-tail boat on the Chao Praya, stop by this unique museum housing the royal barges. These elaborately decorated sailing vessels, the largest over 46m (50 yd.) long and rowed by up to 60 men, are used by the royal family on state occasions or for high religious ceremonies. The king's barge, the *Suphanahong,* is decorated with red-and-gold carvings of fearsome mythological beasts, like the garuda and dragon on the bow and stern. (If you can't make it to the royal barges, there is a smaller display of barges at the National Museum.)

On Klong Bangkok Noi (canal), north of the Phra Pinklao Bridge, Thonburi. ℂ 02424-0004. Admission 30B (75¢) adults, children free; additional fees for cameras. Daily 8:30am–4:30pm. Take a taxi over the Phra Pinklao Bridge or take a ferry to Tha Rot Fai ("Railway Landing"), walk west along the street parallel to and between the tracks and the klong until you come to a bridge over the klong, cross the bridge and follow the wooden walkway.

Vimanmek Mansion Museum 𝒻

Built in 1901 by King Chulalongkorn the Great (Rama V) as the Celestial Residence, this large, beautiful, golden teakwood mansion was restored in 1982 for Bangkok's bicentennial and reopened by Queen Sirikit as a private museum with a collection of the royal family's memorabilia. An intriguing and informative hour-long tour takes you through a series of apartments and rooms (81 in all) in what is said to be the largest teak building in the world—the thought of all that gorgeous teakwood employed is staggering. The original **Abhisek Dusit Throne Hall** houses a display of Thai handicrafts, and nine other buildings north of the mansion display photographs, clocks, fabrics, royal carriages, and other regalia. Classical Thai dance, folk dance, and martial art demonstrations are given daily at 10:30am and 2pm.

193/2 Ratchavitee Rd., Dusit Palace grounds (opposite the Dusit Zoo, north of the National Assembly Building). ℂ 02281-8166. Admission 50B ($1.20); free if you already have a 200B ($4.90) ticket to the Grand Palace and Wat Phra Kaeo. Daily 9:30am–4pm.

Wang Suan Pakkard

Wang Suan Pakkard ("Palace of the Lettuce Garden") is one of Bangkok's most delightful retreats. This peaceful oasis was the home of Princess Chumbhot of Nakhon Sawan. Five 19th-century teak houses were moved from Chiang Mai in

1952 and rebuilt in a beautifully landscaped garden on a private klong, separated by a high wall from the tumult of Bangkok's streets. The **Lacquer Pavilion** (actually an Ayuthaya house, moved here in 1958) was a birthday present from the prince to the princess.

Princess Chumbhot was an avid art collector and one of the country's most dedicated archaeologists—credited with having partly financed the excavations at Ban Chiang I in 1967. There is an entire room of objects from that site, including pottery and jewelry, surpassed only by the prehistoric findings exhibited at the National Museum. The balance of the collection is diverse, with Khmer sculpture, ivory boxes, perfume bottles, nielloware, marvelous prints by European artists depicting their images of Siamese people before the country opened to the Western world, a superb Buddha head from Ayuthaya, and a royal barge. Be sure to ask to see the pavilion housing the princess's collection of Thai and Chinese ceramics. The gift shop at Wang Suan Pakkard offers ceramics, some genuine and some reproductions, and prices are quite reasonable.

352 Si Ayuthaya Rd. (between Phayathai and Ratchaprarop rds.). (C) **02245-4934**. www.suanpakkad.com. Admission 100B ($2.45) adults, 50B ($1.20) children, including material for a self-guided tour of grounds and collections. Daily 9am–4pm. 10-min. walk from Phaya Thai BTS station.

Wat Phra Kaeo ★★★   The "Temple of the Holy Jewel Image," or as it is commonly known, the Temple of the Emerald Buddha, is the royal chapel and probably the shrine most revered by the Thai people. It sits within the grounds of the Grand Palace, surrounded by walls more than a mile long, and contains some of the finest examples of Buddhist sculpture, architecture, painting, and decorative craft in the country.

Central to the Wat is the **Emerald Buddha** itself, a rather small, dark statue, a little more than .6m (2 ft.) tall, made of green jasper or perhaps jadeite ("emerald" in Thai refers to intense green color, not the specific stone) that sits atop a huge gold altar. Legend says it came from Sri Lanka, but most art historians believe that it was sculpted in the 14th century in northern Thailand, as it is in the Chiang Saen (Lanna Thai) style.

The Buddha, like many others in Thailand, is covered in a seasonal cloak, changed three times a year to correspond to the summer, winter, and rainy months. The changing of the robes is an important ritual, performed by the king, who also sprinkles water over the monks and well-wishers to bring good fortune during the upcoming season.

The Emerald Buddha is housed in an equally magnificent *bot* (the central shrine in a Buddhist temple), used by monks for important religious rituals. The interior walls are decorated with late Ayuthaya–style murals depicting the life of the Buddha, steps to enlightenment, and the Buddhist cosmology of the Worlds of Desire, Being, and Illusion. The cycle begins with the birth of the Buddha, which can be seen in the middle of the left wall as you enter the sanctuary, and the story continues counterclockwise. Also note the exquisite inlaid mother-of-pearl work on the door panels.

The surrounding portico of the *bot* is an example of masterful Thai craftsmanship. On the perimeter are 12 open pavilions, built during the reign of Rama I. The inside walls of the compound are decorated with murals depicting the entire Ramakien, the Thai national epic, painted during the reign of Rama I and last restored in 1982, in 178 scenes beginning at the north gate and continuing clockwise.

Subsequent kings built more monuments and restored or embellished existing structures. Among the most interesting of these are the three pagodas to the immediate north of the *ubosoth,* representing the changing centers of Buddhist influence: The first, to the west, is **Phra Si Ratana Chedi,** a 19th-century Sri Lankan–style stupa housing ashes of the Buddha; second, in the middle, is the library, or **Phra Mondop,**

"Mai, Khòp Khun," Means "No, thank you."

You will be hassled and harried going in and out of the major sites in and around the Grand Palace. Do not get into a tuk-tuk in this area, period. These guys are famous for telling visitors that this or that site is closed and suggesting alternate destinations. They'll offer rides as low as 10B (25¢) but the sum total is that you are being scammed into a "shopping tour" to outlets that pay commission to drivers. Even if you don't buy the silk suit that is pushed on you or the plastic marbles that you'll be told will fetch a minor fortune back in your home country, you will be wasting your precious time. If you do ride the tuk-tuks near the main sites, make sure you've agreed with the driver on your next destination for a reasonable fee (from 30B/75¢) with no extra stops: say, "No shopping." Avoid frustrations by avoiding these characters, and if you have any problems, don't hesitate to call the Tourist Police at ✆ 1155.

---

built in Thai style by Rama I, known for its excellently crafted Ayuthaya-style mother-of-pearl doors, bookcases containing the *Tripitaka* (sacred Buddhist manuscripts), human- and dragon-headed *nagas* (snakes), and statues of Chakri kings; and third, to the east, is the **Royal Pantheon,** built in Khmer style during the 19th century—it's open to the public in October for 1 day to commemorate the founding of the Chakri dynasty. To the immediate north of the library is a model of Angkor Wat, the most sacred of all Cambodian shrines, the model constructed by King Mongkut as a reminder that the neighboring state was under the dominion of Thailand. To the west of the *bot,* near the entry gate, is a black stone statue of a hermit, considered a patron of medicine, before which relatives of the ill and infirm pay homage and make offerings of joss sticks, fruit, flowers, and candles.

Scattered around the complex are statues of elephants, thought to represent independence and power. Thai kings went to battle atop elephants, and it is customary for parents to walk their children around an elephant three times to bring them strength. You can rub the head of an elephant statue for good luck, and notice how smooth it is from the touch of millions.

In the Grand Palace complex. ✆ **02222-0094.** Admission included in the Grand Palace fee, 200B ($4.90). Daily 8:30am–3:30pm. Take the Chao Praya Express Boat to Tha Chang Pier, then walk east and south.

3 The Wats

The many temples of Bangkok are each unique and inspiring. If you can only see a few, pay attention to the star ratings and hit the highlights (Wat Phra Kaeo is listed in the above section due to its location within the Grand Palace Compound). But while the big temples of Bangkok are highly recommended, don't pass up smaller neighborhood temples where you have a good chance of learning about Buddhism in daily practice. Early morning is a good time to visit temples: the air is cool, monks busy themselves with morning activities, and the complexes are generally less crowded.

Thai people make regular offerings to temples and monasteries as an act of merit-making. Supporting the *sangha,* or monkhood, brings one closer to Buddhist ideals and increases the likelihood of a better life beyond this one. Many shops near temples sell saffron-colored pails filled with everyday supplies such as toothbrushes, soap, and other common necessities, and Thais bring these and other gifts as offerings to Buddhist mendicants as a way of gaining good graces. You may even see an early-morning *Pintabat* or column of barefoot monks carrying their bowls on morning begging rounds.

Small monetary contributions (the amount is up to you) are welcome at any temple. Devotions at a temple involve bowing three times, placing the forehead on the ground at the foot of the Buddha, as well as lighting candles and incense and chanting. Tourists are welcome to participate in any capacity, whether doing the full "do" of kneeling and bowing or just lighting a candle for the suffering in this world, and all are welcome at the temple.

Erawan Shrine ✿✿   Built in 1956 as a way to appease the supposed evil forces that were taking the lives of construction workers and causing other calamities in the early stages of building what is now the Grand Hyatt Erawan, one of Bangkok's top hotels along Sukhumvit Road, the Erawan Shrine is not old but an interesting testament to the faith (or superstition, perhaps) in Thai society. It is a simple statue of the four-faced Hindu god Brahma, named Than Tao Mahaprom, and sits in an unassuming corner of the hotel grounds, but the curative effect of building the monument (construction deaths stopped and the hotel grew very prosperous) meant that the shrine became, and is, one of the most revered spots in the kingdom. The area is crowded with worshippers day and night and always wafting with incense smoke. It is common to see people bowing as they pass by bus, taxi, or above by Skytrain. Don't miss it on the northwest corner of the Grand Hyatt Erawan property, near the Chit Lom stop on the Skytrain. The Hyatt has just built a new shopping area, and a luxurious Burberry outlet overlooks the shrine site. The store has even sponsored sun umbrellas for all the vendors, which makes it look like the site is Burberry-sponsored.

On the corner of Rama I and Ratchadamri Rd. (near the Grand Hyatt Erawan). Open daily dawn to 8pm. No entrance (from 20B/50¢ for incense and flowers).

Wat Arun (Temple of Dawn) ✿✿✿   The 79m-high (260-ft.), Khmer-inspired tower, the centerpiece of the "Temple of Dawn," rises majestically from the banks of the Chao Praya, across from Wat Po. This religious complex served as the royal chapel during King Thaksin's reign (1809–24), when Thonburi was the capital of Thailand.

The original tower was only 15m (50 ft.) high, but was expanded during the rule of Rama III (1824–51) to its current height. The exterior is decorated with flower and decorative motifs made of ceramic shards donated to the monastery by local people, at the request of Rama III. At the base of the complex are Chinese stone statues, once used as ballast in trading ships, gifts from Chinese merchants.

You can climb the central *prang,* but be warned: The steps are treacherously tall, narrow, and steep—and even more precarious coming down. If you go up, notice the caryatids and the Hindu gods atop the three-headed elephants. The view of the river, Wat Po, and Grand Palace is well worth the climb. Be sure to walk to the back of the tower to the monk's living quarters, a tranquil world far from the bustle of Bangkok's busy streets. Wat Arun is a sight to behold shimmering with the sunrise, but despite its name, a late afternoon visit is better so that you can enjoy the sunset. Temple of the dusk, maybe?

West bank of the Chao Praya, opposite Tha Thien Pier. ✆ 02465-5640. 20B (50¢) admission. Daily 8am–5:30pm. Take a water taxi from Tha Tien Pier (near Wat Po), or cross the Phra Pinklao Bridge and follow the river south on Arun Amarin Rd.

Wat Benchamabophit (the Marble Wat)   Wat Benchamabophit, called the Marble Wat because of the white Carrara marble of which it is constructed, is an early-20th-century temple designed by Prince Narai, the half-brother of Rama V. It is the most modern and one of the most beautiful of Bangkok's royal wats. Unlike the older complexes, there's no truly monumental *wihaan* or *chedi* dominating the grounds. Many smaller buildings reflect a melding of European materials and designs with traditional Thai religious architecture. Even the courtyards are paved with polished white marble. Walk inside the compound, beyond the main *bot,* to view the many Buddha images that represent various regional styles. During the early mornings, monks chant in the main chapel, sometimes so intensely that it seems as if the temple is going to lift off.

Si Ayuthaya Rd. (south of the Assembly Building near Chitralada Palace). ✆ **02281-2501.** 20B (50¢) admission. Daily 8am–5pm.

Wat Mahathat (Temple of the Great Relic)   Built to house a relic of the Buddha, Wat Mahathat is one of Bangkok's oldest shrines and the headquarters for Thailand's largest monastic order. Also the home of the Center for Vipassana Meditation at Buddhist University, the most important center for the study of Buddhism and meditation, Wat Mahathat offers some programs in English. (See "Cultural Pursuits," below, for more information about courses.)

Adjacent to it, between Maharaj Road and the river, is the city's biggest **amulet market,** where a fantastic array of religious amulets, charms, talismans, and traditional medicine is sold. Each Sunday hundreds of worshipers squat on the ground studying tiny images of the Buddha with magnifying glasses, hoping to find one that will bring good fortune or ward off evil. Each amulet brings a specific kind of luck—to get the girl, to pass your exams, to keep bugs out of your rice stock, or to ward off your mother-in-law—so if you buy one, choose carefully. (The newer amulet market is part of Wat Ratchanada, off the intersection of Mahachai and Ratchadamnoen Klang roads, across from the Golden Mount at Wat Saket.)

Na Phra That Rd. (near Sanam Luang Park, between the Grand Palace and the National Museum). ✆ **02222-6011.** Donations welcome. Daily 9am–5pm.

Wat Po   Also known as the Temple of the Reclining Buddha, Wat Po was built by Rama I in the 16th century and is the oldest and largest Buddhist temple in Bangkok. The compound, divided into two sections by Chetuphon Road, is a 15-minute walk south of the Grand Palace. The northern area contains the most important monuments, and the southern portion is where monks reside.

Most people go straight to the enormous Reclining Buddha in the northern section. It is more than 43m (140 ft.) long and 15m (50 ft.) high, and was built during the mid-19th-century reign of Rama III. The statue is brick, covered with layers of plaster, and always-flaking gold leaf; the feet are inlaid with mother-of-pearl illustrations of 108 auspicious *laksanas* (characteristics) of the Buddha. Twenty baht (50¢) buys you a small cup full of coins and, along the spine of Wat Po's reclining Buddha, you'll find a long row of black begging bowls. One coin in each (takes about 2 min.) and you're all filled with luck and good karma.

Outside, the grounds contain 91 *chedis* (*stupas* or mounds), four *wihaans* (halls), and a *bot* (the central shrine in a Buddhist temple). Most impressive, aside from the Reclining Buddha, are the four main *chedis* dedicated to the first four Chakri kings and, nearby, the library. Wat Po is among the most photogenic of all the wats in Bangkok.

Of all the major temples in Bangkok, this is one of the most active. The temple is considered Thailand's first public university, because many of its monuments and artworks explain principles of religion, science, and literature. Visitors still drop 1-satang coins in 108 bronze bowls—corresponding to the 108 auspicious characteristics of the Buddha—for good fortune, and to help the monks keep up the *wat*.

Wat Po is home to the leading school for Thai massage in the country. You can learn about traditional Thai massage and medicine at the **Traditional Medical Practitioners Association Center,** an open-air hall to the rear of the wat compound. You can also receive a Thai massage here for 200B ($4.90) an hour (but there are better places in town; see "Thai Massage" under "Cultural Pursuits," below). True Thai massage, such as that taught here, involves chiropractic manipulation and acupressure, as well as stretching, stroking, and kneading, and is something to be endured for its sensational salubrious effects. Massage courses of 7 to 10 days are available, with details given later in this chapter.

You can hire a well-informed and entertaining English-speaking guide for about 200B ($5), depending on the number in your party. There are also a few astrologers and palm readers available for consultation. For a small donation you can receive a blessing from a monk and a bracelet of braided colored string to commemorate the occasion. (Donations go toward upkeep and renovations.)

Maharaj Rd., near the river (about 1km/⅔ mile south of the Grand Palace). © 02222-0933. 20B (50¢) admission. Daily 8am–5pm; massages offered until 6pm.

Wat Saket (The Golden Mount) ✦

Wat Saket is easily recognized by its golden *chedi* atop a fortresslike hill near busy Ratchadamnoen Road and Banglampoo. King Rama I restored the wat, and 30,000 bodies were brought here during a plague in the reign of Rama II. The hill, which is almost 80m (262 ft.) high, is an artificial construction begun during the reign of Rama III. Rama IV brought in 1,000 teak logs to shore it up because it was sinking into the swampy ground. Rama V built the golden *chedi* to house a relic of Buddha, said to be from India or Nepal, given to him by the British. The concrete walls were added during World War II to keep the structure from collapsing.

The Golden Mount, a short climb, is interesting for its vista of old Rattanakosin Island and the rooftops of Bangkok. Every late October to mid-November (for 9 days around the full moon) Wat Sakhet hosts Bangkok's most important temple fair, when the Golden Mount is wrapped with red cloth and a carnival erupts around it, with food and trinket stalls, theatrical performances, freak shows, animal circuses, and other monkey business.

Just north of Wat Saket is where you can catch canal boats back to the town center, Siam, or further up Sukhumvit. A stinky but memorable ride.

Ratchadamnoen Klang and Boripihat rds. Entrance to wat is free; admission to the *chedi* is 10B (25¢). Donations welcome. Daily 9am–5pm.

Wat Suthat and the Giant Swing

This temple is among the oldest and largest in Bangkok, and Somerset Maugham declared its roofline the most beautiful. It was begun by Rama I and finished by Rama III; Rama II carved the panels for the *wihaan's* doors. It houses the beautiful 14th-century Phra Buddha Shakyamuni, a Buddha image that was brought from Sukhothai; and the ashes of King Rama VIII, Ananda Mahidol, brother of the current king, are contained in its base. The wall paintings for which it is known were done during Rama III's reign.

Outside the *wihaan* stand many Chinese pagodas, bronze horses, and figures of Chinese soldiers. The most important religious association, however, is with the Brahman priests who officiate at important state ceremonies, and there are two Hindu shrines nearby. To the northwest across the street is the Deva Sathan, which contains images of Shiva and Ganesh, and to the east, the smaller Saan Jao Phitsanu is dedicated to Vishnu.

The huge teak arch—also carved by Rama II—in front is all that remains of an original giant swing, which was used until 1932 to celebrate and thank Shiva for a bountiful rice harvest and to ask for the gods' blessing on the next. The minister of rice, accompanied by hundreds of Brahman court astrologers, would lead a parade around the city walls to the temple precinct. Teams of men would ride the swing on arcs as high as 25m (82 ft.) in the air, trying to grab a bag of silver coins with their teeth. Due to injuries and deaths, the dangerous swing ceremony has been discontinued, but the thanksgiving festival is still celebrated in mid-December after the rice harvest.

Sao Chingcha Sq. (near the intersection of Bamrung Muang. and Ti Thong rds.). (© **02222-0280**. Donations welcome. Daily 9am–9pm.

Wat Traimit (The Golden Buddha)   Wat Traimit, which is thought to date from the 13th century, would hardly rate a second glance if not for its astonishing Buddha image, which is nearly 3m (10 ft.) high, weighs over 5 tons, and is believed to be cast of solid gold. It was discovered by accident in 1957 when an old stucco image was being moved from a storeroom by a crane, which dropped it and shattered the plaster shell, revealing the shining gold beneath. This powerful image has such a bright, reflective surface that its edges seem to disappear, and it is truly dazzling. The graceful seated statue is thought to have been cast during the Sukhothai period and later covered with plaster to hide it from the Burmese or other invaders. Pieces of the stucco are on display in a case to the left.

Traimit Rd. (west of Hua Lampong Station, just west of the intersection of Krung Kasem and Rama IV rds.). Donations welcome. Daily 9am–5pm. Walk southwest on Traimit Rd. and look for a school on the right with a playground; the wat is up a flight of stairs overlooking the school.

4 Cultural Pursuits

Culture isn't just dusty old buildings and aging collections; culture is in the daily activities, festivals, ceremonies, events, and practices that weave the fabric of a society, and there are ample opportunities to take part in life in Thailand. Check with the **TAT** (© **1155**) or the **Bangkok Tourism Bureau** (see their information offices around the city or call © **02225-7612**) and keep an eye on magazines like *Metro* or local newspapers, *The Nation* and *The Bangkok Post,* for major events during your stay (also see the holidays listed in chapter 2, "Planning Your Trip to Thailand"). The best part of Thai festivals is that, whether getting soaked by buckets of water on Song Kran or releasing candle floats down river on Lòy Krathong, foreign visitors aren't usually left to observe but always invited to join. Thais are very proud of their cultural heritage, and opportunities abound to learn and participate.

THAI COOKING

Fancy a chance to learn cooking techniques from the pros? Thai cooking is fun and easy, and there are a few good hands-on courses in Bangkok. You'll learn about Thai herbs, spices, and unique local veggies. You'll never look at a produce market the same again. Lectures on Thai regional cuisine, cooking techniques, and menu planning complement classroom exercises to prepare all your favorite dishes. The best part is afterwards, when you get to eat them.

- **The Blue Elephant** *☆☆* is the best in town. A large Belgian-based Thai restaurant chain popular throughout Europe, they have just opened this latest branch in a turn-of-the-20th-century Thai mansion adjacent to Surasak BTS station. Classes begin at 8am with a visit to the market to pick up fresh ingredients for the day.

Back in the classroom, you'll first watch demonstrations before stepping-up to your own deluxe cooking station to practice what you've learned under the watchful eye of a teacher. It is all fun and learning at the stoves before sharing your creations with the rest of the class in a delicious lunch spread. The course is open to anyone from beginner to expert. Different dishes are taught each day, so you could attend for a week and always learn something new. Visit them at 233 South Sathorn Road, just below BTS Surasak station, or call © **02673-9353** (www. blueelephant.com). One-day courses cost 2,800B ($68); group rates are available.

• **The Oriental Cooking School** ✦, located in a quaint campus across the river from the famed hotel, holds one day courses every day but Sunday starting at 9am, with lunch afterwards. The cost is 6,150B ($150) per person per day. Very expensive, but their chef is tops and you'll learn, through demonstration and hands-on practice, every aspect of Thai cooking. Call them at © **02437-6211** for booking and information. The hotel also offers combined cooking, study, and accommodation packages.

THAI MASSAGE

A traditional **Thai massage** is a must-do for visitors in Thailand and is quite unique. You don't just lie back and passively receive a Thai massage; instead, you are an active participant as masseurs manipulate your limbs to stretch each muscle, then apply acupressure techniques to loosen up tense muscles and get energy flowing. It has been described as having yoga "done" to you, and your body will be twisted, pulled, and sometimes pounded in the process. Talk to any hotel concierge, as most hotels have in-house services or can otherwise make arrangements.

The home of Thai massage, **Wat Po** is school to almost every masseuse in Bangkok, and has cheap massages in an open-air pavilion within the temple complex—a very interesting, but not necessarily relaxing, experience (see "The Wats," above; © **02221-2974;** 200B/$4.90 per hr.). Here you can arrange day courses if you are interested in learning Thai massage.

Bangkok, like most tourist destinations in Thailand, supports some fine **spas,** most in the larger hotels. **Le Banyan Tree Spa** (© **02679-1054;** www.banyantree.com) and **The Oriental's** spa (see "On the River" under "Where to Stay & Dine in Bangkok"; © **02439-7613;** www.mandarin-oriental.com) are two of the finest places going if price is less of an issue. These are just two of the many fine spas in town (in hotels and out). For a more budget spa experience, stop by the newly opened **Chivit Chiva** (16/1-2 Sukhumvit Soi 19; © **02253-0607;** near the Asoke BTS station), a fancy little getaway with services starting at just 600B ($15).

There are countless massage places around Bangkok, and many offer fine services at very reasonable rates (where else can you get an hour of massage for 200B/$4.90?). Be aware that certain massage parlors cater to gentlemen, with services beyond the standard massage: aim for places offering "traditional massage" and open storefront areas instead of backrooms. Many places have "no sex" or other blatant signs indicating the place is hanky-panky free (and if you're looking for hanky-panky, those signs are just as blatant). Try Po Thong Thai Massage, in the basement of the **Fortuna Hotel,** Sukhumvit Soi 5 (© **02255-1045;** 300B/$7.30 per hr.), or **Arima Onsen** (37/10–11 Soi Surawong Plaza near Sala Daeng BTS station; © **02235-2142;** 220B/$5.40 per hr.). According to the experts, 2 hours is the minimum to experience the full benefits of Thai massage, but 1 hour treatments are common. These places, and the many like them, also offer foot massage, but honestly, this bone-grinding process can be pretty painful (ask for a gentle foot massage, unless you can handle the pain).

THAI BOXING

Muaythai, or **Thai Boxing,** is Thailand's national sport, and a visit to the two venues in Bangkok, or the many fight-nights in towns all over Thailand (as much festival as sport), is a fun window into Thai culture. The pageant of the fighters' elegant pre-bout rituals, live musical performances, and the frenetic gambling activity are a real spectacle. In Bangkok, catch up to 15 bouts nightly at either of two stadiums. The **Ratchadamnoen Stadium** (Ratchadamnoen Nok Ave.; © **02281-4205**) hosts fights on Monday, Wednesday, Thursday, and Sunday, while the **Lumphini Stadium** on Rama IV Road (© **02251-4303**) has bouts on Tuesdays, Fridays, and Saturdays. Tickets are 1,500B ($37) for ringside seats, 800B ($20) for second class, and all the way down to 500B ($12) for nose-bleed seats behind a cage. Ringside is not worth it. It is best to go second class or cheaper, where you still have a good view of the action in the ring and are close-up to the gambling action: guys with multiple cellphones scream, shout, and often overshadow the action in the ring as they swap wagers. A memorable night, though a bit much for the squeamish.

Keen to try some kicks and punches yourself? Look for the small alley-side boxing school in Khao San Road, **Mr. Sor. Vorapin's Thai Boxing Training Center** (© **02243-3651;** www.thaiboxings.com). A 1-hour lesson will run you just 400B ($9.75), less per hour for longer courses, at one of their rural facilities.

MEDITATION

Wat Mahathat, or the Temple of the Great Relic (see "The Wats," earlier in this chapter), serves one of Thailand's largest Buddhist Universities and has become a popular center for **meditation lessons and practice,** with English-speaking monks overseeing students of Vipassana, also called Insight Meditation. Meditation instruction is held daily, and call ahead (© **02222-6011**) to get the schedule and to make an appointment. It is a good introduction to basic technique.

THAI LANGUAGE STUDY

So you've learned your "Sawadee-krup" or "Sawadee-ka," but want to take it a little further from here. Thai people are very gracious and welcoming with foreigners comically butchering their language (the tones make you pronounce the most mundane phrases in laughable ways), and there are a few good schools in Bangkok (though maybe taking a seat in the market is your best bet). Among the many try **Siri-Pattana Thai Language School** (13 Sathorn Tai Rd., 5 Fl. YMCA; © **02/213-1206;** siri_pattanathai@yahoo. com) or the notoriously intensive **Unity Thai Language School** (15 Fl.-01 Times Square Building, 246 Sukhumvit Rd.; © **02653-1538;** www.utl-school.com).

OTHER

If you're traveling through Bangkok during February through April, you can't beat the fantastic sights of the **kite-fighting** competitions held at Lumphini Park in the center of the city and at Sanam Luang near The Grand Palace. Elaborate creations in vivid colors vie for prizes, and "fighting," a team spectator sport complete with sponsors, thrills onlookers. The TAT will have all the information you need about exact dates, or you can check the local papers or travel publications.

Okay, so it is not exactly culture per se, but you'll have a hard time getting out of Thailand without encountering some kind of snake show. Bangkok's biggest venue is at the **Red Cross Snake Farm,** 1871 Rama IV Rd. (© **02252-0161**). Located in the heart of Bangkok opposite the Montien Hotel, this institute for the study of venomous snakes, established in 1923, was the second facility of its type in the world (the first was in Brazil). There are slide shows and snake-handling demonstrations weekdays at 10:30am and 2pm; on weekends and holidays at 10:30am. You can also watch the handlers work with deadly cobras and equally poisonous banded kraits and green pit vipers, with demonstrations of venom milking. The venom is later gradually injected into horses, which produce antivenin for the treatment of snakebites. The Thai Red Cross sells medical guides and will also inoculate you against such maladies as typhoid, cholera, and smallpox in their clinic. The farm is open daily Monday to Friday 8:30am to 3pm, Saturday and Sunday 8:30am to noon; admission is 70B ($1.70). It is at the corner of Rama IV Road and Henri Dunant.

5 Staying Active

FITNESS

Most hotels, certainly the finest five-star properties, support quality fitness centers complete with personal trainers and top equipment. **California,** just along Silom Road near Patpong at Liberty Square (© **02631-1122**), is a large convenient facility open to day visitors. The riotous **Hash House Harriers** (the drinking club for people with a running problem) holds regular events and is very active throughout Thailand. Check their website at www.bangkokhhh.com.

GOLF

Enthusiasts will be happy to know that you don't have to go far to enjoy some of Thailand's best courses; there are a number of courses, some of championship quality, in or near the city center.

- **Kantarat,** Thai Airports Authority Gate, 1km (⅔ mile) south of the airport domestic terminal (© **02534-3840**), also known as Don Muang or the Old Royal Thai Air Force course, because this long 18-hole course sits between the two primary runways at Bangkok's Don Muang International Airport. As if putting isn't nerve-wracking enough, you'll have planes landing and taking off all around. Tough course, and full of potential laughs. It's best to make reservations for weekend play (greens fees: weekdays 600B/$15; weekends 800B/$20).
- **Pinehurst Golf & Country Club,** 73 Pahonyothin Rd., Klong Luang, Pathom Thani (© **05321-1911**), sports three 9-hole courses at par 27 each. This prestigious club served as the venue for the 1992 Johnnie Walker Classic (greens fees: 1,500B/$37 weekdays, 2,000B/$49 weekends).
- **Rose Garden Golf Club,** 53/1 Moo 4, Petchkasem Highway, Sam Phran, Nakhon Pathom (© **02253-0295**), an esteemed par-72 course, offers a pretty game, with scenery enhanced by wooded surrounds (greens fees: weekdays 450B/$11; weekends 1,110B/$27).
- **Royal Thai Army Golf Club,** 459 Ram Indra Road, Bang Kaen, Bangkok, (© **02521-1530**), has both an old course and a new course to choose from. This well-maintained course was host to the Thai Open (greens fees: weekdays 600B/$15; weekends 800B/$20).
- **Unico Golf Club,** 47 Moo 7, Krungthep Kretha Road, Prawet, Bangkok (© **02377-9038;** fax 02379-3780), is a well-established city course with many challenging holes (greens fees: weekdays 535B/$13; weekends 1,070B/$26).

HORSE RACING

The prestigious and private **Royal Bangkok Sports Club** holds horse-racing events that are open to the public every second Sunday of the month. It occupies a prime spot on Henri Dunant Road, opposite Chulalongkorn University, north of Rama IV Road (© **02251-0181**). Admission is 150B ($3.65), and betting begins at 50B ($1.20) on a win-place basis only.

YOGA

Bikram Yoga, the famous "sweaty yoga" of athletic Hatha postures done in a room heated-up like a sauna, has a branch in central Bangkok. There are numerous daily classes from 10am until evening. They also offer courses in strenuous **power yoga.** Walk-ins for the rigorous 1½-hour sessions pay 500B ($12). Wear loose workout duds and bring a big bottle of water (or buy one there) and be ready to sweat buckets. The studio is at 29/1 14th Fl., Soi Langsuan, Ploenchit Rd (© **02652-1333**), near the Chit Lom station on the BTS Skytrain.

6 Shopping

Bangkok is a shopper's paradise, with shops ranging from street-side stalls to ultrachic boutiques. Bargain-hunters will find unusual, high-quality goods at very reasonable prices. If you encounter problems with merchants, contact the **Tourist Police** (© **0694-1222,** ext. 1, or the hot line at © **1155**).

WHAT TO BUY

ANTIQUES

Buying antiques in Thailand is tricky. Any real antiques are less than 200 years old, dating from the beginning of the Chakri Dynasty in Bangkok, but most are fakes, new pieces that have been carefully "worried" and aged despite any "Certificate of Authenticity." If you do find something real, remember that the Thai government has an interest in keeping authentic antiquities and sacred items in the country, and will require special permission for export.

By law, Buddha images are prohibited from export, except for religious or educational purposes, and even in these instances you'll still have to obtain permission from the **Department of Fine Arts** to remove them from Thailand, but this rule is little-enforced and the focus is more on antique Buddhas than those you'll find in tourist markets. Details on how to contact the Department of Fine Arts and file for permission is provided in chapter 2. The law is to protect national treasures stolen from temples, so if you're thinking about an amulet or a small image that could fit in your pocket, don't sweat it.

CRAFTS

Brass, bronze, and pewter items, as well as fine celadon pottery are available in many outlets on Sukhumvit and Charoen Krung. Other gifts and crafts, carvings, and castings from throughout the region are sold at comparable prices to where they are made (in places like Chiang Mai and Chiang Rai), and Thai craftsmanship is quite impressive. Try lesser-known areas like Chinatown to avoid the same old tourist gear.

FASHION

Bangkok is internationally known for its designer look-alike fashions, counterfeit clothing bearing the famous labels "knocked off" at substantially lower prices than the original. Less-known are the small, independent designers with their own Thai fashions that look good in Asia and back home. Quality runs the gamut, as do prices and service at Bangkok's many small tailoring storefronts. They're everywhere, really, in tourist towns all over Thailand, and you won't have to walk far to get that new suit made in the Big Mango. Along Sukhumvit (Soi 11 in particular), Riverside Charoen Krung, and Khao San all have similar services, for tailor-made orders. Expect very fast service (even 24-hr.), but be sure to schedule at least two fittings.

GIFTS & SOUVENIRS

Street vendors throughout the city are a good source of affordable and fun souvenirs. The best stalls are along Silom Road, along Sukhumvit Road beginning at Soi 4, on Khao San Road, and in Chinatown. Some stuff is quite unique, and the prices are right to stock up for Christmas.

JEWELRY

Any discussion of gems shopping in Thailand begins with an important warning.

Sapphires, rubies, garnets, turquoise, and zircons are mined in Thailand, and nearly every other stone you can think of is imported and cut here, and Thai artisans are among the most skillful in the world. Work in gold and silver is generally of high quality at very good value. If you're interested in a custom setting, bring a photo or drawing of what you'd like along and discuss your ideas at length.

Warning Jewelry Scams

For every reputable gems dealer in Bangkok, there are at least 100 crooks waiting to catch you in the latest scam. To avoid being ripped off, follow these rules.

1. If a kind person approaches you on the street and offers to take you to a special shop (or anywhere for that matter), always refuse.
2. If a tuk-tuk or taxi driver wants to take you shopping, say, "No thanks" (or "*Mai, khòp kun.*").
3. If anyone approaches you in a temple or at an attraction and offers to take you sightseeing, do not accept.
4. Be suspect of strangers in these situations who flash TAT, Tourist Police, or any other "badge."
5. There is no such thing as a government auction, government clearinghouse, or anything "government" related to the gems industry.
6. There is no such thing as a tax-free day for gemstones purchases.
7. Do not agree to let any gem purchases be shipped to your home address.
8. As with any purchase you make, if you use a credit card, instruct them to keep the card in your sight at all times and watch them make one print of it.
9. If anyone tells you that your purchase can be resold back home for more than you paid for it in Thailand, you are without a doubt being sucked into somebody's shell game. These guys are clever; working in groups they can trap even the most street-smart consumer.

The TAT and the **Thai Gem and Jewelry Traders Association** created an organization called the Jewel Fest Club. Talk to the TAT about their booklet listing shops that are members of this reputable organization. They also provide guidelines for purchasing gems.

You'll find jewelry stores in every part of town, but try Mahesak Road off of Silom for wholesale goods. The whole Silom area is a good bet, in fact. The **Asian Institute of Gemological Sciences** (11th floor, Jewelry Trade Center at 919/1 Silom Rd.; © 02267-4315) is useful for verifying the quality of cut stones (although it's not an appraiser). If you have any problems with vendors, contact the tourist police at © **1155.**

SILK & COTTON

There are numerous silk outlets throughout the city, in the many shopping areas, and in the lobbies of international hotels. Synthetics are frequently sold as silk, and if you're in doubt about a particular piece, select a thread and burn it; silk should smell like singed hair or feathers. Sometimes only the warp (lengthwise threads) is synthetic because it is more uniform and easier to work with, but as this isn't seen or felt, it is a less important consideration. For outlets, try: **Jim Thompson Thai Silk Company,** the town's most famous (see "Jim Thompson's House" under "Bangkok's Historical Treasures," earlier in this chapter), and with many outlets in hotels all over Thailand (main store is at 9 Surawong Rd., near Silom; © 02632-8100); **T. Shinawatra Silk** (94 Sukhumvit Soi 23; © 02258-0295); and **H. M. Factory Thai Silk** (45 Promchai, Sukhumvit Soi 39; © 02258-8766).

WHERE TO BUY

Shopping is a real adventure in the Big Mango. The big markets are a visual onslaught (don't miss the Sat–Sun Weekend Market, see below), and there are great upmarket gift and antique dealers as well as small souvenir stalls scattered about town. Below is a breakdown of some of the best areas.

Nancy Chandler's *The Market Map and Much More* is available at bookstores throughout the city for 160B ($3.90) and has detailed insets of places like Chinatown and the sprawling Weekend Market.

ON THE WATER

One of the finest collections of art and antique dealers anywhere in the kingdom is set at **River City** in a large convention hall at riverside just alongside some of Bangkok's finest accommodations (the Oriental and Peninsula). Sticker-shock is the rule, but you get what you pay for, and what you get at River City are artful copies and stunning original art and antiques. All shops arrange shipping.

Riverside **Charoen Krung/New Road** features lots of high-end shopping venues, from jewelry to antiques, carpet, and fine tailoring.

Lek Gallery, at 1124-1134 New Road (© 02639-5870), is not far from the River City Shopping Complex and has new decorative items and furniture that are just downright sexy.

Both the **Peninsula Plaza** arcade and the **Oriental Hotel** arcade have some of the finest shops in town. Don't miss the Peninsula's luxury **Prasart Collection** (© 02253-9772) of fine Benjarong porcelain.

SUKHUMVIT ROAD

This area is lined with shops from one end to the other, as well as some of Bangkok's biggest shopping malls (see "Department Stores & Shopping Plazas" below).

For fine silk, stop in at **T. Shinawatra** (94 Sukhumvit Soi 23; © 02258-0295), a large chain and close rival of Jim Thompson silks. For antiques, try **L'Arcadia** (12/2 Sukhumvit Soi 23; © 02259-1517), where you'll find fine Burmese and Thai furniture and carvings. **Celadon House,** on 85 Ratchadaphisek (near Sukhumvit; *Ⓒ* **02253-9237**), carries fine displays of attractive celadon ceramic. **Siamese D'Art** (264 Sukhumvit Rd.; *Ⓒ* **02253-9237**) carries similar fine pottery stock.

For gems, try **Uthai's Gems** down Ruam Rudee, a busy short-cut *soi* parallel to Wireless just south of Phloen Chit (28/7 Soi Ruam Rudee; *Ⓒ* **02253-8582**). They have great custom gems and jewels at higher prices, but guaranteed real.

For fine tailoring, try the many shops along Sukhumvit Soi 11. Most ship your order off to have clothes made in a factory, but you can get good deals if you bargain. **Ambassador Fashion** (28–28 Sukhumvit Soi 19; *Ⓒ* **02253-2993**) has been in the business for years and provides affordable, reliable, friendly, and efficient service from their large showroom near the Asoke BTS Skytrain station.

SILOM ROAD

This area is packed with outdoor shopping (see the Patpong Night Market in "Markets," below), and there are any number of fine jewelry shops, silk retailers, and tailors. Try **Chartered Gems Ltd.** (92 Silom Soi 24; *Ⓒ* **02233-9320**) for fine jewelry, and the famed **Jim Thompson Thai Silk Company** (9 Surawong Rd., just behind the busy Night Market area and Patpong; *Ⓒ* **02234-4900**), a famed Bangkok institution offering fine silks based on the legacy of Bangkok's most famous businessman (for more information, see "Jim Thompson's House" under "Bangkok's Historical Treasures," earlier in this chapter).

MARKETS

Visiting Bangkok's many markets is as cultural as it is a consumer experience; the markets are where the Thai economy happens, where goods come in from all corners of the kingdom and where the bargaining is fast and furious. Smaller markets with fewer tourists are great for wandering. Try these: **Bangrak Market** is behind the Shangri-La Hotel, a compact and unique little meander. **Pratunam Market,** at the intersection of Phetchaburi and Ratchaprarop roads, is a big wholesale center, with a vast array of inexpensive clothing. **Pak Klong Talaat** is home to Bangkok's cut-flower market, with huge bushels of cut flowers and vegetables passing through here; it is near the Memorial Bridge, on Chakrapatch Road along the Chao Praya at Luk Luang.

Khao San Road Area   Not an official market, the nighttime stalls on Khao San Road cater to young travelers and, as such, this is where you'll find the funkiest do-dads and trinkets in town. From hip-hop fashions and cool T-shirts, to small original artworks, souvenirs, and lots of pirate CD and DVD stalls (you didn't hear it from me), you'll find it all on Khao San (and much the same stuff as in other markets in Thailand at good prices). It is worth the trip for the atmosphere alone—bass-thumping clubs, busy bars, and Internet shops, and all the tattooed, pierced, and idealistic young travelers going or coming from all corners of Asia. The area just north of Khao San is a maze of small department stores, shops, and very affordable retail goods, from clothes to furniture to food. In Banglampoo, just north of the Grand Palace area and Ratchadamnoen Road.

Patpong Night Market   The Patpong area is famous for its bars, neon lights, girls, sex shows, girls, and massage parlors, but in recent years has spawned a bustling Night Market along the central streets (hemmed-in on all sides by go-go bars and sex-show clubs). This popular Night Market has lots of faux brands: pirated CDs and tapes, designer knockoffs, copy watches (including fake "Rolexes" that we've gotten some good reports on), leather goods stamped with desirable logos (sure to hold up better than cardboard)—not especially cheap, but lively and fun, especially if you enjoy crowds and the challenge of hard bargaining. Open daily after sundown. Patpong Soi 1, between Silom and Surawong rds.

Suan Lum Night Market ✿   Bangkok's newest night market is just east of Lumpini Park, not too far from Silom Road. The new subway will mean easier access here. Suan Lum has many of the same Thai trinkets and souvenirs you'll find in other Bangkok markets, but here they're under covered walkways and with a few bars, restaurants, and a huge covered food court, with live bands nightly. Well worth a wander. Just east of Lumpini Park on Rama IV road (next to the Lumpini Stop on the subway).

Weekend Market (Chatuchak) ✿✿   If you're in Bangkok on a weekend, don't miss the Weekend Market adjacent to the Mo Chit BTS stop at the northern terminus of the Skytrain. Chatuchak covers a vast area with rows of stalls selling everything—souvenirs, "antiques," fresh and dried seafood, vegetables and condiments, blue-and-white pottery, pets of every sort (from guppies to Rottweilers), orchids and other exotic plants, clothing, and a host of strange exotic items on top of the usual array of T-shirts, trinkets, and souvenirs. It is a great way to introduce yourself to the exotic sights, flavors, and colors of Thai life. And it is a great way to get all of those souvenirs you didn't buy yet. The market looks like chaos, but there is some organization present, with similar shops forming small clusters (Nancy Chandler's illustrated *Market Map* has a color-coded insert), but it is a fun place to get lost (and you will). Open on Saturdays and Sundays. Try to get there early in the morning before the heat. *Hint:* Hop off the Skytrain at Saphan Khwai and walk the one stop to the main market area, staying on the left (or west) side of the train. All along here you'll find some great antique and jewelry stalls. Chatuchak Park at Mo Chit BTS.

DEPARTMENT STORES & SHOPPING PLAZAS

Bangkok's downtown looks more and more like urban Tokyo these days, particularly near Siam Square, the hub of the two BTS Skytrain lines and an area chockablock with shopping. The size and opulence of Bangkok's many malls and shopping areas are often a shock to those who imagine Bangkok an exotic, impoverished destination. Sipping cappuccino at a Starbucks overlooking a busy city street may not be what you've come to Asia to find, but to many it is a comfort (especially after long trips in more rugged parts of the kingdom). The truth is, Thai malls are where the rubber meets the road with old and new in Siam, and are closer to the pulse of the nation than the many temples and ancient history that foreign visitors are keen to experience. You're sure to visit Thai mall culture if only briefly in your travels in Thailand, even in real rural parts. Below are just of a few of Bangkok's many malls:

- **The Emporium** (622 Sukhumvit Soi 24; ✆ **02664-8000**), Bangkok's finest shopping area, has all of the designer outlets of similar places in big cities the world over, from Gucci to Prada, Sony to Walt Disney (there's a big cinema on the top floor). They've got it all, and this place attracts expats with a yearning for the familiar: the food court on the top floor just about covers any craving.
- **Siam Discovery Center** (on Rama 1 Rd.; ✆ **02658-1000**) is opposite the Siam stop on the BTS Skytrain and adjoins **Siam Center** for some of the largest acreage of high-end shopping in Bangkok. The top-floor cinema plays current Western films.
- **Mah Boon Krong,** or **MBK,** and **Tokyu Department Store** (444 Phayathai Rd., at the intersection of Rama 1 and Phayathai; National Stadium BTS station;

ℂ 02217-9111) are a real trip to teeny-bopper Thailand, and support lots of more affordable local shops. This is more an exercise in "how Bangkok shops" than for finding great merchandise.

- **World Trade Center,** on the corner of Rama I and Ratchadamri roads (ℂ **02255-9400**), is like your average mall in the U.S.
- **Panthip Plaza** is a mall dedicated to computers and electronics. It is located on Petchaburi Road about a 10-minute walk east from the Ratchathewi BTS Station. Panthip used to be where you'd find lots of bootleg software, but a sincere crackdown means that software is sold surreptitiously and can result in problems with the police. Best to be avoided. You can, however, find very affordable computer components and great services.

7 Bangkok After Dark

One night in Bangkok, right? Well, you better move fast, because new legislation means that the bars close promptly at 2am, and further legislation has put some limits on some of the racier nightlife in places like Patpong. But the action is still fierce and furious in Thailand's hedonistic capital, and a rollicking good time can be had by those who seek it out.

If the Bangkok debauch isn't your scene, it is important to note that the town is not all red-light by any means: There are cultural and artistic events, as well as all kinds of discos and bars.

For the hippest nightlife update, check out *Metro Magazine* (100B/($2.45), available at bookstores. Featuring monthly listings of musical and artistic events as well as up-to-date info about the club scene, it is the best entertainment source in Bonkers. Both the *Bangkok Post* and *The Nation* offer daily listings of cultural events and performance schedules. The **TAT** (in Bangkok, ℂ **1672**) will also provide schedule information. Your hotel concierge will also have listings.

THE PERFORMING ARTS

Although the large shopping malls and international hotels often sponsor a cultural show, most travelers experience the Thai classical performing arts at a commercially staged dance show accompanying a Thai banquet; several hotels and restaurants offer this program. Generally there's a fixed-menu dinner of Thai favorites accompanied by a small orchestra, followed by a dance performance. Combined, you won't get the best food or the best dance. (See "Dinner with Thai Dance," in chapter 5, "Where to Stay & Dine in Bangkok," for specific recommendations.)

For a different experience, visit the **Erawan Shrine,** at the corner of Ratchadamri and Ploenchit roads (near the Grand Hyatt Erawan Bangkok and Sogo Department Store). In front of the large, white marble altar to Brahma, the Hindu god of creation, you'll often find musicians and beautifully costumed dancers commissioned to amuse Brahma by a grateful or hopeful worshipper.

There are two major theaters for Thai and international performances, the National Theater and the Thai Cultural Center. The **National Theater,** 1 Na Phra That Rd. (ℂ **02224-1342**), presents demonstrations of Thai classical dancing and music by performers from the School of Music and Dance in Bangkok, which are generally superior to those at the tourist restaurants and hotels. There are also performances by visiting ballet and theatrical companies. Call the TAT or the box office for the current schedule.

The **Thailand Cultural Center,** Thiem Ruammit Road off Ratchadaphisek Road, Huai Khwang (✆ **02247-0028**), is the newest and largest performance center in town, offering a wide variety of programs. The Bangkok Symphony performs here during its short summer season. Other local and visiting companies also present theater and dance at the center. If you're to see the *Ramayana* performed in Bangkok, this is probably the place you'll see it. Call for the current schedule.

The **Joe Louis Theater,** located in the Suan Lum Night Market (adjacent to Lumpini Park), holds nightly **puppet theater** performances of stories from the *Ramakien* (the Thai national epic), as well as comic vignettes of rural Thai life. Complex puppets are manipulated by up to three puppet masters, and the theater is also a training facility for Thai kids interested in the ancient art. Shows are nightly at 7:30 and 8:30pm. Tickets start at just 250B ($6.10). Located at the Suan Lum Night Market along Rama IV Road (✆ **02252-9683**).

For a bit of tongue-in-cheek theater, a couple of Cabaret shows in Bangkok feature Katoeys (aka "Lady-Boys") in 6-inch heels and feather boas performing to pop hits— rather hilarious extravaganzas, really. The best is **Calypso Cabaret** at the Asia Hotel (296 Phayathai Rd.; ✆ **02261-6355**), which features performances that are more creative than the standard drag parades at cabarets in Phuket or Pattaya. (Shows nightly at 8:15 and 9:45pm; tickets 700B/$17.) A more typical show for Thailand, featuring much of the same routine as at the resorts, is **Mambo** (Washington Square, Sukhumvit Soi 22; ✆ **02259-5128**), with shows nightly at 8:30 and 10pm (tickets 800B/$20).

CINEMA

Bangkok offers lots of venues showing the latest Hollywood films with Thai subtitles. It is a popular place to kick back in some pop culture and catch up on the latest movies, especially if you've been out in the sticks for a while in Thailand or elsewhere in the region.

Apex Cinema (✆ **02252-6498;** www.apexsiam-square.com) has outlets in Siam square; **EGV** (✆ **02812-9999;** www.egv.com) has a complex at the top of Big C across from the World Trade Center on Rajdamri; and **SF Cinema** (✆ **02937-2111;** www.sfcinemacity.com) has two large theaters (the best in town) at the **Emporium Shopping Center** (Sukhumvit Soi 24 near the Phrom Phong BTS station; ✆ **02894-4000**) and at **MBK Shopping Center** (on Phayathai Rd. opposite the National Stadium BTS Skytrain stop; ✆ **02611-6444**).

Bangkok also hosts a large **International Film Festival** annually (www.bangkok film.org).

THE CLUB & BAR SCENE

Bangkok is huge, and there are nighttime adventures to be found down any *soi* in the town. If you'd just like to unwind with an evening cocktail, check out what's happening at your hotel's lobby bar; many set up jazzy live music to entertain folks. For the best lobby bar atmosphere head for the **Bamboo Bar at the Oriental Hotel** (Oriental Lane off Charoen Krung Rd.; ✆ **02236-0400**), with classy live jazz—some of the best in the city. For the infamous Bangkok sex-show scene, check out "Silom Road & Patpong," below. Bars and discos are all over the city, and the main areas are listed below, but small nightclubs pop up here and there around town (and many disappear just as quickly). If you're looking for Bangkok's gay scene, start at Silom Soi 4 (see "Silom Road & Patpong," below).

SILOM ROAD & PATPONG

Most visitors won't leave Bangkok without a stroll around Patpong, the infamous sex strip and Night Market with myriad street-side market vendors and blocks of bars and clubs. The Patpong scene centers on Soi Patpong 1 and Soi Patpong 2, between Surawong and Silom roads. Even if you're not exactly after any risqué entertainment, most visitors come to wander the Market area (lots of knock-off goods and pirate recordings), and at least just peek in the doors of the go-go dens and hit a casual bar or club. It is a good little wander, but be prepared for big crowds and beware of pickpockets.

Visitors walking through the busy market will be harried by grinning touts with menu-boards telling of "ping-pong ball shows" and other circuslike spectacles. These upstairs **"sex-show"** places charge an entrance fee or have a one- or two-drink minimum; if you're interested, be sure to negotiate for exactly what you'll pay, as many visitors get lured upstairs and end up with large surcharges added to the bill. If there are problems, just pay up, get a receipt, and go to the Tourist Police on Surawong Road. The Tourist Police here are a force to be reckoned with, and have helped many a traveler out of just such a scam (see "The Sex Scene," below). **Go-go bars** are open to the street and passers-by get a peak at the groups of scantily clad young ladies crowding together on a central catwalk (and looking pretty bored, really). You won't pay an entrance fee, but it is more or less a "drink or leave" policy, and the ladies will circulate from stage to the bar area (see "The Sex Scene," below, for more information).

Despite its rep as a go-go center, there are lots of good bars in Patpong. **O'Reilly's Irish Pub,** 62 Silom Rd., on the corner of Soi Thaniya just east of Patpong (✆ 02632-7515), is a lively bar full of locals and travelers. **The Barbican** (9/4–5 Soi Thaniya off Silom Rd.; ✆ 02234-3590) is a stylish hangout with great food, and they feature some nice live music. **The Irish Exchange** across from Patpong on Convent Road (next to Silom Complex at 1/5–6 Sivadon Building; ✆ 02266-7160) caters to Bangkok yuppies and foreign expatriates with Irish pub style and live music after office working hours. Head to **Silom Soi 4** (between Patpong 2 and Soi Thaniya off Silom Rd.), where you'll find small home-grown clubs spinning great music, as well as the city's prominent gay clubs: **Telephone Bar** (114/11–13 Silom Soi 4; ✆ 02234-3279) and **The Balcony** (86–8 Silom Soi 4; ✆ 02235-5891), foremost among them.

Between Silom and the River, find **Hu'u Bar Bangkok** (1st and 2nd floor of the Ascot; ✆ 02676-6677; www.huuinasia.com), a hip new joint and another very popular haunt (BTS Surasak station).

SIAM SQUARE

Siam Square, on Rama I Road between Henri Dunant Road and Phayathai Road, houses quite a few popular joints. Here's where you'll find **Bangkok's Hard Rock Café,** featuring good live bands, at 424/3–6 Siam Square Soi 11 (✆ 02254-0830). At the **Hartmannsdorfer Brauhaus,** 2nd floor, **Siam Discovery Center,** Rama I Road (✆ 02658-0223), you'll find home brews in a nice atmosphere—with special beer discounts on Sundays.

A great disco, **Concept CM²** goes nightly with live or DJ music—a very popular place in the basement of the **Novotel Siam** (Siam Square Soi 6; ✆ 02255-6888). **Spasso,** in the Grand Hyatt Erawan Hotel (494 Ratchadamri Rd.; ✆ 02254-1234), is a great Italian restaurant (see "Where to Stay & Dine in Bangkok," in chapter 5) that turns upscale club featuring live music acts nightly.

A little bit north of this area (a short cab ride away), near the Victory Monument BTS station (a cab ride up Phayathai Rd.), check out live jazz and blues at **Saxophone**

Pub and Restaurant. They're at Phayathai Road on the southeast corner of the Victory Monument traffic circle (© **02246-5472**).

KHAO SAN ROAD

Over on Rattanakosin Island in Old Bangkok, the backpackers on Khao San Road still party on despite more and more restrictions. Start at **Gulliver's** on the corner of Khao San and Chakrabongse roads, then explore the back lanes off Khao San for small dance clubs (some the size of broom closets) and hang outs. You'll find lots of travelers in their 20s, and the atmosphere is always laid-back and anything goes. In the middle of Khao San, look for **Silk Bar** (129–131 Khaosan Rd.; © **02281-9981**), a dolled-up little hideaway set back from the road a hitch and just across from the Krung Thai Bank. Also try **Khao San Center** (at the middle, of course), and don't miss **Lava** (249 Khao San Rd.; © **02281-6565**), a popular basement dance club. For a more laid-back evening, head west of Khao San to riverside **Phra Athit Road,** where there are any number of small cafes with live folk, blues, and rock cover acts, and lots of small venues full of Thai college students going "beat." Acts change nightly, so walk the road's length, have a peek in each spot to find the Thai Joan Baez or young Pete Seeger yet to be discovered. Down the small *sois* surrounding the temple compound (on the river end of Khao San) look for lots of little open-air places; a good place to meet fellow travelers. Try **Bangkok Times** (12 Soi Rongmai; © **02629-1596**).

SUKHUMVIT ROAD

One of the most happenin' areas of Bangkok, the small *sois* along busy Sukhumvit play host to a wide range of bars as well as Bangkok's top clubs. You can hop the Skytrain from one to the next or, after midnight when the Skytrain stops, hop a tuk-tuk or taxi.

Q Bar (34 Sukhumvit Soi 11; © **02252-3274**) is *the* place for the slick urban hip of Bangkok, its only rival is the similarly ab-fab **Bed Supper Club** (see "Where to Stay & Dine in Bangkok," in chapter 5; 26 Sukhumvit Soi 11; © **02651-3537**). Both are ultramodern, have great expat DJs, and boom-boom-boom late into the night 7 days a week. The newly built **Conrad Hotel** (87 Wireless Road, just across from the U.S. Embassy; © **02690-9999**) hosts two of Bangkok's newest and best spots: **87** is an ultra-chic, ultra-exclusive club, and their **Diplomat Bar** fills with, well, diplomats from the U.S. Embassy, as well as Bangkok's hip and happenin' hobnobbers (it gets so crowded that the bar often spills over into the lobby). Call ahead to any of these for the latest events and, wherever possible, wear black and bring your posse.

For bars along Sukhumvit, try **The Bull's Head** (Sukhumvit Soi 33/1; © **02259-4444**), a fun local pub that draws crowds with frequent theme parties and a clubhouse vibe. **Larry's Dive Bar** (8/3 Sukhumvit Soi 22; © **02663-4563**) is a laid-back little place, like a little island getaway in the busy city and just as affordable. **Brauhaus Bangkok** (President Park, at the end of Sukhumvit Soi 24; © **02661-1111**) is a popular brewpub, as is **Taurus Brew House** (Sukhumvit Soi 26; © **02661-2207**), which packs them in—especially on weekends—for home brews and live pop music. Taurus also boasts one of the better discos in the Sukhumvit area, just across from the Brew House, this hip and huge "complex" has live music, a giant disco, and good food. For the best live music, however, head for **Riva's,** Sheraton Grande Sukhumvit Hotel, 250 Sukhumvit Rd. (© **02653-0333**), with international bands and lots of dancing (open 'til nearly 2am).

For a quick drink at a unique little outdoor bar, try **Cheap Charlie's,** in a little alleyway off of Soi 11 (near Suk 11 guesthouse). It is like a small beach bar, but in the middle of Bangkok and drinks are "affordable," and it is a fun after-work atmosphere. Tell them Charlie sent you, and they will charge you double.

Similar to the Patpong sex-show scene, Sukhumvit hosts a few small go-go bar areas that are "same-same but different," like Patpong without all the hype. Check out **Nana Plaza** just on Sukhumvit Soi 4, or **Soi Cowboy** (the oldest go-go scene, dating from Vietnam War days) between Soi Asoke (Sukhumvit Soi 21) and Sukhumvit Soi 23. The girls are not shy and business is brisk, and attracts more of an expat clientele than touristy Patpong.

THE SEX SCENE

Since the 1960s—and particularly since the Vietnam War—Bangkok has been the sin capital of Asia, with sex clubs, bars, massage parlors, and prostitutes concentrated in the **Patpong, Nana Plaza,** and **Soi Cowboy** districts. Sex is for sale in many quarters in Bangkok, and many first-time visitors experience surprise at seeing the many older Western gentlemen strutting about town with lovely young Thai ladies.

A startling increase in HIV-positive cases in the last 20 years brought on mandated as well as grass-roots efforts to educate sex workers about the use of condoms. And it is working. AIDS is still a major concern among sex workers, but the tide of new cases has slowed somewhat. Recent crackdowns in Patpong means that some of the raunchier shows and more overt venues for prostitution have closed, but in other cases, the focus has shifted to younger and younger women. The picture certainly isn't rosy.

Go-go bars and clubs are really little more than fronts for prostitution, and very thinly veiled fronts at that. The men and women in the clubs are all available to take out of the bar. You'll be required to pay a "bar fine" (about 400B/$9.75), and you can take the companion of your choice out to other clubs, or to someplace more private. Sex is negotiated directly with him or her. If this is your scene, take great care: Apart from the condom thing (use one), the prostitutes are known to slip you drugs (which happens), rob your hotel room while you're sleeping (which happens), or get you mixed up with illegal activities (which happens).

If you're staying in a very expensive upmarket hotel, many times you will not be allowed to bring prostitutes through the lobby. Most hotels require guests to register visitors, and will bump you up to the next pay category. There are cheaper hotels popular with punters where overnight or short-term visitors can register separately at a security desk. Otherwise ask any "new friend" about cheap "short-time" hotels near the go-go bars.

While prostitution is technically illegal in Thailand, this law is never enforced. International reports about poor farmers selling their children into prostitution are true—many children are held in brothels against their will. However, the majority of sex workers are adults who enter the industry of their own free will out of basic economic necessity, and often support many people on their earnings. Remember that child prostitution, slavery, and violence against sex workers still happens; if you encounter any of these activities, please report them to the **Tourist Police** (**⌒ 1155**).

MASSAGE PARLORS

Though suffering from official pressure to close, Bangkok has hundreds of giant massage facilities, advertised in neon as "modern" or "physical" massage parlors, that offer something quite different from traditional Thai massage (more or less just direct sex for sale).

Physical massage involves a masseuse first washing the client and then, covered in soap (or oil), using her entire body for a "body-body" massage (sometimes a "sand-wich" of two masseuses). Nearly all massage parlors are organized along the same lines. Guests enter the lobby where there's a coffee shop/bar and several waiting rooms where young Thai women wearing numbers pinned to their blouses sit on bleachers. Guests choose a woman from behind the glass, and then proceed to a private room for between 1 and 2 hours. It is all negotiable, but rates for a physical massage start at about 1,500B ($37) and increase for different services.

8 Side Trips from Bangkok

There are plenty of easy day trips from Bangkok. Favorites include various cruises along the Chao Praya to the more distant klongs and to the ancient capital of Ayuthaya, north of Bangkok, with a stop at the Bang Pa-In Summer Palace. There's also a large floating market south of Bangkok. Also try Thailand-in-miniature Ancient City, the Rose Garden's performance arts show, at the temples of Nakhon Pathom, or the Samutprakarn Crocodile Farm and the Elephant Grounds. Kids will enjoy most of these.

EASY 1-DAY EXCURSIONS
FLOATING MARKET AT DAMNOEN ✿ Kids

The **Floating Market at Damnoen Saduak,** Ratchaburi, is about 40 minutes south of Nakhon Pathom. This market is popular for photographers. Some tours combine the Floating Market with a visit to the Rose Garden or with the River Kwai sights (see below for more on each). If you choose to go via organized tour, such as **World Travel Service** (✆ 02233-5900), expect to pay about 1,500B ($37) for the 1-day trip combo with the Rose Garden.

THE ANCIENT CITY (MUANG BORAN)

This remarkable museum is a giant scale model of Thailand, with the country's major landmarks built full-scale or in miniature and spread over 81 hectares (200 acres). It was built over the last 20 years by a local millionaire who has played out his obsession with Thai history on a grand scale.

Because it is far from the heart of Bangkok, the Ancient City is best visited by organized tour, though you can certainly go on your own. It is at kilometer 33 on the old Sukhumvit Highway in Samut Prakan Province.

All travel agents offer package tours that combine the Rose Garden with other attractions in the area, such as the Crocodile Farm or the huge Buddhist *chedi* in nearby Nakhon Pathom. Admission to the Ancient City is 300B ($7.30) and includes bicycle rental or a tram ride around the sites. Muang Boran is open daily from 8am to 5pm. Contact them at ✆ 02709-1644 (www.ancientcity.com).

A CROCODILE FARM

Only 3km (2 miles) from the Ancient City you'll find the **Samutprakarn Crocodile Farm and Zoo,** at kilometer 30 on the Old Sukhumvit Highway (✆ 02387-0020). The world's largest, it has more than 40,000 snappers, both fresh- and saltwater. At the hourly show, handlers wrestle the crocs in murky ponds. A great outing for families! Admission is 300B ($7.50) for adults, 200B ($4.90) for kids. Daily from 7am to 5pm; feedings take place every hour.

ROSE GARDEN COUNTRY RESORT

Besides its rose garden, this attractive if somewhat touristy resort is known for its all-in-one show of Thai culture that includes Thai classical and folk dancing, Thai boxing, sword fighting, and cock fighting—a convenient way for visitors with limited time to digest some canned Thai culture. It is located 32km (20 miles) west of Bangkok on the way to Nakhon Pathom on Highway 4 (℘ **03432-2588;** www.thai culturalshow.com). Surprisingly, the resort's restaurant is very appealing and not expensive. Admission is 10B (25¢) for the grounds; 220B ($5.40) for the show. It is open daily from 8am to 6pm; the cultural show is at 2:45pm and 4pm.

SAMPHRAN ELEPHANT GROUNDS & ZOO

Located 1 kilometer (⁹⁄₁₀ mile) north of the Rose Garden Country Resort in Yannowa (30km/18½ miles from the city), the **Samphran Elephant Grounds and Zoo** (℘ **02284-1873**) is a lush 9-hectare (22-acre) garden complex offering an entertaining elephant show, plus thousands of crocodiles, including the world's largest white crocodile. Admission is 300B ($7.30) for adults, 200B ($4.90) for children. The zoo is open daily from 9am to 6pm; crocodile wrestling shows—12:45 and 2:20pm; elephant show times—1:45 and 3:30pm; additional shows on Saturday, Sunday, and holidays at 10:30am.

A WATER PARK

If the heat and the kids have gotten to you, consider a trip to one of two water parks. The closest is **Suan Siam (Siam Park),** 101 Sukhapibarn 2 Rd., Bangkapi (℘ **02517-0075**), a 30-minute drive east of town (or an hour on bus no. 26 or 27 from the Victory Monument). It is a large complex of water slides (try the Super Spiral—about .2km/⅛-mile long), enormous swimming pools with artificial surf, waterfalls, landscaped gardens, playgrounds, beer garden, and more. There is a fishing farm on the way, which the kids might also enjoy.

Admission is 200B ($4.90), including rides. Siam Park is open weekdays 10am to 6pm; weekends 9am to 7pm.

SITES FARTHER AFIELD
KANCHANABURI
120 kilometers (74 miles) NW of Bangkok

Really more than a 1-day trip (best as an overnight), Kanchanaburi is home of the famed Bridge over the River Kwai and the notorious internment camps for Allied troops forced into servitude (and death) by the Japanese during World War II in an effort to link Burma and Thailand by rail. Made legendary by the film of the same name, "The Bridge over the River Kwai" lives on in name only; the existing bridge is just a little rattle-trap trestle that crosses not the River Kwai but a tributary (but that doesn't stop souvenir hawkers and the tourist infrastructure that has grown up around the bridge). There are, however, lots of good excursions in the area, many caves and waterfalls in the surrounding hills, and a few good hotels and riverside guesthouses: a popular escape from the heat, traffic, and pollution of Bangkok.

Getting to Kanchanaburi

You can connect by railway from Bangkok's **Hua Lampong Station** (℘ **1690**) on regular weekend junkets starting in the early morning, or go by daily ordinary trains from **Bangkok Noi Station** (℘ **02411-3102**) with slow, daily connections to Kanchanaburi

Station (© **03456-1052**); rail trips here are quite scenic and a great experience (though a long, hot ride). There are also frequent regular buses from the **Southern Bus Terminal** (© **02434-5557**), but, if by road, it is perhaps best by rented car (see "Getting Around" in chapter 4 for more information).

Accommodations

The best place to stay is **The Felix River Kwai Resort** (9/1 Moo 3 Tambon, Kanchanaburi; © **03451-5061;** www.felixriverkwai.co.th.). The Felix has rooms starting at 2,000B ($49) and is the best for comfort, but places like the **Jungle Raft Resort** (Lam Khao Ngu; © **02377-5556**), which is just as it says—a bunch of jungle rafts— are certainly far more atmospheric and adventurous. There are guesthouses and many services along central **Mae Nam Road** and adjacent to the bridge.

Attractions

The town's sites focus on the World War II history of the area. Start any tour of Kanchanaburi at **The Bridge Over the River Kwai,** the very mention of which purses my lips and has me whistling "Hi-ho Hi-ho, it's off to work we go," as the indentured World War II POW bridge-builders were depicted doing in the film of the same name. The bridge is about 5km north of the business district of Kanchanaburi.

The **Kanchanaburi War Cemetery** is home to many of the nearly 7,000 POWs who died, and graves are marked and organized by country. The site is just 1.5km from the train station. Daily 8:30am to 6pm. No entry fee.

Adjacent to the cemetery is the Thailand–Burma Railway Center (© **03451-0067;** www.tbrconline.com), an organized and interesting collection of photos and memorabilia with ample English descriptions, maps, and histories, as well as good film screenings, telling the history of Allied POWs during World War II. Nearby (just south of the cemetery along the river) find the older **Jeath War Museum** (Wat Chaichumpol, Bantai, Kanchanaburi; © **03451-5203;** daily 8:30am–4:30pm; 30B/75¢), a collection of photos and artifacts in a rustic bamboo museum adjacent to Wat Chaichumpol. JEATH is an acronym for Japan, England, Australia/America, Thailand, and Holland. Most interesting at Jeath are the letters and faded photos of the many GIs who've returned since the end of the war.

Some 45km (28 miles) north of Kanchanaburi, and made popular by a recent series of Discovery Channel specials, find **Wat Pa Luangta Bua Yannasampanno,** the famed **Tiger Temple,** a huge nature preserve with deer, wild boar, and various jungle animals, as well as a clutch of large tigers, most rescued from the wild as cubs (most were left on the temple doorstep by poachers). The costs of feeding the animals each day is a steep 10,000B ($245), and various international agencies have contributed to help, but visitors here are asked to give donations, and many are given the opportunity to pose with the tigers close up. The temple is open to visitors daily from 8:30am to 5pm, but it is best to go between 1:30pm and 5pm to meet the tigers close up. The temple is in Tambon Singh, 45km (28 miles) north of the city. Go Rt. 323 to Saiyok Dist. and pass the entrance to the Muang Singh Park; go 6km and turn right off the main street after 2km.

Other sites further afield from Kanchanaburi include the **Hellfire Pass,** which can be visited by train, as well as the Erawan National Park, north of town.

KHAO YAI NATIONAL PARK

The first official national park in Thailand (circa 1962) and located 3 hours from the big city near Nakon Ratchasima on the western edge of Isan, Thailand's rural Northeast, the park is home to high peaks (some over 1,000m) that offer cooler temperatures year-round. A good place to witness local wildlife, from golden gibbons to wild elephants congregated around roadside salt-licks, barking deer to any of a wide variety of birds (birders visit here from far and wide). Lots of good day hikes.

AYUTHAYA & 1-DAY RIVERBOAT TRIPS
76km (47 miles) NW of Bangkok

The temple town of Ayuthaya and nearby Bang Pa-In are both popular day trips from Bangkok. Ayuthaya was the capital of Thailand from 1350 until it was sacked in 1767 by the Burmese; thereafter the capital was Thonburi, just across the Chao Praya from present-day Bangkok. The Ayuthaya temples are magnificent, both Khmer and more Thai-style ruins at riverside in what was once Thailand's greatest city. It is a great place to rent a bicycle and truck around town (it's flat), and certainly worth an overnight and a great 1-day boat trip. Nearby Bang Pa-In is home to the ancient palace and is visited as part of most 1-day tours to Bangkok. For more specific information on Ayuthaya (how to get there and where to stay and dine if you choose), see the first section of chapter 10, "Central Thailand."

All-day river cruises are a popular option to and from Ayuthaya. Contact **River Sun Cruises** (© 02266-9125) directly or book through any riverside hotel: departure points are the **Oriental Hotel** (© 02236-0400), **Shangri-La Hotel** (© 02236-7777), or River City pier, daily at approximately 7:30am (and include a stop at Bang Pa-In). Most day trips include a return by air-conditioned coach or vice versa (trip time: all day; 1,600B/$39). For a super-luxury option, the *Manhora Song* does the same trip as a multiday, high-end cruise on a traditional rice barge (from 40,000B/$976 for two). Only on Sundays, a much cheaper, self-guided boat trip can be arranged through the **Chao Praya Express Co.** (© 02222-5330). The unguided, all-day excursion is very popular with locals and costs 350B ($8.55) per person (meals exclusive).

Also look for the many 1-day boat-trip options to **Ko Kret,** an island in the mouth of the Chao Praya famed for its population of indigenous Mon people, early immigrants to Thailand. **Chao Praya Express Co.** (see above) runs Sunday day trips to the island, and many Bangkok tour operators run special trips.

7

The Eastern Seaboard

Tracing the coastline directly east of Bangkok along the Gulf of Thailand, there are a few resort spots that are attractive as much for their proximity to Bangkok as anything. Closest is Pattaya, one of Thailand's earliest holiday developments and famous (or infamous) for its wild nightlife, its sea of amber-lit, open-air beer bars, go-go spots, and hostess clubs. The town is always hoppin' late into the night and guys come from all over the world to live it up. But there's a dark side: The skin trade in Pattaya lures some pretty nasty elements, such as child prostitution and drug activity.

As such, much of Pattaya is too seedy for family vacations, but there are some fine resorts, plenty of shopping, and good golf courses. The main Pattaya beach is still overcoming the effects of years of pell-mell construction and the spilling of pollutants directly into the bay (there's now a sewage treatment plant). The beach is also just a thin strip of coarse sand with too many motorboats buzzing offshore; but nearby Jomtien, just south of town, is good for swimming, and day trips to outlying islands are popular. Pattaya is a crazy love-it-or-hate-it kind of place, and the proverbial "One Night in Bangkok" pales in comparison.

Continuing east from Pattaya, **Ko Samet,** in Rayong Province, is a small island with loads of affordable, makeshift bungalow resorts. It is a low-luxe, laid-back little retreat reached by a short ferry ride from the mainland at the town of Ban Phe (via Rayong). Though isolated, Ko Samet is popular with foreigners on a budget and gets very crowded on weekends with young Thai vacationers from Bangkok.

Ko Chang, the last stop before Cambodia to the east, is growing into a popular international resort destination with some recent developments and more planned. Ko Chang now boasts a few large, international-style resorts, as well as a host of good mid-range and budget choices, and Thailand's second largest island is rising in the pecking order of Thailand's most popular beach destination (just after Phuket and Koh Samui). By road, Ko Chang is some 5 hours east of Bangkok, but there are an increasing number of flights to Trat, the small town on the coast, making it a much more manageable trip.

1 Pattaya

147km (91 miles) E of Bangkok

The current incarnation of Pattaya claims its founders' day as June 29, 1959, when a few truckloads of American troops stationed in nearby Isan arrived, rented houses along the beach, and had such a hoot that they told their friends. Word spread and, over time, the town became the R&R capital for war-weary American troops for the next many years. The legacy of those early visitors is today's adult playground with hundreds of go-go clubs, beer bars, and massage parlors at beachside.

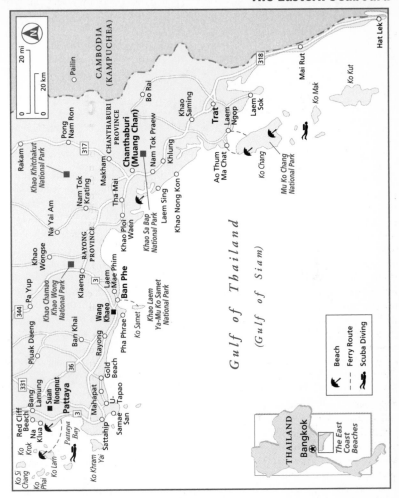

Tourism boomed in the 1980s, and unchecked resort development was not accompanied by infrastructure upgrades such that beaches became veritable toilets of raw sewage. Recent years have seen a few civil projects to clean up the bay with some success, but the beach is not at all pleasant.

Despite this, Pattaya now supports a collection of large, sophisticated international resorts, retreats set in sprawling, manicured seaside gardens. Pattaya would like to be a family destination, and, along with fine accommodations, there are some family activities, but Pattaya's mammoth sex-tourism industry kind of puts the kibosh on any wholesome family fun (parents may not be able to field all of the questions the town raises in the little ones).

Neighboring Jomtien is a popular alternative to Pattaya. Less seedy activities and cleaner beaches (though just a long, thin stretch of coarse sand), Jomtien's best accommodations are private condominiums, but it is good for day visits.

ESSENTIALS
GETTING THERE

By Plane   There is no airport in Pattaya, the nearest being in U Tapao, an hour east of the city (© **03824-5595**) and served by **Bangkok Airways** with a daily flight from Koh Samui (trip time: 1 hr.). They also fly four times a week to and from Phnom Penh in Cambodia. Make reservations through their offices at Bangkok (© **02229-3456**). They have an office in Pattaya at Royal Garden Plaza, 218 Beach Rd., 2d floor (© **03841-1965**). To get to and from the airport to Pattaya, arrange private transfer through your resort (a limo can be as steep as 1,000B/$24), or take the Bangkok Airways minivan for 150B ($3.65). It is so close to Bangkok, however, that it is a cinch to go overland.

By Train   Once-a-day train service leaves from **Bangkok's Hua Lampong station** at 6:55am and returns from Pattaya at 2:50pm. The 5-hour trip through the countryside is pleasant and costs only 31B (75¢). Call **Hua Lampong** in Bangkok (© **02223-7010** or 1690) or the train station in Pattaya at © **03842-9285.** The Pattaya train station is east of the resort strip off Sukhumvit Road and shared-ride *songtao* (minitruck) connect with all destinations on the main beach for just 20B (50¢).

By Public Bus   The most common and practical form of transportation to Pattaya is the bus. Buses depart from **Bangkok's Eastern Bus Terminal** on Sukhumvit Road (opposite Soi 63 at the BTS Ekkamai Station; © **02391-2504**) every half-hour beginning from 5am until 10pm every day. For air-conditioned coach the fare is 90B ($2.20). There's also regular bus service from **Bangkok's Northern Bus Terminal,** on Kampaengphet 2 Road (Mo Chit) (© **02936-2841**), which is a good way to avoid Bangkok rush-hour traffic.

   The bus station in Pattaya for air-conditioned buses to and from Bangkok is on North Pattaya Road (© **03842-9877**). From there, catch a shared ride on a *songtao* to your resort or hotel for about 20B (50¢), more for private taxi.

By Private Bus   Major hotels or travel agencies in both Bangkok and Pattaya operate private shuttles, so be sure to inquire when booking. **Rung Reung Tour** (© **03842-9877**) has air-conditioned bus service every 2 hours from 7am to 5pm (trip time: 3 hr.) to and from Bangkok's Don Muang International Airport, and minibuses also depart from Khao San Road (any agent can make good discount arrangements).

By Taxi   Taxis from the Don Muang International Airport taxi counter go for 1,250B ($30), and any hotel concierge can negotiate with a metered taxi driver to take you to or from Pattaya resort, door to door, for about 1,500B ($37).

By Car   Take Highway 3 east from Bangkok.

VISITOR INFORMATION

The **TAT office** (609 Moo 10, Pratamnak Rd.; © **03842-8750**) is inconveniently located south of Pattaya City, up the mountain on the road between Pattaya and neighboring resort Jomtien. Better info is available in most hotel lobbies: free local maps and publications like *What's On Pattaya* and *Explore Pattaya and the East Coast. Pattaya Mail* is the local English-language paper (25B/60¢).

ORIENTATION

Pattaya Beach road is the heart of the town, a long strip of hotels, bars, restaurants, and shops overlooking Pattaya Bay. Pattaya 2nd and Pattaya 3rd roads run parallel to

Pattaya

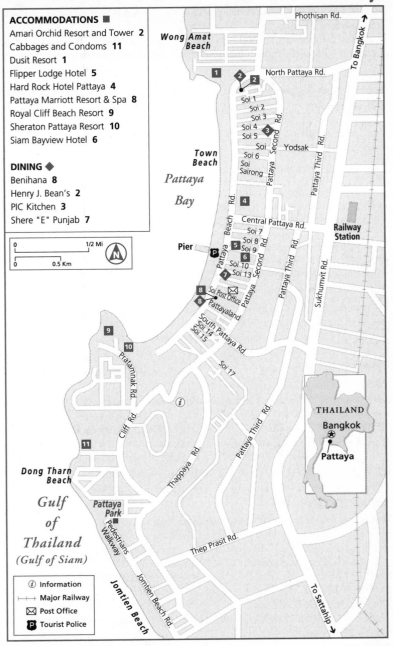

ACCOMMODATIONS ■
Amari Orchid Resort and Tower **2**
Cabbages and Condoms **11**
Dusit Resort **1**
Flipper Lodge Hotel **5**
Hard Rock Hotel Pattaya **4**
Pattaya Marriott Resort & Spa **8**
Royal Cliff Beach Resort **9**
Sheraton Pattaya Resort **10**
Siam Bayview Hotel **6**

DINING ◆
Benihana **8**
Henry J. Bean's **2**
PIC Kitchen **3**
Shere "E" Punjab **7**

0   1/2 Mi
0   0.5 Km

Phothisan Rd.

To Bangkok

Wong Amat Beach

North Pattaya Rd.

Soi 1
Soi 2
Soi 3
Soi 4
Soi 5
Soi 6
Soi Sairong

Pattaya Second Rd.

Pattaya Third Rd.

Yodsak

Town Beach

Pattaya Bay

Central Pattaya Rd.

Railway Station

Pattaya Beach Rd.

Soi 7
Soi 8
Soi 9
Soi 10
Soi 13

Pier

P

Post Office

Pattayaland

South Pattaya Rd.

Soi 14
Soi 15

Soi 17

Sukhumvit Rd.

THAILAND
Bangkok
Pattaya

Pratamnak Rd.

Cliff Rd.

Dong Tharn Beach

Gulf of Thailand
(Gulf of Siam)

Pattaya Park

Pedestrians Walkway

Thappaya Rd.

Pattaya Third Rd.

Thep Prasit Rd.

Jomtien Beach Rd.

Jomtien Beach

To Sattahip

ⓘ Information
├─┼─┤ Major Railway
✉ Post Office
🅿 Tourist Police

163

Beach Road and form a busy central grid of small, crowded *sois* bound by North Pattaya Road and South Pattaya Road, and bisected by Central Pattaya Road. At both the far northern (Dusit Resort) and southern (Royal Cliff Beach Resort) ends of the strip are two bluffs. Due south is condo-lined Jomtien Beach, a 15-minute ride from Pattaya.

GETTING AROUND

By Minibus or Songtao   *Songtaos* (called baht buses here) are covered pickup trucks with wooden benches that follow regular routes up and down the main streets. Fares within Pattaya start at 10B (25¢). To far-flung beaches such as Jomtien, they're 30B (75¢). Drivers will try to charge you a taxi-rate (especially if empty), but don't have any of it (bargain hard and wait for a full truck). Some hotels operate their own minibuses.

By Car   There are plenty of car-rental agencies, and you can negotiate the price with most, especially outside the high season. **Avis** is at the **Dusit Resort** (© **03836-1628**), with self-drive rates from about 1,500B ($37) per day for a Suzuki Caribian 4WD sport vehicle to 2,000B ($49) and up for a compact sedan. **Budget Car Rental** has an office at Liabchayhard Beach Road (© **03871-0717**) and offers comparable rates. **VIA Rent-a-Car,** 215/15–18 Pattaya 2nd Road, opposite Royal Garden Plaza (© **03872-3123**), has a good reputation and, like the many along Pattaya Beach Road, offers better rates (from 900B/$22), but be sure to read all contracts and check vehicles closely before renting.

By Motorcycle   Let's be honest, Pattaya's busy roads are full of drunk and reckless foreign drivers on motorbikes, but the brave (or foolish) can rent 150cc motorcycles for 200B ($4.90) a day (no insurance). Big choppers and Japanese speed bikes (500cc) will go for from 500B to 900B ($12–$22) per day. Demand a helmet, and as always, "renter beware."

FAST FACTS

There are many independent **money-changing booths,** bank exchanges (with better rates) open 24 hours, and ATMs at every turn in town. The post office is on **Soi Post Office** near the Royal Garden Plaza (© **03842-9341**). **Bangkok Pattaya Hospital** (© **03842-7751**) has full services and English-speaking staff. In Pattaya, the number for the **Tourist Police** is © **03842-9371** or 1155. Internet service in Pattaya costs 2B per minute ($3/hr.; expensive for Thailand) and there are a number of cafes along the water (try Soi Yamato).

WHAT TO SEE & DO

Wat Khao Prayai is a small temple complex high above town to the south (go by songtao toward Jomtien, then hop off and climb the steep hill). The temple has excellent vistas and a 10m (32½-ft.) gold Buddha serenely surveying the western sea.

If you don't have time to visit all of Thailand's many architectural wonders, **Mini Siam** (387 Moo 6 Sukhumvit Rd., North Pattaya City; © **03842-1628**) offers a comprehensive tour of the kingdoms highlights in miniature (an example of scale: Bangkok's huge Grand Palace is waist high). Open daily 7am to 8pm; admission 200B ($4.90) adults, 100B ($2.45) children. It is 14km (8½ miles) north of Pattaya City and best reached by taxi or private car.

For something completely unusual, the **Ripley's Believe It or Not** showcase, 3rd Floor, Royal Garden Plaza, 218 Beach Road (© **03871-0294**), open 10am to midnight daily (admission 320B/$7.80), is hilarious, with unusual exhibits and odd facts from around the globe. Just next-door is the Ripley's Motion Master simulator ride. Both are highly recommended for kids of all ages.

The **Pattaya Elephant Village** (see the Elephant Desk at Tropicana Hotel, Beach Rd.; ℂ **03842-8158**) stages elephant shows daily at 2:30pm. You can also arrange for a little jungle trekking on elephant back; a half-hour trek is about 500B ($12) per adult and 200B ($5) per child. If that's not quite your speed, check out Pattaya Go-Kart, Sukhumvit Road next to Mini Siam (ℂ **03842-2044**), with a 400m (1,312 ft.) track that is also suitable for children. Rates run between 100B ($2.45) and 200B ($4.90) per 10 minutes, depending on the power of your cart.

Also some 18km (11½ miles) from Pattaya is **Nong Nooch** (ℂ **03842-9321**), a giant botanical garden and elephant park with daily performances—with elephants performing alongside some 100 dancers, musicians, and performers for spectator crowds of up to 1,000. Cultural performances, music, Thai boxing, audience participation, and dozens of funny photo ops make this really touristy activity a load of laughs. Make your booking directly and they can arrange shuttles from Pattaya at either 8:30am or 1:15pm with return.

WHERE TO STAY

Busy central Pattaya features a range of accommodation, from seedy to stylish, and the town supports a few more isolated, peaceful getaways. During the high season, reservations are recommended at least 2 weeks in advance, especially December through January.

EXPENSIVE

Amari ⋆ On the northern end of busy Pattaya, just out of the fray but close enough to walk there, the Amari provides comforts typical of its many properties throughout Thailand. Rooms are clean, with all the right amenities, and the staff is helpful: a great choice for the family (but not particularly luxurious). The open-air lobby is inviting and guest rooms are large, trimmed in dark wood with parquet floors with pleasing, contemporary lines. There's a playground and lots of space in the grassy central area. They have good in-house dining (see Henry J. Bean's in "Where to Dine," below), and can help arrange any eventuality during your stay.

Pattaya Beach, Pattaya 20150 (on the very northernmost end of the beachfront road). ℂ **02255-3767**. Fax 02255-3718. 236 units. 9,000B–9,800B ($220–$240) double; from 11,000B ($270) suite. **Amenities:** 3 restaurants; 3 bars; outdoor pool; 9-hole mini-golf; 2 tennis courts; fitness center; Jacuzzi; playground and kids' club; tour desk; business center w/Internet; gift shop; salon; 24-hr. room service; babysitting; laundry and dry-cleaning; nonsmoking rooms. *In room:* A/C, satellite TV, minibar, fridge, safe, IDD phone.

Dusit Resort ⋆ This sprawling, landscaped resort straddles the bluff on the north end of the main beach and is choc-full of fine amenities: watersports, two fine pools, access to two small but well-kept sandy beach coves, several dining outlets, and a small shopping arcade. Most of the balconied rooms overlook Pattaya Bay, but the garden view rooms are a great value. Tasteful, modern rooms are trimmed with stained wood and each has fine furnishings and all-marble bathrooms. While you may get an overall "chain-hotel feel" here, the accommodations are very clean and comfortable, and there is a unique Zodiac theme throughout. Larger rooms and suites have outdoor showers on large balconies.

240/2 Pattaya Beach Rd., Pattaya 20150, Chonburi (north end of Pattaya Beach). ℂ **03842-5611**. Fax 03842-8239. www.dusit.com. 462 units. 6,000B–6,800B ($146–$166) double; from 9,300B ($227) suite. AE, DC, MC, V. **Amenities:** 3 restaurants; lobby bar w/live music; 2 large free-form pools; 2 outdoor tennis courts; small fitness center; spa w/massage, sauna, steam; watersports equipment/rentals; games; concierge; tour desk; car-rental desk; limousine service; small business center w/Internet; shopping arcade; 24-hr. room service; babysitting; same-day laundry service/dry cleaning; nonsmoking rooms. *In room:* A/C, satellite TV, minibar, fridge, coffeemaker, hair dryer, safe, IDD phone.

Hard Rock Hotel Pattaya 🎸🎸 New and ultra-modern Hard Rock Hotel is a rollicking, good-time oasis in the heart of sordid Pattaya. This is one place in town you might feel okay bringing the kids, and they're sure to have a ball in the fun sandy-edged pool, game area, and Internet cafe. Rooms are compact and purposely sparse in immaculate whites set against bright blue or orange. Each room features larger-than-life murals of your favorite rock-and-roll idols, from Elvis to John Lennon. Media mavens will be pleased with the in-room CD players and in-house movies. Large family suites are a good option. The lobby and adjoining Hard Rock Cafe features the chain's typical minimuseum of musical memorabilia; their Lil' Rock Kid's Club is one of the best going; the poolside spa is tops; and the pool area is compact but has lots of shady areas and massage *salas,* a kind of low, Thai-style pavilion that is a better alternative than the beach. Don't miss their big "foam parties" on weekends.

Beach Road, P.O. Box 99, Pattaya 20260 (next to Montien Hotel). © **03842-8755.** Fax 03842-1673. www.hardrock hotels.net. 320 units. $125 superior double; $145 deluxe double; from $155 club rooms and suites. AE, MC, V. **Amenities:** 3 restaurants; Hard Rock Cafe with live rock music; huge outdoor lagoon-style pool; fitness center; spa w/massage, Jacuzzi, sauna, and steam; watersports equipment and activities; "Lil' Rock" club for kids; game room; tour desk; limousine service; "e-bar" Internet lounge; shopping arcade; salon; 24-hr. room service; babysitting; same-day laundry service/dry cleaning; nonsmoking rooms; executive-level rooms. *In room:* A/C, satellite TV, CD players, fridge, minibar, coffeemaker, hair dryer, safe, IDD phone.

Pattaya Marriott Resort & Spa 🎸🎸 Right in the center of Pattaya Beach and adjoining the Royal Garden Plaza shopping complex, you really can't get a better location than the Marriott. In the hotel's quiet courtyard garden and landscaped pool area you'd hardly know Pattaya City was just beyond the walls. Spacious balconied rooms have views of the gardens or the sea and are done in a tidy, upscale chain style with lots of nice little Thai touches. This resort makes for a great retreat full of all of the requisite creature comforts. The adjoining Royal Garden Plaza means access to fine dining, and entertainment and the hotel pool is the largest in Pattaya, a veritable oasis.

218 Beach Rd., Pattaya 20150, Chonburi. © **03841-2120.** Fax 03842-9926. 300 units. 6,000B–8,250B ($146–$201) double; from 17,000B ($415) suite. AE, DC, MC, V. **Amenities:** 3 restaurants; lounge; pool with swim-up bar; 2 lighted grass tennis courts; large fitness center; spa w/Jacuzzi, sauna, and steam; Thai herbal spa; watersports equipment/rentals; children's programs; game room; Ripley's Believe It Or Not Museum; Motion Master Theater; tour desk; limousine service; shopping mall with more than 50 shops; salon; 24-hr. room service; babysitting; same-day laundry service/dry cleaning; nonsmoking rooms; executive-level rooms. *In room:* A/C, satellite TV w/in-house movies, minibar, fridge, coffee/tea-making facilities, safe, IDD phone.

The Royal Cliff Beach Resort 🎸🎸🎸 Comprising the Royal Cliff Grand, The Royal Wing and Spa, and The Royal Cliff Resort (and Terrace), this large, luxurious compound provides a range of accommodation and is by far the best choice in Pattaya. Each property has its own charm. High-end Royal Cliff Grand and Royal Wing are the top choices and cater to the well-heeled business traveler. Everything is luxurious: from the columned public spaces, chandeliers, and fountains, to large and opulent guest rooms. The Grand's spacious rooms are set in a contemporary, scallop-shaped tower and have deluxe appointments like marble bathrooms with separate shower stalls and twin sinks. Classic furniture and coffered ceilings are tribute to the era of King Rama V, who inspired the Victoriana/Siam design. The Royal Club on the sixth floor boasts a private spa with massage, Jacuzzi, and sun deck.

The Royal Cliff Beach Hotel, the most affordable of the Royal Cliff properties, is Pattaya's top family resort. Rooms are spacious with bleached wood and pastel decor and large terraces, most with bay views. Two-bedroom suites are perfect for families.

Even the more modest rooms in this cliff-top perch look out over the bay of Pattaya, and the hotel amenities are without rival: a fine health club, pool, spa, and great dining, as well as an enormous convention center on the grounds. The Royal Cliff is far above the beach and far removed from busy Pattaya: quiet, luxurious, and welcoming.

353 Phra Tamnuk Rd., Pattaya, Chonburi 20150 (on cliff, south end of Pattaya Bay). ℭ 03825-0421. Fax 03825-0514. www.royalcliff.com. 1,072 units. $99–$159 range of deluxe double rooms; from $309 suite. AE, DC, MC, V. **Amenities:** Full facilities sharing with all Royal Cliff Beach Resort properties, including 10 restaurants; 6 bars (many with live music); 5 outdoor landscaped pools; golf course or nearby 3-hole putting green; 6 outdoor lighted tennis courts; large completely equipped fitness center with spa, sauna, steam, and massage; Jacuzzi; watersports equipment rental (catamaran for rent); concierge; tour desk; limousine service; business center; salon; 24-hr. room service; babysitting; same-day laundry/dry cleaning; nonsmoking rooms. *In room:* A/C, satellite TV, minibar, fridge, hair dryer, safe.

Sheraton Pattaya Resort ✺✺   New on the scene in 2005, the Sheraton is a luxury campus of terraced gardens and groovy pool nooks surrounded by stunning private villas, pavilions, and large hotel blocks. Spacious pavilion rooms, with large Jacuzzi tubs, comfy divans, and high-peaked private salas, or balconies, overlooking the sea are well worth the upgrade. A very romantic choice, with pools divided into separate nooks for privacy, and good dining options and a good activity desk meaning you don't even have to dip a toe into Pattaya far below. The resort is high on the hill above town, near the Royal Cliff (above).

437 Phra Tamnak Rd., Pattaya 20150. ℭ 03825-9888. Fax 03825-9899. www.sheraton.com/pattaya. 156 units. $140–$180 Deluxe; $210–$240 Pavilion; $510–$810 suite. **Amenities:** 3 restaurants (Fusion, Italian, Poolside); 2 bars; 3 outdoor pools; tennis courts; health club; Jacuzzi; bike rentals; Wireless Internet and DVD rentals; library and lounge; children's center; tour desk; car-rental desk; courtesy car or limo; 24-hour room service; massage; babysitting; laundry service; dry cleaning. *In room:* A/C, satellite TV, fridge, minibar, coffeemaker, hair dryer, safe, phone.

MODERATE

Cabbages & Condoms   A fun, inviting resort built by Khun Mechai and the same folks who support sustainable rural development and health education throughout Thailand (see their restaurants in both Bangkok and Chiang Rai). Rooms are cozy here, and the resort is a luxurious oasis in the far south of Pattaya, far from the maddening crowds and isolated on a quiet hilltop overlooking the sea. An atmospheric, affordable escape. There are fun wishing wells, a local herb garden, and you can even ride special exercise bikes designed to irrigate them.

366/11 Moo 12 Phra Tamnak 4 Road, Nongprue, Banglamung, Chonburi (south of town on the hilltop, not far from Royal Cliff). ℭ 03825-0556. Fax 03825-0034. 56 units. 3,500B–4,500B ($85–$110) double; from 5,800B ($141) 1- and 2-bedroom suites. AE, MC, V. **Amenities:** Restaurant; large outdoor pool; spa w/massage; tour desk; limited room service; laundry. *In room:* A/C, satellite TV, minibar, fridge.

Siam Bayview Hotel   Managed by the same people as the nearby Siam Bayview Resort (ℭ 03842-8678), a comparable property, larger and more removed on the south end of Pattaya, the Siam Bayview is set in a spacious garden at the town center and features some basic beachfront activities. But Bayview is more city hotel than resort, though, and rooms are bland but comfortable and convenient to in-town activities. Some rooms have balconies, but cheaper rooms with city views are not special—go for the seaview rooms on upper floors. Their hotels have landscaped pools as well as tennis, good dining, and a helpful staff.

Beach Rd., Pattaya, Chonburi 20260 (center of beach, between Sois 9 and 10). ✆ **03842-3871.** Fax 03842-3879. www.siamhotels.com. 270 units. 3,000B–4,500B ($73–$110) double; from 8,000B ($195) suite. AE, MC, V. **Amenities:** 3 restaurants; lounge; 2 outdoor pools; 2 lighted tennis courts; fitness center; tour desk; business center; limited room service; babysitting; same-day laundry service/dry cleaning. *In room:* A/C, satellite TV, minibar, fridge, coffeemaker, hair dryer, IDD phone.

INEXPENSIVE

Budget lodgings in Pattaya attract a rough clientele and can be pretty unpleasant, but you'll find a range starting as low as 400B ($9.75). In the center of it all, and each with counters for registering lady visitors, **Flipper Lodge Hotel** (✆ **03842-6401**) and nearby **Sunshine Hotel** (✆ **03842-9247**), both on Soi 8 not far from the beach, have clean and comfortable air-conditioned rooms starting at 800B ($20), accept credit cards, and offer just the basic services (each has a small pool). The **Sawasdee Pattaya** (367 M. Soi Dianna, Pattaya 2 Rd., Pattaya 20260; ✆ **03872-0563;** www.sawasdee-hotels.com) is another good budget choice near the city center.

WHERE TO DINE

Busy Pattaya is chockablock with small storefront bars and eateries. You'll find the big fast-food chains well represented (including two Starbucks along the beachfront road and a Subway Sandwich shop), and the Royal Garden Shopping Complex (south of town) as well as the large Big C Festival Center (on Pattaya 2 Rd., north end of town) support a number of very familiar restaurants. Local dining is best at open-air joints down any soi. Pattaya's mass influx of CSWs (Commercial Sex Workers) from Isan, the far northeast of Thailand, means that you can find good, authentic (i.e. fiery hot) Isan fare, including papaya salad, barbecued chicken with chili, and grilled pork, all eaten with sticky rice.

MODERATE

Benihana JAPANESE/AMERICAN   Most American readers are thinking, "Benihana? In Thailand?" Well, if you've had your fill of *tom yam* and pad thai, this place is a welcome respite. It has got all the fun of any Benihana's—teppanyaki grill displays performed by chefs who have as much humor as skill, and the food is just great. Come for a good time and a lot of laughs.

2nd Level, Royal Garden Plaza. ✆ **03842-5029.** Set menus 150B–500B ($3.65–$12). AE, DC, MC, V. Daily 11am–10pm.

Henry J. Bean's TEX-MEX   Part of the Amari resort complex, Henry J. Bean's is a big, busy bar and restaurant at beachside (on the very north end of the beachside strip). There are live bands nightly and the food is a delicious mix of good Western fare, burgers, steaks and fries, and good Tex-Mex of anything from flaming fajitas to tasty quesadillas. Good margaritas and a range of fine cocktails too.

Pattaya Beach Road (north end). ✆ **03842-8161.** Main courses 190B–350B ($4.65–$8.55) AE, MC, V. Daily 11am–1am.

PIC Kitchen ✦ THAI   Named for the Pattaya International Clinic PIC Hospital next door (don't worry, they're unrelated), PIC has a warm atmosphere of small Thai teak pavilions, both air-conditioned and open-air, with Thai-style, floor seating and romantic tables. Delicious and affordable Thai cuisine is served a la carte or in lunch and dinner sets. The spring rolls and deep-fried crab claws are mouthwatering. Other dishes come pan-fried, steamed, or charcoal-grilled, with spice added to taste. At night, groove to a live jazz band from 7pm to 1am.

Soi 5 Pattaya 2nd Road. (✆ **03842-8374**. 75B–320B ($1.85–$7.80). AE, DC, MC, V. Daily 8am–midnight.

Shere "E" Punjab NORTHERN INDIAN   An inviting little storefront right along the main beach road at town center, Shere "E" Punjab has candle-lit tables in air-conditioned comfort. They offer a range of northern Indian cuisine and tandoori grilled dishes. Everything is cooked to order with fresh ingredients, and everything is authentic, a far better choice than the faux-Western eateries in town.

216 Soi 11 Beach Road. (✆ **03842-0158**. Main courses 120B–280B ($2.95–$6.85). AE, MC, V. Daily noon–1am.

OUTDOOR ACTIVITIES IN PATTAYA
GOLF
The hills around Pattaya are known as the "Golf Paradise of the East," with many international-class courses in a short 40km (25-mile) radius of the city.

- **Bangphra International Golf Club,** 45 Moo 6, Tambon Bang Phra, Sri Racha, (✆ **03834-1149**), is the finest course in Pattaya, although it is a long drive (greens fees: weekdays 840B/$20; weekends 1,500B/$37).
- **Laem Chabang International Country Club,** 106/8 Moo 4 Tambon Bung, Sri Racha, (✆ **03837-2273**), is a 9-hole course designed by Jack Nicklaus with very dramatic scenery (greens fees: weekdays 1,500B/$37; weekends 2,500B/$61).
- **Siam Country Club,** 50 Tambol Poeng, Banglamung, (✆ **03824-9381;** Fax 03824-9387), is a short hop from Pattaya and believed to be one of the country's most challenging courses (greens fees: all days 1,100B/$27).

WATERSPORTS
Efforts at clean-up are ongoing, but the bay in Pattaya is still quite polluted. Sad that development ruined the one thing that drew travelers here in the first place. Beach sand is coarse, and swimming, if you dare, is best either at the very north of Pattaya Beach or a 15-minute drive south, over the mountain, to Jomtien Beach. The bay is full of boats ready to take you to **outlying islands** like Ko Khrok, Ko Lan, and Ko Sok for a day of private beach lounging or snorkeling starting at 500B ($12) per head on a full boat (more for a private charter). To far-flung Bamboo Island or Ko Man Wichai will cost you a bit more, some 2,000B ($49). **Paragliding** around the bay behind a motorboat is a popular beachfront activity and a 5-minute flight costs from 250B ($6).

Jomtien beach hosts **windsurfing** and **sea-kayaking;** boards and boats are rented along the beach for from 200B ($4.90) per hour.

Scuba diving is popular, and there are a few dive-sites near the islands just off-shore in Pattaya Bay, as well as Ko Si Chang to the north, once famous as the summer play-ground of foreign ambassadors to Siam during the 19th century, and Sattahip to the south, with diving to a depth of 40m (131 ft.). There are a number of good dive shops with PADI- and NAUI-certified instructors in the area. **Adventure Divers,** 219/56 Soi Yamato (✆ **03871-0899;** www.pattayadivers.com), is one of many PADI-certified companies offering daily trips and courses for all levels.

PATTAYA AFTER DARK
Pattaya is all flashing neon and blaring music down even the smallest *soi,* an assault on the senses. Places like the South Pattaya pedestrian area, "Walking Street," are lined

with open-air watering holes with bar girls luring each passerby: The nightlife finds you in this town with an imploring, "You, mister, where you go?" Go-go bars are everywhere and red-light "Bar Beer" joints are springing up as fast as local officials can close them down. The city is a larger version of Bangkok's Patpong, complete with "Boyz Town," a row of gay go-go clubs in south Pattaya. The same debauchery that brings so many to Pattaya is pretty sad in the light of day, though, when bleary-eyed revelers stumble around streets once glowing with neon, now bleak and strewn with garbage.

Sex for money in Pattaya is a simple and direct business. Pattaya's "physical" massage parlors are on Pattaya Second Road in northern Pattaya. Typically, dozens of girls wearing numbered buttons wait to be selected by clients, and then it is off to private massage rooms and negotiations for services. All-night companionship is a matter of a small payment to a club owner (a bar fine) and simple negotiations. Most hotels have security desks where girls must register with security guards before coming up to guest rooms (often for a fee). There's also a very active *Katoey* (transvestite) scene. Stories of laced drinks and theft (or worse) abound, and AIDS and other STDs are a concern, as in all of Thailand (See "Sex for Sale," in chapter 2.).

If the sex scene is not your thing, there are a few spots without the sleaze. **Hopf Brewery,** 219 Beach Rd. (✆ **03871-0650**), makes its own fine brand of suds, and their in-house Hopf Band plays everything from old Herb Alpert tunes to newer jazzy sounds. **Shenanigan's** is a fun Irish bar hangout at the Royal Garden Complex (near the Marriott), with the front entrance on Pattaya 2nd Road (✆ **03871-0641**); and **Henry J. Bean's** (on the beach near the Amari Hotel; ✆ **03842-8161;** see "Where to Dine") has a live band and a light, friendly atmosphere.

The town's campy cabaret shows are touristy good fun. Pattaya's most beautiful *Katoeys* (transsexuals) don sequined gowns and feather boas to strut their stuff for packed houses nightly. Both **Tiffany's** (464 Moo 9, 2nd Rd.; ✆ **03842-9642**) and **Alcazar** (78/14 Pattaya 2nd Rd., opposite Soi 5; ✆ **03841-0505**) have hilarious shows much like those in other tourist towns in Thailand.

2 Ban Phe & Ko Samet ⍟

220km (136 miles) E of Bangkok on Highway 3 via Pattaya, or 185km (115 miles) on Highway 3 via the Pattaya bypass. Ban Phe is 35km (22 miles) east of Rayong City.

Tiny Ko Samet first became popular with Thais from the poetry of Sunthon Phu, a venerated 19th-century author and Rayong native who set his best-known epic on Samet. The island is a national park (you'll pay 200B/$5 at all ferry landings), but with all the beachside lodging and resort development no one is quite sure what's being protected. Just 1km (⅔-mile) wide, the island is split by a rocky ridge.

Reaching Samet by ferry in the north end at Na Dan, the island's main port, it is a 10-minute walk south to Hat Sai Kaeo, or Diamond Beach, on the northeast cape, the island's most developed and crowded beach. From Diamond Beach, you can rent a motorbike to travel the bumpy, dirt roads, or go by *songtao* to any of the many small beach developments, most along the east coast: Ao Pai and Vong Deuan are popular choices and quite basic, though better than most (budget stops here are one step up from camping). Many bungalows on Ao Prao (on the west side of the island) and Vong Deuan on the east run direct ferries to their resorts from Ban Phe. Contact them directly or at booking offices near the ferry. It is best to arrive on a weekday to avoid the busy weekend rush, but it can be fun to join in with big groups of young Thai weekenders.

Ko Samet's peak season follows Pattaya—with July through October bringing fewer travelers, so bungalow prices are discounted accordingly. Weekends get busy, however, so discounts may not apply.

ESSENTIALS
GETTING THERE

By Bus   Buses leave Bangkok every hour between 5am and 7pm for the 3½-hour journey, departing from **Ekkamai,** Bangkok's Eastern Bus Terminal on Sukhumvit Road opposite Soi 63 (© **02391-2504**). The one-way trip to Rayong costs 120B ($2.95), and from there it is a 20B (50¢) shared songtao to Ban Phe and the ferry landing (some buses go directly to Ban Phe). From Pattaya, you'll have to flag down passing public buses from far out on the main road and they're often full, so you'll be standing (see the minibus option, below).

By Minibus   **Samet Island Tour** (109/22 Moo 10 Pratamnak Rd. Pattaya; © **03871-0676**) runs regular routes from Pattaya (trip time: 1 hr.; 300B/$7.30 round-trip). They also book affordable lodging at their Vong Deuan Resort, Malibu (see "Where to Stay" below). Private cars can also be arranged.

By Car   Take Highway 3 east from Bangkok along the longer, more scenic coastal route (about 3½–4 hr.), or the quicker route: via Highway 3 east to Pattaya, then Highway 36 to Rayong, then the coastal Highway 3 to Ban Phe (about 3 hr.).

GETTING TO KO SAMET

By Ferry   Connect by bus from central Rayong to the ferry pier at Ban Phe. From there, ferries leave for the island's northern ferry terminal at Na Dan, every half hour (trip time: 40 min.; 40B/$1) or when full. The first boat departs at 9:30am and the last at 5pm. Several agents at the pier in Ban Phe sell passage directly to Vong Deuan beach for as little as 50B/$1.20. Special boats to Ao Prao Resort can be booked at their dockside office in Ban Phe.

After arriving at the ferry terminal on the northern tip of Samet Island you can catch a *songtao* (pickup truck) to other beaches for between 10B and 50B (25¢–$1.20). There is one road on Samet connecting the main town, Samet Village, halfway down the eastern shore of the island to Vong Deuan. Beyond that you won't find more than footpaths, and you can rent cool scooters that have been upgraded with good suspension for off-road riding; on the weekends, they rent for 400B ($9.75) per day or 100B ($2.45 per hour).

FAST FACTS

Ko Samet has no banks or ATMs but any resort can change money. The post office is at the Naga Bar along the main road south of Diamond Beach. (See how laid-back this place is? The post office is in a bar.)

WHERE TO STAY

If you don't book ahead, have no fear; several travel agents and "helpful" locals hover at the Ban Phe pier with photo albums showing off their rooms to rent. With few exceptions, budget accommodations are basic, though rates are higher than at other "undeveloped" island resorts because food and water must be imported from the mainland. On the far southern tip of the island, keep an eye out for **Paradee** (© **02438-9771** in the busy weekend rush, but it can be fun to join in with big groups of young Thai weekenders.

Ko Samet's peak season follows Pattaya—with July through October bringing fewer travelers, so bungalow prices are discounted accordingly. Weekends get busy, however, so discounts may not apply.

ESSENTIALS
GETTING THERE

By Bus   Buses leave Bangkok every hour between 5am and 7pm for the 3½-hour journey, departing from **Ekkamai,** Bangkok's Eastern Bus Terminal on Sukhumvit Road opposite Soi 63 (© **02391-2504**). The one-way trip to Rayong costs 120B ($2.95), and from there it is a 20B (50¢) shared songtao to Ban Phe and the ferry landing (some buses go directly to Ban Phe). From Pattaya, you'll have to flag down passing public buses from far out on the main road and they're often full, so you'll be standing (see the minibus option, below).

By Minibus   Samet Island Tour (109/22 Moo 10 Pratamnak Rd. Pattaya; © **03871-0676**) runs regular routes from Pattaya (trip time: 1 hr.; 300B/$7.30 round-trip). They also book affordable lodging at their Vong Deuan Resort, Malibu (see "Where to Stay" below). Private cars can also be arranged.

By Car   Take Highway 3 east from Bangkok along the longer, more scenic coastal route (about 3½–4 hr.), or the quicker route: via Highway 3 east to Pattaya, then Highway 36 to Rayong, then the coastal Highway 3 to Ban Phe (about 3 hr.).

GETTING TO KO SAMET

By Ferry   Connect by bus from central Rayong to the ferry pier at Ban Phe. From there, ferries leave for the island's northern ferry terminal at Na Dan, every half hour (trip time: 40 min.; 40B/$1) or when full. The first boat departs at 9:30am and the last at 5pm. Several agents at the pier in Ban Phe sell passage directly to Vong Deuan beach for as little as 50B/$1.20. Special boats to Ao Prao Resort can be booked at their dockside office in Ban Phe.

After arriving at the ferry terminal on the northern tip of Samet Island you can catch a *songtao* (pickup truck) to other beaches for between 10B and 50B (25¢–$1.20). There is one road on Samet connecting the main town, Samet Village, halfway down the eastern shore of the island to Vong Deuan. Beyond that you won't find more than footpaths, and you can rent cool scooters that have been upgraded with good suspension for off-road riding; on the weekends, they rent for 400B ($9.75) per day or 100B ($2.45 per hour).

FAST FACTS

Ko Samet has no banks or ATMs but any resort can change money. The post office is at the Naga Bar along the main road south of Diamond Beach. (See how laid-back this place is? The post office is in a bar.)

WHERE TO STAY

If you don't book ahead, have no fear; several travel agents and "helpful" locals hover at the Ban Phe pier with photo albums showing off their rooms to rent. With few exceptions, budget accommodations are basic, though rates are higher than at other "undeveloped" island resorts because food and water must be imported from the mainland. On the far southern tip of the island, keep an eye out for **Paradee** (© **02438-9771** in

Bangkok; www.samedresorts.com), the island's newest and most upmarket destination, which was just completing construction at the time of this publication.

AO PRAO

This is the only beach on the west coast and home to the island's best accommodation. Ao Prao Resort (below) has a private, direct ferry, but you can also get there by pickup or motorbike from the public ferry at Na Dan.

Ao Prao Resort   Ao Prao is a collection of mid-range bungalows on a quiet hillside overlooking the sea on the only west-facing beach on the island. The resort offers good basic amenities, and the highest standard rooms are worth the outlay. They have direct connections from their office just north of the main ferry pier. Contact the resort directly for arrangements. **Le Vinara Cottages** (✆ **03864-4104**) is Ao Prao's more upscale, boutique sister property just next door. There's a pool and more luxurious bungalows start at 8,000B ($195). These are quaint little honeymoon retreats, and there is a small spa adjoining.

60 Moo 4 Tumbong Phe, Rayong 21160 (on the NW end of the island, best by direct boat, otherwise rough island road far from Diamond Beach and the ferry landing). ✆ **03861-6881**. Fax 03861-6885. 52 units. 5,200B–5,800B ($127–$141) deluxe; from 6,700B ($163) suite. MC, V. **Amenities:** Restaurant/bar; watersports rentals; tour desk; massage; laundry. *In room:* A/C, satellite TV, minibar, fridge.

HAT SAI KAEW/DIAMOND BEACH

Sai Kaew Beach Resort (✆ **01874-8081**) dominates Hat Sai Kaew, but there are any number of simple budget numbers, basic bungalows, starting at 600B ($15), as well as the biggest concentration of restaurants and bars. Nearby, on the north end of Diamond Beach, find **White Sand Resort** (✆ **03864-4000**), a popular place with Bangkokians on the weekend and often packed with revelers.

Just a short jaunt south of Diamond Beach, you'll reach Ao Phai; there, try **Ao Phai Hut** (✆ **03874-4075**) for cozy, rustic bungalows set on a hillside (from 500B/$12). Ao Phai is considerably more quiet and toned down than Diamond. Also check out **Silver Sand Resort** (✆ **06530-2417;** www.silversandresort.com) with small but very tidy bungalows done in white clapboards; they offer good services (dining, tours) and are right on the beach.

VONG DEUAN

This area is the most happenin' beach in Samet. Busy, with lots of bungalows and open-air eateries, Vong Deuan has a good vibe in the evening and is a fun party spot on the weekend. The beach is about halfway down the island and can be reached by ferry directly from Ban Phe for just 60B ($1.45) one-way (contact Samet Tour at Malibu Garden Resort below, or in Ban Phe look for the Chok Krisda Pier; ✆ **03865-1790**). If the bungalow resorts below are full, there are many other options, with bungalows starting at just 600B ($15).

Malibu Garden Resort   These clean concrete motel-style rooms are in a quiet, grassy compound just off the beach. There's a thatch dining pavilion, a small swimming pool, and little else: rooms are basic but clean, and most have air-conditioning and hot water. The staff is friendly as all get-out, and their in-house tour company, **Samet Island Tour,** can arrange direct transport and tours.

77 Vong Deuan Beach, Samet Island, Ban Phe, 21160 Rayong. ✆/Fax **03842-7277-8** or contact Samet Island Tour in Pattaya at ✆ **03871-0676**. www.malibu-samet.com. 74 units. 1,550B–3,000B ($38–$73) double with A/C.

Amenities: Restaurant; small pool; watersports rentals; boat transfer available; convenience shop; laundry. *In room:* No phone.

Vong Deuan Resort   Book ahead, because this one is popular and often full. Just simple, solid, wooden bungalows scattered among a sprawling, hillside grove of trees at beachside. They have all the basic services you could want.

Vong Deuan Beach (office near 7-Eleven in Ban Phe), P.O. Box 9, Ban Phe 21160. © **03864-4171**. 1,500B–3,500B ($37–$85). Cash only. 40 units. **Amenities:** Restaurant; tour desk; boat transfer available; convenience shop; laundry. *In room:* no phone.

WHERE TO DINE

All of the bungalows offer some sort of eating experience, mostly bland local food and beer, with some Western breakfast offerings. In the evenings on Vong Deuan beach, tables are set up under twinkling lights alongside big seafood barbecues brimming with the day's catch (your best bet). Try **Sea Horse.**

In Ao Pai just south of Diamond Beach, **Naga Bar** is a popular hangout and serves a fine menu of local eats and serves good baked goods. **Jep's Bungalows** (© **03864-4112**), just south of Naga Bar, has a fairly decent menu, a good beer selection, and a bakery that has surprisingly fresh goods in the mornings. Most bungalows on Samet have their own dining areas for inexpensive, fresh seafood (don't miss the locally caught squid and cuttlefish, which are barbecued on skewers), and standard Thai rice and noodle dishes. All restaurants on the island turn into all-night party affairs at beachside (depending on the crowd), and Vong Deuan Beach in particular hosts a good little selection of cozy bars with floor seating and mats out on the sand.

3 Chanthaburi Province

Travelers heading east to beautiful Ko Chang (see "Trat & Ko Chang," below) will pass through Chanthaburi province and its capital city, Chanthaburi Town (Muang Chan). This region is known for its gem mines (a lucrative export industry) and tropical fruit production. Durian, custard apple, longan, and rambutan are grown in large plantations, but small family farms are much in evidence. Don't be startled by the roadside 7.9m-high (26-ft.) durian sculpture, or the many watermelon and fruit stands alongside the highway.

Chanthaburi Town (Muang Chan) is a large city built on both sides of the Chanthaburi River. In central Taksin Park, there's a statue of King Taksin on horseback, surrounded by sword-brandishing troops, to commemorate his victory over Burmese invaders in 1767, after the fall of Ayutthaya. The city's main avenue is Tha Chalab Road. The taxi stand and bus station (to Trat or Bangkok) are just west of the Chanthaburi Hotel on this street; both flank the central produce market and night market.

The 17,000-hectare (42,000-acre) **Namtok Philu National Park** is a popular day trip from Chanthaburi, as is **Laem Sadet,** a stunning beach and rocky cape located some 35km (22 miles) southwest of the city. Both sites can be visited by private car or arranged taxi only.

Gem Shopping is one of the few draws to commercial Chanthaburi, and some say there are bargains to be found on Gem Street, near the main market.

WHERE TO STAY

There's no reason to spend the night in Chanthaburi town, but if you must, **K. P. Grand** (35/200–201 Trirat Rd.; © **03932-3201**) is by far the most modern facility in town, with comfortable rooms starting at 1,250B ($30). It is a typical provincial capital business hotel, simple and comfortable enough.

4 Trat & Ko Chang

400km (248 miles) E of Bangkok

Trat Province is the gateway to the tranquil, unspoiled acres of Ko Chang National Park, 52 heavily wooded islands, most popular of which is Ko Chang Island, which has developed into a major international resort locale. Ko Chang is scenically beautiful, and offers daytime adventures in the mountainous interior, trips by elephant or jeep, as well as good scuba and snorkeling, and long sandy beaches. Despite limits on construction because of the island's national-park status, large-scale development is expected, so get there before the place has its own Chaweng Beach (a la Koh Samui) or Patong (a la Phuket).

ESSENTIALS
GETTING THERE
By Plane   An increasingly popular option, **Bangkok Airways** (© 02265-5678) has daily flights between Bangkok and Trat. Minibus transfers to and from the airport in Trat and Ko Chang start at about 250B ($6.10), but if you are booking with a specific resort, be sure to ask about any inclusions or special arrangements.

By Public Bus   There are numerous daily departures from Bangkok's Eastern or **Ekkamai Bus Terminal** to Trat (© 02391-2504; trip time: 5–6 hr.; 190B/$4.65). From Pattaya, you'll have to flag down west-bound buses along Sukhumvit Road and it is a 3½-hour trip (Pattaya tour companies can arrange direct minivans).

By Car   Take Highway 3 east from Bangkok to Chonburi, then Highway 344 southeast to Klaeng (bypassing Pattaya and Rayong), then the coastal Highway 3 east through Chanthaburi and south to Trat (about 5 hr.).

GETTING TO THE ISLAND FROM TRAT
From Trat you'll hop a shared *songtao* (pickup) to the pier at Ao Thammachat, Center Point, or Laem Ngop for just 30B (75¢). Seven ferries depart Ao Thammachat daily from 7am to 7pm (trip time, 30 minutes; 30B/75¢), and land at Ao Sapparos ferry terminal on Ko Chang. Less frequent boats leave from Center Point Pier (50B/$1.20) and Laem Ngop and connect with Ko Chang at Dan Kao Cabana Pier just a few clicks east of Ao Sapparos in the north end of the island. From wherever you land on Ko Chang you can hop a *songtao* to your destination starting at 40B ($1) for a 15-minute shared ride (to White Sand Beach). Negotiate a rate for a private car with taxi touts, but don't pay much more than 200B ($4.90) from the ferry pier to your resort. Touts from the many bungalows will offer free rides if you stay (or just look) at their bungalows. If you are booking with one of the larger resorts, ask about affordable minivan pickup from either the airport or one of the island piers.

VISITOR INFORMATION
The **TAT** has an office in Trat (Moo 1 Trat-Laem Ngop Rd.; © 03959-7259) and provides information about the nearby islands. On Ko Chang, look for *Koh Chang Trat and the Eastern Islands,* a free local advertising circular with good maps and info.

ORIENTATION

Ko Chang, Thailand's second largest island after Phuket, is the anchor of the 52-island Mu Ko Chang National Park. Thickly forested hills rise from its many rocky bays, forming a swaying hump reminiscent of a sleeping elephant (*chang* means elephant). Pineapple and coconut palms dominate the landscape, with a few scattered fishing villages and sparsely populated islands. Cambodia is visible from the eastern shore. Most of the island's resort development is on the west coast. **Hat Sai Khao (White Sand Beach)** is the closest and most popular of the western beaches, with the majority of Ko Chang's bungalow housing set in a narrow ribbon along its kilometer- (⅔-mile) long, fine-sand strand. A 10-minute ride south is (**Hat) Khlong Phrao Beach** with a number of resorts, and further south is **Kai Be Beach.** Furthest south on the west side of the island is **Bangbao Fishing Village,** a popular spot for dinner or setting off on boat tours and diving trips. On a map it looks like you could drive around the island, but the southern end of the island is mountainous jungle. There are a number of waterfalls and vantage points on the east side of the island, but you'll have to drive all the way around.

WHERE TO STAY IN TRANG

If you're arriving in the late evening and get stranded in Trat, the **Muang Trad Hotel** is at 4 Sukhumvit Road (© **03951-1091**), 1 block south of the bus terminal, and has 144 very basic rooms: A double with fan costs 450B ($11) and 650B ($16) for a double with air-conditioning. They accept MasterCard and Visa.

WHERE TO STAY ON KO CHANG

There are more and more large resorts on Ko Chang, and the best are of the self-contained destination variety (you don't have to go anywhere but the beach). Dining is best at your resort of choice, but White Sand Beach in particular hosts lots of little open-air joints, and fresh seafood from Bang Bao pier in the far south is tops.

HAD SAI KHAO (WHITE SAND BEACH)

The busiest beach area on Ko Chang, White Sand is still one of the best beaches, with acres of wide open, you guessed it, white sand, shade trees slung with hammocks, and lots of beach activity. That means pesky touts and salesman on one hand, and lots of good services (waitresses, even) on the other.

Expensive

Aiyapura ⚐   Just a short ride from the pier on the far north end of the island, Aiyapura sits on its own little isolated peninsula just to the north of White Sand Beach. The tidal flats out front aren't particularly spectacular, but the resort offers a great selection of very cozy, atmospheric rooms and bungalows set on a cool hillside campus (they have golf carts to shuttle you around). The pool villas and suites are absolutely over-the-top, large and luxuriant, and what smaller wooden bungalows lack in size and over-the-top amenities they make up for in pure charm. A good, romantic getaway and very self-contained with fine dining options, a cozy pool area, and good options for local touring.

29 Moo 3 Klong Son Beach, Ko Chang Island District, Trat 23170. © **03955-5119**. Fax 03955-5118. www.aiyapura. com. 84 units. 5,800B–8,000B ($141–$195) superior/deluxe double; from 9,000B–16,000B ($220–$390) villas. MC, V. **Amenities:** 2 restaurants (Thai, seafood/BBQ); pool bar; outdoor pool; small fitness center; small spa pavilion; Jacuzzi; bike rentals; tour desk; car-rental available; salon; limited room service; massage; laundry service. *In room:* A/C, satellite TV, fridge, minibar, safe, IDD phone.

Moderate

Banpu   Atmospheric bungalows, casual open-air *salas* for dining and relaxing, a small pool, a friendly staff, and good, basic services, as well as a central location on busy White Sand Beach means that Banpu is still one of the best choices on the island. Free-standing bungalow rooms have a campy, Catskills holiday feel, but are quite large with fine bamboo ceilings and rustic island touches in local material (some are a bit musty though, so check first). Right in the heart of White Sand Beach.

9/11 Moo 4, White Sand Beach, Ko Chang 23120 (on the west coast, just a short ride from any ferry pier). *C* **03955-1234**. Fax 03955-1237. 35 units. 1,500B–2,500B ($37–$61) double in hotel block; 2,000B–3,500B ($49–$85) double freestanding bungalow; from 5,000B ($122) suite. AE, MC, V. **Amenities:** Restaurant; small outdoor pool; watersports equipment rentals; tour desk; laundry. *In room:* A/C, TV, minibar, fridge, safe.

Mac Resort   Less "resort" than "beachside mini-hotel," Mac Resort is a good, centrally located budget option on White Sand Beach. Rooms are set in a simple, tidy hotel block around a small central pool. Some units have good sea views or overlook the pool. Friendly staff.

7/3 Moo 4 White Sand Beach, Ko Chang 23170. *C* **03955-1124**. Fax 03955-125. www.mac-resorthotel.com. 24 units. 1,700B–4,500B ($41–$110). MC, V. **Amenities:** Restaurant; outdoor pool; watersports equipment rental; car and motorbike rental; tour desk; laundry service. *In room:* A/C, TV, fridge, minibar, phone.

KLONG PRAO & KAI BAE BEACH

Just south of White Sand Beach, Klong Prao is named for the narrow canal *(klong)* that connects with the island interior; Kai Be is just a hitch south of Klong Prao. The beaches are of coarser sand, but still a fine place to dip your toes and swim. There are lots of budget services along this strip (motorbike rentals, open-air restaurants, and cafes, etc.) and more development to come.

Expensive
Amari Emerald Cove Resort *GG*   The best of Ko Chang's resorts, the Amari Emerald Cove is a study in style and comfort. Three-story room blocks form a quiet courtyard around the hotel's long, luxurious seaside pool and good central dining venues. Rooms are simple and elegant, in rosewood and tile with silk hangings and local artwork, the most civilized going with large, well-appointed bathrooms and cozy balcony spaces, many overlooking the sea. The sandy beach is inviting and, though not private, usually very quiet. Their Thai restaurant, *Just Thai,* serves delicious local fare tempered to the Western palate, their Italian venue is the real deal, and the resort covers all the bases with a "can do" spirit to service, efficient and helpful. Their lobby lounge area rocks late into the evening with a raucous Philippine band.

88/8 Moo 4, Tambol Ko Chang 23170. *C* **03955-2000**. Fax 03955-2001. www.amari.com. 165 units. $170–$396 superior/deluxe double; from $350 suite. **Amenities:** 3 restaurants (international, Thai, Italian); 2 bars; large seaside pool; health club; spa; Jacuzzi; sauna; bike rentals; tour desk; car-rental desk; courtesy car or limo; business center limited room service; massage; babysitting; laundry service. *In room:* A/C, satellite TV, fridge, minibar, coffeemaker, hair dryer, safe, phone.

Panviman *G*   Like its sister resort on Kok Pha Ngan, the Panviman is hard to get to but quite cozy. Connected by a rutted track from the main road, the resort's rooms are set in high-peaked, Thai-style buildings with arching *naga* roofs on the spacious, manicured grounds at seaside, and the pool is a beautiful little meander flanked on one side by a casual bar and the resort's fine dining venue. Rooms are tidy affairs of tile and teak, each with canopy bed, large sitting area, balcony, and large stylish bathrooms. Bathrooms have huge tubs and, get this, a small waterfall. It is not a private beach, but the resort is far south of central White Sand Beach, so even in high season you might have a vast stretch of sand to yourself. Dining is tops, tasty European and Thai dishes served in their open-air pavilion overlooking the sea. Traditional massage is available in a lovely old teak building at seaside.

8/15 Klong Prao Beach, Ko Chang Trat 23120 (a short ride south of White Sand Beach on the west coast of the island). ℂ 03955-1290 or 02910-8660 in Bangkok. Fax 03955-1283. 50 units. 5,000B–6,000B ($122–$146) double. MC, V. **Amenities:** Restaurant; bar; outdoor pool; fitness center; Jacuzzi; watersports equipment rentals; car rental; tour desk; transfer services; Internet; limited room service; massage; laundry service. *In room:* A/C, satellite TV, minibar, fridge, coffeemaker, safe, IDD phone.

Moderate

Ko Chang Resort One of the oldest developments, Ko Chang resort is recently renovated and has both free-standing bungalows (of varying size and quality) as well as more modern hotel-block rooms. Resort accommodation is clean but not particularly luxurious. The beach is the attraction, and there are good shady spots in the sand as well as a tidy little pool. There's good in-house dining and helpful tour services. Spring for the beachfront bungalows with delightful verandas and sea views, and you'll have arrived.

Just south of White Sand Beach (Bangkok office: 118 Viphavadee-Rungsit Rd.). www.kohchangresortandspa.com. ℂ 02277-5256. 126 units. 1,900B–2,800B ($46–$68) double. MC, V. **Amenities:** Restaurant; outdoor pool; some watersports equipment; tour desk; laundry service. *In room:* A/C, TV, minibar, no phone.

HAT THA NAM (LONELY BEACH) & BANG BAO PIER

At the far southern end of the west coast Ko Chang Road, below are just a few of the many far-flung resorts popping up here and there.

Bhumiyama Beach Resort Quite far to the south along Ko Chang's busy west coast, in an area popular for budget accommodations called "Lonely Beach," Bhumiyama is a cozy mid-range resort popular with European groups. Rather uninspired blocky hotel rooms are set in a lush little garden area around a small but inviting central pool. Rooms have terra-cotta tile, most with balcony, and best are the freestanding bungalows nearest the beach.

Tah Nam (Lonely) Beach, Ko Chang. ℂ 01860-4623. Bangkok office: 439 Soi Kaewfar, Sipraya Rd., Bangrak; ℂ 02266-4388. Fax 02266-4389. www.bhumiyama.com. 46 units. 3,200B–3,500B ($78–$85) superior room; 3,600B–4,700B ($88–$115) bungalows. MC, V. **Amenities:** Restaurant; outdoor pool; Jacuzzi; watersports rentals; tour desk; laundry service. *In room:* A/C, TV, fridge, minibar, phone.

Nirvana Resort About as far off the track as you can get in Ko Chang, little Nirvana is all the way at the southern tip of the island near Bang Bao pier. This simple bungalow resort has a high standard of rustic, stylish rooms, a small restaurant, and two inviting pools overlooking the pier and the beach. Popular for honeymooners, the place has chic style and nice decor throughout. A good, simple escape. Nirvana? That is up to you. Dig the free wireless at poolside.

12/4-5 Moo 1 Bangbao, Ko Chang. ℂ 03955-8061. Fax 03955-8065. www.nirvanakohchang.com. 11 units. $90–$115 bungalow; $116–$140 1-bedroom bungalow; $179–$231 2-bedroom bungalow. V, MC. **Amenities:** Restaurant and bar; 2 outdoor pools; watersports equipment rentals; tour desk; laundry service. *In room:* A/C; TV; fridge, minibar; IDD phone.

DINING

The best dining options are at your resort of choice; the likes of the Amari, Panviman, and Aiyapura resorts (see above) all offer great in-house dining. None of Ko Chang's freestanding restaurants really stands out. At the center of White Sand Beach, look for second story **Sfizioso** (7/33 Moo 4, White Sand Beach; ℂ 09587-8527), which

8

Southern Peninsula:
The East Coast & Islands

Thailand's slim Malay peninsula extends 1,250km (775 miles) south from Bangkok to the Malaysian border at Sungai Kolok. The towns of Cha Am and the royal retreat of Hua Hin are just a short hop south of Bangkok, and the ancient temples of Phetchaburi, the last outpost of the Khmer Empire, are a good day trip from there. Passing through coastal towns like Prachuap Kiri Khan and Chumphon, heading further south you come to Surat Thani, the jumping-off point for islands in the east: Koh Samui, Ko Pha Ngan, and Ko Tao. If the beach resorts of Phuket dominate the tourist landscape on the west coast, so too Koh Samui, a heavily developed resort island in the Gulf of Siam,

dominates the east. Nearby Ko Pha Ngan, famed for its wild full-moon parties, is gaining prominence as a rustic resort destination, as is Ko Tao for its access to some of Thailand's best dive sites.

With its fine islands and beaches, the Gulf of Siam is the Thai paradise of legend and, whether armed with little money and lots of time or lots of money and little time (it's always one or the other, no?), there's an adventure and a little bit of heaven for everyone among palm-draped beaches, lacy coral reefs, or in small mainland towns, Muslim fishing villages, and even Buddhist temples that welcome foreign spiritual seekers.

1 Hua Hin/Cha-Am

Hua Hin is 265km (164 miles) S of Bangkok; 223km (138 miles) N of Chumphon
Cha-Am is 240km (149 miles) S of Bangkok; 248km (154 miles) N of Chumphon

Hua Hin and Cha-Am, neighboring towns on the Gulf of Thailand, are together the country's oldest resort area. Developed in the 1920s as a relaxing getaway for Bangkok's elite, the beautiful seaside of "Thailand's Riviera" was a mere 3 or 4 hours' journey from the capital by train, thanks to the southern railway's completion in 1916. The royal family was the first to embrace these two small fishing villages as the perfect location for both summer vacations and health retreats. In 1924, King Vajiravudh (Rama VI) built the royal Mareukatayawan Palace amid the tall evergreens that lined these stretches of golden sand. At the same time, the Royal Hua Hin Golf Course opened as the first course in Thailand. As Bangkok's upper classes began building summer bungalows along the shore, the State Railways opened the Hua Hin Railway Hotel for tourists, which stands today as the Hotel Sofitel Central, and to this day the King of Thailand spends much of his time at his regal residence just north of town (note the constant presence of Coast Guard cutters and battleships just off shore).

When Pattaya, on Thailand's eastern coast, hit the scene in the 1960s, it lured vacationers away from Hua Hin and Cha-Am with promises of inexpensive holidays with spicier nightlife. Since then, Pattaya's tourism has grown to a riotous, red-light din, and quiet Hua Hin and Cha-Am are a good alternative for relaxing getaways and health retreats. The clean sea and beaches support some unique resorts, and there are a few good day trips in the area.

Plan your trip for the months between November and May for the most sunshine and least rain, but note that from about mid-December to mid-January, Hua Hin and Cha-Am reach peak levels, and bookings should be made well in advance (at a higher rate). Low season means more rain, but rarely all day long.

ESSENTIALS
GETTING THERE
By Plane   While there is a domestic airport in Hua Hin, no airlines have serviced it for years.

By Train   Both Hua Hin and Cha-Am are reached via the train station in Hua Hin. Ten trains make the daily trek from Bangkok's **Hua Lampong Railway Station** (© **02223-7010** or 1690). For an idea of the fare, a second-class seat from Bangkok to Hua Hin is 262B ($6.40). The trip is just over 4 hours.

The **Hua Hin Railway Station** (© **03286-1505**) is at the tip of Damnoenkasem Road, which slices through the center of town straight to the beach. Pickup truck taxis (*songtao*) and tuk-tuks wait outside to take you to your hotel starting at 50B ($1.20).

By Bus/Minibus   Going by road is the best choice from Bangkok to Hua Hin. Best are the minibuses that connect with Central Cha-Am and Hua Hin. You can arrange **minivan connections** from your hotel in the city, or go to the busy traffic circle at the base of the **Victory Monument** (a stop on the BTS Skytrain) and look for the minivans that depart when full throughout the day, which cost just 140B ($3.40) to Hua Hin.

Regular buses depart from **Bangkok's Southern Bus Terminal** (© **02434-7192**) every 20 minutes from 5am to 10pm (130B/$3.20). There are also 5 daily buses to Cha-Am between 5am and 2pm (113B/$2.75).

Buses from Bangkok arrive in **Hua Hin** at the air-conditioned bus station (© **03251-1230**) on Srasong Road, 1 block north of Damnoenkasem Road. From here it is easy to find a *songtao* or tuk-tuk to take you to your destination. The **Cha-Am bus station** is on the main beach road (© **03242-5307**).

By Car   From Bangkok, take Route 35, the Thonburi–Paktho Highway, southwest and allow 2 to 4 hours, depending on traffic.

SPECIAL EVENTS
The annual **King's Cup Elephant Polo Tournament** comes to Hua Hin each September. Teams from as far away as Europe and Sri Lanka play three-a-side polo, much like equine polo only with longer mallets on a smaller field. Sponsored by the **TAT** at **Anantara Resort & Spa** (© **03252-0250;** see "Where to Stay," below), the event raises money for the National Elephant Institute. There are parades and events, but the pachyderms out on the pitch are the highlight.

ORIENTATION
Despite all the tourist traffic, Hua Hin is easy to navigate. The main artery, Petchkasem Road, runs parallel to the waterfront about 4 blocks inland. The wide Damnoenkasem Road cuts through Petchkasem and runs straight to the beach. On

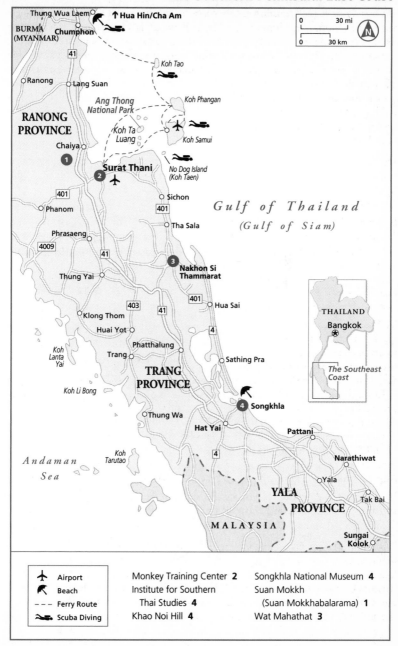

0   30 mi

0   30 km

Thung Wua Laem ○
BURMA
(MYANMAR)   **Chumphon** ○
↑ **Hua Hin/Cha Am**

41

○ Ranong   ○ Lang Suan

Koh Tao

*Ang Thong
National Park*

Koh Phangan

**RANONG
PROVINCE**

*Koh Ta
Luang*

Koh Samui

Chaiya ○   ❶

Surat Thani
❷ ✈

*No Dog Island
(Koh Taen)*

○ Sichon

401

○ Phanom

401

○ Tha Sala

Gulf of Thailand
(Gulf of Siam)

Phrasaeng ○

4009

41

❸

**Nakhon Si
Thammarat**

Thung Yai ○

401 ○ Hua Sai

403   41

Klong Thom ○

4

Huai Yot ○

Phatthalung ○

*Koh
Lanta
Yai*

Trang ○

○ Sathing Pra

**TRANG
PROVINCE**

Koh Li Bong

❹ ☂ **Songkhla**

○ Thung Wa

Hat Yai ○

○ Pattani

*Andaman
Sea*

*Koh
Tarutao*

4

Narathiwat
○

○ Yala

**YALA
PROVINCE**

○ Tak Bai

MALAYSIA

**Sungai
Kolok** ○

THAILAND
Bangkok
✪

*The Southeast
Coast*

✈ Airport
☚ Beach
- - - Ferry Route
🌊 Scuba Diving

Monkey Training Center **2**
Institute for Southern
   Thai Studies **4**
Khao Noi Hill **4**

Songkhla National Museum **4**
Suan Mokkh
   (Suan Mokkhabalarama) **1**
Wat Mahathat **3**

the north side of Damnoenkasem toward the waterfront, you'll find a cluster of guest-houses, restaurants, shopping, and nightspots lining the narrow lanes. Across Petchkasem to the west are the bus terminals, railway station, and night market.

Smaller Cha-Am is a 25-minute drive north of Hua Hin along Petchkasem Road. Ruamchit Road, also known as Beach Road, hugs the shore and is lined with shops, restaurants, hotels, and motels. Cha-Am's resorts line the 8km (5-mile) stretch of beach that runs south from the village toward Hua Hin.

GETTING AROUND

By *Songtao* *Sontaos* follow regular routes in Hua Hin, passing the railway station and bus terminals at regular intervals. Flag one down that's going in your direction. Fares range from 10B to 20B (25¢–50¢) within town, while stops at outlying resorts will be up to 50B ($1.20). Trips between Hua Hin and Cha-Am cost between 100B and 200B ($2.45–$4.90).

By Tuk-Tuk   Tuk-tuks rides are negotiable, as always, but expect to pay as little as 20B (50¢) for a ride within town.

By Motorcycle Taxi   Within each town, motorcycle taxi fares begin at 20B (50¢). The taxi drivers, identifiable by colorful numbered vests, are a good way to get to your resort if you're in Cha-Am after hours (about 100B/$2.45).

By Samlor   Trishaws, or *samlors,* can be hired for short distances in town (from 20B/50¢). You can also negotiate an hourly rate.

By Car or Motorcycle   **Avis** has a desk at both the Hotel Sofitel Central in Hua Hin (© 03251-2021) and the Dusit Resort and Polo Club in Cha-Am (© 3252-0008). **Budget** has an office at the Grand Hotel (© 03251-4220). Self-drive rates start at 1,500B ($37). Call ahead to reserve at least 1 day in advance. A cheaper alternative is to rent from one of the smalltime agents near the beach on Damnoenkasem Road. A Suzuki Caribian goes for around 1,000B ($24) per day. 100cc motorbikes are available for 200B ($4.90) per day.

On Foot   Hua Hin is a labyrinth of busy streets and narrow alleys with little guest-houses, colorful local bars, and a wide assortment of casual eating venues. Most everything in town is accessible on foot.

VISITOR INFORMATION

The **Hua Hin Tourist Information Center** (© 03251-1047 or 03253-2433) is in the center of town, tucked behind the city shrine at the corner of Damnoenkasem and Petchkasem roads. Opening hours are from 8:30am to 4:30pm daily. In Cha-Am, the **TAT office** (© 03247-1005 or 03247-1006) is inconveniently located on the corner of Petchkasem and Narathip roads (the main Beach Road is about 1km/⅔-mile away). There are lots of free local event calendars and maps.

FAST FACTS

IN HUA HIN   All major banks are along Petchkasem Road to the north of Dam-noenkasem, and there are many money changers throughout the town. The **main post office** (© 03251-1350) is on Damnoenkasem Road near the Petchkasem intersection. Both Hua Hin and Cha-Am have Internet cafes along the more-traveled shopping streets. The **Hua Hin Hospital** (© 03252-0371) is located in the north of town along Petchkasem Road. Call the **Tourist Police** for either town at © 03251-5995.

IN CHA-AM   Banks are centered along Petchkasem Road, and the post office is on Beach Road. The **Thonburi Cha-Am Hospital** (© **03243-3903**) is off Narathip Road. Internet access is available in a few places along Beach Road.

WHAT TO SEE & DO

The stunning Khmer-style temples of **Phetchaburi** (see "Side Trips from Hua Hin & Cha-Am" at the end of this section) are the most significant cultural sites near Hua Hin and Cha-Am, but really what attracts so many to this area is what first attracted the Thai royal family: proximity to the capital, lovely beaches, watersports, and activities like golf and scuba, or even horseback riding. Hua Hin supports fine resorts with services from great spa treatments to dining, golf, and many sporting activities.

One of the most important in-town sites is the 80-year-old **Sofitel Hotel** originally built for Thai royals and their guests. Visitors are welcome to wander the lush grounds amid the grand colonial buildings and fun topiary (don't miss the giant elephant). **High Tea at the Sofitel** is perhaps the most high-brow cultural thing you could do in Hua Hin and highly recommended. For just 370B ($9) you can sip tea and nibble scones and desserts from a splendid array and get downright lazy and colonial in a quaint garden-side area, the lobby of the original hotel. The buffet and atmosphere are well worth it. Daily 3:30pm until 5pm.

Don't miss the town's **Night Market** (on Decha Nuchit Rd. on the northern end at town center), which is busy from dusk to late with small food stalls and vendors. There are also lots of shops in and around the central beachfront, and Hua Hin, not unlike most resort areas in Thailand, is a good place to get that suit made or buy your brother a Buddha.

The big Buddha and viewpoint from spiky **Khao Takiap,** or the **Chopstick Peaks,** a small cape just a few clicks south of Hua Hin (hop a tuk-tuk for 50B/$1.20) is a pretty area worth a visit. Also near Hua Hin is the **Mareukatayawan Palace,** or the Teakwood Mansion (daily 8:30am–4pm, free admission). Built and designed in 1924 by King Rama VI, it served for many years as the royal summer residence, and is now open to the public.

Horseback riding is popular along the busy beaches at Hua Hin. Sturdy, spirited ponies can be rented by the hour (from 500B/$12) for either guided rides, with a groom holding the horse's reins, or free riding along with a mounted guide. If you're interested, take a walk down to the beach and you'll be besieged by riders eager to rent their horses, almost like cowboy tuk-tuk drivers.

See "Side Trips from Hua Hin & Cha-Am" at the end of this section for trips to natural sites.

WHERE TO STAY IN HUA HIN
VERY EXPENSIVE

Chiva-Som International Health Resort 🐟🐟🐟   Chiva-Som is a new beginning for many. One of the finest high-end health resorts in the region, this ultrapeaceful campus is a sublime collection of handsome pavilions, bungalows, and central buildings dressed in fine teak and sea-colored tiles nestled in landscaped grounds just beyond a pristine beach. Fine accommodation aside, what brings so many to Chiva-Som are their spa programs: From Chi Gong to chin-ups, muscle straining to massage, a stay at Chiva-Som is a chance to escape the workaday world and focus on the development of body and mind. Leave the kids at home, turn-off the cellphone, and change your suit for loose-fitting cotton because, whether just to relax or to start a new chapter in life, a visit to Chiva-Som is proactive. Upon check-in, you'll fill out an extensive survey, have a brief medical check, and meet with a counselor who can tailor a program to fit your needs, goals, budget, or package you have booked (there is a wide range). From there, guests might focus on early-morning yoga, stretching and tough workouts, or go for gentle massages, aromatherapy, even isolation chambers and past-life regression workshops. The choices are many, and personal trainers, staff, and facilities are unmatched in the region.

The resort's spa cuisine is not all granola and oats, but simple, healthy fare, and there is a nice bond that develops between guests and staff in weekly barbecues and frequent mocktail parties. The spa treatments are fantastic: don't pass up their signature Chiva-Som Massage. Day spa visitors welcome. It all comes with a high price tag, but it is worth it.

73/4 Petchkasem Rd., Hua Hin, 77110 Thailand (5-min. drive south of Hua Hin). ✆ **03253-6536.** Fax 03251-1615. www.chivasom.com. 57 units. All double rates are quoted per person. Contact the resort directly about spa and health packages. 13,800B ($337) ocean-view double; 16,000B ($390) pavilion; from 24,000B ($585) suite. Nightly rate includes 3 spa cuisine meals per day, health and beauty consultations, daily massage, and participation in fitness and leisure activities. Contact the resort about other packages. AE, DC, MC, V. **Amenities:** 2 restaurants; 1 ozonated indoor swimming pool and 1 outdoor swimming pool; golf course nearby; amazing fitness center w/personal trainer and exercise classes; his-and-hers spas w/steam and hydrotherapy treatments, massage, beauty treatments, floatation, medical advisement; watersports equipment; bike rental; library; concierge; tour desk; limousine service; salon; 24-hr. room service; same-day laundry service/dry cleaning; nonsmoking rooms. *In room:* A/C, satellite TV, minibar, fridge, safe, IDD phone.

EXPENSIVE

Anantara Resort & Spa ✸✸   A series of elegantly designed Thai-style pavilions usher you through the public areas at this "village" just north of Hua Hin. A lovely Kaliga tapestry hangs prominently in the open-air sala-style lobby, which is tastefully decorated with ornately carved teak wooden lanterns, warm wood floors, and oversize furniture with Thai cushions. The Lagoon is an area of teak pavilions surrounded by lily ponds, and from the hotel's most luxurious rooms you can hear chirping frogs and watch buzzing dragonflies from wide balconies. Other rooms cluster around a manicured courtyard. Consistent with the lobby, rooms are furnished Thai style with teak-and-rattan furniture. Superior rooms have a garden view and deluxe rooms overlook the sand and sea. Beach terrace rooms have large patios perfect for private barbecues. Junior Suite rooms have enormous aggregate bathtubs that open to guest rooms by a sliding door. Fine dining options are many, and the resort's spa is large and luxurious. The Anantara holds the annual Elephant Polo in Hua Hin, an event gaining worldwide attention.

43/1 Petchkasem Beach Rd., Hua Hin 77110. ✆ **03252-0250.** Fax 03252-0259. www.anantara.com. 197 units. 6,800B–7,600B ($166–$185) double; 8,400B ($205) terrace double; suite from 9,000B ($220). AE, DC, MC, V. **Amenities:** 4 restaurants; lounge; outdoor pool with children's pool; outdoor lighted tennis courts; fitness center; spa w/sauna, steam, massage; Jacuzzi; watersports equipment and instruction; bike and motorcycle rental; children's playground; concierge; tour desk; car-rental desk; limousine service; shopping arcade; salon; 24-hr. room service; babysitting; same-day laundry service/dry cleaning; nonsmoking rooms. *In room:* A/C, satellite TV, minibar, fridge, coffee/tea-making facilities, hair dryer, safe.

Hilton Hua Hin Resort and Spa ✸   Right in the heart of downtown Hua Hin, this massive tower overlooks the main beach. It is a Hilton, which means a fine, familiar room standard. Staff is courteous and professional. The marble lobby with quiet reflection pools is welcoming, the beachside pool is luxurious, and everything is well-maintained and sparkling clean. A top international standard and the best location for strolling the main beach area, in-town shopping, and nightlife.

33 Narsdamri Rd., Hua Hin 77110 (on the main beach and in the heart of downtown shopping). © 03251-2888. Fax 02250-0999. www.huahin.hilton.com. 296 units. 7,500B–9,500B ($183–$232) double; from 11,800B ($288) suite. AE, DC, MC, V. **Amenities:** 3 restaurants; 2 bars; outdoor pool; 2 tennis courts; health club; spa w/massage, Jacuzzi, sauna, steam; concierge; tour desk; car-rental; shopping arcade; salon; 24-hr. room service; laundry and dry cleaning; babysitting. *In room:* A/C, satellite TV w/in-house movies, minibar, fridge, coffeemaker, hair dryer, safe, IDD phone.

Hua Hin Marriott Resort & Spa 𝒜

From the giant swinging couches in the main lobby to the large central pavilions, the hotel is done in a grand, if exaggerated, Thai style. The Marriott attracts large groups, but is a good choice for families. Ponds, pools, boats, golf, tennis, and other sport venues dot the junglelike grounds leading to their open beach area. There is a good kids' club. The hotel is relatively far from the busy town center and provides shuttle service. Deluxe rooms are the best choice—large, amenity-filled, and facing the sea. Terrace rooms at beachside are worth the bump up. The spa is luxurious, too.

107/1 Petchkasem Beach Rd., Hua Hin 77110. © **800/228-9290** in the U.S., or 03251-1881. Fax 03251-2422. www.marriot.com. 216 units. 6,400B ($156) double; 7,300B–8,800B ($178–$215) beach terrace; from 14,300B ($349) suite. AE, DC, MC, V. **Amenities:** 3 restaurants; lounge; outdoor pool; golf course nearby; outdoor lighted tennis courts; fitness center; spa; watersports equipment; bike rental; children's playground and zoo; concierge; tour desk; car-rental desk; limousine service; shopping arcade; salon; 24-hr. room service; massage; babysitting; same-day laundry service/dry cleaning; nonsmoking rooms. *In room:* A/C, TV w/satellite programming, minibar, coffee/tea-making facilities, hair dryer, safe.

Sofitel Central Hua Hin Resort 𝒜𝒜𝒜

It is one of the town's main sites, really. A stay at the Sofitel Central is a luxurious romp into another time. The Hua Hin Railway Hotel opened in 1922 and is the classiest, most luxurious accommodation going. There's a cool, calm, colonial effect to the whitewashed buildings, shaded verandas and walkways, fine wooden details, red-tile roofs, and immaculate gardens with topiaries. There is a small hotel museum of photography and memorabilia, and the original 14 bedrooms are preserved for posterity. Subsequent additions and renovations over the years have expanded the hotel into a large and modern full-facility hotel without sacrificing a bit of its former charm. The original rooms have their unique appeal, but the newer rooms are larger, brighter, and more comfortable. With furnishings that reflect the hotel's old beach resort feel, they are still modern and cozy. Sofitel's three magnificent outdoor pools are finely landscaped and have sun decks under shady trees. The new Spa Health Club, in its own beachside bungalow, provides full-service health and beauty treatments, and the fitness center is extensive. They have wireless Internet in public spaces, and there is a can-do attitude to service. The adjoining **Central Hua Hin Village** (© **03251-2021**) is now under Sofitel management and features luxurious private bungalows (41 in total) at seaside. Come for **High Tea** at least, and don't miss their popular Japanese restaurant, **Hagi,** which is streetside on Damnoenkasem Road and popular with outside guests.

1 Damnoenkasem Rd., Hua Hin 77110 (in the center of town by the beach). © **800/221-4542** in the U.S., or 03251-2021. Fax 03251-1014. www.sofitel.com. 248 units (including Central Hua Hin Village). 6,400B–7,600B ($156–$185) double; from 10,000B ($244) suite. DC, MC, V. **Amenities:** 5 restaurants; lounge and bar; 3 outdoor pools; putting green and miniature golf; golf course nearby; outdoor lighted tennis courts; new fitness center; spa w/massage; watersports equipment; bike rental; kids' club; daily craft and language lessons; nature tours; billiards room; concierge; tour desk; car-rental desk; limousine service; business center; shopping arcade; salon; 24-hr. room service; babysitting; same-day laundry service/dry cleaning; nonsmoking rooms; executive-level rooms. *In room:* A/C, satellite TV, minibar, fridge, hair dryer, safe, IDD phone.

MODERATE

There are lots of mid- and low-range choices in and around central Hua Hin. **City Beach Resort** (16 Damnoenkasem Rd.; © **03251-2870;** www.citybeach.co.th) abuts the Hilton, and is not bad in a pinch (rooms from 1,700B/$41), and nearby **Sirin Hotel** (© 03251-1150) has basic rooms from 1,500B ($37) comparable to those below.

PP Villa   Tile entries, parquet floors in basic rooms with balconies, proximity to the central beach, and shopping are the hallmarks of PP Villa. It is not the Ritz, but it is comfortable. The staff is super-friendly and there's a pool. Little else.

11 Damnoenkasem Rd., Hua Hin 77110 (near the central beach area and shopping). © 03253-3785. Fax 03251-1216. 52 units. 1,200B–1,500B ($29–$37). V, MC. **Amenities:** Restaurant, outdoor pool, laundry service. In room: A/C, TV, fridge.

Jed Pee Nong Hotel   This recently renovated hotel is a clean and comfy budget choice less than 100m from the Sofitel. There is a small pool, and the simple balconied rooms are carpeted and have air-conditioning. The higher-priced rooms have better decor and hug the pool, cabana-style.

17 Damnoenkasem Rd., Hua Hin 77110 (on the main street near the town beach). © 03251-2381. Fax 3253-22036. www.jedpeenonghotel-huahin.com. 25 units. 1,200B–1,500B ($29–$37). No credit cards. **Amenities:** 1 restaurant (international), pool, laundry service. In room: Minibar.

WHERE TO STAY IN CHA-AM

Along the quiet stretch between Hua Hin and Cha-Am there are a number of fine resorts (and a growing number of condos). Cha-Am village itself is a bit raucous (the Ocean City, NJ, to Hua Hin's the Hamptons) and most stay outside of town; for in-town lodging, try the Methavalai, below.

EXPENSIVE

Dusit Resort and Polo Club ✸   A "Polo Club" in theme only, the Dusit has all the amenities of a fine resort. The elegant marble lobby features bronze horses, hunting-and-riding oil paintings, and hall doors have polo mallet handles and other equine-themed artwork and decor. Guest rooms carry the same theme and are spacious with big marble bathrooms. Room rates vary with the view, although every room's balcony faces the lushly landscaped pool. Ground floor rooms are landscaped for privacy with private verandas leading to the pool and the beach. Suites are enormous with elegant living rooms, full pantry area, and dressing area. For all its air of formality, the resort is great for those who prefer swimsuits and T-shirts to riding jodhpurs, and a relaxed holiday air pervades. All sorts of watersports are available on the quiet beach. It is a bit far from both Hua Hin and Cha-Am, but the resort is completely self-contained.

1349 Petchkasem Rd., Cha-Am 76120. © 03252-0009. Fax 03252-0296. www.dusit.com. 300 units. 5,500B–6,000B ($134–$146) double; from 12,000B ($293) Landmark suite. AE, DC, MC, V. **Amenities:** 5 restaurants; lounge; huge outdoor pool; minigolf; golf course nearby; outdoor lighted tennis courts; squash courts; fitness center; Jacuzzi; sauna; equestrian center and horseback riding; watersports equipment; bike and motorcycle rental; billiards and game room; concierge; tour desk; car-rental desk; limousine service; business center; shopping arcade; salon; 24-hr. room service; massage; babysitting; same-day laundry service/dry cleaning; nonsmoking rooms; executive-level rooms. In room: A/C, satellite TV, minibar, fridge, coffee/tea-making facilities, hair dryer, safe, IDD phone.

MODERATE

The Cha-Am Methavalai Hotel   The Methavalai is the best of the rag-tag collection in busy Cha-Am town. Large, clean, and on the main Beach Road in Cha-Am, it is convenient to the restaurants, shopping, and small nightlife scene in town. Guest rooms are painted from a pastel palette and are peaceful, all with balconies and sun deck, and clean but not luxurious bathrooms. Rooms look out over the good-size central pool (front-facing rooms can be a bit noisy, though). If you want to stay in downtown Cha-Am, this is the best choice of the lot.

220 Ruamchit Rd., Cha-Am 76120. ⓒ **03247-1028**. Fax 03247-1590. www.methavalai.com. 118 units. 3,440B ($84) double; from 4,000B ($98) pavilion and suite. AE, DC, MC, V. **Amenities:** 2 restaurants; lounge and karaoke; pool; golf course nearby; tour desk; salon; limited room service; massage; babysitting; same-day laundry service. *In room:* A/C, satellite TV, minibar, fridge.

The Regent Cha-Am ⭐ No relation to the Regent chain, the Regent Cha-Am is a sprawling property, the combination of three resorts for a total of some 708 rooms (at the Regent Resort, and more luxurious Regency Wing and Regent Chalet). There are lots of services, large pools, watersports, squash, and a small fitness area. The main resort is a massive courtyard, and the Chalet is a separate, quieter bungalow facility (the best choice). Standard rooms are comfortable and affordable, done up like the average chain hotel. The resort is on the road between Hua Hin and Cha-Am and a long ride to either. Come with your own wheels or you will be stuck. The Regent is busy year-round, mostly on the weekends.

849/21 Petchkasem Rd., Cha-Am 76120. ⓒ **03245-1240**. Fax 03245-1277. www.regent-chaam.com. 708 units. 4,000B–4,800B ($98–$117) double; from 5,600B ($137) suite. AE, MC, V. **Amenities:** 3 restaurants; lounge; 3 pools; outdoor lighted tennis courts; squash courts; fitness center; Jacuzzi; watersports equipment; bike and motorcycle rental; game room; tour desk; limousine service; business center; salon; 24-hr. room service; massage; babysitting; same-day laundry service/dry cleaning. *In room:* A/C, satellite TV, minibar, fridge.

WHERE TO DINE IN HUA HIN

If you wake up at about 7am and walk to the piers in either Hua Hin or Cha-Am, you can watch the fishing boats return with their loads. Workers sort all varieties of creatures, packing them on ice for distribution around the country. In both Hua Hin and Cha-Am, look for the docks at the very north end of the beach; nearby open-air restaurants serve fresh seafood at a fraction of prices inland.

The Night Market, on Dechanuchit Road west of Petchkasem Road in the north end of town, is a great place for authentic local eats for very little. The Resorts have more restaurants than there is room to list, and no matter where you stay you'll have great dining options in-house. In town there are lots of small storefront eateries and tourist cafes as well.

An old expat favorite, **Il Gelato Italiano** (ⓒ **03253-3753**) on Damnoenkasem Road, near Jed Pee Nong Hotel, serves the real deal: home-made Italian gelato. A real treat and a good place to meet, greet, and people-watch.

Itsara ⭐ THAI In a two-story seaside home built in the 1920s, this restaurant has a real laid-back charm, from the noisy, open kitchen to the terrace seating and views of the beach—quite atmospheric and a good place to get together with friends, cover the table with dishes, and enjoy the good life. Specialties include a sizzling hot plate of glass noodles with prawns, squid, pork, and vegetables. A variety of fresh seafood and meats are prepared steamed or deep-fried, and can be served with either salt, chili, or red curry paste.

7 Napkehard St., Hua Hin (seaside, a 50B/$1.20 *samlor* ride north from the town center). ⓒ **03253-0574**. Reservations recommended Sat dinner. Main courses 60B–290B ($1.50–$7.10). MC, V. Mon–Fri 10am–midnight; Sat–Sun 2pm–midnight.

Meekaruna Seafood SEAFOOD This small family-run restaurant serves fresh fish prepared as you like. They're located on a wooden deck overlooking the main fishing pier in Hua Hin and in among many other large seafood places. There are fewer flashing lights and no carnival barker out front to drag you in, and such a lack of hype alone is refreshing. They have great *tom yam goong*—also try fried crab cakes, fish served in any number of styles, and my favorite, baby clams fried in chili sauce.

26/1 Naratdamri Rd., Hua Hin (near the fishing pier). ℂ **03251-1932**. Main courses 120B–500B ($2.95–$12). AE, DC, MC, V. Daily 10am–10pm.

ACTIVITIES
GOLF

Probably the most popular activity in Hua Hin and Cha-Am is **golf,** and the town boasts some fine courses. Reservations are suggested and necessary most weekends. Many of the hotels run FOC (free of charge) shuttles, and most clubs can arrange pickup and drop-off to any hotel.

- **Royal Hua Hin Golf Course,** Damnoenkasem Road near the Hua Hin Railway Station (ℂ **03251-2475**), is Thailand's first championship golf course, opened in 1924. Don't miss the many topiary figures along its fairways (greens fees: 1,400B/$34; open daily 6am–6pm).
- **Springfield Royal Country Club,** 193 Huay-Sai Nua, Petchkasem Road, Cha-Am (ℂ **03247-1303**), designed by Jack Nicklaus in 1993, is in a beautiful valley setting—the best by far (greens fees: 2,700B/$66; open daily 6am-6pm).
- **Palm Hills Golf Resort and Country Club,** 1444 Petchkasem Road, Cha-Am; (ℂ **03252-0800**), just north of Hua Hin, Palm Hills is a picturesque course set among rolling hills and jagged escarpments (greens fees: 2,000B/$49 open daily 6am-6pm).

WATERSPORTS

While most of the larger resorts will plan watersports activities for you upon request, you can make arrangements with small operators on the beach (for a significant savings). Most resorts forbid noisy **jet skis,** but the beaches are lined with young entrepreneurs renting them out for 500B ($12) per hour. Windsurfers and Hobie Cats are for rent at most resorts or with small outfits along the beach (starting at 300B/$7.30 and 600B/$15 per hr., respectively).

Call **Western Tours** at ℂ **03253-3303** and ask about their **snorkeling trips** to outer islands for about 1,500B ($37) per person. Their office is at 11 Damnoenkasem Road, in the city center.

SPAS

Hua Hin is famous for its fine spas, and each of the top resorts (see the Marriot, Anantara, and Hilton in "Where to Stay in Hua Hin," above) features excellent services. There are lots of small massage storefronts in Hua Hin, but this is a great place to go upscale and get the royal treatment.

The best choice for a day of pampering is at **Chiva-Som** (73/4 Petchkasem Rd., Hua Hin; 5-min. drive south of town; ℂ **03253-6536**), where you pay a lot and get a lot. There's nothing like it.

Far south of town, luxury **Evason Resort and Spa** (9 Paknampran Beach, Pranburi 77220; 30km/19 miles south of Hua Hin; ℂ **03263-2111**) is a destination spa worth visiting in and of itself, but also a fine stop for high-end day treatments. Very atmospheric, and comparable in quality with Chiva-Som.

SHOPPING

It's a popular tourist town close to the country's largest city, and the result is all of the good shopping services you would find in Bangkok, from fine tailors and jewelers to souvenir shops. The Day Market along Damnoenkasem Road near the beach features local crafts made from seashells, batik clothing, and many other handicrafts. At night the 2-block-long **Night Market** on Dechanuchit Road west of Petchkasem Road is a great stop for tasty treats and fun trinkets.

NIGHTLIFE

For nightlife, your best bet is Hua Hin. A 15-minute stroll through the labyrinth of *sois* between Damnoenkasem, Poolsuk, and Dechanuchit roads near the beach reveals all sorts of small places to stop for a cool cocktail and some fun.

SIDE TRIPS FROM HUA HIN & CHA-AM
PHETCHABURI ★★

Phetchaburi, one of the country's oldest towns, possibly dates from the same period as Ayutthaya and Kanchanaburi, though it is believed to have been first settled during the Dvaravati period. After the rise of the Thai nation, it served as an important royal military city and was home to several princes who were groomed for ascendance to the throne. Phetchaburi's palace and historically significant temples highlight an excellent day trip. It is just 1 hour from Hua Hin.

The main attraction is **Phra Nakhon Khiri** (© **03242-8539**), a summer palace in the hills overlooking the city. Built in 1858 by King Mongkut (Rama IV), it was intended as not only a summer retreat for the royal family, but for foreign dignitaries as well. Combining Thai, European, and Chinese architectural styles, the palace buildings include guesthouses and a royal Khmer-style *chedi,* or temple. The Phra Thinang Phetphum Phairot Hall is open for viewing and contains period art and antiques from the household. Once accessible only via a 4km (2½-mile) hike uphill, you'll be happy to hear there's a funicular railway (called a "cable car," but not really) to bring you to the top for 40B ($1). Open Monday through Friday 8:15am to 5pm and Saturday and Sunday from 8:15am to 5:50pm. The site is open daily from 9am to 4pm and admission is 40B ($1).

Another fascinating sight at Phetchaburi, the **Khao Luang Cave,** houses more than 170 Buddha images underground. Outside the cave, hundreds of noisy monkeys descend upon the parking lot and food stalls looking for handouts. Sometimes you'll find a guide outside who'll escort you through the caves for a small fee.

Wat Yai Suwannaram is a stunning royal temple built during the Ayutthaya period. The teak ordination hall was moved from Ayutthaya after the second Burmese invasion on the city (don't miss the axe-chop battle scar on the building's carved doors). Inside there are large religious murals featuring Brahmans, hermits, giants, and deities.

Another wat with impressive paintings is **Wat Ko Keo Suttharam,** also built in the 17th century. These representational murals, painted in the 1730s, even depict some Westerners: There are several panels depicting the arrival in the Ayutthaya court of European courtesans and diplomats (including a Jesuit dressed in Buddhist garb).

Another fabulous wat is **Wat Kamphaeng Laeng,** originally constructed during the reign of Khmer ruler King Jayavarman VII (1157–1207) as a Hindu shrine. Made of laterite, it was once covered in decorative stucco, some of which still remains. Each of the five *prangs,* or towers, was devoted to a deity—the center *prang* to Shiva is done in a classical Khmer style. During the Ayutthaya period, it was converted to a Buddhist temple.

The temples of Petchaburi are best visited during daylight hours, from early morning until 5pm.

Lastly, the **Phra Ram Raja Nivesana,** or **Ban Puen Palace** (✆ 03242-8506; daily 8am–4pm, free admission), is a nice stop. A royal palace built by Rama V, the German-designed grand summer home comes alive with colorful tile work, neoclassical marble columns, and floor motifs. Today it sits on military grounds and is a popular venue for ceremonies and large occasions.

Western Tours, 11 Damnoenkasem Rd. (✆ 03253-3303), has day excursions for 700B ($17) per person, and it is a good day trip by rented car.

KHAO SAM ROI YOT NATIONAL PARK

Just a 40-minute drive south of Hua Hin, Khao Sam Roi Yot, or the "Mountain of Three Hundred Peaks," is comparatively small in relation to the nation's other parks, but offers great short hikes to panoramic views of the sea. There is abundant wildlife here (seen only if you're lucky). Of the park's two caves, Kaew Cave is the most interesting, housing a *sala* pavilion that was built in 1890 for King Chulalongkorn. For more information, call the park services at (✆ 02561-2919). To arrange a tour, call **Western Tours** (✆ 03253-3303; 700B/$17 per person). A half-day trip to the Pala-U waterfall close to the Burmese border (63km/39 miles west of Hua Hin) is another nature trekking option. Nature trails take you through hills and valleys until you end up at the falls. Western Tours does the trip for 900B ($22) per person. The driver can stop at the **Dole Thailand pineapple factory** for a tour and tasting (✆ 03257-1177; daily 9am–4pm; 200B/$4.90 admission), and the Kaew Cave.

PRACHUAP KHIRI KHAN

If you've had enough of Thailand's many overdeveloped beach areas, the small town and beaches near Prachuap Khiri Khan (just a 1-hr. drive south of Hua Hin) might just be the answer. Some of the kindest people in Thailand live here, the beaches are lovely and little-used, and the town begs a wander. There is little in the way of fine dining and accommodation, but it is a good stop on the way south to Chumphon.

2 Chumphon

463km (287 miles) S of Bangkok; 193km (120 miles) N of Surat Thani

There isn't much of interest to travelers in tiny Chumphon: just a brief stop on the way south and a good jumping-off point for Ko Tao, which offers some of the best scuba diving in Thailand. There is, however, a growing resort and diving area on the mainland Thung Wua Laem, 12km (7½ miles) northeast of town. The town of **Ranong** straddles the Burmese/Thai border west of Chumphon, and is a popular day trip to enjoy the **hot springs** or a boat trip to Burma.

ESSENTIALS
GETTING THERE

By Plane   Air Andaman runs flights three times a week from Bangkok, stopping in Chumphon then heading to Phuket. In Bangkok make reservations at ✆ 02535-6231. For 80B ($1.95), you can catch a minivan into town.

By Train   Ten daily trains stop in Chumphon from Bangkok. Book tickets through the **Hua Lampong Railway Station** in Bangkok at ✆ 02223-7010 or 1690. A second-class sleeper to Bangkok is 284B ($6.95). The Chumphon Railway Station is on Kromluang Road (© **07751-1103**), a wide thoroughfare lined with restaurants, hawkers, and guesthouses. A *songtao* or motorcycle taxi can bring you where you need to go for 20B to 40B (50¢–$1).

By Bus   Four standard air-conditioned buses depart from Bangkok's Southern Bus Terminal (© **02435-1199**). The trip time is 7 hours and costs 425B ($10). The main bus terminal is far north of the town center (accessible by tuk-tuk for 80B/$1.95), and the in-town bus terminal on Thatapao Road (© **07757-0294**) is near many travel agencies, but bus services here are infrequent.

By Ferry   Songserm Travel Center runs the daily FerryLine service connecting Chumphon with Ko Tao, Ko Pha Ngan, Koh Samui, and Surat Thani. On Ko Tao, their office is at Mae Had Beach (© **07745-6274**); on Koh Samui in Nathon (© **07742-0157**); in Surat Thani (© **07720-5418**); and in Chumphon (© **07750-6205**).

VISITOR INFORMATION

There is a Tourist Information Center on Paraminmankha Road in the city's Provincial Hall, but better information is found at any of the tour operators in town. Try **Kiat Travel** (115 Thatapao Rd.; © **07750-2127**).

GETTING AROUND

By *Songtao*   They cruise the main roads, and charge about 20B to 40B (50¢–$1) for rides.

By Motorcycle Taxi   Look for the men in colored vests, and they'll take you where you need to go for as little as 10B (25¢) a trip.

ORIENTATION

Chumphon is small enough to walk around easily. The main spots for travelers are Kromluang Road, running from the railway station, with dining options and cheap accommodations, and Thatapao Road, where there is a small bus terminal (another is out on the highway), as well as many tour operators.

FAST FACTS

Numerous **banks** are all on Saladaeng Road, running parallel to Thatapao. The main **post office** is outside of the town center and a bit hard to reach—I recommend posting from your hotel's front desk. For **Internet service,** check around the Ocean Shopping Complex area, and inside the guesthouses and travel agencies along Kromluang Road. For **police** assistance call © **07751-1505.**

WHAT TO SEE & DO

Most people who come through Chumphon are on their way to Ko Tao, an island near Koh Samui in the Gulf of Thailand—a favorite destination for scuba divers (see the section later in this chapter for information on getting there).

For day trips, contact **Kiat Travel** (115 Thatapao Rd.; © **07750-2127**) or **Ekawin Tours** (Kromluang Rd.; © **07750-1821**). There are sometimes local rafting trips, and these agencies can put together tours to local waterfalls, caves, and beaches, or onward to Ko Tao or other islands in the Gulf of Siam.

Some head out for the beaches near Chumphon, the nicest one being Thung Wua Laen Beach. See **Chumphon Cabana Resort and Diving Center,** below.

WHERE TO STAY

MODERATE

Chumphon Cabana Resort and Diving Center Located on Thung Wua Laen Beach some 30 minutes from Chumphon town, Chumphon Cabana Resort is a basic bungalow resort, but a good spot for affordable fun in the sun. Both bungalow and hotel-style rooms are clean and nicely appointed but sparse. The folks here can organize windsurfing, sailing, and mountain biking; you can take trips to nearby coral reefs with their dive master; or you can just laze by the small outdoor pool. They have a good little restaurant dishing-up fine seafood.

69 Moo 8, Saplee, Pathui, Chumphon 86230. ✆ **07756-0245.** Fax 07756-0247. www.cabana.co.th. 100 units. 1,400B ($34) double; 1,800B ($44) cottage. AE, MC, V. **Amenities:** Restaurant; lounge; small outdoor pool; watersports equipment and dive center; bike rental; laundry service. *In room:* TV w/satellite programming, minibar.

INEXPENSIVE

The **Jansom Chumphon** (118/138 Saladaeng Rd.; ✆ **07750-2502**) is your best bet for in-town accommodation, with basic air-conditioned rooms starting at 500B ($12). Other basic in-town hotels include **Suriwong Chumphon Hotel** (✆ **07751-1203**) and **Chumphon Palace Hotel** (328/15 Pracha-Uthit; ✆ **07757-1715**) near the new market at the town center, both with basic rooms from just 250B/$6.10).

WHERE TO DINE

Though there's nothing in the way of fine dining in Chumphon, there are lots of small storefronts serving good Thai and seafood, especially along Thatapao and Kromluang Road near the train station: try **PaPa** (Kromluang Road; ✆ **07751-1972**), a popular, affordable seafood restaurant, among them.

3 Surat Thani

644km (399 miles) S of Bangkok

Surat Thani was an important center of the Sumatra-based Srivijaya Empire in the 9th and 10th centuries. Today, it is known to foreigners as the gateway to beautiful Koh Samui, and to Thais as a rich agricultural province.

Surat is the main jumping-off point for the eastern islands, **Koh Samui, Ko Pha Ngan,** and **Ko Tao,** as well as the jungles of **Khao Sok National Park.** Also popular near Surat is **Suan Mohk,** an international meditation center (see "Side Trips" at the end of this section).

Surat is known for its **oysters,** farmed in Ka Dae and the Tha Thanong Estuary (30km/18 miles south of town), where more than 6,475 hectares (16,000 acres) are devoted to aquaculture. Fallow rice paddies now support young *hoi takram,* or tilam oysters, which cling to bamboo poles submerged in brackish water. After 2 years they can be harvested; the summer months yield the best crop. Surat Thani's other famed product is the Rong Rian rambutan (*ngor* in Thai), a fruit with a spiky rind hiding a sweet, pitted fruit not unlike litchi. In 1926, a breed of the spine-covered fruit grown in Penang was transplanted here, and now more than 50,590 hectares (125,000 acres) of the Nasan district (40km/24 miles south of town) are devoted to plantations. Each August (the harvest is Aug–Oct) a Rambutan Fair is held, with a parade of fruit-covered floats and performances by trained monkeys.

Surat Thani

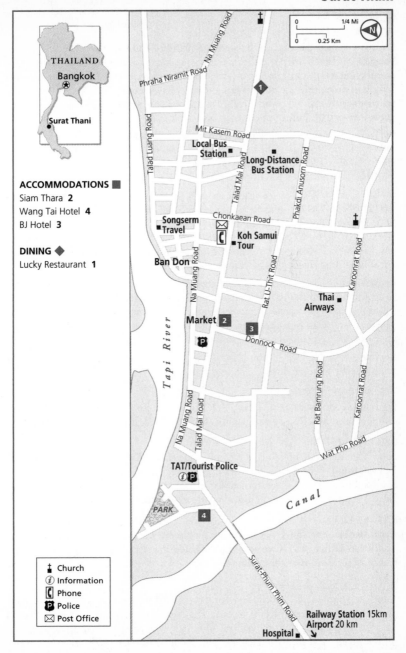

THAILAND

Bangkok ★

Surat Thani •

ACCOMMODATIONS ■
Siam Thara **2**
Wang Tai Hotel **4**
BJ Hotel **3**

DINING ◆
Lucky Restaurant **1**

Phraha Niramit Road

Na Muang Road

Talad Luang Road

Mit Kasem Road

Talad Mai Road

Local Bus Station

Long-Distance Bus Station

Phakdi Anusorn Road

Chonkaean Road

Songserm Travel ■

Koh Samui Tour ■

Ban Don

Na Muang Road

Rat U-Thit Road

Karoonrat Road

Thai Airways ■

Market 2

3

P

Donnock Road

Tapi River

Rat Bamrung Road

Karoonrat Road

Na Muang Road

Talad Mai Road

Wat Pho Road

TAT/Tourist Police
ⓘ P

Canal

PARK

4

Surat-Phum Phim Road

Railway Station 15km
Airport 20 km

Hospital ■ ↘

✝ Church
ⓘ Information
Ⓒ Phone
P Police
✉ Post Office

0 — 1/4 Mi
0 — 0.25 Km
N

ESSENTIALS
GETTING THERE

By Plane **Thai Airways** (in Bangkok, © 02535-2084) has two daily flights from Bangkok to Surat Thani (trip time: 70 min.). If you've rolled into Surat Thani on the morning train you can just hop on one of the travel agent buses to the ferry—either Songserm or Panthip has buses waiting. Otherwise you can grab a shared minivan to town for 80B ($1.95). The Thai Airways office is at 3/27–28 Karoonrat Road (© 07727-2610), just south of town.

By Train Ten trains leave daily from **Bangkok's Hua Lampong station** (© 1690) to Surat Thani (trip time: 13 hr.); second-class sleeper 480B ($12), second-class seat 290B ($7.10). The Surat Thani train station is very inconvenient, but minitrucks meet trains to transport you to town for 20B (50¢) shared ride.

By Bus Two VIP 24-seater buses leave daily from **Bangkok's Southern Bus Terminal** (© 02434-7192; trip time: 10 hr.; 590B/$14). Air-conditioned buses leave daily from Phuket's Bus Terminal off Phang-nga Road opposite the Royal Phuket City Hotel (© 07621-1977; trip time: 5 hr.; 150B/$3.65). Also from Phuket, minivans travel to Surat Thani daily (trip time: 4 hr.; 160B/$3.90). The Surat Thani Bus Terminal is on Kaset II Road, a block east of the main road.

By Minivan The best way to travel between southern cities is by privately operated air-conditioned minivans. They are affordable and run regular schedules from Surat Thani to/from Chumphon, Ranong, Nakhon Si Thammarat, Hat Yai, and beyond. The best way to arrange these trips is to consult your hotel's front desk. You can go door-to-door to the hotel of your choice, usually for little more than 100B ($2.45).

By Car Take Highway 4 south from Bangkok to Chumphon, then Highway 41 south directly to Surat Thani.

VISITOR INFORMATION

For information about Surat Thani, Koh Samui, and Ko Pha Ngan, contact the **TAT** office, 5 Talad Mai Rd., Surat Thani (© 07728-8818), near the Wang Tai Hotel.

ORIENTATION

Surat Thani is built up along the south shore of the Tapi River. Talad Mai Road, 2 blocks south of the river, is the city's main street, with the TAT office at its west end, and the bus station and central market at its east end. Frequent *songtaos* run along Talad Mai; prices are based on distance but rarely exceed 20B (50¢).

FAST FACTS

Major **banks** along Talad Mai Road have ATMs and will perform currency exchanges. The **Post Office** and **Overseas Call Office** are together on Na Muang and Chonkasean roads, near the center of town.

WHAT TO SEE & DO

Surat is a typical small Thai city and, for most foreign visitors, little more than a transportation hub to the islands (Samui and Pha Ngan). Most people will want to press on. If it is your only stop in Thailand (on the way to Samui, for example), give the town a wander and see what Thai life is all about (go explore small streets and find a wat). Those with an extra day or two may want to organize a visit to a local Monkey

Training Center, where monkeys are taught how to harvest ripe coconuts, or to the small town of Chaiya and Suan Mokkh Monastery, a renowned Buddhist retreat with meditation study programs in English (see "Day Trips from Surat Thani," below).

Monkeys have been trained to harvest fruit from south Thailand's particularly tall breed of coconut palm since the 1950s. In that time, dozens of private schools have opened, each accepting up to about 50 monkeys per year. At the **Monkey Training College,** 24 Moo 4, Tambon Thungkong (𝄐 07722-7351), watch how monkeys are trained to distinguish ripe from unripe or rotten fruit, how to spin coconuts around their stems to break them off the tree, and how to pitch them into receptacles below. The college is on Talad Mai Road about 30 minutes east of town; daily shows begin at 9am (the best time to come) until 6pm, and cost about 300B ($7.30) per person. The TAT (see "Visitor Information," above) can assist in making travel arrangements.

WHERE TO STAY
MODERATE
Wang Tai Hotel   The best quality choice is a bit inconvenient, but only 25B (60¢) by tuk-tuk from the bus terminal or ferry company offices. This newer hotel tower features a coffee shop, where acceptable Thai food and good salads are served at tables overlooking the Tapi River, and a pleasant pool and sun deck. There's also a lobby cafe with coffee and pastries, for a quick bite while you're running to catch your morning ferry to Samui. Spacious rooms are clean and comfortable, a great value for the money (rates vary according to view).

1 Talad Mai Rd., Surat Thani 84000 (south side of town near TAT). 𝄐 07728-3020. Fax 07728-1007. 238 units. 950B–1,000B ($23–$24) double; from 2,000B ($49) suite. AE, MC, V. **Amenities:** Restaurant; lounge; pool; limited room service; same-day laundry service. *In room:* A/C, satellite TV, minibar, fridge, IDD phone.

INEXPENSIVE
For years the **Siam Thara** (1/144 Donnok Rd.; 𝄐 07727-3740) was a popular budget standby, but the place has gone down hill. It is convenient to the bus station, though, and not bad in a pinch with rooms for as little as 350B ($8.55).

BJ Hotel   Simple but clean tile rooms with small shower-in-room baths are what's offered at this new block building just a short walk south and east of the town center. Staff can help with travel arrangements and there's a small restaurant, but otherwise it is just a place to lay your head, and a clean one at that.

17/1 Donnok Rd. Surat Thani 84000 (about 1km/½-mile south of the bus station and on a side-road east of central Talad Mai Rd.). 𝄐 07721-7410. Fax 07721-7414. 72 units. 500B ($12). MC, V. **Amenities:** Restaurant; laundry service. *In room:* A/C, TV, minibar, fridge.

WHERE TO DINE
You can sample Surat Thani's famous oysters at any streetside cafe, and there is a small cluster of open-air eateries along Talad Mai near the turn to BJ Hotel.

In the north end of town near the bus station, **Lucky's Restaurant** (452/84–85 Talad Mai Rd.; 𝄐 07727-3267) has an open-air dining room and an air-conditioned hall, both filled with locals enjoying the inexpensive, well-cooked food. Pork curry with coconut milk, ginger, and peppers is a spicy but tolerable brew, and deliciously tender, and the *tom yam* soups are delicious but spicy enough to take off paint unless you say *"kaw, mai phet"* ("not spicy, please").

DAY TRIPS FROM SURAT THANI
CHAIYA TOWN & SUAN MOKKH

Suan Mokkhabalarama (the Grove of the Power of Liberation, better known as Suan Mokkh) was founded in 1932 by Ajahn Buddhadasa, a widely published monk and scholar, venerated by Thais, whose knowledge of English (among other languages) brought him many Western students in the 1970s and 1980s. Although he has passed away, Ajahn Buddhadasa left a legacy of a large forest monastery for Dharma study (characterized by giant Dharma ships, boat-shaped buildings in concrete) as well as a nearby retreat center, Wat Suan Mokkh Nanachat (International). From the 1st to the 10th of each month, foreigner visitors are invited to practice meditation, learn about Thai Buddhism, and experiment with austere living (up at 4am, long hours sitting, chores, study, no talking, no meals after noon). Retreats ask visitors to focus an inward eye through the technique of Anapanasati, a method of concentration through mindfulness of breathing and the baby-steps of Vipassana, or "Insight" meditation, where the calm and concentrated mind goes to work on our wavering emotions and develops compassion for all sentient beings. Sounds simple (right?), but for most it is a matter of years of effort. The 10 days at Suan Mokkh, though rigorous, are accessible for beginners: The sitting times are many but short, and, despite the rule of silence, there are opportunities to voice questions to monks, nuns, and lay volunteers.

Applicants are accepted on a first-come basis at the end of each month (it's good to come a few days early, on the 29th/30th, in high season) and all are expected to stay the full 11 days from the night of the 31st to the morning of the 11th. Visitors check in at the main forest monastery, a popular tour stop (follow signs to "information"), and then walk or ride the 1km (⅔-mile) to the retreat center. For 10 days of dorm lodging and meals, the recommended donation is 1,200B ($29).

Day visitors are welcome at the main forest monastery where you can wander the many forest paths among monk's "kutees" (small bungalows). Don't miss the unique **Spiritual Theater** of didactic Buddhist imagery. The monastery is just south of the town of Chaiya, 50km (31 miles) north of Surat Thani on Highway 41; long-distance buses and minitrucks pass by the entrance throughout the day and can drop you off as requested, and *songtaos* (pickups) connect to and from Chaiya (you have to wave them down) for 20B (50¢).

The **town of Chaiya** itself is a little-visited stop on the southern railroad line, a kind of "Main Street, Thailand," if you will. There's an active central market, small stores by the dozen, Chinese teashops, and there always seem to be school kids running about in bright uniforms. The people of Chaiya are used to lots of wild-eyed foreign meditators wandering the town before and after Suan Mohk retreats, and there are a few Internet cafes along the main drag and a cafe that seems to shift from place to place on a whim (opens and closes with the season). **Chaiya National Museum** (© 07743-1066; Wed–Sun 9am–4pm; 10B/25¢) contains 5th and 6th century relics and tells the story of the area from pre-history to the present, and nearby 7th century **Wat Boromthat** is an elaborate compound of stupas and temples, the only mark of a time when tiny Chaiya was a powerful monastic center.

A short ride north of Chaiya, the town of **Pum Riang** is a Muslim fishing village where there are many small storefront weaving factories still in operation.

KHAO SOK NATIONAL PARK

One of the largest jungle parks in the south, Khao Sok is know for its stunning scenery and exotic wildlife. The park is a convenient stop between Surat Thani (and the islands of Samui and Pha Ngan) and Phuket, and the main east–west road (Rte. 415) passes the park headquarters.

The park is some 646 sq. km (249 sq. miles) in area and is traced by jungle waterways and steep trails among craggy, limestone cliffs—imagine the jutting formations of Phangnga Bay or Krabi, only inland. Rising some 1,000m (3,280 ft.), and laced with shaggy patches of forest, the dense jungle habitat of the park is literally crawling with life. Among the dense underbrush and thick vines hanging from the high canopy, tigers, leopards, golden cats, and even elephants still wander freely, but you may be hard-pressed to actually spot any. More commonly seen are guar, Malaysian sun bear, gibbons, magur, macaques, civets, flying lemur, and squirrels. Keep your eye peeled for the more than 200 species of birds like hornbills, woodpeckers, and kingfishers. As for the flora, there is every variety, and the *Rafflesia,* the largest flower in the world (and a parasite), finds vines from which to draw its nourishment (the largest are up to 1m/3¼ ft. wide).

Well-marked trails lead you through the park to central **Rajprabha Dam** and reservoir where you can go boating, rafting, and fishing among the **limestone cliffs** that act as islands in the swelling waters. The park office provides camping equipment and arranges accommodations in simple bungalows or bamboo huts. Guides will offer their services and help plan your itinerary.

One of the best ways to get up close with the varied fauna of the park is by kayak along the nether reaches of the large reservoir. Jungle animals are skittish, and your chances of seeing something rare by noisily tromping through the bush are slim at best. Kayaks are silent and get you deep into the bush where no paths tread, and going by boat with a knowledgeable guide offers the best chances of sighting anything from black bears to large monkey troupes and even rare tapirs and sloths. Contact the folks at **Paddle Asia** in Phuket (53/80 Moo 5, Thambon Srisoonthon, Thalang, Phuket, 83110; ✆ **07631-1222;** fax 07631-3689; www.paddleasia.com) for details.

The Park's **Natural Resources Conservation office** (Royal Forestry Department, 61 Pahonyothin Rd., Chatuchak, Bangkok 10900; ✆ **02579-7223**), or the TAT offices in Phuket Town or Surat Thani, have good maps and info.

4 Koh Samui

644km (399 miles) S of Bangkok to Surat Thani; 84km (52 miles) E from Surat Thani to Koh Samui

The island of Koh Samui lies 84km (52 miles) off the east coast in the Gulf of Thailand, near the mainland commercial town of Surat Thani. Since the 1850s, Koh Samui has been visited by Chinese merchants sailing from Hainan Island in the South China Sea to trade coconuts and cotton, the island's two most profitable products.

In the 1970s, though, the island's early merchant visitors were replaced by a strange, camera-toting breed, whose patronage has swollen the ranks of hotels and guesthouses to a phenomenal number along the popular beaches. Once a hippie haven of pristine beaches, idyllic bungalows, and thatched eateries along dirt roads, Samui is an international resort area with all of the attendant comforts and crowding. If you came here as a backpacker in the past, you may not want to come back to see the McDonald's outlets where hammocks once hung, or large Wal-Mart-style shopping malls where island jungle once grew, but if you are coming back with the kids, the backpacker days long over, you might be pleasantly surprised at the comforts afforded on this once "alternative" island. Up to 20 flights land at Samui's international airport, and the island hosts some very fine upmarket resorts and affordable mid-range choices.

Koh Samui is still in some places an idyllic tropical retreat with fine sand beaches and simple living—in fact, many Western visitors are settling in for their retirement on the island, and talk of good real estate deals and vacation time-shares is all the buzz. Comparisons with Phuket, on the west coast, are apt.

The high season on Koh Samui is from mid-December to mid-January. January to April has the best weather, before its gets hot. October through mid-December are the wettest months, with November bringing extreme rain and winds that make the east side of the island rough for swimming. August sees a brief increase in visitors, a mini-high season, but the island's west side is often buffeted by summer monsoons from the mainland.

More than 2 million coconuts, reputedly the best in the region, are shipped to Bangkok each month—a massive island industry. Much of the fruit is made into coconut oil, a process that involves scraping the meat out of the shell, drying it, and pressing it to produce sweet oil. To assist farmers with Koh Samui's indigenous breed of tall palm trees, monkeys are trained to climb them, twist loose the ripe coconuts, and gather them for their master. (See "Surat Thani," above, and "What to See & Do," below, for info on monkey training schools.)

ESSENTIALS
GETTING THERE
By Plane   Up to 17 flights depart daily from Bangkok on **Bangkok Airways** (© **02265-5555** in Bangkok), one every 40 minutes between 6:20am and 7:20pm. Two daily flights from Phuket (Bangkok Airways Phuket office; © **07622-5033**), and another daily from the U-Tapao airport near Pattaya (Bangkok Airways Pattaya office; © **03841-1965**) connect these major beach destinations, with additional Bangkok Airways flights connecting the northern cities through Bangkok. From Singapore, **Silk Air** (© **02236-5301-3** in Bangkok) flies daily, and **Bangkok Airways** (© **07742-2512** in Samui) three or four times each week.

Koh Samui Airport is a little slice of heaven—open-air pavilions with thatch roofs surrounded by gardens and palms. For **airport information** call © **07742-5012.** If you're staying at a larger resort, airport minivan shuttles can be arranged when you book your room. There's also a convenient minivan service. Book your ticket at the transportation counter upon arrival and you'll get door-to-door service for 100B ($2.45).

If you're unable to book a flight directly to the island, **Thai Airways** operates two daily flights to the nearby mainland at Surat Thani (© **02525-2084** for domestic reservations in Bangkok). From the airport, it is a shuttle to the town of Surat Thani and then connecting ferry to the island (see Songserm Travel, below).

By Ferry   If you're traveling overland, **Songserm Travel** (© **07728-7124** in Surat Thani) runs a convenient ferry loop from Surat Thani with stops in Koh Samui, Ko Pha Ngan, and Ko Tao, finishing at Chumphon (and back again). The total trip is about 4 hours, while the Surat–Samui leg is 2 hours. Rates are as follows: Surat–Samui 150B ($3.65); Samui–Pha Ngan 130B ($3.20); Pha Ngan–Ko Tao 250B ($6.10); Ko Tao–Chumphon 400B ($9.75). The morning boat leaves at 8am. There are a number of smaller companies that make boat connections (also speedboats), but Songserm is the best.

Another popular choice, **Seatran** runs regular routes from Donsak pier and arranges connection from their riverside office in the center of Surat Thani (© **07125-1555;** www.seatranferry.com). It costs 130B ($3.20) from Surat to Samui, and 220B ($5.35) from Surat on to Ko Pha Ngan.

Koh Samui

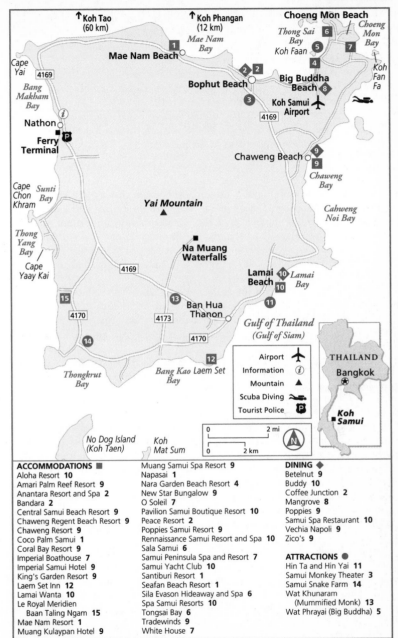

Koh Tao (60 km)
Koh Phangan (12 km)

Mae Nam Beach — Mae Nam Bay

Choeng Mon Beach
Thong Sai Bay
Koh Faan
Choeng Mon Bay

Cape Yai
4169
Bang Makham Bay

Bophut Beach

Big Buddha Beach

Koh Fan Fa

Nathon

Ferry Terminal

Koh Samui Airport
4169

Cape Chon Khram
Sunti Bay

Chaweng Beach
Chaweng Bay

Yai Mountain

Cahweng Noi Bay

Thong Yang Bay
Cape Yaay Kai

Na Muang Waterfalls

4169

Lamai Beach — Lamai Bay

15
4170

13
Ban Hua Thanon
4173
4170

14

12

Gulf of Thailand
(Gulf of Siam)

Bang Kao Laem Set Bay

Thongkrut Bay

Airport	✈
Information	ⓘ
Mountain	▲
Scuba Diving	
Tourist Police	P

THAILAND
Bangkok
Koh Samui

No Dog Island (Koh Taen)
Koh Mat Sum

0   2 mi
0   2 km
N

You can book with any of the ferry companies from small storefront places in Surat. Try **Koh Samui Tour** (346/36 Talat Mai; © 07728-2352) just south of the bus station in the center of Surat. Many who go the ferry route book a bus ticket with ferry included from Bangkok or other points in Thailand.

If you book ahead at a resort, most will arrange transport from the Samui ferry pier at Nathon to your hotel, otherwise *songtaos* make the trip to most beaches on the east coast for as little as 30B (75¢) if they can get a packed truckload from the boat landing (and it can be very packed). If you have no accommodations booking, songtaos will even make a few stops along the way so you can check a few places out before deciding. There are also private taxis at the pier; expect to pay about 200B ($4.90) from Nathon pier to Chaweng.

ORIENTATION

Though Koh Samui is the country's third-largest island, with a total area of 233 sq. km (90 sq. miles), its entire coastline can be toured by car or motorcycle in about 2½ hours. The island is hilly, densely forested, and rimmed with coconut palm plantations. The Koh Samui airport is in the northeast corner of the island. The hydrofoils, car ferry, and express boats arrive on the west coast, in or near (depending on the boat) Nathon. The island's main road (Hwy. 4169, also called the "ring road") circles the island.

Samui's best beaches are on the north and east coasts. The long east coast stretch between Chaweng and Lamai beaches is the most popular destination for visitors and, consequently, where you'll find the greatest concentration of hotels and bungalows. The south coast has a few little hideaways and the west coast has a few sandy strips, but few amenities for tourists.

Nathon, the aforementioned ferry arrival point on the west coast, is just a tiny town; here you'll find a few banks, the TAT office, and main post office, but few visitors spend much time here.

THE BEACHES

Clockwise from Nathon, **Mae Nam Bay** is 12km (7½ miles) from the ferry pier, at the midpoint of Samui's north shore, facing nearby Ko Pha Ngan. The beach is long and narrow, with coarse sand shaded by trees. The water is deep enough for good swimming (on some beaches the water is shallow unless you walk out very far). This bay is often spared the fierce winds that whip during the stormy months, making it popular during the winter. Mae Nam is relatively isolated, and there are a number of simple, charming beach bungalows on unpaved roads off Highway 4169. Ban Mae Nam, the commercial center, is just east of the Santiburi Resort and has lots of good little restaurants and shops.

Bophut Beach, on the north coast just east of Mae Nam, is one of the island's fastest developing areas. Find many small restaurants, businesses, shops, and an increasing number of new resorts and taxis, which creates a busier pace than is evident at other, more removed beaches. Bophut's very long (usually crowded in the high season) sand beach narrows considerably in the monsoon season, but the water remains fairly calm year-round. The sand is coarse. Fisherman's Village is the sign that marks entrance to the busiest area of Bophut, where you'll find cheap restaurants and guesthouses among a pier-side clutch of small houses and shops worth a wander.

Big Buddha Beach is just east of Bophut and has a fairly clean, coarse sand beach (narrow in the monsoon months) and a calm, shallow swimming bay. Some small hotels and many simple bungalows look out over Ko Faan, the island home of Koh Samui's huge seated Buddha. Fishing boats and long-tail water taxis connect with Ko Pha Ngan from here, popular during Full-Moon Party time (see "Ko Pha Ngan," later in this chapter).

Koh Samui juts out at the northeastern tip in a rough, irregular coastline. Bold rock formations create private coves and protected swimming areas, though from mid-October to mid-December the monsoon whips up the wind and waves, creating a steep drop-off from the coarse sand beach and strong undertow. **Tongsai Bay** is a beautiful cove dominated by one resort (reviewed later in this chapter); its privacy is a plus and a minus.

Southeast of Tongsai Beach, at the foot of high, craggy cliffs, is the fine sand beach of **Choeng Mon,** a gracefully shaped crescent about 1km (⅔ miles) long. Palm trees shading sunbathers reach right to the water's edge; swimming is excellent, with few rocks near the central shore. Across the way is Ko Fan Fa, a deserted island with an excellent beach. You can swim or, if the tides are right, walk there, but be careful of the rocks at low tide. Choeng Mon is isolated, but there are many small hotels and bungalows, and it's just a short ride to the busier beach areas.

The two Chaweng beaches (the main **Chaweng** and south **Chaweng Noi**) are the busiest destinations on Koh Samui. The benefits of Chaweng are the many tourist conveniences: money changing, Internet, laundry, travel and rental agencies, medical facilities, shopping, restaurants, and nightlife, not to mention more choices for accommodations. Chaweng can be a blast if you don't mind a little hustle and bustle. If you've come to get away from the familiar—from McDonald's and Starbucks—Chaweng is to be avoided, but even if you don't stay here, most visitors at least take a wander of an evening. The beaches of Chaweng and Chawng Noi are by far the longest on the island. The more recently developed north end of the strip abuts rocky coast, but to the south the swimming is good (though a bit shallow near shore).

The long sand beach on **Lamai Bay** is comparable to Chaweng's, and with the exception of a few upper-range (and one high-end) resorts caters to more budget travelers. The wide range of services, cafes, and nightlife make Lamai the best budget choice and a popular spot.

Laem Set Bay is a small rocky cape on Samui's southeast coast, with dramatic scenery that has prompted the construction of a few well-known hotels.

On the west coast, from Laem Phang Ka, you'll find one of Samui's better beaches on the island's southwest tip, where the highway cuts inland, heading north past **Ban Taling Ngam** and the cutoff running west to the car-ferry jetty. These beaches are the most isolated on the island, with few facilities to support resorts and waters filled with rocks, making the beaches barely swimmable. Many Thai families stop for picnics at Hin Lat Falls, a rather uninteresting, littered site 2km (1¼ miles) south of Nathon, which supplies the town with its drinking water.

VISITOR INFORMATION

The **TAT Information Center** is on Thawiratchaphakdi Road just north of the main fairy terminal in Nathon (© **07742-0504**). A good place to stop before you head out to the beach, they distribute, in addition to TAT pamphlets, the thin *Accommodations Samui* guidebook, a free booklet packed with information on hotel, dining, and activity options. You'll find a host of free small-press magazines in Samui: Bangkok Airways produces the free *Samui Guide,* a color magazine with advertisements and information about the island; and *What's On Samui* is similar (but different). *Samui*

Dining Guide (www.samuidiningguide.com) lists the best restaurants on the island. You can also pick up any of a number of free maps with lots of adverts and info.

GETTING AROUND

By *Songtao* *Songtaos* are the easiest and most efficient way to get around the island. They advertise their destinations—to such beaches as Lamai, Chaweng, and Mai Nam—with colorfully painted signs, and all follow Rte. 4169, the ring road, around the island. For many trips, you have to change trucks between north and south routes. You can hail one anywhere along the highway and along beach roads. To visit a site off the beaten track (or one other than that painted on a truck's sign), ask the driver to make a detour. Most stop running regular routes after sundown, after which some will hang around outside the discos in Chaweng to take night owls home to other beaches. The cost is 30B to 40B (75¢–$1) one-way, with steep fares (up to 300B/$7.30) after hours.

By Rental Car Koh Samui's roads are narrow, winding, and poorly maintained, with few lights at night to guide you. Road accidents are many, and renting a car is a far-better idea than going on a motorcycle. Your defensive driving skills will be required to navigate around slow-moving trucks and motorcycles at the side of the road, not to mention the occasional wandering dog.

Budget Car Rental (② 07742-7188) has an office at the Samui Airport. Contact **Avis** (② 07742-5031) at the airport or at the Santiburi Resort (② 07742-5031). **Hertz** is at the Central Samui Beach Resort (② 07723-0500). All offer a range of vehicles, starting as low as 1,500B ($37), and do pick-up and delivery.

Local rental companies and travel agents have great deals for car rentals, and while vehicles are sometimes a little beat up, they're generally sound. Look for bargains as low as 900B ($22) per day, but don't expect insurance coverage. Read all the fine print, and make sure, if you don't have an international driver's license, that your local license is acceptable under the agreement.

By Motorcycle Road accidents injure or kill an inordinate number of tourists and locals each year on Samui, mostly motorcycle riders; but still, two-wheels and a motor is still the most popular way to get around the island. The roads on Samui are busy, so stay left and close to the shoulder of the road to make way for passing cars and trucks, and go easy. It is a 500B ($12) fine for not wearing a helmet (but enforced irregularly), and there are infrequent checks for international licensing (have one, from AAA in the U.S., or pony up 200B/$4.90). Travel agencies and small operators rent motorcycles in popular beach areas. A 100cc Honda scooter goes for as little as 150B ($3.65) per day, while a 250cc chopper is as expensive as 700B to 900B ($17–$22) a day. For the best big bikes, look for **Ohm Cycles** on the far southern end of Chaweng (on the road heading to Lamai; ② 07723-0701).

FAST FACTS

All the major **banks** are in Nathon along waterfront Thawiratchaphakdi Road. In Chaweng you'll find numerous money-changers and ATMs: Try Krung Thai Bank's (opposite Starbucks). Hotels and guesthouses also accept traveler's checks. The main **post office** (② 07742-1013) is on Chonwithee Road in Nathon, but you'll probably not hike all the way back to the main pier for posting. Any hotel or guesthouse will handle it for you, and stamps can be purchased in small provision shops in beach areas. For **Internet service,** there are a number of options in Chaweng. Try the kind folks at **Multi Travel and Tour** (164/3 Moo 2 Chaweng; ② 07741-3969) among the many. **Bandon International Hospital** (② 07742-5382) is a fine facility with

English-speaking physicians who make house calls. Located in the north of Chaweng. For **tourist police** emergencies, dial ⓒ **1155** or ⓒ **07742-1281.**

WHAT TO SEE & DO

Busy Samui supports all kinds of activities, from scuba diving to bungee jumping, jungle trekking to cooking schools. Most folks come here for beach fun and frolic, and you'll find all kinds of activities, sailing, jet skis, and parasailing among them, at beachside. Have a look at "Exploring Koh Samui" at the end of this section for more outdoor activities and happenings.

Na Muang Trekking (ⓒ 07741-8681) is one of many small tour and trekking agencies arranging day trips to the sites below; however self-drive, best by car rather than motorbike, will get you there just as easily.

The gold-tiled **Wat Phrayai (Big Buddha),** more than 24m (80 ft.) tall, sits atop Ko Faan (Barking Deer Island), a small islet connected to the shore by a dirt causeway almost 305m (1,000 ft.) long. Though of little historic value, it is an imposing presence on the northeast coast and is one of Samui's primary landmarks. It is open all day (no admission, but donations accepted). It is easy to reach, just hop on any *songtao* going to Big Buddha Beach. You can't miss it.

Koh Samui's famed **Wonderful Rocks**—the most important of which are the unique **Hin Ta and Hin Yai,** or Grandfather and Grandmother Stones, shaped like the male and female anatomy—are located at the far southern end of Lamai Beach. To get there, flag-down any minitruck to Lamai Beach.

The **Mummified Monk** at Wat Khunaram is certainly worth a visit if your bend is to roadside oddities. He died in the meditation mudra, legs folded lotus style, and he was embalmed that way; you can see him behind glass in a small pavilion at the right as you enter Wat Khunaram, itself a worthy example of a typical Thai town temple. At the entrance to the monks' pavilion, a few coins are the cost of the resident monk's blessing with water. Take off your shoes, smile, and kneel, and he will put water on your head and say a few good words, for whatever it's worth. The site is along the main road, Rte. 4169, as it shoots inland far south of Lamai.

Just across Rte. 4169 from the Wat Khunaram is the dirt track leading up to **Na Muang Falls,** a pleasant waterfall once visited by many kings of the Chakri dynasty. After the rainy season ends in December, it reaches a height of almost 30m (100 ft.) and a width of about 20m (66 ft.). Na Muang is a steamy 5km (3-mile) walk from the coast road and makes for a nice bathing and picnic stop. You can even trek to the falls on the back of an elephant (contact the many agencies there).

For something a little more tranquil, visit the **Butterfly Garden** (ⓒ 07742-4020), off the 4170 Road near Laem Din on the southeast corner (daily 9am–5pm; adults 50B/$1.20, children 20B/50¢).

Along Samui's main roads, you'll find little hand-painted signs along the lines of MONKEY WORK COCONUT. These home-grown tourist spots show off monkey skills involved in the local coconut industry—they're trained to climb the trees, spin the coconuts to break them off their stems, and collect them from the bottom when they're finished. The **Samui Monkey Theater** (ⓒ 07724-5140) is just south of Bophut village on 4169 Road. Shows are a little more vaudeville than the "working" demonstrations—with costumes and goofy tricks—and are a lot more fun for kids than for adults. Show times are at 10:30am, 2pm, and 4pm daily, and cost 150B ($3.65) for adults, 50B ($1.20) for children.

I defy you to find a Thai tourist spot without the requisite **snake farm,** where young men harass dangerous snakes (many reputedly drugged; the snakes, that is) and taunt audiences by catching the slithering animals in their bare hands (and sometimes their teeth). It is a lot of laughs, though, to see the audience squirming in semi-amused horror. Samui's snake farm is at the far southwest corner of the island on 4170 Road (© **07742-3247**), with daily shows at 11am and 2pm; tickets cost 250B ($6.10).

Samui's traditional **buffalo fights** now take place only on holidays. This equitable sport, popular in south Thailand, pits male water buffaloes in a contest of locked horns. Endurance, chutzpah, and brute strength determine the winner; the loser usually lies down or runs away. (Buffalo rarely hurt one another, though fans have been trampled!) Authorities have tried to curb gambling, but the event is still festive; shamans are called in to rile up the bulls, ribbons are hung around their necks, and buffalo horns are decorated with gold leaf. Contact the TAT office about when and where specific bouts will be held.

WHERE TO STAY ON KOH SAMUI

Twenty years ago there were but a few makeshift beachside bungalow compounds along the nearly deserted coast of Samui. Today, luxury resorts stand shoulder-to-shoulder with homey guesthouses, chic modern facilities next to motel cellblocks, and all are vying for supremacy for the choicest beachside real estate. Even if your budget is tight, you can still enjoy the same sand as those in the more exclusive joints.

For more detailed information on each beach, check out "The Beaches" section above; the list below is but a selection from each area, the best of the many options on this fast-developing island.

MAE NAM BAY
VERY EXPENSIVE

Napasai ✸✸   Santiburi (below) was the first high-end property in the area but now has lots of competition. Napasai is just such an upstart from Pansea Orient-Express (they have many boutique properties throughout the region). The resort is a collection of rustic-themed luxury bungalows overlooking a rocky promontory and beach on the farthest western end of Mae Nam. Pansea style pervades, and a high service standard and lots of comfort does not come without the constant reminder that you are in old Siam (with a hint of French colonial style). Choose from cozy cottages in teak with high ceilings, some with large aggregate bathtubs overlooking the sea, all with balconies. Pool villas are over the top. The place is a bit isolated, but thoroughly self-contained. The seaside pool is large and inviting; they have a top spa and good in-house dining.

65/10 Moo 5, Maenam, Koh Samui 84330. © **07743-9200.** Fax 07742-9201. www.pansea.com. 55 units. 14,000B–15,200B ($341–$371) sea view cottage; from 19,200B ($468) villas. **Amenities:** Restaurant and bar; outdoor pool; tennis courts; fitness center; spa; Jacuzzi; watersports rentals; tour desk; car-rental; limited room service; massage; laundry. *In room:* A/C, satellite TV, fridge, minibar, tea and coffeemaker, safe, IDD phone.

Santiburi Resort ✸✸✸   The Santiburi (formerly part of the Dusit chain) is the ultimate in relaxed luxury on the island. The resort design is influenced by late Thai royal architecture, with spacious and airy interiors—a simplicity accented with luxurious Jim Thompson Thai silks and tidy floral arrangements. The gardens and beachfront are picturesque and quiet, and the staff is motivated to please. The resort's top villas front the beach, while the others are set among lush greenery around a central pool and spa. Each bungalow is a luxe suite, with living and sleeping areas divided by glass and flowers. The bathroom is masterfully fitted in wood and black tiles, the centerpiece a large, round sunken tub. Standard features such as a video player and stereo system make each villa as convenient as your own home. Guests can take advantage of windsurfing and sailing on the house. They also have their own gorgeous Chinese junk anchored in the bay for dinner cruises or for hiring out to tour surrounding islands. Santiburi now has a new, more affordable companion in nearby Bophut called the **Bophut Resort and Spa,** at a similar high standard, with 61 luxury villas at seaside. Santiburi also hosts the island's only golf course, **Santiburi Golf,** near the resort.

12/12 Moo 1, Tambol Mae Nam, Koh Samui, Surat Thani 84330. ✆ 07742-5031. Fax 07742-5040. www.dusit.com. 71 units. 16,000B–20,000B ($390–$488) deluxe suites; from 20,000B ($488) villas; AE, DC, MC, V. **Amenities:** 2 restaurants; 2 bars and a lounge; outdoor pool; golf course (nearby, connected by free shuttle); outdoor lighted tennis courts; fitness center; spa; Jacuzzi; sauna; watersports equipment; concierge; car-rental desk; limousine service; Internet; salon; 24-hr. room service; massage; babysitting; same-day laundry service/dry cleaning. *In room:* A/C, satellite TV and DVD with disc library, wireless Internet, stereo system, minibar, fridge, hair dryer, safe, IDD phone.

MODERATE/INEXPENSIVE

Coco Palm Samui   A good budget choice, Coco Palm's bungalows are basic and comfortable, all with air-conditioning, minibar, and TV. They attract lots of families on a budget, but still it is quite peaceful. Deluxe bungalows are worth a bump-up; though still with just shower-in-room baths, they are airy with vaulted ceilings. Seaside bungalows are worth the next bump-up in price for their location.

26/4 Moo 4, Maenam Beach, Koh Samui 84330. ✆ 07724-7288. Fax 07742-5321. www.cocopalmsamui.com. 86 units. 800B–1,000 ($20–$24) double; 1,100B–1,800B ($27–$44) deluxe; from 2,500B ($61) beachfront. MC, V. **Amenities:** Restaurant; small outdoor pool; Jeep and motorcycle rental; tour desk; transfer service; laundry service. *In room:* A/C, minibar, no phone.

Mae Nam Resort ✦ *Value*   A quiet bungalow village, Mae Nam Resort has bungalows with teak paneling and floors, rattan furnishings, small bathroom, and a small deck in front. Beachfront bungalows will have you stepping off your balcony right into the silky, palm-shaded sand for very little considering the neighboring Santiburi Dusit Resort's beachfront villa run about 32,800B ($800). Okay, Mae Nam Resort can't compare to five-star luxury, but it is the same sand and view.

Mae Nam Beach, Koh Samui, 84330 Surat Thani (next to the Santiburi Dusit). ✆ 07724-7287. Fax 07724-5116. www.maenamresort.com. 41 units. 1,200B ($29) double w/fan; from 1,800B ($44) A/C bungalow. AE, MC, V. **Amenities:** Restaurant; Jeep and motorcycle rental; transfer service; limited room service; laundry service. *In room:* no phone.

Seafan Beach Resort   With Thai ambience and low-key elegance, these semi-deluxe beach bungalows are connected by wooden walkways covering 3 hectares (8 acres) of landscaped grounds fronting the bay. Each rustic rattan and coconut-wood house has two queen-size beds, an extra rattan daybed, built-in bamboo furnishings, and a large, all-tiled bathroom with nice robes and slippers for padding about. Bungalows are well spaced and private. A small pool with kiddy pool and a snack bar overlook the beach. The restaurant features Thai, Continental, and good seafood. Ask about special rates.

Mae Nam Beach, Koh Samui 84330, Surat Thani (west end of beach). ✆ 07742-5204. Fax 07742-5350. www.samui-hotels.com/seafan. 36 units. 4,500B ($110) double, slightly more for seafront; special rates available. AE, DC, MC, V. **Amenities:** Restaurant; lounge; outdoor pool and children's pool; watersports equipment; children's playroom; tour desk; limousine service; massage; same-day laundry service/dry cleaning. *In room:* A/C, minibar, hair dryer, safe.

BOPHUT BEACH
EXPENSIVE

Anantara Resort and Spa ✦✦   Like its other properties in Thailand (see Hua Hin and the Golden Triangle), the Anantara on Samui looks like an old royal compound, complete with elephant enclosures (and elephants, of course), and public spaces done on a grand, lavish scale. Rooms are like luxe city suites done up in local themes, with large baths open to rooms by sliding doors, and fun touches like fighting fish in bowls on the dresser. Suites are huge, with a pivoting entertainment console separating sleeping and living quarters. The private villas of the spa are also something from another time, with heavy wooden doors leading to sumptuous suites.

101/3 Bophut Bay, Koh Samui 84320. ✆ **07742-8300.** Fax 07742-8310. www.anantara.com. 106 units. 8,200B–8,800B ($200–$215) deluxe double; from 19,400B ($473) suite. AE, MC, V. **Amenities:** 2 restaurants (Thai, Italian); bar; outdoor pool; tennis court; fitness center; spa; Jacuzzi; watersports rentals; library with Internet and games; shopping arcade; limited room service; massage; laundry. *In room:* A/C, satellite TV, fridge, minibar, tea and coffeemaker, safe, IDD phone.

Bandara One of the many new resorts in Bophut, Bandara is a rather tame mid-range standard of rooms set around a sprawling courtyard around a good-size raised pool. Slick and contemporary without sparing good Thai touches, standard and deluxe rooms flank the main courtyard, and seaside units are over the top, some quite luxurious with private pools.

178/2 Moo 1, Bophut, Koh Samui 84320. ✆ **07724-5795.** Fax 07724-7340. www.bandararesort.com. 151 units. 5,500B–6,500B ($134–$159) double superior/deluxe; 8,500B ($207) grand deluxe; from 12,000B ($293) pool villa. MC, V. **Amenities:** 2 restaurants; bar; outdoor pool; fitness center; watersports rentals; tour desk; car-rental; limited room service; massage; laundry. *In room:* A/C, satellite TV, fridge, minibar, safe, IDD phone.

MODERATE

Peace Resort 🐾🐾 The Peace Resort is a cozy clutch of mid-range freestanding bungalows. All have vaulted ceilings with design schemes that are either finely crafted wood or cooler, almost Mediterranean numbers in pastel tiles with designer flat-stone masonry and smooth stucco. Spring for the larger seaside rooms. The central pool is not particularly large but cozy and near the beach. There's a small, open-air restaurant where you can enjoy a cool drink, the company of good friends, and the calm of this tranquil bay with the Big Buddha winking from the next beach. Peace, indeed.

Bo Phut Beach, Koh Samui 94320 (central Bo Phut). ✆ **07742-5357.** Fax 07742-5343. www.peaceresort.com. 102 units. 2,850B–3,500B ($70–$85) garden bungalow; 3,800B–4,900B ($93–$120) beach-view bungalow. MC, V. **Amenities:** Restaurant; bar; outdoor pool; spa (across the road); kids' club and playground; tour desk; car and motorbike rental; Internet; babysitting; limited room service (6am–11:30pm); laundry service. *In room:* A/C, satellite TV, minibar, fridge, safe, no phone.

BIG BUDDHA BEACH

Nara Garden Beach Resort The Nara is one of the island's older inns, with attached rooms as similar to an American motel as you'll come in Koh Samui. A well-kept lawn leads to the beach and quiet bay. The Nara has large connecting rooms for families. Spring for a superior. She's getting a bit old, but it's not a bad choice. Next door **Samui Mermaid Resort** (34/1 Moo 4; ✆ **07742-7547**) is a similar mid/low-end choice.

81 Moo 4, Bophut, Koh Samui 84320, Surat Thani (Big Buddha Beach). ✆ **07742-5364.** Fax 07742-5292. naragarden@sawadee.com. 43 units. 1,800B ($44) standard; 2,100B–2,700B ($51–$66) superior–deluxe; 3,000B ($73) suite. MC, V. **Amenities:** Restaurant; bar; outdoor pool; tour desk; transfer service; babysitting; laundry service. *In room:* A/C, satellite TV, minibar, fridge.

TONGSAI BAY

The Tongsai Bay 🐾🐾 Built amphitheatrically down a hillside, the white stucco, red-tile-roofed bungalows and buildings remind one of the Mediterranean, though the palm trees are pure Thai. Between the half-moon cove's rocky bookends, the coarse sand beach invites you to idle away the days. This all-suite resort has some very unique touches that set it apart—each unit has plenty of outdoor terrace space, most with sea views. Terrace suites have outdoor bathtubs, while the Grand Tongsai Villas have not only tubs but also gazebos. The villas are designed in a unique harmony with nature; some even have small stands of trees growing though the middle of them, and you'll find plenty of spots to hide out with a hammock under a shade tree. The experience is casual luxury in the outdoors with service that is very attentive yet not stuffy. The only drawback: The many steps between the hilltop reception area, the bungalows, and the beach. Advance reservations are required in high season.

84 Moo 5, Ban Plailaem, Bophut, Koh Samui 84320, Surat Thani (northeast tip of island). © 07742-5015. Fax 07742-5462. Bangkok reservations office 02254-0056. Fax 02254-0054. www.tongsaibay.co.th. 83 units. 11,000B–13,000B ($268–$317) beachfront or cottage suite; 22,000B ($537) Tongsai Grand Villa; from 25,000B ($610) pool villa. AE, DC, MC, V. **Amenities:** 3 restaurants; 2 bars; outdoor pool; outdoor lighted tennis court; fitness center; spa w/massage and beauty treatments; watersports equipment; snooker room; tour desk; car-rental desk; limousine service; Internet center; limited room service; same-day laundry service/dry cleaning. *In room:* A/C, TV w/satellite programming, DVD player (disks available at small library), minibar, fridge, coffee/tea-making facilities, hair dryer, safe, IDD phone.

TONGSON BAY

On the very northeastern tip of Samui, just around the promontory that shelters Tongsai Bay, Tongson Bay hosts a few high-end choices. A good getaway.

Sala Samui ✿ Hip, slick, and cool, that's the vibe at Sala Samui. Stylish rooms, just being completed at the time of our research, all with a view to private courtyards or the sea, and many with private pools. The place has a cool, boutique vibe, with colored concrete accented in Thai silk hangings and canopy beds. Good beach area. Construction is ongoing here (one to watch).

10/9 Moo 5, Baan Plai Lam Bo Phut, Koh Samui Suratthani 84320. © 07724-5888. Fax 07724-5889. www.sala samui.com. 69 units. $225 deluxe; from $300–$550 pool villa; $700 presidential villa. AE, MC, V. **Amenities:** Restaurant and bar/wine lounge; 2 outdoor pools; fitness center; spa; watersports rentals; tour desk; car-rental; limited room service; massage; laundry. *In room:* A/C, satellite TV, fridge, minibar, coffeemaker, safe, IDD phone.

Sila Evason Hideaway and Spa ✿✿ A luxe campus of private villas and suites tucked along the craggy hilltop overlooking Tongson Bay, Sila Evason Hideaway is a unique high standard, a great choice for that second honeymoon or a special occasion splash-out. Service is tops, and everything from their fine dining options, sumptuous spa facilities, stylish rooms, and great service makes this a great choice. You're far removed from it all, and that is the point.

9/10 Moo 5, Baan Plai Laem Bophut, Koh Samui 84320. © 07724-5678. Fax 07724-5671. www.sixsenses.com. 66 units. 15,000B–40,000B ($366–$976) villas; from 20,000B–50,000B ($488–$1,220) pool villas; from 30,000B ($732). AE, MC, V. **Amenities:** 2 restaurants; 2 bars; outdoor pool; health club; spa; Jacuzzi; sauna; watersports rentals; tour desk; car-rental; 24-hr. room service; massage; laundry. *In room:* A/C, TV, fridge, minibar, coffeemaker, hair dryer, safe, phone.

CHOENG MON
VERY EXPENSIVE

Samui Peninsula Spa and Resort ✿✿ You'll be treated like royalty at Samui Peninsula, in a fine private suite or your own luxury pool villa with incredible views from this rocky promontory on the cusp of Choeng Mon and Bophut. It is a long walk to the beach proper, but you may not want to leave this ultra-comfy compound. Rooms are sanctuaries done in dark wood, silk, and brimming with Thai features and classical style. The central pool has scenic views, and resort dining and services are tops. A honeymooner's delight.

24/73 Moo 5, Bo Phut Beach, Koh Samui 84320 (on the rocky point between Mae Nam and Bo Phut). ✆ 07742-8100. Fax 07742-8122. www.samuipeninsula.com. 68 units. 11,000B–15,000B ($268–$366) suite; from 24,000B ($585) villa. AE, MC, V. **Amenities:** 2 restaurants; bar; outdoor pool; watersports equipment rental; tour desk; car rental; limousine service; Internet; 24-hr. room service; massage; same-day laundry and dry cleaning. *In room:* A/C, satellite TV w/in-house movies; minibar, fridge, safe, IDD phone.

EXPENSIVE

The Imperial Boathouse ✿ You've a pretty unique concept here—34 authentic teak rice barges have been dry-docked and converted into charming free-standing suites: one of a kind. The less-expensive rooms in the three-story buildings are fine but not nearly as atmospheric. Hotel facilities are extensive, and if you can't get a boat suite, you can swim in their boat-shaped swimming pool.

83 Moo 5, Tambon Bophut, Koh Samui 84320, Surat Thani (southern part of beach). ✆ 07742-5041. Fax 07742-5460. www.imperialhotels.com. 210 units. 4,000B–4,500B ($98–$110) double; 6,400B–8,000B ($156–$195) boat suite. AE, DC, MC, V. **Amenities:** 2 restaurants; bar; 2 outdoor pools; fitness center; spa; Jacuzzi; sauna; watersports equipment; concierge; tour desk; car-rental desk; limousine service; business center; 24-hr. room service; massage; babysitting; same-day laundry service/dry cleaning. *In room:* A/C, satellite TV, minibar; fridge, hair dryer, safe, IDD phone.

The White House ✿✿ This resort's graceful Ayutthaya-style buildings surround a garden with lotus pond and swimming pool, a familiar and affordable standard of rooms and comforts overlooking Choeng Mon on a good swimming beach. Each building houses four large rooms, all with separate sitting areas, huge beds, fine furnishings, and large bathrooms. By the beach there's a pool with a bar and an especially graceful teak *sala.* The intimate size of this place is quite comfortable, and the White House is still a fine choice in Choeng Mon.

59/3 Moo 5, Choeng Mon Beach, Koh Samui 84320, Surat Thani. ✆ 07724-5315. Fax 07724-5318. www.samui dreamholiday.com. 40 units. 5,000B–5,600B ($122–$137) double; from 6,200B ($151) suite. AE, MC, V. **Amenities:** 2 restaurants; bar; outdoor pool; Jacuzzi; Jeep and motorcycle rental; tour desk; transfer service; massage; laundry service. *In room:* A/C, TV w/satellite programming, minibar, fridge, coffee/tea-making facilities, safe.

MODERATE/INEXPENSIVE

O Soleil It's just spick-and-span bungalows well-spaced for extra quiet at affordable prices. Down a small dirt road, the villas are on a large lawn with lots of flowering plants. There is also a basic bamboo bar and dining pavilion at seaside. Large rustic bungalows with bamboo porch furniture have comfortable beds, and tidy shower-in-room tile bathrooms.

Choeng Mon Beach (down a dirt track at the north end of beach, past White House Hotel). ✆ 07742-5160. osoleil@loxinfo.co.th. 27 units. 1,000B–1,200B ($24–$29) double with A/C. MC, V. **Amenities:** Restaurant; laundry service. *In room:* No phone.

CHAWENG & CHAWENG NOI BAYS
Expensive
Amari Palm Reef Resort ✿✿ This is the finest of Amari's many hotels in Thailand by virtue of their luxury suites at beachside and the comfortable design of the ocean-side pool and dining. Older accommodation in the main block is not particularly luxurious, though very clean with parquet floors. New suite rooms face the sea and are designed in a seamless marriage of contemporary and traditional Thai, with large decks giving way to huge glass sliders, lovely sunken seating areas, massive, plush beds situated in the center of the rooms, and behind which you'll find designer bathrooms with a separate shower, tub, and his-and-her sinks. There is a new block of mid-range units

in a small "village" location across the road from the beach with separate pool. The central beachside pool area is lovely, their new spa is sumptuous, and the staff is kind and helpful. The rocks and coral along the beach mean you'll have to take a bit of a walk for swimming, but the scenery is great. The resort is far enough from Chaweng strip to be quiet and comfortable (but close enough to party). Check out their popular new Italian restaurant, Prego, on the strip in Chaweng. Great for families.

Chaweng Beach, Samui 84320 (north end of the main strip). (C) **07742-2015**. Fax 07742-2394. www.amari.com. 187 units. 6,000B ($146) superior; 7,200B ($176) deluxe; 10,000B ($244) suite. AE, MC, V. **Amenities:** 3 restaurants; 2 outdoor pools; squash court; spa w/massage, Jacuzzi, sauna, and steam; bike rental; kids' club; tour desk; car rental; small boutique shopping; babysitting; same-day laundry/dry cleaning service; nonsmoking rooms. *In room:* A/C, satellite TV, minibar, fridge, coffeemaker, hair dryer, safe, IDD phone.

Central Samui Beach Resort 🗡

A sprawling resort right in the heart of Samui, Central has all the big amenities, and even when choc-a-block with groups there is always some room for privacy. Public areas are spacious, and amenities, like their fine spa and cozy pool area, are inviting. Rooms are rather bland, but in a comfortable contemporary style. They host a unique Brazilian dining outlet just across the street, Zico's (see "Where to Dine in Koh Samui," later), and are attached to a large shopping compound (the Central group also owns huge shopping malls throughout Thailand).

38/2 Moo 3, Chaweng Beach, Koh Samui 84320. (C) **07723-0500**. Fax 07742-2385. www.centralhotelsresorts.com. 208 units. 4 restaurants; 2 bars; outdoor pool; tennis courts; health club; spa; Jacuzzi; sauna; watersports rentals; tour desk; car-rental; shopping arcade; limited room service; massage; laundry. *In room:* A/C, TV, fridge, minibar, safe, IDD phone.

Chaweng Regent Beach Resort

A good mid-range option in the very center of Chaweng, Chaweng Regent was built in 1990 (early for Samui) and is popular with group tours. They cover all the bases in amenities, including both seaside and garden pool areas, and rooms are a cool international standard, not fancy but cozy. Their seaside dining is good, as is their Red Snapper Restaurant, which faces the main drag in Chaweng and is popular for outside guests.

155/4 Chaweng Beach, Koh Samui 84320. (C) **07744-2389**. Fax 07742-2222. www.chawengregent.com. 141 units. 4,000B–7,000B ($98–$171) double. **Amenities:** 2 restaurants; 2 bars; outdoor pool; health club; spa; Jacuzzi; sauna; watersports rentals; tour desk; car-rental; limited room service; massage; laundry. *In room:* A/C, TV, fridge, minibar, safe, IDD phone.

Coral Bay Resort 🗡🗡

Far from the boom-boom bass of Chaweng but close enough to commute easily, the Coral Bay crests a picturesque hill on the northern end of Chaweng and is a collection of large, upscale thatch bungalows. Rooms are in rows along the hillside (it takes a bit of trudging to get to some), and each has a large balcony, some shared with adjoining rooms. Room decor is lavish with bamboo and coconut inlaid cabinets, intricate thatch, fine hangings, and some rooms feature unique, graphic mosaics: nothing like it on Samui. Spring for a deluxe room with canopy bed. Baths are small garden landscapes with waterfall showers and designer flat-stone masonry. The central pool area is high above the rock and coral beach below (not good for swimming), and large thatch pavilions house the open lobby and fine dining. A good standard of comfort and service throughout, and they provide good information about self-touring (or can make arrangements for you). Rooms do not have TVs, lending to the escape quality of the place, and there is a library and video lounge if you are jonesin'. Their small spa is very professional and affordable, with internationally trained staff and a roster of excellent treatments.

9 Moo 2, Bophut, Chaweng Beach, Koh Samui 84320 (north end of Chaweng as the road crests the first big hill).
© **07742-2223**. Fax 07742-2392. www.coralbay.net. 53 units. 3,300B–9,000B ($80–$220) double bungalow (based on season and location); from 9,000B ($220) family units and suites. AE, MC, V. **Amenities:** 2 restaurants; bar; pool; spa; Jacuzzi; sauna; kids' club; tour desk; car rental; Internet; library and video lounge; small shop; massage; babysitting; laundry service; nonsmoking rooms. *In room:* A/C, minibar, fridge, safe, IDD phone.

Imperial Samui Hotel ♠ A member of the large, Thai-owned Imperial group, the hotel is set in a sprawling hill-top grove of coconut palms a short drive south of busy Chaweng. You can't walk it, but they do have frequent shuttle service to town, and the resort, unlike most on or near Chaweng, is quiet. Their large, salt-water pool has an organic design with large boulders, a central island, and a vanishing edge overlooking the bay below. Spacious rooms have large balconies with sea views, lots of floral prints and rattan, large bathrooms with potted plants, and easy access (via steps) to the beach. The sprawling hillside location means a bit of hill hiking to some of the furthest rooms, but for seclusion and comfort, this is a good choice.

86 Moo 3, Ban Chaweng Noi, Koh Samui 84320, Surat Thani (middle of Chaweng Noi Beach). © **07742-2020**. Fax 07742-2396. www.imperialhotels.com. 155 units. 5,600B ($137) double; 7,000B ($171) premiere sea-facing; from 7,600B ($185) suite. AE, DC, MC, V. **Amenities:** 2 restaurants; lounge; 2 outdoor pools; 1 freshwater and 1 seawater; outdoor lighted tennis courts; Jacuzzi; watersports equipment and dive center; bike rental; snooker and badminton; concierge; tour desk; car-rental desk; limousine service; 24-hr. room service; massage; babysitting; same-day laundry service/dry cleaning. *In room:* A/C, satellite TV with free in-house movies, minibar, fridge, coffeemaker, hair dryer, safe, IDD phone.

Muang Kulaypan Hotel ♠ Like a museum "installation" as much as a hotel, the rooms of the Muang Kulaypan are gracefully simple in natural woods and rich local textiles and clean, contemporary minimalist lines. The name is derived from an ancient Thai-Javanese tale and pieces of the story are spelled-out in calligraphy on some room walls. The design can be almost harsh, it is so spartan, but you are meant to like it that way, and the overall effect of the interiors is not displeasing. Almost all rooms have sea views. That same clean-lined minimalism of the rooms only works when it is in fact "clean," though, and the sprawling public spaces and central courtyard are getting a bit run-down. The black-tiled pool is lovely, and their Budsaba Restaurant serves fine Thai cuisine in private thatched *salas*. The staff is smartly dressed and snaps to. A good place for that post-modern honeymoon.

100 Moo 2, Chaweng Beach Rd., Koh Samui 84320, Surat Thani (northern end of Chaweng Beach). © **07723-0850**. Fax 07723-0031. www.kulaypan.com. 41 units. 3,600B–6,000B ($88–$146) double; from 8,500B ($207) suite. AE, DC, MC, V. **Amenities:** Restaurant; lounge; outdoor pool; small fitness center; tour desk; car and motorcycle rental; limousine service; limited room service; massage; babysitting; same-day laundry service/dry cleaning. *In room:* A/C, minibar, fridge, safe.

Muang Samui Spa Resort ♠ A slightly fancier (pricier) central Chaweng address, the Muang Samui is a sumptuous little boutique affair (you won't know you're in the heart of Chaweng). Large luxury suites are decked out in teak and fine silk, and resort service is tops. Their two freestanding restaurants are just across the street and popular choices in busy Chaweng.

13/1 Moo 2, Chaweng, Koh Samui. © **07742-9700**. Fax 07741-3225. www.muangsamui.com. 53 units. 12,000B–25,000B ($293–$610) suites. AE, MC, V. 2 restaurants (International, Seafood); bar; outdoor pool; fitness center; spa; Jacuzzi; watersports rental; tour desk; car-rental; limited room service; massage; laundry. *In room:* A/C, satellite TV, fridge, minibar, safe, IDD phone.

Poppies Samui Resort ♠♠ The famed Balinese resort features this popular annex in Samui. On the south end of busy Chaweng, Poppies is indeed an oasis. Luxury cottages, all the same, have thatch roofs and Thai-Balinese appointments. Privacy and service is the hallmark here. Rooms are set close together but well situated for optimum privacy. This is a popular honeymoon choice, and the service and standards throughout are tops. Their central pool is small but cozy, and the hotel dining is some of the best going (see "Where to Dine in Koh Samui," below).

P.O. Box 1, Chaweng, Koh Samui 84320 (on the south end of the Chaweng strip). ✆ 07742-2419. Fax 07742-2420. www.poppies.net. 24 units. From 8,000B ($195) double with seasonal fluctuations. AE, MC, V. **Amenities:** Restaurant, pool, spa, tour desk, shopping, limited room service, massage, laundry. *In room:* A/C, satellite TV, minibar, fridge, coffee and tea, safe, IDD phone.

Moderate

Chaweng Resort   The Chaweng Resort just finished a cosmetic facelift and the old gal is looking pretty good: the grounds are nicely landscaped and the carved concrete lobby is as ornate as a Hindu temple (or a wedding cake), and there are lots of fun Thai touches and statues throughout. Chaweng Resort is two columns of freestanding bungalows leading to the sea. Cottages are basic but spacious, with lots of overdone filigree. Bathrooms are plain but spotless. The larger suites are a good value for families. The central pool is small but cozy, and their Thai/Continental restaurant overlooks the beach. The place is not luxurious, but a good family choice bustling with activity.

Chaweng Beach, Koh Samui, 84320 Surat Thani (middle of Chaweng Beach). ✆ 07742-2230, or 02651-0016 in Bangkok. Fax 07751-0018. www.chawengresort.com. 70 units. 1,600B–3,400B ($39–$83) double; from 3,900B ($95) beachfront bungalows and suites. AE, DC, MC, V. **Amenities:** Restaurant; pool; tour desk; Internet; massage; laundry service. *In room:* A/C, satellite TV, minibar, fridge.

New Star Bungalow   Far to the south of busy Chaweng on a quiet hilltop out of the fray, New Star has good, basic, freestanding villas with private decks and views of a quiet stretch of beach. Deluxe bungalows are larger and further uphill with better sea views and charming stonework in the bathrooms. Smaller superior rooms line up suburban style (in rows) at seaside (only the front row rooms have good views . . . oh, those Joneses!). Many rooms have both a double bed and small alcove single bed, ideal for small families.

Chaweng Noi Beach, Koh Samui 84320, Surat Thani (south of Chaweng on a hilltop near the Imperial Resort). ✆ 07742-2407. Fax 07742-2325. 50 units. 2,000B–2,500B ($49–$61) superior double; from 3,000B ($73) deluxe bungalow. MC, V. **Amenities:** Restaurant; watersports equipment; bike rental; transfer service; same-day laundry service. *In room:* A/C, fridge, minibar.

Tradewinds   Tradewinds was one of the earliest hotels in Chaweng and still a good choice on the south end of the strip. From the higher priced bungalows you can step right off your front porch into the sand, while standard bungalows are in a secluded garden not far from the beach. Rooms are not particularly luxurious but have large beds and rattan furnishings, good for travelers who want the intimate feeling of a bungalow village but don't want to sacrifice modern conveniences. They've just opened a new motel-style block, but stick to the bungalows. Tradewinds is also home to Samui's catamaran sailing center, under the tutelage of longtime islander John Stall.

17/14 Moo 3, Chaweng Beach, Koh Samui 84320, Surat Thani. ✆ 07723-0602. Fax 07723-1247. www.tradewinds-samui.com. 29 units. 2,500B–3,500B ($61–$85) double. AE, DC, MC, V. **Amenities:** Restaurant; bar; catamaran sailing center; laundry service. *In room:* A/C, minibar, fridge.

Inexpensive

King's Garden Resort   These simple bungalows are the last of a dying breed along busy Chaweng. They've gone and gotten themselves air conditioners for all rooms, but the price is still right and the vibe still mellow. Simple and spartan, but close to town on a nice stretch of beach.

12 Moo 2, Chaweng Beach, Koh Samui 84320, Surat Thani (middle of Chaweng Beach). (*C* 07742-2304. Fax 07742-0430. 32 units. 1,000B–2,500B ($24–$61) double with A/C; 350B–800B ($8.55–$20) double with fan. No credit cards. **Amenities:** Restaurant; massage; laundry service. *In room:* No phone.

LAMAI BAY
Very Expensive
Renaissance Samui Resort and Spa *★★*   Opened in the fall of 2003 as privately owned Buriraya, the resort has recently reopened as a Renaissance Resort, part of the Marriott chain, and now offers all the benefits of that brand. The resort is the height of luxury and service in the hills high above busy Lamai Beach. Rooms in the larger tower block are very chic and comfortable with large puffy beds covered in sumptuous silk, rich wood floors, and fine Thai appointments. Larger, freestanding villas set in the resort's verdant gardens (all with private Jacuzzi and pool) are luxurious hideaways with fine traditional decor done on a grand scale. The pool is lovely, the spa is luxurious, and there are great fine-dining options. The views of sand and sea from this exclusive perch are breathtaking, and everything is new and orderly.

208/1 Moo 4, T. Maret, Lamai, Koh Samui 84310 (on the north-east end of Lamai, on the hilltop). (*C* 07742-9300. Fax 07742-9333. www.buriraya.com. 79 units. 8,000B–14,000B ($195–$341) deluxe double; 12,000B–15,000B ($293–$366) pool villa; from 16,600B ($405) suite. AE, DC, MC, V. **Amenities:** 3 restaurants; outdoor pool; health club; spa w/Jacuzzi, sauna, steam; sea kayak & bicycles free of charge; watersports rentals; children's center; tour desk; car-rental; business center; shopping; limited room service; babysitting; same-day laundry and dry cleaning. *In room:* A/C, satellite TV w/DVD and CD, minibar, fridge, coffeemaker, safe, IDD phone.

Expensive
Pavilion Samui Boutique Resort *★*   Applying the term "boutique" is usually left to travel agents and writers, but at the Pavilion they've just cut out the middleman. What is boutique, anyway? It's style on a small scale with top service; the newly renovated Pavilion is more the rococo of a small-time mafia Don's private sanctuary, but they're pretty close and the service is good. Public spaces are chic and upscale, surrounded by lots of greenery. Rooms run the gamut from Mediterranean-style bungalows to grand honeymoon suites, and spa rooms with huge luxury bathrooms, some even with a courtyard area where guests can enjoy a Jacuzzi and shower under the stars. They have a fine new spa, the small pool and dining pavilion are right on the surf, and proximity to Lamai's nightlife is a plus for most guests.

124/24 Moo 3, Lamai Beach, Koh Samui 84310, Surat Thani (north end of Lamai Beach). (*C* 07742-4030. Fax 07742-4029. www.pavilionsamui.com. 62 units. 6,000B–7,500B ($146–$183) bungalow double; from 10,000B ($244) suite. AE, DC, MC, V. **Amenities:** Restaurant; bar; outdoor pool; spa; Jacuzzi; steam bath; tour desk; car-rental desk; transfer service; limited room service; laundry service. *In room:* A/C, TV, minibar, safe.

Moderate
Aloha Resort   One of a few midsize, mid-range resorts in the heart of the Lamai strip at oceanside. The location is attractive and accommodation is utilitarian, not stylish. They have a good pool and cover all of the basic amenities. A good choice for basic comforts in the heart of Lamai. Popular with groups.

128 Lamai Beach, Koh Samui 84310. (*C* 07742-4014. www.alohasamui.com. 73 units. 2,400B–3,600B ($59–$88) double; from 3,800B ($93) suite. AE, MC, V. **Amenities:** 2 restaurants; 1 bar; outdoor pool; Jacuzzi; watersports equipment rentals; tour desk; car-rental; limited room service; massage; laundry. *In room:* A/C, TV, fridge, minibar, IDD phone.

Samui Yacht Club   This tidy bungalow complex, a yacht club in name only, has an almost exclusive access to a small cove north of Lamai Beach. It is very quiet. The rocky beach is not for swimming, but there's good snorkeling further out. Each bungalow has a porch, canopy beds with mosquito netting (for effect), clean tiled floors, and rattan furnishings. Best are the beachfront bungalows right on the sand. The restaurant is fine for breakfast, but go out for dinner. This place is best for people who want to be left alone and aren't looking for many services.

Ao Tongtakian, between Chaweng and Lamai Beaches (3km/2 miles north of Lamai), Koh Samui 84320, Surat Thani. © 07742-2225. Fax 07742-2400. www.samuiyachtclub.com. 43 units. 2,100B–3,100B ($51–$76) garden bungalow; 3,600B–4,100 ($88–$100) beachfront bungalow. AE, MC, V. **Amenities:** Restaurant; outdoor pool; motorcycle rental; laundry service. *In room:* A/C, satellite TV, minibar, fridge, safe.

Spa Samui Resorts ★ *Value*

For long-term stays or just a daytime spa visit, The Spa Samui Resorts is a unique choice offering a "healthy good time." Their popular cleansing and fasting series rejuvenates your system with prepared detox drinks and tablets, plus twice daily colonic enemas. It is really two resorts: first the original laid-back spa resort on the sea, called **Spa Beach,** just north of Lamai, a rustic grouping of old bungalows and open-air dining and massage pavilions (recent upgrades mean a pool and some cosmetic improvements); second is the **Spa Village,** a more comfortable property in the south of Lamai, high in the hills above town. Rooms at both locations range from simple, affordable bungalows to large private suites with large balconies. All rooms are fitted with a colonic board for daily enemas. The new spa has a cozy pool, herbal steam bath in a large stone grotto, massage, body wraps, and facial treatments. Classes and workshops on yoga, meditation, and massage techniques can fill your day, or you can just put your feet up, colon all sparkling clean, and have a go at that novel you've been lugging around (or writing). All of the spa services are available for day visitors. Their vegetarian restaurants at both locations serve excellent dishes, with particular care to cleansing out the body (see "Where to Dine in Koh Samui," below).

Spa Village: Lamai Beach, Koh Samui 84320, Surat Thani (just south, in the hills over Lamai Beach). © 07723-0855. Fax 07742-4126. www.spasamui.com. 39 units. 1,200B–2,500B ($29–$61) double. **Spa Beach:** Lamai Beach (on the north end of the main strip in Lamai). 32 units. 500B–2,000B ($12–$49). MC, V. **Amenities:** Restaurant; juice bar; pool; spa; sauna; massage; laundry service. *In room:* A/C, minibar, fridge, safe.

Inexpensive

Lamai Wanta

Beachside on the north end of Lamai, the Lamai Wanta is a small campus of simple, clean-lined, contemporary cottages and a cluster of rooms in a two-story hotel block. There is little in the way of service here, but the small seaside pool is an oasis, and you are close to town for services. Tidy rooms have terra-cotta tile, high ceiling, dark wooden trim, and all come with small balconies. There's nothing like it in Lamai at this price (ask about seasonal discounts).

124/264 Moo 3, Tumbon Maret (north end of Lamai beach). © 07742-4550. Fax 07742-4218. www.lamaiwanta. com. 50 units. 1,200B ($29) double in hotel block; 1,600B–2,000B ($39–$49) bungalow. MC, V. **Amenities:** Tour desk; Internet; laundry. *In room:* A/C, satellite TV, minibar, fridge, safe, IDD phone.

LAEM SET BAY

Laem Set Inn ★★

Unique in a landscape of cookie-cutter, high-end resorts, the Laem Set Inn is a cozy hideaway, a collection of uniquely designed Thai suites ranging from rustic thatch bungalows to private pool villas, many built from salvaged rural teak homes. Family suites have bunk beds, private baths for kids, and small family dining nooks. Large porches bookend all villas, and provide a perch for drinking in the views beyond the pounding surf to nearby No Dog Island. Kayaks, mountain bikes, and snorkel gear are available to explore this location's stunning scenery. Wireless

Internet comes standard in all areas, free of charge. The elevated pool seamlessly blends with the gulf, reflecting sea and sky, and the pavilion restaurant serves gourmet fare and delicious Thai seafood. This boutique inn is true rustic luxury, far from the crowds and intimate. Friendly staff cater to any need—an ideal getaway.

110 Moo 2, Hua Thanon, Laem Set, Koh Samui 84310, Surat Thani. © **07742-4393**. Fax 07742-4394. www.laemset. com. 30 units. 4,900B–8,800B ($120–$215) standard double; from 9,000B ($220) suite. MC, V. **Amenities:** 2 restaurants; bar; outdoor pool; fitness center; Jacuzzi; sauna; watersports equipment; bike and motorcycle rental; children's programs; concierge; tour desk; car-rental desk; limousine service; business center; limited room service; massage; babysitting; same-day laundry service. *In room:* A/C, wireless Internet, minibar, fridge, coffee/tea-making facilities, hair dryer, safe, IDD phone.

WEST COAST

Le Royal Meridien Baan Taling Ngam ⟨★★★⟩   The Le Royal Meridien is a peaceful hideaway on the western side of the island some 40 minutes' drive from the Samui Airport. Built on the side of a hill, the resort's accommodations include deluxe rooms and suites, as well as one- to three-bedroom beach and cliff villas. The hilltop lobby and restaurant, as well as the guest rooms, have fantastic views of the sea and resort gardens, and the main pool appears to spill over its edges into the coconut palm grove below. Guest rooms combine Thai furniture, fine textiles, and louvered wood paneling, including the sliding doors to the huge tanning terrace. Bathrooms feature oversized tubs and sophisticated black slate and wood paneling. The two-bedroom villas afford the most value and convenience for families. The resort's only detractor is that the beach is small, and while some may seek out the privacy this resort promises, the cost is isolation from the "action" on the other parts of the island—at least a 30-minute drive away. They have kayaks, catamarans, snorkeling gear, and Windsurfers for rent, as well as tennis, mountain bikes, a fine spa, PADI dive school, and no fewer than seven outdoor swimming pools, so no one will get bored. Dining at the hilltop Lom Talay is as gorgeous as the Thai and Asian cuisine served, while the Promenade serves locally caught fresh seafood by the beach.

295 Moo 3, Taling Ngam Beach, Koh Samui, Surat Thani 84140. © **800/225-5843** in the U.S., or 07742-3019. www. lemeridien.com. 72 units. 18,000B–20,500B ($439–$500) double; 31,150B ($760) suite; 31,150B–90,600B ($760–$2,210) villa. AE, DC, MC, V. **Amenities:** 3 restaurants; lounge; 7 pools; outdoor lighted tennis courts; fitness center; spa with massage; Jacuzzi; sauna; watersports equipment and dive center; bike rental; concierge; tour desk; car-rental desk; limousine service; salon; 24-hr. room service; babysitting; same-day laundry service/dry cleaning. *In room:* A/C, satellite TV, minibar, fridge, IDD phone.

WHERE TO DINE IN KOH SAMUI
CHAWENG BEACH

Chaweng is lined with eateries, with anything from McDonald's to fine dining. Below are merely a few. A new trend is for the larger resorts to set up freestanding restaurants for both in-house and outside guests. See **Zico's,** listed below, and look for the likes of **Samui Seafood** (sponsored by Muang Samui Resort), **Red Snapper** (sponsored by the Chaweng Regent), and **Prego** (from Amari).

Betelnut ⟨★⟩ INTERNATIONAL   California cuisine anyone? Down a quiet *soi* off the south end of Chaweng, you'll be greeted at the door by Jeffrey Lord, owner, proprietor, and rollicking raconteur, who hands out fine wit and witticisms along with good victuals. The menu is divided into "Eats Big" and "Eats Small," not necessarily apps and main courses but they could be, and runs the gamut from "Buddha Jumped Over the Wall" (an ostrich steak) to clam chowder with green curry. I had a delicious sesame-encrusted salmon katsu, indicative of the international fare here. The blackened tuna with salsa, and soft-shell crabs with green papaya and mango salad are also good choices. Come with friends, order a spread of tapas choices, and pick from among their fine wines for a great evening.

46/27 Chaweng Blvd. down Soi Colibri, Chaweng (across from Central Resort). © 07741-3370. Main courses 475B–650B ($12–$16). MC, V. Daily 6pm–last order.

Poppies THAI/INTERNATIONAL   Known for its Balinese flare, Poppies is equally famous for fresh seafood by the beach. The romantic atmosphere under the large thatch pavilion is enhanced by soft lighting and live international jazz music. Guest chefs from around the world mean the menu is ever-changing, but you can be sure their seafood selections are some of the best catches around. A good place, especially if you're romancing someone special.

South Chaweng Beach. © 07742-2419. Reservations recommended during peak season. Main courses 80B–240B ($1.95–$5.85). AE, MC, V. Daily 7am–10pm.

Vecchia Napoli ⊛ ITALIAN   The simple authentic Northern Italian cuisine at this restaurant fits the bill for a casual evening. Tomato and mozzarella with a splash of pesto, a glass of red, and good conversation; you won't believe you're just a stone's throw from busy Chaweng (down a little alley with seedy massage places and bars, but that somehow lends to the atmosphere). They have it all here: great pastas, grilled specials, pizza, and the house special is the shellfish soup with king prawns, fresh crab, mussels, and clams, done in a special Neapolitan broth. Follow it up with a real gelato or tiramisu and espresso. Also ask about their new upmarket venue, **Bellini** (46/26 Chaweng Beach, Soi Calibri; © **07741-3831;** www.bellini-samui.com), on the south end of Chaweng opposite Central Resort.

166/31 Moo 2, Chaweng Beach, Koh Samui 84320 (central Chaweng). © 07723-1229. Main courses 120B–420B ($2.95–$10). MC, V. Daily 11am–11pm.

Zico's ⊛ BRAZILIAN   Here's a guaranteed wild night. Zico's, run by the folks at Central Resort across the street, is a unique Brazilian-themed restaurant. It is a one-price dining experience where roving waiters, called *Passadors,* come around with massive skewers of meat and trays of delicacies (also choose from the massive salad bar). You choose what you like and as much as you like by laying a small coin on the table with the green side up for "More please," and the red side up for "Enough for now, thanks." And the place is a riot of music, drink, and dance, with Brazilian performers shaking their tail feathers from table to table.

38/2 Moo 3, Chaweng Beach (on the south end of Chaweng across from the Central Resort). © 07723-1560. 680B ($17) for unlimited buffet. MC, V. Daily 7pm–10:30pm. Dance shows at 8pm, 9:30pm, and 10pm.

LAMAI BEACH
Buddy   Like a little backpacker franchise, the Buddy Beer folks have put up another large restaurant on the beach in the north end of Lamai (see their lodge and restaurant on Khao San Rd. in Bangkok). The place is open 24 hours, and is more or less a party by the sea. They even have a pool which is open to diners. The food is the usual mélange of Thai tempered to Western tastes and facsimile American and continental grub, but the prices are right, the place is always busy, and no one is going to shout "last call."

Route 4169 on the north end of Lamai Beach. © 07745-8080. Main courses 50B–250B ($1.20–$6.10). MC, V. Open 24 hours.

The Spa Restaurant VEGETARIAN   Not just for veggies here at The Spa Restaurant (they serve a few seafood and chicken dishes as well), but to anyone who'd like to enjoy a healthful, tasty dish. Go for the delicious curries, or try the excellent local dishes. But leave plenty of time for an herbal steam and massage at their Health Center. I think for a vacation activity, this is tops for relaxation—an afternoon of pure indulgence, and it's good for you! Try either their new mountain-top retreat or the older resort just north of Lamai.

Route 4169, between Chaweng and Lamai beaches. ℂ 07723-0855. Reservations recommended in peak season. Main courses 30B–250B (75¢–$6.10). MC, V. Daily 7am–10pm.

BOPHUT BEACH

Little Bophut's Fisherman's Village area, near the ferry jump-off, is lined with lots of little semi-luxe restaurants, most like little shooting stars that open, burn brightly, close, and are replaced. Nearby high-end resorts, the likes of Santiburi and Banburi, run regular shuttles. A good place to take in an affordable seaside meal, but none are particularly easy to recommend. There is the **Samui French Bakery** (6/1 Moo 1, Bophut; ℂ **07743-0408**) at the far end of town, as well as stylish **Starfish and Coffee** (51/7 Moo 1, Bophut; ℂ **07742-7201**) at the town center overlooking the water. Just a few of the many little dining venues here. Also try:

Coffee Junction　　Just a little corner coffee shop overlooking the busy ferry pier area (but across the street from the beach), the Coffee Junction is a good place to put your feet up and people-watch in the very heart of the Fisherman's Village of Bophut. They serve great little sandwiches (create your own) and western treats, best followed-up by a hearty cup of chai. A good base for a day of shopping and exploring little Bophut.

37 Moo 1, Bophut, Koh Samui 84320. ℂ **09866-1085**. Main course 80B–250B ($1.95–$6.10). No credit cards. Daily 8am–9pm.

The Mangrove ✿✿ INTERNATIONAL　　For romantic, elegant dining, the Mangrove is the best on Samui. They're on a quiet stretch of rural road (near the airport), and although far from the bustling tourist areas like Chaweng, that is in fact the very appeal here, and the restaurant is but a short ride from Chaweng (near Bophut Beach). The casual, cozy, open-air dining area overlooks a grove of mangroves, of course, and echoes with the sounds of forest and jungle. The menu changes monthly to cater to their oft-returning expatriate clientele. For a starter, try the crab salad, and ask about any daily specials. I had a delicious lamb chop marinated in herbs de Provence. The place is run by a friendly young (but very experienced) French/Belgian couple who go to great lengths. Don't scrimp on dessert; try the rich chocolate mousse and follow it up with a Rum Ginger, their signature after-dinner drink. Ask about their new outlet in central Chaweng, to open in 2006.

32/6 Moo 4, Bophut, Koh Samui 84320 (on the airport road between Bophut and Big Buddha). ℂ 07742-7584. Main courses 280B–520B ($6.85–$13). Daily 5pm–last order. (**Note:** They're closed on the last 3 days of each month.)

WEST COAST BEACHES
Big John Seafood ✿ SEAFOOD　　This is worth the ride across the island, or a worthy goal at the end of a day of exploring, especially if you like fresh seafood. The atmosphere is so-so, but you overlook a pretty stretch of coconut palm–lined beach and can take in the sunset just as the barbecues are firing up. Order the day's catch as you like, and accompany it with any of a myriad of good Thai curries and sides. A longtime popular spot on the island, and there's great live music most nights.

95/4 Moo 2, Lipanoi Beach. ℂ **07741-5537**. www.bigjohnsamui.com. Seafood by the kilogram. Daily 11am–10pm.

EXPLORING KOH SAMUI
SCUBA & SNORKELING

Local aquanauts agree that the best **scuba diving** is off Ko Tao, a small island north of Ko Pha Ngan and Koh Samui, and many of the operations on Samui coordinate with larger on-site dive centers there, while also offering good day trips from Samui. Conditions vary with the seasons (best from October to March). The cluster of tiny islands south of Samui, in Mu Ko Angthong National Park, are often more reliable destinations. Follow the advice of a local dive shop on where to go, because many have schools on Samui and offer trips ranging further afield. The few shops listed below are good choices among many on the island. *Note:* There is a decompression chamber on Samui.

Samui International Diving School (at the Malibu Resort, Chaweng Beach; ℂ 07742-2386; www.planet-scuba.net) is a good bet for full-services. **Easy Divers,** open since 1987, has locations in Chaweng (ℂ **07741-3373**; www.easydivers-thailand. com) and other beaches, and offers good deals for beginners. Both outfits offer all sorts of PADI courses and daily dive tours, and have international safety standard boats, good equipment, and complete insurance packages. Daily dives (two dives per day) start from about 3,000B ($73) per person including land transportation, breakfast, equipment, lunch, and drinks.

Big Blue (ℂ 07745-6179) caters custom trips to divers of any skill-level and is a good choice for a small group or those seeking private attention.

Some of the finest **snorkeling** off Koh Samui is found along the rocky coast between Chaweng Noi and Lamai Bays. Several shops along Chaweng Beach rent snorkeling gear for about 100B ($2.45) per day.

GOLF

Samui now boasts its own course, the picturesque **Santiburi Golf Course** sponsored by the Santiburi Resort (12/12 Moo 1, Mae Nam; ℂ **07742-5040**; www.santiburi. com), and high in the hills on the north end of the island. Greens fees start from 3,350B ($82) for 18 holes.

KAYAKING

Blue Stars Sea Kayaking, at the Gallery Lafayette next to the Green Mango in Chaweng (ℂ **07723-0497**), and easy to contact through most booking agents, takes people kayaking and snorkeling to the Marine National Park. The rubber canoes are perfect for exploring the caverns underneath limestone cliffs. If you can't get to Phang Nga for the most fantastic sea cave scenery, this trip is a fun alternative. The 4-hour trip costs 2,000B ($49) per person.

CRUISING & SAILING

The *June Bahtra* is a stunning Chinese junk new to the waters of Samui (the same company also sails out of Phuket), and their 1-day or moonlight cruises around the island are a guaranteed highlight. Contact them at their office in Bophut: ℂ 07742-2738; www.junebahtra.com. Ask at hotel activity desks for connection with other junkets, mostly small cruise yachts and snorkeling day trips, that start from Samui.

For **catamaran sailing,** check out **Tradewinds Resort** in Chaweng (ℂ **07723-0602**; www.sailingkohsamui.com). Owner and long-time resident John Stall offers courses and guides day-sailing.

COOKING COURSES

For daily Thai cooking and fruit-carving lessons, **Samui Institute of Thai Culinary Arts (SITCA;** www.sitca.com) is a professional operation and a great way to have fun—especially if your beach plans get rained out. A lunchtime course goes for 995B ($24), and a dinner course is 1,400B ($34; they accept major credit cards). Call *C* **07741-3172** for more details or stop in on Chaweng Beach across from the Central Samui Resort (on the same street as Betelnut, see "Where to Dine in Koh Samui," above).

KOH SAMUI SPAS

The spa scene on the island has really taken off. All of the big resorts offer "spa" services of varying quality, and there are a number of good day spas on the island. Whether as an escape from the kids on a rainy day or as part of a larger health-focused mission in Thailand, Samui has all the services.

Ban Sabai (at Big Buddha Beach; *C* **07724-5175;** www.ban-sabai.com) is a great choice for relaxing seaside massage and offers all treatments, from aromatherapy to body waxing, in their lush, Thai-style compound. Personal attention is their hallmark, and a well-informed staff can tailor a program to your every need. Treatments start at just 1,000B ($24) for a 1-hour massage.

Heavena Spa just north of Chaweng (follow signs to the Chaba Resort; *C* **07723-0771**) is another oasis of calm, a hotel-block compound of full-facility massage rooms offering all treatments.

Down in Lamai, **The Spa Resort** (*C* **07723-0855;** www.spasamui.com) has been a leader on the island for years and continues to provide good, affordable day-programs, as well as their signature fasting retreat and all-inclusive packages.

Tamarind Retreat is a more exclusive choice set apart in a jungle area just off the beach at Lamai. They offer the standard services at slightly inflated prices and practice paparazzi prevention (they allow no visitors). Call ahead: *C* **07723-0571** (www. tamarindretreat.com).

Traditional massage is available in any number of storefronts in Chaweng and everywhere along the beach. Expect to pay between 200B and 400B ($4.90–$9.75) per hour for services much the same as the average spa, but without the pomp, circumstance, and incense.

SHOPPING

There is very little in terms of local crafts production on the island—most everything is imported from the mainland, so save the big purchases for Bangkok or Chiang Mai. **Pearls** are cultivated locally, and you'll see some good examples in a few shops. Ask local tour operators about trips to nearby pearl-diving areas.

KOH SAMUI AFTER DARK

Any given evening along the Chaweng strip is certain to be disrupted at least a few times by roaming pickup trucks with crackling PA systems blaring out advertisements in Thai and English for local **Thai boxing bouts.** Grab one of their flyers for times and locations, which vary.

The same infernal trucks advertise the **"Freedom Beach Party!"** which takes place on the beaches north of Chaweng on full moon nights, mostly. Party music, flashing lights, and drinks dispensed from great big coolers all add up to your average fraternity party, but it can be fun. When not doing the old "over-bite boogie," kick back on big straw mats, gaze at the stars, and get metaphysical.

Many of the hotels and resorts have cultural shows featuring Thai dance that are worth seeing, and it wouldn't be a Thai beach without Koh Samui's drag queen review. **Christy's Cabaret** (© 01676-2181 cellular) on the north end of Chaweng puts on a hilarious show that's free of charge. Come well before the show starts at 11pm to get a better seat, and be prepared to make up for that free admission with their cocktail prices.

For **bars and discos,** Chaweng is the place to be. A mainstream kind of fun seems to always be happening at **The Reggae Pub** (indicated on just about every island map—back from the main road around the central beach area). A huge thatch mansion, the stage thumps with some funky international acts, the dance floor jumps (even during low season they do a booming business), and the upstairs pool tables are good for sporting around. Just outside is a collection of open-air bars, also found along Chaweng's beach road.

The **Green Mango** has its own street just off the beachfront road in the northern end of Chaweng and boom-boom-booms late every night as the town's number one dance location. Don't think of going before 10 or 11pm.

Irish-owned and managed **Tropical Murphy's** (across from McDonald's in the south of Chaweng; © 07741-3614) is indeed a slice of Ireland along the Chaweng strip. It is always full and open late, and the best place to have a friendly pint without having to scream over the thumping base of house music. They have good Irish bands visit from time to time.

Zico's, a unique Brazilian restaurant, has a slick, big-city kind of bar glowing with neon. Zico's modern facade looks over the busy main drag in the south of Chaweng near the Central Resort compound (© 07723-1560).

For **live music** on Chaweng, go no further than **Coco Blues Company** (171/9 Moo 2 Chaweng Beach Rd.; © 07741-4354; www.cocobluescompany.com), which hosts great international acts nightly (until 2am), and even hosts an annual festival (Canned Heat was in town when I was there).

Over at Lamai Beach, there are some open-air bars geared to budget backpackers, but many are the sleazier bar-beer variety. **Bauhaus,** located in the center of town on the beach road, is at its best a stompin' club and at its worst hosts only a few tables of the lads there to watch English football. It is usually going strong in high season.

On Bophut Beach, be sure to stop by friendly and laid-back **Frog and Gecko Bar** (in Fisherman's Village; © 07742-5248), especially for their popular pub quiz on Wednesday evenings.

Sunday afternoons, be sure to truck on over to **The Secret Garden Pub** ✿✿ on Big Buddha Beach (© 07724-5253) for live music and a barbecue on the beach. Many a famous performer (Gerry played here, man!) has jumped up on stage, and there have been times where the pub has hosted thousands. It's not exactly "secret," but highly recommended.

SIDE TRIPS FROM KOH SAMUI
ANG THONG NATIONAL MARINE PARK ✿

Forty islands northwest of Koh Samui have been designated a national park. **Ang Thong National Marine Park** is known for its scenic beauty and rare coral reefs. Many of these islands are limestone rock towers (similar to Phang Nga Bay off Phuket), once used by pirates marauding in the South China Sea.

Ko Wua Ta Lap (Sleeping Cow Island), the largest of the 40, is home to the **National Park Headquarters,** where there are some very basic accommodations (book only through the park headquarters at Ⓒ **07728-6025**), but most just visit for the day. The island has freshwater springs and a park service restaurant as well.

Mae Ko (Mother Island) is known for both its beach and Thale Noi, an inland saltwater lake that is mysteriously replenished through an undiscovered outlet to the sea. Known to the Thais as **Ang Thong,** or **Golden Bowl,** this yellowish-green lagoon gave its name to the entire archipelago.

The best way to get to Ang Thong is on the new day junkets by luxury boat with **Seatrans** (Ⓒ **07742-6000**). A 1-day trip takes you to the main sites and includes snorkel gear and use of kayaks (2,800B/$68 for adults; 2,300B/$56 for kids). You can also arrange private tours through any front desk or travel agent. For special kayak trips to Ang Thong, contact **Blue Stars** in Chaweng (Ⓒ **07723-0497**).

5 Ko Pha Ngan

644km (399 miles) S of Bangkok to Surat Thani; 75km (46½ miles) E from Surat Thani to Ko Pha Ngan

Ko Pha Ngan is a more rustic alternative to busy and developed Koh Samui. Like the kids in Alex Garland's *The Beach,* many come to Thailand to find that island paradise that has been unspoiled by the tacky trappings of mass tourism. The message of that novel is a perfect example of what eventually happens—paradise seekers inevitably bring their own standards of comfort and values, ironically turning their utopia into what they have strived to escape. Ko Pha Ngan still attracts an adventurous young crowd, but is following the said-same model of development.

Easily visible from Koh Samui and about two-thirds its size with similar terrain and flora, Ko Pha Ngan has beautiful beaches. and the further reaches of the island—the rugged north and west coast areas accessible only by bumpy road or chartered boat—feature a few cozy resorts and a measure of rustic tranquillity.

The southeastern peninsula of **Haad Rin** is the locus of the monthly **Full Moon Party,** a multiday beachside rave with all the day-glow, strobe-lights, and debauchery you can handle; attendance at the raves, especially in high season, numbers in many thousands of partyers moving to the mix of a European DJ, gobbling tabs of Ecstasy and magic mushrooms, and letting loose, very loose: something like Ibiza meets a Fish show at the beach. The aftermath of the party is a beautiful white-sand beach strewn with party garbage and buzzing with flies ("Has anyone seen my shoes?"). Efforts at clean-up are often inadequate.

If you're interested in attending, boats from piers at either Big Buddha Beach or Bophut on Koh Samui leave at regular intervals all day and night (stopping at around 1am) and many revelers just make a night of it, crash on the beach, and come back to Samui in the morning. *A word of warning:* Beware of theft at Full Moon parties—do yourself a favor and lock all your valuables in a hotel safe.

At other times, when not filled with wild-eyed revelers, the small area of Haad Rin is busy with young travelers. Find New Age crystal, trinket, and T-shirt shops, vegetarian restaurants, bars playing DVD films, masseurs, cheap beers, and $10 bungalows just a Frisbee throw away from a white-sand beach.

Don't be too put-off by Pha Ngan's party reputation. Haad Rin can be avoided altogether and, even during the full moon, you can find peace in any of a number of cozy hideaways on the island.

Just say "Mai!"

"Mai" means "no," and Nancy Reagan's ardent, much-parodied plea couldn't be more apt. Thai authorities hope to put the kibosh on Haad Rin's monthly Full Moon (and other "Half-moon" and "No-moon" excuses to rage). This means undercover drug busts by the very guy who just sold you that bag of oregano, and having to bribe your way out of a stripe-suited homestay or worse. It's not worth it, even if it seems all the other kids are doing it (insert Mom's hyperbole about bridges and foolish conformity).

GETTING THERE

By Boat   Frequent boats link Surat Thani, Koh Samui, Ko Pha Ngan, Ko Tao, and Chumphon, and back again. From Samui's Nathon Pier, the trip to Ko Pha Ngan takes just over an hour with the **Songserm Ferry** and costs 130B ($3.20). Contact them in Koh Samui (© 07742-0157). *Note:* Unfortunately, the muster point in Pha Ngan is not well organized. Come armed with the patience of Buddha, especially any time near Full Moon.

The fastest way to Pha Ngan from Samui is by **Lomprayah High Speed Catamaran** (on Samui: © **07742-7765;** on Pha Ngan: © **07723-8412;** www.lomprayah. com), which leaves from Bophut and takes about 20 minutes and costs 250B ($6.10). Lomprayah also makes daily connections on to Ko Tao and back to the mainland at Chumphon (but not to Surat Thani).

Boats can also be chartered from Samui's Big Buddha Beach or Bophut Beach on a sliding scale (during Full Moon Parties at greatly inflated rates).

FAST FACTS

The tourist police operate a small information kiosk on the north end of the ferry offices at Thong Sala pier; contact them at © **07742-1281** for info or © **1155** in an emergency. There are Branches of Siam City Bank with **exchange and ATM service** along both the main street of Thong Sala and in Haad Rin. Internet service is chockablock around the island; prices are an inflated 2B (5¢) per minute.

GETTING AROUND

Jeep and motorbike rental on Ko Pha Ngan is available anywhere in Haad Rin or near the ferry pier at Thong Sala (Carabineer Jeeps from 900B/$22; regular motorbikes from 150B/$3.65). The island roads are steep and treacherous, especially the popular southern reaches east of Thong Sala near Haad Rin. Many interior roads, including the trek to the secluded Thong Nai Pan area in the north, are hilly, muddy tracks. You can rent motorbikes with good suspension, a jazzed-up version of the standard scooter, for about 300B ($7.30) per day. *Songtaos* follow regular routes between Thong Sala ferry pier and Haad Rin, as well as up the west coast, and cost from 30B(75¢), more at night or during party time.

WHAT TO SEE & DO

The rugged roads of Pha Ngan beg to be explored, and interior roads connect small towns worth seeing as a window into a way of laid-back island living that is slowly disappearing.

Wat Kow Tahm is a well-known international meditation center and temple compound just north of the road connecting Thong Sala pier and busy Haad Rin. Since

1988, Steve and Rosemary Weissmann (from the U.S. and Australia, respectively) have been offering courses in Insight Meditation, or Vipassana, as practiced in the Thai Theravada tradition. The emphasis is on the development of compassionate understanding through the practice of formal walking and sitting meditation. There are frequent Dhamma talks, and introductory 10-day intensive retreats are open to meditators of all experience levels (4,000B/$98). The temple is also open to day visitors and has an overlook with one of the best views on the island. Check their informative website at www.watkowtahm.org, or write for information to: RETREATS, Wat Kow Tahm, P.O. Box 18, Ko Pah Ngan, Surat Thani 84280.

WHERE TO STAY
BAAN TAI BEACH

No one stays in busy Thong Sala, the ferry town; at the least, visitors head due east to nearby Ban Tai Beach, a quiet stretch of sand just to the east of the ferry pier and readily accessible by *songtao*. The water is shallow and not great for swimming, but the beaches are lovely, and there are a few convenient little resorts far from the hubbub of Haad Rin but close enough to visit.

First Villa   First in what? We're not sure, but it's a good choice (maybe #3). They have a small pool, which sets this place ahead of the pack, and rooms are very clean and comfortable; some high-end units even come with a private Jacuzzi. Just east of the ferry pier, the beach is picturesque here but not great for swimming. The central dining area is a large, Thai pavilion, and the staff is on the ball.

145/1 Moo 1, Bantai Beach, Ko Pha Ngan 84280 (2km/1¼ miles east of Thong Sala). ✆ 07737-7225. Fax 07723-8352. 29 units. 1,200B–2,050B ($29–$50) garden double; 2,255B–4,100B ($55–$100) seaview double. MC, V. **Amenities:** Restaurant; pool; Jacuzzi; tour desk; car rental; Internet; massage; laundry. *In room:* A/C, TV, minibar, fridge, safe.

Mac Bay Resort   Mac Bay is comfortable, on a nice stretch of isolated beach. Basic rooms are clean and adequate but are just tiled cells, really; larger air-conditioned rooms are a better choice. All have small shaded balconies and look onto the sea. There are limited services, but a friendly, helpful staff.

Baan Tai Beach, Ko Pha Ngan 84280 (down a small lane south of the main east–west road). ✆ 07723-8443. 25 units. 300B–450B ($7.30–$11) double w/fan; 700B ($17) double w/A/C. MC, V. **Amenities:** Restaurant; tour desk; motorbike rental; laundry. *In room:* Fan or A/C.

HAAD RIN

Haad Rin is a narrow peninsula on the island's southeast tip, with a large number of bungalows on both the west and east sides and busy shopping streets and footpaths leading between them. On the busier west side of the peninsula, also called Sunset Beach, try **Coral Bungalows, Sunset Bay Resort,** or **Rin Bay View Bungalow,** all with rustic bungalows from 600B to 800B ($15–$20).

If in an effort to transcend it all, hilltop **Sea Breeze Bungalow** might be the ticket (94/11 Moo 6, Haad Rin; ✆ 07737-5162). It is a quiet, lofty perch high enough above town for a bit of quiet but close enough to walk down and join the festivities. Rooms start at 500B ($12) for fan only (double at Full Moon).

The Sanctuary ✸   This funky little hippie haven is just a short boat ride to the north of Haad Rin. Though not a retreat center, the Sanctuary offers all kinds of healthy activities like yoga, massage, fasting, and a whole list of treatments and programs. The place has a good, laid-back approach to healthy living at beachside. They have accommodations ranging from 70B ($1.70) dorms, to tidy, basic bungalows from 400B ($9.75), to large scenic theme houses, a model of outdoor living with small kitchen, outdoor bath, and open to the jungle. You'll need to arrange a taxi boat from Haad Rin to Haad Tien (70B/$1.70 if shared, 300B/$7.30 if alone). A good place to tune in, turn on, and drop out for a while.

Contact them at: P.O. Box 3, Ko Pha Ngan 84280. ℂ **01271-3614**. www.thesanctuarythailand.com. 30 units. 70B ($1.70) dorm; 400B–1,100B ($9.75–$27) basic bungalows; 1,250B–2,700B ($30–$66) theme houses. No credit cards. **Amenities:** Restaurant and bar; spa; sauna; watersports rentals; laundry service. *In room:* No phone. Theme suites with small kitchens.

WEST COAST

The west coast has good beaches and is far from the monthly "do" at Haad Rin, a relief for many. Resorts here are quiet and affordable, and growing in number and quality of amenities.

Green Papaya A mellow little courtyard resort at beachside, the bungalows of Green Papaya remind one of Mr. and Mrs. Howell's residence on Gilligan's Island, rustic luxury at beachside that makes brilliant use of local material. Okay, so they've got more than a malfunctioning radio here; in fact, all rooms are equipped with all the comforts of home, but the style of the place is special, and each deluxe bungalow has a big hammock in the shade of a private porch. If Bob Denver (as Gilligan) came stumbling down the path in his ill-fitting red-and-white get-up, floppy hat and all, you wouldn't bat an eye.

Haad Salad, Ko Pha Ngan, 84280 (on the far northwest of the island, about 16km/10 miles north of the ferry). ℂ and fax **07737-4230**. 18 units. 2,700B–4,000B ($66–$98). MC, V. **Amenities:** Restaurant and bar; tour desk; laundry. *In room:* A/C, TV.

Haad Son Resort A respectful (but not isolated) distance from town and good hilltop views of the sea are the hallmarks of this grouping of bungalows. Ever under expansion, Haad Son Resort has a range of accommodations, from bungalow basics in wood and bamboo to concrete room blocks and private bungalows at seaside. A good escape, but not too far from the action.

Moo 8 Ko Phangan 84280. ℂ **07734-9104**. Fax 07734-9103. www.phangan.info/haadson. 36 units. 400B–1,050B ($9.75–$26) fan bungalow; 1,000B–3,500B ($24–$85) A/C bungalow. MC, V. **Amenities:** Restaurant and bar; outdoor pool; tour desk; car-rental; massage; laundry. *In room:* A/C (some), TV, fridge, IDD phone.

Long Bay Resort Contact them in advance of arrival and the friendly folks at Long Bay, on the west coast north of the ferry pier, can make all the arrangements. This is a large campus of bungalows, and the resort is constantly under construction, expanding in increments. They offer a comfortable international standard of room and lots of good local adventure (rentals and tour services), as well as good eats along a quiet beach good for swimming.

Haad Yao, Ko Pha Ngan 84280 (11km/7 miles north of Thong Sala along the west coast). ℂ **07737-7289**. 37 units. 600B ($15) double w/fan; 1,600B–2,750B ($39–$67) double w/A/C. MC, V. **Amenities:** Restaurant; bar; tour desk; car and motorbike rental; shuttle service; Internet; mini-mart; massage; laundry. *In room:* A/C, TV, minibar, fridge.

Salad Beach Resort 🖈 Just next to Green Papaya (above) on the far reaches of Pha Ngan's west coast, Salad Beach is a lovely, sandy cove, and Salad Beach Resort is the most luxurious choice here by far. Only recently opened, they have a small but lovely pool (quite special for Pha Ngan), and rooms are in a central courtyard of fine masonry buildings and have all the top comforts: air-conditioning and TV, stylish sleeping areas, and designer baths in layered shale stone and black tile. A good, semi-luxe romantic getaway with fine basic services.

Haad Salad, Ko Pha Ngan 84280 (on the far northwest of the island, about 16km/10 miles north of the ferry). ℂ 07734-9274. Fax 07723-8242. 49 units. From 2,200B ($54) double. MC, V. **Amenities:** Restaurant; bar; pool; tour desk. *In room:* A/C, TV, minibar, fridge.

NORTHEAST/THONG NAI PAN

Secluded on its own stretch of beach 17km (10½ miles) from the ferry pier and north of busy Haad Rin, this area features great beaches with a few budget stops, as well as the island's best resort. Thong Nai Pan is a scenic choice, easily reached by boat (contact Panviman below) or, less easily, by bumpy dirt road.

Panviman ✿   Rustic-style bungalows outfitted with all the comforts of a high-end hotel cluster along the hills here high above Thong Nai Pan. The service is good, the pool is lovely (a multi-tiered affair with gorgeous views of the bay below), and they have all you need for a good hideaway vacation. Hotel block rooms are also well appointed. You're a long hike from the hilltop to the beach, but they have convenient shuttles, and their good dining options mean you don't have to leave for any reason.

22/1 Moo 5, Thong Nai Pan Noi Bay, Ko Pha Ngan 84280. ℂ and fax **07723-8543.** www.panviman.com. 42 units. 2,000B ($49) hotel block double; 3,000B–4,400B ($73–$107) bungalows. MC, V. **Amenities:** 2 restaurants; bar; pool; Jacuzzi; watersports rental; snooker; tour desk; library and video lounge; limited room service; laundry. *In room:* A/C, satellite TV, minibar, fridge, IDD phone.

WHERE TO DINE

Cheap eats abound in busy Haad Rin, your best bet for a good meal outside of your chosen resort, but there are mostly budget storefronts blaring DVD movies at high decibels. One bright spot is **Om Ganesh** (ℂ 07737-5123) near the main ferry pier; they have great curries and set menus (all you can eat Indian *thali* meals) for little. Authentic, delicious, and very popular.

6 Ko Tao

Tiny **Ko Tao** is a diver's paradise offering easy access to some of Thailand's best coral sites, but with some chic new resorts, the island is not just for divers anymore. True, the bulk of visitors are there for affordable and very professional dive training, and the island is dominated by the many all-inclusive dive resorts and a busy beach party scene among diving expats, but there are still lots of rustic budget choices on the island, as well as a growing number of rustic boutique resorts (see "Where to Stay & Dine," below). The island is a rocky hump shaped like a turtle shell—the name "Ko Tao" meaning "Turtle Island"—and you can explore the island in a day, finding some quiet coves or relaxing along Sai Ree Beach. Avoid Ko Tao in the stormy November to December season, when the monsoon whips up and winds cloud the normally transparent seas.

GETTING THERE

Songserm Travel connects from nearby islands: from Chumphon the fare is 400B ($9.75), from Koh Samui 300B ($7.30), and from Ko Pha Ngan 250B ($6.10). Contact Songserm in Samui (ℂ 07742-0157).

Lomprayah High Speed Catamarans (ℂ 07742-7765; www.lomprayah.com) also make the connection from Samui via Ko Pha Ngan and on to Chumphon twice daily: from Chumphon the fare is 550B ($13); from Koh Samui 550B ($13); and from Ko Pha Ngan 300B ($7.30). A fast and smooth connection.

ORIENTATION & GETTING AROUND

All boats arrive in **Mae Haad Village** on the west of the island, and apart from the few resorts and restaurants scattered along the rocky southern end of this tiny rock, most of the activity centers in busy Mae Haad, and just north of there along the west coast at Sai Ree Beach, up to little Sai Ree Village. It is less than a click from the ferry to the first few dive resorts of Sai Ree Beach, and touts will take you to check out their hotel for no fee; otherwise hop a songtao or a scooter (or rent one for 200B/$4.90 per day) at Mae Haad. Touts from resorts and scuba operators alike line the strip at Mae Haad, and if you haven't booked ahead (and can be flexible) you can find good deals by bargaining.

WHERE TO STAY & DINE

Mae Haad offers lots of budget accommodation with all of the attendant noise of bars and busy traffic in the evening. Most popular are the many mid-range dive resorts lining Sai Ree Beach, just north of the ferry terminal. There are also some new high-end choices scattered across the island.

EXPENSIVE/MODERATE

Charm Churee Villa   Rustic lodging sits on a forested hummock overtop a secluded cove. Rooms are tidy and basic, with a few dolled-up numbers worth the upgrade (and more villas under construction), but what sets this little resort apart is the cozy beach and private cove, a great spot to hang in the hammock and have drinks ferried to you, or explore the blue waters with snorkel and mask.

30/1 Moo 2, Jansom Bay (just south of the ferry landings at Mae Haad Village), Ko Tao 84280. © 07745-6393. Fax 0288-40045. www.charmchureevilla.com. 30 units. 5,900B–6,990B ($144–$170) double; from 7,990B ($195) suite. Amenities: 2 restaurants; spa; tour desk; car-rental; massage; laundry. In room: A/C, TV, fridge, minibar, safe, IDD phone.

Jamahkiri Spa & Resort ⚘   The hideaway of hideaways on Ko Tao, luxurious little Jamahkiri is accessible by precipitous mountain track that would make you reconsider the return trip, but the good news is that you might not mind being stranded at this unique boutique gem. Overlooking Shark Bay are a clutch of high-end pavilions and suites, some with two levels, all with balconies. There is a luxurious little spa area and fine dining outlet, and public spaces are grand with grottos and lots of steep steps, the kind of hideaway where a James Bond villain would be right at home. The best choice on the island, but far from the action.

Overlooking Thian Og Bay (Shark Bay) on the southern end of the island. © 07745-6400. www.jamahkiri.com. 12 units. 5,900B–7,900B ($144–$193) pavilion; from 8,900B ($217) suite. MC, V. Amenities: Restaurant and bar; spa; Jacuzzi; tour desk; massage; laundry. In room: A/C, TV, fridge, minibar, coffeemaker, safe, IDD phone.

Koh Tao Cabana ⚘   A collection of upmarket bungalows line this high rocky outcrop on the northeastern end of the island (they'll pick you up at the pier in their VW microbus). Amenities are light (no pool), but they do have good in-house dining, and the place is an ideal romantic escape. Rooms are either large pavilions at seaside or raised jungle bungalows high above the beach, all arranged for privacy and quiet. Friendly staff can make any arrangements.

16 Moo 1, Baan Haad Sai Ree (on the far north end of Sai Ree Beach), Ko Tao 84280. © 07745-6505. www.kohtao cabana.com. 33 units. 2,900B–5,100B ($71–$124) double. MC, V. Amenities: Restaurant and bar; tour desk; car-rental; massage; laundry. In room: A/C, TV, fridge, minibar, safe, IDD phone.

INEXPENSIVE

Hat Sai Ree is lined with budget bungalows, all available to walk-in guests but mostly booked through budget scuba packages, popular choices for long-staying guests getting more extensive Scuba certification. Try **Big Blue** (© 07745-6415; www.bigblue diving.com) among the many.

On the far south end of the island, a popular all-inclusive scuba and stay resort is **Big Bubble Dive Resort** (© 07745-6669; www.bigbubble.info).

WHERE TO DINE

The ferry terminal area on the west side of the island is choc-a-bloc with small local eateries and tourist feedbags, nothing too spectacular (and all wildly overpriced because of the remote island location). On the far southern tip of the island and worth the trip for the view alone is little **New Heaven Restaurant** (© 07745-6462), which serves good Thai and Western food (heavy on fresh seafood) from a deck overlooking a spectacular bay. **Sairee Beach** and **Sairee Village** are both busy with small resorts and their attendant dining outlets. Look for **New Heaven Home Bakery** (© 07745-6554) on the north end of Sairee Beach, a popular sandwich and breakfast stop for divers. One freestanding standout in Sairee Beach is:

Papa's Tapas 🌶🌶   In the heart of busy Sairee Village, Papa's Tapas is the brainchild of a group of expat entrepreneurs (they're also at work on a large resort nearby). The concept is simple: innovative international cuisine, a constantly evolving menu of specials, served with good wine and enjoyed at your pace in a casual, candlelit, open-air pavilion. I had a taste of spare ribs, rich garlic bread, and lamb kebabs with tzadziki. There's also a great wine list, and it's the only absinthe bar in Thailand.

In Sairee Village on the north end of Sairee Beach. No phone. 80B–130B ($1.95–$3.20) 1 tapas course (expect to spend about $12 per person). Daily 6pm until late.

NIGHTLIFE

The island nightlife is big on beer-soaked braggadocio about brushes with sharks or unruly dive-shop managers that plague the large expat diving community. You can always find a good late-night rollicking romp somewhere on the island; try **Choppers Bar and Grill** (14/43 Moo 1, Sairee Village; © 07745-6641, www.choppers-sportsbar.com) on the north end of Sai Ree Beach.

DIVING

It's a real international scene on Ko Tao, and in high season the expat community swells as dive masters the world over make their way to the busy little isle. The west coast of the island just north of the ferry landing is lined with small operators, most with adjoining accommodation. Many travelers book ahead from home or from Bangkok or Koh Samui. I've listed just a few of the many.

- **Big Blue Diving Koh Tao** in Mae Haad Town; © 07745-6415 (www.bigblue diving.com).
- **Easy Divers** in Mae Haad Town (at catamaran jetty); © 07745-6010 (www.thai dive.com).
- **Big Bubble** in the south end of the island; © 07745-6669 (www.bigbubble.info).

Note that every hotel on the island can book dive tours. A great place to get a very affordable start with the sport.

Also look into unique dive-and-stay packages at Nangyuan Resort, an isolated island location just off the northwest tip of Ko Tao (see www.nangyuan.com) with rooms starting as low as 1,200B ($29).

7 The Far South & on to Malaysia

From Surat Thani going south, Thailand slowly gives way to Malay culture and Buddhism—predominant elsewhere in the kingdom—and is replaced by rich Islamic influence, a more gradual process than about any precise border line. Nakhon Si Thammarat is an ancient Buddhist city of note with many temples worth visiting. Far southern Hat Yai is a major transport hub and a destination more popular with Malay and Singaporean tourists, and mostly a stopover for onward travel to (or connecting from) Malaysia.

Important Note: The far southern region of Thailand has seen some unrest from violent separatist insurgents in recent years. Few travelers are making their way much past Nakhon Si Thammarat, except for those going on to Malaysia or Singapore via Hat Yai. Stay abreast of events.

NAKHON SI THAMMARAT

Nakhon Si Thammarat, one of the oldest cities in south Thailand, has long been its religious capital. **Wat Mahathat** houses a hair of the Buddha and is the town's central attraction and important pilgrimage point for Thai Buddhists. This region is the locus for traditional Thai puppet-plays, and **Ban Nang Thalung Suchart Subsin** (Mr. Subsin's House of Shadow Plays) at 110/18 Si Thammasok Soi 3 (© **7534-6394**), makes for an interesting visit.

Thai Airways and **PB Air** each connect Nakhon with Bangkok. All north–south trains make a stop, and affordable minivans can be arranged from any hotel (the best way to get around the south).

Thai Hotel, 1375 Ratchadamnoen Road (© **7534-1509**), is a basic standard, and convenient with rooms starting at 390B ($9.50).

HAT YAI

It's a town full of tourists behaving badly, really, mostly men from nearby Malaysia and Singapore attracted by this rowdy, slightly sleazy, inexpensive, consumer playground. For Westerners, Hat Yai is mostly a gateway to Malaysia by train or bus or a stepping-off point for rugged Tarutao National Park. Hat Yai's busy Night Market is certainly worth a wander, and the beaches at nearby Songkhla are not a bad day trip.

Hat Yai International Airport welcomes flights from Malaysia and Singapore frequently throughout the week via Silk Air, Malaysia Airlines, and Thai Airways, and there are available connections to Bangkok and Phuket.

A major rail hub, five trains depart daily from **Bangkok's Hua Lampong Station** to Hat Yai (for info, call © **2223-7010** or 1690), and there are daily connections with Malaysia. Minibuses connect from other parts of the region, and long-distance buses connect with the **Bangkok Southern Bus Terminal** (© **2435-1199**).

A number of fine hotels cater to Malay tourists. Try **The Regency Hotel,** 23 Prachathipat Rd. (© **7423-4400**), with rooms from 900B ($22); or the popular backpacker haunt, **Cathay Guest House,** 93/1 Niphat Uthit 2 Rd. (© **7424-3815**), with dorms from 100B ($2.45) and reasonable singles from 160B ($3.90).

9

Southern Peninsula: The West Coast & Islands

The west coast of Thailand was hit hard by the Christmas Tsunami on December 26, 2004. The coastal area of Khao Lak as well as the island of Koh Phi Phi were devastated, and parts of the heavily developed west coast of Phuket were heavily damaged. Many travelers balk at the thought of returning to the scene of such tragedy, but most of the coastal resorts in the area were up and running just months after the disaster and are now desperate for tourists, the heart of the economy in this region. A sophisticated earthquake and tsunami warning system is now in place in the Indian Ocean to detect the unlikely case of another massive quake and rogue wave, and many hotels even have a tsunami alarm, as well as marked escape routes to high ground. The Thai government has made a quick job of cleanup and revitalization, and the best assistance we can offer as tourists is to return to the region with our tourist dollars.

The island of **Phuket** was one of the earliest tourist developments in the kingdom, and from humble origins has grown into a top international resort area: the best choice for comfort and services on the west coast. Phuket may be the largest and best known, but is but one of many in the brilliant blue Andaman Sea; rocky islets, atolls, and leafy jungle coastline play host to a roster of island resorts and getaways. The Southern Peninsula is a great area to island-hop by bus and ferry connections, and there are opportunities for snorkeling, trekking, and laid-back luxury in every quarter.

The province of **Krabi** encompasses all the land east of Phuket, including Koh Phi Phi and Koh Lanta, but "Krabi" typically refers to the small port town and nearby beaches of the **Krabi Resort Area** and **Ao Nang Beach.** In places like Raillay Beach, you'll find dynamic stone-tower landscapes (famous for rock climbing), great beaches, and a range of resorts. It is a popular alternative to busy Phuket.

Koh Phi Phi, despite damage from the tsunami, still greets guests with some fine resorts scattered in the lee of Phi Phi Don, the main island. The small backpacker town on Phi Phi Don is slowly rebuilding, but the land is officially national park land and there is talk that Phi Phi will become a day-trip destination only. Snorkeling trips around Phi Phi Don are very popular.

Koh Lanta is a large island southeast of Krabi Town populated mostly by Muslim fisherman, but Lanta now hosts a bevy of mid- and high-end resorts, as well as some good budget choices.

The high season on the west coast is from November to April—bookings must be made in advance, especially on Phuket, and discounted rates are hard to come by. Still, Western winter months are the time for water activities, when the Andaman is calm and the skies clear (when the snow falls thick in many parts of the world). During super peak season,

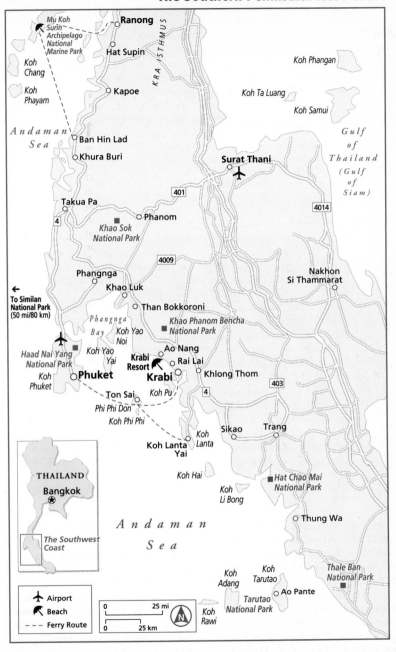

Mu Koh Surin Archipelago National Marine Park

Ranong

K R A   I S T H M U S

Hat Supin

Koh Chang

Koh Phayam

Kapoe

Koh Phangan

Koh Ta Luang

Koh Samui

A n d a m a n
S e a

Ban Hin Lad

Khura Buri

G u l f
o f
T h a i l a n d
(G u l f
o f
S i a m)

Surat Thani

Takua Pa

401

4

Phanom

Khao Sok National Park

4009

4014

Phangnga

Khao Luk

Than Bokkoroni

Nakhon Si Thammarat

Phangnga Bay

Koh Yao Noi

Khao Phanom Bencha National Park

Ao Nang

Krabi Resort

Rai Lai

Koh Yao Yai

Haad Nai Yang National Park

Phuket

Krabi

Khlong Thom

Koh Phuket

Ton Sai

Koh Pu

4

403

Phi Phi Don

Koh Phi Phi

Sikao

Trang

← To Similan National Park (50 mi/80 km)

Koh Lanta Yai

Koh Lanta

Koh Hai

Hat Chao Mai National Park

A n d a m a n
S e a

Koh Li Bong

Thung Wa

THAILAND

Bangkok

The Southwest Coast

Koh Adang

Koh Tarutao

Tarutao National Park

Ao Pante

Thale Ban National Park

Koh Rawi

✈ Airport

✦ Beach

--- Ferry Route

0   25 mi

0   25 km

N

from the Christmas holiday through New Year's to about January 10, most places tack on steep surcharges.

The monsoon winds strike from about May through October; during the period from late June through August, the "promotional season," many hotels and other establishments offer discounts up to 50%. While the monsoon does bring rains, they rarely last all day, and the weather can even be completely clear for long stretches. One constant of the monsoon, however, is rough seas. Even swimming becomes dangerous with heavy surf and a strong undertow. Islands in the eastern Gulf of Thailand, Koh Samui, Koh Pha Ngan, and Koh Tao, are more sheltered from the monsoon weather, so are a better bet, but the big off-season discounts at the more luxurious properties in places like Phuket are worth considering.

1 Phuket

The 2004 Christmas Tsunami struck a devastating blow to the resorts on the west coast of Phuket, but most are operating at full capacity; many in fact used the disaster as an opportunity to renovate and upgrade. While no one wants to forget the tragedy, tourists are the mainstay of the economy and are more welcome than ever.

At its best, Phuket is idyllic: It has long sandy beaches (some with dunes), warm water, excellent snorkeling and scuba diving at the Similan Islands, ideal windsurfing conditions, mountains, fine resorts, and some of the best seafood in all of Thailand. At its worst, it is overdeveloped, overrun with tour groups, and areas like busy Patong's pulsing commercial strip and raucous nightlife can be a bit too much for families in search of beachside tranquillity. As groups pour in from Singapore, Hong Kong, and Europe, backpackers head off to the eastern Gulf islands and lesser known atolls.

Many of Phuket's fine resorts, however, are elegant and designed to give you the illusion of tropical solitude even in busier areas. It is nearly impossible to find a totally secluded beach, but there are a number of very attractive and comfortable facilities with a high level of service—not a bad trade-off for those in search of all the luxuries. If you're on a family holiday, Phuket is a good choice.

The name "Phuket" is derived from the Malay "Bukit," meaning hill, and hills dominate much of the island's interior. There are still some rubber plantations and a few open-pit mining operations going on. Going by rented car or taking a fun but touristy "safari" is a good way to get into the jungle or up the hills, from which you'll have great views of the beaches below and the many surrounding islands and islets. Most folks come for the beaches, though, and Phuket's are indeed some of the best in Thailand. Take your shoes off, find a hammock, and relax.

ARRIVING

BY PLANE   **Thai Airways** (© 02525-2084 domestic reservations in Bangkok) flies more than a dozen times daily from Bangkok from 7am to 9:30pm (trip time: 1 hr. 20 min.); and a daily flight from Hat Yai (trip time: 45 min.). In Hat Yai, its office is at 190/6 Niphat Uthit Rd. (© 07423-3433). Thai Airways' office in Phuket is at 78 Ranong Rd. (© 07621-1195 domestic, or 07621-2499 international).

Bangkok Airways (© 02229-3434 in Bangkok or 07724-5601 on Koh Samui) connects Phuket with Koh Samui at least two times daily. The Bangkok Airways office in Phuket is at 158/2–3 Yaowarat Rd., Phuket Town (© 07622-5033, or 07632-7114 at Phuket Airport).

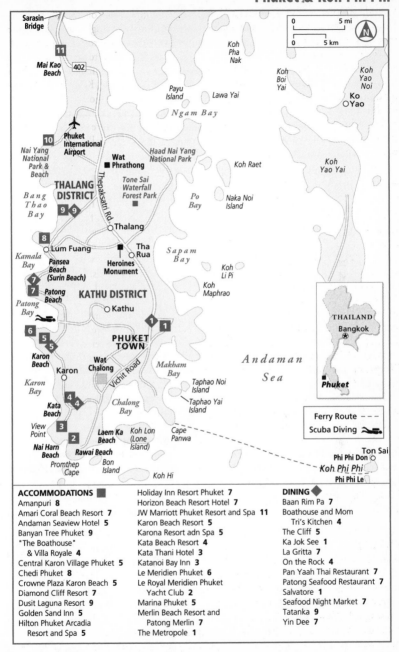

Phuket & Koh Phi Phi

ACCOMMODATIONS ■
Amanpuri **8**
Amari Coral Beach Resort **7**
Andaman Seaview Hotel **5**
Banyan Tree Phuket **9**
"The Boathouse"
& Villa Royale **4**
Central Karon Village Phuket **5**
Chedi Phuket **8**
Crowne Plaza Karon Beach **5**
Diamond Cliff Resort **7**
Dusit Laguna Resort **9**
Golden Sand Inn **5**
Hilton Phuket Arcadia
Resort and Spa **5**

Holiday Inn Resort Phuket **7**
Horizon Beach Resort Hotel **7**
JW Marriott Phuket Resort and Spa **11**
Karon Beach Resort **5**
Karona Resort adn Spa **5**
Kata Beach Resort **4**
Kata Thani Hotel **3**
Katanoi Bay Inn **3**
Le Meridien Phuket **6**
Le Royal Meridien Phuket
Yacht Club **2**
Marina Phuket **5**
Merlin Beach Resort and
Patong Merlin **7**
The Metropole **1**

DINING ◆
Baan Rim Pa **7**
Boathouse and Mom
Tri's Kitchen **4**
The Cliff **5**
Ka Jok See **1**
La Gritta **7**
On the Rock **4**
Pan Yaah Thai Restaurant **7**
Patong Seafood Restaurant **7**
Salvatore **1**
Seafood Night Market **7**
Tatanka **9**
Yin Dee **7**

Phuket Airlines (✆ **02535-6382**) also has daily flights (leaving in the morning, returning in evening). Thailand's newest budget airline, **Air Asia** (www.airasia.com; ✆ **02515-9999**), flies between Bangkok and Phuket for about the same price as the train.

Thai Airways (✆ **02525-2084**) connects Phuket with international flights to and from Frankfurt, Hong Kong, Perth, Singapore, and Tokyo. **Silk Air** (✆ **02353-6000** in Bangkok) has daily connections with Singapore.

The attractive, modern **Phuket International Airport** (✆ **07732-7230,** information) is located in the north of the island, about 40 minutes' drive from town or from Patong Beach. There are banks, money-changing facilities, car-rental agents (see "Getting Around," below), and a post office. The Phuket Tourist Business Association booth can help you make hotel arrangements if you haven't booked a room.

Many resorts will pick you up at the airport upon request for a fee, usually steep, though some include this with your booking. The airport limousine counter, operated by **Tour Royale** (✆ **07634-1214**), offers many options for getting to your hotel from the airport. The cheapest way is the minibus, which operates every hour on the hour from 9am to 11pm daily. Stopping between Patong, Kata, Karon, and Phuket Town, prices start at 150B ($3.65), depending on how far you're going; 180B ($4.40) gets you as far south as Kata Beach (*Note:* This van will stop at a small travel agent and make sure that everyone is pre-booked, and removing any stragglers can mean a long wait). **Taxi service** from the airport, also arranged at the limousine counter, will cost between 400B ($9.75) to Phuket Town and 600B ($14.65) to Kata Beach. There are many VIP options as well, and a new airport bus connecting with Phuket Town bus terminal for just 52B/$1.25.

BY BUS   Three air-conditioned 24-seat VIP buses leave daily from **Bangkok's Southern Bus Terminal** (✆ **02434-7192**), best as an overnight, and cost from 750B ($18) for a VIP bus (fewer seats and more room, a movie, hostesses, and snacks). Numerous regular air-conditioned buses go each day and cost as little as 275B ($6.70). Standard buses make frequent connections to Surat Thani and nearby towns on the mainland (to Surat is 6 hrs. and 105B/$2.55).

The intercity bus terminal is at the **City Park Complex** on Phang-nga Road (✆ **07621-1480**), east of Phuket Town just opposite the Royal Phuket City Hotel. For information on how to get from here to the beaches, see "Getting Around," below.

BY MINIVAN   Minivans to and from Surat Thani, Krabi, Nakhon Si Thammarat, Ranong, and other southern cities leave on regular schedules throughout the day. In each city, minivan operators work with the hotels and arrange free pickup, so it is best to book through your hotel front desk or a travel agent (also, the operators who man the phones at minivan companies rarely speak English). Tickets to destinations in the south, to places like Surat Thani or Hat Yai, go for between 100B and 250B ($2.45–$6.10).

VISITOR INFORMATION

The **Tourism Authority of Thailand** has an office in Phuket Town at 73–75 Phuket Rd. (✆ **07621-2213**), but there is far better information at any hotel concierge or tour desk. There are lots of free maps on offer (all are full of advertisements), and for driving around the island, pick up the very detailed *Periplus Editions Map of Phuket* at bookstores. Restaurants and hotel lobbies are good places to pick up any of a number of free local publications: *Phuket Food-Shopping-Entertainment* is packed with dining suggestions and ads for many of the island's activities; *What's on South* has some useful information on Phuket, Koh Phi Phi, and Krabi; and there a few fun ultraglossy local magazines for sale.

ISLAND LAYOUT

If you arrive by car or coach, you'll cross over to Phuket from the mainland at the northern tip of the island via the Sarasin Bridge along Rt. 402. Phuket Town, the island's commercial center, is in the southeast of the island at the terminus of Rte. 402; local buses stop near Phuket Town. Phuket's picturesque stretches of sand dot the stretch of western coast from Nai Harn, on the southern tip, to Bang Tao, about 30km (19 miles) north. Beginning in the south, you'll find Kata Noi, Kata, Karon, Patong, Surin, and a number of smaller beaches all along this corridor. A busy coastal road links the popular tour towns in the south, but stops north of Patong require short detours from the main highway. Inland Phuket, with its winding mountain roads, buzzes with traffic, and many visitors rent vehicles to tour the island's smaller byways or make the trip to jungle parks like Khao Phra Thaeo Wildlife Park in the northeast of the isle, famed for diverse flora and fauna. The western beaches have all the services visitors might need, but everything comes with resort prices and is very westernized and modern. For a taste of Thai life, affordable services, and a few restaurants, hit Phuket Town (especially recommended if this is your only destination in Thailand).

THE BEACHES   There's a beach for everyone in Phuket, from exclusive hideaways with luxury hotels to backpacker towns and even campgrounds. Each beach is distinct, and selecting the appropriate area makes all the difference.

Nai Harn, the southernmost bay on the west coast, is home to only one major resort and just a few scattered bungalows, and, although the beach here is not as grand, it is more laid back and quiet. The sand is fine and the water deep. As a public beach, with a few small, local eateries, it makes for a great day trip if you're staying at a more populated beach and want to run away for the day (a good long motorbike/car ride south of Kata/Karon).

Rawai Beach and **Chalong Beach** are the island's two eastern facing beaches, both hosting a few resorts and restaurants.

North of Nai Harn are the more popular developed beaches: **Kata, Kata Noi,** and **Karon Beaches.** Developed, but not overwhelmingly so (far from over-the-top Patong), along these beaches you'll find resorts large and small. In general this is the least expensive area on Phuket, with still a few hold-out budget places that haven't been bulldozed and made high-end yet. Sandy beaches are long and picturesque, and the water is deep with some nice wave breaks. This beach area has more restaurants than the remote bays, and some shopping, nightlife, and travel agent options as well. But you won't find rowdy crowds here and, even with all the development, the area manages to maintain a laidback character.

North of the Kata and Karon bays you'll pass through **Relax Bay,** a small cove with a few resorts, before rolling down the mountain to **Patong Beach,** the most famous (perhaps infamous) strip on the island. Patong's draw is its raucous nightlife, busy shops, and restaurants, and brash neon-radiating pulse: can you hear the bass? Accommodation runs the gamut from five-star resorts to budget motels. Love it or hate it, the town has the most diverse selection of dining facilities and highest concentration of tour and dive operators, watersports activities, shopping, and nightlife, and most visitors end up spending a few nights on the shiny strip. The drawbacks—the town is a parade of tourists and touts, and hassling streetside tailors and souvenir salesmen are on your every move. Also the nightlife can be risqué, even sleazy, so nighttime isn't best for the kids. If you love to be in the center of it all, stay in Patong; if you want some peace, stay away.

Still north of Patong, **Kamala Bay, Surin Beach,** and **Pan Sea Beach** have more secluded resorts on lovely beaches for those who still want the convenience of nearby Patong, but cherish the serenity of a quiet resort.

About two-thirds of the way to the northern tip of the island, **Bang Tao Beach** is home to the Laguna Resort Complex, a partnership of five world-class resorts sharing excellent facilities and a fabulous beach. While this area is rather far from both Patong Beach and Phuket Town, the many dining and activity options make this area quite self-sufficient for those with the means.

Far north of the main resort areas, **Haad Nai Yang National Park** has limited facilities and may not appeal to most, but for real beach lovers it is a dream come true. There is a coral reef just 1,400m (4,592 ft.) off shore, and if you are looking to get back to nature, Haad Nai Yang is your best bet.

Mai Khao is the northernmost beach in Phuket and is famed for the annual hatching of giant sea turtles. This stunning stretch of desolate beach hosts just one luxe resort: the JW Marriott Phuket.

GETTING AROUND

Public transportation is a problem on Phuket that never seems to get solved. If you've spent any time in other parts of the country, you'll know that the covered pickup trucks that cruise the streets picking up and dropping off passengers are called songtaos, while the noisy motorized three-wheel demon vehicles are known as tuk-tuks. Not so on Phuket! Here, the people call the minitrucks "tuk-tuks," while songtaos are the giant colorful buses that ply the main roads (also called "baht buses").

Here's the problem: Tuk-tuk drivers, the guys in the minipickups, have exclusive rights to transport people *between* beaches and have set up a price fix: at night they'll charge an arm and a leg and are the only game in town. *Songtao* buses are only permitted to travel from each beach to Phuket Town (not from beach to beach).

BY *SONGTAO*   The local bus terminal is in front of the Central Market on Ranong Road in Phuket Town. Fares to the most popular beaches range from 20B to 30B (50¢–75¢). *Songtaos* leave when full, usually every 30 minutes, from 7am to 6pm between Phuket Town and the main beaches on the west coast. They do not operate routes between beaches.

BY TUK-TUK & DAIHATSU MINI   Within Phuket Town, tuk-tuks cost about 20B to 40B (50¢–$1) for in-town trips: a good way to get to the bus station or to Phuket Town's restaurants.

In the west-coast beaches, tuk-tuks and small Daihatsu minitrucks roll around town honking at any tourist on foot, especially in Patong. It is the only way to travel between beaches. Bargain hard and beware that these guys will try to eke every baht out of you. Expect to pay about 400B ($9.75) from town to the airport, 150B ($3.65) from town to Patong Beach, and 120B ($2.90) from Patong Beach to Karon Beach. It costs more late at night, and unless you can bargain ruthlessly you'll have to pay through the nose, usually double the normal day rates (but remember that you're choosing from tens of drivers, so walking away, or to the next vehicle, when the price isn't right, is an effective tactic).

BY MOTORCYCLE TAXI   Drivers, identifiable by colored vests, make short trips within Phuket Town or along Patong Beach for 20B–40B (50¢–$1). Don't let them talk you into any but short in-town rides; in other words, the winding roads between beaches, unless you're looking for a hair-raising adventure.

BY CAR   Self-driving is popular in Phuket, but extreme caution applies. Roads between the main beaches in the west and connecting with Phuket Town across the center of the island are dangerously steep, and winding with more than a few hairpin turns and lots of unpredictable traffic. As in other parts of the kingdom, drivers pass aggressively, even on blind curves, and self-driving visitors will want to be very defensive and alert at all times.

Avis has a counter at **Phuket Airport** (© 07653-1243). Plan on spending around 1,500B to 1,800B ($37–$44) per day for a Suzuki Caribian 4WD sport vehicle. **Budget** (© 07620-5396) is a bit cheaper, and has an airport location as well as counters at a number of hotels (JW Marriott, Evason Resort, and Club Andaman Beach Resort in Patong). **Hertz** also has a counter at the airport (© 07635-1166). All international renters offer sedans, and have sound insurance coverage available, which is highly recommended.

Inexpensive Suzuki Caribians can be rented from almost all travel agents and from hotels at the beach areas. Prices start at 1,200B ($29) per day. Independent agents hang around under umbrellas along Patong Beach and offer great bargains if you negotiate (as little as 1,000B/$24 per day). Independent dealers have the same product for less money, but don't count on them having an insurance policy.

BY MOTORCYCLE   Also along the Patong strip, the same car-rental guys will provide you with a bike for cheap. A 100cc Honda scooter goes for 200B ($4.90) per day, while a 400cc Honda Shadow chopper will set you back at least 600B ($14.65) per day. Significant discounts can be negotiated if you plan to rent for a longer time. Wear your helmet (sometimes-enforced fines of 500B/$12 for going without), keep to the left, and let cars pass. You're sure to meet up with a few road-rashed travelers in any beach area, and there is no quicker way to end a vacation than on slippery, treacherous roads, especially for inexperienced riders, so practice caution. For the best big bikes, try **The Big Bike Company** (103 Rachauthid Rd., Patong © 07634-5199; www.bigbikecompany.com).

FAST FACTS: Phuket

Banks   Banks are located in Phuket Town, with many larger branches on Ranong and Rasada roads. There are bank offices at the airport, as well as branches of major Thai banks at Kata, Karon, and Patong beaches. See each section for more complete information. **Money changers** are in major shopping areas on each beach, and at most resorts. Banks offer the best rates.

Bookstores   There are lots of small book shops on the small lanes off of Kata Beach. Also look for **The Books** in Patong at 198/2 Rat-U-Thit Rd. (© 07634-2980).

Post Office   The General Post Office in Phuket Town (© 07621-1020) is at the corner of Thalang and Montri roads.

Hospitals The **Bangkok Phuket Hospital** at 2/1 Hongyok-Uthit Rd. (off Yaowarat Rd. in Phuket Town) (© **07625-4421**) has English-speaking staff and high-quality facilities. Also with clinics at Patong (Soi Patong Beach Hotel, © **07634-4699**; and Laguna Canal Village, Laguna Phuket, © **07632-5442**).

Internet Internet service is fairly easy to find on the island. There are cafes aplenty in Patong, the best are further away from the beach. Along Rat-u-thit Road in the center of Patong (a 5-min. walk east, away from the beach) you'll find 1B per minute ($1.45 per hour) service. In Kata and Karon, a number of small storefronts have good connections. Try **Lionchai Cyber** (204/30 Rat-u-thit Rd.; © **06946-6412**; www.liontchai.com).

Police The emergency number for the **Tourist Police** is fast-dial four digit © **1155**.

SPECIAL EVENTS

If you are on Phuket in October, don't miss the **Vegetarian Festival.** The name is misleading—it is not about animal rights or being health consciousness, but a Thai Chinese tradition on Phuket (and now celebrated widely throughout Thailand) that corresponds with the Buddhist Lent. For 9 days not only do devotees refrain from meat consumption, many also submit to physical self-mutilation through extreme body-piercing with long skewers or swords and walk over coals. The festival began as an act of penance to the spirits to help early inhabitants ward off malaria, but these days the rituals are more for young men to prove themselves and for gaining other kinds of merit and good luck. Early morning processions follow through the streets of Phuket Town, with onlookers clad in white for the occasion. During this time you can also feast on terrific vegetarian buffets at just about any restaurant in Thailand.

THINGS TO SEE & DO

If Phuket is your only destination in Thailand, you'll certainly want to get to some of the small rural temples and Phuket Town, but touring Phuket pales in comparison to culturally rich areas like Bangkok or Chiang Mai. Beach and outdoor activities top the list of things to do, and there's certainly something for everyone (see section 4, "Exploring Phuket"). Opportunities to tour the island's rustic bays and many beaches or take day-trips to scenic **Phang Nga Bay** to the north or the islands jungle interior abound.

Thalang National Museum, in the east just off Highway 402 at the Heroine's Monument (© **07631-1426;** daily 9am–4pm; 30B/75¢), exhibits Phuket's indigenous cultures, the history of the Thais on Phuket, and crafts from the southern Thai regions as well as a 9th century statue of the Hindu deity Vishnu—evidence of early Indian merchants on the burgeoning kingdom.

There are a few Buddhist temples on the island that are quite notable: the most unique is **Wat Pra Tong,** located along Highway 402 in Thalang just south of the airport. Years ago, a boy fell ill and dropped dead after tying his buffalo to a post sticking out of the ground. It was later discovered that the post was actually the top of a huge Buddha image that was buried under the earth. Numerous attempts to dig out the post failed—during one attempt in 1785, workers were chased off by hornets. Everyone took all this failure to mean that the Buddha image wanted to just stay put, so they covered the "post" with a plaster image of The Buddha's head and shoulders and built a temple around it. Nearby **Wat Pra Nahng Sahng** houses three very interesting Buddha images made of tin, a local natural resource once considered semiprecious. Each image has a smaller Buddha in its belly.

The most famous temple among Thai visitors is **Wat Chalong.** Chalong was the first resort on Phuket, back when the Thais first started coming to the island for vacations. Nowadays, the discovery of better beaches on the west side of the island has driven most tourists away from this area, but the temple still remains the center of Buddhist worship. While the temple compound itself is pretty standard in terms of modern temples, the place comes to life during Buddhist holy days. The temple is on the Bypass Road, about 8km (5 miles) south of Phuket Town.

Sea Gypsies, considered the indigenous people of Phuket, are fast disappearing from the island and surrounds. Commercial fishing interests and shoreline development continue to threaten their livelihood of subsistence fishing. Related to Malaysian **Orang Laut** and the southern Thai **Sakai** tribes, Phuket and Pha Nga's Sea Gypsies form a few small settlements on Phuket island, one on Koh Sirey east of Phuket Town, and another at Rawai Beach just south of Chalong Bay. The villages are simple, floating shacks and long-tail boats. Visits to some of the larger settlements in Phang Nga Bay are included in many island day trips. It is an enlightening experience to visit these people and their disappearing culture. Be prepared for panhandling children.

2 Where to Stay

The island's hotels, resorts, and restaurants below are divided into beach areas to simplify choice. Phuket is thick with development, so the list below is but a selection, the best of each category on each beach. Prices are listed by the high-season rack-rate, an almost fictitious fee but a good point of departure for gauging price. Expect to pay from 30% and as much as 50% below the listed rate, especially in low season (see "Tips on Accommodations," in chapter 2).

NAI HARN BEACH

Far to the south, Nai Harn Beach is a good escape. Adjacent beaches on the eastern side of the island, **Rawai** and **Chalong,** are home to a few good high-end resorts: **Evason Phuket Resort and Spa** (100 Vised Rd.; © **07638-1010;** Fax 07638-1018; www.sixsenses.com) is a luxury enclave (and popular day-spa destination); and **Mangosteen** (99/4 Moo 7, Soi Mangosteen; © **07628-9399;** Fax 07628-9389; www. mangosteen-phuket.com) is a newer high-end choice (both with rooms starting at around $170). On Nai Harn try:

EXPENSIVE

Le Royal Meridien Phuket Yacht Club 🐾🐾   Perched above the northern edge of Nai Harn Beach, overlooking the public beach and yachts beyond, the Yacht Club is one of the earliest luxury accommodations in Phuket yet still rivals nearly anything on the island for setting and comfort. Staff members in pith helmets greet with heel-clicking salutes and, as you enter, the pagoda-style foyer gives way to the terraced gardens overflowing with pink and white bougainvillea. Common areas are terra-cotta tile and open air with views. All rooms have large balconies for viewing the beach, the Andaman Sea, and Promthep Cape from every angle. Interiors are spacious and decorated with cheerful fabrics and wicker furniture; bathrooms are huge, many with sunken tubs, and feature luxury amenities. The resort is more sedate and romantic than the many noisy family resorts on the island, exemplified by the Yacht Club's sister property, Le Meridien Phuket.

23/3 Viset Rd., Nai Harn Beach, Phuket 83130 (above Nai Harn Beach, 18km/11 miles south of Phuket). ⓒ 0800/ 225-5843 or 07638-1156. Fax 07638-1164. www.lemeridien.com. 110 units. 9,600B–12,400B ($234–$302) double (varies with view); from 14,800B ($361) suite. AE, DC, MC, V. **Amenities:** 3 restaurants; patio lounge; outdoor pool; 2 outdoor lighted tennis courts; small fitness center; spa w/Jacuzzi, steam, massage, face and body treatments; extensive watersports equipment; tour desk; car-rental desk; limousine service; business center; small boutique; salon; 24-hr. room service; babysitting; same-day laundry service/dry cleaning; nonsmoking rooms. *In room:* A/C, TV w/pay movies and satellite programming, minibar, fridge, coffee/tea-making facilities, hair dryer, safe, IDD phone.

INEXPENSIVE

Just up the road from the Le Meridien you'll find rustic bungalows at **Baan Krating Jungle Beach Resort** (11/3 Viset Rd.; ⓒ and fax **07638-1108**). There are no services to speak of, but it is a good getaway. Rooms start at 800B ($20).

KATA BEACH

Arguably one of the best beaches in Phuket, Kata is a wide strip of soft sand and rolling surf. Rent an umbrella for 100B ($2.45) per day, get a massage or grab a kayak or surfboard and hit the waves (okay, the small waves mostly, but a good little rip from May to October). Unfortunately, the choicest real estate near the beach is taken up by the sprawling **Phuket Club Mediterranee** (ⓒ **07633-0455**), a branch of the famous "love it or leave it" luxury chain of all-inclusive club style resorts (for info see www.clubmed.com), but the beach is open to all.

EXPENSIVE

Kata Beach Resort ⭐　Having completed major cosmetic renovations, the new-and-improved, sprawling Kata Beach dominates the southern end of Kata. With its soaring granite-and-marble lobby and fine rooms, it is the most formal facility on the Kata coast and attracts not only individual tourists looking for comfort, but a burgeoning international conference market. Go for a deluxe sea-view room in the central building—the slightly higher-priced choice, but the view really is lovely. All rooms have balconies and are attractively decorated, and while the seaside location is great, the group experience is sometimes not.

1 Pakbang Rd., Tambon Karon, Phuket 83100 (south end of the Kata Beach strip). ⓒ 07633-0530, or 02939-4062 in Bangkok. Fax 07633-0128. www.katagroup.com. 200 units. 6,600B ($161) superior double; 7,200B ($176) deluxe double; 8,160B ($199) deluxe sea view; from 14,800B ($361) suite. AE, DC, MC, V. **Amenities:** 2 restaurants; 2 bars; 2 outdoor pools; fitness center with sauna and massage; watersports; children's center; concierge; tour desk; limousine service; business center; shopping arcade; salon; limited room service; babysitting; same-day laundry service/dry cleaning. *In room:* A/C, TV w/satellite programming, minibar, fridge, hair dryer, safe.

Katathani Hotel ⭐⭐　The Katathani is the best option on the cul-de-sac of lovely Kata Noi Beach, a haven of quiet luxury. Recent major renovations mean a much higher standard for the same good value. Rooms are a very cozy contemporary style, all with large balconies and cozy indoor sitting areas. Wide, well-groomed lawns surround sizable pools and lead to the graceful curve of the pristine cove. There is a nightly poolside buffet. The Katathani's best feature is that it is right on the beach, rare on Phuket, and all rooms have good sea views. Kata Noi is a bit out of the fray, a few clicks south of the main Kata beach and far from the raucous strip at Patong, but the hotel is self-contained (with great dining options), and they can arrange transport for any excursion (including day diving trips with their in-house dive center).

3/24 Patak Rd., Kata Noi Beach, Phuket 83100 (north end of Kata Noi Beach). © 07633-0124. Fax 07633-0426. www.katathani.com. 530 units. 7,200B–13,600B ($176–$332) junior suite (varies with seasons); from 10,400B ($254) suite. AE, DC, MC, V. **Amenities:** 5 restaurants; lounge and library; 5 outdoor pools; golf course nearby; 2 out-door lighted tennis courts; fitness center; aromatherapy spa; Jacuzzi; sauna; watersports equipment/scuba diving; game room; tour desk; car-rental desk; limousine service; salon; 24-hr. room service; massage; babysitting; same-day laundry service/dry cleaning. *In room:* A/C, TV w/satellite programming, minibar, coffee/tea-making facilities, hair dryer, safe.

Mom Tri's Boathouse (aka "The Boathouse") & Villa Royale ✦✦

At the qui-eter south end of Kata Beach, the small inn called The Boathouse is a long-time favorite with many returning visitors. More inn than resort, there's a real home-style feeling here. Comfortable, attractive rooms all face the sea, each with a terrace over-looking a courtyard pool and beach beyond, but not particularly luxurious (though clean and adequate). The hotel had a direct hit from the tsunami (the only property that did along Kata Beach), and took the opportunity to upgrade some units and open up their dining area to the sea. Nothing about the hotel calls attention to itself, really; instead, it is the friendly, attentive staff, fine dining, and laid-back setting that makes a stay at The Boathouse very special. The Boathouse Wine and Grill, the first-floor restaurant, is a long-time favorite for the visiting connoisseur (see "Where to Dine," later in this chapter). For a very special stay, stop in to their latest venture, **Villa Royale,** a collection of super-luxe suites, now 26 units in all. These large, luxury rooms are perched over a steep cliff with stunning views of the sea, and are sumptu-ously decorated in a unique mix of local materials: dark teaks, mosaics of bamboo and coconut, black tile with stone inlay, and elegant weavings. **Mom Tri's Kitchen,** the hotel companion restaurant, offers some of the best dining on the island (see "Where to Dine," later in this chapter). They offer good cooking classes, too.

The Boathouse: 182 Koktanod Rd., Kata Beach, Phuket 83100. © 07633-0015. Fax 07633-0561. **Villa Royale:** 12 Kata Noi Rd, Kata Noi Beach, Phuket 83100. www.boathousephuket.com. 36 units at The Boathouse; 26 units at the Villa Royale. 7,500B–9,500B ($183–$232) Boathouse double; from 14,000B ($341) Boathouse Suite; from 12,000B–25,000B ($293–$610) Villa Royale Suite. AE, DC, MC, V. **Amenities:** 3 restaurants; lounge and library; out-door pool; golf course nearby; fitness center; Jacuzzi; limousine service; limited room service (7am–10:30pm); mas-sage; babysitting; same-day laundry service/dry cleaning. *In room:* A/C, TV w/satellite programming, minibar, fridge, coffee/tea-making facilities, hair dryer, safe, IDD phone.

MODERATE

Sawasdee Village

Just a short walk from Kata Beach you'll pass a small portico of stone with some Khmer statuary; walk in and you've found a little Eden among the budget resorts of Kata. Everything is done small but ornate. You are greeted by the hotel's new dining and spa before reaching the rooms at the central courtyard. The garden surrounds a small pool with ornate fountains bordered in fine masonry and overflowing with greenery. There are lots of Thai *salas* for relaxing or getting a mas-sage, and they have free wireless Internet (and lend laptops), so you can relax in the shade and tell the folks back home all about it. Rooms are midsize and stylish in wood with fine canopy beds. Bathrooms are shower only and not too big. There are no TVs. Sliding doors connect each room to the courtyard, a bit too intimate (crowded) for some. There are lots of Thai touches throughout, and the place is kitschy but com-fortable at cost.

68/69 Patak Rd., Kata Beach 83100 (down a small road north of the sprawling Club Med). © 07633-0979. Fax 07633-0905. www.phuketsawasdee.com. 46 units. 2,200B–7,000B ($54–$171). MC, V. **Amenities:** Restaurant; bar; small outdoor pool; spa; tour desk; Internet; massage; laundry/dry cleaning service. *In room:* A/C, minibar, fridge, no phone.

INEXPENSIVE

Katanoi Bay Inn   Just basic, motel-style rooms adjacent to the Kata Thani Hotel, most with balconies and firm beds. There is little in the way of facilities, but there's quiet Kata Noi Beach just across the road.

4/16 Moo 2 Patak Rd., Kata Noi Beach, Phuket 83100 (Kata Noi is south of Kata Beach). ℭ and fax **07633-3308.** www.phuket.com/katanoibayinn. 28 units. 1,200B ($29) double. MC, V. **Amenities:** Restaurant; tour desk; car-rental desk; Internet terminal; same-day laundry service/dry cleaning. *In room:* Fridge, no phone.

KARON BEACH

Karon Beach is a long, straight stretch of beach lined with upper and mid-range hotels and resorts. You'll find heaps of tailors, gift-shops, small restaurants, Internet service, and mini-marts on the north end of the beach.

WHERE TO STAY IN KARON BEACH
EXPENSIVE

Andaman Seaview Hotel ★★   A real Karon Beach gem, Andaman Seaview has bright and airy public spaces done in Mediterranean hues of light-blue and white, a Sino-Portuguese theme, flanked by ponds and a large central courtyard with a garden and meandering pool. Rooms overlook the pool area and are large and nicely appointed, better than most in this category. There is a charm throughout that is less about luxury than the warm welcome, tidy appearance of the place, and the friendly crowd this attracts. The restaurant is a hotel coffee shop de rigueur, but you'll want to dine at poolside: In fact, do everything at poolside. There's a small spa, and you're just across the street from Karon Beach.

Karon Rd., Phuket 83100 (along the main strip at Karon Beach). ℭ **07639-8111.** Fax 07639-8177. www.andaman phuket.com. 161 units. 6,900B ($168) superior double; 8,800B ($215) deluxe double (big discounts available). AE, MC, V. **Amenities:** Restaurant; bar (poolside); 2 outdoor pools; small fitness center; spa; Jacuzzi; Internet corner; gift shop; tailor; 24-hr. room service; massage; same-day laundry/dry cleaning service. *In room:* A/C, satellite TV, minibar, fridge, coffee/tea-making service, safe, IDD phone.

Central Karon Village Phuket ★★   You'll find Central Hotels in every corner of Thailand, and the longstanding Central Karon Village is one of best. Set on its hill-side perch on the north end of Karon Beach—along the crest of hill between Karon and Relax Bay—the resort is a hillside hideaway of freestanding, luxury bungalows. You'll need to get to your room by golf cart along a narrow switchback road. Many of the large bungalows—all the same standard—overlook the crashing surf at Karon. Brash purple and loud floral accents in guest rooms are quite unique, and bathrooms are done in a slick, colored concrete. Unique are the retractable shades over the toilet area, as well as the large guppy bowl in each bath. Their Cliff Restaurant is tops (see "Dining" below for more info), and this self-contained gem has a friendly staff who can handle any eventuality, including a Hertz rental car office and handy tour desk. Their small outdoor pool overlooks the sea and is a good little escape, and their outdoor spa salas are a great place to learn the word "Sabai."

701 Patak Rd., Tambon Karon, Phuket 83100. ℭ **07628-6300.** Fax 07628-6315. www.centralhotelsresorts.com. 72 units. 4,000B–6,000B ($98–$146) suite. **Amenities:** Restaurant and bar; 2 outdoor pools; tour desk; car-rental desk; limited room service; massage; babysitting; laundry service. *In room:* A/C, satellite TV, minibar, fridge, coffeemaker, hair dryer, safe, IDD phone.

Crowne Plaza Karon Beach ★   Just opened at the time of our research, the Crowne Plaza in Karon flanks the north end of large Hilton Phuket (below) and offers a run for the money, a similar sprawling campus of fine rooms, villas, and a full host of resort facilities on the main strip of Karon Beach. Rooms are a studied, plain contemporary, large and all far from the sea. They have a good spa, a busy kid's club, and lots of activities. The rates listed here are for its soft opening, and a big discount from what you might actually pay in the future. One to watch.

509 Patak Rd., Karon Beach Phuket 83100 ✆ **07639-6139.** Fax 07639-6122. www.phuket.crowneplaza.com. 332 units. 3,500B ($85) deluxe double; from 5,000B ($122) suite/villas. AE, MC, V. **Amenities:** 3 restaurants; 2 bars; outdoor pool; tennis courts; health club; spa; Jacuzzi; kid's club; business center; shopping arcade; 24-hr. room service; massage; babysitting; laundry; dry cleaning. *In room:* A/C, satellite TV, minibar, fridge, coffeemaker, hair dryer, safe, IDD phone.

Hilton Phuket Arcadia Resort and Spa ★★

Recent rebranding as a Hilton property has been a real breath of fresh air for this long-time Karon Beach campus resort. Set in acres of sprawl, the Hilton Phuket Arcadia is a modern, full-facility resort, with stylish guest rooms, many overlooking the Karon Bay. The resort is the largest on the island. Rooms are set in three wings (one currently under construction), all high towers overlooking central Karon Beach and the sea beyond. Upgraded rooms are luxurious, with cool Thai touches, like artfully painted sliding doors to bathrooms, and many units have rounded edges at the corner of each rounded tower, a cool look, and great Thai contemporary furnishings throughout. The hotel sports a large new spa village with luxury spa suites connected by raised wooden platform in a mellow, wooded glen at the heart of the resort. Their in-house dining choices are great (go for the Thai restaurant), and everything about the place is classy, with snappy service that doesn't leave out a genuine Thai smile of welcome. The hotel sponsors an elephant conservation project for the many animals used for labor and tours throughout the south.

78/2 Patak Rd., Karon Beach, Phuket 83100 (middle of Karon Beach Rd.). ✆ **07639-6433.** Fax 07639-6136. www.hilton.com. 685 units. 3,000B–11,800B ($73–$288) double. AE, DC, MC, V. **Amenities:** 5 restaurants; lounge and karaoke; large outdoor pool; golf course nearby and putting green on the premises; outdoor lighted tennis courts; fitness center with Jacuzzi, sauna, steam, and massage; game room; tour desk; limousine service; salon; 24-hr. room service; babysitting; same-day laundry service/dry cleaning. *In room:* A/C, TV w/satellite programming, minibar, coffee/tea-making facilities, safe.

Thavorn Palm Beach Hotel ★

Near the beach and just south of the Hilton Arcadia (above), this large resort covers a lot of territory and has all the amenities. Recent room renovations are an improvement, but this 19-year-old hotel is showing her age. Public spaces are grand, oversized really, and the resort is dripping with baroque Ramayana-themed statuary and Thai-style touches. Room decor is simple but pleasant, with tiled floors, rattan furnishings, and small balconies. Suites are decorated in Thai style featuring teak woodcarvings and local textiles. The hotel is across the busy beach road from Karon Beach.

128/10 Moo 3, Karon Beach, Phuket 83110 (in mid–Karon Beach area). ✆ **07639-6091.** Fax 07639-6555. www.thavornpalmbeach.com. 210 units. 4,000B–9,600B ($98–$234) double; from 14,000B ($341) suite. AE, DC, MC, V. **Amenities:** 5 restaurants; lounge; 4 outdoor pools; golf course nearby; outdoor lighted tennis courts; fitness center; watersports equipment; game room; concierge; tour desk; car-rental desk; limousine service; 24-hr. room service; massage; babysitting; same-day laundry service/dry cleaning. *In room:* A/C, TV w/satellite programming, minibar, hair dryer.

MODERATE

Karon Beach Resort This is the only Karon Beach property with direct beach access (from all others you'll have to walk across the road). They've just undergone a major cosmetic renovation (the lobby is downright glittery now), and it is a good, cozy choice at beachside; great for young couples. Rooms are midsize, with dark wooden entries, clean tile floors, and some Thai touches in décor, but are most noteworthy for their orientation to the sea: Balconies are stacked in receding, semi-circular tiers and all look on the pool below (first floor with direct pool access) or to the beach and sea beyond.

51 Karon Road, Tambon Daron, Phuket 83100 (the south end of Karon Beach, just as the road bends up to cross to Kata). ⓒ 07633-0006. Fax 07633-0217. www.katagroup.com. 81 units. 5,000B ($122); from 6,300B ($154) suite. AE, MC, V. **Amenities:** 2 restaurants; 2 outdoor pools; tour desk; car rental; courtesy car and airport transfer; Internet corner; massage; laundry service. *In room:* A/C, satellite TV, minibar, fridge, safe (charge of 50B/ $1.25), IDD phone.

Marina Phuket ⚐ These simple cottages, tucked in the jungle above a scenic promontory between Kata and Karon beaches, are quite comfortable, and the best choice of the many mid-range choices nearby. Rates vary according to the view, but all have a jungle bungalow charm, connected by hilly walkways and boardwalks past the lush hillside greenery (keep your eyes peeled for wildlife). Guest rooms are decorated in Thai style but are not particularly luxurious: standard rooms are just plain tile floors and basic built-in furniture; superior rooms are just a bit larger with more flourish, like fine Thai fabrics, higher ceilings, and good views. It is a hike down to the rocky shore and the swimming isn't great, but they have a good seaside restaurant, On the Rock (see "Where to Dine," later), and their in-house **Marina Divers** (ⓒ **07638-1625**) is a PADI International Diving School, which conducts classes, rents equipment, and leads good multiday expeditions. A good, convenient, atmospheric choice.

47 Karon Rd., Karon Beach, Phuket 83100 (on bluff at south end of Karon Beach Rd.). ⓒ 07633-0625. Fax 07633-0516. www.marinaphuket.com. 92 units. 4,800B–6,500B ($117–$159) double. From 8,800B ($215) villas. MC, V. **Amenities:** Restaurant; pool; dive center; limited room service; same-day laundry service. *In room:* A/C, TV w/satellite programming, minibar, no phone.

Phuket Orchid Resort Another of the Kata Group properties (see Karon Beach Resort and Kata Beach Resorts, above), this is a popular stop for big tour groups, with affordable rooms and some good family amenities, but not incredibly luxurious. The place is huge, too, and constantly under renovation, but the large central areas are a plus: The kid's pool has fun slides, and the adult pool features a giant reproduction of the famous heads from the Bayon at Angkor Wat, quite impressive (only here the mouths squirt water and underneath is not a temple but a swim-up bar). Rooms are large and very clean, all with balcony, but quite plain. They have connecting rooms and family suites as well as first-floor deluxe rooms with "swim-up" access along the hotel pool's long meandering pool. They have good dining choices and a helpful tour desk. Even when overrun by groups, the front desk handles things with aplomb.

34 Luangphochuan Rd., Karon Beach, Phuket 83100 (just inland of the beach road in the south of Karon). ⓒ **07639-6645** www.katagroup.com. 525 units. 4,400B ($107) superior double; 5,680B ($139) deluxe double; from 6,360B ($155) family suite. AE, MC, V. **Amenities:** 3 restaurants; bar; 3 outdoor pools; Jacuzzi; tour desk; car rental; Internet; shopping; massage; babysitting; same-day laundry/dry-cleaning service. *In room:* A/C, satellite TV, minibar, fridge, safe, IDD phone.

INEXPENSIVE

Golden Sand Inn One of only a few acceptable budget accommodations on this part of the island (they're either getting converted into swanky digs or falling into disrepair, as in Patong), the Golden Sand is clean and quiet, located on the northernmost end of Karon and not far from all the town services and the beach. Rooms are large and little like a beat-up roadside motel. They do have a nice coffee shop, though, and a small swimming pool. Off-season rates are cheap-cheap.

Karon Beach, Phuket 83100 (across highway from north end of beach, above traffic circle). ⓒ **07639-6493.** Fax 07639-6117. www.katakaron.com. 88 units. 1,800B–2,500B ($44–$61) double. AE, DC, MC, V. **Amenities:** Restaurant; pool; laundry. *In room:* A/C, TV, minibar, fridge, safe.

Karona Resort and Spa ⭐ Tucked in a little side street where Karon and Kata beaches meet, the Karona Resort is a low-luxe find, with basic but cozy rooms surrounding a tiered central pool, all just a short walk from Karon Beach and the busy Kata strip. Deluxe rooms in a block overlooking the pool are worth the upgrade. They also have good, affordable spa treatments, and the place is quite stylish and the service good for the price (and the prices below are negotiable).

6 Karon Soi 2, Karon Beach, Phuket 83100. ⓒ **07628-6406.** Fax 07628-6411. www.karonaresort.com. 92 units. 1,600B–3,000B ($39–$73) superior double; 3,400B ($83) deluxe double. MC, V. **Amenities:** Restaurant and bar; outdoor pool; spa; Jacuzzi; tour desk; car-rental desk; limited room service; massage; laundry. *In room:* A/C, satellite TV, minibar, fridge, safe (deluxe), IDD phone.

RELAX BAY

Le Meridien Phuket ⭐ *Kids* Le Meridien Phuket is tucked away on secluded Relax Bay, with a lovely 549m (600-yd.) beach and 16 hectares (40 acres) of tropical greenery, one of the largest resorts on the island. Hit hard by the tsunami, the resort has been renovated in grand style and opened in the summer of 2005 just in time for the busy season (and this place is always busy). The advantages of this large resort are its numerous facilities—two big swimming pools, watersports, four tennis courts, putting green and practice range, and a fine fitness center; the disadvantage is the crowds. The resort caters to families, and there are lots of activities and a good day-care center that kids just seem to love. The large building complex combines Western and traditional Thai architecture, and one of the advantages to its U-shape layout is that it ensures that 80% of the rooms face the ocean. The modern furnishings in cheerful rooms are of rattan and teak, each with a balcony and wooden sun deck chairs. No fewer than 10 restaurants give you all kinds of choice.

8/5 Tambol, Karon Noi, P.O. Box 277, Relax Bay, Phuket 83000. ⓒ **0800/225-5843** or 07634-0480. Fax 07634-0479. www.lemeridien.com. 470 units. 11,500B–13,500B ($280–$329) double; from 18,000B ($439) suite. AE, DC, MC, V. **Amenities:** 10 restaurants; 4 pubs with games and live shows; 2 large outdoor pools; golf driving range and on-site pro; minigolf; outdoor lighted tennis courts; squash courts; fitness center; watersports equipment and dive center; bike rental; excellent children's center; game room; concierge; tour desk; car-rental desk; limousine service; business center; shopping arcade; salon; 24-hr. room service; massage; babysitting; same-day laundry service/dry cleaning; nonsmoking rooms. *In room:* A/C, TV w/satellite programming, minibar, fridge, coffee/tea-making facilities, hair dryer, safe.

PATONG

Patong's got it all, but it is all stacked in a heap and glowing with neon. The area pulses with activity, shopping, dining, and nightlife late into the evening. In the downtown it is touts catcalling and the beeping horns of passing tuk-tuks wanting to take you for a ride (quite literally); but Patong has tons of services and some good accommodations (the best find creative ways to make you feel like you're not in Patong). Patong was the area of Phuket hardest hit by the Christmas Tsunami of 2004, but the damage was limited to a thin strip at oceanside, and international reports often confused Patong with areas like Khao Lak, north of Phuket, which were completely wiped out. With few exceptions, hotels on this busy strip were up and running soon after the tsunami. Most continue to offer significant discounts to attract travelers.

EXPENSIVE

Amari Coral Beach Resort ⭐⭐ The Amari Coral Beach stands on the rocks high above the southern end of busy Patong, well away from the din of Patong's congested strip, but close for access to the mayhem. The beachfront below is rocky, but the whole resort, from the very grand terraced lobby, guest rooms, and fine pool, is oriented to the incredible views of the grand bay below. The rooms have sea-foam tones, cozy balconies, and all the comforts of home. The massive colonnaded lobby space is a grand picture frame for the sea beyond, and the whole place has a busy and welcoming feel. There is live music nightly and the hotel's Italian restaurant, La Gritta (see "Where to Dine," later), is tops. The Amari is a very good, affordable, atmospheric choice.

2 Meun-ngern Rd., Phuket 83150 (south and uphill of Patong Beach). © **07634-0106.** Fax 07634-0115. www.amari. com. 200 units. 7,000B ($171) double (low-season and special discounts available); from 10,000B ($244) suite. AE, DC, MC, V. **Amenities:** 3 restaurants; lounge; 2 outdoor pools; outdoor lighted tennis court; fitness center; brand-new spa; dive center; game room; tour desk; car-rental desk; limousine service; salon; 24-hr. room service; massage; babysitting; same-day laundry service/dry cleaning. *In room:* A/C, TV w/satellite programming, minibar, safe.

Diamond Cliff Resort 🐾

The Diamond Cliff is a gleaming hilltop resort, with rooms done in soothing sea greens, blues, and light wood trim, and all command great ocean views. The grounds are attractively landscaped and common areas are luxurious. They have irregular shuttle service to cover the distance down the hill and into town; after the one long walk you take on their special boardwalk to Patong that winds through the rocky coastline, you'll want to get some wheels. The hotel does have quite a selection of good facilities and the place is in tip-top shape. Comparable to Novotel next door. Check their website for significant discounts when booking directly.

284 Prabaramee Rd., Patong, Phuket 83150 (far south end, on the road to Kamala Beach). © **07634-0501.** Fax 07634-0507. www.diamondcliff.com. 330 units. 10,500B–11,000B ($256–$268) double; from 12,500B ($305) suite. AE, DC, MC, V. **Amenities:** 8 restaurants; lounge; outdoor pool; minigolf; outdoor lighted tennis courts; fitness center; small spa; dive center; game room; concierge; tour desk; car-rental desk; limousine service; salon; 24-hr. room service; massage; babysitting; same-day laundry service/dry cleaning. *In room:* A/C, TV w/satellite programming, minibar, safe.

Holiday Inn Resort Phuket 🐾🐾 (Kids)

Holiday Inn took advantage of damage from the tsunami to improve itself, and massive new renovations were just being completed at the time of this writing. The best choice is a room in the Busakorn Wing, which is the hotel's newest (for now) and stylish area, with rooms done in Thai decor with teak appointments, carving, and pottery. What distinguishes the Holiday Inn is their excellent offerings for traveling families. The central pool areas have elaborate fountains and a fun meandering pool suited to kids of all ages, and the hotel has active kids' programs and a children's center, not to mention babysitting for when mom and dad need a night out. There are lots of family activities and excursions to choose from. There are even Family Suites, with separate "kids rooms" that have a jungle- or pirate-theme decor, TV with video and PlayStation, stocked toy boxes, and some with bunk beds. The hotel also has a self-service launderette, so you don't have to pay hotel laundry prices for the bio-mass of play clothes your kids will rip through: quite unique. Also unique is the hotel's minibar scheme, whereby rooms have just a bare fridge and guests visit a small convenience store in the lobby and choose what they would like and have it delivered to their room at a cost of only a small bump-up from retail price.

52 Thaweewong Rd., Patong Beach, Phuket 83150 (Patong Beach strip). © **0800/HOLIDAY** or 07634-0608. Fax 07634-0435. www.holiday.phuket.com/. 369 units. 7,000B–10,000B ($171–$244) main wing double or suite; 9,000B–12,000B ($220–$293) Busakorn studio or family suite (good low-season discounts and Internet rates available). AE, DC, MC, V. **Amenities:** 3 restaurants; lounge; 4 outdoor pools; fitness center; spa with massage, sauna, and steam; tip-top children's center and programs; tour desk; car-rental desk; limousine service; business center; 24-hr. room service; massage; babysitting; same-day laundry service/dry cleaning and self-service launderette. *In room:* A/C, TV w/satellite programming, choose-your-own minibar, fridge, coffee/tea-making facilities, hair dryer, safe, IDD phone.

Merlin Beach Resort and Patong Merlin 🐾

The Merlin Group maintains two massive compounds, one in central Patong, the other more choice property is 3km

(2 miles) south on scenic Merlin Beach, a small horseshoe of sand in an isolated bay (the beach is all coral, though not for swimming). Both are popular with Australian tourists, and feature particularly attractive common areas, spacious open-plan lobbies with oversize rattan furniture, and rooms with balconies and views of the pool or seaside. Both facilities feature stunning lagoon-style swimming pools, each with a pool bar, and some rooms even have private "swim-up" access. There are nicely manicured gardens throughout. Both are all-inclusive, with facilities ranging from a fine fitness club, watersports, game room, gym, sauna, and snooker. The Merlin Beach resort, with its private beach access, is the better of the two with newer rooms just a hitch higher standard. The resort is somewhat remote from the action of Patong, but for some that is its greatest asset.

Patong Merlin: 99/2 Moo 4, Patong Beach, Phuket 83150 (on Patong strip near south end of town). © 07634-0037. Fax 07634-0394. www.merlinphuket.com. 386 units. 4,800B ($117) double; from 9,000B ($220) suite. AE, DC, MC, V. **Amenities:** 3 restaurants; lounge; 3 pools; outdoor lighted tennis courts; fitness center; watersports equipment; game room; tour desk; limousine service; 24-hr. room service; massage; babysitting; same-day laundry service/dry cleaning. *In room:* A/C, satellite TV, minibar, fridge, IDD phone.

Merlin Beach Resort: 158 Jawaraj Rd., Phuket 83000 (3km/2 miles south and west of Patong). © 07621-2866. Fax 0762-16429. www.merlinphuket.com. 414 units. 7,000B–7,500B ($171–$183) deluxe double; from 20,000B ($488) suite. AE, DC, MC, V. **Amenities:** 4 restaurants; bar and lounge; 2 outdoor pools; tennis; small fitness center; spa with massage, Jacuzzi, sauna, steam; tour desk; car-rental desk; business center w/Internet; shopping arcade; limited room service; babysitting; same-day laundry/dry-cleaning service; ballroom and meeting rooms; nonsmoking rooms. *In room:* A/C, satellite TV, minibar, fridge, coffeemaker, safe, IDD phone.

Novotel Coralia Phuket ✪

Just next to the Diamond Cliff Resort (above) and a similar standard on the north end of Patong, the Novotel is a lovely hilltop hideaway. It is typical of Accor hotels anywhere: good service and comfortable rooms done in a local style. What sets this apart is the three-tiered pool at the center of the property and its dynamic view of the beach and sea from this towering point. The lobby is under an enormous steep Thai roof, and from their luxury massage pavilions to their many fine dining choices, you are constantly reminded of Thai culture and wrapped in comfort.

Kalim Beach Rd., Patong Beach 83150 (on the hill north of town, just as the road heads uphill). © 07634-2777. Fax 07634-2168. www.novotelphuket.com. 215 units. 6,500B–8,500B ($159–$207); from 11,000B ($268) suite. AE, MC, V. **Amenities:** 3 restaurants; 3 bars; pool (with multiple tiers); 2 tennis courts; fitness center; sauna; tour desk; car-rental desk; business center w/Internet; shopping; 24-hr. room service; massage; kids' club; babysitting; laundry/dry-cleaning service. *In room:* A/C, satellite TV, minibar, fridge, safe, IDD phone.

MODERATE

Budget accommodation is best along Kata and Karon beaches in the southern end of the island. In Patong, budget hotels are generally run-down, even seedy, owing to the hostess bar and go-go scene, but below are the best of the bunch.

Horizon Beach Resort Hotel ✪

The top mid-range hotel in the middle of busy Patong, the Horizon is a compact little oasis with cozy, affordable rooms and friendly, efficient service. They have two pools, and most rooms are right at pool's edge. Plain tile rooms are clean, with hard beds and simple tile baths (shower only). The place attracts lots of individual European travelers, and the place is festive without being too wild.

Thaweewong Rd., Soi Kep Sap, Patong Beach, Phuket 83150. © 07629-2526. Fax 07629-2535. www.horizonbeach.com. 127 units. 2,300B–2,800B ($56–$68). From 3,100B ($76) suites. MC, V. **Amenities:** 2 restaurants; 2 bars; 2 outdoor pools; tour desk; car-rental desk; limited room service; massage; babysitting; laundry service. *In room:* A/C, satellite TV, minibar, fridge, safe, IDD phone.

Royal Palm Resortel If you want to be in the center of it all, Royal Palm is smack-dab in the middle of the crazy main thoroughfare at beachside. Rooms are not bad—with king-size beds, small closets, and a bathroom with bathtub. It is noisy and busy, but affordable. The first floor of this little hotel was gutted by the tsunami (see the photos in the lobby), and they've used the reconstruction as an excuse to renovate, now sporting a tidy, upscale lobby area and a better room standard.

66/2 Thaweewong Rd., Patong Beach, Phuket 83150 (in the middle of the Patong Beach strip). ✆ **07629-2510.** Fax 07629-2510. www.theroyalpalm.com. 43 units. 2,300B–3,500B ($56–$85) double; from 4,300B ($105) suite. MC, V. **Amenities:** Restaurant; small rooftop pool; limited room service; same-day laundry service/dry cleaning. *In room:* A/C, satellite TV, minibar, fridge.

THE NORTHWEST COAST
PANSEA BEACH (SURIN BEACH)
Also known as Surin Beach, the Pansea area has coconut plantations, steep slopes leading down to the beach, and small, private coves dominated by two of the most secluded and divine hotels on the island.

Very Expensive
Amanpuri ✿✿✿ The discreet and sublime Amanpuri is the Phuket address for international celebrities. It was the first of the many Aman properties in the region, and rooms that were over-the-top in the 90s are looking rather small in the light of today's swing to ultra-luxe, oversized private villas in the region, but Aman was the first, and the hotel retains a chin-high dignity and ultra-high standard of service. It is the most elegant and secluded resort on the island and priced accordingly. The lobby is an open-air pavilion with an elegant black-tile swimming pool and stairs leading to the beach. Freestanding pavilion suites dot the dense coconut palm grounds; each is masterfully designed in a traditional Thai style, with teak and tile floors, sliding teak doors, exquisite built-ins, and well-chosen accents, including antiques. Private *salas* (covered patios) are perfect for romantic dining or secluded sunbathing. The Aman spa is one of the finest in the region, with six large spa suites, a grand herbal steam bath and sauna; services are over-the-top. The resort has a fleet of fine yachts, including a refitted rice barge, great for day cruising and sailing. "Ask and it will be done," is the service policy. There's nothing else like it. They're the only private beach on Phuket.

Pansea Beach, Phuket 83110 (north end of cove). ✆ **07632-4333.** Fax 07632-4100. www.amanresorts.com. 53 units. $680 garden view pavilion; from $920 sea-view pavilion; from $2,100 2-bedroom villa. AE, DC, MC, V. **Amenities:** 2 restaurants; pool; golf course nearby; outdoor lighted tennis courts; squash courts; fitness center; spa; sauna; watersports equipment and instruction; private yacht fleet; library; concierge; limousine service; limited room service; babysitting; same-day laundry service/dry cleaning. *In room:* A/C, minibar, fridge, hi-fi.

The Chedi Phuket ✿✿ Like its august neighbor, Amanpuri (listed above), the Chedi commands an excellent view of the bay and has its own private stretch of sand. From the exotic lobby (with columns and lily pond) to sleek and handsome private bungalows, it is one of the most handsome properties on the island. It is quality with a big price tag, but this romantic getaway has all the details down. Each room is a thatched mini-suite with a lovely private sun deck and top amenities. The black-tile swimming pool is large and luxurious. The snappy staff can arrange any watersports, sightseeing tour, or activity. The fine service here caters to the likes of honeymooners and celebrities, and everyone is treated like a VIP. While it may not be as outwardly impressive as its extraordinary neighbor, The Chedi is quiet, comfortably informal, and very relaxing, with fine dining options. They have a new, top-notch cooking school as well.

118 Moo 3, Choeng Talay, Pansea Beach, Phuket 83110 (next to the Amanpuri). (*) 07632-4017. Fax 07632-4252. www.ghmhotels.com. 108 units. $400 Hillside cottage; $470 Superior cottage; $540 Deluxe cottage; $620 Beach cottage (discounts available in low-season). AE, DC, MC, V. **Amenities:** 3 restaurants; bar; outdoor pool; 2 outdoor lighted tennis courts; volleyball and badminton; spa; watersports equipment; children's center; game room; concierge; tour desk; car-rental desk; limousine service; 24-hr. room service; massage; babysitting; same-day laundry service/dry cleaning. *In room:* A/C, TV w/satellite programming, minibar, coffee/tea-making facilities, safe.

Treetops Arasia ★★   Fancy hillside suites, ultra-contemporary and popular with regional guests from Hong Kong, the rooms at the Treetops feel like you are suspended high on a clifftop (and you are), but there are snappy golf carts to take you to your rooms, and once there you won't want to leave. All units are private villas or suites, many with private plunge pools. A good little honeymoon hideaway, and their fine-dining outlet is tops.

125 Moo 3 Srisoonthon Rd., Cherngtalay, Thalang, Phuket 83110. (*) 07627-1271. Fax 07627-1270. www.treetops-arasia.com. 48 units. $500–$1,000 suites. V, MC, AE. **Amenities:** Restaurant and bar; outdoor pool; health club; spa; Jacuzzi; sauna; concierge; tour desk; car-rental desk; 24-hr. room service; massage; babysitting; laundry service. *In room:* A/C, satellite TV, minibar, fridge, coffeemaker, hair dryer, safe, IDD phone.

BANG THAO BAY (THE LAGUNA RESORT COMPLEX)

Twenty minutes south of the airport and just as far north of Patong Beach on the western shore of Phuket, this isolated area is Phuket's high-end, "integrated resort" of five high-end properties that share the island's most top-rated facilities. Among them you'll find world-class health spas, countless restaurants, and the island's best golf course. The grounds are impressively landscaped, and the hotel properties are scattered among the winding lagoons, all navigable by boat. The best thing about staying here is that you can dine at any of the fine hotel restaurants, connecting by boat or free shuttle, and be charged on one simple bill at whatever resort you choose. The three below are the best, but also consider the original **Laguna Beach Resort** ((*) 07632-4352; www.lagunabeach-resort.com), with a similar high standard of rooms and services (popular with groups).

VERY EXPENSIVE

Banyan Tree Phuket ★★★   Banyan Tree is a famous hideaway for honeymooners and high society (paparazzi-free for your protection). There is nothing like it for people of means who need an escape. Private villas with walled courtyards (many with private pool or Jacuzzi) are spacious and grand, lushly styled in teakwood with outdoor bathtubs. Style throughout is low Thai pavilions, and there are good Thai touches like platform beds and large Thai murals depicting the *Ramakien,* an ancient Thai saga. The resort can arrange private barbecues at your villa, and private massage in the room or in outdoor pavilions. The reception area is a large open *sala* with lovely lotus pools. A small village in itself, the spa provides a wide range of beauty and health treatments in luxurious rooms. Their Tamarind Restaurant serves delicious, light, and authentic spa cuisine. The main pool is truly impressive—a free-form lagoon, landscaped with greenery and rock formations—with a flowing water canal. There's a top-notch golf course on-site and private tour office. The Banyan Tree garners many international awards and is a member of the Leading Small Hotels of the World.

33 Moo 4, Srisoonthon Rd., Cherngtalay District, Amphur Talang, Phuket 83110 (north end of beach). (*) 800/525-4800 or 07632-4374. Fax 07632-4375. 121 units. 22,000B–64,000B ($537–$1,561) villas; 104,000B ($2,537) presidential suite (**Note:** higher rates during peak holiday season). AE, DC, MC, V. **Amenities:** 6 restaurants; lounge; outdoor lagoon-style pool; golf course; 3 outdoor lighted tennis courts; fitness center; award-winning spa w/spa pool; sauna, steam, massage; watersports equipment; tour desk; car-rental desk; limousine service; 24-hr. room service;

babysitting; same-day laundry service/dry cleaning. *In room:* A/C, TV w/pay movies and satellite programming, mini-bar; fridge; coffeemaker; safe; IDD phone.

Dusit Laguna Resort ✴ The Dusit hotel group has some fine properties in Thailand, and the Dusit Laguna is no exception. The rooms are midsize and done with pastel tiles, faux columns and bathrooms that open to the living area by wide, wooden doors. Spring for a deluxe room with a balcony and ocean view for not much more than standard. Suites are large and luxurious. There are lots of Thai touches throughout, some tacky, others, like some of the large, traditional hangings, are quite pleasing. The hotel features some fine dining options, particularly of note is their quaint Italian restaurant, La Trattoria, serving authentic Italian cuisine in a chic but laid-back gardenside pavilion decorated in cool whites and blues. The well-landscaped gardens at seaside have an especially delightful waterfall and an excellent pool, and the grounds open onto a long, wide, white-sand beach flanked by two lagoons. Facilities for kids are great: a Kids Corner; babysitting; a playground, and computer games.

390 Srisoonthon Rd., Cherngtalay District, Phuket 83110 (south end of beach). ℂ 07632-4320. Fax 07632-4174. www.dusit.com. 226 units. 7,400B–14,000B ($180–$341) double; from 18,600B ($454) suite. AE, DC, MC, V. **Amenities:** 4 restaurants; lounge; free-form outdoor pool; golf course nearby and pitch and putt on premises; outdoor lighted tennis courts; fitness center; spa w/Jacuzzi, sauna, steam, massage; watersports equipment/rentals; bike rental; tour desk; car-rental desk; limousine service; business center; shopping arcade; salon; 24-hr. room service; babysitting; same-day laundry service/dry cleaning; nonsmoking rooms. *In room:* A/C; satellite TV; minibar; fridge; coffee/tea-making facilities; safe; IDD phone.

Sheraton Grande Laguna Phuket ✴✴ The granddaddy of the lagoon in terms of size, the Sheraton is a sprawling, luxury campus of two- and three-story hotel-style pavilions. Rooms are quite large and luxurious with tile floors, cozy sitting areas, large balconies, and some bathrooms have sunken tubs. On a large island, the hotel design carefully traces the natural lines, the coves and jetties, of the surrounding lagoon, and the area is quiet and very private. The pool is a long, winding meander and there are good amenities for kids of all ages, from a kids' club (called VIK or Very Important Kids) to beach games and sailboat rental at their private, sandy put-in at the lagoon. With both fine dining and more casual eateries and cafes (including a good bakery) and a very professional staff, the Sheraton is a fine, reliable, familiar choice.

10 Moo 4, Bang Tao Bay, Phuket 83110. ℂ 07632-4101. Fax 07632-4108. www.starwood.com. 335 units. 8,400B–14,000B ($205–$341) double; from 15,000B ($366) suite. AE, DC, MC, V. **Amenities:** 6 restaurants; bar and lounge; free-form outdoor pool; golf course nearby; 2 outdoor lighted tennis courts; fitness center; spa; watersports equipment/rentals; bike rental; kids' club; tour desk; car-rental desk; limousine service; business center w/Internet; shopping; 24-hr. room service; babysitting; same-day laundry service/dry cleaning; nonsmoking rooms. *In room:* A/C; satellite TV; minibar; fridge; coffeemaker; hair dryer; safe; IDD phone.

NAI YANG BEACH & NAI THON

Nai Yang National Park is a long stretch of shoreline peeking out from underneath a dense forest of palms, casuarina, and other indigenous flora. It is good for leaving the crowds behind, but be warned that it is isolated and, short of Pearl Village (below), quite rustic (there are basic bungalows or you can rent a tent for a stay in a campground).

Nai Yang is known for its annual release of sea turtles back into the Andaman Sea. The turtles weigh from 100 to 1,500 pounds and swim the waters around Phuket, unprotected from fishermen. If not for the efforts of the Marine Biological Center, these creatures would probably be locally extinct. April 13, during the Songkran holiday, is the day of release. You'll have to pay 30B (75¢) to enter the park, and there is a small information kiosk and restaurant at the park headquarters. Tent accommodation begins at 20B (50¢) if you bring your own gear, 100B ($2.45) for a small tent, and up to 1,200B ($29) for a four-man rustic bungalow. For more information, contact **Sirinath Park Campground,** 89/1 Moo 1, Talang, Phuket 83110; ✆ **07632-8226.**

   Nai Thon is just south of Nai Yang (closer to Laguna) and is home to one luxe resort: Trisara.

NAI THON
Very Expensive
Trisara ✿   Another uber-luxe villa resort comes to Phuket. Trisara is a small boutique property some 15 minutes from the airport. The price tag is high, but affords the most kingly comforts in a clutch of private, contemporary pool villas at seaside. Private spaces are large and over-the-top, most with pools overlooking the blue water below. Precise in every detail.

60/1 Moo 6, Srisoonthon Road, Cherngtalay, Talang, Phuket 83110. ✆ 07631-0100. Fax 07631-0300. www.trisara.com. 42 units. $695–$1,380 pool villa (price varies with sea proximity); from $1,600 multi-bedroom villas. AE, V, MC. **Amenities:** Restaurant and bar; all units have private outdoor pool, also large seaside public pool; tennis courts; health club; spa; Jacuzzi; sauna; watersports equipment/rentals; bike rentals; library with Internet; concierge; tour desk; car-rental desk; shopping arcade; salon; 24-hr. room service; massage; babysitting; laundry service; dry cleaning. *In room:* A/C, satellite TV, fax, minibar, fridge, coffeemaker, hair dryer, iron/ironing board, safe, IDD phone.

NAI YANG
Moderate
Pearl Village ✿   One of the earliest resorts to go up on Phuket (the idea was that more might follow in the area, but didn't), the Pearl Village is an aging property but nevertheless holds its own due to its location, facilities, and friendly atmosphere. On the periphery of the national park, the hotel is isolated from the ravages of over-development characterizing the rest of tourist Phuket. The facilities are good, especially for families; "Cottage" suites are private, connecting rooms, and there's a central play area, games, and babysitting services that make it a good place to bring the brood. The one drawback is that you're out in the sticks here. For some, that is just what they're looking for, and the nearby coral beaches at Nai Yang are enough of an amusement; for others (like teenagers), it means banishment from the action of Patong.

Nai Yang Beach and National Park, Amphur Talang, Phuket 83104 (5 min. south of the airport). ✆ 07632-7006. Fax 07632-7338. www.pearlvillage.co.th. 243 units. 4,500B ($110) double; 5,300B ($129) cottage; from 5,500B ($134) suite. AE, DC, MC, V. **Amenities:** 4 restaurants; lounge; pool; outdoor lighted tennis courts; fitness center; spa; Jacuzzi; watersports and dive center; bike rental; children's center; game room; tour desk; car-rental desk; limousine service; Internet center; limited room service; babysitting; same-day laundry service/dry cleaning. *In room:* A/C, satellite TV w/in-house movies, minibar, fridge, coffee/tea-making facilities, hair dryer, safe, IDD phone.

MAI KHAO BEACH & THE FAR NORTH OF PHUKET
Mai Khao is a wide sweep of beach on the northeastern shore close to the airport. It is Phuket's longest beach and is the site where sea turtles lay their eggs during December and January. The eggs are coveted by Thai and Chinese people, who eat them for the supposed life-sustaining power, but large-scale efforts are underway to assist these glorious animals and protect their potential hatchlings.

VERY EXPENSIVE
JW Marriott Phuket Resort and Spa ✿✿✿   The clean-lined luxury of the Marriott could make a haiku poet out of anyone. Along the windswept stretch of sand and roaring surf along desolate Mai Khao Beach, this resort is a masterpiece of luxury and

service. Arrivals at night will awe to the opulence of oversized torches lining the circular drive, and the wide, low pavilions of the lobby surround an enormous, black reflecting pool that sparkles with torchlight. There are no services outside of the hotel, and it is a 30-minute drive to the nearest tourist area, but the resort facilities are complete and guests needn't leave. Rooms are private getaways with open-plan bathrooms, a small meditation and reading corner with Thai cushions, and lovely balconies that give way to sumptuous gardens: a hidden Eden. Service at the Marriott is impeccable. Come to the Marriott to leave it all behind, enjoy fine spa treatments, sports, activities, and fine dining. The hotel can arrange transport anywhere on the island, and there are a host of fine excursions to choose from at their helpful tour desk. The hotel supports annual efforts to preserve turtle breeding grounds.

231 Moo 3, Mai Khao, Talang, Phuket 83110. ✆ **07633-8000**. Fax 07634-8360. www.marriott.com. 21,500B–24,000B ($524–$585) deluxe double; from 55,300B ($1,349) suite. AE, DC, MC, V. 265 units. **Amenities:** 5 restaurants; 3 bars; 2 outdoor pools; 2 tennis courts; top-notch fitness center w/lots of activities; extensive spa; Jacuzzi; sauna; watersports equipment rentals (Hobie Cat and runabouts); bicycles (free to guests); children's center; kids' club; teen activity center w/computers; concierge; tour desk; car-rental desk; limousine service; business center; shopping arcade; salon; 24-hr. room service; massage; babysitting; same-day laundry/dry cleaning; nonsmoking rooms; executive level rooms w/private check-in. *In room:* A/C, satellite TV w/in-house movies, dataport (modem connection), minibar, fridge, coffeemaker, hair dryer, safe, IDD phone.

PHUKET TOWN

Most just pass through the island's commercial hub, but there are some high-class facilities if you're stuck, and a few restaurants that are worth the trip, especially if Phuket Island is your only destination (see "Where to Dine," later in this chapter).

If you're in a pinch and looking for a budget spot, **The Tavorn Hotel** (74 Rasada Rd., Amphur Muang, Phuket 83000; ✆ **07621-1333**) is an old standby at the town center with rooms starting at 550B/$13. The hotel has seen better days, though; in fact it has seen much better days, and there is a little museum in the beat old lobby that testifies to the fact. A careful renovation could bring the old gal back to her former glory, days when she was the choice of kings, but for now it is pretty rough. **Phuket Island Pavilion** (133 Satoon Rd.; ✆ **07621-0444**) has better rooms starting at just 1,500B/$37.

EXPENSIVE

The Metropole Just around the corner from the Royal Phuket City Hotel, the Metropole is a fine business hotel. Public spaces are all spit-and-polish (though not especially grand), and the rooms are large and fully appointed (if bland) with good black-and-white tile bathrooms. Service is professional but curt.

1 Soi Surin, Montri Rd., Phuket Town 83000. ✆ **07621-5050**. Fax 07621-5990. www.metropolephuket.com. 248 units. 3,200B–3,800B ($78–$93) double; 6,000B ($146) suite. AE, MC, V. **Amenities:** 2 restaurants; lounge and bar; pool; small fitness corner; tour desk; business center; shopping; salon; 24-hr. room service; laundry and dry cleaning. *In room:* A/C, satellite TV, minibar, fridge, safe, IDD phone.

Royal Phuket City Hotel ✦ For a small town like Phuket, this hotel is surprisingly cosmopolitan. A true city hotel, Royal Phuket's facilities include one of the finest fitness centers going, a full-service spa with massage, large outdoor swimming pool, and a very professional executive business center. Above the cavernous marble lobby, guest rooms are smart, in contemporary hues and style, but dull with views of the busy little town below that pale in comparison to the beachfront just a short ride away. Pickles Restaurant serves international cuisine, and the Chinatown Restaurant is one of the most posh in town. Few indeed stay in Phuket Town, but if you're stuck here, go for style.

154 Phang-Nga Rd., Amphur Muang, Phuket 83000 (located to the east of Phuket Town, across from the intercity bus terminal). ℂ 07623-3333. Fax 07623-3335. www.royalphuketcity.com. 251 units. 4,100B–5,000B ($122–$122) double; from 6,000B ($146) suite (discounts available). AE, DC, MC, V. **Amenities:** 2 restaurants; lobby lounge; outdoor pool; golf course nearby; fitness center w/sauna, steam, massage, spa; tour desk; limousine service; business center; 24-hr. room service; babysitting; same-day laundry service/dry cleaning; nonsmoking rooms; executive-level rooms. *In room:* A/C, TV w/satellite programming, dataport, minibar, fridge, hair dryer, safe, IDD phone.

3 Where to Dine

From tip-to-tip, north to south, it is over an hour's drive on Phuket, but hired tuk-tuks, hotel transport, or even self-drive vehicles mean that for dining and nightlife, you can choose from any on the island. The beach areas in the west are chockablock with small, storefront eateries, and Patong features everything from the obligatory McDonald's and Starbucks to small designer sushi chains. Look for the spicy local noodle specialty, *Kanom Jin,* best at streetside stalls or in Phuket town.

KATA & KARON

The busy road between Kata and Karon (as well as the many side streets) are chockablock with small cafes and restaurants serving affordable Thai and Western food. Stop by **Euro Deli** (58/60 Karon Rd.; ℂ 07628-6265) for a good sandwich (open 8am–1am) or a coffee (just one of many). Also note the area of outdoor beer bars and travelers cafes on the far southern end of Kata beach, just behind the Club Med. These places rock late; also a good spot to grab a quick bite local style. On the north end of Karon, look for **Karon Café** (down a busy beer bar *soi* off of Prajak Rd.; ℂ 07628-6400; www.karoncafe.com) with good, casual Western dining (great Aussie steaks).

EXPENSIVE

The Boathouse and Mom Tri's Kitchen ✵✵✵ THAI/INTERNATIONAL   So legendary is the Thai and Western cuisine at The Boathouse that the inn where it resides offers popular holiday packages for visitors who wish to come and take lessons from its chef. A large bar and dining area were recently renovated after damage from the tsunami, and the cool updates make the space more light and airy, with huge picture windows perfect for watching the sun set over a watery horizon. Cuisine combines the best of East and West, and chefs use only the finest ingredients. If you're in the mood for the works, the Phuket lobster is one of the most expensive dishes on the menu, but is worth every baht. The Boathouse also has an excellent selection of international wines—420 labels. Mom Tri's is a veritable island institution, and its popularity has spawned a new outlet, along with a luxury resort, just up the hill from the original; **Mom Tri's Kitchen** is the latest upscale venture from the folks at The Boathouse, and serves similar fine cuisine from its luxury perch. Bon appétit.

The Boathouse Inn, 114 Patak Rd. ℂ 07633-0557. Reservations recommended during peak season. Main courses 280B–850B ($6.85–$21); seafood sold at market price. AE, DC, MC, V. Daily 7am–10:30pm.

MODERATE/INEXPENSIVE

The Cliff ✵ INTERNATIONAL   High above Karon on the rise heading toward Patong, the Cliff is part of the Central Hotel complex. Serving delicious contemporary Thai and Mediterranean dishes from atop their hilltop perch, this is a great escape from town. Try the thinly sliced tuna for an appetizer. They have good grill items, from Aussie tenderloin to roast lamb, and a long list of good Thai curries, all artfully presented. A romantic spot overlooking the sea far below.

701 Patak Rd., Tambon Karon, Phuket 83100. ⓒ **07628-6300**. www.centralhotelsresorts.com. Main courses 180B–650B ($4.40–$16). V, MC. Daily 6pm–11pm.

On the Rock ⏣⏣ THAI/SEAFOOD Part of the Marina Phuket (see "Where to Stay" earlier in this chapter), this little unassuming restaurant serves tip-top Thai meals from their scenic deck high above the south end of Karen beach. Just opened after renovations, the new restaurant is still laid-back and rustic, at night overlooking the pounding surf (lit by flood lights) along the southern end of Karon Beach. Try the Seafood Basket, a medley of grilled and fried ocean critters. They have steaks and French entrees like Chicken Cordon Bleu, but stick with the better Thai dishes for a great meal in a great atmosphere. Staff is friendly and playful, and the restaurant is a great choice for a candlelit evening.

47 Karon Rd., Karon Beach, Phuket 83100 (on bluff at south end of Karon Beach Rd.). ⓒ **07633-0625**. Fax 07633-0516. www.marinaphuket.com. Main courses 120B–580B ($2.95–$14). AE, MC, V. Daily 8am–11pm.

PATONG

Some of the best seafood dining in busy Patong doesn't come from any upscale restaurant, but at the small **Seafood Night Market** in the north end of Patong along busy, central Rat-u-thit Road. It is really just a collection of outdoor restaurants sharing a large open-air dining area. Visitors who approach or show any interest will be attacked with menus and implored to choose from among the restaurants. This can be a bit off-putting, but just pick a menu or a kind face (the others will disperse) and order from a wide selection of fresh seafood as you like it (all the seafood is displayed on iced countertops, so have a look). Good food at a fraction of restaurant prices.

One popular little breakfast place is **Sabai-Sabai** (100/3 Thaweewong Rd.; ⓒ **07634-0222**); the name means "relaxed" and they are indeed so, just a laid-back storefront in a small *soi* off of busy Patong Beach Road. Also look for little **Orchid** on the next *soi* south (78/304 Thaweewong Rd., Soi Perm Pong; ⓒ **07634-0462**) for good, affordable Thai and European.

Scruffy Murphy's (Soi Bangla; ⓒ **07629-2590**) is a popular Irish pub (see Nightlife) that also serves good pub grub and fry-ups (great hangover chow).

Also look for little **Zen** (ⓒ **07629-3053**), a popular Thai sushi chain with a busy outlet on the main beach road in Patong. Here also find lots of international fast food chains, overpriced coffee, and, of course, the obligatory 7-Eleven.

Baan Rim Pa ⏣⏣ THAI In a beautiful Thai-style teak house, Baan Rim Pa has dining in a romantic indoor setting or with gorgeous views of the bay from outdoor terraces. Among high-end travelers, the restaurant is one of the most popular stops on the island, so be sure to reserve your table early. Thai cuisine features seafood, with a variety of other meat and vegetable dishes, including a rich duck curry and a sweet honey chicken dish. The seafood basket is a fantastic assortment of prawns, mussels, squid, and crab. The owner of Baan Rim Pa has opened up a few other restaurants on the cliffside next to Baan Rim Pa, including a Japanese restaurant, **Otowa** (ⓒ **07634-4254**), and a new Italian restaurant, **Da Maurizio Bar and Ristorante** (ⓒ **07634-4079**).

223 Kalim Beach Rd. (on the cliffs just north of Patong Beach). ⓒ **07634-0789**. www.baanrimpa.com. Reservations necessary. Main courses 250B–1,200B ($6.10–$29). AE, DC, MC, V. Daily noon–2:30pm and 6–10pm.

La Gritta ⏣ ITALIAN Similar to the Amari chain's other fine Italian restaurants of the same name, this one is notable for it is views of Patong Beach below, the best in town, really. It is classic Northern Italian cuisine—antipasti, salads, soup, grilled entrees, and pastas, accompanied by an extensive wine list. They use all fresh ingredients and serve a colorful antipasto plate that makes a great shared appetizer while watching the fireworks of a Phuket sunset.

At the Amari Hotel; 2 Meun-ngern Rd., Phuket 83150 (south and uphill of Patong Beach). © 07634-0106. Main courses 170B–520B ($4.15–$13). AE, MC, V. Daily 11am–10pm.

Pan Yaah Thai Restaurant THAI   Here is a good escape from busy Patong and some real Thai home cooking. The restaurant is a wooden deck overlooking the bay some 2km north of central Patong. The menu is classic Thai, with some one-dish meals like fried rice or noodles, but best enjoyed with friends sharing a number of courses, with some spicy *tom yam* soup with prawns, great stir-frys, and whole fish done to order. Prices are low and service is friendly and laid back.

249 Prabaramee Rd., Patong, Phuket 83150 (2km north of Patong along the coast). © 07634-4473. Main courses 90B–150B ($2.20–$3.65). V, MC. Daily 11am–11pm.

Patong Seafood Restaurant SEAFOOD   Take an evening stroll along the lively Patong Beach strip and you'll find quite a few open-air seafood restaurants displaying their catch of the day on chipped-ice buffet tables out front. The best choice of them all is the casual Patong Seafood, for the freshest and best selection of seafood, including several types of local fish, lobster, squid (very tender), prawn, and crab. The menu has a fantastic assortment of preparation styles—with photos of popular Thai noodles and Chinese stir-fry dishes. Service is good, and they're popular enough that they don't employ a carnival barker like most along the strip; they just attract with their food rather than promote with ploys.

Patong Beach Rd., Patong Beach. © 07634-0247. Reservations not accepted. Main courses 80B–250B ($1.95–$6.10); seafood at market price. AE, DC, MC, V. Daily 7am–11pm.

Yin Dee ⚔ THAI   The name means "Welcome," and this hilltop boutique resort hosts an in-house restaurant good enough (and with a great location overlooking Patong from a hill to the south) to attract bevies of outside guests. Try their grilled dishes, like the white snapper Picasso with fried fresh fruit and potato, or something light like a green or Niçoise salad. They have daily specials, and the place is very romantic, with chic outdoor dining at poolside with a few tables overlooking the sea. Great apple pie.

7/5 Muean Ngen Rd., Kathu, Phuket 83150 (on the hill high above the Amari Hotel on the south end of Patong Beach). © 07629-4108. www.baanyindee.com. Main courses 295B–550B ($7.20–$13). V, MC. Daily 11am–10pm.

BANG THAO BAY (THE LAGUNA RESORT COMPLEX)

The many hotel restaurants of the five-star properties in the Laguna Complex could fill a small guidebook of its own. You can't go too wrong in any of the hotels, really, and here, more than anywhere, it is a question of getting what you pay for; from super-luxurious fine-dining to laid-back hotel grills or snack corners, they cover it all. One restaurant just outside the complex is worth mentioning (it is where all the hotel managers eat when they get out of work).

Tatanka ⚔⚔ INTERNATIONAL   Billed as "Globe-trotter Cuisine," dining at Tatanka is indeed a foray into the realm of a culinary nomad. Harold Schwarz, the young owner and well-traveled chef, puts to use his many years in hotel restaurants around the world (his resume is written on the bathroom wall; each tile features another of Harold's many stops). "Fusion" is a battered and broken term in restaurant parlay, but dishes here are a creative melding of Mediterranean, Pan-American, and Oriental influences. The emphasis is on variety, and selections from the tapas menu include vegetable quesadillas, California crab cakes, stuffed Calamari cups, wanton wafers, and moo shu rolls. The menu is updated frequently and depends on what is fresh that day, but features anything from Peking duck to pizza, gazpacho to Thai *tom yam* (hot and sour soup with shrimp). Ask what's good and enjoy.

382/19 Moo 1, Srisoonthon Rd., Cherngtalay, Phuket 83110 (at the entrance of the Laguna Resort in Bangtao Bay). 🕿 and fax **07632-4349**. Main courses 150B–420B ($3.65–$10). MC, V. Daily 6pm–last order.

CHALONG BAY

One good bet for fresh seafood is in the far south of the island in Chalong Bay at **Kan Eang Seafood** (9/3 Chaofa Rd., Chalong Bay; 🕿 **07638-1323**). Whole fish and specials like Phuket Lobster just jump out of the nets and onto your plate. If you've rented wheels, a ride down this way makes for a fun day.

PHUKET TOWN

A long ride from the west coast beach areas, a night out in Phuket Town is worth it for some fine meals and a taste of local culture.

Ka Jok See 🐟🐟 *Finds* THAI   This is one of those special finds in Thailand. A classy, exclusive restaurant peopled by hotel big-wigs and local businessmen hides behind an unassuming storefront hanging with ivy—there is no sign (look for the small Indian restaurant next door). Wood-beamed ceilings, antiques lit by candlelight, and classic jazz set the stage. Ka Jok See is smart and chic, cozy, and intimate. They prepare fabulous dishes like the house specialty, *goong-saroong*—vermicelli-wrapped shrimp, fried quick and light and served with a velvety mustard dipping sauce. There are great daily specials, and entrees like smoky grilled eggplant and shrimp salad or stir-fried beef curry. This place is well worth a venture from the beach for an evening.

26 Takuapa Rd., Phuket Town (a short walk from central Rasada Rd.). 🕿 **07621-7903**. Reservations recommended. Main courses 150B–380B ($3.65–$9.25). No credit cards. Tues–Sun 6pm–midnight (kitchen closes around 11pm); closed Mon.

Salvatore 🐟 ITALIAN   *"Va bene!"* This is the real thing: pasta, grilled dishes, huge salads, and great pizza in a large air-conditioned dining room at the town center. The wine list is great, and Salvatore himself comes to your table and will make you something special. There are lots of Italian restaurants in all of the resort areas of Thailand, but this one is the best, with an unpretentious atmosphere and good food that brings many regular customers. Fine pasta, lasagna, steaks, cacciatore dishes, and a range of daily specials are all made with fresh ingredients and all the extras, like the important spices, garnish, even prosciutto, and, of course, the wine, are imported. Don't miss the dessert of Limoncello Truffle, a liqueur meringue that will melt your palate and goes great with their strong coffee.

15 Rasada Rd., Tambol Taladyai, Phuket (central Phuket Town). 🕿 and fax **07622-5958**. Main courses 140B–650B ($3.40–$16). AE, MC, V. Open daily 11:30am–3pm; 6–11pm.

Watermark 🐟 THAI/INTERNATIONAL   An old expat favorite, the Watermark serves fine international fare from their very refined seaside dining area, overlooking Phuket's luxury marina just north of Phuket town. Popular dishes include a seared ahi tuna appetizer, great pasta dishes, grilled specials, and a whole roster of contemporary Thai dishes. Worth the drive.

Phuket Boat Lagoon. 22/1 Moo 2 Thepkasattri Rd., Koh Kaew, Phuket 83000 (10 minutes north of Phuket Town, 30 minutes from the west coast beaches). ✆ **07623-9730.** www.watermarkphuket.com. Main course 175B–700B ($4.25–$17). MC, V. Daily 11am–10pm.

4 Exploring Phuket

You can spend a lot of time on Phuket and still not do everything. Thanks to years of resort growth, there are a host of activities here, and there's certainly something for everyone. The beachfront areas are full of tour operators, each vying for your business and offering similar trips (or copycat tours). Below are listed the most reputable firms, but still ask lots of questions before signing up for anything (everything from safety precautions to the lunch menu) so there are no surprises.

BEACHFRONT WATERSPORTS

Most of the noisier watersports activities are concentrated along Patong Beach—so swimmers can enjoy other beaches without the buzz of a jet ski or power boat. **Jet skis** are technically illegal, but can still be rented out for 30 minutes at 700B/$17 (if you can't beat 'em, join 'em). A 10-minute **parasailing ride** is 600B ($14.65), and you can rent outboard runabouts by the hour or the day. You'll also find **Hobie Cats** for around 600B ($14.65) per hour, as well as **windsurf boards** for 200B ($4.90) per hour. On Patong, there are no specific offices to organize these activities, just small operators with hand-painted signs usually hanging around under umbrellas.

You'll find small sailboats and kayaks for rent along all of the beaches. Kata is a good place to rent a kayak and play in the waves for 200B/$4.90 per hour.

DAY-CRUISING & YACHTING

The crystal blue waters of the Andaman Sea near Phuket are an Old Salt's dream. Every December Phuket hosts the increasingly popular **King's Cup Regatta,** in which almost 100 international racing yachts compete. For more information check out: www.kingscup.com.

For a different view of the gorgeous Phang Nga Bay, book a trip aboard one of Asian Oasis' three luxury Chinese junks, the *June Bahtra 1, 2,* and *3.* Full-day trips include lunch and hotel transfers. Passage on an all-day cruise in stunning Pha Nga Bay, to the likes of James Bond Island and among the sea gypsies, starts as low as 1,000B ($24) per person, depending on the number in a group (alcoholic beverages not included). Contact **East West Siam** at their booking office in Bangkok at ✆ **02651-9078,** or book through their websites: www.ewsiam.com or www.asian-oasis.com.

There are more and more options for chartering yachts in Phuket. Contact **Thai Marine Leisure** for details (c/o Phuket Boat Lagoon, 20/2 Thepkasattri Rd., Tambon Koh Kaew, Phuket 83200; ✆ **07623-9111;** www.thaimarine.com) or **Sunsail Asia Pacific** (Phuket Boat Lagoon, 20/5 Moo 2, Thepkasattri Rd., Phuket 83200; ✆ **07623-9057;** www.sunsail.com).

Many of the high-end resorts, foremost among them the **Amanpuri** (✆ **07632-4333;** www.amanresorts.com), have their own fleet of pleasure boats for in-house guests or can make arrangements.

FISHING

Blue Water Anglers are deep-sea fishing experts with well-equipped boats. They'll take you out for marlin, sailfish, swordfish, and tuna, and also have special night-fishing programs, but be warned that if you're new to the sport, it ain't cheap—the trip will set you back thousands of baht. Stop by at 35/7 Sakadidet Road, Phuket Town, or call ℂ **07639-1287.** Or you can check out www.bluewater-anglers.com.

GOLF

There are some fine courses on Phuket and golf junkets bring vacationing expats and international tourists alike.

- The best course is the **Banyan Tree Club & Laguna,** 34 Moo 4, Srisoonthon Road, at the Laguna Resort Complex on Bang Tao Bay (ℂ **07627-0991;** fax 07632-4351), a par-71 championship course with many water features (greens fees: 2,900B/$71; guests of Laguna resorts receive a discount).
- The **Blue Canyon Country Club,** 165 Moo 1, Thepkasattri Road, near the airport (ℂ **07632-7440;** fax 07632-7449; www.bluecanyonclub.com), is a par-72 championship course with natural hazards, trees, and guarded greens (greens fees: from 2,900/$71).
- An older course, the **Phuket Country Club,** 80/1 Vichitsongkram Road, west of Phuket Town (ℂ **07632-1038;** fax 07632-1721; www.phuketcountryclub.com), has beautiful greens and fairways, plus a giant lake (greens fees: 2,400B/$59).

HORSEBACK RIDING

A romantic and charming way to see Phuket's jungles and beaches is on horseback. The **Phuket Laguna Riding Club,** 394 Moo 1, Bangtao Beach (ℂ **07632-4199**), welcomes riders of all ages and experience levels, and can provide instruction for beginners and children. Prices start at 500B ($12) per hour.

SEA KAYAKING

Phang Nga Bay National Park, a 1½-hour drive north of Phuket (3 hr. by boat) hosts great day-trips by sea kayak. The scenery is stunning, with limestone karst towers jutting precariously from the water's surface, creating more than 120 small islands. These craggy rock formations (the backdrop for the James Bond classic, *The Man with the Golden Gun*) look like they were taken straight from a Chinese scroll painting. Sea kayaks are perfect for inching your way into the many breathtaking caves and chambers that hide beneath the jagged cliffs. All tours include the hour-plus ride to and from Pha Nga, the cruise to the island area, paddle-guide, kayak, and lunch. The company to pioneer the cave trips is **Sea Canoe** (main office in Phuket Town, P.O. Box 276, Muang Phuket 83000; ℂ **07621-2252;** www.seacanoe.net). They're much imitated, but still the best choice for day trips through island caves to central lagoons (called "Hongs"). The standard day trip runs 3,500B ($85) per adult (1,750B/$43 per child). It is touristy, and you'll be sitting two to an inflated boat and be paddled by a guide going in and out of the caves (frustrating if you like to actually paddle), but the scenery is great and the caves are stunning (and there's free time for paddling on your own later). They also offer multiday and more adventurous "self-guided" tours.

The folks at **Paddle-Asia** (53/80 Moo 5, Thambon Srisoonthon, Thalang, Phuket, 83110; ℂ **07631-1222;** fax 07631-3689; www.paddleasia.com) make Phuket their home and do trips throughout the region, with a focus more on custom adventure travel, not day junkets. They have great options for anyone from beginner to expert, and on any trip you'll paddle real decked kayaks, not inflatables. A highlight is their trip to **Khao Sok National Park** (see "Day Trips from Surat Thani," in chapter 8), a 3-day adventure in which you're sure to see some amazing jungle wildlife. In Phuket they can arrange offshore paddling to outlying islands, kayak-surfing on Kata Beach, or any custom adventure ranging as far as Laos.

SCUBA DIVING

World renowned for its access to nearby **Similan Islands,** scuba diving is a huge draw to the island of Phuket. Thailand is one of the most affordable (and most importantly, safe) places to get into this other-worldly sport, and Phuket is a top choice. There are three decompression chambers on the island and a strong dive-community ensures good quality outfits. The problem is, there are something like 40 companies on Phuket, so it becomes difficult to choose. All companies can arrange day trips to the nearby coral wall and wrecks, as well as overnight or long-term excursions to the Similan Islands (also PADI courses, Dive Master courses, or 1-day introductory lessons and open-water certification). Multiday open-water courses can cost as little as 10,000B ($244).

In selecting a company, be sure they are certified with PADI. Many of the storefront operations are just consolidators for other companies (meaning you get less quality care and pay a fee to a middle-man), so ask if they have their own boats and make sure you'll be diving with the folks you meet behind the counter. Also check about the ratio of divers to instructor or divemaster; anything more than five to one is not acceptable, and it should be more like two to one for beginner courses. Below are a few of the best choices in Phuket.

- The folks at **Scuba Cat** (94 Thaweewong Rd., Patong; ℂ **07629-3120;** www.scubacat.com) have got the best thing going in Phuket. With some 10 years of experience, a large expatriate staff, and their own fleet of boats, it is a very professional outfit offering the full range of trips for anyone from beginner to expert (and at competitive prices). You can't miss the small practice pool in front of their beachside Patong office (in fact, you have to cross a small bridge to get in the place), and the staff is very helpful and welcoming.
- **Fantasea Divers** is another reputable firm on Phuket. Their main office is at Patong Beach at 219 Rat-U-Thit Rd. (ℂ **07634-0088;** fax 07634-0309; www.fantasea.net). Dive packages include live-aboard trips to the Burmese coast and 4-day PADI certification courses, in addition to full-day dives around Phuket.
- **Sunrise Diving** (49 Thaweewong Road, Patong Beach; ℂ **07629-3034;** www.sunrisediving.net) is new on the scene and provides good services from the only seaside dive shop on the island. They have their own boats.
- **Sea Bees Diving** (1/3 Moo 9, Viset Road, Chalong Bay; ℂ and fax **07638-1765;** www.sea-bees.com) is another good outfit offering day trips.
- **Dive Master's EcoDive 2000** has mostly live-aboard trips, with a focus on education and marine biology. Contact 75/20 Moo 10, Patak Road, Chalong (ℂ **07628-0330**).
- **Dive Asia** (P.O. Box 70, Kata Beach, Phuket 83100; ℂ **07633-0598**) offers similar services, dive training, day trips, and live-aboard trips.

SNORKELING

In the smaller bays around the island, such as Nai Harn Beach or Relax Bay, you'll come across some lovely **snorkeling** right along the shore. For the best coral just off the shoreline, trek up to **Haad Nai Yang National Park** for its long reef in clear shallow waters. Nearby Raya Island is popular, and many venture further to the **Similan Islands** or **Koh Phi Phi.** The best times to snorkel are from November to April before the monsoon comes and makes the water too choppy. Almost every tour operator and hotel can book day trips by boat that include hotel transfers, lunch, and gear for about 1,000B ($24) per person.

TREKKING & OTHER ACTIVITIES

To experience the wild side of Phuket's interior, try a **rainforest trekking journey** through the Khao Phra Thaew National Park. **Phuket Nature Tour** takes small groups through 3.5km (2¼ miles) of jungle paths past waterfalls and swimming holes. A typical half-day excursion includes hotel transfers, English-speaking jungle guides, and drinks. Call ℂ **07625-5522.**

Then there's **elephant trekking,** a perennial favorite for children, and a great time for adults, too. Elephants are not indigenous to Phuket, so what you get here is more-or-less a pony ride, but arguments over captive elephant-tour programs aside, the kids dig it (and the elephants do better here than when paraded around city streets for owners to collect coins). **Siam Safari Nature Tours** coordinates daily treks on elephants, Land Rovers, and river rafts. Their three-in-one Half-Day Eco-Adventure includes 4 hours of elephant treks through jungles to rubber estates, Jeep tours to see local wildlife, and a light river-rafting journey to Chalong Bay. A full day tour is the three-in-one plus a trek on foot through Khao Pra Thaew National Park and a Thai lunch. Siam Safari's office is at 70/1 Chaofa Road in Chalong (ℂ **07628-0116;** www. phuket.com/safari). **Siam Adventures** (60/4 Rat-u-thit Rd., Patong Beach; ℂ **07634-1799**) arranges similar adventures and is a leader in Phuket.

OTHER ACTIVITIES

The **Jungle Bungy Jump** awaits. If you have the nerve to jump out 50m (150 ft.) over the water, call their "Bungy Hotline" at ℂ **07632-1351.** They're in Kathu near Patong. They charge 1,400B ($34) per jump.

NATURAL TREASURES

Haad Nai Yang National Park, 90 sq. km (35 sq. miles) of protected land in the northwest corner of the island, offers a peaceful retreat from the rest of the island's tourism madness. There are two fantastic reasons to make the journey out to the park. The first is for Phuket's largest coral reef in shallow water, only 1,400m (460 ft.) from the shore. The second is for the giant leatherback turtles that come to nest every year between November and February. Park headquarters is a very short hop from Phuket Airport off Highway 402.

Playful **monkeys** add a fun dimension to bars, restaurants, and guesthouses around Thailand, where the adorable creatures are kept as pets. Many times, however, these gibbons are mistreated. Raised in captivity on unhealthful food in restricted living conditions, and subjected to human companionship exclusively, many develop psychological problems. Depression and despondency become common for maladjusted monkeys, with violent outbursts occurring sometimes. Bar monkeys end up drinking alcohol, and are force-fed uppers to keep them awake and lively—to the delight of tourists who aren't aware of the inevitable destruction it causes. **The Gibbon Rehabilitation Project,** off Highway 4027 at the Bang Pae waterfall in the northeastern corner of the island (ℂ **07626-0492**), cares for mistreated gibbons, placing them in more caring and natural surroundings (among other gibbons). Volunteer guides offer tours. Open daily from 10am to 4pm, admission is free, but donations are accepted and appreciated.

The Phuket Aquarium at the **Phuket Marine Biological Center** seeks to educate the public about local marine life and nature preservation. Unfortunately most of the signs throughout are in Thai (very disappointing). Open 8:30am to 4pm daily, admission is 20B (50¢). Call ✆ **07638-1226** for more information.

The **Butterfly Garden & Aquarium,** Soi Phaniang, Samkong, Phuket Town (✆ **07621-5616**), captures and breeds hundreds of gorgeous butterflies in a large, enclosed garden. Photo ops are great, so bring film. The aquarium may not be as large as the Marine Biology Center's, but here the tanks are filled with great "show fish," fascinating for their beautiful or unusual appearances rather than for marine education. Open daily from 9am to 5pm, adult admission 150B ($3.65), children below 10 years of age 60B ($1.50).

You'd never think seashells were so fascinating until you visit the **Phuket Shell Museum.** The largest shell museum in the world, this rare collection is simply beautiful. The gift shop sells a range of high-quality shell products like big, beautiful whole shells that make great gifts (if you can carry them). Open daily from 8am to 7pm, the museum is at 12/2 Moo 2, Viset Road, Rawai Beach (just south of Chalong Bay; ✆ **07638-1266;** admission 100B/$2.45, free for kids).

PHUKET'S SPAS 𝕶𝕶𝕶

If you've come to Phuket to escape and relax, there's no better way to accomplish your goal than to visit one of Phuket's spas. Even the smallest resort now offers full spa services (of varying quality), and you can find good, affordable massage along any beach and in storefronts in the main tourist areas.

For luxury treatments, the most famous and exclusive facility here is **The Spa at the Banyan Tree Phuket** (see its listing earlier). In secluded garden pavilions you'll be treated regally, and may choose from many types of massage, body and facial treatments, or health and beauty programs. To make reservations call ✆ **07632-4374** (ww.lagunaphuket.com/spa). Expect to pay for the luxury—figure at least 2,000B ($49) per individual treatment.

Another high-end resort in the furthest southeast of the island, **Evason,** makes for a great day-spa experience. They are a full-featured five-star resort with all the trimmings, and their spa is renowned (similar to Banyan Tree's prices). They're at 100 Vised Road, Rawai Beach, Phuket 83130 (✆ **07638-1010;** fax 07638-1018; www.sixsenses.com).

Hilton Phuket Arcadia Resort and Spa (Karon Beach; ✆ **07639-6433**) is home to one of the finest new spas on the island, a Thai village complex of individual spa suites connected by a meandering boardwalk. A great choice for luxury treatments.

Mom Tri's Villa Royale (12 Kata Noi Rd.; ✆ **07633-0015;** www.boathouse phuket.com) is now home to a chic new spa area at their luxury hilltop resort.

Let's Relax is a more affordable little day-spa in and among many similar services (some are a bit dodgy, really, but this one is okay) just off of Patong (Rat-u-thit Rd.; ✆ **07634-0913**). One hour Thai massage begins at 350B ($8.55).

SHOPPING

Patong Beach is the center of handicraft and souvenir shopping in Phuket, and the main streets and small *sois* are chockablock with storefront tailors, leather shops, jewelers, and ready-to-wear clothing boutiques. Vendors line the sidewalks selling everything from batik clothing, T-shirts, pirated CDs, local arts and handicrafts, northern hill-tribe handicrafts, silver, and souvenir trinkets. Vendors everywhere in Patong have the rotten habit of hassling every passerby. The prices are inflated compared to Bangkok or other tourist markets in Thailand, but some hard bargaining can get you the right price. Many items, northern handicrafts, for example, are best if purchased closer to the source, but if this is your only stop in Thailand, everything is cheap compared to the West, and you can stock-up with all the goodies you need to bring home for friends and family. There are a few boutiques in Phuket Town: try **Ban Boran Antiques** (24 Takuapa Rd.; © 07621-2473) or **The Loft** (36 Thalang Rd.; © 07625-8160).

In Phuket Town, and with outlets at a few hotels around the island, the **Soul of Asia** (37-39 Ratsada Rd., Taladyai; © 07621-1122; www.soulofasia.com) sells some of Asia's finest artist's works. If you like good, original artwork, this place is worth the trip (just down the street from Salvatore's Restaurant). They have a comprehensive collection, and effusive owner Mr. Eric Smulders knows his stuff.

Phuket is also home to a number of large mall venues, most notable the new **Central Festival,** about 10km (6 miles) inland from Patong and 3km (2 miles) inland from Phuket town on Chalermprakiet Road (© 07629-1111), with all the goods (kitchen sinks, too).

PHUKET AFTER DARK

Phuket Fantasea ★★ From the huge billboards and glossy brochures, **Phuket Fantasea** (www.phuket-fantasea.com), the island's premiere theme attraction, seems like it could be touristy and ridiculous. Surprise—it is!! But it is fun in the same way Atlantic City can be fun. Phuket Fantasea is a big theme park with a festival village lined with glitzy shops, games, entertainment, and snacks. A wander here will keep you busy until the show starts. They serve a huge buffet in the palatial Golden Kinaree Restaurant, and then visitors proceed to the Palace of the Elephants for the show. Frankly, the shopping is expensive and the dinner is just so-so (you can buy a ticket for the show only, no dinner), but the big spectacle is incredibly entertaining and very professional. There are posters for this place everywhere, and you can buy a ticket, including transport, in any hotel lobby or travel agent. The show is at Kamala Beach, north of Patong, on the coastal road. Call © 07638-5111 for reservations. The stage is dark on Thursdays. The park opens at 5:30pm; the buffet begins at 6:30pm, and the show at 9pm. Tickets for the show are 1,000B ($24) for adults and 750B ($18) for children, while dinner and transfer fees usually add 500B ($12) for adults and 300B ($7.30) for children. Ask about the rates at any hotel concierge; they often have deals.

Kamala Beach, Kathu, Phuket 83150. © 07638-5111. www.phuket-fantasea.com. Site open daily 5:30pm–11:30pm; daily show 9pm (arrive earlier for dinner). Cash.

Phuket also has a resident cabaret troupe at **Simon Cabaret,** 100/6-8 Moo 4, Patong Karon Road (© 07634-2011). There are shows at 7:30 and 9pm nightly; the cost is 600B ($14.65); they're on the south end of Patong. It is a featured spot on every planned tour agenda that draws busloads. This glitzy transsexual show caters mostly to Asian tourists, and lip-sync numbers of popular Asian pop songs keep the audience roaring. It can be a lot of fun. In between the comedy are dance numbers with pretty impressive sets and costumes.

Sphinx is a slick new show nearer the heart of Patong (120 Rat-U-thit Rd.; © 07634-1500; www.sphinxthai.com). Something like Simon Cabaret (above), but with not just transsexuals but female dancers as well. The dinner is the best dinner-show meal on the island. Set menus are from 550B to 700B ($13–$17); it costs 300B ($7.30) for the show alone (V, MC accepted). Performances start at 9pm and 10:30pm nightly except Tuesdays. Dining opens from 6pm.

Every night you can catch Thai boxing at **Vegas Thai Boxing** in Patong at the Patong Simon Shopping Arcade on Soi Bangla. Bouts start every night from 7pm and last until 3am. Fight-night info is all over town and admission is free.

Patong nightlife is wild. Lit up like a little Las Vegas, the beach town hops and it is Saturday every night of the week. Shops and restaurants stay open late, and there are an array of bars, nightclubs, karaoke lounges, snooker halls, massage parlors, go-go bars, and dance shows a la Bangkok's Patpong or the streets of Pattaya. Bangla Road, perpendicular to the beach road on the north end of Patong, is the little red-light district in town, and the hostess girls line up and reel in passersby (this goes something like: "Hey handsome man, where you go?"). It is pretty seedy, and you might want to keep the little ones away to avoid any lengthy explanations later, but it is an entertaining scene. A few bars about halfway down the road are always packed for views of the informal tabletop dancing. The curvaceous, costumed dancers are mostly transsexuals (*Important:* No photos!).

Scruffy Murphy's (© 07629-2590), along the main strip in Patong, is the obligatory beachside Irish pub with only a few scruffy ones wandering about, mostly young U.K. tourists revving up to make a night of it, and a good place to get your evening started. There are a few discos in town; just ask around to find out what's going on.

Dino Park Mini Golf *Kids* (© 07633-0625; www.dinopark.com) is a great one for bored teenagers or unruly whippersnappers. A good place to let them loose, and adults can even enjoy some grown-up time in the outdoor Flintstone-inspired gallery bar and restaurant while the kids hit the links (the course is a narrow pathway). Eighteen holes cost 260B ($6.35) for big kids (over 12) and 200B ($4.90) for whippersnappers. Find the course in the heart of Kata Beach, adjoining the popular Marina Phuket Hotel (see "Where to Stay," earlier).

Near the center of the island on the road between Kata/Karon beaches and Phuket Town, find **The Green Man** (82/15 Moo 4, Patak Rd., Rawai; © 07628-1445; www.the-green-man.net), an old English pub complete with exterior timber framing and a smoky interior filled with glib expats. Open until 2am.

5 Side Trips from Phuket

There are lots of adventure outfitters and travel agents on Phuket, all offering a variety of day trips and overnights. Phang Nga Bay is popular for adventure travel, and see the "Side Trips from Surat Thani" in chapter 8 for information about great trips to **Khao Sok National Park,** best by kayak.

Just north of the island of Phuket on the mainland, the **Khao Lak** and **Pha Nga** areas were hardest hit by the Christmas Tsunami of 2004. Rebuilding is ongoing, and subsidies and help arrived fast. Phang Nga Bay, with its arching karst limestone spires, made famous in the James Bond film *The Man With the Golden Gun,* is a very popular day trip by luxury boat or kayak. Khao Lak is a burgeoning resort destination hosting a number of fine, upmarket resorts, some new and some rebuilt. Many make it a day trip or an overnight from Phuket. For overnights, consider luxury **Le Meridien Khao Lak Beach & Spa Resort** (9/9 Moo 1, Tambol Kuk Kak, Amphur Takuapa Pa, Phang Nga 82190; © 07642-7500; www.lemeridien.com), which is just finishing rebuilding; or the newer **Merlin Khao Lak** (7/7 Moo 2, Petchkasem Road, Khao Lak Beach, Lamkan, Taimuang, Phang-Nga 82210; © 0764-28300; fax 07644-3200; www.merlinphuket.com), both on the high end.

Or, on the budget end, try **Khaolak Tropicana Beach Resort** (36 Mu 6, Petchakasem Road, Tambon Kukkak, Takuapa District, Phang Nga, 82190; © **07642-0231;** fax 07642-0240; www.khaolak-tropicana.com), with rooms starting at 1,600B ($39).

Ko Phi Phi is another popular day trip for snorkeling, or commonly an overnight from Phuket. See section 8, after Krabi, for info on Phi Phi.

6 Krabi (Ao Nang, Raillay & Khlong Muang Beaches)

814km (505 miles) S of Bangkok; 165km (109 miles) E of Phuket; 42km (26 miles) E of Koh Phi Phi; 276km (171 miles) N of Satun; 211km (131 miles) SW of Surat Thani

Krabi has become a popular alternative to busy Phuket and Koh Phi Phi (or at least a stop along the way). The town of Krabi isn't much to see, but as a main hub, everyone ends up here at least for a few minutes. Ferries and minivans from other destinations connect via *songtao* and boats to the nearby beach and tourist strip at Ao Nang and to the farther-flung beaches: Haad Raillay, the famed "climbers beach" with its stunning karst towers, is accessed by boat (from either Krabi town to the northeast or Ao Nang Beach from the west); and Khlong Muang Beach, only recently developed, just north of Ao Nang by car.

The best time to visit the Krabi area is November through April, with January and February the ideal months. The rainy season runs May through October.

ESSENTIALS
GETTING THERE

There are boat and bus connections between Krabi and Phuket. Krabi Town and nearby beaches are convenient to Phuket and connect via Surat Thani with the east coast islands (Samui, Pha Ngan).

By Plane   **Thai Airways** flies at least twice daily from Bangkok (© **02535-2084**). **Air Andaman** has a daily flight via Phuket (© **02251-4905,** Bangkok reservations). From the airport you can catch a minivan to town for 60B ($1.45), more for further beaches. Taxis start at 300B ($7.30).

By Boat   Thrice-daily trips leave from Koh Phi Phi to Krabi (trip time 2 hr.; 200B/$4.90). There are two daily boats from Koh Lanta to Krabi in the high season (trip time: 2½ hr.; 150B/$3.65).

By Bus   Two air-conditioned VIP 24-seater buses leave daily from **Bangkok's Southern Bus Terminal** (© **02435-1199;** trip time: 12 hr.; 710B/$17) to Krabi Town. Frequently scheduled air-conditioned minibuses leave daily from Surat Thani to Krabi (trip time: 2¾ hr.; 150B/$3.65). Three air-conditioned minibuses leave daily from Phuket Town to Krabi (trip time: 3½ hr.; 200B/$4.90).

VISITOR INFORMATION

There's a small branch of the TAT on the north end of the esplanade along the river in Krabi Town (© **07561-2740**). Check in the small shops around town for a copy of the local free map of the resort area, town, and surrounding islands.

ORIENTATION/FAST FACTS

Most services in Krabi town are on Utarakit Road, paralleling the waterfront (to the right as you alight the ferry). Here you'll find the **TAT Office** (© **07562-2163**) and a number of **banks** with ATM service. The **post office** and **police station**

(© **07563-7208**) are located south on Utarakit Road, to the left as you leave the pier. There are a few banks in Ao Nang, near the Phra Nang Inn.

GETTING AROUND

Krabi Town is the commercial hub in the area, but few stay. There is frequent *song-tao* service between Krabi Town and Ao Nang Beach; just flag down a white pickup (the trip takes 30 min. and costs 20B/50¢).

Raillay Beach is not an island but is cut off by its high cliffs from the mainland and reached only by boat: from the pier in Krabi Town for 80B/$1.95 (45 min.), or from the beach at Ao Nang (at the small pavilion across from the Prah Nang Inn) for 50B ($1.20) (just 20 min.).

Khlong Muang beach is some 25km (16 miles) northwest of Krabi Town. Expect to pay at least 250B ($6.10) for a taxi.

If you're checking in at any resort, ask about transportation arrangements (which are often included).

WHAT TO SEE & DO

Krabi has a number of sites, but most head straight for the beaches to relax. Popular activities are day boat trips, snorkeling, and rock-climbing at Raillay.

Just north and east of Krabi Town, though, you will find **Wat Tham Sua (The Tiger Temple),** a stunning hilltop pilgrimage point. A hearty 30- to 40-minute climb brings you to the rocky pinnacle where Buddhist statuary overlook panoramic views of the surrounding area, from Krabi Town to the rock towers near Raillay and Ao Nang. There is a large monastery and temple compound built into the rock at the bottom of the mountain where you may chance upon a monk in silent meditation or chat with one of the friendly temple stewards (most are eager to practice English). Ajahn Jomnien, the abbot, speaks English, and welcomes foreign meditators. If you decide to climb the steep temple mountain, go either in the early morning or late afternoon to beat the heat. The more than 2,000 steep concrete steps do a job on your knees, but the view is worth it (not to mention all the good karma you can accrue). *Note:* Be careful of the many monkeys here. Don't look them in the eye, just go about your business, and don't hold anything tempting in your hands or it will be taken.

The beaches and stunning cliffs of **Raillay Beach** are certainly worth a day trip even if you don't stay there (see "Where to Stay," below). Long-tail boats wait just off-shore at Ao Nang, and boat drivers consolidate passengers at a small pavilion just across from the Phra Nang Inn for the 50B ($1.20) ride (20 min). From the docks in Krabi Town it costs 80B ($1.95) (40 min). Daytime only.

The craggy karst cliffs of Raillay make it one of the best-known **rock climbing** spots in the region (if not the world). It is "sport climbing" done on mapped routes with safety bolts already drilled into the rock, and there are a number of companies offering full and half-day courses, as well as good rental equipment for experienced climbers. There are many routes suitable for beginners, and climbing schools all set up "top rope" climbing for safety (climbers are attached by a rope through a fixed pulley at the top and to a guide on the other end holding you fast). The schools all offer similar rates and have offices scattered around Raillay Beach, with posters and pamphlets everywhere. Try **King Climbers** (© **07563-7125;** www.railay.com) or **Cliffs Man** (© **07562-1768;** www.cliffsman.com). Half-day courses (and this may be all you'll want to try at first) start at about 800B ($20), and full-day courses are from 1,500B ($37). You won't believe what you can do until you try this!

For non-climbers, the beaches of Raillay are also worth the trip. Be sure to make your way to **Prah Nang Beach,** a secluded section of sand that is either a short 20B (50¢) boat trip from Raillay proper or a cliffside walk east, past Rayavadee Resort and south along a shaded cliffside path (watch for monkeys). Masseuses and salespeople will hassle you here, but not too badly. Right offshore you can swim (sometimes walk) to **Happy Island** (I never found out what's "happy" about it), and don't miss **Prah Nang Cave,** a small crevice at the base of a tall cliff which is much revered. The cliffs are stunning and the sunsets spectacular.

It is also along the path to **Prah Nang Beach** that you'll find the **secluded lagoon** at Raillay; look for signs pointing up to a small cleft in the rocks, and come prepared for a short hike up a steep escarpment before a treacherous, wet, muddy down-climb (with some old fray ropes to guide) to a shallow, salty lagoon. Keep an eye out for monkeys. This is a very adventurous little jaunt, but fun.

Full-day boat trips and snorkeling can be arranged from any beachfront tour agent or hotel near Krabi, which will take you to a few small coral sites as well as any number of secluded coves starting at 800B ($20) for a half-day or 1,500B ($37) for a full day. Rent snorkel gear from any of the tour operators along Ao Nang or Raillay for about 50B ($1.20) per day.

There are some dive operators, but it is a better idea to save your money and time for Koh Phi Phi or Phuket—from Krabi you'll have to travel farther to reach the better sites.

Day **kayak tours** to outlying islands or the mangroves near **Ao Luk** are becoming popular for visitors to Ao Nang. Contact **Sea, Land and Trek Co.** (21/1 Moo 2, Ao Nang; ✆ **07563-7364**) or **Sea Kayak Krabi** (40 Maharach Soi 2, Krabi; ✆ **07563-0270**). Rates begin at 1,500B ($37).

WHERE TO STAY
KRABI TOWN
Few stay in Krabi Town, but if you're stuck or are too tired to leave, the best is **Krabi City Seaview Hotel** (77/1 Longkha Rd.; ✆ **07562-2885**), with basic air-conditioned rooms starting at 500B ($12). There are also a number of small guesthouses.

RAILLAY BEACH
Very Expensive
Rayavadee ✿✿✿   Rayavadee is one of the finest resorts in Thailand. Handsome two-story rounded pavilions are large and luxurious, offering every modern convenience and utmost privacy—first-floor sitting areas have a central, hanging lounger with cushions, second-story bedrooms are all silk and teak, and private bathrooms have big Jacuzzi tubs and luxury products. The resort grounds lie at the base of towering cliffs on the island's most choice piece of property, a triangle of land where each point accesses the island's beaches: Phra Nang, Nam Mao, and Raillay. Their central dining outlet is excellent, and only overshadowed by the more romantic and relaxed atmosphere of their seaside Thai restaurant, Raitalay. The resort is a peaceful village with paths meandering among private lotus ponds and meticulous landscaping (you won't be bothered by meandering tourists). The sunsets at the big, beautiful pool at beachside or on Raillay Beach itself are sensational. Resort staff covers all services here, even arranging rock climbing and day trips, and they offer transfers to and from Krabi Town by private speedboat (and a small tractor will ferry you to the resort doorstep at low tide). The price is high, but the location, luxury, and privacy is unique.

214 Moo 2, Tambol Ao Nang, Amphur Muang, Krabi 81000 (30 min. northwest of Krabi Town by long-tail boat or 70 min. from Phuket on the resort's own launch). ⓒ 07562-0740. Fax 07562-0630. 100 units. 24,000B–34,000B ($585–$829) deluxe pavilion; 40,000B ($976) hydro-pool pavilion; 50,000B ($1,220) family pavilion; from 140,000B ($3,415) specialty villas. AE, DC, MC, V. **Amenities:** 2 restaurants; lounge and library; outdoor pool with children's pool; outdoor lighted tennis courts; air-conditioned squash court; fitness center; spa w/massage; Jacuzzi; sauna; watersports equipment and scuba center; concierge; 24-hr. room service; massage; same-day laundry service. *In room:* A/C, satellite TV, minibar, fridge, safe, IDD phone.

Moderate
Sand Sea Resort   Just down the beach from Rayavadee's pool area along Raillay beach (great sunsets from here), Sand Sea is a good little bungalow haven along this busy beachfront. Flowering bushes surround putting-green lawns, and bungalows line the garden paths. Rooms have air-conditioning and offer the comfort of your average hotel room (many opt to open the screened windows and turn on the room fan, though). They have a small pool and a good restaurant right on the busy beach. Step right out front and join a game of soccer or rent a kayak and travel around the craggy coast. A good, simple choice.

39 Moo 2, Raillay Beach, Ao Nang, Krabi 81000 (on western-facing Raillay Beach, long-tails from Ao Nang pull up on shore out front). ⓒ 07562-2170. Fax 07562-2608. 68 units. 900B–1,900B ($22–$46) double w/fan; 1,900B–4,000B ($46–$98) double w/A.C. MC, V. **Amenities:** Restaurant; pool; watersports rentals (kayaks); tour desk; mini-mart; massage; laundry service. *In room:* A/C (some), TV, minibar, fridge, no phone.

Inexpensive
Diamond Cave Resort   Okay, "resort" is pushing it a bit here, but it is not uncommon to use the term loosely at island properties in the south. The hallmark of Diamond Cave is their clean, cozy, tile-floor bungalows set in shady rows in a little suburban neighborhood, each with a small, shaded veranda. Their adjoining "Private Resort" has a small pool, but the affordable bungalows are the best choice, and a nice place to escape the vagaries of life and enjoy some nearby climbing. Diamond Cave is at the far end of Raillay Beach East, and far from the good sandy beaches, but cozy in and among lots of budget dining and bars.

36 Moo 1, Ao Nang Krabi (north end of Raillay East Beach). ⓒ 07562-2589. Fax 07562-2590. 32 units. From 1,000B ($24) double. MC, V. **Amenities:** Restaurant; bar; pool; tour desk; mini-mart; laundry. *In room:* no phone.

AO NANG BEACH
Moderate
Ao Nang Villa 🌸   The best standard on Ao Nang Beach, the calculated cool of Ao Nang Villa is unique in the area. It is a fine collection of semi-luxe rooms at poolside and has an inviting, listless atmosphere, but can be a bit insular, even sterile (it's hard to believe you're in Ao Nang). It is quiet, though, and well away from the busy road. The modern, colonnaded walkways, open-plan lobby, and laid-back pool areas are peaceful if a bit studied, and rooms are similarly comfortable though unremarkable.

113 Moo 2, Ao Nang, Krabi (east of the main strip in Ao Nang). ⓒ 07563-7270. Fax 07569-5072. www.aonang villa.com. 157 units. 3,500B–4,000B ($85–$98) double; from 4,200B ($102) suite. AE, DC, MC, V. **Amenities:** 2 restaurants; bar; 2 outdoor pools; Jacuzzi; sauna; tour desk; car-rental desk; shopping arcade; limited room service; massage; laundry. *In room:* A/C, satellite TV, minibar, fridge, safe, IDD phone.

Golden Beach Resort   Comparable service and standards as the nearby Phra Nang Inn (below), the Golden Beach's deluxe rooms are a slightly higher standard, the pool is large and inviting, and the resort is just a short hop down a cul-de-sac and away from busy, central Ao Nang. Their free-standing, pagoda suites make masterful use of curved lines inside and out, and feature luxurious canopy beds and indoor/outdoor bathrooms. Standard rooms are cozy.

254 Moo 2, Ao Nan, Krabi 81000 (the east end of Ao Nang, down a dead-end at beachside behind the boat pavilion for trips to Raillay). ⓒ 07563-7870. Fax 07563-7875. 66 units. 4,500B ($110) double; from 6,000B ($146) suite. AE, MC, V. **Amenities:** Restaurant; bar; large outdoor pool; tour desk; car-rental desk; limited room service; massage (poolside); laundry. *In room:* A/C, satellite TV, minibar, fridge, IDD phone.

Krabi Resort The Krabi Resort is the only property in Ao Nang with direct beach access. It is a compound of two hotel blocks and an array of freestanding beachside bungalows. Tidy grounds surround a fine swimming pool, but other resort amenities are unused and aging. More private sea-view bungalows are the best choice: large and clean with parquet floors, high ceilings, rattan furnishings, and lots of little Thai touches. It is just north of the main shopping and restaurant area at Ao Nang, but a lovely beach walk. Ask about their overnight trips to rustic bungalows on nearby Poda Island.

53–57 Patthana Rd., Ao Nang Beach, Krabi 81000 (overlooking beach at Ao Nang). ⓒ 07563-7051. 75 units. 4,600B–6,100B ($112–$149) bungalow priced according to view; 4,000B–8,800B ($98–$215) suite. MC, V. **Amenities:** Restaurant; lounge; pool; outdoor lighted tennis courts; fitness center; watersports equipment; bike rental; tour desk; limited room service; massage; same-day laundry service. *In room:* A/C, satellite TV, minibar, fridge, safe, IDD phone.

Phra-Nang Inn ✿ The outside of the eccentric Phra-Nang Inn looks like a rustic woodland lodge, built with pine and palms, with papasans (those round comfy sink-in chairs) arranged overlooking central gardens. Inside, the rooms are more or less an upscale guesthouse standard, but furnished in a unique mix of Chinese tiles, concrete furnishings built into the walls, seashell and stucco mosaics, and a twisted wood canopy bed hung with strands of shells. Even the bathroom is odd, with a concrete and slate built-in shower and vanity. The hotel's two wings are on either side of the busiest intersection in Ao Nang (where the beachfront road turns inland toward Krabi Town), but oriented away from the road to private courtyards, one forming a U around a tiny pool and restaurant area. You're right in the thick of it here, though, and the helpful staff can help arrange tours and onward boat travel (from right across the street).

119 Ao Nang Beach (P.O. Box 25), Krabi 81000 (overlooking beach at Ao Nang-Raillay boat dock). ⓒ 07563-7130. Fax 07563-7134. 88 units. 2,000B–4,000B ($49–$98) double; from 5,000B ($122) suite. DC, MC, V. **Amenities:** 2 restaurants; 2 bars; small pool; spa w/massage; sauna; tour desk; Internet; 24-hr. room service; laundry service. *In room:* A/C, satellite TV w/in-house movies, minibar, fridge, safe, IDD phone.

Inexpensive

Ao Nang has lots of budget guesthouses to choose from. The friendly folks at **J. Mansion** (302 Moo 2, Ao Nang; ⓒ 07569-5130) have clean, air-conditioned rooms starting at 350B ($8.55), with satellite TV and a safety box. They're a 5-minute walk up the hill from the beach.

KHLONG MUANG BEACH

Following the coast north of the busy Ao Nang strip you'll come to quiet Klong Muang with a long stretch of quiet beach and a few good resorts from which to choose.

Expensive

Nakamanda A collection of luxurious private villas, Nakamanda is an opulent choice on the far northern end of Krabi (just past the Sheraton). The name means the "Dragon of the Andaman," and this stylish outcrop does in fact look otherworldly, like an emerging Atlantis or a lost ancient city. Public spaces are spartan and done in a cool contemporary style, with large block walls and meticulous gardens. All villas are aligned for optimal privacy, and inside everything is sumptuous bleached wood and granite. Rooms range from anything like a basic villa, like your average suite room elsewhere, to over-the-top private pool villas with sea views. The spa is inviting, their seaside pool an oasis, and the resort restaurant is great. Nakamanda is a member of the Small Luxury Hotels of the World. A tip-top boutique destination spa and great honeymoon choice.

Klong Muang Beach, Tambol Nongtalay, Amphur Muang, Krabi 81000. © 07562-8200. Fax 07564-4389. www. nakamanda.com. 39 units. 15,000B ($366) sala villa; 35,000B ($854) Jacuzzi villa; 65,000B ($1,585) pool villa. AE, MC, V. **Amenities:** Restaurant and bars; outdoor pool; health club; spa; Jacuzzi; sauna; watersports rentals; library with Internet; tour desk; car-rental; limited room service; massage; laundry. *In room:* A/C, satellite TV, fridge, minibar, coffeemaker, hair dryer, safe, IDD phone.

Sheraton Krabi Beach Resort ★★   A large circular drive and luxurious modern lobby pavilion ushers you into this expansive resort. Rooms are set in large blocks, a U-shaped configuration connected by boardwalks above mangrove flats that flood with the daily tide. Moderate-size rooms are luxurious in fine tile and dark wood furnishings, and appointments that are an unlikely but pleasant fusion of Zen simplicity and Art Deco. Services range from fine dining choices, whether laid-back at poolside or a more formal set-piece in the main building, a large, luxurious beachside pool and fine health and fitness area with a variety of good programs (from kick-boxing to meditation). The spa, too, is a real treat. So, whether to get the edge back in your tennis game, relax by the pool all day, or bob in the tepid sea while watching a fireworks sunset, there is something for everyone here.

155 Moo 2, Baan Khlong Muang Beach, Nong Talay, Krabi 81000 (15km/9 miles north of Ao Nang, 26km/16 miles from Krabi Town). © 07562-8000. Fax 07562-8028. www.sheraton.com. 246 units. 10,600B–11,700B ($259–$285) double; 24,000B ($585) suite. AE, DC, MC, V. **Amenities:** 3 restaurants; 3 bars; outdoor pool; tennis court (shoe and racket rental available); fitness center; spa w/massage; Jacuzzi; sauna; sailboat and kayak rental (no motorboats); mountain bike rental; kids' club; library area w/games, video, and Internet; tour desk; car-rental desk (Avis); shopping arcade; babysitting; 24-hr. room service; laundry; nonsmoking rooms; meeting facilities. *In room:* A/C, satellite TV, dataport, minibar, fridge, coffeemaker, hair dryer, safe, IDD phone.

Moderate

Andaman Holiday Resort   Set between the Sheraton and Nakamanda, the Andaman Holiday is a cozy alternative at a fraction of the price (okay, and a fraction of the luxury). Rooms are large and clean, a range from older chain hotel-style rooms to small bungalows and large family suites that are more rustic lodge than resort. There is a good central pool and a large garden area near the sea. The beach is a wide, open stretch of sand and often deserted. The lobby is an exposed timber pavilion and the grounds invite meandering and offer cool shaded rest areas. Hotel services are limited but adequate (it's a long ride to any alternative).

98 Moo 3, Klong Muang Beach, Tambon Nongtalay, Krabi 81000 (16km/10 miles north of Ao Nang, 27km/17 miles from Krabi Town). © 07562-8300. Fax 07564-4320. www.andamanholiday.com. 116 units. 3,000B–7,000B ($73–$171) double; from 5,000B ($122) villa. AE, DC, MC, V. **Amenities:** 3 restaurants; bar; 2 outdoor pools; small fitness center (open-air); tour desk (scuba trips); car-rental desk; shopping; salon; massage; laundry. *In room:* A/C, satellite TV, minibar, fridge, coffeemaker, IDD phone.

WHERE TO DINE

Apart from the good dining choices at the many resorts listed above, there are no restaurants worth mentioning in or around Krabi. Everywhere you go, you'll find small storefront eateries and tourist cafes, though. In the north end of Krabi Town, the **Night Market** just off Utarakit riverside road on Maharaj Soi 10 has good local specials like deep fried oysters and Pad Thai. Many of the stalls have signs in English (you'll find great desserts and fresh fruit here, too). In Ao Nang, the little beachside tourist street will likely grow up to be like Patong in nearby Phuket, and is well on the way; there are lots of neon-lit shops and storefront eateries: Try **Ao Nang Cuisine** for good Thai fare or any of the small beachside eateries. On Raillay, all of the bars and bungalows at beachside serve good Thai and Western.

7 Koh Phi Phi

814km (505 miles) S of Bangkok, then 42km (26 miles) W of Krabi; 160km (99 miles) SW of Phuket

Koh Phi Phi and the thin isthmus of Tonsai Bay on the main island of Phi Phi Don, once chockablock with hotels, guesthouses, and shops, was literally wiped off the map by the tsunami of December 26, 2004. What is left is the fallen down shell of the Phuket Cabana Hotel, and an open field between the ferry and the beach. As of fall 2005, some businesses had returned and, with the help of many international volunteers, the island has cleaned up all debris and rebuilding is under way. Where elsewhere, on Phuket or in Khao Lak, the Thai government has subsidized rebuilding, the businesses on the island of Phi Phi Don were in fact built by squatters on National Park land, and the government will offer them no help. There is talk of making the now empty strip at the island center into a public park space, encouraging day trippers from Phuket or Krabi instead of overnighters on the busy backpacker ghetto that is slowly reemerging after the devastation, but only time (and the Thai government) will tell. Phi Phi supports a number of high-end resorts on more far-flung stretches of beach, none of which were affected by the tsunami. Look for the small memorial garden that is coming together on the land near where Charlie's Bungalows once stood (to the right and across the isthmus as you alight the ferry).

Phi Phi is a popular choice for day trips, snorkeling, and scuba junkets from Krabi. Tourists flock to the site where filmmakers chose to stage the Hollywood version of Utopia in the film *The Beach,* with Leonardo DiCaprio, and day trips take you to the remote cove where crews filmed.

Phi Phi is two islands. Phi Phi Don is the main barbell-shaped island whose central isthmus (the barbell handle) was hit by the tsunami; all visitors arrive at the busy ferry port in Phi Phi Don's Loh Dalam Bay, and the sandy beaches at Tonsai (just opposite) are good for sunbathing. Smaller Phi Phi Lei is south of the main island and famed for its coveted swallow nests and the courageous pole-climbing daredevils who go get them (the nests fetch a hefty price for the making of a gourmet Chinese soup). The smaller island is protected as a natural park, but is visited as part of most day trips.

Small beachfront outfits rent snorkel gear and conduct long-tail boat tours to quiet coves with great views of coral reefs and sea life for as little as 500B ($12) for an all-day trip (packing your own lunch). You can rent kayaks and do a little exploring on your own, hike one of the island viewpoints, or just enjoy the sea and sand on busy Tongsai Bay.

HOW TO GET THERE

Ferries make regular connections from both Phuket and Krabi. Boats from the pier in central Krabi Town run three times daily: 9am, 10:30am, and 1pm (more in high season) for 300B ($7.30). From Phuket there are a number of ferry services leaving from the pier near Phuket Town with rates as low as 450B ($11) for the 2-hour trip.

WHERE TO STAY

The scene on Phi Phi Don during our recent visit was bleak. Just a few smaller hotels have been rebuilt, and it is uncertain to what extent the precious low-lying isthmus will in fact be repopulated. The decimated hulk of the Phi Phi Island Cabana stands out like a sore thumb on the left as you alight the ferry. The **Phi Phi Hotel** and **Phi Phi Banyan Villa** (near the ferry dock; © 07561-1233; www.phiphi-hotel.com) are the best choices on the main beach (from 1,500B/$37), and bungalows and small restaurants are being rebuilt or built anew all along the beach and hills to the right of the ferry pier in the little backpacker neighborhood. The best accommodation is on further-flung parts of Phi Phi Don, reached only by boat, and best if pre-arranged to avoid the rabid touts at the pier.

Expensive

Holiday Inn Phi Phi   The Holiday Inn is part of further expansion of resort development on the farther-flung shores of Koh Phi Phi (you can only get here by boat, just past Phi Phi Island Village, below). Bungalows cluster along a thin stretch of beach, a fine high standard, and the resort covers all the amenities and can arrange smooth transport from their hotel in Phuket.

Laem Tong Beach, Koh Phi Phi, Krabi. Phuket Office: 100/435 Moo 5 Chalermprakiet Rama 9 Rd., T. Rassada, Phuket 83000. © 07626-1860. Fax 07626-1866. www.holiday-inn.com. 77 units. 4,000B–6,000B ($98–$146). **Amenities:** 2 restaurants; 1 bar; outdoor pool; health club; Jacuzzi; watersports rentals; tour desk; limited room service; massage; laundry. *In room:* A/C, satellite TV, fridge, minibar, IDD phone.

Phi Phi Island Village ❧   This is the top choice among the islands more far-reaching resorts. You'll need to get here by boat, a 30-minute ride (they have regular shuttles and arrange pickup from the ferry pier), but you'll be glad that you did; it is a quiet little beachfront campus of deluxe, raised bungalows, all quite large and comfortable with big private balconies and designer, open-plan bathrooms done in stone and tile (shower only). This is a popular choice for families and young couples/ honeymooners, and even a few backpackers blowing the budget for a few days. The resort has a luxury spa in a separate area high on a hill, two large pools, fine dining, shopping, a mini-mart, and good tour programs and a scuba school; it's all very self-contained, which is essential here, because, apart from a few nearby jungle walks, there's nowhere to go. The beachfront at high tide is lovely and sunset is inspiring.

Phuket Office: 89 Satoon Rd. Phuket 83000 (in Loh Ba Kao Bay in the NE end of the island, 30 min. by long-tail boat). © 07621-5014. Fax 07621-4918. www.ppisland.com. 100 units. 4,500B–7,500B ($110–$183) double; from 10,000B ($244) villas. AE, MC, V. **Amenities:** 3 restaurants; 3 bars; 2 outdoor pools; spa w/massage; Jacuzzi; sauna; scuba school; watersports rentals; tour desk; courtesy boat transport to main beach area; Internet service; babysitting, laundry service. *In room:* A/C, satellite TV, minibar, fridge, no phone.

WHERE TO DINE/NIGHTLIFE

Dining at your resort of choice is best on Phi Phi, but there are a few fried rice-and-noodles joints near the central beach area on Phi Phi Don. **PP Bakery** amazingly survived the tsunami and still offers good sandwiches, cakes, and cheap Thai food from their longtime storefront outlet (surrounded on all sides by copycats); they are always full. You'll also find a few little halal food stands, and vendors with wheeled carts making southern-style sweet roti with banana.

Once a Muslim village, Phi Phi now parties into the night at places like the **Reggae Bar,** an old standby which was quick to rebuild post-tsunami, but there aren't as many places as before. Time will tell.

ACTIVITIES

Snorkeling trips around the island are popular and can be arranged with any hotel or with any of the many beachfront travel agencies for as little as 500B ($12) per day.

Scuba diving is quite popular, too, and **Aquanauts Scuba,** among other full-service, professional outfits, offers anything from day trips to multiday adventures as well as all the requisite PADI course instruction. Their office is a short walk to the right as you alight the ferry (℃ **07421-2640**). Also look for **Visa Diving** on the main strip just east of the ferry pier (℃ **07561-8106;** www.visadiving.com).

Some rock-climbing outfits on Krabi's Raillay Beach (see the Krabi section, above) arrange day trips and overnights to scramble the gnarled cliffs around the two Phi Phi islands; climbers are often belayed by boat.

8 Koh Lanta

About 70km (43 miles) SE of Krabi

Small Muslim fishing villages dot the east coast of Lanta Yai (Big Lanta) and carry on with their traditional economy, ignoring the rolling cement trucks and bang-bang of bungalow building hammers over on the west coast. I stopped in a small town and talked with a fisherman who was keen to know how much my hotel cost; he cracked up, pointing out how I'd been duped and paid a year's rent for him for 1 night. You cross Lanta Noi (Small Lanta) coming from the north to get to the main beach areas of Lanta Yai. The west coast of Lanta Yai has seen a real boom in fine accommodation, led by Pimalai to the far south, and now covering every budget range. Lanta is going international.

GETTING THERE

Minivans from Krabi Town and Trang make connections to Lanta (cost is from 150B/$3.65 for bus/boat/bus door-to-door). To get to the beaches along the west coast of Lanta Yai, you'll make two ferry crossings: one from the mainland to Lanta Noi (Small Lanta), then across the island by car before another ferry to Lanta Yai (Big Lanta). Most transport stops in the small town of **Saladan** near the ferry pier on the northern tip of Lanta Yai. Minibuses stop at tour agencies to try and coax you into this resort property or that for a small fee (not a bad choice, really). From Saladan, it is a pickup truck ride free of charge to the resort of your choice (whether you book with them or not, it is part of the minivan fee). Contact **Kanokwan Tour** (Lanta office: ℃ **07568-4419,** or Krabi office: ℃ 07563-0192) or **Lanta Transport Co.** (℃ **07568-4482**) to make budget transportation arrangements.

There are chartered boat options from Krabi Town or even Phuket and Phi Phi in the high season (see individual chapters for private boat charter information), and Pimalai Resort (below) arranges luxury boat transport when you make your reservation.

WHERE TO STAY
VERY EXPENSIVE

Pimalai Resort and Spa ⭑⭑⭑   From Krabi Town or the airport you can ride in style: first by luxury van, then a picturesque private boat ride directly to the resort in high season (a short 4×4 ride to another pier in low season). Pimalai Resort is a fine marriage of comfort and proximity to nature. Large, freestanding villas are partly walled compounds with rooms done in hardwoods, with luxurious bathrooms with outdoor showers. Each room has a large veranda, some overlooking the sea or at least in earshot of the crashing surf of the picturesque beach below (a good swimming beach). High-end suites are spectacular, and the resort just opened a new wing of sumptuous private pool villas. Resort services like the spa, pool, and fine dining, as well as a library and gym for those rainy days, makes Pimalai sufficiently self-contained. Design throughout, from the unique spa set in a small ravine with simple but luxurious thatched treatment *salas* and trickling waterfall, to the many Thai pavilions as well as small touches, like hangings and carvings, reminds you where you are—not heaven, but Thailand. They arrange great day trips, and there's also a cooking school.

99 Moo 5, Ba Kan Tiang Beach, Lanta Yai Island, Krabi 81150 (on the far SE coast of Lanta Yai). © 07560-7999. Fax 07560-7998. www.pimalai.com. 118 units. 8,500B–15,000B ($207–$366) double (priced to view and season); 15,000B–18,000B ($366–$439) beach villa; from 20,000B ($488) pavilion suite. AE, DC, MC, V. **Amenities:** 3 restaurants; bar; pool; spa w/massage; Jacuzzi; watersports rentals; mountain bike rentals; dive center; library w/good book selection; tour desk; car-rental desk; limousine transfer; business center w/Internet; 24-hr. room service; same-day laundry service. *In room:* A/C, satellite TV (some with CD and DVD players), fridge, minibar, safe, IDD phone.

EXPENSIVE

Layana ⭐⭐ A new boutique resort, little Layana is a real find. Contemporary rooms and suites are all situated toward a lovely stretch of ocean. They have a grand central pool that is uniquely calibrated to the same salinity as human tears, so you'll have no chlorine eyes. Each room has an open, airy feel with lush decor of hard woods, silks, and local art. Great open-plan baths have windows open to a private garden (windows even surround the loo in some). All units have large balconies and cozy designer wood slat-deck chairs. Expat-owned and -managed, the place has it right in all the details, a truly boutique experience.

272 Moo 3 Saladan, Phra-Ae Beach, Koh Lanta, Krabi 81150. © 07560-7100. Fax 07560-7199. www.layana resort.com. 50 units. $163–$338 double priced by location and season; $273–$448 suite. AE, MC, V. **Amenities:** 2 restaurants; 2 bars; outdoor pool; health club; spa; Jacuzzi; sauna; watersports rentals; bike rentals; library with Internet; tour desk; car-rental; limited room service; massage; laundry. *In room:* A/C, satellite TV, fridge, minibar, coffeemaker, safe, IDD phone.

MODERATE

Lanta Casuarina A good mid-range choice, Lanta Casuarina is popular with European groups and Thai conventioneers. Rooms are a comfortable mid-range standard, airy and clean but not distinct, and the hotel has good basic services, a friendly coffee shop, and good seaside pool. A good choice right in the center of Lanta's west coast strip (near Layana, above).

288 Moo 3, Phra Ae Beach, Saladan, Koh Lanta Yai, Krabi 81150. © 07568-4685. Fax 07568-4689. www.hmhotels-resorts.com. 51 units. 3,500B–4,000B ($85–$98) double; from 5,500 ($138) villa. MC, V. **Amenities:** Restaurant and bar; outdoor pool; watersports rentals; car-rental; massage; laundry. *In room:* A/C, satellite TV, fridge, minibar, IDD phone.

INEXPENSIVE

Andaman Lanta Resort An older resort, but a good budget choice with either simple hotel-style rooms in a two-story block, or small rustic bungalows, some at seaside, all surrounding a midsize central pool. Very basic in-house dining and tour services make Andaman Lanta self-contained, and the low price means you don't "have to" have a perfect time; just put your feet up and learn "Thai time" and "Sanook." The mid-range bungalows are the best choice.

142 Moo 3, Klong Dow Beach, Koh Lanta Yai, Krabi 81150. © 07568-4200. Fax 07568-4203. www.andaman lanta.com. 79 units. 800B–1,800B ($20–$44) double in hotel block; 1,000B–2,300B ($24–$56) bungalow double;

from 3,000B ($73) suite. MC, V. **Amenities:** Restaurant and bar; outdoor pool; watersports rentals; car-rentals; tour desk; massage; laundry. *In room:* A/C, satellite TV, fridge, IDD phone.

Moonlight Bay Resort   Long popular in the far south of Lanta, Moon Light Bay is typical of the many bungalow resorts here and offers rustic but cozy accommodations on a hilltop overlooking the beach below. The place has enough amenities, from dining to recreation and travel service, to be a comfortable self-contained destination. Ask for a bungalow facing the sea and put your feet up.

69 Moo 8, Klongtob, Koh Lanta Yai, Krabi 81150. © **07568-4401.** Fax 07561-8097. www.mlb-resort.com. 30 units. 2,000B–6,000B ($49–$146) double (varies with location and size). **Amenities:** Restaurant and bar; small outdoor pool; Jacuzzi; tour desk; car-rental; massage; laundry. *In room:* A/C, satellite TV, fridge, minibar, IDD phone.

Southern Lanta Resort and Spa   Oddly, Southern Lanta Resort is on the north end of the island, but who's splitting hairs at an affordable little retreat like this? It is a basic but cozy bungalow suburb at beachside that is easy on the wallet and convenient to the small town of Saladan and the ferry pier. Rooms vary, the best being the basic bungalows with balconies at beachside. Larger suites are worth the small outlay and are airy with raised bathtub areas, and most with good ocean views. They have a small spa facility, a cozy central pool, and good in-house dining. A convenient budget choice.

105 Moo 3, Saladan, Koh Lanta Yai, Krabi 81150. © **07568-4175.** Fax 07568-4174. www.southernlanta.com. 90 units. 800B–2,400B ($20–60) garden view double; 1,000B–4,500B ($24–$110) beach-view double; from 4,000B ($98) suite. MC, V. **Amenities:** 2 restaurants; bar; outdoor pool; spa; Jacuzzi; watersports rentals; tour desk; car-rental; massage; laundry. *In room:* A/C, satellite TV, fridge, IDD phone.

9 Trang

"Shhh . . ." You heard it here, but don't tell anybody. Tiny Trang is where it's at if you're looking for a real Thai-style beach in the south. Trang City is the capital of this large province, an area ripe for exploration and replete with national parks and lots of wide-open spaces. Most tourists head first for Ha Pak Mieng Beach, then to outlying islands by ferry. Day snorkeling tours are a ball and affordable, and the scenery is much like nearby Krabi without as many tourists. The main beach at Ha Pak Mien, a long stretch, is crowded with Thai tourists, especially on weekends and holidays, and is a great place to meet locals (though not a particularly beautiful beach).

GETTING THERE

Trang city is connected by train with Bangkok on the main north–south line. Two daily departures make the 16-hour trek. Ask for details at **Bangkok's Hua Lampong Station** (© **1690**), and there are frequent buses from Bangkok's Southern Bus terminal (© **02434-7192**), and minibus connection from Krabi and Surat Thani. When you arrive in Trang, connect by minibus with Ha Pak Mieng for 50B/$1.20 (a 30-min. ride). Ferry boats to the outlying islands leave regularly all day from the pier on the north end of the beach. It costs 500B ($12) for an all-day tour by boat (including lunch), and they can drop you off at any number of islands (Koh Ngai, Koh Mook, or Koh Kradung). Try **Chao Mai Tour** (© **07521-4742**), just one among many at the port, or contact any of the hotels below and they can help with arrangements.

WHERE TO STAY

Amari Trang Resort   The overall effect of this newly opened resort is a fine harmony with nature: water flows here, light reflects from pools there. The pool is huge, the rooms are well-appointed, and everything is new and efficient. They've made some recent additions and upgrades, making this a true five-star (by standards set by the TAT), and Amari Trang, with its fine dining, great spa facility, and cozy room design, is attracting folks tired of busy beach areas in other parts of Thailand. The hotel hosts a luxe little day resort on nearby Koh Kradung, where you can dig your toes in the sand on a private beach for the day.

Changlang Beach, Trang 92150. ✆ 07520-5888. Fax 07520-5889. www.amari.com. 128 units. 10,200B–13,000B ($249–$317) double; from 16,400B ($400) suite. AE, V, MC. **Amenities:** 3 restaurants, 2 bars, outdoor pool, spa, fitness-center, kayak and bicycle rental, tour desk, limited room service, same-day laundry service. *In room:* A/C, satellite TV, fridge, minibar, safe, IDD phone.

Near the Amari is the **Pakmeng Resort** (60/1 Moo, Tambol Maifad, Trang; ✆ 07527-4111), rustic but cozy and quiet in a grove near the concrete sea-wall: a mangrove oasis. Rooms are from 350B to 1,400B ($8.55–$34).

On the islands, go for **Charlie Beach Resort** on Koh Mook (✆ 07521-7671 or 07520-3281), affordable but cozy, starting at 1,400B ($34).

10

Central Thailand

Going north from Bangkok, travelers tracing the route of the Chao Praya River travel back in time as they push upstream and beyond. Starting with the ruins of Ayuthaya, the towns as you go north are the successive historical capitals of old Siam: Ayuthaya (capital from 1350–1760) to tiny Lop Buri, then further north to the vast Central Plains and the nation's greatest architectural wonder, Sukhothai, the very founding point of the Thai kingdom in 1238. Beyond Sukhothai to the north is the land of Lanna and the distinct ancient kingdom centered on Chiang Mai (see chapters 12–14).

While it is a good area to discover Thailand's historical past, Central Thailand's smaller work-a-day towns provide a window into rural culture and lifestyles of another time.

It's a short ride from the current Thai capital to nearby Ayuthaya, and many go by train and make the short hop to Lop Buri before going onward to Phitsanulok, the commercial hub of the Central Plains. A vast area, known as the "Great Rice Bowl" for its agricultural abundance, the Central Plains are washed by rivers, including the Chao Praya, tessellated with rice fields, and dotted by architectural sites like the temples at Sukhothai. Further west, tiny Mae Sot is a Thai–Burmese bordertown worth a visit. Many travelers continue north to Chiang Mai by bus or train from the Central Plains at Phitsanulok.

Accommodation in the area runs the gamut. Riding the trains is a good adventure, rent bicycles wherever you can, try some different food at the night markets, and bring your curiosity and a phrase book.

1 Ayuthaya

76km (47 miles) N of Bangkok

Ayuthaya is one of Thailand's historical highlights. Many travelers take the day tour from Bangkok, which allows about 3 hours at the sites, but for folks with an interest in archaeological ruins, Ayuthaya justifies an overnight or more.

From its establishment in 1350 by King U-Thong (Ramathibodi I) until its fall to the Burmese in 1767, Ayuthaya was Thailand's capital and home to 33 kings and numerous dynasties. At its zenith and until the mid–18th century, Ayuthaya was a majestic city with three palaces and 400 splendid temples on an island threaded by canals—a site that mightily impressed European visitors.

Then, in 1767, after a 15-month siege, the town was destroyed by the Burmese, and today there are but groups of crumbling ruins and rows of headless Buddhas where once an empire thrived. The temple compounds are still awe-inspiring even in disrepair, and a visit here is memorable and a good beginning for those drawn to the relics of history.

The architecture of Ayuthaya is a fascinating mix of Khmer, or ancient Cambodian style, and early Sukhothai style. Cactus-shaped obelisks, called *prangs,* denote Khmer

Ayuthaya

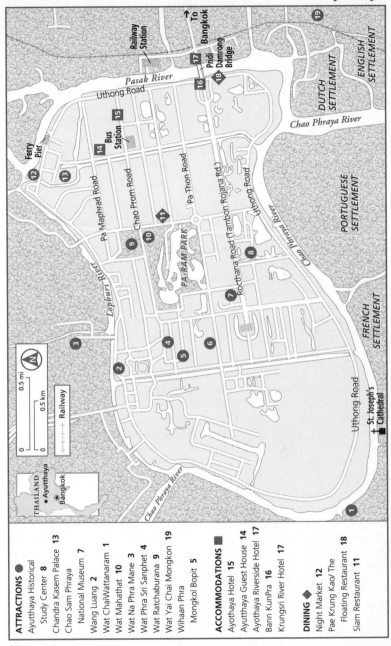

ATTRACTIONS ●
Ayutthaya Historical
  Study Center **8**
Chandra Kasem Palace **13**
Chao Sam Phraya
  National Museum **7**
Wang Luang **2**
Wat ChaiWattanaram **1**
Wat Mahathat **10**
Wat Na Phra Mane **3**
Wat Phra Sri Sanphet **4**
Wat Ratchaburana **9**
Wat Yai Chai Mongkon **19**
Wihaan Phra
  Mongkol Bopit **5**

ACCOMMODATIONS ■
Ayothaya Hotel **15**
Ayutthaya Guest House **14**
Ayothaya Riverside Hotel **17**
Bann KunPra **16**
Krungsri River Hotel **17**

DINING ◆
Night Market **12**
Pae Krung Kao/ The
  Floating Restaurant **18**
Siam Restaurant **11**

influence, and look something like the famous towers of Angkor Wat. The more pointed *stupas* are ascribed to Sukhothai. If you've just arrived and have confined your stay to Bangkok, you might note similarities with the riverside Wat Arun, an 18th-century structure that was built in the so-called Ayuthaya style, a melding of Sukhothai Buddhist influences and Hindu-inspired Khmer motifs.

ESSENTIALS
GETTING THERE

By Train   Trains depart 15 times daily from **Bangkok's Hua Lampong Railway Station** (© **1690**) starting at 4:30am (trip time: 1½ hr; 15B/35¢ third class). Look for the good Express Trains with 2nd Class A/C cars with seats from 75B ($1.80).

By Bus   Buses leave every 20 minutes from **Bangkok's Northern Bus Terminal,** on Kampaengphet 2 Rd. Mo Chit (© **02936-2841**), beginning at 5:40am (trip time: 1½ hr.; 50B/$1.20).

By Boat   All-day river cruises are a popular option to and from Ayuthaya and there are a number of companies making the connection. Contact **River Sun Cruises** (© **02266-9316**) directly or book through any riverside hotel: departure points are the **Oriental Hotel** (© **02236-0400**), **Shangri-La Hotel** (© **02236-7777**), or River City pier daily at approximately 7:30am (and include a stop at Bang Pa-In). Day trips include a cruise on the Chao Praya, tour of the ancient city, and return by air-conditioned coach or vice versa (trip time: all day; 1,600B/$39).

If you really want to turn your trip to Ayuthaya into an adventure, travel aboard the *Manhora Song.* Trips leave every Monday and Thursday and passengers enjoy the height of luxury for 3 days and 2 nights on this renovated 60-year-old teak rice barge. Four state rooms, with en suite bathrooms, are appointed in warm teak and mahogany. The ship's crew serves cocktails, snacks, and delicious Thai meals on a shaded deck or sun deck lounge area. The trip includes a stop at Wat Bang Na temple, among others. Inclusive of all fine meals, tours and transfers, the trip runs $1,000 for two. For reservations, call © **02476-0021** or fax 02476-1805.

A much cheaper, self-guided boat trip can be arranged through the **Chao Praya Express Co.** (© **02222-5330**), which offers service on Sundays at 8am from the Maharat Pier to Bang Pa-In, where you can have lunch. The unguided, all-day excursion is very popular with locals and costs 350B ($8.55) per person, meals not included.

ORIENTATION

The town is encircled by water with perimeters defined by the Chao Praya on the southern and western sides, the Lopburi River to the north, and the Pasak to the east. The main ferry pier is located on the east side of town, just opposite the train station. The Bangkok bus makes its last stop at the station adjacent to the Siam Commercial Bank Building, off Chao Prom Road in the downtown area (there is another stop before this that lets travelers off near the bridge). Buses from Phitsanulok stop 5km (3 miles) north of town; you'll need to take a 10B (25¢) local bus to the center.

VISITOR INFORMATION

There is a **TAT** office at Si Sanphet Road opposite the National Museum (© **03532-2730**). Stop by for maps and other information.

GETTING AROUND

A tuk-tuk from the train station into town will cost about 40B ($1), but about 50m (150ft) from the station is a small river ferry, which will take you to city-island for 3B (10¢) and runs from 5:30am until 9pm daily. Tuk-tuks from the island will take you to your hotel, and there are even a few *samlors* (pedicabs), a unique way to get around (from 20B/50¢ for a short ride). Better yet, hire a long-tail boat to see the city the leisurely way for about 200B/$4.90 per hour (look for the small independent operators on the northeast end of the island, near the night market). There is regular minibus service between Ayuthaya and Bang Pa-In, departing from Chao Prom Market on the road of the same name (trip time: 50 min.; 20B/50¢).

FAST FACTS

Siam City Bank has a branch on U-Thong Road just south of the ferry terminal on the temple side of the river (across from the train station). The **post office** is on Rojana road in the south of town near the main police station (any hotel or guesthouse can help with posting mail). Fof good Internet service try **Phone Net** (look for the "High Speed Internet" sign on Naresuan; ℂ **03523-1253**) with DSL for 30B (75¢) per hour.

WHAT TO SEE & DO

The central island area of Ayuthaya is itself the site: modern buildings and busy canal-side streets are in and among the ruins of this once-great city. The sites below are but of a few of the many, and having a guide is a good idea (contact any hotel front desk). The TAT (at the museum) has a detailed map, and most hotels and guesthouses publish small maps to augment the one in this section.

MUSEUMS

Ayuthaya Historical Study Center 🐾🐾   As a resource for students, scholars, and the public, the center presents displays of the ancient city including models of the palace and the port area and reconstructions of ships and architectural elements, as well as a fine selection of historical objects. There's an interesting section about the earliest foreigners in Ayuthaya. A good overview.

Rojana Rd. ℂ **03524-5124**. Admission 100B ($2.45). Mon–Fri 9am–4:30pm; Sat–Sun 9am–5pm.

Chandra Kasem Palace 🐾   A branch of the National Museum (above), the splendid Chandra Kasem Palace was built in 1577 by King Maha Thamaraja (the 17th Ayuthaya monarch) for his son, who became King Naresuan. It was destroyed but later restored by King Mongkut, who stayed there whenever he visited Ayuthaya. On display are gold artifacts, jewelry, carvings, Buddha images, and domestic and religious objects from the 13th through 17th centuries.

Northeast part of old city. Admission 30B (75¢). Wed–Sun 9am–noon and 1–4pm.

Chao Sam Phraya National Museum 🐾🐾   Thailand's second largest museum houses impressive antique bronze Buddha images, carved panels, religious objects, and other local artifacts. Close to the Ayuthaya Historical center (above) and across from the TAT office. A comprehensive collection and a must-see in Ayuthaya.

Rojana Rd. (1½ blocks west of the center near the junction of Sri Sanphet Rd.). ℂ **03524-1587**. Admission 30B (75¢). Wed–Sun 9am–4pm.

THE WATS (TEMPLES) & RUINS

Ancient Palace (Grand Palace)   Sometimes called Wang Luang, the palace lies in ruins, having been completely destroyed by the Burmese in the late 1700s. Located in the northwestern section of the city, the foundations of the three main buildings can still be made out, and the size of the compound is impressive.

Northwestern quadrant of the city overlooking the Lopburi River. Daily 8am–6pm.

Wat Chai Wattanaram A long bike ride from the other main temple sites just across the river to the southwest of the city, Wat Chai Wattanaram is an excellent example of Khmer architecture in the Ayuthaya period, and is still in good shape. You can climb to the steep steps of the central *prang* and have a beautiful view of the surrounding countryside. It is so intact that you get a good idea what a working temple might have been like some 300 years ago.

On the opposite bank of the Chao Praya river, far southwest of the town center. Admission 30B (75¢). Daily 8am–6pm.

Wat Mahathat ★★ The most striking of all of the temples in Ayuthaya and at the very heart of the city, Wat Mahathat, built in 1384 during the reign of King Rachatirat, is typical of the Ayuthaya ruins. Large crumbling stupas are surrounded by low laterite walls and rows of headless Buddhas. A great place at sunset, and also where you can see the Buddha head in the tree trunk.

Opposite Wat Mahathat stands **Wat Ratachaburana,** built in 1424 and splendidly restored—the towering monuments (both rounded Khmer-style *prangs* and Sukhothai-style pointed *chedis*) have even retained some of their original stucco. In the two crypts, excavators have found bronze Buddha images and votive tablets, as well as golden objects and jewelry, many of which are displayed in the Chao Sam Phraya Museum. There are also murals, as well as a frieze of heavenly beings and some Chinese scenes. Both wats remain severely damaged despite restoration.

Along Sikhun Road, near the terminus of Horattanachai and Naresuan. Admission 30B (75¢). Daily 8am–6pm.

Wat Na Phra Mane Located on the Lopburi side of the river, Wat Na Phra Mane survived Ayuthaya's destruction and is worth visiting to see the black stone Buddha dating from the Mon (Dvaravati) period, as well as the principal Buddha decorated in regal attire. The building has stunning vaulted ceilings supported by ornate pineapple-shaped columns. It was the site of Thai-Burmese peace talks ending the years of aggression in the late 1700s.

Across the river, north of the Grand Palace area. Admission 20B (50¢). Daily 8am–5pm.

Wat Phra Sri Sanphet Originally built in 1448 as the king's private chapel (the equivalent of the Wat Phra Kaeo, Temple of the Emerald Buddha, in Bangkok), Sri Sanphet is just south of the raised Grand Palace area. The buildings were renovated in the 16th and 17th centuries. The 17m (55 ft.) bronze standing Buddha was originally cast and covered in gold in 1500 during the reign of the ninth king, Ramathibodi. In 1767, the Burmese tried to melt the gold, causing a fire that destroyed the image and the temple; the one you see today is a replica. Nearby are three Sri Lankan–style *chedis*, built during the 15th century to enshrine the ashes of three Ayuthaya kings.

Just south of the Grand Palace ruin in the northwest end of the island. Admission 30B (75¢).

Wat Yai Chai Mongkon Visible for miles around, the gold *chedi* of Wat Yai is surrounded by sitting Buddhas and one of the most stunning sites in town (though most of what is striking are recent additions). A long walk (or a short 20B/50¢ tuk-tuk ride) southeast of ancient Ayuthaya (across the river and out of town) gets you there. King U-Thong founded the temple in 1357 as a center for monks returning from study in

Sri Lanka. The recently restored white reclining Buddha near the entrance was built by King Naresuan. The massive pagoda celebrates the defeat of the Burmese at Suphanburi in 1592, and King Naresuan's defeat of the crown prince of Burma in an elephant joust.

East of Ayuthaya, across the Pridi Damrong Bridge and NW of the train station. Admission 20B (50¢). Daily 8am–6pm.

Wihaan Phra Mongkol Bopit   Wihaan Phra Mongkol Bopit is home to Thailand's largest seated bronze Buddha. It is housed in a somewhat cramped wihaan, built in 1956 in the style of the original, which was destroyed in 1767. This Buddha image was either brought from Sukhothai or copied from a Sukhothai image and was erected here in 1615 by King Ekatosarot, in honor of his brother Naresuan, who drove the Burmese from Sukhothai.

West of Wat Mahathat and just south of the Grand Palace area. Free admission. Daily 8am-6pm.

WHERE TO STAY
MODERATE
Ayothaya Hotel   The Ayothaya Hotel (same city, different spelling) is a basic low-end business standard in the center of town near the popular backpacker street, Naresuan Road. Facilities are limited, but a convenient location makes for easy in-and-outs of Ayuthaya for a day of temple touring. Be sure to check rooms first as they can be quite musty, and avoid their very basic rooms out back.

12 Moo Tessabarn Soi 2, Ayuthaya 13000 (just west of the ferry on the main street, across from the market). ℭ 03523-2855. Fax 03525-1018. 117 units. 1,200B–1,500B ($29–$37) double; 3,500B ($85) suite. MC, V. **Amenities:** Restaurant; small pool; Internet; massage; laundry. *In room:* A/C, TV, minibar, fridge, IDD phone.

Ayothaya Riverside Hotel   Just across from the train station (on the way to Krungsri River Hotel, above), this is a mid/low standard well worth the upgrade from the town's many small guesthouses, but not particularly special. Their riverside restaurant is a good spot for a drink, and they have a good collection of large, clean rooms, a Thai business-hotel standard, many overlooking the river.

91/1 Moo 10 Wat Pako Rd. (across from the train station). ℭ 03523-8737. Fax 03424-4139. ayothaya_riverside@ hotmail.com. 102 units. 1,180B ($29) superior double; 2,000B ($49) deluxe double. **Amenities:** 2 restaurants (both serve Thai, 1 is floating at riverside); tour desk and rentals available; laundry. *In room:* A/C, satellite TV, fridge, IDD phone.

Krungsri River Hotel ℛ   This hotel is within walking distance of the train station and provides the best standard of comfort in town (and has a spiffy lobby, to boot). Rooms are ample-sized, clean, and comfortable, with large bathrooms—and some rooms look over the river. You'll need to go by shuttle to the main sights, across the river, but this is a good base and has a clean and familiar coffee shop and a small pool. *Note:* Be sure to ask for a nonsmoking room.

7/2 Rojana Rd., Ayuthaya 13000 (northeast side of Pridi Damrong Bridge). ℭ 03524-4333. Fax 03524-3777. 212 units. 1,750B–2,350B ($43–$57) double; from 3,500B ($85) suite. AE, DC, MC, V. **Amenities:** 3 restaurants; beer garden and pub; pool; fitness center with sauna; game room; bowling alley; tour desk; small business center w/Internet; salon; 24-hr. room service; babysitting; same-day laundry service/dry cleaning; nonsmoking rooms. *In room:* A/C, satellite TV, minibar, fridge, safe, IDD phone.

INEXPENSIVE
Ayuthaya Guesthouse   On busy Naresuan Road, a small backpacker ghetto, Mr. Hong and family offer some of the best low-budget beds in Ayuthaya: a good place to meet other travelers headed north. If they're full they'll point you to something comparable.

They now have two great A/C rooms from 400B ($9.75) per night. They have a good little restaurant and can rent bikes. They even have their own in-house tour company, **The Sun Tours** (✆ 03523-2510).

12/34 Naresuan Rd., Ayuthaya 13000 (a short walk north of the in-town bus station). ✆ 03523-2868. 20 units. From 150B ($3.65) double w/fan; from 500B ($12) double w/A/C. No credit cards. **Amenities:** Restaurant; bike rental; tour information; laundry service. *In room:* No phone.

Bann KunPra   Bann KunPra is a beautiful riverside teak house converted into comfortable if very basic guest quarters. These traditional fan-only rooms are small with high ceilings and, set around a small common area, exude a certain old-time Siamese rustic charm. Their fine open-air restaurant is lit by candlelight and overlooks the river. Friendly staff can handle any eventuality.

48 Moo 3 U-Thong Rd., Ayuthaya 13000 (west bank of Pasak River, north of Pridi Damron Bridge, across from train station). ✆ 03524-1978. www.bannkunpra.com. 6 units. 500B–600B ($12–$15) double with shared bathroom. No credit cards. **Amenities:** Riverside restaurant; tour information. *In room:* No phone.

All along Naresuan you'll find good budget accommodations, and the street gets pretty busy in backpacker high season (winter). If the Ayuthaya Guesthouse is full try **Tony's Place** (12/18 Soi Naresuan; ✆ 03525-2578), which is a constantly buzzing backpacker warren of budget rooms with a large restaurant, bar with pool table, and two special units with A/C.

WHERE TO DINE

Particularly if this is your first stop outside of Bangkok, don't miss the town's **Night Market** along the river in the northeast of town near the pier. Fresh produce, delicious Thai dishes (some stalls have English signs), and tasty Thai desserts are not to be missed. There is also a **New Night Market** just south of Wat Mahathat at the town center (the old Night Market is getting overcrowded). All of the guesthouses along Naresuan (see "Ayuthaya Guesthouse," above) serve good Thai fare geared to foreigners, and now **Naresuan** hosts a few **open-air restaurants** right on the street, a great place to meet, greet, eat, and party late.

Pae Krung Kao/The Floating Restaurant ✷ THAI/CHINESE   On low-floating pallets at riverside, diners have great views of passing boats and river life and the food is tops: typical Thai/Chinese stir-fry and curries. The atmosphere is just dreamy: a peaceful Chinese garden, a strumming balladeer who knows every song the Eagles ever sang, and candlelight at waters edge.

4 Moo 2, U-Thong Rd. (west bank of Pasak River, north of Pridi Damrong Bridge). ✆ 03525-1807. Main courses 60B–200B ($1.50–$4.90). MC, V. Daily 5–10pm.

Siam Restaurant THAI   Just across from the large temple of Wat Mahathat, Siam Restaurant is a good spot to beat the mid-day heat in air-conditioning, have a drink, and enjoy a light meal while temple touring or, at day's end, to visit a Wat Mahathat sunset and enjoy a cool drink after.

11/3 Pratuchai Rd, Ayuthaya 10003 (across from Wat Mahathat). ✆ 03521-1070. Main courses 70B–250B ($1.70–$6.10). MC, V. Daily 10am–10pm.

SIDE TRIPS FROM AYUTHAYA
BANG PA-IN

Only 61km (38 miles) north of Bangkok, this royal palace is usually combined with Ayuthaya in most 1-day tours and is accessible by minivan. Much of the palace isn't open to the public so, if pressed for time, stick to Ayuthaya.

The 17th-century temple and palace at Bang Pa-In were originally built by Ayuthaya's King Prasat Thong, later abandoned when the capital moved in the late 1700s, and then rebuilt again by King Chulalongkorn in the late 1800s.

The architecture is Thai with strong European influences. In the center of the small lake, **Phra Thinang Aisawan Thippa-At,** is an excellent example of classic Thai style. Behind it, in Versailles style, are the former **king's apartments,** which today serve as a hall for state ceremonies. The **Phra Thinang Wehat Chamrun,** also noteworthy, is a Chinese-style building (open to the public) where court members generally lived during the rainy and cool seasons. Also worth visiting is the **Phra Thinang Withun Thatsuna,** an observatory on a small island that affords a fine view of the countryside.

2 Lop Buri

77km (48 miles) N of Ayuthaya; 153km (95 miles) N of Bangkok; 224km (139 miles) S of Phitsanulok.

Lop Buri is as famous for its 14th to 17th century temple ruins as it is for the mischievous band of monkeys that call them home. The town hosted kings and emissaries from around the world some 400 years ago, and archaeological evidence posits a model of a highly developed Buddhist society as early as the 11th century. Lop Buri is a popular day trip from Ayuthaya or a good matinee stopover on the way north by train.

ESSENTIALS
GETTING THERE
Lop Buri is along Highway 1 just past Saraburi (connect with Lop Buri via Highway 3196 to Rte. 311). Numerous trains make daily connection with Lop Buri via Ayuthaya from Bangkok's **Hua Lampong Railway Station** (✆ **1690**). It is 30B (75¢) for third-class from Ayuthaya (a colorful experience). Regular buses connect via Ayuthaya from Bangkok's **Northern Bus Terminal** (✆ **02936-2841**).

INFORMATION & ORIENTATION
The **TAT Office** is in a teak house built in the 1930s just a short walk from the train station (follow the signs) on Rop Wat Phra That Road (✆ **03642-2768**). They have a useful map and can point you to sites within walking distance.

WHAT TO DO & SEE
Do Lop Buri in a clockwise circle. From the train station hit **Wat Phra Sri Rattana Mahathat** just out front. Built in 1257, Mahathat is a stunning ruin much like the temples of Ayuthaya (entrance 30B/75¢; daily 7am–5pm). On a small side street just north of the temple, stop in at the TAT office and pick up a map and advice.

Directly west of the TAT, the large complex of **King Narai's Palace** was built in 1666 and combines a large museum of Lop Buri antiquities with the wats and palace of the king. When nearby Ayuthaya was little more than a bog, King Narai hosted emissaries from around the world (note the many Islamic-style doorways). The museum houses displays of Thai rural life and traditions from weaving and agriculture to shadow puppetry (admission 30B/75¢; daily 8am–5pm).

Exiting Narai's palace, head north through the town's small streets and market areas to **Wat Sao Thong Thong,** which houses a large golden Buddha and fine Khmer and Ayuthaya period statues. Further north brings you to the ruins of **Ban Vichayen,** the manicured ruins of the fine housing built for visiting dignitaries (admission 30B/75¢; Wed–Sun 7am–5pm).

Going east along Vichayen Road toward the town center, **Phra Prang Sam Yod** is a stunning example of the Khmer-influenced, Lop Buri style in its three connected pagodas. Sam Yod is also the temple where you'll find Lop Buri's famous **band of monkeys** most hours of the day (admission 30B/75¢; Wed–Sun; 7am–5pm; you can see this one just fine from the outside). Take care around these mischievous critters: you can get close and take pictures, but don't carry food, and it is a good idea to have a stick with you (available at the entrance).

Reaching Sam Yod (above) brings you full-circle, back to the train tracks just north of the station. If you're in Lop Buri in late spring, ask about the occasional monkey banquets, where a formal table is set for the little beasts who tear it to bits, no manners at all. Most days, monkeys are fed at a temple just east of Sam Yod, called **Wat Phra Khan** (across the train tracks), and it is worth seeing. Twice a day, a band of mischievous monkeys trapezes along the high wires and swoops down on town shop owners armed with sticks who keep a close eye on outdoor merchandise: a different kind of rush hour altogether.

WHERE TO STAY & DINE

Few stay in little Lop Buri, instead making it a day trip from Ayuthaya or a brief stopover on the way to points north. If you do get stuck here, try the **Lop Buri Inn** (28/9 Naraimaharat Rd.; ✆ **03641-2300**) with rooms from 500B ($12).

There are lots of small open-air restaurants in and around town; the best restaurant going is friendly, air-conditioned **Taisawan Vietnamese Food** (11/8 Sorasak Rd.; ✆ **03641-1881**), just southeast of the main entrance to King Narai's Palace. Delicious, spicy Vietnamese dishes like Bun Hoi, noodles and pork, or shrimp kebabs start at just 60B ($1.45).

3 Phitsanulok

377km (234 miles) N of Bangkok; 93km (58 miles) SE of Sukhothai

Phitsanulok is a bustling agricultural center, with a population of 80,000, on the banks of the Nan River. Roughly equidistant from Chiang Mai and Bangkok, the city is hectic, noisy, and just a stopover on the way to Sukhothai for most.

Outside of town, the terrain is flat and the rice paddies endless, their vivid green especially delightful in the late spring. In winter, white-flowering tobacco and pink-flowering soybeans are planted in rotation. Rice barges, houseboats, and long-tail boats ply the Nan and Song Kwai rivers, which eventually connect to the Chao Praya and feed into the Gulf of Thailand (Gulf of Siam).

Phitsanulok is the birthplace of King Naresun (the Great), the Ayuthaya king who, on elephant-back, defended Thailand from the Burmese army during the 16th century. Other Ayuthaya kings used Phitsanulok as a staging and training ground for battles with the Burmese, and for 25 years it served as the capital.

When a tragic fire burned most of the city in 1959, one of the only buildings to survive was Wat Yai, famed for its unique statue of Buddha; the temple is now a holy pilgrimage site for Thai people. For travelers, Wat Yai is worth a visit on the way west to Sukhothai or further to the Burmese border.

Phitsanulok is famous for the Bangkaew Dog, a notoriously fierce and faithful breed prized throughout Thailand.

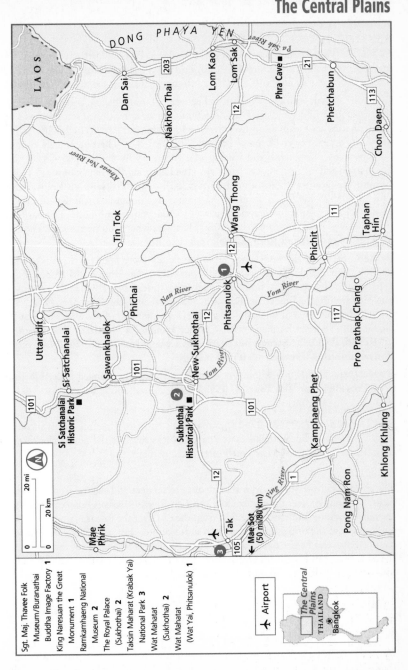

The Central Plains

THAILAND

Bangkok

✈ Airport

LAOS

DONG PHAYA YEN

Dan Sai

Nakhon Thai

Lom Kao

Lom Sak

Phra Cave

Phetchabun

Chon Daen

Pa Sak River

203

12

21

113

Khwae Noi River

Tin Tok

Wang Thong

11

Taphan Hin

Phichit

12

Phitsanulok

Nan River

Yom River

Phichai

117

Pro Prathap Chang

Uttaradit

Si Satchanalai

Sawankhalok

New Sukhothai

101

Yom River

Kamphaeng Phet

Si Satchanalai Historic Park ■

Sukhothai Historical Park ■

12

101

Khlong Khlung

101

Ping River

1

Pong Nam Ron

Mae Phrik

Tak

105

Mae Sot (50 mi/80 km)

20 mi

20 km

N

Sgt. Maj. Thawee Folk
Museum/Buranathai
Buddha Image Factory **1**
King Naresuan the Great
Monument **1**
Ramkamhaeng National
Museum **2**
The Royal Palace
(Sukhothai) **2**
Taksin Maharat (Krabak Yai)
National Park **3**
Wat Mahatat
(Sukhothai) **2**
Wat Mahatat
(Wat Yai, Phitsanulok) **1**

ESSENTIALS
GETTING THERE

By Plane **Thai Airways** has three flights each day to Phitsanulok from Bangkok (flying time: 45 min.). Taxis cost 50B ($1.20) into town from the airport. The Thai Airways office in Phitsanulok is at 209/26–28 Boromtrailokanart Rd. (© 05528-0060).

By Train About 10 trains per day travel between Phitsanulok and Bangkok. The trip time is about 6 hours and costs 200B/$4.90 for an air-conditioned second-class seat. Sleeper berths start from 325B ($7.95). "Rapid" trains can take up to 9 hours, so it is worth the expense to go "Express" or even "Sprinter" class. There are 6 daily connections between Phitsanulok and Chiang Mai (7 hr.; 190B–330B/$4.65–$8.05). For information and reservations, call Bangkok's **Hua Lampong Railway Station** (© 1690), **Chiang Mai Railway Station** (© 05324-5363), or the **Phitsanulok Railway Station** (© 05525-8005). In front of the station in Phitsanulok, throngs of *samlors* (pedicabs) and regular motorcycle taxis wait to take you to your hotel. The station is right in town, so expect to pay just 40B ($1) to get where you need to go. The bidding will start at around 100B ($2.45); smile and haggle.

By Bus Standard air-conditioned buses leave daily every hour for the trip to Phitsanulok from Bangkok from 7am to 4:30pm (trip time: 6 hr.; 218B/$5.30). Buses depart from Chiang Mai in similar numbers (trip time: 6 hr.; 216B/$5.25). Frequent non-air-conditioned buses connect with Sukhothai and cost just 38B (95¢). The intercity bus terminal in Phitsanulok is 2km (1¼ miles) east of town on Highway 12 (about 40B/$1 by tuk-tuk or taxi). Contact **Bangkok's Northern Bus Terminal** (© 02936-2841), the **Arcade Bus Station in Chiang Mai** (© 05324-2664), or the **Phitsanulok Bus Terminal** (© 05524-2430).

By Minivan Travel to Sukhothai or on to Mae Sot can be arranged with **Able Tour** (© 05524-3851) or **Win Tour** (© 05523-0541).

VISITOR INFORMATION

The **TAT office** (© 05525-2742) has maps and basic information, but is inconveniently located on Boromtrailokanart Road, 2 blocks south of the central clock tower down a small side-street. Most hotels offer free city maps.

ORIENTATION

The town is fairly compact, with the majority of services and sights for tourists concentrated along or near the east bank of the Nan River. Naresuan Road extends from the railway station and crosses the river from the east over the town's main bridge. Wat Yai is north of the bridge and just a hitch north of busy Hwy. 12. The main market, featuring trinkets in the day and food stalls at night, is just south of the bridge on riverside Buddhabucha Road. One landmark is the clock tower at the southern end of the commercial district, Boromtrailokanart Road.

GETTING AROUND

By Tuk-Tuk & Songtao Tuk-tuks (called taxis here) collect near the bus and train stations. Negotiate for an in-town fare, usually about 40B ($1). Songtao (covered pickup trucks) follow regular routes outside of town.

By Bus There's a well-organized city bus system with a main terminal south of the train station on A-Kathotsarot Road. There are five main routes: no. 1 goes to the intercity bus terminal and Wat Yai; no. 2 serves the southeast sector of the city; no. 3

goes west across the river; no. 4 goes to the airport; and no. 5 goes north to the Topland Plaza, across Highway 12. Trips are between 5B and 10B (10¢–20¢), but you would do just as well to hire tuk-tuks or taxis.

There are frequent (every half-hour 6am–6pm) buses from the intercity bus terminal east of town to **New Sukhothai** (trip time: 1 hr.; 40B/$1).

By Hired Minivan   Any hotel in Phitsanulok can arrange minivan tours in the area and to Sukhothai. Expect to pay at least 1,500B ($37) with driver.

By Rental Car   **Budget** has a small operation at the airport. Call ☎ **05525-8556** for reservations and information. **Avis** operates out of an office adjoining the Phitsanulok Youth Hostel (see "Where to Stay," below).

SPECIAL EVENTS
The **Buddha Chinarat Festival** is held annually on the sixth day of the waxing moon in the third lunar month (usually late Jan or early Feb). Then, Phitsanulok's Wat Yai is packed with well-wishers, dancers, monks and abbots, children, and tourists, all converging on the temple grounds for a 6-day celebration.

FAST FACTS
Several **banks** are located along central Boromtrailokanart Road. The **General Post Office** (☎ 05525-8013) is on Buddhabucha Road, along the river 2 blocks north of Naresuan Road. The **Overseas Call Office** is on the second floor of the post office. Internet access service is mostly in small storefront video game centers and costs 15B (35¢) per hour.

WHERE TO STAY
MODERATE
Amarin Lagoon Hotel ✿   If you've got your own wheels, the best and most attractive resort hotel in the area is the Amarin, a few short clicks east of town on Highway 12. The location is a drawback, but rooms are spacious, attractive, and quiet. I recommend Topland (below) over the Amarin just in terms of location.

52/299 Moo 6, Praongkhao Rd., Amphur Muang, Phitsanulok 65000 (on Hwy. 12 east of town). ☎ 05522-0999. Fax 05522-0944. 301 units. 1,200B–2,000B ($29–$49) double. AE, MC, V. **Amenities:** Restaurant; lounge; pool; fitness center; car-rental desk; 24-hr. room service; babysitting; same-day laundry service. *In room:* A/C, TV w/satellite programming, minibar, fridge.

Pailyn Phitsanulok Hotel   A good choice for in-town lodging, but this is more or less a business hotel that services the occasional large tour group. The bright marble lobby gives the place some panache, and rooms are clean, fairly quiet for the location, and done in textured wallpaper and rattan decor. Rooms are priced according to size; upper standards have slightly vaulted ceilings with a wooden veneer. Bathrooms are small and plain. *Note:* There are no double beds in any rooms.

38 Boromtrailokanart Rd., Phitsanulok 65000 (2 long blocks north of the road extending west from the train station, Naresuan Rd.). ☎ 05525-2411. Fax 05525-8185. www.pailynhotel.phitsanulok.com. 247 units. 1,100B ($27) single; 1,200B ($29) double; 2,200B–3,500B ($54–$85) suite. AE, MC, V. **Amenities:** 2 restaurants; bar; sauna; tour desk; car-rental desk; limited room service; massage; babysitting; same-day laundry service/dry cleaning; disco. *In room:* A/C, TV w/satellite programming, minibar, fridge, IDD phone.

Phitsanulok Thani Hotel ✿   The Phitsanulok Thani is clean and comfortable: an international business hotel standard convenient to the airport. Rooms are spacious and clean but bland. Bathrooms are neat but small. Suites are just larger versions of standard rooms. It is a popular stop for big tour groups, and though it is located a bit out of the center of town, they provide shuttle service and it is a short tuk-tuk ride from anywhere. Helpful staff can make any arrangements.

39 Sanambin Rd., Phitsanulok 65000 (4km/2½ miles southeast of clock tower, about 1km (⅔ mile) from airport). *C* 05521-1065. Fax 05521-1071. 110 units. 800B–1,200B ($20–$29) double; 2,000B–4,000B ($49–$98) suite. AE, DC, MC, V. **Amenities:** Restaurant; lounge and karaoke pub; pool; limousine service; business center; limited room service; massage; babysitting; same-day laundry service/dry cleaning executive-level rooms. *In room:* A/C, TV w/satellite programming, minibar, fridge, coffee/tea-making facilities, safe.

Topland Hotel and Convention Center ★★ Adjoining the town's largest shopping center of the same name and ownership, the busy Topland is in fact the "top land" and number-one standard in Phitsanulok. Just a stone's throw from Wat Yai, the hotel caters mostly to domestic business travelers but is a familiar and comfortable enough standard. Service is snappy, but the lobby can be a pretty busy place at check-out time. Deluxe rooms are tidy, with crown molding linking capped columns that augments bland wallpaper and floral prints for a classier look. Bathrooms are large and done in marble counters and wood trim.

68/33 Akathodsarod St., Phitsanulok 65000. *C* 05524-7800. Fax 05524-7815. www.toplandhotel.com. 253 units. 2,000B ($49) superior double; 4,000B ($98) business suite. AE, MC, V. **Amenities:** Restaurant; 2 bars (pub and snooker area); outdoor pool; small fitness center; spa; Jacuzzi; sauna; steam; tour desk; limousine service; shopping mall adjoining; salon; 24-hr. room service; meeting rooms; laundry service; dry cleaning; meeting rooms. *In room:* A/C, satellite TV, minibar, fridge, hair dryer, safe, IDD phone.

INEXPENSIVE

There are lots of budget places in and around the station, none really worth the savings. South of town, near the airport and the Phitsanulok Thani Hotel (above), the **Phitsanulok Youth Hostel** (38 Sanambin Rd.; *C* 05524-2060) has very basic rooms starting from 200B ($4.90) for a fan room and 300B ($7.30) for A/C.

WHERE TO DINE

No real fine-dining options exist in Phitsanulok, but there are lots of small local eateries in and around the train station. Be sure to try the local specialty, *khaew tak,* delicious sun-dried banana baked with honey; small packages are sold everywhere and cost just 30B (75¢). The newly renovated **Night Bazaar** at riverside is a great place to test your charade skills; point and smile and try to order what you want (or practice/learn some Thai). Many enjoy the "flying vegetables"—morning-glory greens sautéed, tossed high in the air, and adeptly caught by the chef. You can order a main dish at one stall, claim a table, and then graze for side dishes and tasty desserts.

Pae Pha Thai Floating Restaurant THAI The best of many similar places along the riverbank just opposite the main tour attraction, Wat Yai, Pae Pha Thai is a friendly, casual eatery with no pretense, just good food and a fine view. Come with friends, cover the table with Thai dishes, and fill the air with laughter. The English language menu is easy to follow. I shared an order of *Tod Mun Plah* (deep-fried fish cakes), *pat kapow* (chicken with basil and chili), *tom yum* soup, and a whole fish encrusted with garlic and lemon: the kind of spread you might find in a Thai home, and all the better at water's edge.

Phuttabucha Rd. (on Nan River across from Wat Yai). *C* 05524-2743. Main courses 70B–150B ($1.70–$3.65). MC, V. Daily 10am–11pm.

You won't find much in the way of nightlife in Phitsanulok, but for a cool drink or a late snack set to noisy Thai Pop music, stop by **The Tree House** (*C* 05521-2587), a small bar with adjoining garden across from the Phitsanulok Thani Hotel.

WHAT TO SEE & DO

Most use Phitsanulok as a jumping-off point for Sukhothai, but there are a few sights in the town proper, Wat Yai the foremost among them (see last entry).

The Sgt. Maj. Thavee Folk Museum ✿   This small campus of low-slung pavilions houses a private collection of antique items from Thai rural life. Farming and trapping equipment, household items, and old photographs of the city are lovingly displayed by the good sergeant major, with good descriptions in English. A good primer for a trip out into the countryside where one still finds many such aged implements in use. Just across the road is the **Buranathai Buddha Image Factory,** where you can see the carving and casting of large Buddhas, mostly copies of the Chinarat Buddha image from Wat Yai (below).

26/43 Wisutkasat Rd. (about a 20-min. walk from the train station and accessed by local bus no. 3). ✆ 05525-8715. Suggested donation 40B ($1). Tues–Sun 8:30am–4:30pm.

Wat Chulamanee   The oldest temple in the Phitsanulok area and the site of the original city, Wat Chulamanee is still an active monastery. The temple was restored in the 1950s and is studied particularly for its fine laterite cactus-shaped *prang* and the elaborate stucco designs decorating the structure.

7km south of the Nakon Sawan Highway on Boromtrailokanart Rd., and accessible by local bus no. 4 (best with your own wheels). Suggested donation 20B (50¢). Daily 6am–7pm.

Wat Yai ✿✿   Its full name is **Wat Phra Sri Ratana Mahathat,** but most know it as Wat Yai, and it is one of the holiest Buddhist temples in the country because of its highly revered image of the Buddha. The late Sukhothai period Phra Buddha Chinarat statue is a bronze image cast in 1357 under the Sukhothai king Mahatmmaracha; its most distinctive feature is its flamelike halo *(mandorla)*, which symbolizes spiritual radiance. Only the Emerald Buddha in Bangkok is more highly revered by the Thai people.

The *wihaan* housing the Buddha is a prize example of traditional Thai architecture, with three eaves, overlapping one another to emphasize the nave, and graceful black and gold columns. Don't miss the excellent late Ayuthaya period, mother-of-pearl inlaid doors leading into the chapel; added in 1576 as a gift from King Borommakot of Ayuthaya. Inside, also note the Italian marble floor, the two painted *thammas* (pulpits) to one side, and murals illustrating the life of Buddha.

Other than the main *bot,* the *wat's* most distinctive architectural aspect is the Khmer-style *prang,* rebuilt by King Boromtrailokanart, that houses the relic from which the wat takes its name; Mahathat means "Great Relic." The gilding on the top half is probably recent, but it complements the Khmer temple decor. The small museum houses a collection of Sukhothai- and Ayuthaya-era Buddhas.

The *wat* is always packed with worshippers paying their respects and making offerings. Conservative dress is suggested. During the winter Buddha Chinarat Festival, it is transformed into a cultural circus (see "Special Events," above).

After your visit here, a short walk south along Buddhabucha Road gives glimpses of river life in **Song Kwai,** a small floating village of houseboats.

1 block north of the Highway 12 bridge and just a short walk east of the river. Suggested donation of 50B ($1.20). Open daily 6am–6pm (during the Buddha Chinarat Festival, 6am–midnight); the museum is open Wed–Sun 9am–4pm.

4 Sukhothai & Si Satchanalai Historical Parks

Sukhothai: 427km (265 miles) N of Bangkok; 58km (36 miles) E of Phitsanulok
Si Satchanalai: 56km (35 miles) N of Sukhothai

The emergence of Sukhothai ("Dawn of Happiness" in Pali) in 1238 as an independent political state signified the birth of the first unified kingdom known as Thailand. It was here that Phor Khun Bangk Klang Hao became the first Thai monarch, as King Sri Indrathit, in what would become the country's most influential religious and cultural center. Today Sukhothai is a world-renowned historical site; it is to Thailand what Angkor Wat is to Cambodia.

The **Sukhothai Historical Park,** the main attraction, is situated 12km (7½ miles) west of the town of Sukhothai, also known as "New Sukhothai." There are a few little guesthouses outside of the park gates, but most will commute to the sites from good accommodation in New Sukhothai.

Si Satchanalai, far north of New Sukhothai, is another legacy of the Sukhothai Kingdom. The ancient city is certainly worth the 1-day detour.

If you're traveling from Phitsanulok, the drive takes you across wide plains of rice paddies, cotton fields, and mango and lemon groves.

ESSENTIALS
GETTING THERE
By Plane   Bangkok Airways has a private airport near Sukhothai. They have four flights per week connecting Bangkok, Sukhothai, and Chiang Mai. Contact them in Bangkok at © **02229-3456,** Chiang Mai at © **05328-1519,** or at the airport at © **05564-7224.** Bangkok Air has an office at Pailyn Sukhothai Hotel and will arrange transport by minivan upon request.

By Train   Phitsanulok (above) is the nearest railroad station.

By Bus   Three daily standard air-conditioned buses leave from Bangkok (trip time: 7 hr.; 256B/$6.25), departing from the **Northern Bus Terminal** (© **02936-2841**). There's also air-conditioned bus service from Chiang Mai six times daily (trip time: 5½ hr.; 171B–220B /$4.15–$5.35) from the **Arcade Bus Station** (© **05324-2664**).

By Local Bus from Phitsanulok   Buses leave hourly for New Sukhothai (trip time: 1 hr.; 40B/$1) from the intercity terminal on Highway 12.

VISITOR INFORMATION
Sukhothai has no **TAT** office; the closest one is in Phitsanulok (© **05525-2742**). New Sukhothai is not large enough to get lost in for long, and you can negotiate your own tour with a tuk-tuk driver (most hotels can also help).

ORIENTATION
New Sukhothai, built along the banks of the Yom River, offers a few good hotels and useful services and is the access point for **Sukhothai Historical Park** (or Muang Kao, Old City) some 12km (7½ miles) east of New Sukhothai center. **Si Satchanalai Historic Park,** also along the Yom River, is 56km (35 miles) north of new Sukhothai.

SPECIAL EVENTS
Lòy Krathong is a visually delightful, 3-day festival held on the full moon of the 12th lunar month (usually Oct/Nov) in honor of the water spirits. Around the country, crowds gather at ponds, *klongs,* rivers, and temple fountains to float small banana-leaf

boats bearing candles, incense, a flower, and a coin. This is done as an offering and to wash away the previous year's sins. Since this festival dates from the Sukhothai era, celebrations (including a parade, fireworks, and beauty pageant) are widespread throughout the province.

WHERE TO STAY
MODERATE
Ananda Museum Gallery Hotel   New on the scene, and located rather out of town to the east (on the opposite side from the temples), Ananda is the town's latest little house of style. Midsize boutique-style rooms and very grand public spaces are its hallmark.

10 Moo 4, Bantum, Muang, Sukhothai. ℂ 05562-2428. Fax 05562-1885. www.ananda-hotel.com/contact.htm. 34 units. 3,500B–4,500B ($85–$110) double; from 6,000B ($146) suite. **Amenities:** 2 restaurants; bar and coffee lounge (in the gallery); small spa with massage; tour services; shopping; limited room services; laundry. *In room:* A/C, TV, fridge, minibar, IDD phone.

Lotus Village ✦   This is the best marriage of convenience and atmosphere in Sukhothai, a very stylish guesthouse with a laid-back, friendly atmosphere. Garden paths connect freestanding bungalow rooms of teak wood, some recently upgraded with stylish baths. Spring for the large, sturdy air-conditioned rooms done in polished wood. The Franco/Thai husband-and-wife owners offer certified guides and drivers for a day at the temples. Though quiet, the Lotus is just a short walk from New Sukhothai's large, local market and town center.

170 Ratchathanee Street, Sukhothai 64000 (short walk north along the river from the main market). ℂ 05562-1484. Fax 05562-1463. www.lotus-village.com. 28 units. 680B ($17) double w/fan; 1,120B–1,350B ($27–$33) A/C room. Cash only. **Amenities:** Small restaurant; tour desk; car rental; laundry service. *In room:* Fridge and minibar in top standard only, no phone.

Pailyn Sukhothai Hotel ✦   About halfway along the 12km (7½ miles) stretch of road between town and temples, this roadside resort is bright, modern, and the most luxurious Sukhothai has to offer. Beyond the rattan-and-granite lobby, carpeted rooms are built in two four-story hexagonal wings, one of which encircles a small pool and sun deck. Rates vary according to room size and amenities; higher rates bring minibars and TVs. The suites are enormous, but their bathrooms are surprisingly small. The food in the Thai/Chinese and Continental restaurant is very good, attracting locals as well as hotel guests.

10/2 Moo 1, Jarodvithithong Rd., Sukhothai 64210 (4km/2½ miles east of historical park, 8km/5 miles from the town center). ℂ 05561-3310. Fax 05561-3317. www.pailynhotel.com. 238 units. 950B–1,400 ($23–$34) double; from 2,600B ($63) suite. MC, V. **Amenities:** 2 restaurants; disco; pool; fitness center; sauna; tour desk; limited room service; massage; same-day laundry service. *In room:* A/C, TV w/satellite programming, minibar, fridge.

INEXPENSIVE
Ban Thai Guesthouse   Ban Thai (Thai house) is the best budget choice in Sukhothai proper, and even if you don't stay here you'll want to drop in, have a fruit shake, and peruse maps and their helpful advice book. A-frame teak bungalows with private toilets and bathrooms (cold water only) are basic but the best choice. They run great mountain-biking tours daily.

38 Pravet Nakhon Rd., Sukhothai 64000 (on the west side of Yom River, 1km/⅔ mile northwest of bus station, 300m/984 ft. south of bridge). ℂ 05561-0163. 17 units. 130B ($3.20) double w/shared bathroom; 200B ($4.90) bungalow. No credit cards. **Amenities:** Restaurant; bike rental; tour desk; laundry service. *In room:* No phone.

In a pinch try **Suwatdipong Hotel** (56/2-5 Singhawat Rd., along the town's main commercial artery paralleling the river; © **05561-1567**), with dull but clean A/C rooms from 500B ($12).

WHERE TO DINE

Like most small cities and towns in Thailand, you can find good eats at the central market from early 'til late. Over and above that, try **Ban Thai Guesthouse** (see "Accommodations," above) for tasty and affordable Thai cuisine. There is one restaurant in town that's just head and shoulders above the rest:

Dream Café ✿ INTERNATIONAL   A cozy little cavern of a place, done in teak and stucco, laced with vines and bathed in warm, soft light. It looks as much like an antique store as a restaurant, and features a funky collection of ceramics, copperware, memorabilia, glass, textiles, and old jewelry. Besides the Thai dishes, including many family recipes, Dream also serves excellent European and Chinese cuisine. Try the Sukhothai Fondue, a "cook-it-yourself" hot-pot of meat, veggies, and noodles. Save room for an ice-cream sundae.

86/1 Singhawat Rd., Sukhothai (center of new city). © 05561-2081. Main courses 80B–200B ($1.95–$4.90). V. Daily 10am–midnight.

EXPLORING SUKHOTHAI ✿✿✿

In 1978, UNESCO named Sukhothai a target for preservation, and the Thai government, with international assistance from preservationists worldwide as well as UNESCO, completed the preservation of these magnificent monuments and consolidated them with an excellent museum in one large park.

GETTING TO THE SIGHT   You can reach the historic park of Sukhothai by public bus, a three-wheeled motorcycle taxi (called a *samlor*), or private car. On Jarodvithithong Road, west of the traffic circle, you can catch an open-air public bus to the park entrance for 15B (35¢). The samlors that cruise around New Sukhothai can be hired to trek you out to the monuments, and for a 3-hour tour around the park for about for 300B ($7.30).

TOURING THE SITE   A basic map is available at the museum, but the best maps are to be found at the bicycle rental shops near the entrance. The historical park is open daily 6am to 6pm; admission is 40B ($1) to the central area within the park walls, with additional charges of 30B (75¢) each to visit the areas outside the walls to the north, east, and west. Purchase a combination ticket with admission to the National Museum, Historic Park (all areas), Si Satchanalai National Park, and Sawanvorangayok National Museum for 150B ($3.65)—good value. You can hit the most central sites, around Wat Mahathat, on foot; otherwise rent a bicycle. Be sure to bring water and go early in the morning to beat the buses.

By Bicycle   The area is flat, and cycling is the best way to go. Rent them from one of the many stalls right outside the park gate (across from the museum) for 30B (75¢) per day.

By Samlor   These motorcycles (unique to Sukhothai) have two bench flatbeds, can seat up to six people, and are noisy but fun. You can hire one in New Sukhothai to take you to and around the site. If you don't hire your *samlor* in New Sukhothai town, you can negotiate with one of the guys hanging around the park entrance, and even get him to take you to your hotel when you're done.

SEEING THE HIGHLIGHTS

A network of walls and moats defines the perfect rectangle that is the central city, and the original moat connected Sukhothai with Si Satchanalai. The Phitsanulok–Sukhothai highway runs right to the entrance gate and museum.

RAMAKHAMHAENG NATIONAL MUSEUM   The museum, located in the center of the old city near the park entrance, houses a detailed model of the area, and an admirable display of Sukhothai and Si Satchanalai archaeological finds. Before exploring the temple sites, stop here for maps and information. Open Wednesday through Sunday 9am to 4pm (closed Mon–Tues, and public holidays); admission is 30B (75¢).

WAT MAHATHAT   Begin your exploration of the ancient city ruins at the central area (5-min. walk west of the museum). Wat Mahathat, part of the royal compound, is the most extraordinary monument in the park, a multi-*chedi* edifice that's dominated by a 14th-century lotus-bud tower and encircled by a moat. Surrounding its unique Sukhothai-style *chedi* are several smaller towers of Sri Lankan and Khmer influence, and a grouping of Buddhist disciples in the adoration pose. An imposing cast-bronze seated Buddha used to be placed in front of the reliquary (this image, Phra Si Sakaya Muni, was removed in the 18th century to Bangkok's Wat Suthat). The *viharn* (the sermon hall of a Wat) that housed this figure was built in 1362 by King Lithai. The small *viharn* to the south contains a fine Ayuthaya-era Buddha. Be sure to examine the large *chedi,* the lowest platform (south side of Wat Mahathat), and its excellent stucco sculpture, the crypt murals, and two elegant Sri Lankan–style stupas (equivalent to Thai *chedi*) at the southeast corner of the site. Some of the best architectural ornamentation in Sukhothai is found on the upper, eastern-facing levels of the niche pediments in the main reliquary tower. Dancing figures, Queen Maya giving birth to Prince Siddhartha, and scenes from the life of Buddha are among the best-preserved details.

THE ROYAL PALACE   Between the museum and Wat Mahathat are the remains of the Royal Palace. Although this once-grand complex contained the throne and stone inscription of King Ramakhamhaeng (there's a copy in the Ramakhamhaeng Museum; the original is in the National Museum in Bangkok), today it is a shambles.

WAT SRI SAWAI   Southwest of the palace you'll come to the 12th-century Wat Sri Sawai, a Hindu shrine later converted to a Buddhist temple. The architecture is distinctly Khmer, with three Lopburi-style *prangs* (cactus-shaped towers) commanding center stage. The *viharns* around the central *prangs* are of more traditional Sukhothai design.

OTHER MONUMENTS IN THE PARK   Circling north, just west of Wat Mahathat, is **Wat Traphang Ngoen,** set in its own pond. Though little remains other than an attractive *chedi,* the vistas of the surrounding monuments are among the most superb in the park. North past Wat Mahathat is **Wat Chana Songkram,** where there's a Sri Lankan–style stupa of note. Nearby is **Wat Sra Si,** with a Sri Lankan *chedi* and *viharn* set on a small island in Traphang Takuan pond. Take a moment to examine the stucco Buddha in the fore viharn.

LUNCH AT THE HISTORICAL PARK   There are a number of small store-front eateries in and among the bike rental shops and souvenir hawkers at the gate of the park (just across from Ramakhamhaeng Museum).

SIGHTS OUTSIDE THE HISTORICAL PARK

Small sites and ruins dot the landscape around the ancient city walls, but the best option is to head to the north and northwest areas. If you didn't buy the combination ticket, you'll have to pay 30B (75¢) entry at each site. The sites are open 8am to 4:30pm.

If you leave the park at the northern San Luang Gate and continue about 150m (500 ft.), you'll arrive at **Wat Phra Phai Luang,** similar to Wat Sri Sawai because of its three *prangs.* However, only the north tower still shows off its exquisite stucco decoration. This monument, originally a Hindu shrine, once housed a lingam, a phallic sculpture representing Shiva. Conversion to a Buddhist sanctuary is evidenced by the mondop, a square building containing a Buddha image illustrating the four postures: sitting, standing, reclining, and walking.

Wat Si Chum houses one of the more astonishing and beautiful monuments in Sukhothai: a majestic 15m (50-ft) -tall seated Buddha, in the mudra (pose) of Subduing Mara (evil). When the narrow passageway to the top was open you could admire the 700-year-old slate reliefs within. Don't let fatigue deter you from seeing this celebrated image. You'll find it on the north end of the compound, and may catch site of the many kiln remains in and among the trees on the way there.

For the adventurous, cycle (or motor) the few kilometers west to **Wat Saphan Hin,** a 198m (660-ft.) hilltop ruin visible for miles. It is well worth the steep, 5-minute climb to study the towering Phra Attaros Buddha, a 12m (41-ft.) -tall figure, his right hand raised in the Dispelling Fear mudra, which towers above the *wat's* laterite remains.

EXPLORING SI SATCHANALAI

Ancient Si Satchanalai developed between the Yom River and the Khao Phra Si Valley, on more than 320 hectares (800 acres) of land. The 91 hectares (228 acres) contained within the old laterite ramparts and moats of the city wall are the focus of sightseeing in the historical park and are best reached as a day trip from Sukhothai.

A LOOK AT THE PAST   Although a stone inscription found at Sukhothai refers to Si Satchanalai as a protectorate of King Ramakhamhaeng (possibly its founder), most historians believe that Rama I expanded a city that was built by Khmer settlers, and which was well established by the 13th century, or even earlier. During the Ayuthaya period the town was named Sawankhalok (now the nearest modern town) because of the area's highly prized product, the famous celadon ceramics, which were exported throughout Asia. Si Satchanalai's riverside site was crucial to the development of the ceramics industry; there were literally more than 1,000 kilns operating along the river. These kilns have been excavated by a Thai-Australian team, led by archaeologists from the University of Adelaide. Their findings contradict the prevailing view that Chinese traders brought the method of producing celadon to Sukhothai in the 13th century. Instead they hypothesize that ceramic manufacture began more than 1,000 years ago at Ban Ko Noi (there's a small site museum 6km/3¾ miles north of Satchanalai), strong evidence that it is an indigenous Thai art form.

TOURING THE SITE   Taking Route 101 north from Sukhothai through sugarcane and tobacco fields, one must cross the Yom River to enter the historical park's central city. The remains of the 22 monuments inside the old city rank well below those of Sukhothai in importance, yet the crumbling grandeur of the buildings and the relative isolation of the site add to its allure.

A taxi, private car, or guided tour is the best way to see the spread-out sites of Si Satchanalai. Your hotel or guesthouse can arrange this trip for around 500B ($12).

However, public buses to **Si Satchanalai** depart every half-hour from the bus stop on Jarodvithithong Road just east of the traffic circle for 20B (50¢). It's not a bad idea to have your hotel or guesthouse make you a Paddington Bear "I am lost" tag saying where you'd like to go. I recommend stopping near the cable bridge some 2km (1¼ miles) from the site. From here, you can rent a bicycle for 30B (75¢) per day. **Wat Mahathat** is located just across the bridge, and they will ask for a 10B (25¢) entrance fee. Enterprising locals have organized an **elephant ride** around the park (three passengers fit in the howdah, one rides the neck, and the mahout sits on the head). It costs 500B ($12) per steed for a 30-minute ride around the main temples.

Admission to the park is 40B ($1) (free if you purchased the combination ticket in Sukhothai), and they offer a useful map and pamphlet for 5B (10¢). It is open daily except national holidays 8am to 5pm.

SEEING THE HIGHLIGHTS

The first two monuments that you'll encounter are the largest and most impressive in the city.

WAT CHANG LOM   This compound, to the right of the entrance, is distinctly Sri Lankan, with a characteristic *stupa* and 39 laterite elephant buttresses. It is unusual to find so many elephant sculptures still intact. You can walk around the base of the *stupas* and admire the 19 Buddhas that are installed in niches above the terrace. The discovery of the Buddha's relics at the site during the reign of King Ramakhamhaeng prompted the construction of this temple, an event described in stone inscriptions found at Sukhothai.

WAT CHEDI CHET THAEW   Opposite Wat Chang Lom to the south, within sandstone walls, is Wat Chedi Chet Thaew. Like Wat Mahathat at Sukhothai, this wat is distinguished by a series of lotus-bud towers and rows of *chedis* thought to contain the remains of the royal family. The *chedis* are adorned with 33 Buddha images and other stucco decorative images.

OTHER MONUMENTS IN THE PARK   The balance of monuments within the ancient city walls can be inspected within an hour. **Wat Nan Phaya,** southeast of Chedi Chet Thaew, is known for the stucco bas-reliefs on the remains of a seven-room *viharn.* It is easily spotted by their tin-roof shelter. Nothing compares to **Wat Phra Si Rattana Mahathat,** located 1km (⅔-mile) southeast of the big bridge and directly adjacent to the rickety cable bridge connecting to the main road. The most prominent feature of this 13th-century temple is the Khmer-style *prang,* thought to date from the renovation of the original Sukhothai design made under the rule of the Ayuthaya King Borommakot in the 18th century. The exterior carving and sculpture are superb, in particular a walking Buddha done in relief.

5 Tak Province: Mae Sot & The Myanmar (Burma) Border

Tak: 426km (264 miles) NW of Bangkok; 138km (86 miles) W of Phitsanulok. Mae Sot: 80km (50 miles) W of Tak

Few travelers visit out-of-the-way Tak Province. The area is known to Thais for the Bhumibol Dam, the country's largest, and for having the hottest weather in Thailand. Cooled by surrounding forested hills, the town of Mae Sot is popular with vacationing Thais in the hot spring weather and draws foreign travelers seeking a dose of Burmese culture and bordertown bustle. There are numerous refugee camps and aid facilities for Burmese fleeing their homeland, and Mae Sot is home to many international aid workers, a unique lot. From Mae Sot you can hop "off the track" to rugged Umpang, just south along the Burma border, for good trekking and even whitewater rafting.

ESSENTIALS
GETTING THERE

By Plane There's an airport in Tak, but these days routes to and from the city aren't running. **Phuket Air** has 5 flights a week to Mae Sot from Bangkok, but at the time of research the company was going belly up. The routes will likely be picked up by another carrier.

By Bus Four buses to Tak leave daily from Bangkok (trip time 7 hr.; 245B/$6), and three buses to Mae Sot (trip time 8 hr.; 310B/$7.55) from the **Northern Bus Terminal** (ⓒ 02936-2841). Government buses leave daily from **Phitsanulok's Bus Terminal** (ⓒ 05524-2430) to Tak (departures every hr.; trip time 3 hr.; 44B/$1.10) and to Mae Sot (eight buses; trip time: 5 hr.; 90B/$2.20). Privately operated minivans connect Tak and Mae Sot, leaving when they get a full van (about every half-hour). Trip time is 1½ hours; 44B ($1.10). There are good buses operated by the **Green Bus Line** (www.greenbusthailand.com) from Mae Sot to Tak and on to Lampang and Chiang Mai (departs 8am from Mae Sot; 6 hrs. to Chiang Mai; 283B/$6.90). There are different stations for all points of the compass in Mae Sot, so ask at your hotel or at **Mae Sot Conservation Tours** (415 Intarakeeree Rd.; ⓒ and fax 05553-2818) to make onward arrangements. From the bus terminals in either Tak or Mae Sot, motorcycle taxis, *samlors,* and *songtaos* wait to take you to your hotel for about 30B to 40B (75¢–$1).

VISITOR INFORMATION

Tak has a new **TAT** office near the bus terminal, 193 Taksin Road (ⓒ 05551-4341), but info is geared to Thai nationals or those with a vehicle (good regional maps). **Krua Canadian** (see "Dining," below) is the de facto tourist information in Mae Sot and a good crossroads to meet up with fellow travelers.

SPECIAL EVENTS

Every January a provincial festival is held in Tak to honor King Taksin the Great. The streets around his shrine (on Taksin Rd. at the north side of town) fill with clothes, produce, and food vendors, and stalls piled high with Thai sweets and cakes. Dancers, musicians, and monks come out to celebrate. The shrine is showered with floral wreaths and decked out in gold fabric to impress the Thais who come from afar to pay their respects.

FAST FACTS

There are many banks and services in Tak. In Mae Sot, Siam Commercial Bank has a branch just opposite the entrance to First Hotel on Sawanwithy (see "Where to Stay," below), and Thai Military Bank (with ATM service) is on the central thoroughfare, Prasawithee Road. A post office is on Intharakiri Road opposite DK Hotel (see below) near the main police station. There are a number of Internet storefronts along Intharakiri at the center of town.

WHERE TO STAY
TAK

Few stay in Tak, and I recommend you push on to Mae Sot if you've come this far. If you somehow get stuck, the best choice in Tak is the **Viang Tak Hotel 2,** a surprisingly plush hotel with all the basic amenities, a restaurant, and small pool. Just a

5-minute tuk-tuk jaunt from the bus terminal at 236 Chumphon Road (© **05551-1910**). Price: 550B to 900B ($13–$22) double. Accepts all cards.

MAE SOT
Moderate
Central Mae Sot Hill Hotel ✦   This contemporary four-story hotel is built in two long wings fanning out from a classy open atrium lobby. This is the best around by far (better than even the hotels in Sukhothai) and a good, comfortable base from which to explore the area (always nice to have a good room and hot shower after, say, a day trip in Burma or multiday adventure in Umpang). Hotel staff is helpful and can arrange tours and onward travel. All comfortable rooms have modern amenities and views of the mist-shrouded, wooded hills.

100 Asia Hwy., Mae Sot, Tak 63110 (17km/10½ miles west of border). © **05553-2601**. Fax 05553-2600. 114 units. 2,000B ($49) double; 2,500B–5,000B ($61–$122) suite. MC, V. **Amenities:** 2 restaurants; disco; lounge; 2 pools; 2 outdoor tennis courts; limited room service; laundry service; nonsmoking rooms. *In room:* A/C, TV w/satellite programming, minibar, fridge.

First Hotel *Finds*   First Hotel is like a constantly evolving piece of artwork. Dull concrete outside, the interior is like a wood-carved wedding cake, with intricate three-dimensional woodwork carvings of crazy flora and fauna creeping up every wall and dripping from paneled ceilings. Rooms have big carved headboards and furnishings, as well as tidy marble baths. A guaranteed memorable stay and a good, mid-end standard A/C room in the town center.

444 Intharakiri Rd., Mae Sot, Tak 63110 (just north of the main intersection in town, across from the Thai Commercial Bank). © **05553-1233**. Fax 05553-1340. 45 units. 450B ($11) double w/A/C; 270B ($6.60) double w/fan. No credit cards. **Amenities:** Restaurant; laundry service. *In room:* A/C, TV, no phone.

Inexpensive
Mae Sot has quite a number of small, dirt-cheap guesthouses lining the main street. **DK Hotel** (298/2 Intharakiri Rd near the police station; © **05553-1378**) is a little local business hotel with fan rooms starting at 250B ($6.10) and 450B ($11) with A/C. **Bai Fern** (660/2 Intharakiri; © **05553-343**) is a longtime popular traveler's center, and nearby **Ban Thai** (740 Intharakiri; © **05553-1590**) also offers cheap eats and very cheap sleep (from 150B/$3.65); good places to meet other travelers.

DINING IN MAE SOT
Khaomao-Khaofang Restaurant ✦ THAI   It doesn't get any more surreal than this little oasis along the Burmese border. Ponds overgrown with lush jungle vegetation surround an enormous central thatched pavilion, itself supported by gnarled old jungle trunks with designs done in natural material (or concrete made to look like natural material), so the whole place is a big faux jungle swamp with moss walls and a central fountain. A wooden walkway and platforms at pond-side overlook the surrounding country. From the outside it is all manicured lawns and heel-clicking guards and valet service. Be sure to go to the bathroom, even if you don't have to; these water closets are large grottos with urinals at odd heights and stalactites hanging from the ceiling. Oh, and there's food. Delicious Thai cuisine, a survey course of the whole country, and heavy on good curries and authentic spice. Portions are small, so order up a few dishes. There are always daily specials. It is worth a visit if only for the novelty.

382 Moo 9, Maepa, Maesod, Tak 63110 (head for the Burma border and turn north just before the checkpoint and follow the highway 2km/1¼ mile). © **05553-2483**. Fax 05553-3607. Main courses 60B–180B ($1.45–$4.40). AE, MC, V. Daily 10am–10pm.

Krua Canadian INTERNATIONAL   The name is Thai for "Canadian kitchen," and that's just how it feels, like you've been invited into the home of Canadian Dave and his wife, Chulee. From this simple, central storefront they serve delicious breakfasts, local coffee, and a unique tofu burger that is messy and delicious. Drop in just for a drink and pick up a map of the town and advice on local happenings.

3 Sripanich Rd. Mae Sot (across from the police station). ℂ **05553-4659**. Main course 50B–150B ($1.20–$3.65). No credit cards. Daily 7am–10pm.

Central Intharakiri is lined with budget eateries. **Bai Fern** (660/2 Intharakiri; ℂ **05553-343**) is a popular choice for humanitarian aid workers, and a good place to pick up a cheap meal and some insider info on the area.

EXPLORING THE AREA

Mae Sot is perched on the Burmese border and the area is always buzzing with trade. There is a dark side to it all, though: trade means not just the movement of produce and crafts, but drugs and precious stones. There's something disquieting about the many European luxury cars parked in front of two-story brick homes lining this village's main street, all the luxury of illegal profiteers.

The border also sees big movements of refugees, and there are a number of camps in the surrounding hills. Dr. Cynthia Maung, known to many as the Mother Theresa of Burma, runs just such a large clinic and refugee camp on the outskirts of Mae Sot, and treats the thousands who cross this border in search of help. The camp is not open to visitors, but there are ways to get involved. Contact them at: P.O. Box 67, Mae Sot, Tak 63110 (ℂ **05553-3644;** www.burmacare.org).

Being a bordertown, though, does mean that Mae Sot has a surplus of Burmese woven cotton blankets, lacquerware items, jewelry, newly made bronze Buddhas, cotton sarongs, and wicker ware. Trade is conducted in Thai baht, U.S. dollars, or Myanmar kyat. Be careful about buying any gems unless you know what you're doing; most come away with only a handful of plastic and a dent in their wallet.

The border between Mae Sot (at the town of Rim Moei) and Myawaddy, Burma, is open daily 8am to 5:30pm, and you can cross the bridge over to Burma on foot or in a car with an on-the-spot day visa for 410B ($10). Many visitors cross for a day just for a glimpse of Burmese culture (and a cool passport stamp).

Highland Farm and Gibbon Sanctuary (no phone; highland_ape@hotmail.com) is along Rte. 1090 on the way south to Umpang, and is often included in day trips of the area. Gibbons can be gentle, playful creatures, and for that very reason are prized as pets or as tour-site mascots. Adult gibbons are commonly poached, and gibbon infants are raised in captivity with no hope of return to the wild. The facility provides a home for gibbons from abusive captivity and from would-be pet-owners who weren't up to the task. You can tour the site and even interact with the animals. They ask only a donation and seek support for their "adoption" program. Email them about their externship program.

Along the Asia Highway, 25km (15½ miles) east of Tak, is the **Taksin Maharat (Krabak Yai) National Park,** known for having Thailand's largest tree: a popular stop for groups and self-drive tours. A rigorous little hike brings you to this colossal Krabak tree beside a stream. It takes some 16 people's stretched arm lengths to wrap around this conifer.

Trekking and rafting in this remote and still unspoiled area is gaining popularity (it won't be unspoiled for much longer, really). Many of the guesthouses and travel storefronts tout magnificent adventures, but Mae Sot is far behind its northern neighbors when it comes to organized trips. The one agency that has its act together is **Mae Sot Conservation Tours,** 415 Intarakeeree Road (© and fax **05553-2818**). They offer 1-day trips for trekking, bamboo rafting, and elephant trekking that can include stops at any other local sites, such as the Gibbon Sanctuary or the border area. Longer-term trips into rugged Uphang feature rubber-raft rides on some good rapids and bamboo rafting in tranquil spots on the Mae Krung River. You'll overnight in jungle tents or in a Karen village set up for trekkers. Uphang's jungle scenery is absolutely breathtaking. Prices are between 800B–1,500B ($20–$37) per day on treks.

Exploring Northern Thailand

Northern Thailand is home to the majority of Thailand's half-million-plus tribal peoples, many of whom emigrated from Laos, southwestern China, Burma, and Tibet, and retain their traditional costumes, religion, art, and way of life. Opportunities to visit these distinctive ethnic enclaves and to enjoy the region's scenic beauty make the rural north one of the country's most popular destinations.

Hill-tribe people traditionally practiced slash-and-burn agriculture: burning forests to clear land, planting poppies as a cash crop, then setting up new bamboo and thatch villages whenever their farmland's soil became depleted. This unsustainable model is slowly changing.

Visitors should practice cultural awareness and encourage only positive models of sustainable tourism (i.e. trek with local guides, and model eco-touring ideals).

Adventurous self-drive trips or guided tours, by car or motorbike, are a great way to get around the area. Hill-tribe tours and trekking are also very popular activities and bring visitors into the most intimate contact with the hospitable indigenous groups of the north. Many use Chiang Mai as a hub for forays into the surrounding hills. A great region to get adventurous and explore.

1 The Land & Its People

THE REGION IN BRIEF

Northern Thailand is composed of 15 provinces, many bordering Myanmar (Burma) to the north and west and Laos to the northeast. This verdant, mountainous terrain, including Thailand's largest mountain, Doi Inthanon, at 2,563m (8,408 ft.), supports nomadic farming and teak logging at high altitudes and systematic agriculture in the valleys. The hill-tribes' traditional poppy crops have largely been replaced with rice, tobacco, soybeans, corn, and sugarcane. North and east of Chiang Mai, lowland farmers also cultivate seasonal fruits such as strawberries, longan, mandarin oranges, mango, and melon; the lush, tended fields and winding rivers make sightseeing, particularly in the spring, a visual treat. Lumber (especially teak), textiles and mining, handicrafts, and tourism-related cottage industries also contribute to the growing northern economy.

A LOOK AT THE REGION'S PAST

In the late 13th century, King Mengrai united several Tai tribes that had migrated from southern China and built the first capital of the Lanna Kingdom in Chiang Rai. Mengrai, whose rule was characterized by strategic alliances, saw a threat in the Mongol emperor Kublai Khan's incursions into Myanmar (Burma), and quickly forged ties with the powerful Kingdom of Sukhothai in the south. The Lanna Thai king vanquished the vestiges of the Mon Empire in Lamphun, and in 1296 moved his new

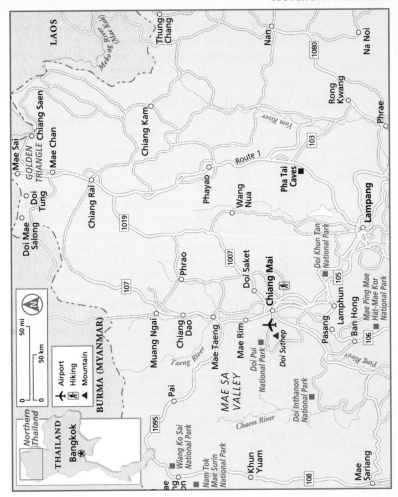

capital south to what is now Chiang Mai. There is a monument to King Mengrai, across from Chiang Mai's Wat Phan Tao, where he is said to have been struck by lightning and killed in 1317.

For the next century, Chiang Mai prospered and the Lanna Kingdom grew, absorbing most of the present-day northern provinces. In alliance Chiang Mai and Sukhothai were able to repulse any significant attacks from Khmer and Mon neighbors. After the Ayuthaya dynasty absorbed Sukhothai, Ayuthaya forces tried repeatedly to take Chiang Mai, but the kingdom did not yield. Instead, Chiang Mai strengthened itself, and from the late 14th century until its eventual fall to the Burmese in 1556, it enjoyed tremendous affluence and influence.

After 2 centuries of relentless warfare, the Burmese captured Chiang Mai in 1556, and for the next 2 centuries the Lanna Kingdom was a Burmese vassal—the Burmese cultural influence is still evident today. After Siam's King Taksin recaptured Chiang Mai from the Burmese in 1775, the city was so weakened that Taksin moved its surviving citizens to nearby Lampang. For 2 decades Chiang Mai was literally a ghost town. Though the city was still nominally under the control of local princes, their power continued to decline, and in 1939 Chiang Mai was formally incorporated into the modern Thai nation.

A PORTRAIT OF THE HILL-TRIBE PEOPLE

The north is a tapestry of the divergent customs and cultures of the many tribes that migrated from China or Tibet to Burma, Laos, and Vietnam, and ultimately settled in Thailand's northern provinces such as Chiang Rai, Chiang Mai, Mae Hong Son, Phayao, and Nan. The six main tribes are the Karen, Akha (also known as the Kaw), Lahu (Mussur), Lisu (Lisaw), Hmong (Meo), and Mien (Yao), each with subgroups that are linked by history, lineage, language, costume, social organization, and religion.

Hill-tribes are divided into two linguistic categories: the Sino-Tibetan and Austro-Asiatic, although only descendants of the Mon-Khmer speak a dialect of the latter category. In addition, tribes are divided geographically into lowland or valley dwellers who grow cyclical crops such as rice or corn and high-altitude dwellers who have traditionally grown opium poppies. The so-called indigenous tribes who have occupied the same areas for hundreds of years are those that tend to inhabit the lower valleys in organized villages of split-log huts. The nomadic groups generally live above 1,000m (3,250 ft.) in easy-to-assemble bamboo and thatch housing, ready to resettle when required.

Highland minorities believe in spirits, and it is the role of the village shaman, or spiritual leader, to understand harbingers and prescribe appeasing rites.

KAREN A quarter million Karen make up the largest tribal group in Thailand, accounting for more than half of all tribal people in the country. In nearby Myanmar (Burma) it is estimated that there are more than four million people of Karen descent (and of Buddhist belief). For years the Burmese government has been battling Karen rebels seeking an autonomous homeland—and many Burmese Karen have sought refuge in Thailand, ranging from Chiang Rai as far south as Kanchanaburi. Practicing an amalgamation of Christianity learned from missionaries and ancient animism, Karen can be easily identified by their method of greeting one another: an exaggerated, hearty handshake.

The Karen are among the most assimilated among the hill-tribes of Thailand, making it difficult to identify them by any outward appearance; however, the most traditional tribespeople wear silver armbands and don a beaded sash and headband, and the single women wear all white.

HMONG (MEO) The Hmong are a nomadic tribe scattered throughout Southeast Asia and China. About 65,000 Hmong live in Thailand, with the greatest number residing in Chiang Mai, Chiang Rai, Nan, Phetchabun, and Phrae provinces; there are approximately four million Hmong living in China. Within Thailand there are several subgroups; the Hmong Daew (White Hmong) and the Hmong Njua (Blue Hmong) are the main divisions, and the Hmong Gua Mba (Armband Hmong) is a subdivision of the Hmong Daew.

Hmong live in the highlands and cultivate opium, although corn, rice, and soybeans are also grown as subsistence crops. The Hmong are also excellent animal breeders, and their ponies are especially prized. Hmong maintain much of their wealth in silver jewelry. Hmong women weave their hair into an enormous bun on the top of their heads.

Hmong are pantheistic and rely on shamans to perform spiritual rites (though their elite is staunchly Catholic). Hmong place particular emphasis on the spirit of doors: doors for entering and exiting the human world, doors to houses, doors to let in good fortune and to block bad spirits, and doors to the afterlife. The Hmong also worship their ancestors, an echo from their Chinese past. Skilled entrepreneurs, Hmong are increasingly moving down from the highlands to ply trades in the lowlands.

LAHU (MUSSUR)   The Lahu people (pop. 40,000) are composed of two main bands: the Lahu Na (Black Lahu) and the Lahu Shi (Yellow Lahu), with a much smaller number of Lahu Hpu (White Lahu), La Ba, and Abele. Most Lahu villages are situated above 1,000m (3.250 ft.) in the mountains around Chiang Mai, Chiang Rai, Mae Hong Son, Tak, and Kamphaeng Phet, where poppies, dry rice, corn, and other cash crops are grown.

Lahu Na, similar to the Tibetan language, is so well accepted that other tribal people and Yunnanese Chinese have adopted it as their common tongue. The Lahu are skilled musicians, and their bamboo and gourd flutes feature prominently in their compositions—flutes are often used by young men to woo the woman of their choice.

Originally animists, the Lahu adopted the worship of a deity called G'ui sha (possibly Tibetan in origin), borrowed the practice of merit-making from Buddhism (Indian or Chinese), and ultimately incorporated Christian (British/Burmese) theology into their belief system. G'ui sha is the supreme being who created the universe and rules over all spirits. Spirits inhabit animate and inanimate objects, making them capable of benevolence or evil, with the soul functioning as the spiritual force within people. In addition they practice a kind of Lahu voodoo, as well as following a messianic tradition. A unique group, the Lahu warmly welcome foreign visitors.

MIEN (YAO)   There are now estimated to be 33,000 Mien living in Thailand, concentrated in Chiang Rai, Phayao, Lampang, and Nan provinces. The Mien are still numerous in China as well as in Vietnam, Myanmar (Burma), and Laos. Like the Hmong, tens of thousands of Mien fled to northern Thailand from Vietnam and Laos after the end of the Vietnam War.

Even more than the Hmong, the Mien (the name is thought to come from the Chinese word for "barbarian") are closely connected to their origins in southern China. They incorporated the Han spoken and written language into their own, and many Mien legends, history books, and religious tracts are recorded in Chinese. The Mien people also assimilated ancestor worship and a form of Taoism into their theology, in addition to celebrating their New Year on the same date (relying on the same calendar system) as the Chinese.

Mien farmers practice slash-and-burn agriculture but do not rely on opium poppies; instead they cultivate dry rice and corn. The women produce rather elaborate and elegant embroidery, which often adorns their clothing. Their silver work is intricate and highly prized even by other tribes, particularly the Hmong. Much of Mien religious art appears to be strongly influenced by Chinese design, particularly Taoist motifs, clearly distinguishing it from other tribes' work.

LISU (LISAW)   The Lisu represent less than 5 percent of all hill-tribe people. They arrived in Chiang Rai province in the 1920s, migrating from nearby Myanmar (Burma). The Lisu occupy high ground and traditionally grew opium poppies as well as other subsistence crops. Lisu frequently intermarry with the Lahu and ethnic Chinese. Lisu clothing is brash, with brightly colored tunics embellished with hundreds of silver beads and trinkets.

The Lisu are achievers who live well-structured lives. Everything from birth to courtship to marriage to death is ruled by an orthodox tradition, with much borrowed from the Chinese.

AKHA (KAW) Of all the tradition-bound tribes, the Akha, accounting for only 3 percent of all minorities living in Thailand, have probably maintained the most profound connection with their past. At great events in one's life, the full name (often more than 50 generations of titles) of an Akha is proclaimed, with each name symbolic of a lineage dating back more than 1,000 years. All aspects of life are governed by the Akha Way, an all-encompassing system of myth, ritual, plant cultivation, courtship and marriage, birth, death, dress, and healing.

The first Akha migrated from Burma to Thailand in the beginning of the 20th century, originally settling in the highlands above the Mae Kok River in Chiang Rai province. Now they are moving down to lower heights in search of more arable land, ranging widely across China and Indochina. They are "shifting" cultivators, depending on subsistence crops planted in rotation and raising domestic animals for their livelihood.

The clothing of the Akha is among the most attractive of all the hill-tribes. Simple black jackets with skillful embroidery are the everyday attire for both men and women. The Akha shoulder bags are adorned with silver coins, baubles, and found beads, and are woven with exceptional skill.

2 When to Go

THE CLIMATE Northern Thailand has three distinct seasons. The **hot season** (Mar–May) is dry with temperatures up to 86°F (30°C). Many Thais vacation in this region to get away from scorching temperatures elsewhere in the hot season. The **rainy season** (June–Oct) is cooler, with the heaviest daily rainfall in September (usually heavy afternoon downpours). While trekking and outdoor activities are still possible, rainy conditions (and mud) should be taken into consideration. The **cool season** (Nov–Feb) is brisk, with daytime temperatures as low as 59°F (21°C) in Chiang Mai town, and 41°F (5°C) in the hills. Bring a sweater and some warm socks. November to May is the best time for trekking, with February, March, and April (when southern Thailand gets extremely hot) usually being the most crowded months. In October and November, after the rainfalls, the forests are lush, rivers swell, and waterfalls are more splendid than usual.

FESTIVALS Northern Thailand celebrates many unique festivals as well as many nationwide festivals in an unusual way. Many Thais travel to participate in these festivals, and advance booking in hotels is a must.

NORTHERN THAILAND CALENDAR OF EVENTS

Many of these annual events are based on the lunar calendar. Contact the **Tourism Authority of Thailand TAT** (© 02694-1222; www.tourismthailand.org) in Bangkok for exact dates.

January

Umbrella Festival, Bo Sang. Held in a village of umbrella craftspeople and painters about 15km (9 miles) east of Chiang Mai, the Umbrella Festival features handicraft competitions, an elephant show, and a local parade.

February

Flower Festival, Chiang Mai. Celebrates the city's undisputed position as the "Flower of the North," with a parade, concerts, flower displays and competitions, a food fair, and a beauty contest at the Buak Hat park.

King Mengrai Festival, Chiang Rai. Known for its special hill-tribe cultural displays and a fine handicrafts market (early Feb).

Sakura Blooms Flower Fair, Doi Mae Salong. Celebrates the sakura of Japanese cherry trees, imported to this northwestern hill village by former members of China's nationalist Kuomintang party (early Feb).

March

Poy Sang Long. A traditional Shan ceremony honoring Buddhist novices, widely celebrated in the northwestern village of Mae Hong Son (late Mar or early Apr).

April

Songkran (Water) Festival. Celebrated over the Lanna Thai New Year, most of the ceremonies take place at the *wats*. Presents and merit-making acts are offered, and water is splashed over Buddhas, monks, elders, and tourists to celebrate the beginning of the harvest and to ensure good fortune. Those who don't want a good soaking should avoid the streets. The festival is celebrated in all northern provinces and throughout the country, but Chiang Mai's celebration is notorious for being the longest (up to 10 days) and the rowdiest. The first day is April 13.

May

Visakha Bucha. Honors the birth, enlightenment, and death of the Lord Buddha on the full moon of this month. Celebrated nationwide, it is a particularly dramatic event in Chiang Mai, where residents walk up Doi Suthep in homage.

Harvest Festival, Kho Loi Park, Chiang Rai. This festival honors the harvest of litchis. There is a parade, litchi competition and display, a beauty contest to find Miss Chiang Rai Litchi Nut, and lots of food (mid-May).

Mango Fair, Chiang Mai. A fair honoring mangoes, the local favorite crop (second weekend).

August

Lamyai or Longan Fair, Lamphun. Celebrates the town's favorite fruit and one of Thailand's largest foreign-exchange earners. Yes, there is a Miss Longan competition, too (first or second weekend).

October

Lanna Boat Races. Nan Province sponsors 2 days of boat racing, with wildly decorated, long, low-slung craft zipping down the Nan River. The Lanna Boat Races are run 7 days after the Rains' Retreat, marking the beginning of the dry season.

November

Lòy Krathong. Occurs around the country over 2 nights of the full moon in the 12th lunar month. Crowds float small banana-leaf boats bearing candles, incense, a flower, and a coin as an offering and to carry away the previous year's sins and bad luck. In Chiang Mai, brightly colored lanterns are strung everywhere; enormous, flaming hot-air balloons are released in the night sky; and there's a parade of women in traditional costumes. The offering boats or *krathongs* are floated on the Ping River.

December

Day of Roses, Chiang Mai. Exhibitions and cultural performances are held in Buak Hat Park (first weekend).

3 Getting There & Getting Around

GETTING THERE

Before the 1920s, when the railway's Northern Line to Chiang Mai was completed, one traveled either by longboat or elephant; it is good to remember when the train-ride gets boring or the flight is crowded that the trip took more than 2 weeks. There are lots of easy, comfortable options these days. For detailed info, be sure to check chapter 12, "Chiang Mai," and chapter 13, "Touring the Northern Hills."

BY PLANE   Thai Airways, Bangkok Air, Orient-Thai, and the new budget carriers Nok Air and Air Asia fly from Bangkok to Chiang Mai, Chiang Rai, Mae Hong Son, Nan, and Phrae. There are also flights between many of these destinations and to or from Phitsanulok in central Thailand. Bangkok Airways connects Bangkok and Chiang Mai with a stop in Sukhothai in the central plains. See destination chapters for details.

BY TRAIN   Express and rapid trains leave Bangkok daily for Chiang Mai, the northern terminus. Sleeper cars are available on certain trains and are highly recommended for the 13-hour overnight trip (reserve as early as possible).

BY BUS   There are dozens of daily and nightly air-conditioned VIP buses to Chiang Mai and other northern cities, as well as cheaper, less comfortable, normal service buses from Bangkok's Northern Bus Terminal. See destination chapters for details.

GETTING AROUND

BY PUBLIC BUS   There's frequent, inexpensive bus service between Chiang Mai and other northern cities. You'll also find *songtaos,* pickup trucks, fitted with long bench seats (also known locally as *seelor* or four-wheels), along the streets of Chiang Mai as well as all the major roads throughout the north, with no fixed schedule, stopping points, or price.

BY CAR   Renting your own car not only allows you freedom, but gives you the chance to see some beautiful countryside at your own pace, parking in rural villages or at friendly road-side stalls or bouncing down scenic tracks as you please. Main roads are well-paved and safe, with frequent petrol stations and restaurants in towns, and there are many side roads varying from packed gravel tarmac to dirt roads with deep mud-ruts. Both **Budget Car Rental** and **Avis** have branches in Chiang Mai and Chiang Rai, and rent out a selection of vehicles, from jeeps to sedans. While these larger rental companies have better insurance policies, they are expensive. Patronizing local companies in Chiang Mai and Chiang Rai will save you money, and some have acceptable insurance and will meet you at the airport. If you'll be driving out to mountain destinations, select the most well-maintained car on the lot (older cars are only for in-town driving). Refer to the "Getting Around" section in chapters 12 and 13 for specific office locations and rates. Consider hiring a car and driver from a smaller private company for as low as an additional 500B/$12 per day.

BY MOTORCYCLE   Motorcycle touring in northern Thailand has become popular, particularly with those who like freedom and experiencing the great outdoors up close. Most use Chiang Mai as a hub for exploring different routes throughout the region. Inexperienced riders should proceed cautiously (maybe start with a few day trips), and all should arm themselves with up-to-date information about road conditions and weather. Keep your ear to the ground in traveler haunts (guesthouses, bars, and coffee shops) to meet up with experienced riders or learn about more rural road information. Stay left, expect the unexpected out on the road (go slow), and carry a map to be sure you don't go straying into Burma. Off-road bikes, such as the 250cc Honda, are commonly available and a good choice because of their added power, good suspension, and large fuel tanks; they rent for about 550B ($13) a day.

4 Tours & Trekking in the Far North

The face of life has changed in the far north, a partial result of the tourist influx, but mainly the growing industrialization and economies of all of Thailand. Northern indigenous peoples have been exposed to the outside world and are being asked by Thai officials to stop slash-and-burn agricultural techniques and participate in the Thai economy by growing crops other than opium. Within the bounds of these influences, indigenous peoples struggle to maintain their cultural identities, livelihoods, and centuries-old ways of life.

Still, many travelers are drawn to the hill-tribe villages in search of a "primitive" culture, unspoiled by modernization, and tour and trekking operators in the region are quick to exploit this; companies advertise their treks as "nontourist," "authentic," or "alternative" in an effort to set them apart from tacky tourist operations or staged cultural experiences. Do not be misled: There are no villages here that are untouched by foreign curiosity. This shouldn't discourage anyone from joining a trek or tour, just be aware and avoid any bogus claims. It is also advisable to leave our preconceptions of "primitive" people to 19th century anthropological journals but rather come to learn how these cultures on the margin of society grapple with complex economic and social pressures to maintain their unique identities. Awareness of our impact as tourists is also important: practice cultural sensitivity. With this as a mission, visitors can have an experience that is quite authentic, but has little to do with our preconceptions and expectations.

TOUR OPTIONS

There are two kinds of hill-tribe operators in northern Thailand: tribal village tours and jungle treks.

Tribal village tours take large and small groups to visit villages that are close to major cities and towns. If you join one of these groups, you'll travel by van or coach to up to three villages, each inhabited by a different tribe, and you'll spend about an hour in each one. These villages have had decades of exposure to foreigners, and, because roads connect them to Chiang Mai, have many modern conveniences. Some overnight trips will put you up in small hotels or hostels that have been built especially for foreigners. Many trips include elephant trekking, visits to roadside craft vendors, and staged cultural performances of costume parades with music and dance. These short trips are great for a closer view of these cultures without undertaking a 3-day hill trek.

Jungle treks are more rugged trips with smaller groups (about 4–10 people) trudging-off to get up-close and personal with tribal people. Treks last anywhere from the usual 3 days and 2 nights up to 2-week special itineraries. Every trek starts with a bumpy road journey before groups head for the hills on foot, accompanied by a local guide. Some tours have bamboo rafting and elephant trekking thrown in for variety.

The guides keep a controlled pace, and even those who aren't particularly fit won't have a problem keeping up. Most guides have some knowledge of a few tribal languages and will serve as your go-between. Good guides will be familiar with the villages they'll take you to, will rehearse you in etiquette and protocol, and will negotiate the terms of your "invitation" with the local village leaders. Your guides will also feed you "jungle

Tips on Jungle Trekking

The problem isn't finding a trek—there are many companies, from small storefronts to hotel concierges, that offer treks out of Chiang Mai, Chiang Rai, Mae Hong Son, and Pai—it's finding the right mix of experienced and knowledgeable guides, an intelligent itinerary, a compatible group, and appropriate timing, all at an acceptable price. Be sure to ask for specifics before departure, because once you're out on the trail there will no longer be any room for debate. Consider the criterion below for any tour.

THE GUIDE   If there's one single element of a trek that will make or break the experience, it is the guide. Few guides are native to these jungles, although some have quite a few years of experience and most can speak the relevant phrases of a few hill-tribe languages (though their command of English is perhaps most important). All guides are required to attend a special 1-month course at Chiang Mai University and must be licensed by the Tourism Authority. Hill-tribe guides are familiar with the best trails, are well informed about the area and people, and are usually pretty interesting characters. Try to meet your prospective guide and ask lots of questions.

THE ITINERARY   Several well-known Chiang Mai agencies offer regularly scheduled routes. Any company can arrange custom tours for a higher fee. Be sure to get specifics about daily schedules. Most treks involve transport to and from the start and end-point of the trek. How long does it take and what are the conditions? Expect from 3 to 6 hours of unhurried walking each day. Gauge your fitness level and adjust to that or adjust the itinerary. When is lunch/dinner each day? What is lunch/dinner? What are the sleeping arrangements, etc. Nearly all trekking itineraries list the various hill-tribe villages visited; try to read as much as you can and decide for yourself which you'd most like to see.

THE GROUP   I've made lifelong friends on trekking trips and, conversely, spent uncomfortably long days and nights in the company of folks with whom I wouldn't want to share a cab-ride, much less days in the jungle. "Life is like a box of chocolates," of course, but if you're planning a long, arduous trip, try to meet your fellow travelers before committing; you might find that their stamina, assumptions, interests, and/or personalities are not compatible with yours. Look for an agency that limits the number of people to about 10 per trek. Having at least 4 in the group minimizes personality clashes and adds conviviality.

THE SEASON   See "When to Go," earlier in this chapter.

WHAT TO BRING   Most trekkers come to Thailand on vacation, totally unprepared for a serious trek, which is just fine. Most routes require good sneakers or walking shoes. A wool sweater for evenings and some outerwear

food," which is usually simple meals of rice and fish. If you're a vegetarian, it is a good idea to discuss this with your guide well in advance. Sometimes villagers will entertain guests with music and dance. All guests are invited to sleep in a separate area of the headman's house, which is usually the largest in the compound but accommodation is to sleep in will come in handy (many trekking companies only provide blankets). It's best to wear long trousers because of dense underbrush, leaches, and mosquitoes. A flashlight, supply of tissues or toilet paper, mosquito repellent, and a basic first-aid kit with blister remedies is also recommended.

Some groups bring gifts for remote villages. Ask your guide for specifics, because he may know the specific needs of the villagers in the places you'll be visiting, and it is important not to give away the likes of pens and sweets.

PRICE   Even the most expensive treks cost less than 1 night at a hotel and three restaurant meals. Some negotiation may be in order, especially if you are traveling with a larger group of people. Expect to pay between 500B to 2000B ($12–$49) per person per night, depending on the itinerary. Typically, food, transport, and equipment (backpack, water bottle, etc.) are included in the fee. Important: be sure to get specifics about what is included. Once on the trail there are no negotiations, and many a trekker comes down from the hills tired, angry, and feeling "taken," because of some often-minor misunderstanding. "You get what you pay for," of course, but be sure that you know what you'll get *before* you pay.

SAFETY   Never set out on your own on a trek. Despite the best efforts of local authorities, it is impossible to police the jungle and there are still some occurrences of banditry on village trails. Do not bring any valuables with you on your trek. You can make arrangements with your hotel or guesthouse in town, or even the trekking company you go with, to stow things safely.

A NOTE ON DRUGS   Travel in this region, so near the famed Golden Triangle and crisscrossed with smuggler trails from nearby Burma, is notorious for the availability of drugs, especially opium. Even with recent government crackdowns and programs to move hill-tribe economies to reliance on more sustainable farming of legal food items instead of poppies, you will still more than likely be offered opium or even invited to the village opium den. That, in fact, was part of the romantic allure of Thai trekking in its earliest inception. If the dangers of smoking opium in a rural village aren't obvious, consider the financial and cultural impact of supporting local drug economies and encouraging poor models of cultural exchange. Be warned that narcotics usage is illegal, and if you do happen to get caught, the penalties are harsh. The current Thai government is cracking down on drug use and the drug trade, and a zero-tolerance policy means that trekking guides, many of whom are addicted to opium, are tested, and tour operators run the risk of being shut down if found promoting drug use on their treks.

very basic (straw mats and blankets). It is unwise to try to go trekking on your own, and in fact it is important to have a guide who can navigate local customs and hospitality. Look for recommended trekking companies listed in each section. Below are some important pointers:

12

Chiang Mai

From 1296 under King Mengrai, Chiang Mai (New City) was the cultural and religious center of the northern Tai. The city was overtaken and occupied by the Burmese in 1556, until King Taksin retook the city in 1775, driving the Burmese forces back to near the present border. Burmese influence on religion, architecture, language, cuisine, and culture, however, remains strong. Local princes, called *chao,* remained in nominal control of the city in the late 18th and early 19th century, but under continued pressure from King Chulalongkorn (Rama V), the Lanna kingdom was brought under the control of the central government in Bangkok. In 1939, the city was formally and fully integrated into the kingdom of Thailand, becoming the administrative center of the north.

These days, Chiang Mai is booming, with an estimated population of 250,000 (in a province of some 1.5 million) and growing, along with the attendant "big city" problems of suburban sprawl, rush-hour traffic, and water shortages (though nothing compared to Bangkok).

It would be difficult to find a city that reflects more of the country's diverse cultural heritage and modern aspirations than Chiang Mai. Massive modern tour buses crowd Burmese-style *wats* ablaze with the color of saffron and humming with the chanting of monks from a bygone era. Hill-tribe groups sell their wares in the busy market next to fast food outlets. Narrow streets lined with ornately carved teak houses lie in the shadow of contemporary skyscrapers. Chiang Mai's heart is its Old City, an area surrounded by vestiges of walls and moats originally constructed for defense; yet Chiang Mai is a modern city with a growing infrastructure of modern shopping malls and condominiums. The contrast is part of the town's charm.

Because of its temperate climate, many Thais choose Chiang Mai as a retreat during March, April, and May, when the rest of the country is wilting under the heat. Chiang Mai is an excellent base for exploring the north.

1 Orientation

ARRIVING

BY PLANE   In planning your trip, keep in mind that Chiang Mai has international links with major cities throughout the region. **Lao Aviation** (*©* **05340-4033**) connects Chiang Mai to Vientiane and Luang Prabang three times each week, while both **Thai Airways** (*©* **05327-0222**) and **Air Mandalay** (*©* **05381-8049**) have limited flights to Yangon and Mandalay, in Myanmar (Burma). **Silk Air** (*©* **05327-6459**), the regional arm of Singapore Airlines, connects Singapore with direct service three times a week. **Thai Airways International** has service directly from Kunming in southern China. For international reservations in Chiang Mai, call *©* **05327-0222**.

Domestically, **Thai Airways** (240 Propokklao Rd.; © 05392-0999) flies from Bangkok to Chiang Mai 10 times daily (trip time: 1 hr., 10 min.). There's a direct flight from Phuket daily, plus a circular route connecting Phitsanulok, Nan, Phrae, and Chiang Mai four times a week. The 35-minute hop up to Chiang Rai departs twice daily, and another 35-minute hop is also the fastest way to get out to Mae Hong Son.

Bangkok Airways has an office at the airport in Chiang Mai (© 05328-1519 or 02229-3434 in Bangkok) and flies numerous daily flights from Bangkok. **Orient Thai** (© 05390-4609) also has regular flights.

For rock-bottom prices, check with new budget carrier, **Air Asia** (© 05392-2170; www.airasia.com). They fly from Bangkok to Chiang Mai for as little as 800B ($20), and budget **Nok Air** (www.nokair.com; © 05392-2183 or © 1318) offers similar budget passage (book both in advance via the Internet).

The **Chiang Mai International Airport** has several banks for changing money, a post and overseas call office, and an information booth.

Taxis from the airport are a flat 100B ($2.45) to town, a bit more for places outside of Chiang Mai proper. Buy a ticket from the taxi booth in the arrival hall, then proceed to the taxi queue with your ticket.

BY TRAIN   Of the seven daily trains from Bangkok to Chiang Mai, the 8:30am Sprinter (11 hr.; 511B/$12.45, second-class air-conditioned seat) is the quickest, but you sacrifice a whole day to travel and spend the entire trip in a seat. The other trains take between 13 and 15 hours, but for overnight trips; second-class sleeper berths are a good choice (781B/$19 upper berth, air-conditioned; 691B/$17 lower berth, air-conditioned). Private sleeper cabins are also available, but at 1,213B ($30) the cost is the same as flying. Purchase tickets at Bangkok's **Hua Lampong Railway Station** (© 02223-7010 or 1690) up to 90 days in advance. For local train information in Chiang Mai call © 05324-5363; for advance booking call © 05324-2094. Reservations cannot be made over the phone, but you can call and check to see if space is available.

BY BUS   Buses from Bangkok to Chiang Mai are many and varied—from rattletrap, open-air numbers to fully reclining VIP buses. The trip takes about 10 hours. From **Bangkok's Northern Bus Terminal,** close to the Mo Chit stop on the Skytrain (© 02936-2841), six daily 24-seater VIP buses provide the most comfort, with larger seats that recline (625B/$15). There is also frequent service between Chiang Mai and Mae Hong Son, Phitsanulok, and Chiang Rai.

Most buses arrive at the **Arcade Bus Station** (© 05324-2664) on Kaeo Nawarat Road, 3km (2 miles) northeast of the Thapae Gate; a few arrive at the Chang Puak station (© 05321-1586), north of the Chang Puak Gate on Chotana Road. Expect to pay 60B to 100B ($1.45–$2.45) for a tuk-tuk, and just 30B/75¢ for a *songtao* to the town center and your hotel.

VISITOR INFORMATION

The **TAT** office is at 105/1 Chiang Mai-Lamphun Road, 400m (1,312 ft.) south of the Nawarat Bridge on the east side of the Ping River (© 05324-8604). There are a couple of free magazines available at hotels and businesses—*Guidelines Chiang Mai, Welcome to Chiang Mai and Chiangrai,* and *What's on Chiang Mai*—which contain maps and fun, useful information. Pick up a copy in any hotel lobby. You can also find any of a number of detailed maps distributed free and chock-full of adverts for local shopping, dining, and events.

CITY LAYOUT

The heart of Chiang Mai is the **Old City,** completely surrounded by a moat (restored in the 19th century) and a few remains of the massive wall, laid out in a square aligned on the cardinal directions. Several of the original gates have been restored and serve as handy reference points, particularly Thapae Gate to the east. The most important temples are within the walls of the Old City.

All major streets radiate from the Old City. The main business and shopping area is the 1km (⅔-mile) stretch between the east side of the Old City and the Ping River. Here you will find the Night Bazaar, many shops, trekking agents, better hotels, guesthouses and restaurants, and some of the most picturesque back streets in the area.

To the west of town and visible from anywhere in the city is the imposing wall of Doi Suthep mountain where, at its crest, you'll find the most regal of all Chiang Mai Buddhist compounds, Wat Phra That Doi Suthep, standing stalwart as if to give its blessing to the city below. The road leading to the temple takes you past a big mall, a strip of modern hotels, the zoo, and the university.

The Superhighway circles the outskirts of the city and is connected by traffic-choked arteries emanating from the city center. If driving or riding a motorbike in Chiang Mai, the many one-way streets in and around town are confounding. The moat that surrounds the city has concentric circles of traffic: the outer ring runs clockwise, and the inner ring counterclockwise, with U-turn bridges between. The streets in and around the Night Bazaar are all one-way, as well. This means that even if you know where you're going, you'll have to pull your share of U-turns.

GETTING AROUND

BY BUS There are no city buses in Chiang Mai.

BY SONGTAO *Songtaos* (covered pickups) cover all routes. From Chang Puak Bus Station, there is frequent, inexpensive bus service to the nearby villages of Sankampaeng and Bo Sang, Lamphun. These red pickup trucks fitted with two long bench seats are also known locally as *seelor* (four wheels). They trace the major roads throughout the city, day and night, with no fixed stopping points. Hail one going in your general direction and tell the driver your destination. (**Tip:** Have your hotel or guesthouse concierge write your destination in Thai before you head out.) If it fits in with the destinations of other passengers, you'll get a ride to your door for only 10B to 20B (25¢–50¢). Some drivers will ask exorbitant fees as if they are a taxi (especially when they're empty); let these guys just drive on. If you can deal with a bit of uncertainty along the confusing twist of roads, it is a great way to explore the city.

Songtaos can also take you up to the top of Doi Suthep Mountain for 35B/85¢, and only 25B/60¢ for the easier downhill return trip.

BY TUK-TUK The ubiquitous tuk-tuk (motorized three-wheeler) is the next best option to the songtao. Fares are negotiable—and you will have to bargain hard to get a good rate—but expect to pay at least 40B ($1) for any ride.

Tuk-tuks are good fun, especially for the first-timer, and whizzing around busy streets brings out the kid in most; many drivers are real characters, too; can speak good English; and offer informal (okay, very informal) info and advice. That said, **be careful:** the same warning for Bangkok applies here—drivers will offer you a low fare and promise a "shopping tour" of their favorite vendors and factories in the hopes of pocketing commissions. The "shopping tour" is a waste of time and lots of frustration, so be sure to negotiate a fare for your destination and be clear: "No shopping." A favorite ploy drivers use is to feign ignorance of a place or tell you the place closed. Don't buy it. When talking prices, it is good to write it down on a scrap of paper so there is no argument when you get there and the driver asks for 200B ($4.90) instead of the 20B (50¢) you agreed on.

BY CAR   **Avis** has an office conveniently located at the airport (© **05320-1798;** www.avisthailand.com). Avis self-drive rental rates for Chiang Mai are the same as they are elsewhere in Thailand, from 2,000B ($49) and up for a compact sedan. **Budget** now has an office at the airport and offers comparable rates and services; contact them at © **05320-2871** (www.budget.co.th). Both companies offer comprehensive insurance and provide good maps—even a miniguidebook.

There are dozens of **local car-rental companies** with sedans for 1,000B to 1,400B ($24–$34) per day, and Suzuki Caribians for as low as 900B ($22) per day. Most travel agents will arrange a car and driver for about 1,600B ($39) per day. **North Wheels,** 127/2 Moonmuang Road (© **05321-6189**), is tops in this category, and does pickup or drop-off service to the airport or your hotel.

BY MOTORCYCLE   Many guesthouses along the Ping River and shops around Chaiyaphum Road (north of Thapae Gate in the Old City) rent 100cc to 150cc motorcycles for about 200B ($4.90) per day (discounts for longer duration). Larger 250cc Hondas (as well as others) with good suspension are commonly available and the best choice for any trips up-country because of their added power and large fuel tanks; they rent for about 550B ($13). Try **Jaguar Rental** (131 Mun Muang Rd.; © **05341-9161**), one of many near Thapae. Make sure you wear a helmet, and expect to leave your passport as security (don't leave any credit cards). Traffic congestion and confusing one-way streets make riding within the city dangerous, so employ defensive driving techniques and take it slow.

BY BICYCLE   Cycling in the city is fun and practical, especially for getting around to the temples within the Old City. Avoid rush hour and take great care on the busy roads outside of the ancient walls. Bikes are available at any of the many guesthouses in or around the old city, and go for about 30B (75¢) per day.

FAST FACTS: Chiang Mai

Airport   See "Arriving," above.

ATMs   For ATMs and money changers, go to Chang Klan and Charoen Prathet roads, around the Night Bazaar, for the most convenient major bank branches.

Bookstores   **Backstreet Books** (© 05387-4143) and **Gecko Books** (© 05387-4066) are neighbors on Chang Moi Kao, a side-street north of eastern Thapae Road just before it meets the city wall. Both have a good selection of new and used books, and do exchanges at the usual rate (two for one, depending on the condition).

Car Rentals   See "Getting Around: By Car," above.

Climate   See "When to Go," in chapter 11, "Exploring Northern Thailand."

Consulates   There are many representative offices in Chiang Mai. Contacts are as follows: **American Consulate General** (© 05325-2629), **Canadian Honorary Consul** (© 05385-0147), **Australian Honorary Consul** (© 05322-1083), and **British Consul** (© 05320-3405).

Dentist/Doctor The American Consulate (see "Consulates," above) will supply you with a list of English-speaking dentists and doctors. There are also several medical clinics; check with your hotel about the best and nearest facility.

Emergencies Dial ℂ 1155 to reach the Tourist Police in case of emergency.

Holidays See "When to Go," in chapter 2, "Planning Your Trip to Thailand," and the "Northern Thailand Calendar of Events," in chapter 11, "Exploring Northern Thailand."

Hospitals In Chiang Mai, hospitals offer excellent emergency and general care, with English-speaking nurses and physicians. The best private hospital is **McCormick** on Kaeo Nawarat Road (ℂ 05324-1311), out toward the Arcade Bus Terminal.

Internet In the Old City, there are numerous small, inexpensive cafes with service sometimes costing only 15B (35¢) per hour. Just outside the city and featuring the speediest service in town for just 1B per minute (about 2¢ per minute) is **NET Generation** at 404/4 Thapae Road (ℂ 01568-7470). In the Night Bazaar area, try **Assign Internet** in Chiang Mai Pavilion at the Night Bazaar on 145/23 Chang Klan Road (ℂ 05381-8911). Just across from the entrance to Gad Suan Kaew/Central Department Store in the northwest corner of the Old City, **Buddy Internet** is at 12 Huaykaew Road (ℂ 05340-4550) and open from 8am to midnight. **Buddy 2** is at 56 Chaiyaphum Road (ℂ 05387-4121), and **Buddy 3** is in the Sompetch Gold Palace on Chaiyaphum Road (ℂ 05323-2970).

Pharmacies There are dozens of pharmacies throughout the city; most are open daily 7am to midnight.

Police For police assistance, call the **Tourist Police** at ℂ 1155, or see them at the TAT office.

Post Office The most convenient branch is at 186/1 on Chang Klan Road (ℂ 05327-3657). The General Post Office is on Charoen Muang (ℂ 05324-1070), near the train station. The Overseas Call Office, open 24 hours, is upstairs from the GPO and offers phone, fax, and telex services. There is a 24-hour branch at the airport (ℂ 05327-7382). **UPS** has an office in the basement of the Night Bazaar (Changklan Road; ℂ 05382-0222; daily 7am–10pm), making it easy to send your finds back home.

2 Accommodations

City accommodations listed below are separated as follows: outside of town; east of town near the Ping River/Night Bazaar area, within the Old City walls, or outside of town on the road to Doi Suthep (near the university).

OUTSIDE CHIANG MAI
VERY EXPENSIVE
The Four Seasons Resort & Spa ✧✧✧   Northern Thailand's finest resort is isolated from the bustle of the city on 8 hectares (20 acres) of landscaped grounds in the Mae Rim Valley. The beautiful central garden includes two small lakes, lily ponds, and terraced rice paddies. There is even a resident family of water buffaloes used to work

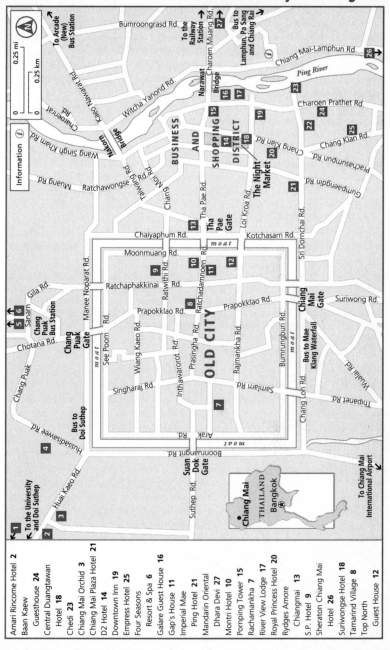

Amari Rincome Hotel **2**
Baan Kaew
  Guesthouse **24**
Central Duangtawan
  Hotel **18**
Chedi **23**
Chiang Mai Orchid **3**
Chiang Mai Plaza Hotel **21**
D2 Hotel **14**
Downtown Inn **19**
Empress Hotel **25**
Four Seasons
  Resort & Spa **6**
Galare Guest House **16**
Gap's House **11**
Imperial Mae
  Ping Hotel **21**
Mandarin Oriental
  Dhara Devi **27**
Montri Hotel **10**
Pornping Tower **15**
Rachamankha **7**
River View Lodge **17**
Royal Princess Hotel **20**
Rydges Amore
  Chiangmai **13**
S.P. Hotel **9**
Sheraton Chiang Mai
  Hotel **26**
Suriwongse Hotel **18**
Tamarind Village **8**
Top North
  Guest House **12**

the fields (perhaps the most pampered beasts of burden in the kingdom). Two-story Lanna-style (northern) pavilions overlook the tranquil scenery. Spacious suites are understatedly elegant with polished teak floors and vaulted ceilings, decorated with traditional Thai fabrics and art, each with an adjoining private *sala* (open-air pavilion). Bathrooms are particularly large and luxurious, with two vanities, separate shower, and a big sunken tub with picture windows on three sides overlooking a secluded, private garden.

The vanishing-edge pool seems to drop off into the paddy fields below and rise into the mountains beyond. At night, torches are lit in the fields, lending a mysterious air to the views from the resort's restaurants. The resort location, though far from Chiang Mai, gives you full access to sites in the Mae Rim valley, and helpful tour staff can arrange day tours and guests are invited to borrow mountain bikes for self-guided exploration of the area (see "Side Trips from Chiang Mai," later in this chapter, about the Mae Sa Valley). If you're worried about being far from Chiang Mai, the resort provides regular shuttles to and from the main business and shopping district. And if you're still twiddling your thumbs you can put them to work at the hotel's fine cooking school. The piece de resistance is the Regent's luxurious Lanna Spa, which offers a standard of luxury and service without rival in the region. A very unique and luxurious resort.

Mae Rim–Samoeng Old Rd., Mae Rim, Chiang Mai 50180 (20 min. north of city, off Chiang Mai–Mae Rim Rd.). ℂ 800/545-4000 in the U.S., or 05329-8181. Fax 05329-8190. www.fourseasons.com. 80 suites. $425–$525 pavilion suite; from $1,050–$1,250 residence suite. AE, DC, MC, V. **Amenities:** 3 restaurants; bar; 2 pools; 2 outdoor lighted grass tennis courts; fitness center w/sauna and steam; spa w/steam, massage, salon; complimentary bicycles available; children's activities; library; concierge w/personalized tour arrangements and car rental; shuttle to town; business center; 24-hr. room service; babysitting; same-day laundry service/dry cleaning. *In room:* A/C, satellite TV w/in-house movies, minibar, fridge, hair dryer, safe.

Mandarin Oriental Dhara Dhevi 🍂🍂🍂

From the same management team that runs the famed Oriental in Bangkok comes this ultra luxury resort. East of Chiang Mai proper on Sankampaeng Road, the Dhara Dhevi is designed like a self-enclosed ancient city, complete with an entry across a small moat (note the purposely noisy wooden bridge to announce visitors' arrival) and a grand city gate that ushers you into the compound. Leave your gas-burning chariot in the parking lot and go by Burmese-style horse-drawn carts to the grand palace and lobby. The resort is just completing the last phase of luxury rooms, but all are sumptuous and oversized suites with every imaginable luxury. Rice villa suites surround a mock-up rice field full of flowers and greenery, and others include pavilion suites and theme suites like their "vegetable garden" quad or the Sipsongpanna rooms influenced by hill-tribe style. All suites have large balcony spaces and two stories of sumptuously decorated interior space. Colonial suites are huge and done in a 19th century style of Burmese and colonial accents, high ceilings and, in their top Mandalay Suite, a high cupola. Style throughout borders on kitsch, but is so over-the-top that it works, and in fact the place is the brainchild of a Thai art collector who hopes the hotel will be like a living museum of art, architecture, and history; he has even commissioned a small department of art and history and filled a small library on site. Their huge luxury spa is a carved wedding cake modeled after the Mandalay Palace in Burma. The resort offers daily courses in cultural studies (basket weaving, etc.), as well as yoga courses, local tours, and a large, upmarket shopping compound at the entrance, this mock-up ancient city's "market." Long-popular is the resort's Grand Lanna Restaurant, and they also offer fine French and international cuisine. Memorable.

51/4 Chiang Mai–Sankampaeng Road, Moo 1 T. Tasala A. Muang Chiang Mai 50000 (10km or 10-min. drive from the airport; 5km or 5 min. from downtown). (✆ **05388-8888**. Fax 05388-8999. www.mandarinoriental.com. 150 units (250 upon completion); $295 villa; $440–$715 deluxe villa; $1,000 2-bedroom deluxe villa. V, MC, AE. **Amenities:** 4 restaurants (Thai, Chinese, French, international); 3 bars; multi-level infinity edge pool; tennis courts; health club; extensive spa; Jacuzzi; sauna; bike rentals; children's center and many cultural programs; concierge; tour desk; limo; business center; shopping arcade; salon; 24-hr. room service; massage; babysitting; laundry service; dry cleaning. *In room:* A/C, satellite TV, free wireless Internet in all rooms, minibar, fridge, coffeemaker, hair dryer, iron/ironing board, safe, phone.

NEAR THE PING RIVER
VERY EXPENSIVE
The Chedi ✦   Opened just a few weeks, The Chedi, like so many along the water's edge, was terribly damaged by major flooding of the Ping River in the fall of 2005. The hotel is set to reopen in the winter of 2005/6. Where for years there have always been luxury hotels on the outskirts of the city (see the Four Seasons, and now, the Dhara Dhevi), The Chedi is a new standard of downtown luxury. A spartan exterior of minimalist wooden slats gives way to a crisp interior of large reflecting pools and aggregate concrete walks. The riverside area and pool pops right out of a fashion shoot. Rooms are a crisp business hotel standard, and the hotel reopening promises some good upgrades. Chedi club suites are enormous and come with lots of included services. In-house dining is at riverside in a lovingly restored old Thai House. The hotel is a luxury oasis facing some beautiful river scenery along the Mae Ping, just south of the Night Bazaar area. They offer extensive spa treatments.

123 Charoen Prathet Rd., T. Changklan, A. Muang Chiang Mai 50100. (✆ **05325-3333**. Fax 05325-3352. www.ghm hotels.com. 84 units. $260 deluxe double; $390 Chedi Club Suite. V, MC, AE. **Amenities:** Restaurant; 3 bars; outdoor pool; health club; spa; Jacuzzi; sauna; concierge; tour desk; car-rental desk; courtesy car or limo; business center; salon; 24-hr. room service; massage; babysitting; laundry service; dry cleaning. *In room:* A/C, satellite TV, fax, data-port, minibar, fridge, coffeemaker, hair dryer, iron/ironing board, safe, IDD phone.

EXPENSIVE
The Imperial Mae Ping Hotel ✦   This imposing, crescent-shaped tower hotel is one of the city's most popular choices for its style and good location—just a short stroll from the Night Bazaar, yet far enough to get a good night's sleep. The unusual two-story lobby interprets Thai architectural elements in bold white-and-gold accents and the decor throughout is a nice mix of modern and traditional. Large, bright guest rooms are modern and feature traditional blond teak furnishings and contemporary Thai elements like sculpted lamp bases, reproductions of temple murals, and Thai weavings. Deluxe rooms have better-than-average amenities for just a small jump in price. Be sure to ask for a room with a mountain view. They have a popular beer garden in the hotel's large courtyard area, and the pool is a good escape after city shopping. A good downtown choice.

153 Sri Dornchai Rd., Chiang Mai 50100 (corner of Kampaengdin Rd., 2 blocks southwest of Night Bazaar). (✆ **05327-0160**. Fax 05327-0181. www.imperialmaeping.com. 371 units. 4,500B–5,500B ($110–$134) double; from 12,000B ($293) suite. AE, DC, MC, V. **Amenities:** 3 restaurants; lounge and beer garden; outdoor pool; fitness center; tour desk; limousine service; business center; salon; 24-hr. room service; massage; babysitting; same-day laundry service/dry cleaning; nonsmoking rooms, executive-level rooms. *In room:* A/C, TV w/satellite programming, minibar, fridge.

Royal Princess Hotel ✦   Under major renovation in 2005, this northern cousin of Bangkok's Dusit Thani is a first-rate city hotel. Guest rooms are done in a mix of cool pastels set against panels, or whole walls, of saturated primary colors, featuring poetry in elegant Thai calligraphy. Upper floor deluxe rooms have an interesting Japanese theme. The downtown location means easy access to shopping and nightlife, and all guest rooms have a good vantage on the glittering lights of the city. You're right in the heart of it here, so be warned that stepping out of the hotel means that touts and tuk-tuk drivers pounce. Don't miss Jasmine Restaurant's excellent dim sum lunch (see "Dining," later in this chapter).

112 Chang Klan Rd., Chiang Mai 50100 (located just south of the Night Bazaar). ✆ 05328-1033. Fax 05328-1044. www.royalprincess.com. 198 units. 3,200B–3,500B ($78–$85) double; from 10,500B ($256) suite. AE, DC, MC, V. **Amenities:** 3 restaurants; lobby lounge and pub; small outdoor pool; concierge; tour desk; limousine service; 24-hr. room service; massage; babysitting; same-day laundry service/dry cleaning. *In room:* A/C, TV w/satellite programming, minibar, fridge, hair dryer, safe.

Sheraton Chiang Mai Hotel ☆☆   Just a short ride out of town, and a popular business and meeting address, the Sheraton (formerly Westin) is a good, familiar choice. From the enormous pillars, chandeliers, frescoes, and filigree of the grand lobby, to their international standard of guest rooms and service, everything is tip-top. What the Sheraton lacks in "local" touches it more than makes up for with comfortable familiarity. Complimentary shuttles to the Night Bazaar and airport help offset the out-of-the-way locale. Rooms, particularly deluxe rooms, are vast; not particularly luxurious, but quite large. Services are extensive, including wireless Internet available on business floors.

318/1 Chiang Mai–Lamphun Rd., Chiang Mai 50007 (south of city center, across Mengrai Bridge on east bank of river). ✆ 05327-5300. Fax 05327-5299. www.sheraton.com. 526 units. 6,200B–7,200B ($151–$176) double; 9,500B ($232) exec. deluxe; from 14,500B ($354) suite. AE, DC, MC, V. **Amenities:** 3 restaurants; lounge; outdoor pool; golf course nearby; fitness center; sauna; concierge; tour desk; car-rental desk; limousine service; business center; 24-hr. room service; massage; babysitting; same-day laundry service/dry cleaning; nonsmoking rooms; executive-level rooms. *In room:* A/C, TV w/satellite programming, minibar, fridge, hair dryer.

MODERATE

Central Duangtawan Hotel   New in the Night Bazaar area, the Central Duangtawan Hotel is the cream of the crop of mid-range hotelier Central's many properties throughout Thailand. More a business hotel than anything, and far more popular with Thai travelers than Westerners, the hotel is still a fine choice with large, somewhat bland, but comfortable rooms, some with great views of the mountain (especially from the top floors of this high tower).

132 Loy Kroh Road, Chiang Mai 50100. ✆ 05390-5000. Fax 05327-5429. www.centralhotelsresorts.com. 500 units. 2,000B–3,200B ($49–$78) double; 4,200B ($102). V, MC. **Amenities:** 2 restaurants; 2 bars; outdoor pool; fitness center; Jacuzzi; sauna; tour desk; car-rental desk; business center; shopping arcade; salon; limited room service; massage; laundry service; dry cleaning. *In room:* A/C, satellite TV, minibar, fridge, safe, phone.

Chiang Mai Plaza Hotel   These two 12-story towers, completed in 1986, are a bland, modern Western hotel, but guest rooms are large, plush, and offer city and mountain views. The lobby is so spacious that the decorative furniture seems almost lost in acres of brilliantly polished granite, and recent renovations give it that extra-glitzy touch. The Plaza is also well located—in town, but just far enough away, toward the Ping River, to be out of the congestion. It is very popular with group tours, but the place is so big you won't know they're there. The swimming pool is surrounded by Lanna-style pavilions, and their newly built spa area is a catacomb in deep umber tones, dim lights, and Thai decoration, where they offer the gamut of affordable but high-quality health and beauty treatments.

92 Sri Dornchai Rd., Chiang Mai 50100 (between Chang Klan and Charoen Prathet rds., midway between Old City and river). ✆ 05327-0036. Fax 05327-2230. 445 units. 2,500B–3,000B ($61–$73) double; from 12,200B ($298)

suite. AE, DC, MC, V. **Amenities:** Restaurant; lounge; outdoor pool; fitness center; spa with massage and sauna; tour desk; car-rental desk; business center; limited room service; massage; babysitting; same-day laundry service/dry cleaning; nonsmoking rooms. *In room:* A/C, TV w/satellite programming, minibar, fridge, hair dryer.

The Empress Hotel ✿ This 17-story tower, opened in 1990, is south of the main business and tourist area, which makes it especially quiet. The hotel has all the amenities, and even when swarming with tourist groups doesn't seem over-run. The impressive public spaces are filled with glass, granite, and chrome, and integrated Thai touches and flairs. Large rooms with picture windows are done in a tasteful, modern interpretation of Asian decor of rose and peach tones. Bathrooms are small but decked-out in marble and offer good complimentary amenities. Ask to be on the mountain side, and there are nice views from upper floors.

199/42 Chang Klan Rd., Chiang Mai 50100 (a 15-min. walk south of Night Bazaar, 2 blocks from river). ✆ 05327-0240. Fax 05327-2467. www.empresshotels.com. 375 units. 3,000B–4,000B ($73–$98) double; from 8,400B ($205) suite. AE, DC, MC, V. **Amenities:** 3 restaurants; lobby lounge and disco; pool; fitness center with sauna; concierge; tour desk; business center; Internet; shopping arcade; salon; 24-hr. room service; massage; babysitting; same-day laundry service/dry cleaning; executive-level rooms. *In room:* A/C, TV w/satellite programming, minibar, fridge, hair dryer.

Pornping Tower Right in the heart of the busy shopping and nightlife area near the Night Bazaar, this 20-story hotel bustles with evening activity. Public spaces are full of polished marble, glass, and mirrors; rooms use cool colors and have a contemporary style. There's an excellent pool with an inviting sundeck, good in-house dining, attentive service, and top location: ingredients that combine to make this one of the best buys in the city. Be sure to check out their happenin' Bubble Disco (when it is happenin', that is—weekend nights, mostly).

46–48 Charoen Prathet Rd., Chiang Mai 50100 (corner of Loy Kroh Rd., 1 block from river). ✆ 05327-0099. Fax 05327-0119. 318 units. 1,500B–2,200B ($37–$54) double; from 5,000B ($122) suite. AE, DC, MC, V. **Amenities:** 3 restaurants; popular disco, lounge and karaoke; outdoor pool; tour desk; 24-hr. room service; babysitting; same-day laundry service/dry cleaning. *In room:* A/C, TV w/satellite programming, minibar, fridge.

River View Lodge ✿✿ An old Frommer's favorite, the River View Lodge has a great location and is the kind of place where people return again and again. The hotel's riverside location makes for a peaceful retreat, and yet it is only a short hop to the city's main business and shopping district. What with the quaint, shady garden, small but cozy riverside pool, open-air cafe, and quiet sitting areas scattered about, there's a good laid-back vibe here. The staff is friendly enough and informed, if a bit "eccentric," to give it a word. Large guest rooms have terra-cotta tile floors with simple wood furnishings and no-fuss decor set against one wall of redbrick facing (some have balconies). Bathrooms have shower stalls only.

25 Charoen Prathet Rd., Soi 4, Chiang Mai 50100 (on river 2 blocks south of Thae Pae Rd.). ✆ 05327-1109. Fax 05327-9019. www.riverviewlodgch.com. 36 units. 1,450B–1,800B ($35–$44) double, priced according to size and view. 2,200B ($54) triple. MC, V. **Amenities:** Restaurant; small pool; laundry service. *In room:* A/C.

Rydges Amore Chiangmai ✿ For years there was a moratorium on high-rise building in and around the old city (all other towers are in the Night Bazaar area). Then (whoops!) the new Rydges Hotel kind of slipped in and there is a twelve-story eye-sore on the edge of the historic, two-story Old City. What this means for you is that rooms on the upper floors offer some of the best views of the Old City and the mountains beyond. Chain-hotel style rooms have no distinguishing features other than their good size and cleanliness. There is a small pool. The place attracts lots of luxury lager louts for its proximity to the beer bars near Thapae gate, and a festive air prevails (that means late-night hall hooting). The Australian chain Rydges has a controlling share for the time being, but the hotel will revert to the Amore name in coming years.

22 Chaiyapoom Road, Chiang Mai 50300 (north of Thapae Gate and just across the moat from the Old City). ℂ **05325-1531.** Fax 05325-1721. www.rydges.com. 204 units. 1,800B–2,400B ($44–$59) double; from 4,000B ($98) suite. AE, MC, V. **Amenities:** Restaurant; lounge; beer garden on top floor, outdoor pool; tour desk; limited room service; babysitting; same-day laundry service/dry cleaning; nonsmoking rooms. *In room:* A/C, satellite TV, minibar, fridge, coffeemaker, safe, IDD phone.

Suriwongse Hotel ✦ For the shopper or party animal looking to be close to the Night Bazaar area, this hotel is tops, but everyone knows it and Suriwongse has been around a while, so it is looking a little worse for the wear. The unique hardwood paneling in the lobby lends warmth to the place, and spacious, teak-trimmed rooms have clean carpet, large, firm beds, and are done in cool off-whites and pastels (if you can ignore the red bordello drapes). This is one of Chiang Mai's better values, but not luxurious. Higher-priced rooms have similar amenities but offer a balcony and better views. The towns McDonald's and Starbucks franchises are both within a stone's throw (if throwing stones is your thing).

110 Chang Klan Rd., Chiang Mai 50100 (corner of Loy Kroh Rd., just southwest of Night Bazaar, halfway between Old City and river). ℂ **05327-0051.** Fax 05327-0063. www.suriwongsehotels.com. 180 units. 2,200B–3,500B ($54–$85) double; from 4,800B ($117) suite (seasonal rates available). AE, DC, MC, V. **Amenities:** 2 restaurants; lounge; pool; tour desk; business center; shopping; limited room service; massage; babysitting; same-day laundry service/dry cleaning; nonsmoking rooms. *In room:* A/C, TV w/satellite programming, minibar, fridge, IDD phone.

INEXPENSIVE

Baan Kaew Guesthouse This motel-style guesthouse, an enclosed compound in a quiet neighborhood just a short walk south of the Night Bazaar, has a well-tended garden and a manicured lawn. Rooms are very simple but spotless, with new floor coverings (guests are asked to remove shoes before entering) and tiled bathrooms with hot-water showers. Breakfast is served in a shaded pavilion. You're close to the market, but the place is quiet.

142 Charoen Prathet Rd., Chiang Mai 50100 (south of Loy Kroh Rd. opposite Wat Chaimongkol; enter gate, turn left, and find guesthouse well back from street). ℂ **05327-1606.** Fax 05327-3436. 20 units. 650B ($16) double. No credit cards. **Amenities:** Restaurant (breakfast only); tour desk; laundry service. *In room:* A/C, IDD phone.

Downtown Inn ✦ A more affordable version of the Empress Hotel (under the same management), little Downtown Inn is a good, simple budget choice close to the action of the Night Bazaar area. Rooms are plain with hard mattresses. Bathrooms are shower only in tidy tile. They have a cozy coffee shop and a simple breakfast is included. The courtyard swimming pool is tiny, but a good little escape. Big discounts are available from the prices below.

172/1-11 Loy-Kroh Road, Anusarn Night Market, Chiang Mai. ℂ **05327-0662.** Fax 05327-2406. www.empress hotels.com. 74 units. 1,900B–2,200B ($46–$54); from 5,500B ($134) suite. V, MC. **Amenities:** Restaurant; outdoor pool; massage; laundry. *In room:* A/C, TV, fridge, IDD phone.

Galare Guest House If the River View Lodge (see "Moderate," above) is booked or you want to save baht, try the smaller Galare, almost next door. It is a Thai-style, three-story, brick-and-wood motel, with broad covered verandas overlooking a pleasant garden and courtyard. Rooms are small but have air-conditioning and king-size beds. It is low-luxe linoleum floors and bamboo catay on the walls, but comfortable. The restaurant serves breakfast, lunch, and dinner on a covered deck overlooking the river. An in-house trekking agency organizes trips to hill-tribe villages, as well as local tours of Chiang Mai. Up to 20% discounts available in the off-season.

7 Charoen Prathet Rd., Soi 2, Chiang Mai 50100 (on river south of Thapae Rd.). © **05381-8887.** Fax 05327-9088. 35 units. 780B–1,050B ($19–$26) double. MC, V. **Amenities:** Restaurant; tour desk; car rental; Internet access; laundry service. *In room:* TV, fridge, no phone.

IN THE OLD CITY

EXPENSIVE

Rachamankha ✦ The highest standard within the city walls, Rachamankha is an ultra-luxe boutique village and a good little escape from the wicked world. Service is professional, and rooms are luxuriant affairs with terra-cotta tile floors, high canopy beds hung with cloth, rattan chairs, and stylish contemporary built-ins and local antiques. Deluxe rooms are just larger versions of superior. Bathrooms are large and well appointed. Hotel dining is in a high-peaked Lanna Thai-style space and the food is excellent The pool is inviting.

6 Rachamankha 9 (on the western edge of the Old City), T. Phra Singh Chiang Mai 50200. © **05390-4111.** Fax 05390-4114. www.rachamankha.com. 23 units. 13,000B ($317) superior double; 17,000B ($415) deluxe double; 22,000B ($537) suite. AE, MC, V. **Amenities:** Restaurant and bar; outdoor pool; tour desk; limited room service; massage; laundry service; dry cleaning. *In room:* A/C, satellite TV, minibar, fridge, coffeemaker, hair dryer, safe, IDD phone.

MODERATE

Tamarind Village ✦✦ Passing down a long, shaded lane lined with new-growth bamboo, follow meandering walkways among the whitewashed buildings of this stylish little hideaway in the heart of the Old City. It is hard to believe that you're in Chiang Mai (though you can still hear the traffic). Rooms at the Tamarind are marvels of concrete flatwork burnished to an almost shining glow and, complimented by straw mats and chic contemporary Thai furnishings, make for a pleasing minimalist feel (if you're a minimalist, that is). Bathrooms are spacious with large double doors connecting with vaulted ceiling guest rooms. There's an almost Mediterranean feel to the whole complex, with all of the arched, covered terra-cotta walks joining buildings in a village-style layout. Short of the fine pool and a dandy restaurant, amenities are sparse, but the staff is helpful and the atmosphere quite unique.

50/1 Ratchadamnoen Rd., Sriphom, Chiang Mai 50200 (a short walk toward the center of the Old City from Thapae Gate). © **05341-8896.** Fax 05341-8900. 40 units. 5,000B ($122) double; 6,000B ($146) deluxe. **Amenities:** Restaurant and bar; outdoor pool; tour desk; same-day laundry/dry cleaning. *In room:* A/C, satellite TV, minibar, fridge, hair dryer, IDD phone.

INEXPENSIVE

Gap's House Gap's House is tucked down a quiet lane just inside the city wall at Thapae. Long popular among budget travelers, the hotel atmosphere is calm with a leafy central garden area surrounding a large, teak, Lanna Thai pavilion. Rooms are in free-standing teak houses and feature woven rattan beds and small tiled bathrooms. Time is taking a toll on the room facilities here, so the rustic charm borders on just plain old, and management is rather indifferent, but it is a good atmospheric choice in the town center. Avoid the budget singles in a separate cement building.

3 Soi 4, Ratchadamnoen Rd., Chiang Mai 50000 (1 block west of Thapae Gate on left). © and fax **05327-8140.** 19 units. 400B–650B ($9.75–$16) double. MC, V. **Amenities:** Restaurant; cooking courses; laundry service. *In room:* A/C, no phone.

Montri Hotel ✦ *Value* The earliest address of note for foreigners in Chiang Mai, the Montri is still a convenient, inexpensive location just inside the Old City and across from Thapae Gate. Newly renovated rooms with built-in cabinets, valances, and new furniture are attractive, comfortable, and a very good value. Be sure to ask for a non-smoking room. Dark parquet floors are standard throughout, and bathrooms are shower-in-room style. *Ask for a back-facing room;* you'll get more peace and from higher floors can see Doi Suthep.

2–6 Ratchadamnoen Rd., Chiang Mai 50100 (just northwest across from Thapae Gate). ✆ **05321-1069.** Fax 05321-7416. www.norththaihotel.com/montri.html. 75 units. 700B–750B ($17–$18) double. MC, V. **Amenities:** Restaurant; tour desk; small business center; laundry service. *In room:* A/C, TV w/satellite programming, fridge, minibar, fridge.

S. P. Hotel   A cozy little courtyard hotel, something like a budget motel in the West, S. P. is a longtime favorite right in the heart of the busy backpacker area near the city center (just inside the moat). Hotel services are limited, but tidy carpeted rooms are convenient to the funky backpacker area and many services (restaurants, cooking schools, and massage) in the Old City. Nothing fancy.

7/1 Moon Muang Rd. Soi 7, Chiang Mai 50200. ✆ **05321-4522.** Fax 05322-3042. www.chiangmaisphotel.com. 40 units. 1,500B ($37). V, MC. **Amenities:** Restaurant; tour services; laundry. *In room:* A/C, TV, fridge, IDD phone.

Top North Guest House   South of Thapae and down one of the Old City's narrow lanes, laid-back Top North is comfortable and affordable. The small central pool is unique in this category and is a popular hangout for backpackers going upscale. There are many room standards. All have high ceilings, and the top category rooms (500B/$12) are large and clean with tile floors and large bathrooms with bathtubs. Time is not kind to budget hotels, though, and indeed some of the room furnishings look like they've gone a few rounds with an angry, caged ape. Rooms on the lower echelon vary in price and amenities (with or without air-conditioning or TV), but all have hot-water showers. Top North has a good tour operation, an Internet cafe on the premises, and shows DVDs in the bar in the evenings. Their sister property, **Top North Hotel,** is an old standby just south of the Thapae Gate within the Old City and offers a slightly higher class of rooms but seems to attract a rougher lot; good in a pinch though, call ✆ **05327-9623.**

15 Moon Muang Rd., Soi 2, Chiang Mai 50100. ✆ **05329-8900.** Fax 05327-8485. 90 units. 500B ($12) double with A/C; 300B ($7.30) double with fan. MC, V. **Amenities:** Restaurant; outdoor pool; bike and motorcycle rental; tour desk; Internet cafe; laundry service. *In room:* A/C, TV, no phone.

WESTSIDE/UNIVERSITY AREA
EXPENSIVE
The Amari Rincome Hotel ✦   This tranquil hotel complex is a favorite because of its elegant, yet traditional, Thai atmosphere. The public spaces are decorated with local handicrafts, and the professional staff wears intricately embroidered costumes. The large, balconied guest rooms are elaborately adorned with Burmese tapestries and carved wood accents in local style, and the bathrooms are plush. There is a gorgeous garden and pool area, the dining at their **La Gritta** (see "Dining," later) is great, and the hotel is located near some of the better upscale shopping and galleries in town. The staff is as professional as they come, will know your name from the moment you cross the threshold, and can help with any eventuality (tours, transport, etc.). A very comfortable choice.

1 Nimmanahaeminda Rd., off Huay Kaeo Rd., Chiang Mai 50200 (near Superhighway northwest of Old City). ✆ **05322-1130.** Fax 05322-1915. www.amari.com. 158 units. 4,300B–5,300B ($105–$129) double; from 10,500B ($256) suite. AE, DC, MC, V. **Amenities:** 3 restaurants; lounge; 2 outdoor pools; outdoor lighted tennis court; concierge; tour desk; limousine service; business center; shopping arcade; salon; 24-hr. room service; massage;

babysitting; same-day laundry service/dry cleaning; nonsmoking rooms; executive-level rooms. *In room:* A/C, TV w/satellite programming, minibar, fridge, hair dryer.

Chiang Mai Orchid 🎯 The Orchid has attractive facilities and friendly service and is located just next to the town's most popular hangout, Gad Suan Kaew Shopping Complex. Spacious, quiet rooms are large, familiar, and pleasantly decorated with local woodcarvings. The lobby and other public spaces are furnished with clusters of chic, low-slung rattan couches and chairs and decorated with flowers. They cover all the bases in amenities, from dining to car rental and a knowledgeable tour desk.

100–102 Huai Kaeo Rd., Chiang Mai 50200 (northwest of Old City, next door to Gad San Kaew/Central Shopping Complex). ✆ 05322-2099. Fax 05322-1625. www.chiangmaiorchid.com. 267 units. 2,800B–3,600B ($68–$88) double; from 9,200B ($224) suite. AE, DC, MC, V. **Amenities:** 3 restaurants; lounge and pub; outdoor pool; car-rental desk; fitness center; sauna; children's playground; tour desk; limited room service; massage; babysitting; same-day laundry service. *In room:* A/C, TV w/satellite programming, dataport, minibar, fridge.

INEXPENSIVE

The Village People were right, you can always "stay at the YMCA," and the budget rooms at Chiang Mai's **YMCA International Hotel** (11 Sermsuk Rd., Mengrairasmi; ✆ **05322-1819**) have attracted missionaries and budget travelers for years. The place is a bit run down these days, but rooms start at just 600B/$15 for a basic double.

3 Dining

Northern-style, called Lanna, Thai cooking is influenced by the Burmese and other ethnic minorities who live in the area. Among the most distinctive northern Thai dishes are *khao miao* (glutinous or sticky rice) often served in a knotted banana leaf, *sai-ua* (Chiang Mai sausage); *khao soi* (a spicy, curried broth with vegetables and glass noodles), as well as many other slightly sweet meat and fish curries. You may be relieved to know that chili peppers are used less than in other Thai regional cuisines.

The formal northern meal is called *khan toke,* referring to the custom of sharing a variety of main courses (eaten with the hands) with guests seated around *khan toke* (low, lacquered teak tables). Most of the restaurants that serve in the *khan toke* style combine a dance performance with the meal. These are covered in the nightlife section later in this chapter.

Chiang Mai is also blessed with good street food and markets. **Anusarn Market** on the corner of Sri Dornchai and Chang Klan roads near the Night Bazaar is a good place for authentic local food. Also try **Somphet Market** on the northeast corner of the city, a good place to pick up snacks like fried bananas or sticky-rice desserts in the daytime or have a good meal for little in the evening when the area bustles with locals and young backpackers alike.

Chiang Mai folks take their *khao soi,* a Chiang Mai specialty of noodles and curry broth, pretty seriously. The best is to be had in **Fa Ham,** an area about 1km (⅔ mile) north of central Nawarat Bridge on Charoenrat Road along the east bank of the Mae Ping River. There are a number of open-air places serving the delicacy for just 20B (50¢), and tasty skewers of chicken and pork satay. Always packed. Say "Fa Ham" to a tuk-tuk driver and pay him with lunch.

NEAR THE PING RIVER
EXPENSIVE
Le Coq d'Or 🎯🎯 FRENCH In a romantic English country house setting, Le Coq d'Or is second to none in Chiang Mai for excellent atmosphere, food, presentation,

and service. Professional waiters serve from a list of imported beef, lamb, and fish pre-pared in French and Continental styles. Presentation is done on fine white linen and real china. Try the chateaubriand, rare, with a delicate gravy and béarnaise on the side. The poached Norwegian salmon is a fine, light choice. For starters, try the foie gras, or a unique salmon tartar wrapped in smoked filet and served with toast, a sour cream and horseradish sauce, and capers. They have a nice wine list to complement your meal. Don't wait for a special occasion.

68/1 Koh Klang Rd. (5-min. drive south of the Sheraton, following the river). ✆ 05328-2024. Reservations recom-mended for weekend dinner. Main courses 320B–1,800B ($7.80–$44). AE, DC, MC, V. Daily 12–2pm and 6–10:30pm.

MODERATE

The Gallery ఴ THAI   Built in 1892 and one of the oldest original wooden struc-tures in Chiang Mai, The Gallery is the most tranquil and romantic of the choice riverside restaurants on the eastern bank of the Mae Ping river. This was the auspicious spot where, during her visit to Chiang Mai in 1996, Hillary Clinton chose to set sail her Krathong, a small decorated bamboo float, as is custom during the Loy Krathong Festival. If the good senator gives her recommendation, it has to be good, right? And it is. I started with a small appetizer plate of "build-your-own" dishes that all required more origami skill than I could muster, but it was fun trying to figure it out with the help of a giggling staff. As an entree, the *hor mok curry*, a popular Chiang Mai dish, was delicious. Candlelight, soft Thai music, and a great view of the river and the city's twinkling lights beyond top off a lovely evening of dining. Bring someone special.

25–29 Charoenrat Rd. (east side of river, north of Nawarat Bridge). ✆ 05324-8601. Main courses 90B–340B ($2.20–$8.30). AE, MC, V. Daily noon–1am.

Good View ఴ THAI/INTERNATIONAL   The newest of the big three along the river (see "The Gallery" and "The Riverside," above and below), this place has a more carefree vibe than either. It is noisy when the live band revs-up, and this is where lots of young Thai people come to have *sanook* (fun), so it is always busy, which is either charming or "too much," depending on the individual. The food is good, especially the Thai portion of the menu. I shared a cover-the-table spread of various Thai cur-ries, stir-fries, and a few whole fish. The picture menu makes it easy and the staff is friendly as all get-out. Come early, around 6pm, enjoy a good, quiet meal overlook-ing the river at sunset, and then stick around for the band and party on.

13 Charoenrat Rd. (east side of river, north of Nawarat Bridge). ✆ 05324-1866. Main courses 70B–250B ($1.70–$6.10). MC, V. Daily 5pm–1:30am.

The House ఴఴ PACIFIC RIM FUSION   This cozy bistro sets a new standard in Chiang Mai: a picturesque, refined dining spot catering to the discerning. Set in an old colonial style edifice that's been lovingly restored and decorated in placid pale tones, the dining room has large windows draped in light curtains and the seating is in rattan chairs around linen-draped tables. An internationally trained and experi-enced Thai chef works his magic on a constantly evolving menu of regionally-influ-enced classical dishes, a medley of grilled items, and imported steaks, lamb, and seafood when available fresh. A good stop for a light lunch when touring or an evening of fine dining. Lots of good candlelit corners to bring that someone special. Also see their boutique next door, Ginger.

199 Moonmuang Rd. (just north of Thapae gate on the inside edge of the city moat). ✆ 05341-9011. Main courses 210B–450B ($5.10–$11). Daily 11am–2:30pm and 6–10:30pm.

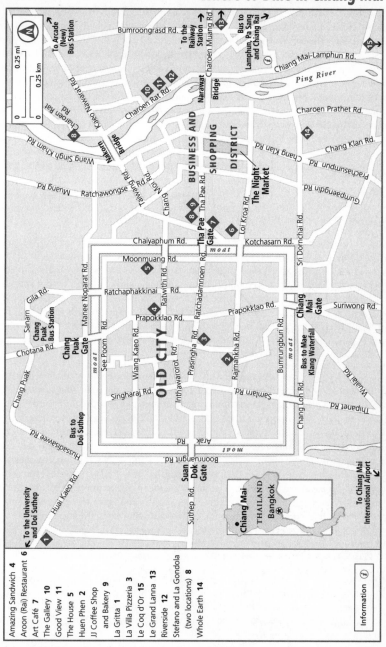

Amazing Sandwich **4**
Aroon (Rai) Restaurant **6**
Art Café **7**
The Gallery **10**
Good View **11**
The House **5**
Huen Phen **2**
JJ Coffee Shop
and Bakery **9**
La Gritta **1**
La Villa Pizzeria **3**
Le Coq d'Or **15**
Le Grand Lanna **13**
Riverside **12**
Stefano and La Gondola
(two locations) **8**
Whole Earth **14**

Information ⓘ

Le Grand Lanna ⍟⍟ THAI   Chiang Mai's most opulent traditional Thai restaurant is indeed grand, but serves meals for very little. Just a 10-minute ride east of town toward the town of Sankampaeng, the restaurant is on a large parcel of lush terrain that promises a first class resort in the coming years. Atmosphere is your choice of deluxe Lanna Thai pavilions, various open deck areas, pond-side courtyards among banyan trees, or in their theme rooms, either French or Chinese. Come for a drink, at least, if you're shopping in Sankampaeng. Evening meals are all candlelight, outdoor torches, and the dulcet tones of traditional music. Presentation is a unique mix of heavy pottery, oversize goblets, and local materials like whole pineapple and coconut husk for sauces and curries. For a main course, try the white fish with lemon coleslaw marinade. Curries are delicious and varied. I had *gaeng hang lan mop,* a dry, fiery red curry that will knock your socks off, which is best mollified by a sweet mango chutney. Don't pass up their signature *sai uai,* or Chiang Mai spicy sausage. Follow up with great homemade ice cream with local litchi or taro flavors.

51/4 Chiang Mai-Sankampaeng Rd., Moo 1 T. Tasala, Chiang Mai 50000 (4km/2½ miles east on Charoen Muang near the end of shopper's row, follow signs and turn right/south down a small lane). ℂ **05326-2569.** Main courses 100B–250B ($2.45–$6.10). AE, MC, V. Daily 11am–10pm.

The Riverside ⍟⍟ THAI/INTERNATIONAL   Casual and cool is what Riverside is all about. It is a tavern with riverside terrace views—make sure you get there before the dinner rush so you get your pick of tables. There's live music, from blues to soft rock, great Thai and Western food (including burgers), and a full bar. Even if you just stop by for a beer, it is a convivial place that always has a jolly crowd of travelers, locals, and expatriates. Riverside also operates a dining cruise at 8pm (boards at 7:15pm) for just 70B ($1.70) per person (drinks and dining a la carte). Call ahead.

9–11 Charoenrat Rd. (east side of river, north of Nawarat Bridge). ℂ **05324-3239.** Main courses 65B–330B ($1.60–$8.05). AE, MC, V. Daily 10am–2am.

Stefano and La Gondola ⍟⍟ ITALIAN   Stefano is in the heart of town in a colorful alley off of Thapae Road, and La Gondola overlooks the Mae Ping River. Under the same owner and management, both take you on a pleasant culinary journey from Lanna to Italy. Both spots are lively and popular and offer an extensive catalogue of Northern Italian cuisine, from steaks to excellent pastas. I had a fusilli with cream sauce and big local mushrooms: a delicious departure from curry, rice, and noodles. Portions are big, the wine list is deep, and there are good daily set menus and specials. La Gondola is a collection of glass aviaries and balcony seating, certainly the more romantic choice of the two. Stefano, at the city center at the terminus of Thapae Road, has its own more raucous allure with brash decor and a younger clientele, mostly backpackers who dust off the credit card for a bit of a splash-out after long journeys.

Stefano is at 2/102 Chang Mai Kao Rd. (just to the east of Thapae Gate). ℂ **05387-4189.** La Gondola is at Rimping Condo 201/6 Charoenrat Rd. (on the east side of Mae Ping River and north of town near Nakhon Ping Bridge). ℂ **05330-6483.** Main courses 90B–300B ($2.20–$7.30). AE, MC, V. Daily 11am–11pm.

The Whole Earth ⍟ VEGETARIAN/INDIAN   Featuring Asian foods, mostly Indian and Thai, prepared with light, fresh ingredients in healthy, creative ways, this 25-year-old Chiang Mai institution is a real find. The restaurant is set in a traditional Lanna Thai pavilion and has an indoor air-conditioned nonsmoking section, and a long open-air veranda with views of the gardens. The menu is extensive, and everything is good. I enjoyed a spicy house vegetarian curry with tofu wrapped in seaweed. Finish off with a fresh mango lassi.

88 Sridonchai Rd., A. Muang. ℂ **05328-2463.** Main course 180B–350B ($4.40–$8.55). Daily 11am–10pm.

AROUND THE OLD CITY
INEXPENSIVE

The Amazing Sandwich WESTERN   The recipe is simple here: create your own "amazing" sandwich for eat-in or take-away. The palette for your masterwork is a list of ingredients, and you simply tick the appropriate boxes to your heart's delight. Even if you are more interested in local food, this is a great place if you want to pack a lunch for any self-guided day trips. So popular among expats and travelers, The Amazing Sandwich now has three locations in Chiang Mai.

252/3 Phra Pokklao Rd. (near the Thai Airways office). ⓒ 05321-8846. 20/2 Huay Kaew Rd. (across from Central Kad Suan Kaew) and 70/9 Chaiyaphum Rd. (across the moat, east side of the city, from the Somphet Market). www.amazingsandwich.com. Main courses 60B–85B ($1.45–$2.10). No credit cards. Mon–Sat 9am–6pm. Sun 11am–2pm.

Aroon (Rai) Restaurant 🍴🍴 NORTHERN THAI   For authentic northern food, adventurous eaters should try this nondescript garden restaurant. Their *khao soi,* filled with egg noodles and crisp-fried chicken bits and sprinkled with dried fried noodles, is spicy and coconut-sweet at the same time. Chiang Mai sausages are served sliced over steamed rice; puffed-up fried pork rinds are the traditional, cholesterol-lover's accompaniment. Dishes are all made to order in an open kitchen, so you can point to things that interest you, including the myriad fried insects and frogs, for which this place is famous. They've added a new attraction—prepackaged spices and recipes for make-it-yourself back at home.

45 Kotchasarn Rd. (2 blocks south of Thapae Gate, outside Old City). ⓒ 05327-6947. Main courses 20B–60B (50¢–$1.45). No credit cards. Daily 9am–10pm.

Art Café INTERNATIONAL   This cheery corner cafe has black-and-white tile floors and cozy booths with picture windows overlooking the busy terminus of Thapae Road: a good spot for people-watching, a rest from city touring, or to pick up free maps and city guides and meet other travelers. I enjoyed a delicious, thin-crust pizza. The menu is ambitious and offers good, familiar fare, from steaks and the aforementioned pizzas to Mexican dishes, meatloaf, cake, and coffee.

291 Thapae Rd. (just opposite Thapae Gate). ⓒ 05320-6365. Main courses 50B–260B ($1.20–$6.35). MC, V. Daily 8am–11pm.

Huen Phen THAI   Just a short walk south and west of Wat Phra Sing, Huen Phen is a good, authentic local choice when temple touring. They have an English menu, but I recommend peeking in the open kitchen and seeing what looks good to you. It is a pretty limited menu, though. They, of course, have *kao soi,* Chiang Mai's famed noodle stew, but try the specialty: Khanom Jeen Namngeua, a beef stew in a hearty broth. It'll keep you warm when those storms come blowing in off of Doi Suthep. One small dining room has air-conditioning. You can't beat the prices here.

112 Rachamankha Rd. ⓒ 05381-4548. Main courses 15B–50B (35¢–$1.20). Cash only. Daily 9am–12:30am.

JJ Coffee Shop and Bakery 🍴🍴 INTERNATIONAL   A Thai-styled diner, JJ's reminds me of an American Denny's, and is in fact a local chain with three locations. Each air-conditioned restaurant has spotless tables and booths and big windows facing the street. The extensive menu includes excellent sandwiches and burgers, good fries, and all things familiar, and the wait staff has personality and can even be a bit caustic and cynical, a comfortable familiarity for the true diner aficionado. Breakfasts are tops and reasonably priced, with tasty baked goods. The Thapae Road branch has a sandwich and salad bar in the evenings—a rare find in Thailand. There's a second branch at the Chiang Inn Plaza off the Night Bazaar, and a third across the river at 129 Lampoon Road.

Thapae Gate, Chiang Mai. © 05323-4007. Main courses 40B–220B ($1–$5.40). V. Daily 6:30am–10:30pm.

La Villa Pizzeria ITALIAN   La Villa is part of a friendly, Italian-run guesthouse, the kind of place where lots of laughter and the occasional "*Ciao, bambina!*" can be heard. Light apps like imported prosciutto and sardines are a treat, and main courses include *fegato alla veneziana* (beef liver fried with onions and butter) and tasty pastas. Wood-fired thin-crust pizzas with authentic tomato sauce and vegetable or meat toppings are light and delicious.

Pensione La Villa, 145 Ratchadamnoen Rd. (west of Propokklao Rd., on left). © 05327-7403. Main courses 80B–200B ($1.95–$4.90). No credit cards. Daily 11am–11pm.

WESTSIDE/HUAI KAEO ROAD

La Gritta ⊛ ITALIAN   Come for their fine lunch or dinner buffets or order from an extensive menu of a la carte entrees ranging from osso buco to home-made pasta. La Gritta is in an elegant Thai-style pavilion adjoining the Amari Hotel to the west of town. The dining room is a feast for the eyes in rich, carved teak, and candlelight conspires with a sultry live jazz band to make for a delightful evening. Authentic Italian dishes include fresh pasta done to order at a pasta station, and a great wine list compliments any entree. A fine meal.

At the Amari Rincome Hotel, 1 Nimmanahaeminda Rd. © 05322-1915. Main courses 190B–520B ($4.65–$12.70); buffet lunch 280B ($6.85); buffet dinner 350B ($8.55). AE, MC, V. Daily 11:30am–2pm and 6:30–10pm.

SNACKS & CAFES

Kalare Food & Shopping Center, 89/2 Chang Klan Road, on the corner of Soi 6, behind the bazaar (© 05327-2067; call for hours), is where you'll find a small food court next to the nightly Thai culture show (buy coupons at a booth and then pick what you want from vendors).

   Bake and Bite is on a small side-street to the south of Thapae Gate (6/1 Kotchasarn Rd. Soi 1; © 05328-5185) and has tasty baked goods, fine bread, and good coffee. (Open Mon–Sat 7am–6pm and Sun 7am–3pm.)

   The Kafe (127-129 Moon Muang Rd.; © 05321-2717; call for hours) is just north of Thapae Gate and a good traveler's crossroads where you can pick up good information, have a great meal of Thai or basic Western food, and throw back a few cold ones.

   Mike's Original (© 01497-1026) serves hot-dogs, burgers, and fries a la an open-air 1950s American hotdog stand. Just north of Thapae Road (and the Amore hotel) on the east edge of the Old City, the storefront is open from 8am until 3am and is a popular stop for a proper drunken feed.

4 Exploring Cultural Chiang Mai

THE WATS

Chiang Mai has more than 700 temples, the largest concentration outside of Bangkok, and unique little sites are around every corner. In 1 very full day you can hit the highlights in Old Chiang Mai if you go by tuk-tuk.

√ **Wat Chedi Luang** ⊛⊛⊛   Because this temple is near the Thapae Gate, most visitors begin their sightseeing here, where there are two *wats* of interest. This complex,

Chiang Mai Attractions

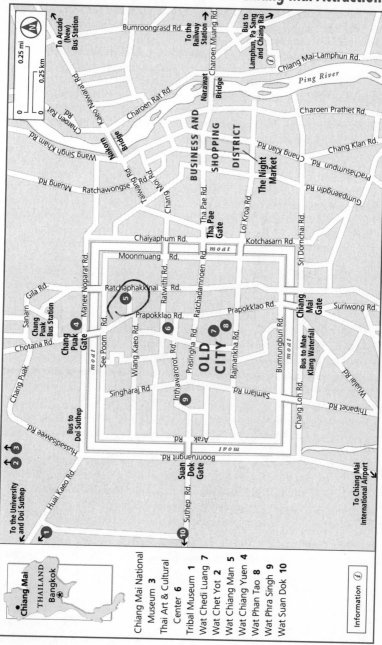

Chiang Mai National Museum **3**
Thai Art & Cultural Center **6**
Tribal Museum **1**
Wat Chedi Luang **7**
Wat Chet Yot **2**
Wat Chiang Man **5**
Wat Chiang Yuen **4**
Wat Phan Tao **8**
Wat Phra Singh **9**
Wat Suan Dok **10**

Information ⓘ

which briefly housed the Emerald Buddha now at Bangkok's Wat Phra Kaeo, dates from 1411 when the original *chedi* was built by King Saen Muang Ma. The already-massive edifice was expanded to 84m (280 ft.) in height in the mid-1400s, only to be ruined by a severe earthquake in 1545, just 11 years before Chiang Mai fell to the Burmese. (It was never rebuilt.) A Buddha still graces its exterior, and it is not unusual to spot a saffron-robed monk bowing to it as he circles the *chedi*.

Wat Phan Tao, also on the grounds, has a wooden *wihaan* (Spirit House) and *bot* (central shrine in a Buddhist temple), reclining Buddha, and fine carving on the eaves and door. After leaving the temple, walk around to the monks' quarters on the side, taking in the traditional teak northern architecture and delightful landscaping.

Propokklao Rd. south of Ratchadamnoen Rd. Suggested donation 20B (50¢). Daily 6am–5pm.

Wat Chet Yot 𝕽𝕽 Also called Wat Maha Photharam, Wat Chet Yot is one of the central city's most elegant sites. The *chedi* was built during the reign of King Tilokkarat in the late 15th century (his remains are in one of the smaller *chedis*), and in 1477, the World Sangkayana convened here to revise the doctrines of the Buddha.

The unusual design of the main rectangular *chedi* with seven peaks was copied from the Maha Bodhi Temple in Bodhgaya, India, where the Buddha first achieved enlightenment. The temple also has architectural elements of Burmese, Chinese Yuan, and Ming influence. The extraordinary proportions, the angelic, levitating *devata* figures carved into the base of the *chedi,* and the juxtaposition of the other buildings make Wat Chet Yot (Seven Spires) a masterpiece.

The Lanna-style Buddha hidden in the center was sculpted in the mid–15th century; a door inside the niche containing the Buddha leads to the roof on which rests the **Phra Kaen Chan (Sandalwood Buddha).** There is a nice vista from up top, but only men are allowed to ascend the stairs.

Superhighway near the Chiang Mai National Museum (north of the intersection of Nimanhemin and Huai Kaeo rds., about 1km/⅔ mile, on the left). Suggested donation 20B (50¢). Daily 6am–5pm.

Wat Chiang Man Thought to be Chiang Mai's oldest *wat,* it was built during the 14th century by King Mengrai, the founder of Chiang Mai, on the spot where he first camped. Like many of the *wats* in Chiang Mai, this complex reflects many architectural styles. Some of the structures are pure Lanna. Others show influences from as far away as Sri Lanka; notice the typical row of elephant supports. Wat Chiang Man is most famous for its two Buddhas: Phra Sritang Khamani (a miniature crystal image also known as the **White Emerald Buddha**) and the marble **Phra Sri-la Buddha.** Unfortunately, the *wihaan* that safeguards these religious sculptures is almost always closed.

North of the intersection of Nimanhemin and Huai Kaeo rds., about 1km (⅔ mile), on the left.

Wat Phra Singh 𝕽𝕽𝕽 This compound was built during the zenith of Chiang Mai's power, and is one of the more venerated shrines in the city. It is still the site of many important religious ceremonies, particularly during the Songkran Festival. More than 700 monks study here, and you will probably find them especially friendly and curious.

King Phayu, of Mengrai lineage, built the *chedis* (mounds) in 1345, principally to house the cremated remains of King Kamfu, his father. As you enter the grounds, head to the right toward the 14th-century library. Notice the graceful carving and the characteristic roofline with four separate elevations. The sculptural *devata* (Buddhist spirits) figures, in both dancing and meditative poses, are thought to have been made

Monk Chat

What do you say to these tonsured men in orange robes one sees piously padding barefoot around Thailand? The answer is: "Hello. How are you?" Monks, especially seniors, deserve a special level of respect, of course, but are quite human, and the best way to find out is to stop by Mahachulalongkorn University (adjoining Wat Suan Dok, east of town on Suthep Road, see above). Every Monday, Wednesday, and Friday, from 5 to 7pm, they welcome foreign visitors for "monk chat," a classroom venue of small, informal discussion groups where visitors and monks come to connect, share culture, and learn about Buddhism from novices eager to explain and, of course, practice their English. It is mostly informal discussion about one's own country or sports (young novices are nuts about David Beckham and English Premiere League Football), but the more senior monks can give you some insights into Buddhist practice and monastic life. They also meet for meditation groups and retreats. Call © **05327-8967** or e-mail thaimonkchat@yahoo.com.

---

during King Muang Kaeo's reign in the early 16th century. They decorate a stone base designed to keep the fragile *saa* (mulberry bark) manuscripts elevated from flooding and vermin.

On the other side of the temple complex is the 200-year-old **Lai Kham (Gilded Hall) Wihaan,** housing the venerated image of the Phra Singh or **Sighing Buddha,** brought to the site by King Muang Ma in 1400. The original Buddha's head was stolen in 1922, but the reproduction in its place doesn't diminish the homage paid to this figure during Songkran. Inside are frescoes illustrating the stories of Sang Thong (the Golden Prince of the Conchshell) and Suwannahong. These images convey a great deal about the religious, civil, and military life of 19th-century Chiang Mai during King Mahotraprathet's reign.

Samlarn and Ratchadamnoen rds. Suggested donation 20B (50¢). Daily 6am–5pm.

Wat Suan Dok   This complex is special less for its architecture (the buildings, though monumental, are undistinguished) than for its contemplative spirit and pleasant surroundings.

The temple was built amid the pleasure gardens of the 14th-century Lanna Thai monarch, King Ku Na. Unlike most of Chiang Mai's other *wats* (more tourist sights than working temples and schools), Wat Suan Dok houses quite a few monks who seem to have isolated themselves from the distractions of the outside world.

Among the main attractions in the complex are the bot, with a very impressive **Chiang Saen Buddha** (one of the largest bronzes in the north) dating from 1504 and some garish murals; the *chedi,* built to hold a relic of the Buddha; and a royal cemetery with some splendid shrines.

There is an informal "monk chat" here each week (see the sidebar, above).

Suthep Rd. (from the Old City, take the Suan Dok Gate and continue 1.6km/1 mile west). Suggested donation 20B (50¢). Daily 6am–5pm

MUSEUMS

Chiang Mai City Arts and Cultural Center   In the building adjacent to the Three Kings Monument in the heart of the Old City, this new museum houses a permanent exhibit that walks visitors through a tour of pre-history to the present. Another section houses short-term local exhibits of all types. More for school trips than anything, a popular choice for those looking for some historical insights.

Propokklao Rd., Chiang Mai 50200. ℃ 05321-7793. Admission 90B ($2.20). Tues–Sun 9am–5pm.

Chiang Mai National Museum   While its collection of historical treasures is not nearly as extensive as that of Bangkok's National Museum, this quick stop does provide something of a historical overview of the region, the city, and historical highlights. The Lanna Kingdom, Tai people, and hill-tribes are highlighted in simple displays with English explanations.

Just off the superhighway northwest of the Old City near Wat Chet Yot. ℃ 05322-1308. Admission 30B (75¢). Tues–Sun 8:30am–4pm.

The Chiang Mai Zoo *(Kids)*   One of Chiang Mai's most popular attractions for locals is the pair of pandas, **Chung Chung and Liu Hui,** the stars of Chiang Mai's tiny zoo. A good one for the kids.

100 Huai Kaeo Rd. (The zoo is west of town on the road to Doi Suthep.) ℃ 05322-1179. 30B (75¢) admission. Daily 9am–5pm.

The Tribal Museum   Formerly part of Chiang Mai University's Tribal Research Institute, this small exhibit showcases the cultures and daily lives of the hill-tribe people of Thailand's north. It is recommended as a good introductory course for those who plan to visit many northern villages.

In Rachamankha Park on Chotana Road. ℃ 05322-1933. Free admission. Weekdays 9am–4pm.

CULTURAL PURSUITS
THAI COOKING SCHOOL
If you love Thai food and want to learn how to make it, book into a class at the **Chiang Mai Cookery School** *(R)*, the oldest establishment of its kind in Chiang Mai. They have five 1-day courses, each designed to teach Thai cooking basics, but with a different menu (up to seven dishes) so you can attend as many days as you like and still gain quite a bit of skill. You'll have hands-on training, and a lot of fun. Classes start at 10am lasting until 4pm, and cost 990B ($24) for the day. Contact them at their main office at 1–3 Moonmuang Road, opposite the Thapae Gate (℃ **05320-6388;** fax 05320-6387; www.thaicookeryschool.com).

MASSAGE SCHOOL
The **Thai massage schools** in Bangkok and Phuket teach the southern style of Thai massage, which places pressure on muscles to make them tender and relaxed. Northern-style Thai massage is something closer to yoga, where your muscles are stretched and elongated to enhance flexibility and relaxation. There are a number of schools in Chiang Mai, and many are no more than small storefronts where, for very little, you'll get individual instruction of varying quality. It is best to go with a more established school: **International Training Massage,** or **ITM,** has popular courses (conducted in English) for anyone from first-timers to experts. Each 5-day course is 2,400B ($59). Contact them at 17/7 Morakot Road, Hah Yaek Santitham (℃ **05321-8632;** fax 05322-4197).

MEDITATION
The **Northern Insight Meditation Center** at Wat Rampoeng (Kan Klongchon-prathan Rd.) is a well-respected center for learning Vipassana meditation. "Are you

ready?" is all they'll ask you upon arrival, because the daily schedule means rising early and many hours spent in concentration. The monks, nuns, and lay volunteers who run the center invite only men and women who bring a certain resolve or at least a willingness to stay for 10 days (though the 26-day course is highly recommended). Volumes have been written about the practice of Vipassana, but the main idea is to develop mindfulness and observe one's body, mind, and emotions, to eventually gain "insight" and to see things as they are, without delusion. Come prepared to "peel the onion" of the ego. Participants are assigned very spartan private rooms, are asked to wear white, loose-fitting togs (available at the temple store), and basic meals are served at 6 and 10:30am only (no evening meal). Rules are drawn from the monastic precept and are thus rigid. There is no charge for the course, but you will be asked to make a contribution to the temple of whatever amount you see fit. Retreats are ongoing, but they try to consolidate first-timer's start dates for orientation purposes. Call ahead (3 weeks advance preferred) at © 05327-8620. The temple also welcomes day visitors, and it might be a good idea for those considering a course to have a look. Located on a rural road south and west of town (past the airport), the temple is best reached by tuk-tuk, *songtao,* or rented motorbike. (Wat Rampoeng, Tambol Suthep, Amphur Muang, Chiang Mai, 50200; © 05327-8620; www.watrampoeng.org.).

5 Chiang Mai Activities

TOURS, TREKS & OUTDOOR ADVENTURE

There are so many tour groups in Chiang Mai that specialize in trekking, that it can seem impossible to choose. Below are some of the better options and most reputable operators for each type of trip. Most of the smaller companies have offices along Thapae Road, in guesthouses, and all along the major tourist routes in the city, and are always happy to talk about what's on offer. Many adventure tours mix mountain biking or motorcycling with tribal village tours. See "Tours & Trekking in the Far North," in chapter 11, for more information on the hill-tribes themselves, descriptions of what to expect on tours, how to select a good operator, and how to prepare for your trip.

For **jungle trekking,** there are a number of small outfits arranging trips from Chiang Mai, but **Contact Travel** (www.activethailand.com) is in a category all its own. Combining treks and village stays with multi-sport adventures by jeep, bicycle, and kayak, the folks at Contact can cater a tour to any needs and price range. They also offer more traditional itineraries with elephant treks, visits to caves, and relaxing bamboo raft river trips, and their English-speaking guides are the best. Treks from Chiang Mai stop at Lisu, Lahu, and Karen villages. A 2-day/1-night trip is 1,300B ($32) per person if you join their regular tour, or 3,900B ($95) per person for a private group trip. A 3-day/2-night trip, which takes you to a greater variety of villages, is 4,300B ($105) per person if you join their regular tour; 5,900B ($144) per person for a private group. For an additional 1,000B ($24) per person you can hire a porter to wrestle your bags along. Their office in Chiang Mai is 73/7 Charoen Prathet Rd. (© 05327-7178; fax 05327-9505).

Small operators that cater to the low-end backpacker market offer trips for as little as 500B ($12) per day. This usually means being in a large group, and care and feeding comes at a lower standard, but that's budget-trekking, and there is a kind of fun in commiseration over post-trek beers. If you want to keep it budget, try the following few companies:

Top North Tours (41 Moonmuang Rd., Chiang Mai; © 05320-8788) offers a range of short tours featuring trekking, bamboo rafting, and elephant riding. They've been around for a while and are a reliable budget choice, but that means big groups and basic services.

Queen Bee Travel Service (5 Moonmuang Rd., Chiang Mai; © 05327-5525) has a whole range of budget trekking services and local cultural tours.

BOAT TRIPS

Within the city, a **long-tail boat trip** along the Mae Ping River is a fun diversion. Head for the boat landing of **Mae Ping River Cruise Co.** (133 Charoen Prathet Rd.; © 05327-4822) at **Wat Chaimongkol** on Charoen Prathet Road, opposite Alliance Française). A tour lasts about 2 hours and costs 400B ($9.75) with fruit and drinks included. Starting in the city center, you'll get good views of old teak riverside mansions behind which arise the tall skyline of this developing burg, while on the outskirts of town, villages offer scenes of more suburban and rural living.

ELEPHANT RIDING

One of Thailand's greatest treasures, the domesticated Asian elephant has worked alongside men since the early history of Siam, and these gentle giants are an important symbol of the kingdom. Elephant training culture is strongest in parts of Isan (the northeast) and the far north.

In and around Chiang Mai alone there are a grand total of 14 elephant camps that try to cash-in on the popularity of these gentle giants, so you're sure to pet a pachyderm somewhere on your travels. Elephant camps can be pretty unpleasant, though, so be warned: at shoddier camps, elephants are drugged to keep them placid, and many animals are kept in poor conditions and often abused in the name of entertainment. Choose your elephant camp wisely. By far the best way to interact with the animals is a visit to the **Young Elephant Training Center** in Lampang (see the Lampang section in "Side Trips from Chiang Mai," later in this chapter). In and around the immediate Chiang Mai area, though, you have your pick of day trips. Just north of town in the Mae Rim Valley you'll find a number of camps offering packaged programs (all similar) that are fun, especially for kids. Most day-tours include a few hours of hill trekking with groups of three or four in a basket on elephant-back, which is followed by ox-cart rides to "primitive" villages set up for tourists, and even bamboo rafting back to camp. Of the many, I recommend **Maetamann Elephant Camp** (535 Rimtai, Mae Rim, Chiang Mai 50180; © 05329-7060).

MOUNTAIN BIKING

Out in the fresh air in the hills outside of town you get a slower, closer look at nature, sights, and people. Many small trekking companies and travel agents offer day trips, but we recommend the folks at **Contact Travel** (73/7 Charoen Prathet Rd.; © 05327-7178) for their 1-day excursions just north of town or for multiday adventures in the region. Day trips start at 1,500B ($37).

OTHER ACTIVITIES

Chiang Mai has a few noteworthy **extreme sports** venues. In fact, it is getting hard to go to a tourist area these days without seeing a big roadside crane and having your bravado challenged by posters and flyers around town offering a bungee jump; Chiang Mai is no exception, and the crane is located north of town in Mae Rim. Just call © 05329-8442 if you have the guts, dude. Rock climbers will be happy to have a place to practice at **The Peak** (28/2 Changklan Rd.; © **05382-0776-8**), a challenging man-made rock wall just at the back of the Chiang Inn Plaza near the Night Bazaar. Single climbs cost 150B ($3.65), and hourly rates are available. They also arrange trips for climbing the real rocks in the surrounding hills.

Ultra-light aircraft flights have come to Chiang Mai. A small but very organized and safe operation, **Chiang Mai Sky Adventures,** has a private airstrip north of the city in Doisaket. A 15-minute flight, more or less like a piggy-back ride on the pilot's shoulders, costs just 1,500B ($37) and takes you on a great loop out over a large damn and reservoir and past a spectacular hilltop temple. Unforgettable! They also do flight instruction and certification. Contact Mr. Chaimongkol at © **05386-8460** (www. skyadventures.info).

HITTING THE LINKS

Golf is the activity du jour in Chiang Mai, especially among the many Western retirees and vacationing Thais. All courses below are open to the public and offer equipment rental. Call ahead to reserve a tee-time.

- **Chiang Mai Green Valley Country Club,** located in Mae Rim, 20 minutes north of town on Rte. 107, 183/2 Chotana Rd., (© **05329-8249;** fax 05327-9386), is in excellent condition with flat greens and fairways that slope toward the Ping River (greens fees: weekdays 1,200B/$29; weekends 2,000B/$49).

- **Lanna Golf Club,** on Chotana Road, 2km (1¼ miles) north of the Old City (© **05322-1911;** fax 05322-1743), is a challenging, wooded 27 holes and a local favorite with great views of Doi Suthep Mountain (greens fees: weekdays 600B/$15; weekends 800B/$20).

- **Chiang Mai–Lamphun Country Club,** Baan Thi Road, 10km (6 miles) east of Sankampaeng (© **05324-8397;** fax 05324-8937), located in a valley to the east, is a fine 18-hole course (greens fees: weekdays 1,400/$34; weekends 1,800B/$44).

SPAS & MASSAGE

The spa industry is taking off all over Thailand and Chiang Mai is no exception. There are a few fine, full-service spas in and around town, and treatments come with a price but are worth it. Many hotels offer massage and beauty treatments, but some new "spa" areas are no more than converted guest rooms with subdued lighting and over-priced services. You can pay a fraction of the cost for the same treatment at one of the many small storefront massage parlors in and around any tourist area of the city. *Note to the lads:* Choosing a "traditional" massage in a place with street-facing windows is just that; while others, with back room oil massage, signify "extra" services, so be sure you know what you're getting into.

There are a few very fine day-spas in and around Chiang Mai:

The Four Seasons Resort (Mae Rim–Samoeng Old Rd., Mae Rim; © **05329-8181**) has some of the finest spa facilities in Thailand and, though it comes with a high price tag, the quality and service is over-the-top.

The spa at the **Mandarin Oriental Dhara Dhevi** (51/4 Chiang Mai–Sankampaeng Road, 5 km east of town; © 05388-8888) offers ultra-luxurious treatments.

Oasis Spa is new on the scene, and offers a unique standard of luxury and service at its two locations in town: at 102 Sirimangkalajarn Rd. and at 4 Samlan Rd. To make a reservation call © **05381-5000.** A luxury campus of private spa villas, Oasis Spa is just that, an oasis, and the roster of treatments is long. They offer free pick up and drop off from hotels in Chiang Mai.

Baan Sabai (on 17/7 Charoen Prathet Rd.; ✆ **05328-5204;** or 216 Moo 9, San Pee Sua; ✆ **05385-4775**) is the bridge between the expensive services of a five-star spa and the affordable street-side places. You get the best of both worlds here: a stylish facility and escape for a few hours at affordable rates, at either their convenient in-town hideaway (near the Night Bazaar) or the more spacious "Village" just northeast of town.

Let's Relax, located in Chiang Mai Pavilion (on the second floor above McDonald's, 145/27 Changklan Rd.; ✆ **05381-8498**) and with another location in the basement of Chiang Inn Plaza (100/1 Changklan Rd.; ✆ **05381-8198**), has affordable massages and is perfect for a quick rest and recharge when shopping the Night Bazaar area.

6 Shopping

If you plan to shop in Thailand, save your money for Chiang Mai. Quality craft pieces and hand-made, traditional items still sell for very little, and large outlets for fine antiques and high-end goods abound in and around the city. Many shoppers pick up an affordable new piece of luggage to tote their finds home and, if you find that huge standing Buddha or oversized Thai divan you've been searching for, all shops can arrange shipping, or look for the **UPS** office in the basement of the Night Bazaar (Changklan Rd.; ✆ **05382-0222;** 7am–10pm).

WHAT TO BUY

Thailand has a rich tradition of handicrafts, developing over centuries of combining local materials, indigenous technology, and skills from Chinese and Indian merchants. Drawing on such ancient technologies and the abundance of hardwoods, precious metals, and stones, raw materials for fabrics and dyes, bamboo, and clay, modern craftsmen have refined traditional techniques and now cater their wares to the modern market. Below is a breakdown of what you might find:

Tribal weaving and craftwork is for sale everywhere in the Lanna capital and you can come away with some unique finds.

Hill-tribe embroidery crafts have been modified over the years, so you can find their delicate styles on anything from chic shoulder bags and backpacks to authentic hill-tribe skirts and shirts.

The hill-tribes' **hand-woven textiles** are rich in texture and natural tones, colored with plants from local sources. Cool, handsomely simple, hill-tribe designs are in ready-made cotton clothing and can be found anywhere for a song.

Some hill-tribe groups are known for their fine **silver jewelry**—necklaces, bangles, and earrings—in unusual traditional ethnic designs or more ordinary Western styles. For all hill-tribe handicrafts, the best place to shop is at the Night Bazaar, and, in fact, you are sure to meet hill-tribe women, covered in bangles and carrying arm-loads of their goods, wandering the market. These ladies are pretty persistent even if you express no interest.

Fine silver works are synonymous with Chiang Mai. Early smiths are believed to have immigrated from Burma with the coming of Kublai Khan, and skills have been passed from generation to generation. While silver is not a local resource, early raw materials were acquired from coins brought by traders. Traditional bowls feature intricate raised floral designs—the deeper the imprint, the higher quality the silver (some up to 80%). Jewelry items are crafted in delicate filigree designs in styles copied by many Western manufacturers. Many families set up shop along Wulai Road, south of the Old City, while outlets on Sankampaeng Road carry large selections.

Gemstones can be good buys here, but like in the rest of Thailand you must be very careful of jewelry scams, overcharging, or the old bait-and-switch. Don't do any shopping with a tuk-tuk driver as a guide. Try the Sankampaeng area.

Thai silk is big in Chiang Mai and outlets on Sankampaeng Road have a larger quantity to choose from.

The early royals commissioned carvers to produce wood furnishings for use in palaces, thrones, temple doors and adornments, carriages, pavilions, howdahs for riding elephant back, and royal barges. The excellent quality of hardwoods in Thailand's forests allowed these items to be adorned with grand and intricate wood carvings. The skills survived, and talented craftspeople still produce furniture, boxes, and all varieties of gift items imaginable. **Wood carving** today is perhaps more influenced by foreign preferences, and most pieces are mass-produced.

Lacquer skills came from China with early migrants. Sap is applied in layers to wooden, clay, or bamboo items and can be carved, colored, and sometimes inlayed with mother-of-pearl for a very elegant finished product. Today it is acknowledged as a traditional Chiang Mai craft, having been perfected over centuries by the Khoen people who live in communities outside the city. **Lacquerware** vases, boxes, bangles, and traditional items are lightweight gifts, practical for carrying home. Larger tiered boxes and furnishings can be shipped.

Celadon pottery is rough finished and elegantly simple in tones of the palest gray-greens. The distinctive color of the glaze comes from a mixture of local clay and wood ash. Chiang Mai has some of the largest and best celadon factories in the country. The best places to purchase celadon are out on Sankampaeng Road, in the large factory outlets.

Authentic antiques are few in the tourist areas of Chiang Mai. As anywhere, the rule is "buyer beware," and if you do get your hands on the genuine article (some shops offer certificates of authenticity) you may have a problem getting it home (see "Export of Antiques or Art in Thailand," in chapter 2).

MARKETS

For many, the **Night Bazaar** is the city's premier attraction, and hours spent wandering amid the cacophony of hawkers, noisy haggling, and all manner of traditional goods and electronic tchotchkes are part and parcel of the city's charms.

Located on north-to-south running Chang Klan Road between Thapae and Loy Kroh roads, the shopping starts around 6pm each night and slows down at about 11pm. The actual Night Bazaar is a modern, antiseptic, three-story building, but the indoor and outdoor market extends south to Sri Dornchai Road and far beyond. Many shops and stalls remain open throughout the day and evening too, especially along Chang Klan Road.

The stalls have grandiose names, like Harrods (with the familiar logo), and most carry Bangkok-produced counterfeits of international name-brand clothing, watches, and luggage. There are thousands of pirated audiotapes and videodiscs, acres of burnished brown "bone" objects, masks, wood carvings, opium pipes, opium weights, you name it.

Inside the Night Bazaar building itself are primarily modern, mass-manufactured goods like low-cost Thai fashions and souvenirs. You'll also find lots of interesting tribal bric-a-brac sold in stalls or by wandering hill-tribe saleswomen. The top floor has booths selling locally produced handicrafts, some "antiques," and decorative arts.

The **Anusarn Night Market,** down Charoen Prathet Road, south of Suriwongse Road, carries more hill-tribe goods in authentic traditional styles.

The **Warowot Market** on Changmoi and Wichayanon roads opens every morning at 7am and stays open until 4pm. This central indoor market is the city's largest. Produce, colorful fruits, spices, and food products jam the ground floor. On the second floor, things are calmer, with dozens of vendors selling cheap cotton sportswear, Thai-made shoes, and some hill-tribe handicrafts and garments. Fun and inexpensive.

SHOPPING IN THE CITY CENTER & OLD TOWN

Small shops and boutiques line the areas around the market and Old Town, luring visitors from the many nearby hotels with unique finds. A short wander in any direction is sure to bring you past a tantalizing shop door. Try: **Ginger** (39/1 Loy Kroh; ✆ 05320-6842), which carries designer clothing and jewelry. Sleek designs steal the show at **Living Space** (276–278 Thapae Rd.; ✆ 05387-4299), with its collection of fine home furnishing and celadon and lacquerware decorative items. **Nova Collection** (201 Thapae Rd.; ✆ 05327-3058) carries a unique line of decorative jewelry in contemporary styles with Asian influences. They make custom pieces and even offer courses in metalwork and jewelry making. **Princess Jewelry** (41 Changklan Rd., near Chiang Inn Plaza; ✆ 05327-3648) offers customized and ready-made jewelry and good personalized service. **Mengrai Kilns** (79/2 Araks Rd., Soi Samlarn 6; ✆ 05327-2063), is in the southwest corner of the old city and specializes in fine celadon and decorative items. There are lots of silk dealers and tailors in and around town of varying quality. Try **City Silk** (336 Thapae Rd., 1 block east of the gate; ✆ 05323-4388) among the many for good selection and affordable tailoring.

WEST SIDE OF THE OLD CITY

At 95 Nimanhemin Rd. across from Amari Rincome Hotel, **Nantawan Arcade** has many notable antiques, crafts, and curio shops that make for fun browsing. Try: **Gong Dee Gallery** (✆ 05321-5768), which has an extensive collection of gifts and original artwork, the most comprehensive collection in Nantawan Arcade. **Design One** (✆ 05335-7204) has an extensive collection of designer teak furnishings. **Tawan Decor** (✆ 05389-4941) features a host of unique knickknacks and furnishings. These are but a few.

WULAI ROAD

Here's the home of Chiang Mai's cottage silver crafts industry, located just south of Chiang Mai Gate. **Siam Silverware** (5 Wua Lai Rd., Soi 3; ✆ 05327-9013) tops the list of many offering fine crafted jewelry and silverwork.

SANKAMPAENG ROAD

Shopaholics will be thrilled by the many outlets along the Chiang Mai–Sankampaeng Road (Rte. 1006). Rent your own wheels or hop on the white songtao that follow this busy road due east of town. After several kilometers you'll reach the many shops, showrooms, and factories extending along a 9km (5½ miles) strip. Talk to any concierge or travel agent about a full or half-day shopping tour. *Important:* Do not arrange a day of shopping with a tuk-tuk driver, as they will collect a commission and drive up the price of your purchases.

The many shops along Sankampaeng feature anything from lacquerware to ready-made clothes, silver to celadon pottery. Among the many, try: **Laitong Lacquerware** (140/1–2 Moo 3, Chiang Mai-Sankampaeng Rd.; ✆ 05333-11178), which carries a host of fine lacquer gifts (among other items). Some of the smaller items, like jewelry boxes, can be quite lightweight, so you won't have to lug 10 tons home with you. *Saa* paper cards (with pressed flowers), stationery, notebooks, and gifts are not only top quality, but they're perfect for light travelers. **Mesa U&P Company's** selection is quite good. Head for 78–78/3 Moo 10, Sankampaeng Road (© **05333-1141**).

For larger housewares and objets d'art, **Pa Ker Yaw Basket & Textile,** 136/1 Moo 2, Sankampaeng Road (© **05333-8512**), deals in fabulous baskets of all shapes and sizes, featuring weaving techniques from hill-tribes in Thailand, Burma, Laos, and Vietnam. For a large selection of celadon ware in traditional Thai designs, **Baan Celadon,** 7 Moo 3, Chiang Mai–Sankampaeng Road (© **05333-8288**); and **Siam Celadon,** 38 moo 13, Chiang Mai–Sankampaeng Road (© **05333-1526**), have the best selections. Smooth and lustrous vases, jars, bowls, and decorative objects spring to life from local hardwoods, you'd almost think these turned wood products were porcelain. **Aroon Colorware,** 67 Moo 4, Baan Sankaokaepgang (© **05388-1605**), turns out mod gifts—very unique.

When you're ready for a little fashion, let **Jolie Femme Thai Silk,** 8/3 Sankampaeng Rd. (© **05324-7222**), hit the spot. Weaving traditional silks in rich colors, they fashion much of their stock into modern ready-to-wear creations. There's also **Shinawatra Thai Silk,** 145/1–2 Sankampaeng Rd. (© **05333-8058**). An outlet of the high-quality Bangkok chain, rivaled only by Jim Thompson's in Bangkok, Shinawatra sells hand-woven and hand-painted silk and cotton by the meter, a wide range of men's and women's conservative silk fashions, cushions, drapery, ties, and dozens of silk accessories.

VILLAGES

Many of the handicrafts you find in town and out at Sankampaeng Road are the fine work of local villagers around Chiang Mai. They welcome visitors to their villages to see their traditional craft techniques that have been handed down through generations. Purchase these items directly from the source, sometimes at a savings.

East of Chiang Mai, **Sri-pun-krua** (near the railway station) specializes in bamboo products and lacquerware. Near Sankampaeng Road, the village of **Tohn Pao** (about 8km/5 miles outside the city) produces *saa* paper products; **Bor Sarng** (10km/6 miles outside the city) is a nationally renowned center for painted paper umbrellas and fans; and **Baan Tohn** (13km/21 miles outside the city) makes fine wood carvings, in addition to umbrellas. Just to the south, **Pa-bong** (about 6km/3¾ miles down Superhighway 11) manufactures furnishings and household items from bamboo.

South of the city, **Muang Goong** (along Hwy. 108) is a center for clay pottery; **Roi-Jaan** (about 8km/5 miles along the same highway) weaves cottons, dying them in natural colors extracted from natural products; while **Tha-wai** (14km/8½ miles south) has families that craft carved wood antique reproductions.

7 Chiang Mai After Dark

Most folks will spend at least 1 evening at the Night Bazaar and, if you get tired and hungry along the way, you'll want to stop at **Kalare Food & Shopping Center,** 89/2 Chang Klan Rd., on the corner of Soi 6, behind the bazaar (© **05327-2067**). Free nightly traditional Thai folk dance and musical performances grace an informal beer garden where shoppers stop for a drink or pick up inexpensive Chinese, Thai, and Indian food from stalls around. Just behind, local singer-guitarists play more modern selections. For an impromptu bar scene, duck into one of the back alleys behind the Night Bazaar mall that are lined with tiny bars.

For a more studied **cultural performance,** the **Old Chiang Mai Cultural Center,** 185/3 Wulai Rd. (© **05327-4093**), stages a good show at 7pm every night for 270B

($6.60), which includes dinner and the show. Live music accompanies female dancers in handsome costumes who perform traditional dances. In between sets, men dance with knives and swords. A *khan toke* dinner is served, and despite the crowds, the wait staff is attentive. Yes, it is touristy—busloads find their way here—but it is a good time. Call ahead, and they'll plan transportation from your hotel.

Most **discos and lounges,** located in major hotels, feature live music, whether it is a quiet piano bar or a rock pub featuring a Filipino band. **Good View** (13 Charoen-rat Rd.; ✆ 05324-1866) and **The Riverside** (9/11 Charoenrat Rd.; ✆ 05324-3239) are both popular restaurants along the Mae Ping River (see "Dining," earlier in this chapter) and feature live music after 8pm and on into the evening. Directly east of the Night Bazaar and in the large compound of the old Diamond Hotel, **River Bar** (33/11 Jarenprathat Rd.; ✆ 05320-6169) has live music nightly and is always full. The Amari Hotel's **La Gritta** (see "Dining," earlier in this chapter; 1 Nimmana-haeminda Rd.; ✆ 05322-1130) has a good jazz band every Saturday night. The small streets in and around Thapae as well as along Loy Kroh Road are the town's small red-light district with red-lit hostess clubs (with girls cooing "Where you go?" from the doorway), small massage storefronts, and lots of street-side bars.

The **Bubble Disco** in Pornping Tower (see "Accommodations," earlier in this chap-ter; 46 Charoen Prathet Rd.; ✆ 05327-0099), and **Crystal Cave Disco** at Empress Hotel, Chang Klan Road (✆ 05327-0240), are two popular haunts, but seem to take turns getting shut down. Pick up a copy of *Welcome to Chiang Mai & Chiang Rai* mag-azine at your hotel for listings of special events.

8 Side Trips from Chiang Mai

If you have time for only one day trip, Wat Phra That Doi Suthep, Chiang Mai's famed mountain and temple, is the best choice. If you have more time, make the jour-ney to Lamphun or to the Elephant Training Camp in Lampang.

WAT PHRA THAT DOI SUTHEP ✦✦✦

The jewel of Chiang Mai, Wat Phra That glistens in the sun on the slopes of Doi Suthep mountain. One of four royal *wats* in the north, at 1,000m (3,250 ft.), it occu-pies an extraordinary site with a cool refreshing climate, expansive views over the city, and the mountain's idyllic forests, waterfalls, and flowers.

In the 14th century, during the installation of a relic of the Buddha in Wat Suan Dok (in the Old City), the holy object split in two, with one part equaling the origi-nal size. A new *wat* was needed to honor the miracle. King Ku Na placed the new relic on a sacred white elephant and let it wander freely through the hills. The elephant climbed to the top of Doi Suthep, trumpeted three times, made three counterclock-wise circles, and knelt down, choosing the site for Wat Phra That.

The original *chedi* was built to a height of 8m (26½ ft.). Subsequent kings con-tributed to it, first by doubling the size, then by adding layers of gold and other orna-mentation to the exterior. The gilded-copper decorative umbrellas around the central *chedi* and the murals showing scenes from the Buddha's life are especially attractive.

Other structures were raised to bring greater honor to the Buddha and various patrons. The most remarkable is the steep 290-step naga (snake) staircase, added in 1557, leading up to the *wat*—one of the most dramatic approaches to a temple in all of Thailand. To shorten the 5-hour climb, the winding road was constructed in 1935 by thousands of volunteers under the direction of a local monk.

Visitors with exposed legs are offered a sarong at the entrance. Most Thai visitors come to make an offering—usually flowers, candles, incense, and small squares of gold leaf that are applied to a favored Buddha or to the exterior of a *chedi*—and to be blessed. Believers kneel down and touch their foreheads to the ground three times in worship. Some shake prayer sticks to learn their fortune.

Wat Phra That is open daily 7am to 5pm; come early or late to avoid the crowds; the suggested donation is 20B (50¢). To get there, take the minibus from Chang Puak (White Elephant) Gate on the north side of the Old City. The fare is 35B (85¢) going up and 25B (60¢) for the descent. The ride can get cool, so bring a sweater or jacket. The bus stops at the base of the *naga* staircase. If you'd rather not climb the 290 steps—a special part of the experience—there's a motorized gondola to the top for 5B (10¢). You can simplify matters by booking a half-day trip though any tour agency for 600B ($15), including a stop at Phuping Palace.

Phuping Palace (Doi Bua Ha) is the summer residence of Thailand's royal family, which is 4km (2½ miles) beyond Doi Suthep, 22km (14 miles) west of the Old City off Rte. 1004. When the royal family isn't present, visitors are allowed to enter and stroll its beautiful gardens. When it is open (check with the TAT), the hours are Friday to Sunday 8:30am to 4:30pm, and admission is free. You really have to dress conservatively for this one. Military guards at the gate act like the fashion police—tuck in your shirt, unroll your trousers, don't tie your sweater around your waist, and anything else they think is unacceptable for a royal palace. The Doi Suthep minibus continues to the Phuping Palace from Wat Phra That (see above).

LAMPHUN ⍟

The oldest continuously inhabited city in Thailand, just 26km (16 miles) south of Chiang Mai, Lamphun was founded in A.D. 663 by the Mon Queen Chammadevi as the capital of Nakon Hariphunchai. Throughout its long history, the Hariphunchai Kingdom, an offspring of the Mon Empire, was fought over, often conquered; yet it remained one of the powers of the north until King Mengrai established his capital in neighboring Chiang Mai.

The best way to get there is by car, taking the old highway Route 106 south to town. The Superhighway no. 11 runs parallel and east of it, but you'll miss the tall *yang* (rubber) trees, which shade the old highway until Sarapi, and the bushy yellow-flowered khilik (cassia) trees. Buses to Lamphun and Pasang leave from the **Chang Puak Bus Station** (© 05321-1586); the 45-minute ride costs 7B (15¢).

The town is legendary for its beautiful women. There are some historical *wats,* including excellent Dvaravati-style *chedis,* and a fine museum. Longan (lumyai) is a native fruit that resembles clusters of fuzzy brown grapes, which peel easily to yield luscious crisp white flesh. The trees can be recognized by their narrow, crooked trunks and large, droopy oval leaves. On the second weekend in August, Lamphun goes wild with its **Longan Festival,** with a parade of floats decorated only in longans and a beauty contest to select that year's Miss Longan. Lamphun and Pasang (to the south) are also popular with shoppers for their excellent cotton and silk weaving.

The highlight of Lamphun is **Wat Phra That Hariphunchai,** one of the most striking temples in all of Thailand. (Wat Phra That Doi Suthep was modeled after it.) The central *chedi,* in Chiang Saen style, is said to house a hair of the Buddha, and is more than 45m (150 ft.) high and dates from the 9th century, when it was built over a royal structure. The nine-tiered umbrella at the top contains 6,498.75 grams of gold, and the *chedi's* exterior is faced with bronze. Also of interest in the temple complex are an immense bronze gong (reputedly the largest in the world), and several *wihaan* (rebuilt in the 19th and 20th c.) containing Buddha images. According to legend, the Buddha visited a hill about 16km (10 miles) southeast of town, where he left his footprints; the site is marked by Wat Phra Bat Tak Pha. During the full-moon day in May, there's a ritual bathing for the Phra That.

The new **Hariphunchai National Museum,** Amphur Muang (© **05351-1186**), is across the street from Wat Phra That Hariphunchai's back entrance. It is worth a visit to see the many bronze and stucco religious works from the *wat.* The museum also contains a fine collection of Dvaravati- and Lanna-style votive and architectural objects. Open Wednesday to Sunday 9am to noon and 1 to 4pm; admission 30B (75¢).

Wat Chammadevi (Wat Kukut) is a large complex located less than 1km (⅔ mile) northwest of the city center. The highlights here are the late Dvaravati-style *chedis,* and Suwan Chang Kot and Ratana, built in the 8th and 10th centuries respectively, and modeled on those at Bodhgaya in India. The central one is remarkable for the 60 standing Buddhas that adorn its four corners. The *wat* itself was built by Khmer artisans for King Mahantayot around A.D. 755. The relics of his mother, Queen Chammadevi, are housed inside, but the gold-covered pagoda was stolen, earning this site its nickname Kukut (topless).

LAMPANG ⨞

The sprawling town of Lampang (originally called Khelang Nakhon) was once famous for its exclusive reliance on the horse and carriage for transportation, even after the "horseless carriage" came into fashion. These buggies can still be rented near the center of town next to the City Hall or arranged through any hotel for about 300B/$7.30 per hour (200B/$4.90 with *hard* bargaining), but they have to share the streets with noisy tuk-tuks and motorcycles, and the modern town offers little in the way of enchantment.

Lampang is graced with some of the finest Burmese temples in Thailand and supports the celebrated Young Elephant Training Camp nearby (see below). Because of the region's fine kilns, there are dozens of ceramics factories producing new and "antique" pottery. For visitor information, contact the **Lampang District Tourist Center,** Boonyawat Road, near the central clock tower (© **05421-8823**).

The easiest way to reach Lampang is by car, taking the old highway Route 106 south to Lamphun, then Superhighway no. 11 southeast for another 64km (40 miles). Buses to Lampang leave regularly though out the day from **Chiang Mai's Arcade Bus Terminal** (© **05324-2664**). The 2½-hour trip costs 60B ($1.45).

For a lunch break or an overnight sojourn, the **Wienglakor Hotel** (138/35 Phaholyothin Rd.; © **05431-6427**) is the best choice in town. Standard rooms start at 1,800B ($44) and are comfortable and clean with all the right amenities, and there's a nice pool and good dining choices in and around the formal lobby area. **Tipchang Hotel** (54/22 Tarkraonoi Rd.; © **05422-6501;** fax 05422-5362) comes a close second.

Lampang's *wats* are best toured by car or taxi. **Wat Phra Kaeo Don Tao** is on Tambon Wiang Nua, 12km (7 miles) southwest of the town center. For 32 years, this highly revered 18th-century Burmese temple housed the Emerald Buddha that's now in Bangkok's Wat Phra Kaeo. Legend has it that one day the prince of Chiang Mai decided to move the Emerald Buddha from Chiang Rai to Chiang Mai. His attendants traveled there with a royal elephant to transport the sacred icon. But when the elephant got to this spot, it refused to go on to Chiang Mai with its burden, and so a *wat* was built here to house the image. There's an impressive carved wooden chapel and Buddha; a 49m-high (162-ft.) pagoda houses a strand of the Buddha's hair. Poke around in the small Laan Thai Museum to the left of the entrance; it contains some fine woodwork and an old *phra wihaan* (Spirit House).

Wat Phra That Lampang Luang is on Tambon Lampang Luang, in Ko Kha, 18km (11 miles) south of the center of Lampang. This impressive complex is considered one of the finest examples of northern Thai architecture. If you mount the main steps toward the older temples, you'll see a site map, a distinguished wihaan (inspired by Wat Phra That Hariphunchai in Lamphun), and behind it to the west, a *chedi* with a fine seated Buddha. Go back to the parking area and cross through the lawn filled with contemporary, painted-plaster Chinese gods. Past the old, old Bodhi tree—whose stems are supported by dozens of bamboo poles and ribbons—you'll see signs for the Emerald Buddha House. The small Phra Kaeo Don Tao image wears a gold necklace and stands on a gold base; it is locked behind two separate sets of gates and is very difficult to see.

The **Young Elephant Training Center** (on the Lampang–Ngao Highway; ✆ 05422-9042) is 54km (33 miles) east of Lampang. It is not a tourist site, per se, and nothing like the pony-ride atmosphere of most elephant camps; instead, the focus at the Young Elephant Training Center is on the animals. Visitors here are not spectators, but participants in a hands-on seminar with these complex and intelligent creatures (be ready to get dirty and be up close with these jumbos). The elephants are not chained but roam free over the grounds and sleep al fresco in the jungle each night, coming to the central area at prescribed times for feeding and training sessions (watch out, because the animals come running to get treats like sugar-cane and bananas). One-day courses show participants the basics of being a mahout, or elephant trainer; first how to climb onto its back and, straddling the neck, to speak the extensive "language" of the elephants (a dialect of the Karen people) and command movement: there is no comparison (nor going back) to sitting in the usual bucket on elephant back at the average elephant camp. Knowledgeable Thai mahouts and a hearty group of expats share their passion for elephants with visitors, and their enthusiasm is infectious. They offer multiday treks (trekkers are assigned their own pachyderm for the journey) and home-stay programs of varying lengths. Many of the elephants are sent here to be rehabilitated after abuse in captivity, and there is an on-site veterinary hospital for elephants with debilitating injuries (many victims of land mines from neighboring Laos). Program costs begin at 1,500B ($37) for 1-day programs and go up to 5,000B ($122) for deluxe multiday treks. It is pricey for Thailand, but more than worth it. Call ahead for info and reservations. Day visitors are welcome and, if the timing is right, you may be able to hop on for a quick 50B ($1.20) ride with the help of a mahout.

DOI INTHANON NATIONAL PARK

Thailand's tallest mountain, **Doi Inthanon**—2,563m (8,408 ft.)—is 47km (29 miles) south of Chiang Mai. It crowns a 932 sq. km (360 sq. mile) national park filled with impressive waterfalls and wild orchids. Doi Inthanon Road climbs 48km (30 miles) to the summit. Along the way is the 30m-high (100-ft.) **Mae Klang Falls,** a popular picnic spot with food stands. Nearby **Pakan Na Falls** is less crowded because it requires a bit of climbing along a path to reach. At the top of the mountain, there's a fine view and two more falls, **Wachirathan** and **Siriphum,** both worth exploring. At the end of the park road you are at the highest point in Thailand. There is a small visitor's center and a short trail into a thick wooded area of mossy overhanging trees; called the

Michael Trail after one of the park's early naturalist researchers, the trail is a short but picturesque walk.

Admission to **Doi Inthanon National Park** is 200B ($4.90). It is open daily from sunrise to sunset. Camping is allowed in the park, but you must check with the TAT or the national park office to obtain permits, schedule information, and regulations.

The area is a popular day-trip destination for residents of Chiang Mai. Day trips organized by Chiang Mai tour companies will cost around 1,400B ($34) including lunch and a few other stops for sightseeing. Not a bad day trip by your own rented car; just take Route 108 south through San Pa Tong; continue south following signs to the national park. You can take a 13km (8-mile) side trip to Lamphun on Route 1015.

THE MAE SA VALLEY

The lovely Mae Sa Valley area, more developed than Doi Inthanon National Park, is about 20km (12 miles) northwest of Chiang Mai. A rash of condo construction and the sprouting of roadside billboards all indicate that Mae Sa Valley is being developed as a rural tourist resort, but it still has an unhurried feel. Current attractions include an elephant show (including rides), a snake show, bungee jumping, and a nature park, as well as orchid nurseries. Most of these attractions are packaged by Chiang Mai tour operators as a half-day trip costing 700B ($17).

CHIANG DAO

The town of Chiang Dao, 56km (35 miles) north of Chiang Mai, and its environs offer several small resort hotels and a few fun activities, but if you don't have a car, the easiest way to sightsee is by joining a day trip organized by Chiang Mai operators, which costs about 1,000B ($24) per person (half-day trips are also offered). The Young Elephants Training Camp in Chiang Dao is rather touristy and not as good as that in Lampang (see above in this section), but it is still a nice treat for kids. The adventure begins as you cross a rope bridge and walk through a forest to the camp. After the elephants bathe in the river (showering themselves and their mahouts) they demonstrate log hauling and log rolling. After the show, you can climb into a howdah and take a safari across the Ping River and through the forest to a Lisu village.

Sixteen kilometers (10 miles) north of the Young Elephants Training Camp is the **Chiang Dao Cave (Wat Tham Chiang Dao),** one of the area's more fascinating sites. Two caverns are illuminated by electric lights, and you can see a number of Buddha statues, including a 4m-long (13-ft.) reclining one. The row of five seated Buddhas in the first cavern is particularly impressive. The cave and two connected caverns extend over 10km (6 miles) into the mountain, but you'll have to hire a local guide with a lantern to explore the unlighted areas. It is open daily from 8:30am to 4:30pm. It can be included with any itinerary that brings you to the elephant camp, but you may have to request it specifically.

13

Touring the Northern Hills

North of Chiang Mai and its satellite cities, travelers enter a stunning mountainous region replete with opportunities for adventure. Rugged landscape, proximity to Myanmar (Burma) and Laos, and the diverse ethnic hill-tribe groups living here distinguish northern Thailand from the rest of the country.

Connected by highways that wind through forested mountains, descend into picturesque valleys, and pass through quaint farming villages, northern points are best explored overland, in a rented vehicle (with driver, if possible). There are lookout viewpoints along the way, and plenty of places to stop and eat, refuel, relax, and stay. Travelers choose from a number of routes: from Chiang Mai to Chiang Rai, north from Chiang Rai to the Burma/Laos/Thai border at the Golden Triangle, or the rugged area northwest of Chiang Mai known as the Mae Hong Son Loop. Any trip in the region means mountain scenery and the opportunity to visit with unique ethnic groups, and trekking by foot, Jeep, elephant back, or boat through the forested hill-tribe homelands—very popular.

1 The Mae Hong Son Loop

Seasoned travelers, given the option, never backtrack, and the "Loop" through the rugged hills north and west of Chiang Mai is gaining popularity for that very reason. Connecting the popular tourist destinations of Pai and Mae Hong Son, the circuit continues to out-of-the way Mae Sariang before returning to Chiang Mai. For all but the adventurous, going by tour or a hired car with driver is recommended, but a self-drive means freedom to take side trips and explore at one's own pace. Give yourself at least 4 days to do it, preferably more, staying 1 night at least in each town. The road, especially on the northernmost points, is serpentine and precipitous and calls for good driving skills; traffic is not too heavy, usually, but drivers must be on the alert for everything from water buffalo to slow-moving, overloaded, smoke-belching trucks and buses.

MAPS & INFORMATION

The most useful resource for a self-guided tour by car or motorbike is a map entitled *Mae Hong Son, The Loop* (published by the adventurous souls at The Golden Triangle Rider and priced at 175B/$4.25; www.gt-rider.com). The GT-Rider map gives exacting details of even the smallest dirt track as well as useful site-maps of each town. You can pick it up in any bookstore in Thailand. The TAT office in Chiang Mai or Mae Hong Son are also good resources for maps and advice on side-trips.

GETTING AROUND

By Car   This is certainly the best option for doing the circuit or even just touring the hills around Pai and Mae Hong Son. See the "Getting Around" section of the Chiang Mai section in chapter 12 for information on rental cars (Avis and Budget have offices at the airport). Travel agents and hotels can arrange a car with driver for about 1,500B ($37) per day, but budget rental agencies (see chapter 12) can go as low as 900B ($22).

By Motorcycle   An increasingly popular option, motorcycle travel around the Mae Hong Son Loop means less traffic than your average Thai byway, but the same warnings apply as anywhere: Wear a helmet, be defensive, and remember that there's not much between you and the road. This route is recommended only for the experienced rider. A variety of good rental bikes are available in Chiang Mai. See the "Getting Around" section in "Chiang Mai," chapter 12, for info.

By Minivan   Travel agents in Chiang Mai can arrange group tours.

By Bus   Regular buses ply the winding tracks between all towns on the loop (Chiang Mai, Pai, Mae Hong Son, and Mae Sariang), but bus travelers are limited in their exploration of the countryside.

2 Pai ⍟

831km (515 miles) NW of Bangkok; 135km (84 miles) NW of Chiang Mai

Halfway between Chiang Mai and Mae Hong Son, the mountain road makes a winding descent into a large green valley carpeted with rice paddies and fruit groves. Mountains rise on all sides, and on warm afternoons, butterflies flit along the streets. Here you'll find a village called Pai, named after the river that runs through the valley. Pai is a speck of a place with main roads (all four of them) littered with homegrown guesthouses, laid-back restaurants and bars, local trekking companies, and small souvenir shops.

The Pai River itself is one of the main attractions here. Outfitters organize rafting adventures on some pretty raucous rapids from July to January. Trekking is also popular, with 2- and 3-day treks to Karen, Lahu, and Lisu villages. The adventurous can find a local map for self-guided hikes to nearby waterfalls and caves, but quite a few wayfarers just lounge in town living simply and enjoying the nightlife. Many local business owners are foreigners or bohemian Thais who come here for a better life than in busy Bangkok or Chiang Mai. The town is a bit too laid back for some, but many are drawn to the languid rhythms of this peaceful spot. In Pai, every day is a lazy Sunday.

Note: Pai was hit with devastating flash floods in September of 2005. Flash flooding and a wall of water flattened the central market, and the overflowing Pai River claimed a few riverside bungalows. Over 20, mostly ethnic hill-tribe people, went missing.

ESSENTIALS
GETTING THERE

By Bus   Five buses a day leave for Pai from Chiang Mai (trip time: 4 hr.; 60B/$1.50). Five buses daily connect Pai and Mae Hong Son (trip time: 4 hr.; 60B/$1.50). The **Chiang Mai Arcade Bus Terminal** is on Kaew Nawarat Road, northeast of the old city across the Ping River (© **05324-2664**). The **bus terminal in Mae Hong Son** is on Khunlumprapas Road (the main street), 2 blocks north of the main intersection. All buses drop off and pick up at this "bus terminal" (more like a vacant lot).

By Minivan   Frequent minivans (called "Rot Too") make connections between Chiang Mai, Pai, and Mae Hong Son for 150B ($3.65) for each leg. Contact any storefront travel agent for details.

By Car   The scenic route is long, with steep, winding roads that make for some very pretty rural scenery: Take Rte. 107 north from Chiang Mai, then Rte. 1095 northwest to Pai.

Touring the Northern Hills

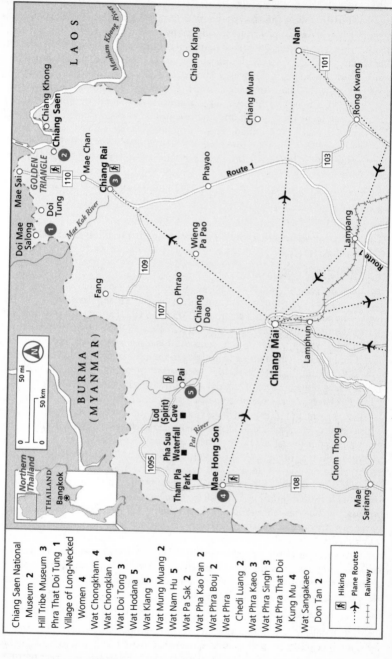

Chiang Saen National
  Museum **2**
Hill Tribe Museum **2**
Phra That Doi Tung **1**
Village of Long-Necked
  Women **4**
Wat Chongkham **4**
Wat Chongklan **4**
Wat Doi Tong **3**
Wat Hodana **5**
Wat Klang **5**
Wat Mung Muang **2**
Wat Nam Hu **5**
Wat Pa Sak **2**
Wat Pha Kao Pan **2**
Wat Phra Bouj **2**
Wat Phra
  Chedi Luang **2**
Wat Phra Kaeo **3**
Wat Phra Singh **3**
Wat Phra That Doi
  Kung Mu **4**
Wat Sangakaeo
  Don Tan **2**

Hiking
Plane Routes
Railway

ORIENTATION & GETTING AROUND

You won't find a tourist information booth in Pai, but restaurateurs, bungalow owners, and fellow travelers aplenty are usually happy to share their knowledge and experience. Most guesthouses and restaurants offer photocopy maps of town and the surrounding areas. Tiny Pai consists of four streets. Route 1095, or the Pai–Mae Hong Son Highway (colloquially known as Khetkelang Rd.), runs parallel to Rangsiyanon Road, which is the main commercial street. Chaisongkram and Raddamrang roads run perpendicular, and many guesthouses and restaurants are in or around this central grid (with many more guesthouses in the surrounding countryside). You can walk the town in 5 minutes. Mountain bikes and motorcycles are available at guesthouses or shops along the main streets for about 50B ($1.20) and 200B ($4.90) respectively. **Rent a motorcycle,** the best choice to go exploring the hills around Pai, at **Aya Service** (22/1 Moo 3, Chaisongkram Rd.; ℂ 05369-9940); 100cc scooters start at just 80B/$1.95 for 24 hours, and 250cc motocross numbers go for as low as 250B/$6.10.

FAST FACTS

There is one **bank** in Pai, on Rangsiyanon Road just next to Charlie House, with an ATM and money-changing services. There are a number of Internet cafes along central Chaisongkram Road.

TREKKING & ADVENTURE

Small trekking companies, operated by locals, are at every guesthouse and all along the main streets. It is hard to choose from the many, but **Duang Trekking** (at Duang Guesthouse across from the bus terminal; ℂ 05369-9101) has a good reputation. Also look for **Outdoor Explorer** (15 Chaisongkram Rd.; ℂ 05369-9815; www.outdoor explorer.info), which is new on the scene and has a strong eco-tour and educational focus. Group treks go for 3 days and 2 nights to Lisu, Karen, Tai Yai, and Lahu villages in the hills around Pai for 1,500B ($37) per person (some trips include bamboo rafting). Trekking offices can tailor any trek or provide private guides according to need.

The **Pai River** is really the most exciting attraction going. Overnight **rafting** trips take you through some exciting rapids as well as more scenic lazy spots, through canyons walled with prehistoric fossilized lime and shell, as well as a **wildlife sanctuary.** A pioneer of the rafting business here, long-time resident Guy Gorias runs **Thai Adventure Rafting** (Rangsiyanon Rd. in the town center; ℂ 05369-9111). There are regular trips from July to January. Two-day adventures begin and end in the town of Pai at a cost of 2,200B ($54) per person. There are many imitators in town, but Thai Adventure is the best outfit by far, with high safety standards and quality equipment, and now a good base-camp on a hill above town in Pai (ask about affordable rooms for rent). They can also make the necessary arrangements for pick-up and drop-off in Mae Hong Son.

You can also do **elephant trekking** out of Pai. There are a number of hourly, all-day, and multiday programs to choose from, and there are a number of elephant camps on the ridge overlooking town; the best is **Thom's Pai Elephant Camp** (5/3 Moo 4, Rangsiyanon Rd.; ℂ 05369-9286).

THINGS TO SEE & DO

There's little in the way of tour sites in Pai (most people come to put their feet up), but it is a great place to stroll along country lanes or even rent a motorbike and buzz around the countryside. There are a few small temples: **Wat Klang** is next to the bus station and has several small pagodas surrounding a central *stupa,* and **Wat Hodana** and **Wat Nam Hu** are west of Route 1095: Nam Hu is known for its Chiang Saen–era Buddha, whose hollow head is filled with holy water. There's a waterfall about 7km (4⅓ miles) west of town past the two *wats,* and a **hot spring** about 7km (4⅓ miles) to the east, past the Pai High School.

Tiny Pai boasts quite a few traditional massage places. The best option is **Mr. Jan's Herbal Sauna and Massage,** where you'll get a Burmese-style massage, which is much kinder and gentler than the rigorous Thai style. Ask around for directions to Mr. Jan's. It is on a narrow *soi* off Chaisongkram Road.

WHERE TO STAY

You won't find a big hotel in Pai yet (a relief for many), but there are loads of guest-houses. Starting at 100B ($2.45) you have your choice of some pretty rough little dives, but there are a few comfortable options for people on any budget.

MODERATE

Belle Villa *Finds* This collection of new, luxury bungalows along a quiet, rural stretch of the Pai River has no rival anywhere along the Mae Hong Son Loop. Large, clean bungalow rooms have contemporary conveniences like digital safes and cable TV without sacrificing the rustic charm of thatched roof and bamboo walls. The bathrooms are resplendent affairs in carefully molded concrete that is dyed a bright yellow and burnished to a sheen. Spacious shower areas are surrounded by small rock gardens and have windows with views to the river. The restaurant is a cozy open-air affair overlooking a small pool and the riverside beyond. You'll be swatting 'skeeters like anywhere in Pai, but the peace, quiet, scenery, and friendly service of this burgeoning little gem are unique.

113 Moo 6, Tumol Viengtai, Pai Mae Hong Son, 58130 (down a small *soi* off the Mae Hong Son Road, 2km/1¼ miles north of Pai). www.bellevillaresort.com. ① **05369-8226**. Fax 05369-8228. 2,943B ($72) double/low season; 4,708B ($115) double/high season. MC, V. **Amenities:** Restaurant; outdoor pool; tour desk; shuttle service; laundry. *In room:* A/C, satellite TV, minibar, fridge, coffeemaker, hairdryer, safe.

Pai River Corner Having lost its budget riverside bungalows to the flash floods in 2005 (no injuries), Pai River Corner is left with only its finest rooms set in two-story, four-unit blocks. Interiors are lavish, with colored textured concrete and lots of local flare. Unique are their two oversized suite rooms, one with an indoor Jacuzzi the size of a duck pond. They have a cozy riverside perch for drinks and dining, and the location is the best in town.

94 Moo 3, Viengtai, Pai, Maehongson 58130. ① **05369-9049**. Fax 05369-9049. www.pairivercorner.com. 9 units. 3,000B ($73) standard double; 4,000B–6,000B ($98–$146) suite. **Amenities:** Restaurant and bar; tour desk; car and motorbike rentals; massage; laundry. *In room:* A/C, phone.

Rim Pai Cottages Simple "cottages" indeed, this unassuming cluster of bungalows occupies some of the best real-estate in the center of Pai Town proper. You'll find lit-tle in the way of luxury, but lots of character in rooms that range from tiny, airless sheds to spacious rustic pavilions on stilts with small balconies and riverside views. Set apart from the rougher budget accommodations by virtue of its airy campus and good location (in town and on the river), Rim Pai has only a few choice amenities: a wel-coming restaurant pavilion and a helpful tour desk.

99 Moo 3, Viengtai, Pai, Mae Hong Son 58130 (right in town at riverside). ① **05369-9133**. Fax 05369-9234. www.rim paicottage.com. 37 units. 600B–1,200B ($15–$29) fan bungalow; 1,200B–4,500B ($29–$110) A/C Bungalow-villas. MC, V. **Amenities:** Restaurant; tour desk; car and motorbike rentals; massage; laundry. *In room:* Fan, no phone.

INEXPENSIVE

Thapai Spa Camping   Located on the banks of the river just a 10-minute drive outside the town, this rustic resort was built to take advantage of the small hot springs nearby. The highlight of this place—the public mineral baths—let you enjoy a healthy mineral soak. Boiling water is piped in and mixed with cool water in various pools (in the actual springs you can boil an egg). Bathing areas with adjoining showers are scattered about the garden. Rooms vary: some are motel-style and plain, others feature fine rock masonry and have large, open-air bathrooms with mineral water showers. It is a popular getaway for large Thai groups and families; a raucous, communal atmosphere pervades.

Chiang Mai reservation office: 58/1 Patanachangpuak Rd., Muang, Chiang Mai (located 6km/3¾ miles from Pai on the way towards Chiang Mai. Look for the sign at the turnoff along Rte. 1095). ℂ 05321-8583. Fax 05321-9610. 20 units. 600B–1,200B ($15–$29) double. No credit cards. **Amenities:** Restaurant; mineral water pool and spa; herbal sauna; bike rental; tour desk; massage; laundry service. *In room:* A/C, no phone.

The proverbial "Cheap Charlies" will be at home in little **Charlie's House** in the middle of town (9 Rangsiyanon Rd.; ℂ **05369-9039**), with basic fan rooms from 200B/$4.90 or A/C units from 400B/$9.75. Charlie's son just built a fancy new restaurant out front.

WHERE TO DINE

Little Pai plays host to a few expat restaurants and bars as well as a whole range of street-side dining. Below are the stars.

Baan Benjarong ✺ THAI   Overlooking mountain rice paddies from this friendly and casual open-air restaurant, choose from a poster-sized menu of delicious Thai dishes. Any of the many hearty stir-fries and spicy soups will do the trick (bring your group after trekking). Try the savory curry made with paddy crabs dipped in a sweet and sour sauce, and do not pass up the *tam long krop,* a unique dish of crispy, deep-fried gourd. Ask for a recommendation and enjoy.

179 Moo 8 (adjacent to Be-bop Bar). ℂ **05369-8010**. Main courses 70B–110B ($1.70–$2.70). Cash only. Daily 10:30am–3pm and 5pm–10pm.

Baan Pai THAI   Right in the center of town is a good choice for authentic Thai at streetside in an open-air Thai house, a good place for people-watching. A good English menu offers up any manner of Thai dish. Everything is good.

7 Moo Rangsiyanon Rd. (around the corner from the bus station). ℂ **05369-9912**. Main courses 80B–200B/ $1.95–$4.90. Daily 8am–11pm.

The most popular spot in town is **Be-bop,** a bar, restaurant, and late-night hangout on the far southern end of town (a 15-min. walk down Khet Klang opposite the Tourist Police); there's an excellent house band, and a young party crowd keeps the place hopping late into the night (about 1am). Live music starts at 9:30pm.

BETWEEN PAI & MAE HONG SON

Either as a day trip from Pai or as a stop on the way to Mae Hong Son, the best little detour going is the **Lod** or **Spirit Cave** off Route 1095 (about 30km/18½ miles NW of Pai on Rte. 1095 in the town of Soppong, then about 8km/5 miles north of the highway). This large, awe-inspiring cave is filled with colorful stalagmites and stalactites, and small caverns will keep you exploring for hours. The cavern was discovered in the 1960s to be filled with **antique pottery** dating from the Ban Chiang culture. There are three caves. The first chamber is a dynamic grotto and the second contains a prehistoric cave painting of a deer (which, unfortunately, has been largely blurred from curious fingers). The third cavern contains **prehistoric coffins** shaped like canoes. A guide to all three caves costs 100B ($2.45), lantern rental included. Be sure to take the canoe ride to the third cave (the ferryman will hit you up for an extra 200B/$4.90, depending on his mood) where, especially in the late afternoon and evening, you can see clouds of bats and swallows vying for space in the high craggy ceiling of the most dynamic cave (and the boat ride is fun, too). Pay another tithe to get back by boat or you can follow the clear jungle path a few clicks back to the parking lot. Bring your own flashlight for self-exploration as well.

There are lots of little guesthouses along the road near the entrance to the Spirit Caves in Soppong; the best is friendly **Little Eden Guesthouse** (295 Moo 1, T. Soppong; ✆ 05361-7054; www.littleeden-guesthouse.com). They have basic bungalows around a postage-stamp pool, as well as a very unique rustic suite overlooking the river (400B–1,200B/$9.75–$29).

As the road curves south heading into Mae Hong Son, **Tham Pla Park** (17km/10½ miles north of Mae Hong Son on Rte. 1095) is a small landscaped park leading up to the entrance of Tham Pla, or fish cave. It is a small grotto crowded with carp (legend says there are 10,000 of them) that mysteriously prefer the cave to the nearby streams. You can buy fish food in the parking lot (10B/25¢ per packet), but the fish don't eat it. Have a look—it is meant to be good luck (also a good leg stretch after the long drive). The grotto, once unsuccessfully explored by Thai Navy divers, is said to be several meters deep and to extend for miles.

Ten kilometers (6 miles) away in the Tham Pla Park interior is the huge **Pha Sua Waterfall,** which tumbles over limestone cliffs in seven cataracts. The water is at its most powerful after the rainy season, in August and September. The Meo hill-tribe village of Mae Sou Yaa is beyond the park on a road suitable for Jeeps, just a few kilometers from the Burmese border.

3 Mae Hong Son

924km (573 miles) NW of Bangkok; 355km (220 miles) NW of Chiang Mai via Pai; 274km (170 miles) NW of Chiang Mai via Mae Sariang

Not far from the Burmese border, Mae Hong Son, the provincial capital of Mae Hong Son province, is the urban center of this large patch of scenic woodlands, waterways, and unique hill-tribe villages. The town's surrounding hills, famed for their eerie morning mist, burst into color each October and November when *tung buatong* (wild sunflowers) come into bloom. The hot season (Mar–Apr) has temperatures as high as 104°F (40°C), and the rainy season is longer (May–Oct), with several brief showers daily, but if you're coming up from the plains, you will find some respite from the heat.

The mountains around Mae Hong Son are scarred by slash-and-burn agriculture and evidence of logged teak forests from departed hill-tribe settlements. Roads, airfields, and public works projects have since opened up the scenic province, and poppy fields gave way to terraced rice paddies and garlic crops. Simultaneously, the surge in tourism brought foreigners trekking into villages where automobiles were still unknown. Although the busy town of Mae Hong Son continues to grow and develop into an urban center, its picturesque valley setting and lovely Burmese-style *wats* are worth a visit.

ESSENTIALS

GETTING THERE

By Plane Three daily Thai Airways flights connect Mae Hong Son to major routes via Chiang Mai (flight time: 45 min.). During the July/August and November/December peak seasons, book in advance as flights fill up early, and in low-season check to see if the flights are actually running (flights also cancel often due to fog). **Thai Airways** in Chiang Mai is at 240 Propokklao Rd. (© **05321-0210** for domestic reservations in Chiang Mai), and in Mae Hong Son at 71 Singhanathbamrung Rd. (© **05361-1297**). The Mae Hong Son Airport is in the northeast section of town.

By Bus Seven non-air-conditioned buses connect with Pai (trip time: 4 hr.; 60B/$1.50) or beyond to the **Chiang Mai Arcade Bus Terminal** (trip time: 4 hr.; 60B/$1.50; © **05324-2664**). Bus service to Mae Sariang to the south leaves in the morning (trip time: 8 hr.; 239B/$5.85). The bus terminal in Mae Hong Son is on Khunlumprapas Road (the main street), 2 blocks north of the main intersection and a short walk from most hotels at town center.

By Car The 6-hour journey to Mae Hong Son from Chiang Mai is a pleasant mountain drive with spectacular views and some fun attractions (see "Between Pai & Mae Hong Son," above). The road is winding but paved and safe, with places to stop for gas, food, and toilets, as well as scenic pull-offs. Take Route 107 north from Chiang Mai to Route 1095 northwest through Pai. For car rental info, see chapter 12, "Chiang Mai."

VISITOR INFORMATION

There is no TAT, but the **Tourist Police** (© **05361-1812**), 1 Ratchathampitak Rd., 3 blocks east of the traffic light on the left, offers 24-hour assistance.

ORIENTATION

Mae Hong Son is small and easy to navigate. Khunlumprapas Road, part of the Pai–Mae Sariang highway (Rte. 108), is the town's main street and home to travel agents, most hotels listed below, and restaurants. **Nong Chongkam Lake** is just east of the main street, and **Wat Phra That Doi Kung Mu** overlooks town from the west.

GETTING AROUND

You can walk to most places in town but there are a few tuk-tuks parked outside the market for longer trips. At some guesthouses you'll find bicycle rental for 50B ($1.20) or 100cc motorbikes for rent at 200B($4.90) per day.

FAST FACTS

There are major **banks** with ATMs and currency exchange along Khunlumprapas and Singhanat Bamrung roads. In addition, several banks open for each flight arrival at the airport. The **Sri Sangawan Hospital** is east of town on Singhanat Bamrung Road (© **05361-1378**). The **post office** is opposite the King Singhanat Rajah statue. There are a few Internet cafes along Khunlumprapas near the Baiyoke Chalet, most with good DSL for 30B (75¢) per hour. The **Tourist Police** are at © **05361-1812** (24 hr.).

WHAT TO SEE & DO

Wat Chongklan and **Wat Chongkham** are reflected in the serene waters of Nong Chongkam Lake, in the heart of town. Their striking white *chedis* and dark teak *viharn* tell of Burmese influence. Wat Chongklan was constructed from 1867 to 1871 as an offering to Burmese monks who made the long journey here to the funeral of

Wat Chongkham's abbot. Inside are a series of folk-style glass paintings depicting the Buddha's life and a small collection of dusty Burmese wood carvings and dolls. The older Wat Chongkham (ca. 1827) was built by King Singhanat Rajah and his queen, and is distinguished by gold-leaf columns supporting its *viharn*. Don't miss the colorful Burmese-style donation boxes; they're like musical arcade games with spinning discs and cups to drop your change in, only the end result is not "game over" but "make merit."

Wat Phra That Doi Kung Mu (also known as Wat Plai Doi) dominates the western hillside above the town, particularly at night when the strings of lights rimming its two Mon pagodas are silhouetted against the dark forest. The oldest part (ca. 1860) of this compound was constructed by King Singhanat Rajah, and a 15-minute climb up its new naga staircase is rewarded by grand views of the mist-shrouded valley, blooming pink cassia trees, and Nong Chongkam Lake below. Each April, the national **Poy Sang Long Festival** honoring Prince Siddhartha's decision to become a monk is celebrated here by a parade of novice monks. Below Wat Phra That, there's a 12m-long (40-ft.) **reclining Buddha** in Wat Phra Non.

For short **1-day hill-tribe treks** in the region, **Rose Garden Tours** (86/4 Khunlumprapas Rd. in the center of town; ℃ and fax **05361-1577**) offers many options including stops at local Meo, Shan, and Karen villages, and adventure activities like elephant trekking and bamboo rafting.

There are two **Padung villages** peopled by the famed **"long-neck Karen" people** close to Mae Hong Son. Rose Garden Tours (above) include village visits in their all-day tours or can arrange special half-day trips. **Huay Sua Tao** village is closest to town and easily reached by car or minivan (entrance is 250B/$6.10), and Nam Phiang Din Village is accessible by boat for 600B ($15).

WHERE TO STAY

The early '90s brought large-scale development to Mae Hong Son and there are a few high-end hotel options downtown and a few rustic resorts in the surrounding hills.

EXPENSIVE

Imperial Tara Mae Hong Son ⋘⋘   The Tara is the top choice for the upscale traveler in Mae Hong Son. Though located some 2km (1¼ miles) out of town, the hotel's style, service, decor, and upkeep set it far above the rest. Guest rooms overlook a teak forest, garden, and stream. All furnishings are in blond wood and wicker on "bowling-alley" shined floors. Most rooms have spacious balconies and suites are large and luxurious. The fine free-form pool is surrounded by a wooden deck, and the open-air restaurant has views of the grounds and garden. They have lots of amenities and the staff is very professional and can help with any eventuality, from day-tours to flat tires.

149 Moo 8, Tampon Pang Moo, Mae Hong Son 58000 (2km/1¼ miles south of town). ℃ **05361-1021.** Fax 05361-1252. 104 units. 4,000B ($98) double; from 5,300B ($129) suite. AE, DC, MC, V. **Amenities:** Restaurant; 2 bars; lounge; outdoor pool; fitness center; sauna; tour desk; limited room service; massage; laundry service. *In room:* A/C, TV w/satellite programming, minibar, fridge, hair dryer, safe.

MODERATE

Bai Yoke Chalet   With the best location, on the main street and in walking distance of everything in town, this hotel offers simple, midsize rooms with high ceilings, hardwood floors, and clean guesthouse-style baths. Rooms overlooking the back are quieter, but the place is often overrun by adventure groups, a young and rowdy crowd sometimes, but that can be a real hoot. The hotel bar and restaurant, Chalet, looks over the main street in town, hosts live bands, and is "where it's at" for locals in Mae Hong Son.

90 Khunlumpraphas, Chong Kham, Amphur Muang, Mae Hong Son 58000 (midtown across from post office). ☏ 05361-1536. Fax 05361-1533. 40 units. 1,150B–1,600B ($28–$39) double. AE, MC, V. **Amenities:** Restaurant; tour desk; laundry service. *In room:* A/C, TV w/satellite programming, minibar, fridge.

Fern Resort ★ (Finds)

Out in the sticks some 8km (5 miles) south of town and just next to the Mae Surin National Park, the Fern Resort rests in a quiet valley along a rushing stream and promises comfort and harmony with nature. Tai Yai (Shan)–style bungalows have *tong tueng* leaf roofs, glass windows and doors, simple but comfortable local-style furnishings, electric lights, and hot water in slate-tiled showers. They have good trail maps of the immediate area, and the resort's friendly bevy of dogs will accompany you on a self-guided tour (borrow a walking stick and just follow the pups). Experienced human guides are also available for more extensive treks. Fern's restaurant offers local, Thai, and international cuisine, or ride the shuttle to town (three times daily) to dine at the market or their in-town restaurant (see "Where to Dine," below).

64 Bann Hua Num Mae Saket, T. Pha Bong, Mae Hong Son 58000 (8km/5 miles south of town). ☏ 05368-0001. Fax 05361-2363. www.fernresort.info. 33 bungalows. 1,200B–2,500B ($29–$61) bungalow w/A/C. MC, V. **Amenities:** Restaurant; bike rental; tour desk; laundry service. *In room:* A/C, no phone.

Golden Pai and Golden Suite Hotel and Resort

Here's one for folks who are traveling with their own car. The Golden Pai is 5km east of town (toward Pai). Suite rooms (the best value) are large and cozy with spacious balconies overlooking a small central pool. Mid/low-end rooms are basic bungalows. Popular for Thai groups. They have a good riverside restaurant, offer some spa treatments and mud baths, as well as local adventure tours. Very friendly staff.

285 Moo 1, Ban Pangmoo, Mae Hong Son 58000. ☏ 05361-2265. Fax 05362-0417. www.goldenpai.com. 70 units. 1,200B–2,500B ($29–$61). V, MC. **Amenities:** Restaurant and bars; outdoor pool; tour desk; laundry. *In room:* A/C, TV, minibar, fridge, phone.

Mae Hong Son Mountain Inn

You can't miss the dynamic angular spire of the oversized Thai Yai–style peaked roofs marking the entrance to this compound. The place has lots of charm and is in a good location just south of the town center. Comfortable guest rooms are arranged in two stories around lush central gardens. The hotel is a bit light on amenities, and you won't find many English speakers on staff, but they're helpful as all get-out. Spring for a deluxe room with parquet floors instead of old carpet, more local do-dads, and a bit of panache. Deluxe bathrooms are large with terra-cotta tile and granite.

112/2 Khunlumpraphas Rd., T. Jongkhum, Mae Hong Son 58000 (on the southern end of the main drag). ☏ 05361-1802. Fax 05361-2284. www.mhsmountaininn.com. 65 units. 2,200B–2,500B ($54–$61) double; from 4,000B ($98) suite; seasonal rates and discounts always available. AE, MC, V. **Amenities:** Restaurant; tour desk; car rental; massage; laundry. *In room:* A/C, satellite TV, minibar, fridge.

INEXPENSIVE

Piya Guest House

This is the best budget choice on beautiful Jong Kham Lake, easily the nicest part of town and a short walk to the two lakeside temples. Piya is a one-story wooden house with a garden courtyard. Basic rooms have private baths, hot-water showers, and air-conditioning, but aren't particularly nice (be sure to check first because many are musty). Piya also runs a trekking service and rents out bikes and motorbikes at reasonable prices.

1/1 Khunlumprapas, Soi 3, Chong Kham, Amphur Muang, Mae Hong Son 58000 (east side of Jong Kham Lake).
℃ 05361-1260. 14 units. 600B ($15) bungalow w/A/C. No credit cards. **Amenities:** Restaurant; bike rental; tour
desk; laundry service. *In room:* no phone.

WHERE TO DINE

The local **Night Market** on central Khunlumprapas is the busiest venue for budget
travelers. Sample noodle soups, crisp-fried beef, dried squid, roast sausage, fish balls,
and other snacks sold by vendors for very little. Open early to late.

Fern Restaurant and Bar THAI/CHINESE/INTERNATIONAL   The biggest
and best restaurant in town serves an especially wide variety of food for this part of
the country—all of it well prepared and pleasantly served. The bar at the entrance has
an inviting quality, and behind it an open-air deck stretches back toward an entertainment area with live music and a karaoke bar. If you come in the early evening, head
for the far back to get a view of the mountain-top temple, Wat Phra That Doi Kung
Mu, in the evening glow.

87 Khunlumprapas Rd. (1½ blocks south of traffic light, on left). ℃ 05361-1374. Main courses 40B–180B ($1–$4.40).
AE, MC, V. Daily 10am–10pm.

Kai-Mook THAI/CHINESE   Kai-Mook is a tin-roofed pavilion with more style
than most: Overhead lights are shaded by straw farmer's hats, and Formica tables are
interspersed between bamboo columns. The Thai and Chinese menu includes Kai-
mook salad, a tasty blend of crispy fried squid, cashews, sausage, and onions, and a
large selection of light and fresh stir-fried dishes.

23 Udom Chaonitesh Rd. (1 block south of traffic light, turn left [east] and find it on right). ℃ 05361-2092. Main
courses 50B–150B ($1.20–$3.65). No credit cards. Daily 9:30am–2pm and 5:30–9pm.

Also look for a little Italian storefront pizza joint, **La Tasca** (88/4 Khunlumprapas;
℃ **05361-1344**), in the town center. A great place for a real coffee and to watch the
world go by (daily 9am–10pm; 120B–200B/$3–$5; cash only).

4 Mae Sariang: Completing the Mae Hong Son Loop

180km (112 miles) W of Chiang Mai; 130km (81 miles) S of Mae Hong Son

The tiny town of Mae Sariang proper boasts no grand museums or shiny hilltop temples; it is just a cozy river-town along the border with Burma and the best halfway
stopover on the long southern link between Mae Hong Son and Chiang Mai. Driving
in the area, along Route 108, takes you past pastoral villages, scenic rolling hills, and
a few enticing side trips to small local temples and waterfalls. Mae Sariang offers only
basic accommodations.

GETTING THERE

By Car   Navigation is a cinch. Just follow Route 108 between Mae Hong Son, Mae
Sariang, and Chiang Mai. Carry a good road map for following side roads.

By Bus   Standard and air-conditioned buses connect Mae Hong Son, Mae Sariang,
and **Chiang Mai Arcade Bus Terminal** (℃ 05324-2664), along the southern leg of
Route 108. Six daily non-air-conditioned buses depart Chiang Mai for the 8- to 12-
hour journey and cost 115B ($2.80) to Mae Hong Son and just 60B ($1.50) to stop
in Mae Sariang. One air-conditioned bus makes the same trip and departs Chiang Mai
at 9am (200B/$4.90 to Mae Hong Son; 100B/$2.45 to Mae Sariang).

WHAT TO SEE

The road is good and the scenery is lush on the long stretch of Route 108 west of Chiang Mai. Don't forget to stop and smell the fertilizer or take side trips wherever possible. Roadside dining and service facilities are limited, but adequate.

Sixty-three kilometers south of Mae Hong Son, in the village of **Khun Yuam,** you'll come to a junction with a road that no longer exists: a ghost trail remembered as "The Road of Japanese Skeletons" and the path of retreat for Japanese soldiers fleeing Burma at the end of WWII. The road lives only in the memory of those who met the starved and dying troops, an estimated 20,000 of whom lie in mass graves in the surrounding area. The **Japanese War Museum** (just south of the junction of Rte. 108 and Rte. 163) commemorates this sorry chapter in history and is worth a visit. The museum features rusting tanks and weaponry, photos, personal effects, and written accounts (in Japanese, English, and Thai) of soldiers' struggles and the kindness of the locals.

Mae Sariang has a few outfits offering day treks and rafting (stop in any of the riverside cafes or hotels), but most just spend a night here before making their way to Chiang Mai.

Between Mae Sariang and Chiang Mai you'll pass near **Doi Inthanon National Park** and the city of **Lamphun.** For details of these, see "Side Trips from Chiang Mai," in chapter 12.

WHERE TO DINE & STAY

There are lots of budget accommodation along the Mae Yuam River in the town center. The best choice is new **Riverhouse Resort** (6/1 Moo 2, Maesarieng 58110; ✆ **05368-3066;** fax 05368-3067; www.riverhousehotels.com), a small resort of cozy wooden pavilions overlooking the Mae Yuam. Rooms start at 1,000B/$25. Riverhouse is also the best bet for dining in their riverside sala, but a short stroll through town will take you past any number of local greasy spoons where the adventurous can find one-dish noodle or rice meals for next to nothing.

5 Chiang Rai

780km (484 miles) NE of Bangkok; 180km (112 miles) NE of Chiang Mai

Chiang Rai is Thailand's northernmost province. The Mekong River makes its borders with Laos to the east and Burma to the west. The smaller, yet scenic Mae Kok River, which supports many hill-tribe villages along its banks, flows right through the provincial capital of the same name.

Chiang Rai City lies some 565m (1,885 ft.) above sea level in a wide fertile valley, and its cool refreshing climate, tree-lined riverbanks, and popular but more subdued Night Market lures travelers weary of traffic congestion and pollution in Chiang Mai. Chiang Rai has some good choices of accommodation, and many travelers use the city as a base for trekking and trips to Chiang Saen and the Golden Triangle.

Note: Some include a stop at the Mae Rim valley on their way north to Chiang Rai (30 minutes north of the city on Rt. 107). Mae Rim is an area popular for elephant trekking, rafting, bungee-jumping, and one of the region's most luxurious properties: the Four Seasons Chiang Mai. See "Side Trips from Chiang Mai," in chapter 12.

Just over 100km north of Chiang Mai on the way to Chiang Rai, look for little **Suanthip Vana Resort** (49 Chiang Mai–Chiang Rai Rd.; ✆ **0572-4226;** www.suanthip resort.com), a semi-luxe property with cool honeymoon bungalows that overlook a river valley. A good little find.

ESSENTIALS
GETTING THERE
By Plane   **Thai Airways** (✆ 05327-0222 in Chiang Mai) has four daily flights from Bangkok to Chiang Rai (flying time: 85 min.), and from Chiang Mai as well (flying time: 30 min.). Thailand's many budget carriers, **Air Asia** (✆ 05392-2170; www.airasia. com), **Nok Air** (✆ 05392-2183 or ✆ 1318; www.nokair.com), and **Orient Thai** (✆ 05390-4609) all make regular connections.

The **Chiang Rai International Airport** (✆ 05379-3048) is about 10km (6 miles) north of town. There is a bank exchange open daily 9am to 5pm and a gift shop. Taxis hover outside expectantly: 150B ($3.65) to town, more to other towns in the province.

By Bus   Three air-conditioned VIP 24-seat buses leave daily from Bangkok's **Northern Bus Terminal** (✆ 02936-2852) to Chiang Rai (trip time: 11 hr.; 700B/$17). Buses leave hourly between 6am and 5:30pm from **Chiang Mai's Arcade Bus Terminal** (✆ 05324-2664) (trip time: 3½ hr.; 66B/$1.60 non-air-conditioned; 119B/$2.90 air-conditioned). Chiang Rai's **Khon Song Bus Terminal** (✆ 05371-1369) couldn't be more conveniently located—on Phrasopsook Road off Phaholyothin Road near the Night Market just in the center of town. Tuk-tuks and *samlors* are easy to catch here for trips around town for 30B to 60B (75¢–$1.50).

By Car   The fast, not particularly scenic, route from Bangkok is Highway 1 North, direct to Chiang Rai. A slow, scenic approach on blacktop mountain roads is Route 107 north from Chiang Mai to Fang, then Route 109 east to Highway 1.

VISITOR INFORMATION
The **TAT** (✆ 05374-4674) is located at 448/16 Singhakai Rd., near Wat Phra Singh on the north side of town, and the Tourist Police are next door. The monthly *Welcome to Chiang Mai and Chiang Rai* is distributed free by most hotels, and has a good, reliable map of the town.

ORIENTATION
Chiang Rai is a small city, with most services grouped around the main north–south street, Phaholyothin Road. There are three noteworthy landmarks: the small clock tower in the city's center; the statue of King Mengrai (the city's founder) at the northeast corner of the city, on the superhighway to Mae Chan; and the Mae Kok River at the north edge of town. Singhakai Road is the main artery on the north side of town, parallel to the river. The bus station is on Prasopsuk Road, 1 block east of Phaholyothin Road, near the Wiang Inn Hotel. The Night Market is on Phaholyothin Road near the bus station.

GETTING AROUND
By *Samlor* or Tuk-Tuk   You'll probably find walking the best method of transport. However, there are *samlors* (pedicabs) parked outside the Night Market and on the banks of the Mae Kok River; they charge 20B to 30B (50¢)–75¢) for in-town trips. During the day there are tuk-tuks, which charge 30B to 60B (75¢–$1.50) for in-town trips.

By Bus   Frequent local buses are the easiest and cheapest way to get to nearby cities. All leave from the bus station (✆ 05371-1369) on Prasopsuk Road near the Wiang Inn Hotel.

By Motorcycle   A good choice to get out of town. **Soon Motorcycle,** 197/2 Trirat Rd. (✆ 05371-4068) charges 180B ($4.40) for a 100cc motorbike.

By Car **Budget** has a branch at the Golden Triangle Inn (see "Where to Stay," below), 590 Phaholyothin Rd. (*©* **05371-1339**), offering the standard rate beginning at 1,500B ($37) for a Suzuki Caribian.

FAST FACTS

Several **bank** exchanges are located on Phaholyothin Road in the center of town and are open daily from 8:30am to 10pm. The **post office** is 2 blocks north of the Clock Tower on Utarakit Road. There are a few **Internet cafes** along the main drag, Phaholyothin Road, with service for as little as 20B/50¢ per hour.

THINGS TO SEE & DO

Wat Phra Kaeo, on Trirat Road on the northwest side of town, is the best known of the northern *wats* because it once housed the Emerald Buddha now at Bangkok's royal Wat Phra Kaeo. Near its Lanna-style chapel is the *chedi,* which (according to legend) was struck by lightning in 1436 to reveal the precious green jasper Buddha. There is now a green jade replica of the image on display.

   Wat Phra Singh is 2 blocks east of Wat Phra Kaeo. The restored *wat* is thought to date from the 15th century. Inside is a replica of the Phra Singh Buddha, a highly revered Theravada Buddhist image; the original was removed to Chiang Mai's Wat Phra Singh.

   The Burmese-style **Wat Doi Tong** (Phra That Chomtong) sits atop a hill above the northwest side of town, up a steep staircase off Kaisornrasit Road, and offers an overview of the town and a panorama of the Mae Kok valley. It is said that King Mengrai himself chose the site for his new Lanna capital from this very hill. The circle of columns at the top of the hill surrounds the city's new *lak muang* (city pillar), built to commemorate the 725th anniversary of the city and King Bhumibol's 60th birthday. It is often criticized for its failure to represent local style. (You can see the old wooden *lak muang* in the *wihaan* of the *wat.*)

   The **Population and Community Development Association (PDA),** 620/25 Thanalai Road, east of Wisetwang Road (*©* **05371-9167**), is a nongovernmental organization responsible for some of the most effective tribal development projects in the region. The popular Cabbages & Condoms restaurants, with branches here and in Bangkok (and now a resort in Pattaya), carry their important message of safe sex and family planning. On the top floor of this office is a small **Hill-tribe Museum** that's heavy on "shop" and light on "museum," but the admission goes to a good cause. Open daily 9am to 8pm; admission 50B ($1.20).

   The **Mae Kok River** is one of the most scenic attractions in Chiang Rai. Hire a long-tail boat to ferry you up and down the river. You'll have the option to stop at the Buddha cave, a temple within a cavern; an elephant camp, for trekking; a hot spring; and a riverside Lahu village. Trips range from 300B to 700B ($7.30–$17), depending on the stops you make. The ferry pier is beyond the bridge across from the Dusit Island Resort. Contact **Maesalong Tours,** 882–4 Phaholyothin Road (*©* **05371-2515;** fax 05371-1011), or ask at your hotel.

TREKKING & HILL-TRIBE TOURS

Most of the **hill-tribe villages** within close range of Chiang Rai have long ago been set up for routine visits by group tours (not recommended). If your time is too limited for a trek, in-town travel agencies offer day trips to the countryside and areas less-traveled. Guided tours with transport are priced on a two-person minimum and greater discounts are available for groups of three or more.

The best operation in Chiang Rai is **Golden Triangle Tours,** 590 Phaholyothin Rd. (© **05371-1339;** fax 05371-3963; www.goldenchiangrai.com). They are professional, experienced, and offer an array of tours or cater to personal interests. For hill-tribe treks, choose anything from a day trip to a week of adventure. **Day trips** to surrounding villages begin at 1,500B ($37) and can include light trekking to villages as well as elephant trekking for groups of two or three people (private tours cost a bit more). **Longer treks** range in price from 1,500B to 3,000B ($37–$73) for anything from multiday trips in the Golden Triangle to 3- to 5-day sojourns among Akha, Hmong, Yao, Karen, and Lahu tribes. Exciting 4×4 treks along the **opium trail** follow new routes cut by government agencies to hurry local produce to market and thus replace community reliance on cultivating opium poppies.

WHERE TO STAY

This city of 40,000 has an impressive 2,000 hotel rooms, but group tours fill them up in high season. With the exception of the resorts across the river, most hotels are within walking distance of the sights and shopping.

EXPENSIVE

Central River House Resort Chiang Rai ☞   New on the scene, River House is a luxurious campus just across the river from town (near Rimkok Resort; see below). Set around a large pool flanked by laughing elephant sculptures, the resort has a full-service spa and dining area. Rooms are all a very high standard, almost like a stylish city hotel with stylish wood built-in cabinetry and fine furnishings. Second floor rooms flank a large veranda overlooking farmer's fields at riverside—great to watch the dragonflies at dusk. River House caters mostly to high-end Thai travelers and an increasing number of European and North Americans. They have regular evening shuttles to town, and the front desk staff is very friendly and helpful.

482 Moo 4, Tambon Rim Kok, Amphur Muang, Chiang Rai 57100. © **05375-0829.** Fax 05375-0822. www.central hotelsresorts.com. 36 units. 6,300B ($154) deluxe in high season ($125 in low season); 8,900B ($217) in high season ($175 in low season). **Amenities:** Restaurant and bar; outdoor pool; health club; tour desk; limited room service; massage; laundry; dry cleaning. *In room:* A/C, satellite TV, minibar, fridge, safe, IDD phone.

Dusit Island Resort Hotel ☞☞   Chiang Rai's best resort hotel occupies a large delta island in the Mae Kok River. The resort offers international comfort at the expense of local flavor and hominess. The dramatic lobby is a soaring space of teak, marble, and glass, as grand as any in Thailand, with panoramic views of the Mae Kok. Rooms are luxuriously appointed in pastel cottons and teak trim. The Dusit Island has manicured grounds, pool, and numerous facilities, making the resort quite self-contained. The hotel's most formal dining room is the semicircular Peak on the 10th floor, with sweeping views and a grand terrace overlooking the Mae Kok (pricey but good). Chinatown is a more casual Cantonese restaurant serving a great dim sum lunch. In the evening stop by the cozy Music Room bar for live entertainment. They offer regular shuttle service.

1129 Kraisorasit Rd., Amphur Muang 57000, Chiang Rai (over bridge at northwest corner of town). © **05371-5777.** Fax 05371-5801. www.dusit.com. 271 units. 4,532B–5,179B ($111–$126) superior/deluxe double; from 7,769B ($189) suite. AE, DC, MC, V. **Amenities:** 3. restaurants; lounge and pub; outdoor pool; lighted tennis courts; fitness center w/Jacuzzi, sauna, steam, massage; game room; concierge; tour desk; car-rental desk; limousine service; 24-hr. room service; babysitting; same-day laundry service/dry cleaning; nonsmoking rooms; executive-level rooms. *In room:* A/C, TV w/satellite programming, minibar, fridge, safe.

The Legend Chiang Rai ⚡ The Legend is a uniquely attractive rural boutique resort. Rooms are private sanctuaries of smooth-finish concrete and stucco walls with bevel edges, a crisp, modern look with many natural touches. Some rooms overlook the river, others line a narrow garden pond, and all have great indoor and outdoor sitting areas, a constant connection with your surroundings. There are a few different configurations, including huge private pool villas and family suites, but all have in common large outdoor shower areas, some with Jacuzzi bath, and large, luxuriant canopy beds. Unique is the small infinity edge pool at the center of the resort. They have a great spa with outdoor salas and indoor treatment rooms, and the resort runs a number of day trips and activities. Adjacent to the Dusit Island Resort, Legend is a great little hideaway.

124/15 Kohloy Rd., Amphur Muang, Chiang Rai 57000. ⓒ 05391-0400. Fax 05371-9650. www.thelegend-chiangrai. com. 76 units. Studio 4,000B–6,700B ($98–$163); Deluxe 5,000B–10,000B ($122–$244); Suite 8,000B–13,000B ($195–$317). MC, V. **Amenities:** Restaurant and bar; outdoor pool; spa; Jacuzzi; tour desk; room service 6am–10pm; massage; babysitting; laundry service; dry cleaning. In room: A/C, satellite TV, minibar, fridge, coffeemaker, safe, IDD phone.

MODERATE
Rimkok Resort Hotel ⚡ Everything is done on a large scale at the Rimkok. Not particularly luxurious, just big. It is a bit distant from town but thoroughly self-contained. Guest rooms are airy with high ceilings and balconies and some Thai touches in an overall bland but comfortable set-up. Public spaces are capped with high-peaked Thai roofs and are grand, featuring Thai decor and artwork. Lushly planted lawns surround the large central pool. The Rimkok Resort offers shuttle service to town (to visit the market). Popular with group tours, the place sometimes gets overrun. Discounts frequently available.

6 Moo 4, Tathorn Rd., Amphur Muang, 57100 Chiang Rai (on north shore of Kok River, about 6km/3¾ miles north of town center). ⓒ 05371-6445. Fax 05371-5859. www.rimkokresort.com. 256 units. 3,000B ($73) double; from 6,000B ($146) suite. AE, DC, MC, V. **Amenities:** 3 restaurants; bar and lounge; large outdoor pool; Jacuzzi; tour desk; limousine service; business center; shopping; salon; limited room service; babysitting; same-day laundry service. In room: A/C, TV w/satellite programming, minibar, fridge.

Wangcome Hotel The Wangcome is located just a stone's throw from the Night Market. Rooms are small but comfortable, detailed with Lanna Thai touches like their fine carved teak headboards. Central rooms face an outdoor swimming pool. There's a lively coffee shop and a moody cocktail lounge, a popular rendezvous spot after the Night Market closes.

896/90 Penawibhata Rd., Chiang Rai Trade Center, Amphur Muang 57000, Chiang Rai (west off Phaholyothin Rd.). ⓒ 05371-1800. Fax 05371-2973. 234 units. 1,600B ($39) double; from 2,000B ($49) suite. AE, DC, MC, V. **Amenities:** Restaurant; lounge; small pool; tour desk; limousine service; business center; massage; laundry service. In room: A/C, TV w/satellite programming, minibar, fridge.

Wiang Inn ⚡ Wiang Inn has a convenient location (just around the corner from the bus station and opposite the Night Market) and with recent renovations is a just a hitch better than the Wangcome Hotel (above). Large rooms are trimmed in dark teak, with pale teak furniture and Thai artwork, including Lanna murals over the beds and ceramic vase table lamps. It is very well maintained, despite the steady stream of group tours, which makes an early booking advisable.

893 Phaholyothin Rd., Amphur Muang 57000, Chiang Rai (center of town, south of bus station). ⓒ 05371-1533. Fax 05371-1877. 256 units. 1,800B–2,200B ($44–$54) double; from 5,000B ($122) suite. AE, DC, MC, V. **Amenities:** 2 restaurants; bar and karaoke lounge; outdoor pool; tour desk; limited room service; massage; babysitting; laundry service/dry cleaning. In room: A/C, TV w/satellite programming, minibar, fridge.

INEXPENSIVE

The Golden Triangle Inn ⋪⋪ A charming little hotel that offers comfort and lots of style and character, Golden Triangle is set in its own quiet little garden patch—once inside you'd never believe bustling Chiang Rai is just beyond the front entrance. Large rooms have terra-cotta tiled floors, traditional-style furniture, and reproductions of Lanna artifacts and paintings. The owners and management are very down-to-earth and extremely helpful; they are the local operators of Budget Car Rental and their in-house travel agency, **Golden Triangle Tours,** is the best choice in town for arranging travel in the area. Their restaurant is excellent (see "Where to Dine," below).

590 Phaholyothin Rd., Amphur Muang 57000, Chiang Rai (2 blocks north of bus station). ℂ 05371-1339. Fax 05371-3963. 30 units. 900B ($22) double. MC, V. **Amenities:** Restaurant; tour desk; car-rental desk; laundry service. In room: A/C, no phone.

WHERE TO DINE

The Night Market is the best for budget eats, but beyond that there are a few good restaurants to choose from. Be sure to sample the town's delicacies, like the huge *ching kong* catfish, caught in April to May; litchis, which ripen in June and July; and the sweet *nanglai* pineapple wine.

Cabbages & Condoms ⋪ THAI Sister restaurant to Cabbages & Condoms in Bangkok, this northern branch was opened by the Population & Community Development Association to promote their humanitarian work in the region. The extensive Thai menu is excellent and features local catfish cooked as you like. They play host to lots of events and live bands, and it is a popular stop for tour groups, which also come for the exhibit upstairs (see "Things to See & Do," above).

620/25 Thanalai Rd. ℂ 05371-9167. Main courses 70B–200B ($1.70–$4.90). MC, V. Daily 10am–11pm.

Golden Triangle Café ⋪ THAI At the entrance to the Golden Triangle Inn (see "Where to Stay," above), one of the best choices in town for accommodation is also where to find the best Thai meal going. Everything is delicious, but perhaps the best reason to eat here is for the menu, which carefully explains the various dishes that make up a standard Thai meal, describing the ingredients and preparation of each. They have the obligatory sandwiches and burgers, but go for regional treats, especially the curry sweetened with local litchis (when in season). After studying the menu, you can order what you like in any restaurant—in Thai, too!

Golden Triangle Inn, 590 Phaholyothin Rd. ℂ 05371-1339. Entrees 80B–250B ($1.95–$6.10). MC, V. Daily 8am–10:30pm.

The Night Market/Food Stalls ⋪⋪ THAI/INTERNATIONAL Every night after 7pm, the cavernous, tin-roofed Municipal Market at the town center comes alive with dozens of chrome-plated food stalls that serve steamed, grilled, and fried Thai treats. It is where locals meet, greet, and eat, and really the heart of the town (a busy mercantile market, as well), so don't miss a wander here even if you're not into street-eats. For standard dining in the market, try **Rattanakosin,** a little market-side edifice done up in contemporary Thai style and serving good local cuisine (mostly for tour groups). And just outside the main entrance to the market on the main drag is **Aye's Restaurant** (869/170 Phaholyothin Rd.; ℂ 05375-2534) serving some familiar, if not all that exciting, European fare. Also try **da Vinci** (879/4-5 Phaholyothin Rd.; ℂ 05375-2535), a new Italian restaurant with good fresh salads, thin crust pizzas, and pasta.

SHOPPING

The recent influx of tourists has made Chiang Rai a magnet for hill-tribe clothing and crafts. You'll find many boutiques in the Night Market near the bus terminal off Phaholyothin Road, as well as some fine shops scattered around the city.

CHIANG RAI AFTER DARK

The main activity is wandering the **Night Market,** which is really just a more toned-down version of the raucous Night Bazaar in Chiang Mai. Like its big-city model, you can find a few bars and clubs (a bit seedy but fun). In Chiang Rai there are the standard "bar beer" storefronts with names like **Patpong Bar, Lobo,** and **Butterfly** lining the road just a short walk west of the market along Punyodyana Road, behind the Wangcome Hotel. There's also a few quiet pubs.

CHIANG RAI TO MAE SAI

A popular "visa run" route where you can cross the border to Myanmar and re-enter Thailand for another 30 days of visa time, most visitor north of Chiang Rai zip through the little border town of Mae Sai on their way to the Golden Triangle and Chiang Saen, but the town is worth a stop. It is the northernmost point in Thailand. Just to the right of the border gate to Myanmar (the end of the highway) you'll find a busy market area with good, affordable gems and silver jewelry brought from Myanmar. There is also a busy hotel, mostly for Thai tourists, called the **Wang Thong Hotel** (299 Phaholyothin Rd.; ✆ **05373-3388;** from 900B ($22) double), but most just pass through (though if it's lunchtime, try their good buffet, and rooms look out over Burmese temples). Also, you can cross the border to the Myanmar border town and market of Tachilek. You exit Thailand (on foot only), leave your passport at a Burmese checkpoint, pay 205B ($5), and then kill time by wandering the market—you'll find lots of Chinese goods, and the hard sell and squalor can be a bit too much. Burmese tuk-tuk drivers will try to finagle you into a 1-day trip inland to temples and a long-neck Karen Village, but it is not really worth it (and these dudes are a bit dodgy).

6 Chiang Saen ⊛ & the Golden Triangle

935km (580 miles) NE of Bangkok; 239km (148 miles) NE of Chiang Mai

The small village of Chiang Saen, the gateway to the Golden Triangle area, has a sleepy, rural charm, as if the waters of the Mekong carry a palpable calm from nearby Burma and Laos. The road from Chiang Rai (59km/37 miles) follows the small Mae Nam Chan River past coconut groves and lush rice paddies. Poinsettias and gladiola decorate thatched Lanna Thai houses with peaked rooflines that extend into Xs like buffalo horns.

Little Chiang Saen, the birthplace of expansionary King Mengrai, was abandoned for the new Lanna Thai capitals of Chiang Rai, then Chiang Mai, in the 13th century. With the Mekong River and the Laos border hemming in its growth, modern developers went elsewhere. Today, the slow rural pace, decaying regal *wats,* crumbling fort walls, and overgrown moat contribute to its appeal.

Once upon a time, the **Golden Triangle** was the center point of many illicit activities. The name was given to the area where Thailand, Laos, and Burma come together—a proximity that facilitated overland drug transportation of opium and heroin in its first steps toward international markets. Thai authorities have mounted a concerted effort to stop the drug traffic here and, while some illegal activity goes unchecked, the area is hardly dangerous. Rather, Ban Sob Ruak, the Thai town at the junction, is a long and disappointing row of souvenir stalls. Still, if you stand at the crook of the river, you can look to the right to see Laos and to the left to see Myanmar (Burma). When the river is low, a large sandbar appears that is apparently unclaimed by any authority.

A common route is to leave from Chiang Rai by car (or motorbike) and travel directly north to the Burmese border town of **Mae Sai,** a great stop for gem and souvenir shopping, then follow the Mekong River going east along the border, making a stop at **The Hall of Opium,** and the town of **Sob Ruak,** before catching the museum and many temples of Chiang Saen. If overnighting in the area, the best stops are in the Golden Triangle proper (west of Chiang Saen).

ESSENTIALS
GETTING THERE

By Bus   Buses from **Chiang Rai's Kohn Song Bus Terminal** leave every 15 minutes from 6am to 6pm (trip time: 1½ hr.; 20B/50¢). The bus drops you on Chiang Saen's main street. The museum and temples are within walking distance. Public *songtaos,* or pickups, make frequent trips between Chiang Saen and the Golden Triangle for about 20B/50¢.

By Car   Take the superhighway Route 110 north from Chiang Rai to Mae Chan, then Route 1016 Northeast to Chiang Saen.

ORIENTATION

Route 1016 is the village's main street, also called Phaholyothin Road, which terminates at the Mekong River. Along the river road there are a few guesthouses, eateries, and souvenir, clothing, and food stalls.

The Golden Triangle and the town of Sob Ruak are just 8km (5 miles) west of the town of Chiang Saen, and the most choice accommodations (the Anantara and the Imperial) are just a few clicks west from there. Mae Sai is some 30 km west of the Golden Triangle.

GETTING AROUND

On Foot   There's so little traffic it is a pleasure to walk; all of the in-town sights are within 15 minutes' walk of each other.

By Bicycle & Motorcycle   It's a great bike ride (45 min.) from Chiang Saen to the prime nearby attraction, the Golden Triangle. The roads are well paved and pretty flat. **Chiang Saen House Rent Motor,** on the river road just east of the main street intersection, has good one-speed bicycles for 30B (75¢) per day, and 100cc motorcycles (no insurance, no helmets) for 150B ($3.65) per day.

By *Samlor*   Motorized pedicabs hover by the bus stop in town to take you to the Golden Triangle for 60B ($1.45) one-way. Round-trip fares with waiting time are negotiable to about 250B ($6.10) for about 2 hours.

By *Songtao*   Songtaos (pickup truck taxis) can be found on the main street across from the market; rides cost only 20B (50¢) to the Golden Triangle.

By Long-tail Boat   Long-tail boat captains down by the river offer Golden Triangle tours for as little as 400B ($9.75) per boat (seating eight) per half-hour. Many people enjoy the half-hour cruise, take a walk around the village of Sob Ruak after they've seen the Golden Triangle, and then continue on by bus.

FAST FACTS

There is a **Siam Commercial Bank** in the center of Phaholyothin Road, Route 1016, the main street, just close to the **bus stop, post and telegram office** (no overseas service and few local telephones), the police station, the many temples, and The Chiang Saen National Museum. There is a **currency exchange** booth at the Golden Triangle.

WHAT TO SEE & DO

Allow half a day to see all of Chiang Saen's historical sights before exploring the Golden Triangle. To help with orientation, make the museum your first stop. There is a good map about local historical sites on the second floor.

The **Chiang Saen National Museum** (702 Phaholyothin Rd.; (℃ **05377-7102**) houses a small but very fine collection of this region's historic and ethnographic products. The ground floor's main room has a collection of large bronze and stone Buddha images dating from the 15th- to 17th-century Lanna Kingdom. Pottery from Sukhothai-era kiln sites is displayed downstairs and on the balcony.

The handicrafts and cultural items of local hill-tribes are fascinating, particularly the display of Nam Bat, an ingenious fishing tool. Burmese-style lacquer ware, Buddha images, and wood carvings scattered through the museum reinforce the similarities seen between Chiang Saen and its spiritual counterpart, Pagan. Allow an hour to go through the museum carefully. It is open Wednesday to Sunday 9am to 4pm, closed holidays; admission 30B (75¢).

Wat Pa Sak, the best preserved, is set in a landscaped historical park that contains a large, square-based *stupa* and six smaller *chedis* and temples. The park preserves what's left of the compound's 1,000 teak trees. The *wat* is said to have been constructed in 1295 by King Saen Phu to house relics of the Buddha, though some historians believe its ornate combination of Sukhothai and Pagan styles dates it later. The historical park is about 201m (660 ft.) west of the Chiang Saen Gate (at the entrance to the village). It is open daily 8am to 5pm; admission 20B (50¢).

The area's oldest *wat* is still an active Buddhist monastery. Rising from a cluster of wooden dorms, **Wat Phra Chedi Luang** (or Jadeeloung) has a huge brick *chedi* that dominates the main street. The *wat* complex was established in 1331 under the reign of King Saen Phu and was rebuilt in 1515 by King Muang Kaeo. The old brick foundations, now supporting a very large, plaster, seated Buddha flanked by smaller ones, are all that remain. Small bronze and stucco Buddhas excavated from the site are now in the museum. It is open daily from 8am to 5pm. Admission is free.

There are several other *wats* of note in and around the town. **Wat Mung Muang** is the 15th-century square-based *stupa* seen next to the post office. Above the bell-shaped *chedi* are four small *stupas*. Across the street, you can see the bell-shaped *chedi* from **Wat Phra Bouj.** It is rumored to have been built by the prince of Chiang Saen in 1346, though historians believe it is of the same period as Mung Muang. As you leave Chiang Saen on the river road, going northwest to the Golden Triangle, you'll pass **Wat Pha Kao Pan,** with some sculpted Buddha images tucked in niches and on its *stupa,* then the unrestored *vihara* mound of **Wat Sangakaeo Don Tan.** Both are thought to date from the 16th century.

THE GOLDEN TRIANGLE

The infamous Golden Triangle (12km/7½ miles northwest of Chiang Saen) is the point where Thailand, Burma, and Laos meet at the confluence of the broad, slow, and silted Mekong and Mae Ruak Rivers. They create Thailand's northern border, separating it from overgrown jungle patches of Burma to the east and forested, hilly Laos to the west. The area's appeal as a vantage point over forbidden territories is quickly diminishing as there is now a legal crossing into Laos from nearby Chiang Khong.

Nonetheless, a "look" at the home of ethnic hill-tribes and their legendary opium trade is still interesting, and there are some good sites to see. In fact, the appeal of this geopolitical phenomenon has created an entire village—Sob Ruak—of thatch souvenir stalls, cheap riverview soda and noodle shops, and very primitive guesthouses. Most interesting is:

The Hall of Opium 𝓡𝓡𝓡   Sponsored by the late Princess Mother as part of a larger effort to educate and find alternatives for hill-tribe peoples of the north, the museum complex covers some 16 hectares (40 acres) of garden overlooking the Mekong. You enter the museum and follow a long corridor through a mountain. In the dark, all you can see are a few murals that portray the pain and anguish of addiction (the kids might get a fright), then emerge in a grand atrium with a large glowing golden triangle (the irony is a bit much). From there it is a multimedia romp of films and light-up displays that tell of the growth of the poppy, its vital importance in British and international trade with China, the many conflicts over opium, the drug's influx into Thailand, and useful information about recent efforts to suppress international smuggling and address rampant addiction throughout the region. Media-savvy exhibits are in both Thai and English. The "Hall of Excuses" at the end highlights (or lowlights?) many of the world's most well-known addicts, and the museum ends in the "Hall of Reflections," where guests are invited to ruminate on their experience. And it *is* an experience (takes about 1½ hours to go through). There's nothing like it anywhere else in Thailand.

10km/6 miles NW of Chiang Saen. ℂ 0578-4444. www.goldentrianglepark.com. Entrance 300B ($7.30). Open Tuesday–Sunday 10am–3:30pm.

Opium Museum   The hand-painted description and battered old display cases pales in comparison to the multi-media extravaganza that is the Hall of Opium (above), but here you can find much of the same info about cultivation, distribution, and opium's place in global trade. There's lots of paraphernalia and a certain battered charm to the place (plus a good little souvenir shop and pee stop on the way to Chiang Saen).

212 House of Opium; Chiang Saen (just opposite the golden Buddha at the very heart of the golden triangle). ℂ 05378-4060. Entrance 20B (50¢). Open daily 7am–7pm.

WHERE TO STAY

There are a few guesthouses in Chiang Saen, and two fine resort hotels in the Golden Triangle area. The area is very scenic and relaxing.

EXPENSIVE

Anantara Resort and Spa Golden Triangle 𝓡𝓡   The newly opened Anantara is a triumph of upscale, local design. Every detail reminds you that you're in the scenic hill-tribe region, and the resort's elegance and style depend on locally produced weavings, carved teak panels, and expansive views of the juncture of the Ruak and Mekong Rivers. The balconied rooms have splendid views and are so spacious and private you will feel like you're in your own bungalow. Tiled foyers lead to large bathrooms and bedrooms are furnished in teak and traditional fabrics. The hotel supports a small elephant camp, and their busy tour desk can arrange any number of trips to far-flung corners of the region (or just across the road to the Hall of Opium). Rooms are a luxurious city hotel standard, many with windows connecting large bathrooms with the main room area. The top choice in the far north hills.

Onward to Laos

Many make Chiang Rai or Chiang Saen their last port of call in the land of Thai and head overland to rugged but inviting Laos. It is possible to travel downriver 70km (43 miles) to Chiang Khong, a small border town (buses and local *songtaos* also make the connection from either Chiang Rai or Chiang Saen). Most travelers head right across the border, but if you are stuck in Chiang Khong, try **Bamboo Guesthouse** (© **5379-1621**), with basic rooms from 150B/$3.65; or **Reuan Thai Sophapham** (© **5379-1023**), on the river with simple rooms, some A/C, from 350B to 600B ($8.55–$15). You'll need to arrange a visa to enter Laos, which is best done in Bangkok or Chiang Mai at any travel agent. Once over the border, the slow boat to Luang Prabang is rugged but memorable (pick up *Frommer's Southeast Asia* or check out www.frommers.com for information on travel in Laos).

229 Moo 1, Chiang Saen 57150, Chiang Rai (above river, 12km/7½ miles northwest of Chiang Saen). © **800/225-5843** in the U.S., or 05378-4084. Fax 05378-4090. www.anantara.com. 90 units. $250–$415 double; $575–$800 suite. AE, DC, MC, V. **Amenities:** 3 restaurants; lounge and bar; outdoor pool; outdoor lighted tennis courts; fitness center w/Jacuzzi, Mandara Spa w/sauna, and massage; bike rental; concierge; tour desk; car-rental desk; limousine service; business center; shopping arcade; salon; limited room service; babysitting; same-day laundry service. *In room:* A/C, satellite TV w/in-house movies, minibar, fridge, coffee/tea-making facilities, hair dryer, safe.

MODERATE

The Imperial Golden Triangle Resort ✦ This five-story hotel block stands in the western corner of the tiny, souvenir village of Ban Sob Ruak. Modern, spacious guest rooms with pastel and rattan decor have large balconies, and the more expensive rooms overlook the Golden Triangle. It is a fine, comfortable choice if you're passing through, but pales in comparison to the nearby Anantara (see above).

222 Golden Triangle, Chiang Saen, 57150 Chiang Rai (in Sob Ruak, 11km/7 miles northwest of Chiang Saen). © **05378-4001**. Fax 05378-4006. www.imperialhotels.com. 73 units. 4,120B–4,700B ($100–$115) double; from 8,000B ($195) suite. AE, MC, V. **Amenities:** Restaurant; lounge; pool; tour desk; laundry service. *In room:* A/C, TV w/satellite programming, minibar, fridge.

INEXPENSIVE

Chiang Saen River Hill Hotel This is the best choice for in-town, budget accommodations in Chiang Saen. The River Hill is about 1km (⅔ mile) east of the main drag. They have bicycle rentals for guests, and it is an easy peddle to the center of town. Guest rooms are concrete block rooms with simple tile floors but are dressed in northern finery, with wood carving details, and funky little Lanna-style seating arrangements—floor cushions around low *khan toke* tables under regal umbrellas. The large and colorful coffee shop (in shades of blue and aqua with little star lights from the ceiling) is open for breakfast, lunch, and dinner, with good selections and a relaxed and refreshing atmosphere.

714 Moo 3, Tambol Viang, Chiang Saen, Chang Rai (5-min. *samlor* ride from bus stop). © **05365-0826**. Fax 05365-0830. 60 units. 800B–1,000B ($18–$23) double. No credit cards. **Amenities:** Restaurant; bike rental; laundry service. *In room:* A/C, TV, no phone.

14

Exploring Isan: Thailand's Frontier

The northeast of Thailand, called Isan (*Eesaan*) in Thai, accounts for roughly one-third of the country's land mass and a quarter of the population. Bordered by Laos to the north and east (along the Mekong) and by Cambodia to the south, the region suffers from a stagnant rural economy and life is hard on the scorched plains of Isan, but the friendly people of this region welcome travelers openly or with unabashed surprise, something like American "Southern hospitality." There is little in the way of jaw-dropping tourist attractions, but all roads lead "off the track" in this rugged region and there are some important archaeological sites (mostly dating from the Khmer period), lovely river towns, finely made craft finds, and fiery hot food. The areas in the far north and along the Mekong are particularly worth the trip.

The weather is especially hot in Isan but follows a pattern much like the rest of Thailand: coolest from November to February; hot and dry from March to May; rain from June to October. Windswept and infertile in parts, verdant along the Mekong, the region attracts few international tourists, but has a few good routes to follow, and Isan is a good jumping off point for trips to Laos.

Indeed, much about Isan, from the weather to the local dialect and culture, resembles Laos and is quite distinct from mainstream Thai culture; as a result, many joke about "Prathet Isan," or "the Nation of Isan," for its unique language, culture, and stubborn pace. As the poorest region of Thailand with little opportunity for young people, Isan experiences an ever-increasing drain on people-power as young folks move to the larger cities. A few learned phrases of the Isan dialect will endear you to a large percentage of the Bangkok cab-driver population, for example, and you'll recognize local Laos-style headscarves on most high-rise construction crews. You are sure to meet kind folks from Isan in every region of Thailand, and the fact that you know the name of their town, much less have been there, will be a source of wonder.

Below I've listed but the highlights.

1 Information & Tours

There are regular buses and train connections throughout Isan, but in remote parts buses are slow and you can't stop and see things of interest. I recommend arranging a tour or going by your own rented vehicle with driver, a relatively affordable proposition (expect to pay about 1,200B/$29 per day plus gas). Contact **North by Northeast Tours** in Nakhon Phanom (746/1 Sunthornvichit Rd., Nakhon Phanom 48000; © 04251-3572; Fax 04251-3573; www.north-by-north-east.com), a small, expat-owned tour company, and they can arrange any private itinerary throughout the region. There are offices of the **Tourist Authority of Thailand (TAT)** in many tour centers through the region (though few are conveniently located). Check out www.tourismthailand.org or call ©1672 for assistance.

2 Nakhon Ratchasima (Khorat)

259km (161 miles) NE of Bangkok; 417km (259 miles) W of Buriram; 305km (189 miles) S of Udon Thani

Nakhon Ratchasima, popularly known as Khorat, isn't a wildly interesting city, but it is close to Bangkok and makes a good base for excursions to beautiful **Khao Yai National Park** (see "Side Trips from Bangkok" in chapter 6) and the temples at **Phimai** and other nearby Khmer sites. It is a rapidly developing industrial city and is called the "Gateway to Isan" because all train lines, bus routes, roads, and communications pass through it. There are some comfortable accommodations in Khorat, and a few temples and city monuments worth seeing.

GETTING THERE
The airport in Khorat is not operational, but there are numerous daily trains from Bangkok's **Hua Lampong Station** (© 1690), and frequent bus connection from Bangkok's Northern Bus Terminal, **Mo Chit** (© 02936-2852). It's about 3 hours by train or bus.

WHAT TO SEE & DO
A trip to **Phimai,** 60km (37 miles) north of town, is worth it if you are interested in Khmer archaeology. Phimai is dominated by the many temple ruins, and there is a large museum. In Khorat, the most interesting temple houses an image of Narayana, a sacred Hindu deity, at **Wat Phra Narai Maharat** along Prajak Road, where you'll also find the **City Pillar.**

WHERE TO STAY
Best is the **Royal Princess Khorat** (1137 Suranarai Rd., northeast of town near the stadium; © 04425-6629), with fine amenities and rooms starting from 2,000B ($49). A close second is **Sima Thani** (Mittraphap Rd., next to the TAT office, west of town; © 04421-3100). **Chomsurang Hotel** (547 Mahatthai Rd. near the Night Market; © 04425-7088) has basic rooms from 900B ($22).

3 Khon Kaen

449km (278 miles) NE of Bangkok; 190km (118 miles) N of Nakhon Ratchasima; 115km (71 miles) S of Udon Thani

For most travelers, Khon Kaen is just a stopover for points north: Udon, Nong Khai, and further to Laos. The town is along Route 2, connects by rail with Bangkok and Nong Khai, and has a large commercial airport.

GETTING THERE
Thai Airways and budget carriers connect with Bangkok. Regular trains run from Bangkok via Khorat, and bus services and connections are many.

WHERE TO STAY
Accommodation choices are many as Khon Kaen is a busy regional convention center. Best is the **Hotel Sofitel Raja Orchid** (9/9 Prachasumran Rd.; © 04332-2155) with stylish rooms from 3,500B ($85), or the **Charoen Thani Princess** (Srichan and Na-Muang rds.; © 04322-0400), both popular convention addresses. Budget **Khon Kaen Hotel** (43/3 Phimpasut Rd.; © 04323-7711) has budget rooms from 500B ($12).

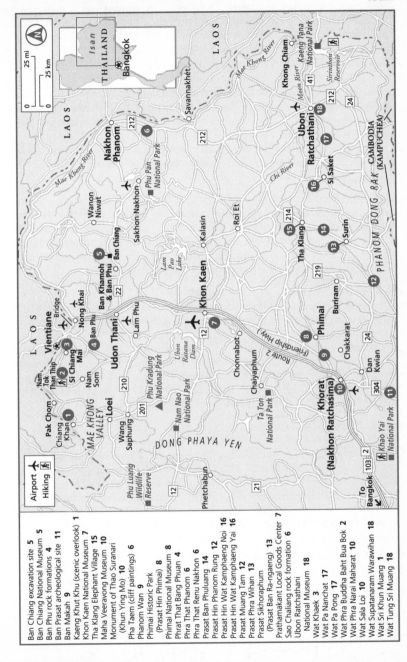

Isan

Ban Chiang excavation site **5**
Ban Chiang National Museum **5**
Ban Phu rock formations **4**
Ban Prasat archeological site **11**
Ban Makah **9**
Kaeng Khut Khu (scenic overlook) **1**
Khon Kaen National Museum **7**
Tha Klang Elephant Village **15**
Maha Veeravong Museum **10**
Monument of Thao Suranari
  (Khun Ying Mo) **10**
Pha Taem (cliff paintings) **6**
Phanom Wan **9**
Phimai Historic Park
  (Prasat Hin Phimai) **8**
Phimai National Museum **8**
Phrat That Bang Phuan **4**
Phra That Phanom **6**
Phra That Renu Nakhon **6**
Prasat Ban Phuluang **14**
Prasat Hin Phanom Rung **12**
Prasat Hin Wat Kamphaeng Noi **16**
Prasat Hin Wat Kamphaeng Yai **16**
Prasat Muang Tam **12**
Prasat Phra Wihan **13**
Prasat Sikhoraphum
  (Prasat Ban Ra-ngaeng) **13**
Sao Chaliang rock formation **6**
Prathamakant Local Goods Center **7**
Ubon Ratchathani
  National Museum **18**
Wat Khaek **3**
Wat Pa Nanchat **17**
Wat Pa Pong **17**
Wat Phra Buddha Baht Bua Bok **2**
Wat Phra Narai Maharat **10**
Wat Sala Loi **10**
Wat Supatanaram Warawihan **18**
Wat Sri Khun Muang **1**
Wat Tung Sri Muang **18**

4 Udon Thani & Ban Chiang

564km (350 miles) NE of Bangkok; 305km (189 miles) N of Nakhon Ratchasima; 115km (71 miles) N of Khon Kaen; 51km (32 miles) S of Nong Khai; 152km (94 miles) E of Loei

"No sweat, man," was the reply from the first tuk-tuk driver I asked to take me to my hotel; the use of 1960s slang keeps it in perspective that Udon Thani, or Udon, was home to a large contingent of U.S. armed forces during the Vietnam War and memories are still fresh. Today you might see a few retired U.S. servicemen around, and each year the area welcomes a contingent of the U.S. military for joint training with Thai forces (mostly the Air Force).

Udon is not very interesting, but a good jumping-off point to small towns like Loei to the west. **Ban Chiang** is a well-know archaeological site east of Udon.

GETTING THERE

By Plane   **Thai Airways** has daily flights, as do other budget carriers; numerous trains (best as an overnight in second-class sleeper) connect from **Hua Lampong** (© **1690**) daily via Korat and Khon Kaen; and there are bus connections from Udon to anywhere in the region. *Note:* There is a **Budget Car Rental** office at the airport (© **04524-0507**), and it is a good idea to fly to Udon and rent a car here to explore the Mekong Valley to the north (see the following sections).

WHERE TO STAY

The hub of the town is the **Charoensri Shopping Complex** around which you'll find many services. The best way to get around is by *samlor* (pedicabs that are, oddly, called "skylabs") or tuk-tuk.

Charoensri Grand Royal Hotel (277/1 Prachak Rd, west of the railway station and adjacent to the mall; © **04234-3555**) is the best choice in town, with cozy rooms, centrally located, from 1,500B ($37). **Charoen Hotel** (549 Phosi Rd, near the train station; © **04224-8155**) has basic rooms from 900B ($22), and older **Udorn Hotel** (81–89 Makkang Rd.; © **04224-8160**) has budget rooms from 400B ($10).

EXPLORING THE AREA

BAN CHIANG NATIONAL MUSEUM   The tiny hamlet of Ban Chiang, approximately 50km (31 miles) east of Udon on the Sakon Nakhon highway, boasts a history of more than 5,000 years, a history that was only stumbled upon (literally) in 1974 and excavated by an international team. The findings at Ban Chiang prove the existence of a distinct and very sophisticated Bronze Age culture in Southeast Asia long before any earlier findings. The museum on-site was funded by the Kennedy Foundation and houses a fine collection of early statuary as well as pottery and ritual implements. The site is open from 8:30am to 4:30pm; admission is 30B (75¢). Ban Chiang is 6km from the main highway between Udon and Nakhon Phanom, best visited by private vehicle, but you can also ask local buses to stop at the Ban Chiang junction and take a tuk-tuk to the site. Along the main road and lining the road to the site look for the many pottery villages producing unique Ban Chiang copy-works.

5 The Mekong Valley Loop

This loop takes you from **Udon** to the west and the little town of **Loei,** then along the Mekong, the natural Thai–Lao border, through **Nong Khai,** on to **Nakhon Phanom,** and with a side trip to **That Phanom** (and a possible stop at Ban Chiang) returns you to Udon, from where you can fly back to Bangkok. You could also amend the route to follow the Mekong all the way south from Nakhon Phanom to **Ubon Ratchathani.** This is adventurous off-the-tour-grid travel, and it's not a bad idea to hire a guide (see "Information & Tours" at the beginning of this chapter) or car and driver.

6 Loei

520km (322 miles) NE of Bangkok; 344km (213 miles) N of Nakhon Ratchasima; 206km (128 miles) NW of Khon Kaen; 202km (125 miles) W of Nong Khai; 269km (167 miles) NE of Phitsanulok

Cool and usually rainy because of its higher elevation (the town is reputedly the coldest spot in the kingdom), little Loei is a lazy riverside burg worth an overnight, but travel up this way is certainly about the beautiful road journey, not the destination. Loei hosts the annual **Pi Tha Khon Festival,** a Thai-style Mardi Gras in which young men dress as spirits and get crazy in the streets. "The devil made me do it!" is the excuse for all kinds of outlandish behavior. Lots of fun. Outside of town is **Phu Kradung National Park,** one of Thailand's most dramatic really, a bell-shaped tabletop mountain of 1,200m/4,000 ft. The park is 82km (51 miles) southwest of Loei and well worth the trip.

GETTING THERE
There is no train line nor airport in Loei, road only, with regular buses from Udon or the most direct route from Khon Kaen.

WHERE TO STAY
Loei Palace Hotel (167/4 Charoenrat Rd.; ✆ **04281-5668;** www.amari.com) is by far the best choice in town, a huge courtyard hotel with lots of amenities and affordable rooms (from 1,200B/$29). **King's Hotel** (1241 Haisoke Rd. at town center; ✆ **04281-1701**) is a basic, affordable choice with rooms from 400B/$9.75.

7 Along the Mekong from Loei to Nong Khai

One of the most scenic areas in Thailand and delightfully secluded, the northwestern perimeter of Isan runs along the wide Mekong River, which forms the border with Laos. The terrain is relatively flat, the road is only lightly trafficked and in a good state of repair, and there are a number of villages where you can stop.

The loop begins in Loei and ends in Nong Khai. Directly north of Loei you'll reach the riverside town of **Chiang Khan,** where you'll find a few riverside guesthouses, a *wat* worth visiting, and a few expatriates who've discovered a simpler life. You can take a short day trip by longtail boat for just 400B ($9.75) for 1 hour (contact any riverside guesthouse).

From Chiang Khan, Route 211 follows the Mekong east to **Pak Chom** and **Si Chiang Mai** before arriving in Nong Khai. Buses and *songtaos* make all of these connections, but it is a hassle, so it's best to have your own transport. The route passes lush banana plantations, terraced fruit farms, and small manganese mines. Cotton and tomato fields fan out along the verdant flood plains of the Mekong basin. Farther inland are lovely waterfalls like **Nam Tok Than Thip** (between Pak Chom and Si Chiang Mai), which are fun for hiking and ideal for picnics.

Don't miss the unique gold tower of the **Prasutham Chedi,** just west of Si Chiang Mai along the main road, and **Wat Hin Mak Peng,** which is some 30km (19 miles) west of Sri Chiang Mai and a glorious temple site overlooking the Mekong.

Si Chiang Mai is opposite Vientiane, the capital of the Lao People's Democratic Republic, and is but 58km (36 miles) due west of Nong Khai. The town is just a quiet Thai backwater. Walks along the long concrete pier or relaxing and watching Lao and Thai long-tail boats load and unload or chugging up and down river is about all that's going on here. In the evenings, join in a game of badminton or a circle of people juggling a *takra* (a small bamboo soccer ball). There are lots of little open-air eateries at riverside and a few small guesthouses along the quay at town center: try **Maneerat Resort** (74 Rimkong Rd., along the eastern end of the quay; © **04245-1311**), with basic but clean air-conditioned rooms starting at 450B ($11) and a friendly and helpful staff.

8 Nong Khai

615km (381 miles) NE of Bangkok; 51km (32 miles) N of Udon Thani; 356km (221 miles) N of Nakhon Ratchasima; 202km (125 miles) E of Loei; 303km (188 miles) W of Nakhon Phanom

The little bordertown of Nong Khai has a certain allure, its sprawling riverside market, **Tha Sadet,** is full of interesting goods from Laos and China, and the place has a palpable calm, with some good laid-back riverside guesthouses. Nong Khai is a popular jumping-off point for travel to Laos.

GETTING THERE

The nearest airport is in Udonthani, but Nong Khai is the terminus of the Northeast train line from Bangkok and is a good overnight journey (best in second class sleeper). Regular buses connect with points throughout the region.

WHAT TO SEE & DO

Tha Sadet, or the **Indochina Market,** located at the heart of town at riverside, is the main attraction in Nong Khai and it is certainly worth a wander. Also check out **Wat Khaek** (about 4km/3 miles east of town on Route 212), where you'll find recently cast concrete Buddhas, Hindu deities, and other fantastic statues of enormous proportions in an attractive garden setting, all the brainchild of the eccentric Mr. Luang Phu Boonlua Surirat, who studied with an Indian guru in Vietnam and later taught in Laos, and whose mummified body can be viewed on a tour of the main temple building (he also built a similar sculpture garden just across the river near Vientiane, Laos). Entry is 10B (25¢), and the site is open daily from 8:30am to 6pm.

The Dragon of the Mekong

Ask around about this mysterious event. In the fall of each year on the full moon days at the end of the Buddhist Lent (usually a few nights in October), the waters of the Mekong ripple and, from their depth rise balls of fire that shoot in a beeline path directly into the sky. This mystical event attracts thousands from all over Thailand. The explanation? The rising *Naga,* or dragon from the river—some say it is the magic of a local monk, others a "mass hallucination." Whether believer or non-believer, the proof is in the pudding (if you can find a place to stay for the night). The event is something like a Thai Loch Ness Monster or Bigfoot, really; lots of speculation, but no one wants to own up to whether it is the truth or not.

Good day trips from Nong Khai include a day (or overnight) across the border to **Vientiane, Laos** (visa available at the border), or head out to **Wat Phra Buddha Baht Bua Bok,** some 70km/43 miles southwest of Nong Khai; the site is a unique grouping of natural sandstone towers that were fashioned into rudimentary cave dwellings and are known for a tragic Romeo-and-Juliet tale.

WHERE TO STAY

Budget accommodations line the small streets all over town. **Mutmee Guesthouse** (111/4 Kaeworawut Rd.; © 04246-0717) is a uniquely comfortable budget choice (from 250B/$6.10) and a great place to get good local info (and great food!). The best hotel in Nong Khai is the **Nong Khai Grand Hotel** (589 Moo 5, Nong Khai-Poanpisai Rd., just south of town on highway; © 04242-0033; www.nongkhaigrand.com), with comfortable air-conditioned rooms from 2,000B/$49. For good local dining, try **Deng Nem Neung** (on a small side-street just off the central market; © 04241-1961), serving a popular do-it-yourself Vietnamese pork spring roll, or stop by **Udomros** (© 04242-1084), serving real Thai right in the heart of the market area overlooking the Mekong.

9 Nakhon Phanom

740km (459 miles) NE of Bangkok; 252km (156 miles) E of Udon Thani; 481km (298 miles) NE of Nakhon Ratchasima; 271km (168 miles) N of Ubon Ratchathani; 303km (188 miles) E of Nong Khai; 93km (58 miles) E of Sakon Nakhon.

It's a rare traveler who makes it out to these parts of the kingdom and, apart from the few good riverside hotels catering to Westerners, the place is pretty quiet. That's the allure. Walk riverside streets, look for the old Vietnamese clock tower, a gift of Ho Chi Minh for Thai aid during the war (Vietnamese soldiers crossed to Nakhon Phanom). South of town is **That Phanom,** an important pilgrimage site for Thai Buddhists; from there pass through Sakhon Nakhon to return to Udonthani (with a possible side trip to Ban Chiang), completing the loop. Many travelers follow the Mekong south from Nakhon Phanom all the way to Ubon Ratchathani, where they can catch a train back to Bangkok.

Nakhon Phanom hosts the famed "Lai Rua Fai" or Fire Boat Festival, where barges float downstream, twinkling with small candles in the night (also dragon boat races by day), all to celebrate the end of the rains.

GETTING THERE

Thai Airways has daily flights, otherwise you'll arrive by road from Sakhon Nakhon or down along the Mekong from Nong Khai.

WHAT TO DO & SEE

Contact **North by Northeast Tours** in Nakhon Phanom (746/1 Sunthornvichit Rd., Nakhon Phanom 48000; © 04251-3572; www.north-by-north-east.com) for good local tours to weaving and silversmith villages in the area. A trip to **That Phanom,** a temple built around a 60m/180 foot rebuilt 9th-century *stupa* which collapsed in 1975, is an important pilgrimage for Buddhists, and the little riverside burg is a unique visit (just an hour south of Nakhon Phanom).

WHERE TO STAY

The Mae Nam Kong Grand View Hotel (527 Soonthornvijitra Rd.; © 04251-3564; fax 04251-1037) has tidy rooms stacked right over the Mekong starting at 1,200B ($29), a good choice.

10 Southeast Isan

Branching off on the eastern spur of the rail-line at Khorat as you head north and east of Bangkok, you trace the edge of the Cambodian border on your way to Laos. First reach **Buriram,** a town with a few notable hilltop Khmer ruins, then **Surin,** an area famous for raising elephants and its annual elephant roundup, before reaching the city of **Ubon Ratchathani.** There are few jaw-dropping sites, but also few Western tourists.

11 Surin

457km (283 miles) NE of Bangkok; 227km (141 miles) W of Ubon Ratchathani; 111km (69 miles) E of Buriram; 198km (123 miles) E of Khorat

Surin is elephant country and famed for it is annual roundup, a nearly 200-year tradition; the city is also a good base for exploring far-flung Khmer ruins.

GETTING THERE

Daily trains connect from Bangkok via the spur line from Khorat (about 8.5 hours), and there are numerous buses.

WHAT TO DO & SEE

If you haven't come with your own guide, the best way to visit the many far-flung sites around Surin is to book a tour with friendly Mr. Pirom at the **Pirom Guest House** (© 04451-5140). Mr. Pirom has been in the business for years and guiding is just an extension of his passion for the ancient history and culture of this rural region. The most popular tours are to the many secluded Khmer temples in the area, and he combines such visits with stops at elephant-training villages, towns of Khmer culture, handicraft villages, and even trips to the weekend market at the Cambodian border. Expect to pay from 1,500/$37 per person for day trips.

WHERE TO STAY

Hotels fill right up and some add a surcharge of up to 50% during the Elephant Roundup. **Thong Tarin Hotel** (60 Sirirat Rd., just east of the bus station and town center; © 04451-4281) is the best accommodation in town, with tidy rooms from 1,300B/$32; nearby **Petchkasem Hotel** (104 Chitbumrung Rd. in the town center; © 04451-1274) is a basic business hotel (from just 600B/$15). **Pirom Guesthouse** (242 Krungsrinai Rd., 2 blocks west of the market; © 04451-5140) is very rustic (rooms start at 180B/$4.40), but a "real guesthouse"—as in you really become a "guest" of Mr. and Mrs. Pirom.

OUTSIDE OF SURIN

Buriram is about halfway between Surin and Khorat (and easily reached by either bus, train, or car), and home to **Phanom Rung,** a stunning Khmer ruin dominated by **Prasat Hin Phanom Rung (Great Mountain),** which was deserted in the late 13th century, rediscovered in 1935, and restored in the 1970s.

Another popular side trip from Surin, best arranged with Mr. Pirom as it is precariously perched along the border with Cambodia, is **Prasat Phra Wiharn,** another stunning Khmer site and a great rugged drive through beautiful country.

Appendix A:
Thailand in Depth

"Thailand in Depth" introduces you to Thailand's history, its people, cultural traditions, and cuisine.

1 The Thai People

Although Bangkok at rush hour feels packed, most of Thailand's 64 million people live in the countryside or in rural villages where they earn a living in agriculture, predominantly rice farming. Under economic strain, rural populations are migrating to the city and, while statistics are unreliable, most estimates put Bangkok's population well past the 10 million mark as a result of the rural influx. Hierarchical Bangkok is divided between native Bangkok Thais, who are educated, often bilingual, and hold more prestigious positions, and up-country workers, mostly uneducated, who speak in rural dialect and have settled here for jobs. It's an important distinction to Thais, who inherited a loose version of the caste system of India, the Thai cultural ancestor. Today's Thai can meet a person, instantly size him up, and know precisely how to treat them according to their relationship within the hierarchy. Interestingly, as a foreigner, you are automatically awarded a position of stature, regardless of your social standing back home.

So, who exactly are the Thai people? It's hard to say. There really are no historically ethnic Thais. Today's Thai people (about 75% of the population) are a hodgepodge from waves of immigrants over the past 10 or so centuries. "A Look at the Past," below, explains these waves in greater detail, but by and large the main bloodline is infused with indigenous people from the Bronze Age, southern Chinese tribes, Mons from Burma, Khmers from Cambodia, Malays, Arabs, and Europeans, plus more recent immigrants from China, Laos, Cambodia, and Myanmar (Burma). Although central Thailand is a true melting pot, you'll find southern Thais have a closer ancestral affinity with Malays, while Thais in the north are more closely related to the Chinese hill-tribes and Burmese people, and likewise in Isan in the northeast, where people trace their heritage to the Lao people. The remaining 25% are divided between Chinese (14%), and Indians, Malays, Karens, Khmer, and Mons (11%).

Statistics aside, the Thai people you will meet throughout the kingdom are a warm and welcoming lot. Locals delight in any foreigner who takes an interest in their heritage, learns a little bit of the language, eats spicy food, and appreciates Thai customs. Above all, the Thai people have an incredible sense of humor. A light spirit and a hearty chuckle go a long way.

ETIQUETTE Thai customs can be a bit confusing and foreigners are not expected to know and follow local etiquette to the letter (in fact it would be odd), but a few small gestures and a general awareness goes a long way to foster a spirit of good will, and Thais appreciate our efforts. First-time visitors are sure to make a few laughable mistakes, but read below carefully in order to avoid the more offensive faux pas.

Thais greet each other with a graceful bow called a *wai*. With hands pressed together, the higher they are held, the greater the show of respect. Younger people are always expected to *wai* an elder first, who will almost always return the gesture. Foreigners are more or less exempt from this custom, as the cultural subtleties are difficult to grasp. In hotels, doormen, bellhops, and waitresses will frequently *wai* to you. Please do not feel compelled to return the greeting; a simple smile of acknowledgment is all that's necessary (otherwise, you'll be bowing all over town). In situations where a *wai* is appropriate, like when meeting a person of obvious status, don't fret about the position of your hands. To keep them level to your chest is perfectly acceptable. Two exceptions—never *wai* to a child, and never expect a monk to *wai* back (they are exempted from the custom).

One of the most important points of Thai etiquette you should remember is that Thais practice, and expect, a certain level of equanimity, calm, and light-heartedness in personal relations. If you are prone to temper, aggravation, and frustration, Thailand can be a challenge of restraint. Anger and confrontational behavior, especially from foreign visitors, is greeted with blank stares. The Thais don't just think such outbursts are rude but an indication of a lesser-developed human being. Getting angry and upset is in essence "losing face" by acting shamefully in front of others, and Thai people will do anything to spare themselves the embarrassment (in other words, walk away). Travelers who throw fits often find themselves abandoned by the very people who could help.

So what do you do if you encounter a frustrating situation? The Thai philosophy says, "*Mai pen rai*," or, "Never mind, no worries." If it's a situation you can't control, like a traffic jam or a delayed flight—*mai pen rai*. If you find yourself at loggerheads with the front desk, arguing with a taxi driver, or in any other truly frustrating situation, keep calm, try a little humor, and find a nonconfrontational, compromising solution that will save face for all involved. The old "catching flies with honey" trick goes a long way in these parts.

The Thais hold two things sacred: their religion and their royal family. In temples and royal palaces, dress with respect— choose long pants or skirts with a neat shirt, and avoid sleeveless tops. Remove your shoes before entering temple buildings if it is the custom (always indicated at entry) and give worshippers their space. Be mindful of your feet—sit with your legs curled beside you, never in front pointing at the Buddha image. While photographing images is allowed, do not climb on any image or pose near it in a way that can be seen as showing disrespect. Women should be especially cautious around monks, who are not allowed to touch members of the opposite gender. If a woman needs to hand something to a monk, she should either hand it to a man to give to the monk, or place the item in front of him. ***Important:*** Never, ever, say anything critical or improper about the royal family, not even in jest.

To an outside observer, Thai society can seem very liberal, but in fact the opposite is true. You'll notice that, with some exceptions, the Thais dress very conservatively. If you're not sure what to wear, look around you. Young Bangkokians dress like any big city in the world, guys in shorts or baggy pants and cut-off shirts, girls in hip-huggers, or postage-stamp miniskirts and bare midriffs or whatever is in fashion, but elsewhere, and certainly among older Thais, covering neck to ankles is more the rule. While you'll see some foreign women sunbathing topless at beach resorts, it is never accepted, merely tolerated, and even shirtlessness among foreign men anywhere but the beach is unacceptable, really (but, of course, tolerated—*mai pen rai*).

Times are changing, but Thais commonly avoid public displays of affection. While members of the same gender often hold hands and walk arm in arm as friends, even the lads, you'll rarely see a Thai couple acting this way. Some Thai women who date foreign men will bend the rules, and you'll see some affectionate younger couples, but as a rule of thumb for couples: don't hold hands, hug, or kiss in public.

Here's the most innocent of insults, but one that most Westerners have a hard time getting used to: Don't use your feet to point at anything or to indicate anything, ever. Especially do not point them at a person, or at a Buddha image. Buddhists believe the feet are the lowest part of the body—such gestures are unbelievably insulting.

In contrast, the head is considered the most sacred part of the body. Don't touch a Thai on the head, tousle a child's hair—instead give that friendly pat on the back or shoulders. Even barbers have to ask permission to touch a customer's crown.

2 A Look at the Past

THE EARLY PEOPLE Archaeologists believe that Thailand was a major thoroughfare for *Homo erectus* en route from Africa to China and other parts of Asia. The earliest evidence of prehistoric life lies in stone tools, dating back some 700,000 years from an excavation site around Lampang in northern Thailand. Cave paintings, found throughout the country, are believed to originate as early as 2,000 B.C., with people dancing, dressed in feathers and kilts, with domesticated animals, popular regional fish such as dolphins (in the south) and catfish (in the north), and wild animals in hunting scenes and grassy patches that appear to be rice paddies. Human remains have been excavated at many sites, the most famous of which, Ban Chiang, contained the first evidence of a Bronze Age in Thailand. Controversy over dating methods suggested that this area may have acquired metallurgy knowledge independent of the few other world centers who'd mastered the skill, but more accurate radiocarbon testing has put Thailand's Bronze Age at about 1500 to 1000 B.C., after China's. It is not known what happened to these early inhabitants.

Modern civilization did not arrive in Thailand until about 1,000 years ago.

There is archaeological evidence that points to an area in central and southern China as a cultural heartland for the descendants of many of the peoples of Southeast Asia. These people began to appear in northern Southeast Asia in the first millennium A.D., and continued to migrate south, east, and west in waves over the following 8 centuries, settling primarily in what is now Vietnam, Laos, Thailand, and Myanmar (Burma). These people, who are called *Tai*, became dispersed over a vast area of space, sharing a cultural and linguistic commonality. Their descendants are the core bloodline of the Thai people of today, the Shan of northern Burma, the Tai people of northern Laos, the Lu of Yunnan province in southern China, as well as groups in Vietnam, on the Chinese island of Hainan, and others in northeastern India. The total number of Tai people today is estimated at 70 million.

The early Tais lived in nuclear families with a dozen or two households forming an independently ruled *muang,* or village. They lived in raised houses in the lowlands, making a living from subsistence agriculture and gathering necessary items from the forest around them. In times of threat, either to economic stability or from outside aggression, many *muang* would combine forces. The organization was usually led by the strongest village or family. What developed were loosely structured feudal states where both lord and villager benefited—the lord from manpower and the villager from stability. The Tais expanded as ruling fathers sent sons out into the world to conquer or colonize neighboring areas, establishing new *muang* in farther regions.

THE DVARAVATI (MON) PERIOD

From the 6th century, Southeast Asia underwent a gradual period of Indianization. Merchants and missionaries from India introduced Brahmanism and Buddhism to the region, as well as Indian political and social values, and art and architectural preferences. Many Tai groups adopted Buddhism, combining its doctrine with their own animistic beliefs. But the true significance of India's impact can be seen in the rise of two of the greatest Southeast Asian civilizations, the Mon and Khmer.

Historians have very little information about the **Mon civilization.** No one knows where these people came from, how far they reached, or where their capital was. What we do know is that around the 6th century A.D., the Mon were responsible for establishing Buddhism in central Thailand. Ancient Mon settlements lined the fringes of Thailand's central plains area, seemingly stretching as far west as Myanmar (Burma), north toward Chiang Mai, northeast to northern Laos and the Khorat Plateau, and east to Cambodia.

THE SRIVIJAYA EMPIRE

In the southern peninsula, the **Srivijaya Empire,** based in Java, began to play an important role in cultural affairs. Before the 9th century A.D., port cities along southern shores had drawn traders from all over the region and beyond. However, the Srivijayas, who had assimilated their own unique brand of Buddhism from India, would leave a lasting impression on these cities, linking them with other Southeast Asian lands and importing Buddhism and Buddhist art. While the empire never actually conquered and ruled the area, its cultural reign is still evident in Nakhon Si Thammarat, and in the southern arts of this period. Some historians argue that Chaiya, near Surat Thani, could have been capital of the empire for a time, but the claim is largely disputed. Srivijaya power, ground by endless warring with southern India, headed into decline and disappeared from Thailand by the 13th century.

THE KHMERS

By the early 9th century A.D., the **Khmer Empire** had risen to power in Cambodia, spreading into surrounding areas. Indravaraman (877–89) saw the kingdom reach the Khorat Plateau in northeastern Thailand. **Suryavarman I** (1002–50) extended the kingdom to the Chao Praya Valley and north to Lamphun, driving out the Mons. **Suryavarman II** (1113–15?) pushed the kingdom even farther, forcing the Mons still deeper into Myanmar (Burma).

With each conquering reign, magnificent Khmer temples were constructed in outposts farther and farther from the Cambodian center of the empire. These early temples were built for the worship of Hindu deities. Brahmanism, having been brought to Cambodia with traders from southern India, influenced not only Khmer religion and temple design (with the distinct corncob shaped *prang,* or tower), but government administration and social order as well. Conquering or forcing villages into their control, the Khmers placed their own leaders in important centers and supplied them with Khmer administrative officers. The empire was extremely hierarchical, with the king as supreme power, ruling from his capital.

The populations of these outposts were largely Tai, and while the Khmers had the authority, Tais were blending in as laborers, slaves, and temple workers. Temple murals in Angkor show quite clearly the Khmer attitude toward what they called *Syam*. The mural shows a stiff orderly regiment of Khmer soldiers following Tais who were shoddy but fierce.

Angkor, Cambodia's great ancient temple city, was built during the reign of Suryavarman II. It is believed the temples of Phimai and Phanom Rung in Isan predated the Khmer's capital temple complex, influencing its style. But by this time the Khmer empire was already in decline. The last great Khmer ruler, **Jayavarman VII** (1181–1219), extended the empire to its farthest limits—north to Vientiane, west to Burma, and down the Malay peninsula. It was he who shifted Khmer ideology toward Buddhism, building temples in Khmer-style, but no longer with a Hindu purpose. His newfound Buddhism inspired him to build extensive highways (portions of which are still evident today), plus more than 100 rest houses for travelers and hospitals in the outer provinces. Jayavarman VII's death in 1220 marks Thailand's final break from Khmer rule. The last known Khmer settlement is at the sight of Wat Kamphaeng Laeng in Phetchaburi.

THE LANNA KINGDOM: THE NORTHERN TAIS

By A.D. 1000, the last of the Tai immigrants had traveled south from China to settle in northern Thailand. Several powerful centers of Tai power—Chiang Saen in northern Thailand, Chiang Hung in southern China, and Luang Prabang in Laos—were linked by a common heritage and the rule of extended families. In the region, *muang* grew stronger and better organized, but infighting remained a problem. In 1239, a leader was born in Chiang Saen who would conquer and unite the northern Tai villages and create a great kingdom.

Born the son of the king of Chiang Saen and a southern Chinese princess, Mengrai ascended the throne in 1259, and established the first capital of the Lanna Kingdom at Chiang Rai in 1263. Conquering what remained of Mon and Khmer settlements in northern Thailand, he assimilated these peoples and cultures. After occupying Lamphun, he shifted his base of power to Chiang Mai in 1296.

Mengrai's Lanna Kingdom became an important empire in the north. Religiously, the Lanna Tais combined traditional animist beliefs with Mon Buddhism. Retaining Mon connections with Ceylon, the Lanna Kingdom saw the rise of a scholarly Buddhism, with strict adherence to orthodox Buddhist ways. Lanna kings were advised by a combination of monks and astrologers, ruling over a well-organized government bureaucracy. Citizens of Lanna enjoyed the benefits of infrastructure projects for transportation and irrigation; developed medicine and law; and heralded the arts through religious sculpture, sacred texts, and poetry. By and large the people were only mildly taxed, and were allowed a great deal of autonomy.

But a rising power threatened Lanna, as well as its neighbors. The Mongols, under the fierce expansionist leadership of Kublai Khan, forced their way into the region. Mengrai, forming strategic alliances with Shan leaders in Myanmar (Burma) and two other Tai kingdoms to the south (one of which, the Sukhothai, would rise as the zenith of Thai culture), succeeded in keeping the Mongols at bay.

SUKHOTHAI: THE DAWN OF SIAMESE CIVILIZATION

While Mengrai was busy building Lanna, a small kingdom to the south was on the verge of stellar power. After the demise of first the Dvaravarti civilization, and later the Khmers, the Tai people who'd made their way into the Chao Praya valley found themselves in small disorganized vassal states. A tiny kingdom based in

Sukhothai would dwell in obscurity until the rise of founding father King Indra-ditya's second son, Rama. Single-hand-edly defeating an invasion from neighboring Mae Sot at the Burmese bor-der, Rama proved himself a powerful force, immediately winning the respect of his people. Upon his coronation in 1279, **Ramakhamhaeng,** or "Rama the Bold," set the scene for what is recognized as the first truly Siamese civilization.

In response to the Khmer's tight grip, Ramakhamhaeng established himself as an accessible king. It is told he had a bell outside his palace for any subject to ring in the event of a grievance. The king him-self would come to hear the dispute and would make a just ruling on the spot. He was seen as a fatherly and fair ruler who allowed his subjects immense freedoms. His kingdom expanded rapidly, it seems through voluntary subjugation, reaching as far west as Pegu in Burma, north to Luang Prabang, east to Vientiane, and south beyond Nakhon Si Thammarat to include portions of present-day Malaysia.

After centuries of diverse influences from outside powers, in Sukhothai, for the first time, we see an emerging culture that is uniquely **Siamese.** The people of the central plains had a heritage mixed with Tai, Mon, Khmer, and indigenous populations, with threads of India and China interwoven in their cultural tapes-try. Ramakhamhaeng was a devout Bud-dhist, adopting the orthodox and scholarly Theravada Buddhism from mis-sionaries from Nakhon Si Thammarat and Ceylon. A patron of the arts, the king commissioned many great Buddha images. While few sculptures from his reign remain today, those that do survive display a refined creativity. For the first time, physical features of the Buddha are Siamese in character. Images have grace-ful, sinuous limbs and robes, radiating flowing motion and delicate energy. Ramakhamhaeng initiated the many

splendid architectural achievements of Sukhothai and nearby Si Satchanalai. In addition, he is credited with developing the modern Thai written language, derived from Khmer and Mon examples. Upon Ramakhamhaeng's death in 1298, he was succeeded by kings who would devote their attentions to religion rather than affairs of state. Sukhothai's brilliant spark faded almost as quickly at it had ignited.

AYUTTHAYA: SIAM ENTERS THE GLOBAL SCENE   In the decades that followed, the central plains area found itself without firm leadership. Along came U Thong; born the son of a wealthy Chinese merchant family, he was also dis-tantly related to the royals of Chiang Saen. Crowning himself Ramathibodi, he set up a capital at Ayutthaya, on the banks of the Lopburi River, and from here set out to conquer what was left of Khmer outposts, eventually swallowing the remains of Sukhothai. The new king-dom incorporated the strengths of its population—Tai military manpower and labor, Khmer bureaucratic sensibilities, and Chinese commercial talents—to cre-ate a strong empire. Ayutthaya differed quite greatly from its predecessor. Follow-ing Khmer models, the king rose above his subjects atop a huge pyramid-shaped administration. He was surrounded by a divine order of Buddhist monks and Brahman sanctities. During the early period of development, Ayutthaya rulers created strictly defined laws, caste sys-tems, and labor units. Foreign traders from the region, China, Japan, and Ara-bia, were required to sell the first pick of their wares to the king for favorable prices. Leading trade this way, the king-dom was buttressed by great riches. Along the river, a huge fortified city was built—with temples that glittered as any in Sukhothai. This was the Kingdom of Siam that the first Europeans, the Por-tuguese, encountered in 1511.

But peace and prosperity would be disrupted with the coming of **Burmese invasion** forces that would take Chiang Mai (thus the Lanna Kingdom) in 1558 and finally Ayutthaya in 1569. The Lanna Kingdom that King Mengrai and his successors built would never regain its former glory. Fortunately Ayutthaya had a happier fate with the rise of one of the greatest leaders in Thai history. **Prince Naresuan,** born in 1555, was the son of the puppet Tai King placed in Ayutthaya by the Burmese. Although Naresuan was directly descended from Sukhothai leaders, it was his early battle accomplishments that served to better distinguish him as a ruler. Having spent many years in Burmese captivity, he returned to Ayutthaya to raise armies to challenge Burmese rule. His small armies were inadequate against the Burmese, but in a historic battle scene, Naresuan, atop an elephant, challenged the Burmese crown prince and defeated him with a single blow.

With the Tais back in control, Ayutthaya continued through the following 2 centuries in grand style. Foreign traders—Portuguese, Dutch, Arab, Chinese, Japanese, and English—not only set up companies and missionaries, but were even encouraged to rise to some of the highest positions of power within the administration. Despite numerous internal conflicts over succession and struggles between foreign powers for court influence, the kingdom managed to proceed steadily. While its Southeast Asian neighbors were falling under colonial rule, the court of Siam was extremely successful in retaining its own sovereignty. It has the distinction of being the only Southeast Asian nation never to have been colonized, a point of great pride for Thais today.

The final demise of Ayutthaya would be two more **Burmese invasions.** The first, in 1760, was led by King Alaunghpaya, who would fail, retreating after he was shot by one of his own cannons. But 6 years later, two Burmese contingents, one from the north and one from the south, would besiege the city. The Burmese raped, pillaged, and plundered the kingdom—capturing fortunes and laborers for return to Burma. The Thai people still hold a bitter grudge against the Burmese for their horrible acts.

THE RISE OF BANGKOK: THE CHAKRI DYNASTY The Siamese did not hesitate to build another kingdom. The Burmese, leaving behind only small strongholds, left themselves open to a Siamese revival. Taksin, a provincial governor of Tak, in the central plains area, rose to power on military excellence, charisma, and a firm belief that he was divinely appointed to lead the land. Rather than build upon the ashes of Ayutthaya, Taksin rebuilt the capital at Thonburi, on the western bank of the Chao Praya River, opposite present-day Bangkok. Within 3 years he'd reunited the lands under the previous kingdom, but his was a troubled rule. Taksin suffered from paranoia and his claims to divinity raised eyebrows in the monastic order and even within his own family. He had monks killed, and eventually his own wife and children. Regional powers were quick to get rid of him—he was swiftly kidnapped, and while covered in a velvet sack was beaten to death with a sandalwood club and buried secretly in his own capital. These same regional powers turned to the brothers Chaophraya Chakri and Chaophraya Surasi, great army generals who'd recaptured the north from Burma, to lead the land. In 1782, Chaophraya Chakri ascended the throne as the first king of Thailand's present dynasty: the Chakri dynasty.

King Ramathibodi, as he was known, moved the capital across the river to Bangkok, where he built a Grand Palace, royal homes and administrative buildings, and great temples. The city was based upon a network of canals, with the river as the central channel for trade and commerce. Siam was now a true melting pot of cultures not limited to the Tai, Mon, and Khmer descendants of former powers, but including powerful Chinese, Arab, Indian, and European bloodlines. The king himself proved to be connected in some way to each major lineage. His early tasks were to reorganize the Buddhist monkhood under an orthodox Theravada Buddhist doctrine, reestablish the state ceremonies of Ayutthaya times without the emphasis of Brahman and animistic sensibility, and revise all laws based upon just and rational arguments. He also wrote the *Ramakien,* based upon the Indian Ramayana, a legend that has become a beloved Thai tale, and a subject for many Thai classical arts.

Despite military threats from all directions, the kingdom continued to grow through a succession of kings from the new royal bloodline. Ramathibodi and his two successors expanded the kingdom to the borders of present-day Thailand and beyond. Foreign relations in the modern sense were developed during this early era, with formal ties to European powers.

King Mongkut (1851–68) had a unique upbringing. As a monk he developed a scholarly character, which throughout his reign would show itself through his leaning toward rational thinking and western learning. With his son, **King Chulalongkorn** (1868–1910), he led Siam into the 20th century as an independent nation, establishing an effective civil service, formalizing global relations, and introducing industrialization-based economics. He united the royal line under the title Rama. Assigning the title Rama I to the dynasty's first king, Mongkut then became Rama IV, and his son Rama V. As an aside, it was King Mongkut who hired Anna Leonowens (recall *The King and I*) as an English tutor for his children. Thai people want everyone to know that Mongkut was not the overbearing, pushover fop described in her account. Historians side with the Thais, for she is barely mentioned in court accounts—the story had its origins more in her imagination than in reality.

The reign of **King Prajadhipok,** Rama VII (1925–35), saw the growth of the urban middle class, and the increasing discontent of a powerful elite. By the beginning of his reign, economic failings and bureaucratic bickering weakened the position of the monarchy, which was delivered its final blow by the Great Depression. To the credit of the king, he'd been pushing for a shift to constitutional monarchy, but in 1932 a group of midlevel officials beat him to the punch with a coup d'état. Prajadhipok eventually abdicated in 1935.

THAILAND IN THE 20TH & 21ST CENTURIES   Democracy had a shaky hold on Siam. Its original constitution, written in 1932, was more a tool for leaders to manipulate rather than a political blueprint to be adhered to. Over the following decades, government leadership changed hands fast and frequently, many times the result of hostile measures. The military had constant influence, most likely the result of its ties to the common people as well as its strong unity. In 1939, the nation adopted the name "Thailand"—land of the free.

During World War II, democracy was stalled in the face of the Japanese invasion in 1941. Thailand gave up quickly, choosing alliance over being conquered, even going so far as to declare war against the Allied powers. But at the war's end, no punitive measures were taken against Thailand, thanks to the Free Thai Movement organized by Ambassador Seni Pramoj in Washington, who had placed the declaration of war in his desk drawer rather than delivering it.

Thailand managed to stay out of direct involvement in the Vietnam War; however, it continues to suffer repercussions from the burden of refugees, as well as reap economic benefits from the infrastructure the U.S. military helped build. The United States pumped billions into the Thai economy, bringing riches to some and relative affluence to many but further impoverishing the poor, especially subsistence farmers, who were hit hard by the accompanying inflation. Communism became an increasingly attractive political philosophy to those ground down by burgeoning capitalism as well as to liberal-minded students and intellectuals, and a full-scale insurrection seemed imminent—which, of course, fueled further political repression by the military rulers.

In June 1973, thousands of Thai students demonstrated in the streets, demanding a new constitution and the return to democratic principles. Tensions grew until October when armed forces attacked a demonstration at Thammasat University in Bangkok, killing 69 students and wounding 800, paralyzing the capital with terror and revulsion.

The constitution was restored, a new government was elected, and democracy once again wobbled on. Many students, however, were not yet satisfied and continued to complain that the financial elite were still in control and resisting change. In 1976, student protests again broke out, and there was a replay of the grisly scene of 3 years before at Thammasat University. The army seized control to impose and maintain order, conveniently spiriting away some bodies and prisoners, and another brief experiment with democracy was at an end. Thanin Kraivichien was installed as prime minister of a new right-wing government, which suspended freedom of speech and the press, further polarizing Thai society.

In 1980, Prem Tinsulanonda was named prime minister, and during the following 8 years he managed to bring remarkable political and economic stability to Thailand. The Thai economy continued to grow steadily through the 1980s, fueled by Japanese investment and Chinese capital in flight from Hong Kong. Leadership since then has seen quite a few changes, including a military coup in 1991, and another student crackdown in 1992.

In July 1997, Thailand became the first victim of the **Asian Economic Crisis** when it floated its currency—a move that caused the baht to devalue 20 percent in the week to follow. A legacy of suspicious government ties to industry, massive overseas borrowing, overbuilt property markets, and lax bank lending practices bubbled to the surface. In November of that year, **Chuan Leekpai** was elected into power to lead the country out of the crisis, but 3 years later Thais were still unsatisfied with the progress being made to change the situation. In January 2001, the Thai people elected populist candidate **Thaksin Shinawatra.**

A telecom tycoon and a member of one of the wealthiest families in the kingdom, Prime Minister Thaksin came into office and raised Thai spirits, promising progress and reform of the economy and an end to corrupt cronyism. Has he delivered? Thaksin's aggressive economic reform has brought the country out of debt and, in November 2003, Thailand paid back its $12 billion loan to the International Monetary Fund, the money borrowed during the 1997 currency crisis. The popular prime minister waged a "War on Poverty and Dark Influence," cracking down on mafia activity and bribe collection (though corruption is still the rule on the local level). Some argue that Thaksin's reforms come at the cost of human liberties; most glaringly, the current administration is responsible for the blacklisting and deadly raids by police and other "silencing" deaths of drug-trafficking suspects (estimates are as high as 3,000 people). PM Thaksin's aggressive response to unrest in Muslim communities in the far south has also come under international censure. But the Thai economy is humming and no one wants to rock this boat.

So what happened to the monarchy and the Chakri dynasty? **King Bhumibol Adulyadej** has been king since 1946 and has seen the dynasty to the new millennium with dignity and noble grace. A compassionate man, while he has no real government power, he is believed by all to be the ultimate upholder of the will of the Thai people. He continues the proud cultural traditions that bind the national psyche to its past while moving toward the future.

3 The Buddha in Thailand

Thai culture cannot be fully appreciated without some understanding of Buddhism, which is practiced by 90% of the population. The Buddha was a great Indian sage who lived in the 6th century B.C. He was born Siddhartha Gautama, a prince who was carefully sheltered from the outside world. When he left the palace walls he encountered an old man, a sick man, a corpse, and a wandering monk. He concluded that all is suffering and resolved to search for relief from that suffering. Sensing that the pleasures of the physical world were impermanent and thus caused us pain, he shed his noble life and went into the forest to live as a solitary ascetic. But, nearing starvation, he was soon to realize this was not the path to happiness, so he turned instead to his "Middle Way," a more moderate practice of meditation, compassion, and understanding. One night, while meditating under a Bodhi (fig) tree and after trials and torment by Mara, the god of death, who sent demons to frighten him and voluptuous dancers to seduce him, Siddhartha Gautama became enlightened: with his mind free of delusion, he gained an intuitive insight into the reality of the nature of the universe and saw things as they are, without defilement, craving, or attachment, but unified and complete. His truth is the Dhamma—his doctrine, which he explained to his first five disciples at Deer Park in India—a sermon now known as "The Discourse on Setting into Motion the Wheel of the Law."

After the death of Buddha two schools arose. The oldest and probably closest to the original is **Theravada** (Doctrine of the Elders), sometimes referred to less correctly as Hinayana (the Small Vehicle), which prevails in Sri Lanka, Myanmar (Burma), Thailand, and Cambodia, and focuses on the enlightenment of individuals, one at a time, with an emphasis on the monastic community and monks who achieve Nibbana (or Nirvana) in this lifetime. The other school, Mahayana (the Large Vehicle), is practiced in China, Korea, and Japan, and posits a model of all of mankind attaining enlightenment at once, not on a case-by-case basis.

The basic document of Thai, or Theravada, Buddhism is the **Pali canon,** which was recorded in writing in the 1st century A.D. The doctrine is essentially an ethical and psychological system in which no deity plays a role. It is a religion without a god, mystical in the sense that it strives for the intuitive realization of the oneness of the universe. Theravada traditions follow no earthly authority, though there is a certain hierarchy based on age among monks and practitioners, and the practice requires that individuals find the truth for themselves, an inward-looking proposition done through meditation and self-examination. Buddha's final words were a plea to "work out your own salvation with diligence."

So, if there is no deity and nothing to worship, then what, you may ask, are the people doing who enter the temple and prostrate themselves before the Buddha, place their hands together in a gesture of worship, light incense, and make offerings of fruit and flowers? Flowers, fruit, and incense are a show of respect, and worshippers bow three times before the image—once for the Buddha himself, once for the sangha (the order of monks), and once for the dhamma (truth). The very orthodox Theravada traditions tend to mingle with local animism and superstition, meaning that practitioners often appeal to the Buddha and to Buddhist images in an effort to improve their lot, which is a bit off the mark, really. That said, Buddhist images and prostrations at the temple are a way to honor the teachers and those who pass on the tradition, show respect for the Buddha's meditative repose and equanimity, and offer reverence for relics of the historical Buddha (many sites, particularly *stupas*, house important relics).

Buddhism has one aim only: to abolish suffering. Buddhist practice offers a path to rid oneself of the causes of suffering, which are desire, malice, and delusion. Practitioners eliminate craving and ill will by exercising self-restraint and showing kindness to all sentient beings. Monks and members of the Buddhist Sangha, or community, are revered as those most diligently working toward enlightenment and the attainment of wisdom.

Theravada Buddhism does not seek converts, nor does it ask practitioners to believe in any truths but those they learn themselves through experience and meditation. Opportunities to study Buddhism or practice meditation in Thailand abound. There are a number of programs designed particularly for foreigners, and this is in fact the best way to better understand the heart of Buddhism, through practice.

Other aspects of the philosophy include the law of *karma,* whereby every action has effects and the energy of past action, good or evil, continues forever and is "reborn." (Some argue, though, that the Buddha took transmigration quite literally.) As a consequence, *tam bun* (merit making) is taken very seriously. Merit can be gained by entering the monkhood (and most Thai males do so for a few days or months), helping in the construction of a monastery or a *stupa,* contributing to education, giving alms, or performing any act of kindness no matter how small.

When the monks go daily with their bowls from house to house, they are not begging, but are giving the people an opportunity to make merit; similarly the people selling caged birds, which people purchase and free, are allowing people to gain merit by freeing the birds. When making merit, it is the *motive* that is all-important—the intention of the mind at the time of the action—which determines the karmic outcome, not the action itself. Buddhism calls for self-reliance; the individual embarks alone on the Noble Eightfold Path to Nirvana following the teachings that include the exhortations "to cease to do evil, learn to do good, cleanse your own heart."

Most Chinese and Vietnamese living in Thailand follow Mahayana Buddhism, and there are numerous temples and monasteries in the country supporting this other tradition.

Other religions and philosophies are also followed in Thailand including Islam, Christianity, Hinduism, and Sikhism. Sunni Islam is followed by more than two million Thais, mostly in the south. Most are of Malay origin and are descendants of the Muslim traders and missionaries who spread their teachings in the southern peninsula in the early 13th century. There are approximately 2,000 mosques in Thailand.

Christianity has spread in Thailand but little since it was first introduced in the 16th century by generations of Jesuit,

Dominican, and Franciscan missionaries from Europe, and later Protestant missionaries from America. Even after centuries of evangelism, there are only a quarter of a million Christians living in the country. Yet Thais have accepted much that has come from the Christian missionaries, particularly ideas on education, health, and science.

4 The Language

Thai is derived principally from Mon, Khmer, Chinese, Pali, Sanskrit, and, increasingly, English. It is a tonal language, with distinctions based on inflection—low, mid, high, rising, or falling tones—rather than stress, which can elude most speakers of Western languages. Among students of Thai, there's a well-known sentence that can be composed of the word *mai* repeated with four variations of tone to say, "Doesn't the green wood burn?" but which, to most, sounds like "Mai mai mai mai."

The grammar of Thai, however, is easily mastered, as there are no verb conjugations; one word says it for everyone. Verb tense indicators are easily learned, or you can stick with the present tense. One interesting aspect of the language that can be confusing to first-time visitors is that the polite words roughly corresponding to our sir and ma'am are not determined by the gender of the person addressed but by the gender of the speaker; females say *ka,* and males say *krup* as an honorific ending to every sentence.

The writing system is derived from Mon and Khmer, from southern Indian models, and is composed of 44 consonants (with only 21 distinct sounds) and 32 vowels (with 48 simple and diphthong possibilities). It reads from left to right, often without breaks between words. For the casual visitor it is best to just pick up a few phrases and go from there (save the ABC's until after the "How are you? I am fine.").

Unfortunately there is no universal transliteration system—so that you will see the usual Thai greeting written in Roman letters as *sawatdee, sawaddi, sawasdee, sawusdi,* and so on. Don't be afraid of getting lost in the different spellings. Derivations of most city names are close enough for anyone to figure out. The model most often used is more like French than English: *th* usually represents our t (as in Thailand); *t* represents our d; *ph* represents our p; *p* sounds more like our b; *kh* represents our k; *k* sounds like g; *r* often sounds like l or is not pronounced at all. (While, contrary to popular belief, there is an r in the alphabet, many Thais are lazy about pronouncing it, and you will hear the river called *Chao Phya* instead of *Chao Praya,* especially by taxi drivers, who are mostly not from Bangkok.) Sometimes *r* is used merely to lengthen a vowel sound (Udon is often written Udorn), and *l* or *r* at the end of a word is pronounced more like our *n* (Ubon is often written Ubol). There is no *v* sound in Thai, and when you see it written, as in Sukhumvit, it should actually sound like our *w*—just the opposite of German. There is also an *ng,* which sounds like those letters in our word sing, used as an initial consonant and difficult for English speakers to hear and pronounce—though the distinction can be important: *noo* means rat or kid (informal for child), but *ngoo* means snake.

Most of the vowel sounds, however, will be familiar to those acquainted with the Romance languages—though the vowel sound in our word see may be written *ee* or *i,* that in our word "moon" may be *oo* or *u,* and that in our word "now" may be written *ow* or even *aew,* as well as the usual *ao.* Doubled vowels most often signify a simple lengthening of the sound, but *i* is usually pronounced as in "hit," and *ii* as in "meet."

Central Thai is the official written and spoken language of the country, and most Thais understand it, but there are three other major dialects: Northeastern Thai, spoken in Isan, and closely related to Lao; Northern Thai, spoken in the northwest, from Tak Province to the Burmese border; and Southern Thai, spoken from Chumphon Province south to the Malaysian border. Each of these dialects also has several variations. The hill-tribes in the North have their own distinct languages, most related to Burmese or Tibetan.

Just as in English, there are various degrees of formality, and words that are acceptable in certain contexts are impolite in others. The most common word for eat is *kin* (also written *gin*), usually *kin khao* ("eat rice"); *thaan* is more polite; *raprathaan* is reserved for royalty.

For some helpful Thai phrases and vocabulary see appendix B, "A Little Bit of Thai to Help You Get By."

5 Thai Architecture 101

The Sukhothai period (13th–14th centuries) is regarded as the zenith of Thai culture, advancing major achievements in Thai art and architecture. One of the lasting legacies of the Sukhothai period is its sculpture, characterized by the graceful aquiline-nosed Buddha, either sitting in meditation or, more distinctively, walking sinuously. These Buddha images are considered some of the most beautiful representations ever produced. Sukhothai, the city, expanded and furthered the layout and decorative style of the Khmer capitals. With the inclusion of Chinese wooden building techniques and polychromatic schemes and Japanese-influenced carved flowing lines, the *wat*, or temple, with its murals, Buddhist sculpture, and spacious religious and administrative buildings, defined the first "pure" Thai Buddhist style. During this period came the mainstays of Thai wat architecture (in order of artistic importance): the *phra chedi* (stupa), *bot, wihaan, phra prang, mondop,* and *prasat,* all of which are explained further.

The dome-shaped *phra chedi*—usually called simply *chedi* and better known in the West as stupa—is the most venerated structure and an elaboration of the basic mound. Originally it enshrined relics of the Buddha—later of holy men and kings. A stupa consists of a dome (tumulus), constructed atop a round base (drum), and surmounted by a cubical chair representing the seated Buddha, over which is the chatra (umbrella) in one or several (usually nine) tiers. There are many different forms extant in Thailand: The tallest, oldest, and most sacred is the **golden *chedi* of Nakhon Pathom.**

The *bot* (*ubosoth* or *uposatha*) is where the *bhikku* (monks) meditate and all ceremonies are performed. It consists of either one large nave or one nave with lateral aisles built on a rectangular plan where the Buddha image is enshrined. At the end of each ridge of the roof are graceful finials, called *chofa* (meaning "sky tassel"), which are reminiscent of animal horns but are thought to represent celestial geese or the **Garuda** (a mythological monster ridden by the god Shiva). The triangular gables are adorned with gilded wooden ornamentation and glass mosaics.

The *wihaan* (*vihara* or *viharn*) is a replica of the *bot* (the central shrine in a Buddhist temple) that is used to keep Buddha images.

The *phra prang,* which originated with the corner tower of the Khmer temple, is a new form of Thai stupa, elliptical in shape and also housing images of the Buddha.

The *mondop* may be made of wood or brick. On a square pillared base the pyramidal roof is formed by a series of receding stories, enriched with the same decoration tapering off in a pinnacle. It may serve to enshrine some holy object as at Saraburi, where it enshrines the footprint of the Lord Buddha, or it may serve as a kind of library and storeroom for religious ceremonial objects, as it does at Wat Phra Kaeo in Bangkok.

The *prasat* (castle) is a direct descendant of the Khmer temple, with its round-topped spire and Greek-cross layout. At the center is a square sanctuary with a domed *sikhara* and four porchlike antechambers that project from the main building, giving the whole temple a steplike contour. The *prasat* serves either as the royal throne hall or as a shrine for venerated objects, such as the *prasat* of Wat Phra Kaeo in Bangkok, which enshrines the statues of the kings of the present dynasty.

Less important architectural structures include the *ho trai* or library, housing palm-leaf books; the *sala*, an open pavilion used for resting; and the *ho rakhang*, the Thai belfry.

The Ayutthaya and Bangkok periods furthered the Sukhothai style, bringing refinements in materials and design. During the Ayutthaya period there was a Khmer revival; the Ayutthaya kings briefly flirted with Hinduism and built a number of neo-Khmer-style temples and edifices. The art and architecture evident in early Bangkok were directly inspired by the dominant styles of the former capital. After the destruction of Ayutthaya in the 18th century, the new leaders, having established their foothold in Thonburi, soon moved across the Chao Praya to Bangkok and tried to copy many of the most distinctive buildings of Ayutthaya. This meant incorporating older Khmer (such as Wat Arun), Chinese, northern Thai, and, to a lesser degree, Western elements into contemporary wats, palaces, sculpture, and murals.

The last major influence in Thailand's architectural and artistic development was Western—and many would say that it is the single most important style today. Beginning with the opening up of the country to Europe during the later days of the Ayutthaya period, Jesuit missionaries and French merchants brought with them decidedly baroque fashions. Although the country was long reluctant in its relations with the West, European influences eventually became evident. Neoclassical elements were increasingly incorporated, notably in the Marble Wat in Bangkok, which was started by King Chulalongkorn in 1900 and designed by his half-brother, Prince Naris. A few decades later Art Deco became an important style, as can easily be seen today at Hualampong Station and along Ratchadamnoen Avenue, and the style is so prevalent that many writers use the term Thai Deco.

Today, much to the consternation of some leading Thai architects, anything goes, and you can see modernism, Greek revival, Bauhaus, sophisticated Chinese, and native Thai elements melded into eclectic designs that are often interesting and sometimes quite pleasing. Much of Bangkok, however, is almost indistinguishable from other fast-growing Asian capitals, such as Hong Kong and Singapore. Typical Thai wooden house blocks are cleared; *klongs* (canals) filled in and replaced by wide thoroughfares; modern high-rise office and apartment complexes, hastily erected—in sharp contrast to the city's vibrant architectural treasures, which are fortunately being well preserved for visitors in search of something truly exotic.

6 Thailand's Exotic Bill of Fare: From Tiger Prawns to Pad Thai

Food is one of the true joys of traveling in Thailand. If you aren't familiar with Thai cooking, imagine the best of Chinese food ingredients and preparation combined with the sophistication of Indian spicing, topped off with red and green chilies. You can find nearly any style of Thai (and international) cooking in Bangkok, from fiery curries from the south to mild northern cuisine. Basic ingredients include a cornucopia of shellfish, fresh fruits, and vegetables—lime, asparagus, tamarind, bean sprouts, carrots, mushrooms (many different kinds), morning glory, spinach, and bamboo shoots—and spices, including basil, lemongrass, mint, chili, garlic, and coriander (cilantro). Thai cooking also uses coconut milk, curry paste, peanuts, and a large variety of noodles and rice.

Among the dishes you'll find throughout the country are: *tom yam goong,* a Thai hot-and-sour shrimp soup; *satay,* charcoal-broiled chicken, beef, or pork strips skewered on a bamboo stick and dipped in a peanut-coconut curry sauce; spring rolls (similar to egg rolls but thinner and usually containing only vegetables); *larb,* a spicy chicken or ground-beef concoction with mint-and-lime flavoring; salads, made with nearly any ingredient as the prime flavor, but most have a dressing made with onion, chili pepper, lime juice, and fish sauce; *pad thai* ("Thai noodles"), rice noodles usually served with large shrimp, eggs, peanuts, fresh bean sprouts, lime, and a delicious sauce; *khao soi,* a northern curried soup served at small food stalls; a wide range of *curries,* flavored with coriander, chili, garlic, and fish sauce or coconut milk; spicy *tod man pla,* fried fish cakes with a sweet honey sauce, served in the north and made from glutinous rice, prepared with vegetables and wrapped in a banana leaf; and Thai fried rice, a simple rice dish made with whatever the kitchen has on hand. ("American fried rice" usually means fried rice topped by a sunny-side-up egg and sometimes accompanied by fried chicken.)

A word of caution: Thais enjoy incredibly spicy food, much hotter than is tolerated in even the most piquant Western cuisine. Protect your palate by saying *"Mai phet, farang,"* meaning "not spicy, foreigner." Also note, most Thai and Chinese food, particularly in the cheaper restaurants and food stalls, is cooked with lots of **MSG** (known locally as *"Ajinomoto"* because of the popular Japanese brand widely used), and it's almost impossible to avoid. If you want them to leave MSG out of your food, say *"Mai sai phong churot."*

Traditionally, Thai menus don't offer fancy desserts. The most you'll find are coconut milk–based sweets or a variety of fruit-flavored custards, but the local fruit is luscious enough for a perfect dessert. Familiar fruits are pineapple (served with salt to heighten the flavor), mangoes, bananas, guava, papaya, coconut, and watermelon, as well as the latest rage, apples grown in the royal orchards. Less familiar possibilities are *durian,* in season during June and July, which is a Thai favorite, but an acquired taste, as it smells like rotten onions; *mangosteen,* a purplish, hard-skinned fruit with delicate, whitish-pink segments that melt in the mouth, available April to September; *jackfruit,* which is large, yellow-brown with a thick, thorned skin that envelops tangy-flavored flesh, available year-round; *litchi; longan,* a small, brown-skinned fruit with very sweet white flesh available July to October; *tamarind,* a spicy little fruit in a pod that you can eat fresh or candied; *rambutan,* which is small, red, and hairy, with transparent sweet flesh clustered round a woody seed, available May to July; and *pomelo,* similar to a grapefruit, but less juicy, available October to December. Some of these fruits are served as salads—the raw green papaya, for example, can be quite good.

The Thai family usually has an early breakfast of *khao tom,* a rice soup (made from leftovers) to which chicken, seafood, or meat may be added. Typically, it's served with a barely cooked egg floating on top and a variety of pickled vegetables, relishes, and spicy condiments to add flavor. It's widely available, even at the poshest hotels.

The Thais take eating very seriously, so businesspeople allow 2 to 3 hours for lunch. A formal business luncheon consists of several dishes, but most casual diners have a one-course rice, noodle, or curry dish. For two people, you'll be fine ordering two hot dishes and perhaps a cold salad (mostly of the "not spicy" variety). Most restaurants throughout the country offer lunch from noon to 2pm; in fact, many close until 6 or 7pm before reopening for dinner.

Thais usually stop at one of the ubiquitous food stalls for a large bowl of noodle soup (served with meat, fish, or poultry), or dine at a department store food court or market where they can buy snacks from many different vendors and have a seat. Snacking from street-side food stalls—some would claim the source of the best Thai food—is popular throughout the day. *A note on etiquette:* You won't see Thais walking down the street munching. Take a seat while you eat.

Dinner is the main meal, and consists of a soup *(gaeng jued);* curried dish *(gaeng ped);* steamed, fried, stir-fried, or grilled dish *(nueng, thod, paad,* or *yaang);* a side dish of salad or condiments *(krueang kiang),* steamed rice *(khao),* and some fruit *(polamai).* Two Thais dining out may share four or five dishes (typically balanced as sweet, salty, sour, bitter, and piquant), always helping themselves to a little portion at a time (so as not to appear gluttonous). Dishes are brought to the table as they're cooked and eaten in any order, family style. Use the serving spoon provided to put a little on your plate.

7 Drinks

Thailand is a drinking culture and every town hosts bars, karaoke and dance clubs, as well as street-side drinking establishments. Liquor and beer are widely available in stores, restaurants, and hotels with few restrictions on sale (though all bars now close at 2am). Several fine varieties of beer are brewed in the country; the best known is **Singha,** and there's locally brewed **Kloster** (German) and **Carlsberg** (Danish), as well as imported **Heineken. Beer Chiang** is a popular malt-liquor that really packs a wallop and costs little. Most vineyard wine is imported and often incredibly expensive—due in part to high import duties—but it's increasingly popular and readily available in

Bangkok, Chiang Mai, and at the beach resorts.

Mekong and **Sang Thip** are two of the more popular local "whiskeys," even though they're actually rum (fermented from sugarcane). Thais will either buy a bottle or bring one to a restaurant where they can buy ice and mixers—usually cola or soda water. Waiters will keep the glasses full all the time, and again, take care with this stuff, as it *does* pack a punch (and some of the cheaper varieties are reputedly laced with some nasty chemicals).

Non-alcoholic drinks run the gamut and you'll find the likes of **Coke** and **Pepsi,** as well as ultra-sweet **Fanta** and fruit drinks, at every turn. Don't miss the fruit shake vendors in most city centers; they offer smoothies done with ice, fresh fruit of your choice, and sugar or sugar-cane juice all spun-up in a blender. Sweet local specials like "Gek Huey," or chrysanthemum juice, are a real treat. Water is also served at most meals, either affordable bottled water or filtered water served in pitchers with ice in glasses.

Appendix B:
A Little Bit of Thai
to Help You Get By

Thai is a tonal language, with distinctions based on inflection—low, mid, high, rising, or falling tone—rather than stress. There are five tonal markings:

low tone: `
falling tone: ^
middle tone (no marking)
rising tone: ˇ
high tone: ´

1 Basic Phrases & Vocabulary

English	Thai Pronunciation
Hello (male)	Sawadee-krup
Hello (female)	Sawadee-ka
How are you?	Sabai-dee rêu?
I am fine	Sabai-dee
My name is (male) . . .	Pôm chê . . .
My name is (female) . . .	Deè-chân chê . . .
I come from . . .	Pôm/Deè-chân ma jàk . . .
Do you speak English?	Khun pût pasâ angkrìt dâi mâi?
I do not understand	Pôm/Deè-chân mâi khâo jai
Excuse me	Khôr tôd. (-krup, -ka)
Thank you	Khòp khun. (-krup, -ka)
No; I do not want . . .	May âo . . .
Where is the toilet?	Hông sûam yù têe nâi?
I need to see a doctor	Pôm/Deè-chân tôngkan mâw
Please call the police	Chwây riâk tam-rùat dûay
Never mind, no problem	Mâi pen rai

2 Getting Around

English	Thai Pronunciation
I want to go to . . .	Pôm/Deè-chân yàk pai . . .
Where is the . . .	Yù têe nâi . . .
taxi stand	têe jòt rót téksêe
bus terminal	satânee rót may

train station	satânee rót fai
airport	sanâm bin
boat jetty	tâ rua
bank	tanakan
TAT office	tông tiâw pràtêt tai
hospital	rong payaban
How much to . . . ?	Pai . . . tâo rai?
What time does it depart?	Kèe mong jà àwk jàk têe nêe?

3 In a Restaurant

English	Thai Pronunciation
coffee	ca-fae
tea	naam-châ
juice	nám-kuá-la-mâi
bottled water	nam kwât
water	naam
wine	wine
bread	ká-nom-pâng
rice	kâo
chicken	kài
beef	núa
pork	môo
fish	pla
shrimp	goông
fruit	kuá-la-mâi
dessert	kong-wan
I am a vegetarian	Pôm/Deè-chân kin jay
I don't like it spicy	Mâi chôp pèt
I like it spicy	Chôp pèt
Delicious!	Ah-lòy!
check	chek-bin

4 Shopping

English	Thai Pronunciation
How much?	Taô rai?
Expensive	Paeng
Any discount?	Lót eèk dâi mâi?
What is your best price?	Raka tàm sùt tâo rai?
Do you have a (smaller/larger) size?	Mee (lék kuà/yài kùa) née mâi?
Do you have another color?	Mee sêe ùn mâi?

5 Numbers

1	neung	6	hok
2	song	7	jed
3	sam	8	pad
4	see	9	gao
5	hah	10	sip

Index

THE NEW TRAVELOCITY GUARANTEE

EVERYTHING YOU BOOK WILL BE RIGHT, OR WE'LL WORK WITH OUR TRAVEL PARTNERS TO MAKE IT RIGHT, RIGHT AWAY.

*To drive home the point,
we're going to use the word "right" in every single sentence.*

Let's get right to it. Right to the meat! Only Travelocity guarantees everything about your booking will be right, or we'll work with our travel partners to make it right, right away. Right on!

Here's a picture taken smack dab right in the middle of Antigua, where the guarantee also covers you.

The guarantee covers all but one of the items pictured to the right.

For example, what if the ocean view you booked actually looks out at a downright ugly parking lot? You'd be right to call – we're there for you. And no one in their right mind would be pleased to learn the rental car place has closed and left them stranded. Call Travelocity and we'll help get you back on the right track.

Now, you may be thinking, "Yeah, right, I'm so sure." That's OK; you have the right to remain skeptical. That is until we mention help is always right around the corner. Call us right off the bat, knowing that our customer service reps are there for you 24/7. Righting wrongs. Left and right.

Now if you're guessing there are some things we can't control, like the weather, well you're right. But we can help you with most things – to get all the details in righting,* visit **travelocity.com/guarantee**.

*Sorry, spelling things right is one of the few things not covered under the guarantee.

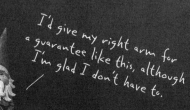

I'd give my right arm for a guarantee like this, although I'm glad I don't have to.

travelocity
You'll never roam alone.